# JUSTICE STATISTICS

## AN EXTENDED LOOK AT CRIME IN THE UNITED STATES

# JUSTICE STATISTICS

## AN EXTENDED LOOK AT CRIME IN THE UNITED STATES

THIRD EDITION
2017

Edited by
Shana Hertz Hattis

Lanham, MD

Published in the United States of America
by Bernan Press, a wholly owned subsidiary of
The Rowman & Littlefield Publishing Group, Inc.
4501 Forbes Boulevard, Suite 200
Lanham, Maryland 20706

Bernan Press
800-462-6420
www.rowman.com

ISBN-13: 978-1-59888-931-4
eISBN-13: 978-1-59888-932-1

∞™ The paper used in this publication meets the minimum requirements of
American National Standard for Information Sciences—Permanence of
Paper for Printed Library Materials, ANSI/NISO Z39.48-1992.
Manufactured in the United States of America.

# Contents

## 119 Part 3. Crimes Against Persons with Disabilities, 2010–2014

## 129    Part 4. Criminal Victimization, 2015

# INTRODUCTION

Bernan Press is pleased to present the third edition of its comprehensive collection of justice statistics in the United States. This volume provides valuable information compiled by the Department of Justice, including its subsidiaries, the Bureau of Justice Statistics (BJS) and the Federal Bureau of Investigation (FBI).

This volume brings together 10 key reports that fall under this category. Topics covered include criminal victimization, correctional populations, crime in the United States, hate crimes, probation, parole, school violence, and law enforcement officers killed and assaulted. Tables in this volume provide a comprehensive account of each of these subjects; for more information, including full-scope methodologies and information about standard errors for each table, please see the full reports at the URLs listed below.

Each section contains statistical tables and figures highlighting the data, as well as a brief summary of the report's methodology and at-a-glance highlights of the most compelling information.

As this book went to press, BJS issued a preview of its *Capital Punishment* 2014–2015 report. The information was insufficient for a full chapter; however, the early data are presented in table format in Appendix B.

The reports:

*Correctional Populations in the United States, 2015*, discusses the trends and changes in the incarcerated populations of the country's prisons. The full report is https://www.bjs.gov/index .cfm?ty=pbdetail&iid=5870

*Crime Against Persons with Disabilities, 2009–2014*, presents estimates of nonfatal violent crime (rape or sexual assault, robbery, aggravated assault, and simple assault) against persons age 12 or older with disabilities. Disabilities are classified according to six limitations: hearing, vision, cognitive, ambulatory, self-care, and independent living. The full report can be found at https://www.bjs.gov/index.cfm?ty=pbdetail&iid=5844

*Crime in the United States, 2015*, provides an introduction to overall crime trends. This report is more fully presented in Bernan Press's companion volume, *Crime in the United States*. However, given the importance of the report in the understanding of justice and crime trends in the United

States, its most relevant tables have been included in this volume. The full report can be accessed at https://ucr.fbi .gov/crime-in-the-u.s/2015/crime-in-the-u.s.-2015/

*Criminal Victimization, 2015*, takes a close look at the victims of violent and property crime in the United States. The full report is accessible at http://www.bjs.gov/index .cfm?ty=pbdetail&iid=5366

*Hate Crime Statistics, 2015*, details the hate crimes committed in the United States throughout 2015. It can be accessed at https://ucr.fbi.gov/hate-crime/2015/home

*Human Trafficking, 2015*, is another report from the FBI's UCR program. In its third year, it has continued to gain state/territory participation, allowing the human trafficking data to become even more useful for shedding light on this type of criminal activity. The full report can be found at https://ucr.fbi.gov/crime -in-the-u.s/2015/crime-in-the-u.s.-2015/additional-reports/ human-trafficking/humantrafficking_-2015-_final

*Indicators of School Crime and Safety, 2015*, which is new to this edition, is an annual report that presents data on crime and safety at school from the perspectives of students, teachers, and principals. Conducted jointly by the Bureau of Justice Statistics and the National Center for Education Statistics, the report's data sources include the National Crime Victimization Survey (NCVS), the School Crime Supplement to the NCVS, the Youth Risk Behavior Survey, and the School Survey on Crime and Safety. The full report can be accessed at http:// www.bjs.gov/index.cfm?ty=pbdetail&iid=5926

*Jail Inmates in 2015*, presents estimates of the inmate populations of jails based on various demographic characteristics. The full report can be accesses at http://www.bjs.gov/content/ pub/pdf/jim14.pdf

*Law Enforcement Officers Killed and Assaulted, 2015*, is the primary resource for data about harm done to law enforcement officers. This volume provides a comprehensive sample of the report; further information can be obtained at https://ucr.fbi .gov/leoka/2015/federal/federal_topic_page_-2015

*Probation and Parole in the United States, 2015*, details data about post-release inmates still in the legal system. The report can be accessed at https://www.bjs.gov/index .cfm?ty=pbdetail&iid=5784

# ABOUT THE EDITOR

Shana Hertz Hattis is an editor with over a decade of experience in statistical and government research publications. Past titles include *State Profiles: The Population and Economy of Each U.S. State, Crime in the United States,* and *The Almanac of American Education.* She earned her bachelor of science in journalism and master of science in education degrees from Northwestern University.

PART 1.

# Correctional Populations in the United States, 2015

# HIGHLIGHTS

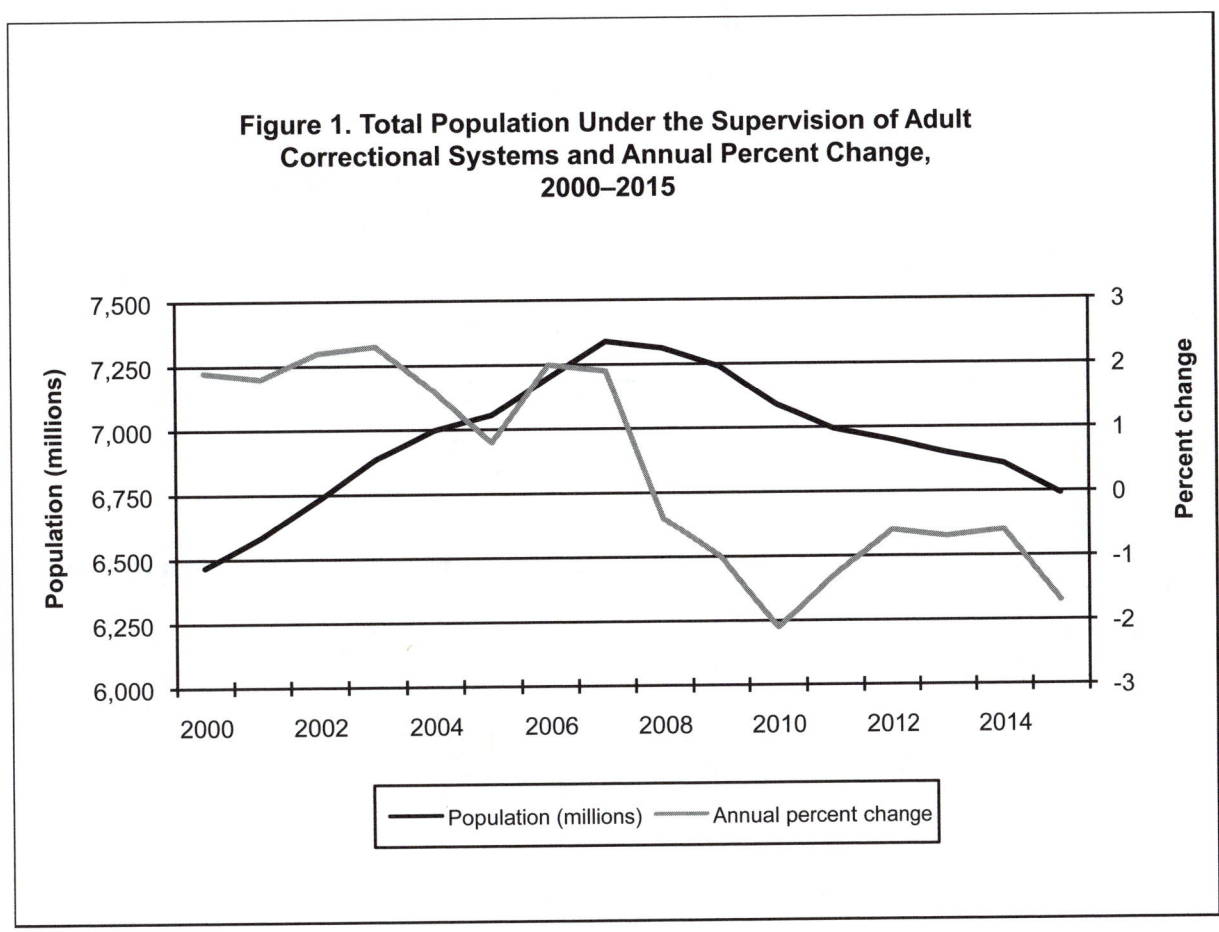

**Figure 1. Total Population Under the Supervision of Adult Correctional Systems and Annual Percent Change, 2000–2015**

- An estimated 6,741,400 persons were supervised by the correctional system at yearend 2015, about 115,600 less than at yearend 2014.

- About 1 in 37 adults (or 2.7 percent of adults in the United States) had some form of correctional supervision at yearend 2015, the lowest rate since 1994; the decreases in the community supervision population (down 1.3 percent) and the incarcerated population (down 2.3 percent) led the U.S. correctional population to a 1.7 percent decline.

- The community supervision population (4,650,900) dropped to its lowest level since 2000 (4,564,900), and the incarcerated population (2,173,800) fell to its lowest level in a decade (2,136,600).

- The 35,500 person drop in the prison population was responsible for the majority (69 percent) of the decline in the incarcerated population.

## Table 1. Number of Persons Supervised by Adult Correctional Systems, by Correctional Status, Selected Years, 2000 and 2006–2015

(Number; percent.)

| Year | Total correctional population[1] | Community supervision | | | Incarcerated[1] | | |
|---|---|---|---|---|---|---|---|
| | | Total[2,3] | Probation | Parole | Total[1] | Local jail | Prison |
| 2000................................ | 6,467,800 | 4,564,900 | 3,839,400 | 725,500 | 1,945,400 | 621,100 | 1,394,200 |
| 2006................................ | 7,199,600 | 5,035,000 | 4,236,800 | 798,200 | 2,256,600 | 765,800 | 1,568,700 |
| 2007................................ | 7,339,600 | 5,119,000 | 4,293,000 | 826,100 | 2,296,400 | 780,200 | 1,596,800 |
| 2008................................ | 7,312,600 | 5,093,400 | 4,271,200 | 826,100 | 2,310,300 | 785,500 | 1,608,300 |
| 2009................................ | 7,239,100 | 5,019,900 | 4,199,800 | 824,600 | 2,297,700 | 767,400 | 1,615,500 |
| 2011................................ | 6,994,500 | 4,818,300 | 3,973,800 | 855,500 | 2,252,500 | 735,600 | 1,599,000 |
| 2012................................ | 6,949,800 | 4,790,700 | 3,944,900 | 858,400 | 2,231,300 | 744,500 | 1,570,400 |
| 2013................................ | 6,899,700 | 4,749,800 | 3,912,900 | 849,500 | 2,222,500 | 731,200 | 1,577,000 |
| 2014................................ | 6,856,900 | 4,713,200 | 3,868,400 | 857,700 | 2,225,100 | 744,600 | 1,562,300 |
| 2015................................ | 6,741,400 | 4,650,900 | 3,789,800 | 870,500 | 2,173,800 | 728,200 | 1,526,800 |
| Average annual percent change, 2007–2015......................... | -1.1 | -1.2 | -1.6 | 0.7 | -0.7 | -0.9 | -0.6 |
| Percent change, 2014–2015 ................ | -1.7 | -1.3 | -2.0 | 1.5 | -2.3 | -2.2 | -2.3 |

Note: Estimates were rounded to the nearest 100 and may not be comparable to previously published BJS reports due to updated information or rounding. Counts include estimates for nonresponding jurisdictions. All probation, parole, and prison counts are for December 31; jail counts are for the last weekday in June. Detail may not sum to total due to rounding and adjustments made to account for offenders with multiple correctional statuses.
[1] Total was adjusted to account for offenders with multiple correctional statuses.
[2] Includes inmates held in local jails or under the jurisdiction of state or federal prisons.
[3] Includes some offenders held in a prison or jail but who remained under the jurisdiction of a probation or parole agency.


## Table 2. Rate of Persons Supervised by U.S. Adult Correctional Systems, by Correctional Status, Selected Years, 2000 and 2005–2015

(Number; rate per 100,000 U.S. residents.)

| Year | Total correctional population[1] | | | Community supervision population | | Incarcerated population[2] | |
|---|---|---|---|---|---|---|---|
| | Number supervised per 100,000 U.S. adult residents[3] | U.S. adult residents under correctional supervision | Number supervised per 100,000 U.S. residents of all ages[4] | Number on probation or parole per 100,000 U.S. adult residents[3] | Number on probation or parole per 100,000 U.S. residents of all ages[4] | Number in prison or local jail per 100,000 U.S. adult residents[3] | Number in prison or local jail per 100,000 U.S. residents of all ages[4] |
| 2000................................ | 3,060 | 1 in 33 | 2,280 | 2,160 | 1,610 | 920 | 690 |
| 2005................................ | 3,160 | 1 in 32 | 2,370 | 2,210 | 1,660 | 990 | 740 |
| 2006................................ | 3,190 | 1 in 31 | 2,400 | 2,230 | 1,680 | 1,000 | 750 |
| 2007................................ | 3,210 | 1 in 31 | 2,420 | 2,240 | 1,690 | 1,000 | 760 |
| 2008................................ | 3,160 | 1 in 32 | 2,390 | 2,200 | 1,670 | 1,000 | 760 |
| 2009................................ | 3,100 | 1 in 32 | 2,350 | 2,150 | 1,630 | 980 | 750 |
| 2010................................ | 3,000 | 1 in 33 | 2,280 | 2,070 | 1,570 | 960 | 730 |
| 2011................................ | 2,930 | 1 in 34 | 2,240 | 2,020 | 1,540 | 940 | 720 |
| 2012................................ | 2,880 | 1 in 35 | 2,210 | 1,980 | 1,520 | 920 | 710 |
| 2013................................ | 2,830 | 1 in 35 | 2,170 | 1,950 | 1,490 | 910 | 700 |
| 2014................................ | 2,780 | 1 in 36 | 2,140 | 1,910 | 1,470 | 900 | 690 |
| 2015................................ | 2,710 | 1 in 37 | 2,090 | 1,870 | 1,440 | 870 | 670 |

Note: Rates were estimated to the nearest 10. Estimates may not be comparable to previously published BJS reports due to updated information or rounding.
[1] Includes offenders in the community under the jurisdiction of probation or parole agencies, under the jurisdiction of state or federal prisons, or held in local jails.
[2] Includes offenders under the jurisdiction of state or federal prisons or held in local jails.
[3] Rates were computed using estimates of the U.S. resident population for persons age 18 or older from the U.S. Census Bureau for January 1 of the following year.
[4] Rates were computed using estimates of the U.S. resident population for persons of all ages from the U.S. Census Bureau for January 1 of the following year..

## Table 3. Number of Persons Supervised by U.S. Adult Correctional Systems, by Correctional Status, 2007 and 2015

(Number; percent.)

| Correctional populations | 2007 | | 2015 | |
|---|---|---|---|---|
| | Population | Percent of total population | Population | Percent of total population |
| Total[1] | 7,339,600 | 100.0 | 6,741,400 | 100.0 |
| Probation[2] | 4,293,000 | 58.5 | 3,789,800 | 56.2 |
| Prison[2] | 1,596,800 | 21.8 | 1,526,800 | 22.6 |
| Parole[2] | 826,100 | 11.3 | 870,500 | 12.9 |
| Local jail[3] | 780,200 | 10.6 | 728,200 | 10.8 |
| Offenders with multiple correctional statuses[4] | 156,400 | : | 174,000 | : |

Note: Counts were rounded to the nearest 100 and include estimates for nonresponding jurisdictions. Detail may not sum to total due to rounding and because offenders with multiple correctional statuses were excluded from the total correctional population.
: = Not calculated.
[1] Adjusted to exclude offenders with multiple correctional statuses to avoid double counting.
[2] Population as of December 31.
[3] Population as of the last weekday in June.
[4] Some probationers and parolees on December 31 were held in a prison or jail but still remained under the jurisdiction of a probation or parole agency, and some parolees were also on probation. In addition, some prisoners were held in jail. They were excluded from the total correctional population to avoid double counting. See Table 6.


## Table 4. Change in the Number of Persons Supervised by U.S. Adult Correctional Systems, 2007–2015 and 2014–2015

(Number; percent.)

| Correctional population | 2007–2015 | | 2014–2015 | |
|---|---|---|---|---|
| | Change in population[1] | Percent of total change[1] | Change in population[1] | Percent of total change[1] |
| Total Change[1] | -598,300 | 100.0 | -115,600 | 100.0 |
| Probation | -503,200 | 84.1 | -78,700 | 68.1 |
| Prison | -70,000 | 11.7 | -35,500 | 30.7 |
| Local jail | -51,900 | 8.7 | -16,300 | 14.1 |
| Parole | 44,400 | -7.4 | 12,800 | -11.1 |
| Offenders with mulitple correction statuses[2] | 17,600 | : | -2,100 | : |

Note: Estimates were rounded to the nearest 100 and include estimates for nonresponding jurisdictions. Detail may not sum to total due to rounding due to adjustments to exclude offenders with multiple correctional statuses from the total to avoid double counting.
: = Not calculated.
[1] Includes the change in the number of offenders with multiple correctional statuses. See Table 6.
[2] Some probationers and parolees on December 31 were held in a prison or jail but still remained under the jurisdiction of a probation or parole agency and some parolees were also on probation. In addition, some prisoners were held in a jail on December 31. These offenders were excluded from the total correctional population prior to calculating change to avoid double counting. See Table 6.

# Table 5. Number and Rate of Persons Supervised by U.S. Adult Correctional Systems, by Jurisdiction and Correctional Status, 2014 and 2015

(Number; rate per 100,000 U.S. residents of all ages.)

| Jurisdiction | Total correctional population, 12/31/14 | | | | | Total correctional population, 12/31/15 | | | | |
|---|---|---|---|---|---|---|---|---|---|---|
| | Number | | | Rate[1] | | Number | | | Rate[1] | |
| | Total[2] | Male | Female | Male | Female | Total[2] | Male | Female | Male | Female |
| U.S. Total[3] | 6,810,800 | 5,560,100 | 1,250,600 | 3,530 | 770 | 6,712,600 | 5,462,700 | 1,249,900 | 3,440 | 760 |
| Federal | 338,000 | 300,600 | 37,400 | 190 | 20 | 328,500 | 292,000 | 36,500 | 180 | 20 |
| State | 6,472,700 | 5,259,500 | 1,213,200 | 3,340 | 750 | 6,384,100 | 5,170,700 | 1,213,400 | 3,250 | 740 |
| Alabama | 103,400 | 86,400 | 17,100 | 3,670 | 680 | 107,500 | 89,200 | 18,300 | 3,780 | 730 |
| Alaska[4] | 14,600 | 12,100 | 2,400 | 3,120 | 700 | 13,900 | 11,400 | 2,500 | 2,930 | 720 |
| Arizona | 133,600 | 111,900 | 21,700 | 3,320 | 640 | 136,300 | 114,100 | 22,200 | 3,340 | 640 |
| Arkansas | 69,400 | 55,800 | 13,600 | 3,820 | 900 | 73,200 | 58,300 | 14,900 | 3,980 | 980 |
| California[4] | 592,500 | 497,900 | 94,600 | 2,570 | 480 | 550,600 | 463,400 | 87,200 | 2,370 | 440 |
| Colorado | 119,800 | 94,000 | 25,800 | 3,460 | 960 | 120,000 | 93,900 | 26,000 | 3,390 | 950 |
| Connecticut | 62,300 | 51,500 | 10,700 | 2,940 | 580 | 61,000 | 50,300 | 10,700 | 2,870 | 580 |
| Delaware | 23,300 | 18,800 | 4,500 | 4,130 | 920 | 22,700 | 18,500 | 4,200 | 4,020 | 870 |
| District of Columbia | 11,900 | 10,200 | 1,800 | 3,210 | 500 | 10,600 | 9,800 | 800 | 3,050 | 230 |
| Florida | 382,800 | 308,900 | 73,900 | 3,150 | 720 | 375,800 | 302,600 | 73,200 | 3,030 | 700 |
| Georgia[5] | 578,000 | 462,300 | 115,800 | 9,330 | 2,220 | 540,000 | 432,900 | 107,100 | 8,650 | 2,030 |
| Hawaii | 28,300 | 22,300 | 6,000 | 3,090 | 860 | 28,300 | 22,400 | 6,000 | 3,070 | 840 |
| Idaho | 48,700 | 37,700 | 10,900 | 4,580 | 1,330 | 48,700 | 37,400 | 11,200 | 4,490 | 1,350 |
| Illinois | 219,000 | 181,000 | 38,000 | 2,860 | 580 | 215,100 | 177,700 | 37,500 | 2,810 | 570 |
| Indiana[4] | 172,500 | 136,900 | 35,600 | 4,200 | 1,060 | 166,000 | 131,300 | 34,700 | 4,020 | 1,030 |
| Iowa | 46,500 | 36,600 | 9,900 | 2,360 | 630 | 46,700 | 36,900 | 9,900 | 2,370 | 630 |
| Kansas[4] | 37,200 | 31,000 | 6,200 | 2,130 | 420 | 37,400 | 31,000 | 6,400 | 2,130 | 440 |
| Kentucky | 103,600 | 77,900 | 25,800 | 3,580 | 1,150 | 103,700 | 77,500 | 26,200 | 3,550 | 1,160 |
| Louisiana | 113,700 | 96,300 | 17,400 | 4,220 | 730 | 114,600 | 97,100 | 17,500 | 4,240 | 730 |
| Maine | 10,100 | 8,400 | 1,700 | 1,290 | 250 | 10,100 | 8,400 | 1,700 | 1,290 | 260 |
| Maryland | 109,700 | 92,100 | 17,700 | 3,170 | 570 | 104,500 | 87,600 | 16,900 | 3,000 | 550 |
| Massachusetts | 90,300 | 75,900 | 14,400 | 2,310 | 410 | 86,900 | 71,400 | 15,500 | 2,160 | 440 |
| Michigan | 256,700 | 203,200 | 53,400 | 4,170 | 1,060 | 250,200 | 199,600 | 50,600 | 4,090 | 1,000 |
| Minnesota | 120,500 | 95,500 | 25,000 | 3,510 | 910 | 121,600 | 95,900 | 25,700 | 3,500 | 930 |
| Mississippi | 69,700 | 58,200 | 11,500 | 4,000 | 750 | 71,900 | 60,400 | 11,500 | 4,160 | 740 |
| Missouri | 108,500 | 88,700 | 19,800 | 2,980 | 640 | 106,000 | 86,100 | 19,900 | 2,880 | 640 |
| Montana | 14,600 | 11,700 | 2,800 | 2,270 | 550 | 14,700 | 11,700 | 3,000 | 2,240 | 570 |
| Nebraska | 22,500 | 17,800 | 4,700 | 1,890 | 490 | 22,300 | 17,600 | 4,600 | 1,860 | 480 |
| Nevada | 37,200 | 31,200 | 6,000 | 2,170 | 420 | 38,300 | 32,100 | 6,200 | 2,190 | 430 |
| New Hampshire | 11,200 | 9,300 | 1,900 | 1,420 | 280 | 10,900 | 9,000 | 1,900 | 1,370 | 280 |
| New Jersey | 164,500 | 137,300 | 27,200 | 3,140 | 590 | 183,500 | 147,800 | 35,700 | 3,370 | 780 |
| New Mexico | 32,400 | 25,900 | 6,500 | 2,510 | 620 | 25,000 | 19,800 | 5,200 | 1,910 | 490 |
| New York | 222,100 | 192,200 | 29,800 | 2,000 | 290 | 216,700 | 187,300 | 29,400 | 1,940 | 290 |
| North Carolina | 153,300 | 123,800 | 29,500 | 2,540 | 580 | 151,200 | 122,200 | 29,000 | 2,490 | 560 |
| North Dakota | 9,300 | 7,300 | 2,000 | 1,900 | 560 | 10,100 | 7,800 | 2,300 | 1,990 | 610 |
| Ohio | 324,200 | 249,400 | 74,800 | 4,390 | 1,260 | 331,500 | 251,500 | 80,000 | 4,420 | 1,350 |
| Oklahoma | 69,500 | 57,600 | 11,900 | 2,990 | 600 | 73,100 | 60,200 | 12,900 | 3,090 | 650 |
| Oregon | 82,700 | 68,200 | 14,500 | 3,450 | 720 | 82,900 | 68,200 | 14,700 | 3,400 | 720 |
| Pennsylvania | 360,900 | 284,800 | 76,100 | 4,550 | 1,160 | 374,200 | 294,300 | 79,900 | 4,690 | 1,220 |
| Rhode Island | 25,100 | 21,300 | 3,800 | 4,160 | 700 | 25,300 | 21,500 | 3,800 | 4,190 | 700 |
| South Carolina | 71,800 | 61,000 | 10,900 | 2,580 | 430 | 70,100 | 59,400 | 10,800 | 2,480 | 430 |
| South Dakota[4] | 14,500 | 11,600 | 2,800 | 2,700 | 660 | 15,000 | 11,900 | 3,100 | 2,750 | 720 |
| Tennessee | 119,800 | 95,800 | 24,000 | 2,990 | 710 | 119,900 | 95,700 | 24,200 | 2,960 | 710 |
| Texas | 697,100 | 562,300 | 134,900 | 4,160 | 980 | 687,300 | 553,500 | 133,800 | 4,020 | 960 |
| Utah | 25,800 | 20,700 | 5,100 | 1,390 | 340 | 25,500 | 20,500 | 5,000 | 1,350 | 330 |
| Vermont | 8,400 | 6,700 | 1,700 | 2,180 | 530 | 8,000 | 6,400 | 1,600 | 2,070 | 520 |
| Virginia | 115,300 | 95,900 | 19,400 | 2,330 | 460 | 114,400 | 94,800 | 19,600 | 2,290 | 460 |
| Washington | 137,200 | 110,500 | 26,700 | 3,100 | 750 | 130,600 | 104,500 | 26,100 | 2,890 | 720 |
| West Virginia | 19,600 | 15,500 | 4,100 | 1,700 | 440 | 20,100 | 15,900 | 4,200 | 1,740 | 450 |
| Wisconsin[4] | 97,300 | 82,300 | 15,000 | 2,870 | 520 | 100,600 | 84,500 | 16,100 | 2,940 | 550 |
| Wyoming | 9,700 | 7,700 | 2,000 | 2,570 | 710 | 9,900 | 7,700 | 2,100 | 2,580 | 750 |

*Note:* Counts were rounded to the nearest 100, and rates were rounded to the nearest 10. Detail may not sum to total due to rounding and because offenders with multiple correctional statuses were excluded from totals. Counts include estimates for nonresponding jurisdictions.

[1] Rates were computed using the U.S state resident population of all ages, by sex. U.S. resident populations of persons age 18 or older were not available by sex at the time this report was published. For this reason, jurisdiction-level rates in other tables of this report may not be comparable to this table.

[2] Excludes, by jurisdiction, an estimated 155,100 males and 18,900 females in 2015 and an estimated 154,100 males and 16,700 females in 2014 with multiple correctional statuses.

[3] Includes local jail counts that are based on December 31, 2015, to produce jurisdiction-level estimates. For this reason, the estimates in this table differ from a significant number f the national estimates presented in other tables and figures.

[4] Excludes about 11,000 inmates that were not held in locally operated jails but rather facilities that were operated by the Federal Bureau of Prisons and functioned as jails.

[5] Includes estimates due to nonresponse for sex.

# Table 6. Estimated Number of Offenders with Multiple Correctional Statuses at Yearend, by Correctional Status, 2000–2015

(Number.)

| Year | Total | Prisoners held in local jail | Probationers | | Parolees | | On probation |
|---|---|---|---|---|---|---|---|
| | | | Local jail | State or federal prison | Local jail | State or federal prison | |
| 2000 | 112,500 | 70,000 | 20,400 | 22,100 | : | : | : |
| 2001 | 116,100 | 72,500 | 23,400 | 20,200 | : | : | : |
| 2002 | 122,800 | 72,600 | 29,300 | 20,900 | : | : | : |
| 2003 | 120,400 | 73,400 | 25,500 | 21,500 | : | : | : |
| 2004 | 130,400 | 74,400 | 34,400 | 21,600 | : | : | : |
| 2005 | 164,500 | 73,100 | 32,600 | 22,100 | 18,300 | 18,400 | : |
| 2006 | 169,900 | 77,900 | 33,900 | 21,700 | 20,700 | 15,700 | : |
| 2007 | 156,400 | 80,600 | 19,300 | 23,100 | 18,800 | 14,600 | : |
| 2008 | 178,500 | 83,500 | 23,800 | 32,400 | 19,300 | 15,600 | 3,900 |
| 2009 | 168,100 | 85,200 | 21,400 | 23,100 | 19,100 | 14,300 | 5,000 |
| 2010 | 170,300 | 83,400 | 21,300 | 21,500 | 21,400 | 14,400 | 8,300 |
| 2011 | 169,300 | 82,100 | 21,100 | 22,300 | 18,000 | 14,900 | 11,000 |
| 2012 | 168,400 | 83,600 | 21,200 | 21,700 | 18,500 | 10,700 | 12,700 |
| 2013 | 170,800 | 85,700 | 22,400 | 16,700 | 21,800 | 11,800 | 12,500 |
| 2014 | 176,100 | 81,800 | 23,500 | 24,600 | 21,800 | 11,600 | 12,900 |
| 2015 | 174,000 | 81,200 | 24,400 | 28,200 | 19,600 | 11,200 | 9,400 |

*Note:* Estimates were rounded to the nearest 100 and may not be comparable to previously published BJS reports due to updated information. Detail may not sum to total due to rounding.
: = Not collected or excluded from total correctional population.

# Table 7. Estimated Number and Rate of Persons Supervised by U.S. Adult Correctional Systems, by Jurisdiction and Correctional Status, 2015

(Number as of 12/31/15; rate per 100,000 adults.)

| Jurisdiction | Total correctional population | | | Community supervision | | | Incarcerated | | |
|---|---|---|---|---|---|---|---|---|---|
| | Total correctional population[1] | Correctional supervision rate, 18 years and over[2] | Correctional supervision rate, all ages[2] | Number on probation or parole[3] | Correctional supervision rate, 18 years and over[2] | Correctional supervision rate, all ages[2] | Number in prison or local jail[4] | Incarceration rate, 18 years and over[2] | Incarceration rate, all ages[2] |
| U.S. Total[5] | 6,712,600 | 2,700 | 2,080 | 4,650,900 | 1,870 | 1,441 | 2,145,100 | 860 | 660 |
| Federal[6] | 328,500 | 130 | 102 | 132,800 | 50 | 40 | 195,700 | 80 | 60 |
| State | 6,384,100 | 2,560 | 1,978 | 4,518,100 | 1,810 | 1,400 | 1,949,400 | 780 | 600 |
| Alabama | 107,500 | 2,850 | 2,210 | 64,600 | 1,710 | 1,330 | 42,900 | 1,140 | 880 |
| Alaska | 13,900 | 2,520 | 1,890 | 8,500 | 1,550 | 1,160 | 5,400 | 970 | 730 |
| Arizona | 136,300 | 2,600 | 1,980 | 83,300 | 1,590 | 1,210 | 54,900 | 1,050 | 800 |
| Arkansas | 73,200 | 3,210 | 2,450 | 51,500 | 2,260 | 1,720 | 24,000 | 1,050 | 800 |
| California | 550,600 | 1,820 | 1,400 | 349,600 | 1,160 | 890 | 201,000 | 670 | 510 |
| Colorado | 120,000 | 2,830 | 2,180 | 89,200 | 2,100 | 1,620 | 31,800 | 750 | 580 |
| Connecticut | 61,000 | 2,150 | 1,700 | 45,300 | 1,600 | 1,260 | 15,800 | 560 | 440 |
| Delaware | 22,700 | 3,050 | 2,390 | 16,100 | 2,150 | 1,690 | 6,700 | 890 | 700 |
| District of Columbia | 10,600 | 1,900 | 1,570 | 9,900 | 1,780 | 1,460 | 1,800 | 320 | 270 |
| Florida | 375,800 | 2,300 | 1,840 | 225,400 | 1,380 | 1,100 | 153,000 | 940 | 750 |
| Georgia[7] | 540,000 | 6,960 | 5,260 | 451,800 | 5,820 | 4,400 | 88,500 | 1,140 | 860 |
| Hawaii | 28,300 | 2,520 | 1,970 | 22,500 | 2,000 | 1,560 | 5,900 | 520 | 410 |
| Idaho | 48,700 | 3,960 | 2,930 | 37,800 | 3,070 | 2,270 | 10,900 | 890 | 660 |
| Illinois | 215,100 | 2,170 | 1,670 | 151,300 | 1,530 | 1,180 | 63,900 | 640 | 500 |
| Indiana | 166,000 | 3,280 | 2,500 | 122,500 | 2,420 | 1,850 | 43,500 | 860 | 650 |
| Iowa | 46,700 | 1,940 | 1,490 | 35,600 | 1,480 | 1,140 | 12,900 | 540 | 410 |
| Kansas | 37,400 | 1,700 | 1,280 | 20,900 | 950 | 720 | 16,600 | 760 | 570 |
| Kentucky | 103,700 | 3,030 | 2,340 | 70,600 | 2,060 | 1,590 | 33,800 | 990 | 760 |
| Louisiana | 114,600 | 3,210 | 2,450 | 71,900 | 2,010 | 1,530 | 49,000 | 1,370 | 1,050 |
| Maine | 10,100 | 940 | 760 | 6,700 | 630 | 510 | 4,000 | 370 | 300 |
| Maryland | 104,500 | 2,240 | 1,740 | 87,400 | 1,870 | 1,450 | 29,700 | 640 | 490 |
| Massachusetts | 86,900 | 1,600 | 1,270 | 66,900 | 1,230 | 980 | 20,100 | 370 | 300 |
| Michigan | 250,200 | 3,240 | 2,520 | 193,900 | 2,510 | 1,950 | 57,700 | 750 | 580 |
| Minnesota | 121,600 | 2,880 | 2,210 | 105,100 | 2,490 | 1,910 | 16,500 | 390 | 300 |
| Mississippi | 71,900 | 3,170 | 2,400 | 44,800 | 1,970 | 1,490 | 28,000 | 1,230 | 940 |
| Missouri | 106,000 | 2,250 | 1,740 | 62,600 | 1,330 | 1,030 | 43,400 | 920 | 710 |
| Montana | 14,700 | 1,810 | 1,410 | 9,700 | 1,200 | 940 | 5,600 | 690 | 540 |
| Nebraska | 22,300 | 1,560 | 1,170 | 13,700 | 950 | 720 | 8,600 | 600 | 450 |
| Nevada | 38,300 | 1,710 | 1,310 | 19,200 | 860 | 660 | 19,100 | 850 | 650 |
| New Hampshire | 10,900 | 1,020 | 820 | 6,300 | 590 | 470 | 4,600 | 430 | 340 |
| New Jersey | 183,500 | 2,630 | 2,040 | 151,300 | 2,170 | 1,690 | 33,900 | 490 | 380 |
| New Mexico | 25,000 | 1,570 | 1,200 | 16,800 | 1,050 | 800 | 15,100 | 950 | 720 |
| New York | 216,700 | 1,390 | 1,090 | 145,600 | 930 | 730 | 75,900 | 490 | 380 |
| North Carolina | 151,200 | 1,940 | 1,500 | 97,400 | 1,250 | 960 | 53,800 | 690 | 530 |
| North Dakota | 10,100 | 1,710 | 1,320 | 6,900 | 1,180 | 910 | 3,200 | 540 | 410 |
| Ohio | 331,500 | 3,680 | 2,850 | 262,000 | 2,910 | 2,250 | 70,700 | 790 | 610 |
| Oklahoma | 73,100 | 2,460 | 1,860 | 33,400 | 1,130 | 850 | 39,700 | 1,340 | 1,010 |
| Oregon | 82,900 | 2,600 | 2,040 | 61,900 | 1,940 | 1,530 | 21,000 | 660 | 520 |
| Pennsylvania | 374,200 | 3,690 | 2,920 | 296,200 | 2,920 | 2,310 | 83,900 | 830 | 650 |
| Rhode Island | 25,300 | 2,990 | 2,390 | 24,400 | 2,870 | 2,300 | 3,200 | 380 | 310 |
| South Carolina | 70,100 | 1,830 | 1,420 | 38,500 | 1,010 | 780 | 31,600 | 820 | 640 |
| South Dakota | 15,000 | 2,310 | 1,740 | 9,800 | 1,500 | 1,130 | 5,300 | 820 | 620 |
| Tennessee | 119,900 | 2,340 | 1,810 | 75,400 | 1,470 | 1,140 | 48,000 | 940 | 720 |
| Texas | 687,300 | 3,360 | 2,480 | 488,800 | 2,390 | 1,760 | 214,800 | 1,050 | 780 |
| Utah | 25,500 | 1,210 | 840 | 15,700 | 750 | 520 | 11,700 | 560 | 390 |

## Table 7. Estimated Number and Rate of Persons Supervised by U.S. Adult Correctional Systems, by Jurisdiction and Correctional Status, 2015—*Continued*

(Number as of 12/31/15; rate per 100,000 adults.)

| Jurisdiction | Total correctional population | | | Community supervision | | | Incarcerated | | |
|---|---|---|---|---|---|---|---|---|---|
| | Total correctional population[1] | Correctional supervision rate, 18 years and over[2] | Correctional supervision rate, all ages[2] | Number on probation or parole[3] | Correctional supervision rate, 18 years and over[2] | Correctional supervision rate, all ages[2] | Number in prison or local jail[4] | Incarceration rate, 18 years and over[2] | Incarceration rate, all ages[2] |
| Vermont ............................ | 8,000 | 1,580 | 1,280 | 6,300 | 1,240 | 1,000 | 1,800 | 350 | 280 |
| Virginia ............................. | 114,400 | 1,750 | 1,360 | 57,000 | 870 | 680 | 57,300 | 880 | 680 |
| Washington ...................... | 130,600 | 2,330 | 1,810 | 104,700 | 1,870 | 1,450 | 29,700 | 530 | 410 |
| West Virginia .................... | 20,100 | 1,370 | 1,090 | 10,100 | 690 | 550 | 10,100 | 690 | 550 |
| Wisconsin ......................... | 100,600 | 2,240 | 1,740 | 65,600 | 1,460 | 1,130 | 35,000 | 780 | 610 |
| Wyoming ........................... | 9,900 | 2,200 | 1,680 | 5,900 | 1,320 | 1,010 | 3,900 | 880 | 670 |

*Note:* Counts were rounded to the nearest 100, and rates were rounded to the nearest 10. Detail may not sum to total due to rounding and because offenders with multiple correctional statuses were excluded from totals. Counts include estimates for nonresponding jurisdictions
[1] Excludes, by jurisdiction, an estimated 81,200 prisoners held in jail, 28,200 probationers in prison, 24,400 probationers in jail, 19,600 parolees in jail, 11,200 parolees in prison, and 9,400 parolees on probation. See Table 6.
[2] Rates were computed using estimates of the U.S. adult resident population of persons age 18 or older and persons of all ages on January 1, 2016, within jurisdiction.
[3] Excludes, by jurisdiction, an estimated 9,400 parolees on probation. See Table 6.
[4] Excludes, by jurisdiction, an estimated 81,200 prisoners held in local jails. See Table 6.
[5] Total correctional population and total number in prison and jail include local jail counts that are based on December 31, 2015 in order to produce jurisdiction-level estimates. For this reason, the totals in this table differ from the national estimates presented in most other data in this report.
[6] Excludes about 11,000 inmates who were not held in locally operated jails but in facilities that were operated by the Federal Bureau of Prisons and functioned as jails.
[7] Total correctional population and community supervision population estimates include misdemeanant probation cases, not individuals, supervised by private companies and may overstate the number of offenders under supervision.

## Table 8. Persons Held in Custody in State or Federal Prisons or in Local Jails, 2000, 2010, and 2014–2015

(Number; percent.)

| Characteristic | Number of inmates | | | | Average annual change, 2000–2014 | Percent change, 2014–2015 |
|---|---|---|---|---|---|---|
| | 2000 | 2013 | 2014 | 2015 | | |
| **Inmates in Custody** ............................ | 1,938,500 | 2,266,500 | 2,217,900 | 2,168,400 | 1.0 | -2.2 |
| Federal prisoners[1] ............................... | 140,100 | 207,000 | 209,600 | 195,800 | 2.9 | -6.6 |
| Prisons .......................................... | 133,900 | 198,300 | 200,100 | 186,700 | 2.9 | -6.7 |
| Federal facilities ......................... | 124,500 | 173,100 | 169,500 | 160,700 | 2.2 | -5.2 |
| Privately operated facilities ...................... | 9,400 | 25,200 | 30,500 | 26,000 | 8.4 | -14.8 |
| Community corrections centers[2] ..................... | 6,100 | 8,600 | 9,500 | 9,200 | 3.2 | -3.2 |
| State prisoners ..................................... | 1,177,200 | 1,310,800 | 1,264,800 | 1,244,400 | 0.5 | -1.6 |
| State facilities[3] ............................... | 1,101,200 | 1,216,700 | 1,173,100 | 1,153,100 | 0.5 | -1.7 |
| Privately operated facilities ........................... | 76,100 | 94,100 | 91,700 | 91,300 | 1.3 | -0.4 |
| Local jails ....................................... | 621,100 | 748,700 | 744,600 | 728,200 | 1.3 | -2.2 |
| Incarceration rate[4] ............................... | 690 | 700 | 690 | 670 | ... | -2.9 |
| Adult incarceration rate[5] ............................. | 920 | 910 | 900 | 870 | -0.2 | -3.3 |

*Note:* Estimates may not be comparable to previously published BJS reports due to updated information. Counts were rounded to the nearest 100 and include estimates for nonresponding jurisdictions. Rates were rounded to the nearest 10. Detail may not sum to total due to rounding. Prison counts are for December 31; jail counts are for the last weekday in June. Total includes all inmates held in local jails, state or federal prisons, or privately operated facilities. It does not include inmates held in U.S. territories, military facilities, U.S. Immigration and Customs Enforcement facilities, in jails in Indian country, or juvenile facilities.
... = Less than 0.05 percent.
[1] After 2001, responsibility for sentenced prisoners from the District of Columbia was transferred to the Federal Bureau of Prisons.
[2] Nonsecure, privately operated community corrections centers.
[3] Excludes prisoners held in local jails in Georgia for 2010, 2014, and 2015 to avoid double counting.
[4] The total number in the custody of local jails, state or federal prisons, or privately operated facilities within the year per 100,000 U.S. residents of all ages.
[5] The total number in custody per 100,000 U.S. residents age 18 or older.

## Table 9. Number of Persons Incarcerated by Other Adult Correctional Systems, 2000, 2010, and 2014–2015

(Number; percent.)

| Characteristic | Number of inmates | | | | Average annual change, 2000–2014 | Percent change, 2014–2015 |
|---|---|---|---|---|---|---|
| | 2000 | 2010 | 2014 | 2015 | | |
| **Other Adult Correctional Systems**............ | 20,400 | 17,600 | 17,800 | 16,800 | -0.9 | -5.7 |
| Territorial prisons[1] .......................................... | 16,200 | 13,800 | 14,000 | 12,900 | -1.0 | -8.1 |
| Military facilties[2]............................................. | 2,400 | 1,400 | 1,400 | 1,400 | -3.9 | -0.8 |
| Jails in Indian country[3].................................... | 1,800 | 2,400 | 2,400 | 2,500 | 2.1 | 5.5 |

Note: Estimates were rounded to the nearest 100 and are for December 31. Total excludes persons held in local jails, under the jurisdiction of state or federal prisons, in U.S. Immigration and Customs Enforcement facilities, or in juvenile facilities.
[1] The 2014 and 2015 totals include population counts that were estimated for some territories due to nonresponse. See *Prisoners in 2015* (NCJ 250229, BJS web, December 2016) for detailed statistics of this population.
[2] See *Prisoners in 2015* (NCJ 250229, BJS web, December 2016) for detailed statistics of this population.
[3] Population counts are for the last weekday in June. See *Jails in Indian Country, 2015* (NCJ 250117, BJS web, November 2016) for detailed statistics of this population.

# METHODOLOGY

## About the Data

The statistics presented in this chapter include data from *Correctional Populations in the United States, 2015*, which itself relies on various Bureau of Justice Statistics (BJS) data collections, each relying on the voluntary participation of federal, state, and local respondents. This report presents statistics on offenders supervised by adult correctional systems in the United States at yearend 2015, including offenders supervised in the community on probation or parole and those incarcerated in prison or local jail. The report provides the size and change in the total correctional population during 2015. It details the slowing rate of decline in the population and the downward trend in the correctional supervision rate. It also examines the impact of changes in the community supervision and incarcerated populations on the total correctional population in recent years. Other information comprises correctional populations, including prisoners under military jurisdiction, inmates held by correctional authorities in the U.S. territories and commonwealths, and jail inmates held in Indian country facilities, and estimates of the total correctional population by jurisdiction and correctional status.

For more information about any of the following data collections, or to see the full report, please see https://www.bjs.gov/content/pub/pdf/cpus15.pdf and http://www.bjs.gov/index.cfm?ty=pbdetail&iid=5870.

## Annual Probation Survey and Annual Parole Survey

Collect administrative data from probation and parole agencies in the U.S. Data collected include the total number of adults on state and federal probation and parole on January 1 and December 31 of each year, the number of adults entering and exiting probation and parole supervision each year, and the characteristics of adults under the supervision of probation and parole agencies. Published data include both national and state-level data. The surveys cover all 50 states, the federal system, and the District of Columbia. They began in 1980 and are conducted annually (except for the year 1991). Probation data are also available dating back to 1977. Through BJS's National Probation Reports, probation data were collected from 1977 to 1979. Parole data are available dating back to 1975. The parole data from 1975 to 1979 were collected through BJS's Uniform Parole Reports.

## Annual Survey of Jails

Collects data from a nationally representative sample of local jails on jail inmate populations, jail capacity, and related information. The collection began in 1982 and has been conducted annually, except for years 1983, 1988, 1993, 1999, and 2005, during which a complete census of U.S. local jails was conducted.

## Census of Jails

The Census of Jail Facilities is part of a series of data collections that study the nation's local jails. To reduce respondent burden and improve data quality and timeliness, the original jail census was split into two parts in 2005: the Census of Jail Inmates (2005) and the Census of Jail Facilities (2006). In 2013, BJS expanded the 2013 Deaths in Custody Reporting Program—Annual Summary on Inmates under Jail Jurisdiction to act as the 2013 Census of Jails. The Census of Jail Facilities collects information on each facility, including admissions and releases, court orders, programs that offer alternatives to incarceration, counts of inmates on hold for other jurisdictions, use of space and crowding, staffing, inmate work assignments, and education and counseling programs. The census provides the sampling frame for the nationwide Survey of Inmates in Local Jails (SILJ) and the Annual Survey of Jails (ASJ).

## Deaths in Custody Reporting Program (DCRP)

Collects inmate death records from each of the nation's 50 state prison systems and approximately 2,800 local jail jurisdictions. In addition, this program collects records of all deaths occurring during the process of arrest. Data are collected directly from state and local law enforcement agencies. Due to concerns regarding data quality and coverage issues, BJS temporarily suspended the arrest-related death portion (ARD) of the DCRP in 2014.

Death records include information on decedent personal characteristics (age, race or Hispanic origin, and sex), decedent criminal background (legal status, offense type, and time served), and the death itself (date, time, location, and cause of death, as well as information on the autopsy and medical treatment provided for any illness or disease).

Data collections covering these populations were developed in annual phases: Annual collection of individual death records from local jail facilities began in 2000, followed by a separate collection for state prison facilities in 2001. Collection of state juvenile correctional agencies began in 2002 but was discontinued in 2006, and collection of arrest-related death records began in 2003. Datasets are produced in an annual format.

## National Prisoner Statistics (NPS) Program

Produces annual national and state-level data on the number of prisoners in state and federal prison facilities. Aggregate data are collected on race and sex of prison inmates, inmates held in private facilities and local jails, system capacity, noncitizens, and persons under age 18. Findings are released in the Prisoners series. Data are from the 50 state departments of corrections, the Federal Bureau of Prisons, and until 2001, from the District of Columbia (after 2001, felons sentenced under the District of Columbia criminal code were housed in federal facilities).

## Survey of Jails in Indian Country

Collects detailed information on confinement facilities, detention centers, jails, and other facilities operated by tribal authorities or the Bureau of Indian Affairs (BIA). Information is gathered on inmate counts, movements, facility operations, and staff. In selected years (1998, 2004, 2007, and 2011), additional information is collected on facility programs and services, such as medical assessments and mental health screening procedures, inmate work assignments, counseling, and educational programs.

## Additional Information

### Counts Adjusted for Offenders with Multiple Correctional Statuses

Offenders under correctional supervision may have multiple correctional statuses for several reasons. For example, probation and parole agencies may not always be notified immediately of new arrests, jail admissions, or prison admissions; absconders included in a probation or parole agency's population in one jurisdiction may actually be incarcerated in another jurisdiction; persons may be admitted to jail or prison before formal revocation hearings and potential discharge by a probation or parole agency; and persons may be serving separate probation and parole sentences concurrently. In addition, state and federal prisons may hold inmates in county facilities or local jails to reduce crowding in their prisons.

In 1998, through the ASPP, BJS began collecting data on the number of probationers and parolees with multiple correctional statuses and has since expanded on the information collected. In 1999, through the NPS, BJS began collecting data on the number of prisoners under the jurisdiction of state or federal prisons that were held in county facilities or local jails. Table 6 includes adjustments that were made to the total correctional population, total community supervision population, and total incarcerated population estimates presented in this report to exclude offenders with multiple correctional statuses to avoid double counting offenders. The estimates from the ASPP are based on data reported by the probation and parole agencies that were able to provide the information within the specific reporting year. Because some probation and parole agencies did not provide these data each year, the numbers may underestimate the total number of offenders who had multiple correctional statuses between 2000 and 2013. Due to these adjustments, the sum of correctional statuses in Tables 1, 2, 3, 4, 5 and appendix table 1 will not equal the total correctional population. In addition, the sum of the probation and parole populations for 2008 through 2013 will not yield the total community supervision population because the total was adjusted for parolees who were also on probation. In addition, the sum of the prison and local jail populations for 2000 through 2013 will not equal the total incarcerated population because prisoners held in local jails were excluded from the total.

### Adjustments for Nonresponse

Probation, parole, jail, and prison population counts were adjusted to account for nonresponse across the data collections. The methods varied and depended on the type of collection, type of respondent, and availability of information. The local jail population counts that were collected through the 2013 Census of Jails to produce the jurisdiction-level estimates that are reported in appendix table 1 were adjusted for unit and item nonresponse. Nonresponse in the 2013 jail census was minimal as the unit response rate was 92.4% and the item response rate for the December 31, 2013, population total was 99.7%. For jails that did not participate in the census or were unable to provide the 2013 yearend count, a sequential hot deck imputation procedure was used to impute values.

### Estimates of Males and Females under Correctional Supervision

The number of males and the number of females on probation or parole were adjusted to account for nonresponse using a ratio adjustment method. For jurisdictions that did not provide data on sex for a portion of their population, the sex distribution of the known portion of the population was used to impute for the unknown portion because it was assumed that the distributions were the same. For states that were unable to provide any data on sex, the state national average was used to impute the number of males and females supervised in those states. Adjusted jurisdiction totals were then aggregated to produce national estimates of the number of males and females on probation and parole. The number of prisoners by sex represents the reported number of males and females under the jurisdiction of state or federal prisons within the reference year. The number of local jail inmates by sex represents the adjusted number of males and females in the custody of local jails within the reference year.

## Definitions

**Adult**—persons subject to the jurisdiction of an adult criminal court or correctional agency. Adults are age 18 or older in most jurisdictions. Persons age 17 or younger who were prosecuted in criminal court as if they were adults are considered adults, but persons age 17 or younger who were under the jurisdiction of a juvenile court or agency are excluded.

**Annual change**—change in a population between two consecutive years.

**Average annual change**—average (mean) annual change in a population across a specific period.

**Community supervision population**—estimated number of persons living in the community while supervised on probation or parole.

**Community supervision rate**—estimated number of persons supervised in the community on probation or parole per 100,000 U.S. residents of all ages (i.e., total community supervision rate) or U.S. residents age 18 or older (i.e., adult community supervision rate).

**Correctional population**—estimated number of persons living in the community while supervised on probation or parole and persons under the jurisdiction of state or federal prisons or held in local jails.

**Correctional supervision rate**—estimated number of persons supervised in the community on probation or parole and persons under the jurisdiction of state or federal prisons or held in local jails per 100,000 U.S. residents of all ages (i.e., total correctional supervision rate) or U.S. residents age 18 or older (i.e., adult correctional supervision rate).

**Imprisonment rate**—estimated number of prisoners under state or federal jurisdiction sentenced to more than 1 year per 100,000 U.S. residents of all ages (i.e., total imprisonment rate) or U.S. residents age 18 or older (i.e., adult imprisonment rate). This statistic does not appear in this report; see *Prisoners in 2015* (NCJ 250229, BJS web, December 2016).

**Incarcerated population**—estimated number of persons under the jurisdiction of state or federal prisons or held in local jails.

**Incarceration rate**—estimated number of persons under the jurisdiction of state or federal prisons or held in local jails per 100,000 U.S. residents of all ages (i.e., total incarceration rate) or U.S. residents age 18 or older (i.e., adult incarceration rate).

**Indian country jail population**—estimated number of inmates held in correctional facilities operated by tribal authorities or the Bureau of Indian Affairs (BIA), U.S. Department of the Interior. These facilities include confinement facilities, detention centers, jails, and other facilities operated by tribal authorities or the BIA.

**Local jail population**—estimated number of inmates held in a confinement facility usually administered by a local law enforcement agency that is intended for adults, but sometimes holds juveniles, for confinement before and after adjudication. These facilities include jails and city or county correctional centers; special jail facilities, such as medical treatment or release centers; halfway houses; work farms; and temporary holding or lockup facilities that are part of the jail's combined function. Inmates sentenced to jail facilities usually have a sentence of 1 year or less.

**Military prison population**—estimated number of service personnel incarcerated under the jurisdiction of U.S. military correctional authorities. (This estimate is presented in appendix table 5.)

**Parole population**—estimated number of persons who are on conditional release in the community following a prison term while under the control, supervision, or care of a correctional agency. Violations of the conditions of supervision during this period may result in a new sentence to confinement or a return to confinement for a technical violation. This population includes parolees released through discretionary (i.e., parole board decision) or mandatory (i.e., provisions of a statute) supervised release from prison, those released through other types of post-custody conditional supervision, and those sentenced to a term of supervised release.

**Prison population**—estimated number of prisoners incarcerated in a long-term confinement facility, run by a state or the federal government, which typically holds felons and offenders with sentences of more than 1 year, although sentence length may vary by jurisdiction.

*Prison jurisdiction population*—estimated number of prisoners under the jurisdiction or legal authority of state or federal correctional officials, regardless of where the prisoner is held. This population represents BJS's official measure of the prison population and includes prisoners held in prisons, penitentiaries, correctional facilities, halfway houses, boot camps, farms, training or treatment centers, and hospitals. Counts also include prisoners who were temporarily absent (fewer than 30 days), in court or on work release, housed in privately operated facilities, local jails, or other state or federal facilities, and serving concurrent sentences for more than one correctional authority.

*Prison custody population*—estimated number of prisoners held in the physical custody of state or federal prisons regardless of sentence length or the authority having jurisdiction. This population includes prisoners housed for other correctional facilities but excludes those in the custody of local jails, those held in other jurisdictions, those out to court, and those in transit from one jurisdiction of legal authority to the custody of a confinement facility outside that jurisdiction.

**Probation population**—estimated number of persons who are on a court-ordered period of supervision in the community while under the control, supervision, or care of a correctional agency. The probation conditions form a contract with the court by which the person must abide in order to remain in the community, generally in lieu of incarceration. In some cases, probation can be a combined sentence of incarceration followed by a period of community supervision. Often, probation entails monitoring or surveillance by a correctional agency. In some instances, probation may not involve any reporting requirements.

**Territorial prison population**—estimated number of prisoners in the custody of correctional facilities operated by departments of corrections in U.S. territories (American Samoa, Guam, and the U.S. Virgin Islands) and U.S. commonwealths (Northern Mariana Islands and Puerto Rico).

PART 2.

# Crime in the United States, 2015

# HIGHLIGHTS

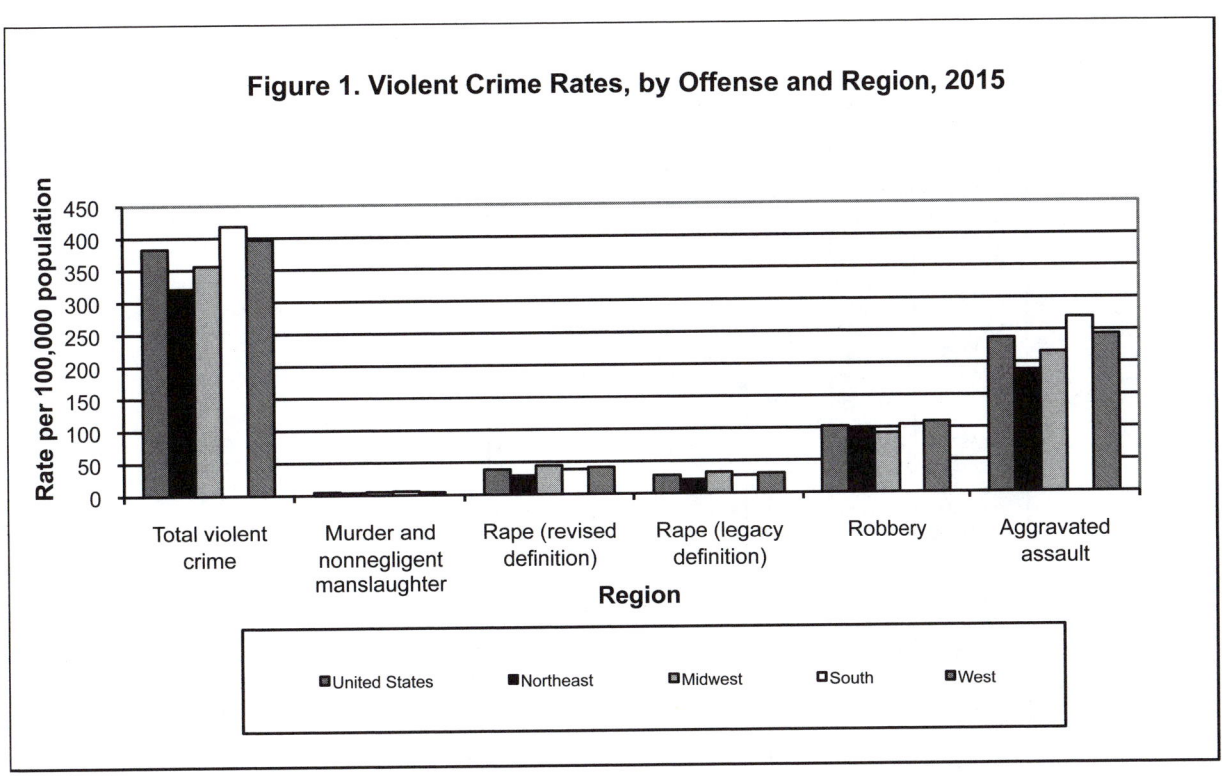

Figure 1. Violent Crime Rates, by Offense and Region, 2015

- In 2015, an estimated 1,197,704 violent crimes occurred nationwide, an increase of nearly 4 percent from the 2014 estimate. Aggravated assaults accounted for 63.8 percent of violent crimes reported to law enforcement in 2015.

- There were an estimated 7,993,631 property crime offenses in the nation in 2015, a 2.6 percent decline from 2014. Of all property crimes in 2014, larceny-theft accounted for 71.4 percent.

- Approximately 46.0 percent of violent crimes and 19.4 percent of property crimes were cleared by arrest or exceptional means.

- Nationwide, law enforcement made an estimated 10,797,088 arrests in 2015. Of these arrests, 505,681 were for violent crimes, and 1,463,213 were for property crimes. The highest number of arrests were for drug abuse violations (estimated at 1,488,707 arrests).

- A total of 13,160 law enforcement agencies provided data on the number of full-time law enforcement employees (sworn officers and civilian personnel) on staff in 2015; nationwide, the rate of sworn officers was 2.3 per 1,000 inhabitants, the same as in 2014.

- White males accounted for 30.6 percent of all reported murder victims in 2015, while White females comprised 12.9 percent of the total. Black males and females accounted for 45.4 percent and 6.9 percent of murder victims, respectively.

- Approximately 39.8 percent of robberies took place on the street or highway, representing the largest number of robberies in a location category.

- Cities with 250,000 to 499,999 inhabitants had the highest arson rate in 2015 (28.5 incidents per 100,000 inhabitants), while nonmetropolitan counties and suburban areas shared the lowest rate (10.1 incidents per 100,000 inhabitants.)

# Table 1. Crime in the United States, by Volume and Rate Per 100,000 Inhabitants, 1996–2015

(Number, rate per 100,000 population.)

| Year | Population[1] | Violent crime[2] Number | Rate | Murder and nonnegligent manslaughter Number | Rate | Rape (revised definition)[3] Number | Rate | Rape (legacy definition)[4] Number | Rate | Robbery Number | Rate | Aggravated assault Number | Rate |
|---|---|---|---|---|---|---|---|---|---|---|---|---|---|
| 1996 | 265,228,572 | 1,688,540 | 636.6 | 19,645 | 7.4 | X | X | 96,252 | 36.3 | 535,594 | 201.9 | 1,037,049 | 391.0 |
| 1997 | 267,783,607 | 1,636,096 | 611.0 | 18,208 | 6.8 | X | X | 96,153 | 35.9 | 498,534 | 186.2 | 1,023,201 | 382.1 |
| 1998 | 270,248,003 | 1,533,887 | 567.6 | 16,974 | 6.3 | X | X | 93,144 | 34.5 | 447,186 | 165.5 | 976,583 | 361.4 |
| 1999 | 272,690,813 | 1,426,044 | 523.0 | 15,522 | 5.7 | X | X | 89,411 | 32.8 | 409,371 | 150.1 | 911,740 | 334.3 |
| 2000 | 281,421,906 | 1,425,486 | 506.5 | 15,586 | 5.5 | X | X | 90,178 | 32.0 | 408,016 | 145.0 | 911,706 | 324.0 |
| 2001 [5] | 285,317,559 | 1,439,480 | 504.5 | 16,037 | 5.6 | X | X | 90,863 | 31.8 | 423,557 | 148.5 | 909,023 | 318.6 |
| 2002 | 287,973,924 | 1,423,677 | 494.4 | 16,229 | 5.6 | X | X | 95,235 | 33.1 | 420,806 | 146.1 | 891,407 | 309.5 |
| 2003 | 290,788,976 | 1,383,676 | 475.8 | 16,528 | 5.7 | X | X | 93,883 | 32.3 | 414,235 | 142.5 | 859,030 | 295.4 |
| 2004 | 293,656,842 | 1,360,088 | 463.2 | 16,148 | 5.5 | X | X | 95,089 | 32.4 | 401,470 | 136.7 | 847,381 | 288.6 |
| 2005 | 296,507,061 | 1,390,745 | 469.0 | 16,740 | 5.6 | X | X | 94,347 | 31.8 | 417,438 | 140.8 | 862,220 | 290.8 |
| 2006 | 299,398,484 | 1,435,123 | 479.3 | 17,309 | 5.8 | X | X | 94,472 | 31.6 | 449,246 | 150.0 | 874,096 | 292.0 |
| 2007 | 301,621,157 | 1,422,970 | 471.8 | 17,128 | 5.7 | X | X | 92,160 | 30.6 | 447,324 | 148.3 | 866,358 | 287.2 |
| 2008 | 304,059,724 | 1,394,461 | 458.6 | 16,465 | 5.4 | X | X | 90,750 | 29.8 | 443,563 | 145.9 | 843,683 | 277.5 |
| 2009 | 307,006,550 | 1,325,896 | 431.9 | 15,399 | 5.0 | X | X | 89,241 | 29.1 | 408,742 | 133.1 | 812,514 | 264.7 |
| 2010 | 309,330,219 | 1,251,248 | 404.5 | 14,722 | 4.8 | X | X | 85,593 | 27.7 | 369,089 | 119.3 | 781,844 | 252.8 |
| 2011 | 311,587,816 | 1,206,005 | 387.1 | 14,661 | 4.7 | X | X | 84,175 | 27.0 | 354,746 | 113.9 | 752,423 | 241.5 |
| 2012 | 313,873,685 | 1,217,057 | 387.8 | 14,856 | 4.7 | X | X | 85,141 | 27.1 | 355,051 | 113.1 | 762,009 | 242.8 |
| 2013 | 316,497,531 | 1,168,298 | 369.1 | 14,319 | 4.5 | 113,695 | 35.9 | 82,109 | 25.9 | 345,093 | 109.0 | 726,777 | 229.6 |
| 2014 [6] | 318,907,401 | 1,153,022 | 361.6 | 14,164 | 4.4 | 118,027 | 37.0 | 84,864 | 26.6 | 322,905 | 101.3 | 731,089 | 229.2 |
| 2015 | 321,418,820 | 1,197,704 | 372.6 | 15,696 | 4.9 | 124,047 | 38.6 | 90,185 | 28.1 | 327,374 | 101.9 | 764,449 | 237.8 |

| Year | Property crime Number | Rate | Burglary Number | Rate | Larceny-theft Number | Rate | Motor vehicle theft Number | Rate |
|---|---|---|---|---|---|---|---|---|
| 1996 | 11,805,323 | 4,451.0 | 2,506,400 | 945.0 | 7,904,685 | 2,980.3 | 1,394,238 | 525.7 |
| 1997 | 11,558,475 | 4,316.3 | 2,460,526 | 918.8 | 7,743,760 | 2,891.8 | 1,354,189 | 505.7 |
| 1998 | 10,951,827 | 4,052.5 | 2,332,735 | 863.2 | 7,376,311 | 2,729.5 | 1,242,781 | 459.9 |
| 1999 | 10,208,334 | 3,743.6 | 2,100,739 | 770.4 | 6,955,520 | 2,550.7 | 1,152,075 | 422.5 |
| 2000 | 10,182,584 | 3,618.3 | 2,050,992 | 728.8 | 6,971,590 | 2,477.3 | 1,160,002 | 412.2 |
| 2001 [5] | 10,437,189 | 3,658.1 | 2,116,531 | 741.8 | 7,092,267 | 2,485.7 | 1,228,391 | 430.5 |
| 2002 | 10,455,277 | 3,630.6 | 2,151,252 | 747.0 | 7,057,379 | 2,450.7 | 1,246,646 | 432.9 |
| 2003 | 10,442,862 | 3,591.2 | 2,154,834 | 741.0 | 7,026,802 | 2,416.5 | 1,261,226 | 433.7 |
| 2004 | 10,319,386 | 3,514.1 | 2,144,446 | 730.3 | 6,937,089 | 2,362.3 | 1,237,851 | 421.5 |
| 2005 | 10,174,754 | 3,431.5 | 2,155,448 | 726.9 | 6,783,447 | 2,287.8 | 1,235,859 | 416.8 |
| 2006 | 10,019,601 | 3,346.6 | 2,194,993 | 733.1 | 6,626,363 | 2,213.2 | 1,198,245 | 400.2 |
| 2007 | 9,882,212 | 3,276.4 | 2,190,198 | 726.1 | 6,591,542 | 2,185.4 | 1,100,472 | 364.9 |
| 2008 | 9,774,152 | 3,214.6 | 2,228,887 | 733.0 | 6,586,206 | 2,166.1 | 959,059 | 315.4 |
| 2009 | 9,337,060 | 3,041.3 | 2,203,313 | 717.7 | 6,338,095 | 2,064.5 | 795,652 | 259.2 |
| 2010 | 9,112,625 | 2,945.9 | 2,168,459 | 701.0 | 6,204,601 | 2,005.8 | 739,565 | 239.1 |
| 2011 | 9,052,743 | 2,905.4 | 2,185,140 | 701.3 | 6,151,095 | 1,974.1 | 716,508 | 230.0 |
| 2012 | 9,001,992 | 2,868.0 | 2,109,932 | 672.2 | 6,168,874 | 1,965.4 | 723,186 | 230.4 |
| 2013 | 8,651,892 | 2,733.6 | 1,932,139 | 610.5 | 6,019,465 | 1,901.9 | 700,288 | 221.3 |
| 2014 [6] | 8,209,010 | 2,574.1 | 1,713,153 | 537.2 | 5,809,054 | 1,821.5 | 686,803 | 215.4 |
| 2015 | 7,993,631 | 2,487.0 | 1,579,527 | 491.4 | 5,706,346 | 1,775.4 | 707,758 | 220.2 |

Note: Although arson data are included in the trend and clearance tables, sufficient data are not available to estimate totals for this offense. Therefore, no arson data are published in this table.
X = Not applicable.
[1] Populations are U.S. Census Bureau provisional estimates as of July 1 for each year except 2000 and 2010, which are decennial census counts.
[2] The violent crime figures include the offenses of murder, rape (legacy definition), robbery, and aggravated assault.
[3] The figures shown in this column for the offense of rape were estimated using the revised UCR definition of rape.
[4] The figures shown in this column for the offense of rape were estimated using the legacy UCR definition of rape.
[5] The murder and nonnegligent homicides that occurred as a result of the events of September 11, 2001, are not included in this table.
[6] The crime figures have been adjusted.

## Table 1A. Crime in the United States, Percent Change in Volume and Rate Per 100,000 Inhabitants for 2 Years, 5 Years, and 10 Years, 2006–2015

(Percent change.)

| Year | Violent crime[1] | | Murder and nonnegligent manslaughter | | Rape (revised definition)[2] | | Rape (legacy definition)[3] | | Robbery | | Aggravated assault | |
|---|---|---|---|---|---|---|---|---|---|---|---|---|
| | Number | Rate | Number | Rate | Number | Rate | Number | Rate | Number | Rate | Number | Rate |
| 2006–2015.................................. | -16.5 | -22.3 | -9.3 | -15.5 | X | X | -4.5 | -11.1 | -27.1 | -32.1 | -12.5 | -18.5 |
| 2011–2015.................................. | -0.7 | -3.7 | +7.1 | +3.8 | X | X | +7.1 | +3.9 | -7.7 | -10.5 | +1.6 | -1.5 |
| 2014–2015.................................. | +3.9 | +3.1 | +10.8 | +10.0 | +5.1 | +4.3 | +6.3 | +5.4 | +1.4 | +0.6 | +4.6 | +3.7 |

X = Not applicable.
[1] The violent crime figures include the offenses of murder, rape (legacy definition), robbery, and aggravated assault.
[2] The figures shown in this column for the offense of rape were estimated using the revised UCR definition of rape.
[3] The figures shown in this column for the offense of rape were estimated using the legacy UCR definition of rape.

| Year | Property crime | | Burglary | | Larceny-theft | | Motor vehicle theft | |
|---|---|---|---|---|---|---|---|---|
| | Number | Rate | Number | Rate | Number | Rate | Number | Rate |
| 2006–2015.................................. | -20.2 | -25.7 | -28.0 | -33.0 | -13.9 | -19.8 | -40.9 | -45.0 |
| 2011–2015.................................. | -11.7 | -14.4 | -27.7 | -29.9 | -7.2 | -10.1 | -1.2 | -4.2 |
| 2014–2015.................................. | -2.6 | -3.4 | -7.8 | -8.5 | -1.8 | -2.5 | +3.1 | +2.2 |

X = Not applicable.
[1] The violent crime figures include the offenses of murder, rape (legacy definition), robbery, and aggravated assault.
[2] The figures shown in this column for the offense of rape were estimated using the revised UCR definition of rape.
[3] The figures shown in this column for the offense of rape were estimated using the legacy UCR definition of rape.

# Table 2. Crime in the United States, by Community Type, 2015

(Number, percent, rate per 100,000 population.)

| Area | Population[1] | Violent crime[2] | Murder and nonnegligent manslaughter | Rape (revised definition)[3] | Rape (legacy definition)[4] | Robbery | Aggravated assault | Property crime | Burglary | Larceny-theft | Motor vehicle theft |
|---|---|---|---|---|---|---|---|---|---|---|---|
| **United States**................................... | 321,418,820 | 1,231,566 | 15,696 | 124,047 | 90,185 | 327,374 | 764,449 | 7,993,631 | 1,579,527 | 5,706,346 | 707,758 |
| Rate per 100,000 inhabitants................. | X | 383.2 | 4.9 | 38.6 | 28.1 | 101.9 | 237.8 | 2,487.0 | 491.4 | 1,775.4 | 220.2 |
| **Metropolitan Statistical Areas ............** | 274,716,919 | | | | | | | | | | |
| Area actually reporting[5].......................... | 98.6 | 1,095,242 | 13,830 | 103,341 | 75,565 | 312,946 | 665,125 | 6,966,601 | 1,334,212 | 4,980,777 | 651,612 |
| Estimated total ..................................... | 100.0 | 1,103,959 | 13,910 | 104,470 | 76,421 | 314,790 | 670,789 | 7,048,081 | 1,349,496 | 5,042,063 | 656,522 |
| Rate per 100,000 inhabitants................. | X | 401.9 | 5.1 | 38.0 | 27.8 | 114.6 | 244.2 | 2,565.6 | 491.2 | 1,835.4 | 239.0 |
| **Cities Outside Metropolitan Areas ......** | 19,048,921 | | | | | | | | | | |
| Area actually reporting[5].......................... | 91.6 | 68,617 | 734 | 9,272 | 6,837 | 8,428 | 50,183 | 543,624 | 107,475 | 412,226 | 23,923 |
| Estimated total ..................................... | 100.0 | 73,978 | 826 | 10,005 | 7,427 | 9,353 | 53,794 | 591,882 | 118,144 | 448,026 | 25,712 |
| Rate per 100,000 inhabitants................. | X | 388.4 | 4.3 | 52.5 | 39.0 | 49.1 | 282.4 | 3,107.2 | 620.2 | 2,352.0 | 135.0 |
| **Nonmetropolitan Counties .................** | 27,652,980 | | | | | | | | | | |
| Area actually reporting[5].......................... | 92.6 | 50,430 | 894 | 8,982 | 5,962 | 2,988 | 37,566 | 332,558 | 104,116 | 204,089 | 24,353 |
| Estimated total ..................................... | 100.0 | 53,629 | 960 | 9,572 | 6,337 | 3,231 | 39,866 | 353,668 | 111,887 | 216,257 | 25,524 |
| Rate per 100,000 inhabitants................. | X | 193.9 | 3.5 | 34.6 | 22.9 | 11.7 | 144.2 | 1,279.0 | 404.6 | 782.0 | 92.3 |

Note: Although arson data are included in the trend and clearance tables, sufficient data are not available to estimate totals for this offense. Therefore, no arson data are published in this table.
X = Not applicable.
[1] Population figures are U.S. Census Bureau provisional estimates as of July 1, 2015.
[2] The violent crime figures include the offenses of murder, rape (revised definition), robbery, and aggravated assault.
[3] The figures shown in this column for the offense of rape were estimated using the revised Uniform Crime Reporting (UCR) definition of rape. See chapter notes for more detail.
[4] The figures shown in this column for the offense of rape were estimated using the legacy Uniform Crime Reporting (UCR) definition of rape. See chapter notes for more detail.
[5] The percentage reported under "Area actually reporting" is based upon the population covered by agencies providing 3 months or more of crime reports to the FBI.

## Table 3. Crime in the United States, Population and Offense Distribution, by Region, 2015

(Percent distribution.)

| Region | Population | Violent crime | Murder and nonnegligent manslaughter | Rape (revised definition)[1] | Rape (legacy definition)[2] | Robbery | Aggravated assault | Property crime | Burglary | Larceny-theft | Motor vehicle theft |
|---|---|---|---|---|---|---|---|---|---|---|---|
| United States[3]..................... | 100.0 | 100.0 | 100.0 | 100.0 | 100.0 | 100.0 | 100.0 | 100.0 | 100.0 | 100.0 | 100.0 |
| Northeast............................ | 17.5 | 14.7 | 12.4 | 13.1 | 13.3 | 17.2 | 13.9 | 11.9 | 10.0 | 12.9 | 8.0 |
| Midwest .............................. | 21.1 | 19.6 | 21.5 | 24.2 | 24.3 | 18.9 | 19.2 | 19.3 | 19.4 | 19.6 | 16.7 |
| South................................... | 37.7 | 41.2 | 45.9 | 37.4 | 36.8 | 38.6 | 42.8 | 42.2 | 45.2 | 42.2 | 35.3 |
| West.................................... | 23.7 | 24.5 | 20.2 | 25.3 | 25.6 | 25.3 | 24.2 | 26.6 | 25.4 | 25.3 | 39.9 |

*Note:* Although arson data are included in the trend and clearance tables, sufficient data are not available to estimate totals for this offense. Therefore, no arson data are published in this table.

[1] The figures shown in this column for the offense of rape were estimated using the revised Uniform Crime Reporting (UCR) definition of rape. See chapter notes for more detail.
[2] The figures shown in this column for the offense of rape were estimated using the legacy Uniform Crime Reporting (UCR) definition of rape. See chapter notes for more detail.
[3] Because of rounding, the percentages may not add to 100.0.

# Table 4. Crime,[1] by Region, Geographic Division, and State, 2014–2015

(Number, rate per 100,000 population, percent.)

| Area | Population[2] | Violent crime[3] Number | Violent crime[3] Rate | Murder and nonnegligent manslaughter Number | Murder and nonnegligent manslaughter Rate | Rape (revised definition)[4] Number | Rape (revised definition)[4] Rate | Rape (legacy definition)[5] Number | Rape (legacy definition)[5] Rate |
|---|---|---|---|---|---|---|---|---|---|
| **United States[6,7,8,9]** .................... | | | | | | | | | |
| 2014................................ | 318,907,401 | 1,186,185 | 372.0 | 14,164 | 4.4 | 118,027 | 37.0 | 84,864 | 26.6 |
| 2015................................ | 321,418,820 | 1,231,566 | 383.2 | 15,696 | 4.9 | 124,047 | 38.6 | 90,185 | 28.1 |
| Percent change .................. | 0.8 | +3.8 | +3.0 | +10.8 | +10.0 | +5.1 | +4.3 | +6.3 | +5.4 |
| **Northeast[6]**................................ | | | | | | | | | |
| 2014................................ | 56,171,281 | 182,139 | 324.3 | 1,873 | 3.3 | 15,703 | 28.0 | 11,391 | 20.3 |
| 2015................................ | 56,283,891 | 180,472 | 320.6 | 1,951 | 3.5 | 16,296 | 29.0 | 11,994 | 21.3 |
| Percent change .................. | 0.2 | -0.9 | -1.1 | +4.2 | +4.0 | +3.8 | +3.6 | +5.3 | +5.1 |
| **New England[6]** ......................... | | | | | | | | | |
| 2014................................ | 14,689,812 | 42,550 | 289.7 | 295 | 2.0 | 4,559 | 31.0 | 3,337 | 22.7 |
| 2015................................ | 14,727,584 | 42,089 | 285.8 | 321 | 2.2 | 4,544 | 30.9 | 3,464 | 23.5 |
| Percent change .................. | 0.3 | -1.1 | -1.3 | +8.8 | +8.5 | -0.3 | -0.6 | +3.8 | +3.5 |
| Connecticut ......................... | | | | | | | | | |
| 2014................................ | 3,594,762 | 8,575 | 238.5 | 89 | 2.5 | 794 | 22.1 | 579 | 16.1 |
| 2015................................ | 3,590,886 | 7,845 | 218.5 | 117 | 3.3 | 773 | 21.5 | 582 | 16.2 |
| Percent change .................. | -0.1 | -8.5 | -8.4 | +31.5 | +31.6 | -2.6 | -2.5 | +0.5 | +0.6 |
| Maine[6] ................................ | | | | | | | | | |
| 2014................................ | 1,330,256 | 1,698 | 127.6 | 21 | 1.6 | 484 | 36.4 | 346 | 26.0 |
| 2015................................ | 1,329,328 | 1,729 | 130.1 | 23 | 1.7 | 474 | 35.7 | 354 | 26.6 |
| Percent change .................. | -0.1 | +1.8 | +1.9 | +9.5 | +9.6 | -2.1 | -2.0 | +2.3 | +2.4 |
| Massachusetts | | | | | | | | | |
| 2014................................ | 6,755,124 | 26,689 | 395.1 | 133 | 2.0 | 2,202 | 32.6 | 1,625 | 24.1 |
| 2015................................ | 6,794,422 | 26,562 | 390.9 | 128 | 1.9 | 2,075 | 30.5 | 1,608 | 23.7 |
| Percent change .................. | 0.6 | -0.5 | -1.1 | -3.8 | -4.3 | -5.8 | -6.3 | -1.0 | -1.6 |
| New Hampshire ................... | | | | | | | | | |
| 2014................................ | 1,327,996 | 2,625 | 197.7 | 16 | 1.2 | 596 | 44.9 | 438 | 33.0 |
| 2015................................ | 1,330,608 | 2,652 | 199.3 | 14 | 1.1 | 627 | 47.1 | 461 | 34.6 |
| Percent change .................. | 0.2 | +1.0 | +0.8 | -12.5 | -12.7 | +5.2 | +5.0 | +5.3 | +5.0 |
| Rhode Island[6] .................... | | | | | | | | | |
| 2014................................ | 1,054,907 | 2,320 | 219.9 | 26 | 2.5 | 366 | 34.7 | 264 | 25.0 |
| 2015................................ | 1,056,298 | 2,562 | 242.5 | 29 | 2.7 | 459 | 43.5 | 338 | 32.0 |
| Percent change .................. | 0.1 | +10.4 | +10.3 | +11.5 | +11.4 | +25.4 | +25.2 | +28.0 | +27.9 |
| Vermont ............................... | | | | | | | | | |
| 2014................................ | 626,767 | 643 | 102.6 | 10 | 1.6 | 117 | 18.7 | 85 | 13.6 |
| 2015................................ | 626,042 | 739 | 118.0 | 10 | 1.6 | 136 | 21.7 | 121 | 19.3 |
| Percent change .................. | -0.1 | +14.9 | +15.1 | 0.0 | +0.1 | 16.2 | +16.4 | +42.4 | +42.5 |
| **Middle Atlantic[6]** .................... | | | | | | | | | |
| 2014................................ | 41,481,469 | 139,589 | 336.5 | 1,578 | 3.8 | 11,144 | 26.9 | 8,054 | 19.4 |
| 2015................................ | 41,556,307 | 138,383 | 333.0 | 1,630 | 3.9 | 11,752 | 28.3 | 8,530 | 20.5 |
| Percent change .................. | 0.2 | -0.9 | -1.0 | +3.3 | +3.1 | +5.5 | +5.3 | +5.9 | +5.7 |
| New Jersey .......................... | | | | | | | | | |
| 2014................................ | 8,938,844 | 23,319 | 260.9 | 352 | 3.9 | 1,280 | 14.3 | 953 | 10.7 |
| 2015................................ | 8,958,013 | 22,879 | 255.4 | 363 | 4.1 | 1,373 | 15.3 | 1,019 | 11.4 |
| Percent change .................. | 0.2 | -1.9 | -2.1 | +3.1 | +2.9 | +7.3 | +7.0 | +6.9 | +6.7 |
| New York[6] ......................... | | | | | | | | | |
| 2014................................ | 19,748,858 | 75,972 | 384.7 | 616 | 3.1 | 6,025 | 30.5 | 4,316 | 21.9 |
| 2015................................ | 19,795,791 | 75,165 | 379.7 | 609 | 3.1 | 6,074 | 30.7 | 4,389 | 22.2 |
| Percent change .................. | 0.2 | -1.1 | -1.3 | -1.1 | -1.4 | +0.8 | +0.6 | +1.7 | +1.5 |
| Pennsylvania ....................... | | | | | | | | | |
| 2014................................ | 12,793,767 | 40,298 | 315.0 | 610 | 4.8 | 3,839 | 30.0 | 2,785 | 21.8 |
| 2015................................ | 12,802,503 | 40,339 | 315.1 | 658 | 5.1 | 4,305 | 33.6 | 3,122 | 24.4 |
| Percent change .................. | 0.1 | +0.1 | * | +7.9 | +7.8 | +12.1 | +12.1 | +12.1 | +12.0 |
| **Midwest[6]** ................................ | | | | | | | | | |
| 2014................................ | 67,762,069 | 232,437 | 343.0 | 2,933 | 4.3 | 28,570 | 42.2 | 20,658 | 30.5 |
| 2015................................ | 67,907,403 | 241,965 | 356.3 | 3,378 | 5.0 | 29,962 | 44.1 | 21,890 | 32.2 |
| Percent change .................. | 0.2 | +4.1 | +3.9 | +15.2 | +14.9 | +4.9 | +4.6 | +6.0 | +5.7 |
| **East North Central[6]** ............... | | | | | | | | | |
| 2014................................ | 46,752,805 | 164,328 | 351.5 | 2,190 | 4.7 | 19,795 | 42.3 | 14,331 | 30.7 |
| 2015................................ | 46,787,011 | 167,783 | 358.6 | 2,428 | 5.2 | 20,604 | 44.0 | 14,879 | 31.8 |
| Percent change .................. | 0.1 | +2.1 | +2.0 | +10.9 | +10.8 | +4.1 | +4.0 | +3.8 | +3.7 |
| Illinois .................................. | | | | | | | | | |
| 2014................................ | 12,882,189 | 47,775 | 370.9 | 690 | 5.4 | 4,329 | 33.6 | 3,182 | 24.7 |
| 2015................................ | 12,859,995 | 49,354 | 383.8 | 744 | 5.8 | 4,821 | 37.5 | 3,549 | 27.6 |
| Percent change .................. | -0.2 | +3.3 | +3.5 | +7.8 | +8.0 | +11.4 | +11.6 | +11.5 | +11.7 |

# Table 4. Crime,[1] by Region, Geographic Division, and State, 2014–2015—*Continued*

(Number, rate per 100,000 population, percent.)

| Area | Robbery Number | Rate | Aggravated assault Number | Rate | Property crime Number | Rate | Burglary Number | Rate | Larceny-theft Number | Rate | Motor vehicle theft Number | Rate |
|---|---|---|---|---|---|---|---|---|---|---|---|---|
| **United States**[6,7,8,9] | | | | | | | | | | | | |
| 2014 | 322,905 | 101.3 | 731,089 | 229.2 | 8,209,010 | 2,574.1 | 1,713,153 | 537.2 | 5,809,054 | 1,821.5 | 686,803 | 215.4 |
| 2015 | 327,374 | 101.9 | 764,449 | 237.8 | 7,993,631 | 2,487.0 | 1,579,527 | 491.4 | 5,706,346 | 1,775.4 | 707,758 | 220.2 |
| Percent change | +1.4 | +0.6 | +4.6 | +3.7 | -2.6 | -3.4 | -7.8 | -8.5 | -1.8 | -2.5 | +3.1 | +2.2 |
| **Northeast**[6] | | | | | | | | | | | | |
| 2014 | 58,779 | 104.6 | 105,784 | 188.3 | 1,021,075 | 1,817.8 | 181,279 | 322.7 | 781,124 | 1,390.6 | 58,672 | 104.5 |
| 2015 | 56,284 | 100.0 | 105,941 | 188.2 | 951,657 | 1,690.8 | 157,909 | 280.6 | 736,844 | 1,309.2 | 56,904 | 101.1 |
| Percent change | -4.2 | -4.4 | +0.1 | -0.1 | -6.8 | -7.0 | -12.9 | -13.1 | -5.7 | -5.9 | -3.0 | -3.2 |
| New England[6] | | | | | | | | | | | | |
| 2014 | 10,699 | 72.8 | 26,997 | 183.8 | 280,035 | 1,906.3 | 53,116 | 361.6 | 208,755 | 1,421.1 | 18,164 | 123.7 |
| 2015 | 9,616 | 65.3 | 27,608 | 187.5 | 256,342 | 1,740.6 | 46,009 | 312.4 | 192,654 | 1,308.1 | 17,679 | 120.0 |
| Percent change | -10.1 | -10.4 | +2.3 | +2.0 | -8.5 | -8.7 | -13.4 | -13.6 | -7.7 | -7.9 | -2.7 | -2.9 |
| Connecticut | | | | | | | | | | | | |
| 2014 | 3,172 | 88.2 | 4,520 | 125.7 | 69,326 | 1,928.5 | 12,017 | 334.3 | 51,195 | 1,424.2 | 6,114 | 170.1 |
| 2015 | 2,892 | 80.5 | 4,063 | 113.1 | 65,066 | 1,812.0 | 10,053 | 280.0 | 48,675 | 1,355.5 | 6,338 | 176.5 |
| Percent change | -8.8 | -8.7 | -10.1 | -10.0 | -6.1 | -6.0 | -16.3 | -16.3 | -4.9 | -4.8 | +3.7 | +3.8 |
| Maine[6] | | | | | | | | | | | | |
| 2014 | 304 | 22.9 | 889 | 66.8 | 26,427 | 1,986.6 | 5,035 | 378.5 | 20,591 | 1,547.9 | 801 | 60.2 |
| 2015 | 311 | 23.4 | 921 | 69.3 | 24,327 | 1,830.0 | 4,684 | 352.4 | 18,829 | 1,416.4 | 814 | 61.2 |
| Percent change | +2.3 | +2.4 | +3.6 | +3.7 | -7.9 | -7.9 | -7.0 | -6.9 | -8.6 | -8.5 | +1.6 | +1.7 |
| Massachusetts | | | | | | | | | | | | |
| 2014 | 6,077 | 90.0 | 18,277 | 270.6 | 125,481 | 1,857.6 | 24,951 | 369.4 | 92,226 | 1,365.3 | 8,304 | 122.9 |
| 2015 | 5,288 | 77.8 | 19,071 | 280.7 | 114,871 | 1,690.7 | 21,890 | 322.2 | 84,912 | 1,249.7 | 8,069 | 118.8 |
| Percent change | -13.0 | -13.5 | +4.3 | +3.7 | -8.5 | -9.0 | -12.3 | -12.8 | -7.9 | -8.5 | -2.8 | -3.4 |
| New Hampshire | | | | | | | | | | | | |
| 2014 | 544 | 41.0 | 1,469 | 110.6 | 26,098 | 1,965.2 | 4,191 | 315.6 | 21,051 | 1,585.2 | 856 | 64.5 |
| 2015 | 468 | 35.2 | 1,543 | 116.0 | 23,229 | 1,745.7 | 3,467 | 260.6 | 18,871 | 1,418.2 | 891 | 67.0 |
| Percent change | -14.0 | -14.1 | +5.0 | +4.8 | -11.0 | -11.2 | -17.3 | -17.4 | -10.4 | -10.5 | +4.1 | +3.9 |
| Rhode Island[6] | | | | | | | | | | | | |
| 2014 | 530 | 50.2 | 1,398 | 132.5 | 22,982 | 2,178.6 | 4,830 | 457.9 | 16,317 | 1,546.8 | 1,835 | 173.9 |
| 2015 | 556 | 52.6 | 1,518 | 143.7 | 20,043 | 1,897.5 | 3,947 | 373.7 | 14,707 | 1,392.3 | 1,389 | 131.5 |
| Percent change | +4.9 | +4.8 | +8.6 | +8.4 | -12.8 | -12.9 | -18.3 | -18.4 | -9.9 | -10.0 | -24.3 | -24.4 |
| Vermont | | | | | | | | | | | | |
| 2014 | 72 | 11.5 | 444 | 70.8 | 9,721 | 1,551.0 | 2,092 | 333.8 | 7,375 | 1,176.7 | 254 | 40.5 |
| 2015 | 101 | 16.1 | 492 | 78.6 | 8,806 | 1,406.6 | 1,968 | 314.4 | 6,660 | 1,063.8 | 178 | 28.4 |
| Percent change | +40.3 | +40.4 | +10.8 | +10.9 | -9.4 | -9.3 | -5.9 | -5.8 | -9.7 | -9.6 | -29.9 | -29.8 |
| Middle Atlantic[6] | | | | | | | | | | | | |
| 2014 | 48,080 | 115.9 | 78,787 | 189.9 | 741,040 | 1,786.4 | 128,163 | 309.0 | 572,369 | 1,379.8 | 40,508 | 97.7 |
| 2015 | 46,668 | 112.3 | 78,333 | 188.5 | 695,315 | 1,673.2 | 111,900 | 269.3 | 544,190 | 1,309.5 | 39,225 | 94.4 |
| Percent change | -2.9 | -3.1 | -0.6 | -0.8 | -6.2 | -6.3 | -12.7 | -12.8 | -4.9 | -5.1 | -3.2 | -3.3 |
| New Jersey | | | | | | | | | | | | |
| 2014 | 10,499 | 117.5 | 11,188 | 125.2 | 154,945 | 1,733.4 | 31,707 | 354.7 | 111,534 | 1,247.7 | 11,704 | 130.9 |
| 2015 | 9,729 | 108.6 | 11,414 | 127.4 | 145,701 | 1,626.5 | 27,960 | 312.1 | 105,963 | 1,182.9 | 11,778 | 131.5 |
| Percent change | -7.3 | -7.5 | +2.0 | +1.8 | -6.0 | -6.2 | -11.8 | -12.0 | -5.0 | -5.2 | +0.6 | +0.4 |
| New York[6] | | | | | | | | | | | | |
| 2014 | 24,036 | 121.7 | 45,295 | 229.4 | 339,113 | 1,717.1 | 50,738 | 256.9 | 272,624 | 1,380.5 | 15,751 | 79.8 |
| 2015 | 23,936 | 120.9 | 44,546 | 225.0 | 317,529 | 1,604.0 | 44,276 | 223.7 | 257,940 | 1,303.0 | 15,313 | 77.4 |
| Percent change | -0.4 | -0.7 | -1.7 | -1.9 | -6.4 | -6.6 | -12.7 | -12.9 | -5.4 | -5.6 | -2.8 | -3.0 |
| Pennsylvania | | | | | | | | | | | | |
| 2014 | 13,545 | 105.9 | 22,304 | 174.3 | 246,982 | 1,930.5 | 45,718 | 357.3 | 188,211 | 1,471.1 | 13,053 | 102.0 |
| 2015 | 13,003 | 101.6 | 22,373 | 174.8 | 232,085 | 1,812.8 | 39,664 | 309.8 | 180,287 | 1,408.2 | 12,134 | 94.8 |
| Percent change | -4.0 | -4.1 | +0.3 | +0.2 | -6.0 | -6.1 | -13.2 | -13.3 | -4.2 | -4.3 | -7.0 | -7.1 |
| **Midwest**[6] | | | | | | | | | | | | |
| 2014 | 61,188 | 90.3 | 139,746 | 206.2 | 1,616,661 | 2,385.8 | 332,691 | 491.0 | 1,160,086 | 1,712.0 | 123,884 | 182.8 |
| 2015 | 61,973 | 91.3 | 146,652 | 216.0 | 1,543,103 | 2,272.4 | 305,689 | 450.2 | 1,119,214 | 1,648.1 | 118,200 | 174.1 |
| Percent change | +1.3 | +1.1 | +4.9 | +4.7 | -4.5 | -4.8 | -8.1 | -8.3 | -3.5 | -3.7 | -4.6 | -4.8 |
| East North Central[6] | | | | | | | | | | | | |
| 2014 | 48,083 | 102.8 | 94,260 | 201.6 | 1,090,300 | 2,332.1 | 232,837 | 498.0 | 776,486 | 1,660.8 | 80,977 | 173.2 |
| 2015 | 47,603 | 101.7 | 97,148 | 207.6 | 1,029,126 | 2,199.6 | 209,751 | 448.3 | 744,226 | 1,590.7 | 75,149 | 160.6 |
| Percent change | -1.0 | -1.1 | +3.1 | +3.0 | -5.6 | -5.7 | -9.9 | -10.0 | -4.2 | -4.2 | -7.2 | -7.3 |
| Illinois | | | | | | | | | | | | |
| 2014 | 15,271 | 118.5 | 27,485 | 213.4 | 269,647 | 2,093.2 | 50,759 | 394.0 | 201,003 | 1,560.3 | 17,885 | 138.8 |
| 2015 | 14,910 | 115.9 | 28,879 | 224.6 | 255,729 | 1,988.6 | 46,443 | 361.1 | 191,634 | 1,490.2 | 17,652 | 137.3 |
| Percent change | -2.4 | -2.2 | +5.1 | +5.3 | -5.2 | -5.0 | -8.5 | -8.3 | -4.7 | -4.5 | -1.3 | -1.1 |

# Table 4. Crime,[1] by Region, Geographic Division, and State, 2014–2015—*Continued*

(Number, rate per 100,000 population, percent.)

| Area | Population[2] | Violent crime[3] | | Murder and nonnegligent manslaughter | | Rape (revised definition)[4] | | Rape (legacy definition)[5] | |
|---|---|---|---|---|---|---|---|---|---|
| | | Number | Rate | Number | Rate | Number | Rate | Number | Rate |
| Indiana[6] | | | | | | | | | |
| 2014 | 6,597,880 | 24,105 | 365.3 | 333 | 5.0 | 2,197 | 33.3 | 1,608 | 24.4 |
| 2015 | 6,619,680 | 25,653 | 387.5 | 373 | 5.6 | 2,404 | 36.3 | 1,789 | 27.0 |
| Percent change | 0.3 | +6.4 | +6.1 | +12.0 | +11.6 | +9.4 | +9.1 | +11.3 | +10.9 |
| Michigan | | | | | | | | | |
| 2014 | 9,916,306 | 42,555 | 429.1 | 544 | 5.5 | 6,364 | 64.2 | 4,500 | 45.4 |
| 2015 | 9,922,576 | 41,231 | 415.5 | 571 | 5.8 | 6,450 | 65.0 | 4,163 | 42.0 |
| Percent change | 0.1 | -3.1 | -3.2 | +5.0 | +4.9 | +1.4 | +1.3 | -7.5 | -7.5 |
| Ohio[6] | | | | | | | | | |
| 2014 | 11,596,998 | 33,130 | 285.7 | 464 | 4.0 | 5,228 | 45.1 | 3,825 | 33.0 |
| 2015 | 11,613,423 | 33,898 | 291.9 | 500 | 4.3 | 5,149 | 44.3 | 4,154 | 35.8 |
| Percent change | 0.1 | +2.3 | +2.2 | +7.8 | +7.6 | -1.5 | -1.7 | +8.6 | +8.4 |
| Wisconsin[6] | | | | | | | | | |
| 2014 | 5,759,432 | 16,763 | 291.1 | 159 | 2.8 | 1,677 | 29.1 | 1,216 | 21.1 |
| 2015 | 5,771,337 | 17,647 | 305.8 | 240 | 4.2 | 1,780 | 30.8 | 1,224 | 21.2 |
| Percent change | 0.2 | +5.3 | +5.1 | +50.9 | +50.6 | +6.1 | +5.9 | +0.7 | +0.5 |
| **West North Central[6]** | | | | | | | | | |
| 2014 | 21,009,264 | 68,109 | 324.2 | 743 | 3.5 | 8,775 | 41.8 | 6,327 | 30.1 |
| 2015 | 21,120,392 | 74,182 | 351.2 | 950 | 4.5 | 9,358 | 44.3 | 7,011 | 33.2 |
| Percent change | 0.5 | +8.9 | +8.3 | +27.9 | +27.2 | +6.6 | +6.1 | +10.8 | +10.2 |
| Iowa | | | | | | | | | |
| 2014 | 3,109,481 | 8,484 | 272.8 | 60 | 1.9 | 1,150 | 37.0 | 829 | 26.7 |
| 2015 | 3,123,899 | 8,936 | 286.1 | 72 | 2.3 | 1,156 | 37.0 | 851 | 27.2 |
| Percent change | 0.5 | +5.3 | +4.8 | +20.0 | +19.4 | +0.5 | +0.1 | +2.7 | +2.2 |
| Kansas | | | | | | | | | |
| 2014 | 2,902,507 | 10,235 | 352.6 | 92 | 3.2 | 1,483 | 51.1 | 1,066 | 36.7 |
| 2015 | 2,911,641 | 11,353 | 389.9 | 128 | 4.4 | 1,615 | 55.5 | 1,251 | 43.0 |
| Percent change | 0.3 | +10.9 | +10.6 | +39.1 | +38.7 | +8.9 | +8.6 | +17.4 | +17.0 |
| Minnesota | | | | | | | | | |
| 2014 | 5,457,125 | 12,505 | 229.1 | 88 | 1.6 | 2,001 | 36.7 | 1,448 | 26.5 |
| 2015 | 5,489,594 | 13,319 | 242.6 | 133 | 2.4 | 2,321 | 42.3 | 1,686 | 30.7 |
| Percent change | 0.6 | +6.5 | +5.9 | +51.1 | +50.2 | +16.0 | +15.3 | +16.4 | +15.7 |
| Missouri | | | | | | | | | |
| 2014 | 6,063,827 | 26,882 | 443.3 | 404 | 6.7 | 2,403 | 39.6 | 1,728 | 28.5 |
| 2015 | 6,083,672 | 30,261 | 497.4 | 502 | 8.3 | 2,553 | 42.0 | 1,854 | 30.5 |
| Percent change | 0.3 | +12.6 | +12.2 | +24.3 | +23.9 | +6.2 | +5.9 | +7.3 | +6.9 |
| Nebraska[6] | | | | | | | | | |
| 2014 | 1,882,980 | 5,201 | 276.2 | 53 | 2.8 | 878 | 46.6 | 645 | 34.3 |
| 2015 | 1,896,190 | 5,212 | 274.9 | 62 | 3.3 | 873 | 46.0 | 652 | 34.4 |
| Percent change | 0.7 | +0.2 | -0.5 | +17.0 | +16.2 | -0.6 | -1.3 | +1.1 | +0.4 |
| North Dakota | | | | | | | | | |
| 2014 | 740,040 | 2,001 | 270.4 | 23 | 3.1 | 382 | 51.6 | 275 | 37.2 |
| 2015 | 756,927 | 1,812 | 239.4 | 21 | 2.8 | 345 | 45.6 | 276 | 36.5 |
| Percent change | 2.3 | -9.4 | -11.5 | -8.7 | -10.7 | -9.7 | -11.7 | +0.4 | -1.9 |
| South Dakota | | | | | | | | | |
| 2014 | 853,304 | 2,801 | 328.3 | 23 | 2.7 | 478 | 56.0 | 336 | 39.4 |
| 2015 | 858,469 | 3,289 | 383.1 | 32 | 3.7 | 495 | 57.7 | 441 | 51.4 |
| Percent change | 0.6 | +17.4 | +16.7 | +39.1 | +38.3 | +3.6 | +2.9 | +31.3 | +30.5 |
| **South[6,7,8,9]** | | | | | | | | | |
| 2014 | 119,795,010 | 491,498 | 410.3 | 6,451 | 5.4 | 44,334 | 37.0 | 31,572 | 26.4 |
| 2015 | 121,182,847 | 506,913 | 418.3 | 7,200 | 5.9 | 46,434 | 38.3 | 33,196 | 27.4 |
| Percent change | 1.2 | +3.1 | +2.0 | +11.6 | +10.3 | +4.7 | +3.5 | +5.1 | +3.9 |
| **South Atlantic[7,8,9]** | | | | | | | | | |
| 2014 | 62,520,247 | 248,962 | 398.2 | 3,360 | 5.4 | 20,400 | 32.6 | 14,378 | 23.0 |
| 2015 | 63,276,764 | 255,164 | 403.3 | 3,766 | 6.0 | 21,271 | 33.6 | 15,078 | 23.8 |
| Percent change | 1.2 | +2.5 | +1.3 | +12.1 | +10.7 | +4.3 | +3.0 | +4.9 | +3.6 |
| Delaware | | | | | | | | | |
| 2014 | 935,968 | 4,568 | 488.1 | 50 | 5.3 | 390 | 41.7 | 274 | 29.3 |
| 2015 | 945,934 | 4,720 | 499.0 | 63 | 6.7 | 341 | 36.0 | 243 | 25.7 |
| Percent change | 1.1 | +3.3 | +2.2 | +26.0 | +24.7 | -12.6 | -13.5 | -11.3 | -12.2 |
| District of Columbia[7] | | | | | | | | | |
| 2014 | 659,836 | 8,199 | 1,242.6 | 105 | 15.9 | 472 | 71.5 | 349 | 52.9 |
| 2015 | 672,228 | 8,531 | 1,269.1 | 162 | 24.1 | 494 | 73.5 | 366 | 54.4 |
| Percent change | 1.9 | +4.0 | +2.1 | +54.3 | +51.4 | +4.7 | +2.7 | +4.9 | +2.9 |
| Florida | | | | | | | | | |
| 2014 | 19,905,569 | 91,345 | 458.9 | 982 | 4.9 | 7,132 | 35.8 | 5,038 | 25.3 |
| 2015 | 20,271,272 | 93,626 | 461.9 | 1,041 | 5.1 | 7,553 | 37.3 | 5,430 | 26.8 |
| Percent change | 1.8 | +2.5 | +0.6 | +6.0 | +4.1 | +5.9 | +4.0 | +7.8 | +5.8 |

(Number, rate per 100,000 population, percent.)

| Area | Robbery Number | Rate | Aggravated assault Number | Rate | Property crime Number | Rate | Burglary Number | Rate | Larceny-theft Number | Rate | Motor vehicle theft Number | Rate |
|---|---|---|---|---|---|---|---|---|---|---|---|---|---|
| Indiana[6] | | | | | | | | | | | | |
| 2014 | 6,894 | 104.5 | 14,681 | 222.5 | 174,909 | 2,651.0 | 36,909 | 559.4 | 124,144 | 1,881.6 | 13,856 | 210.0 |
| 2015 | 7,111 | 107.4 | 15,765 | 238.2 | 171,847 | 2,596.0 | 34,410 | 519.8 | 123,918 | 1,872.0 | 13,519 | 204.2 |
| Percent change | +3.1 | +2.8 | +7.4 | +7.0 | -1.8 | -2.1 | -6.8 | -7.1 | -0.2 | -0.5 | -2.4 | -2.8 |
| Michigan | | | | | | | | | | | | |
| 2014 | 8,037 | 81.0 | 27,610 | 278.4 | 202,692 | 2,044.0 | 44,328 | 447.0 | 137,142 | 1,383.0 | 21,222 | 214.0 |
| 2015 | 7,796 | 78.6 | 26,414 | 266.2 | 187,101 | 1,885.6 | 40,041 | 403.5 | 131,296 | 1,323.2 | 15,764 | 158.9 |
| Percent change | -3.0 | -3.1 | -4.3 | -4.4 | -7.7 | -7.8 | -9.7 | -9.7 | -4.3 | -4.3 | -25.7 | -25.8 |
| Ohio[6] | | | | | | | | | | | | |
| 2014 | 12,780 | 110.2 | 14,658 | 126.4 | 322,517 | 2,781.0 | 79,466 | 685.2 | 224,942 | 1,939.7 | 18,109 | 156.2 |
| 2015 | 12,554 | 108.1 | 15,695 | 135.1 | 300,525 | 2,587.7 | 69,303 | 596.7 | 213,993 | 1,842.6 | 17,229 | 148.4 |
| Percent change | -1.8 | -1.9 | +7.1 | +6.9 | -6.8 | -7.0 | -12.8 | -12.9 | -4.9 | -5.0 | -4.9 | -5.0 |
| Wisconsin[6] | | | | | | | | | | | | |
| 2014 | 5,101 | 88.6 | 9,826 | 170.6 | 120,535 | 2,092.8 | 21,375 | 371.1 | 89,255 | 1,549.7 | 9,905 | 172.0 |
| 2015 | 5,232 | 90.7 | 10,395 | 180.1 | 113,924 | 1,974.0 | 19,554 | 338.8 | 83,385 | 1,444.8 | 10,985 | 190.3 |
| Percent change | +2.6 | +2.4 | +5.8 | +5.6 | -5.5 | -5.7 | -8.5 | -8.7 | -6.6 | -6.8 | +10.9 | +10.7 |
| **West North Central[6]** | | | | | | | | | | | | |
| 2014 | 13,105 | 62.4 | 45,486 | 216.5 | 526,361 | 2,505.4 | 99,854 | 475.3 | 383,600 | 1,825.9 | 42,907 | 204.2 |
| 2015 | 14,370 | 68.0 | 49,504 | 234.4 | 513,977 | 2,433.6 | 95,938 | 454.2 | 374,988 | 1,775.5 | 43,051 | 203.8 |
| Percent change | +9.7 | +9.1 | +8.8 | +8.3 | -2.4 | -2.9 | -3.9 | -4.4 | -2.2 | -2.8 | +0.3 | -0.2 |
| Iowa | | | | | | | | | | | | |
| 2014 | 1,047 | 33.7 | 6,227 | 200.3 | 65,100 | 2,093.6 | 14,363 | 461.9 | 46,594 | 1,498.4 | 4,143 | 133.2 |
| 2015 | 1,047 | 33.5 | 6,661 | 213.2 | 63,957 | 2,047.3 | 14,892 | 476.7 | 44,723 | 1,431.6 | 4,342 | 139.0 |
| Percent change | 0.0 | -0.5 | +7.0 | +6.5 | -1.8 | -2.2 | +3.7 | +3.2 | -4.0 | -4.5 | +4.8 | +4.3 |
| Kansas | | | | | | | | | | | | |
| 2014 | 1,361 | 46.9 | 7,299 | 251.5 | 80,029 | 2,757.2 | 15,921 | 548.5 | 57,169 | 1,969.6 | 6,939 | 239.1 |
| 2015 | 1,818 | 62.4 | 7,792 | 267.6 | 79,199 | 2,720.1 | 15,362 | 527.6 | 56,880 | 1,953.5 | 6,957 | 238.9 |
| Percent change | +33.6 | +33.2 | +6.8 | +6.4 | -1.0 | -1.3 | -3.5 | -3.8 | -0.5 | -0.8 | +0.3 | -0.1 |
| Minnesota | | | | | | | | | | | | |
| 2014 | 3,687 | 67.6 | 6,729 | 123.3 | 125,377 | 2,297.5 | 20,773 | 380.7 | 96,237 | 1,763.5 | 8,367 | 153.3 |
| 2015 | 3,771 | 68.7 | 7,094 | 129.2 | 121,984 | 2,222.1 | 19,299 | 351.6 | 94,704 | 1,725.2 | 7,981 | 145.4 |
| Percent change | +2.3 | +1.7 | +5.4 | +4.8 | -2.7 | -3.3 | -7.1 | -7.6 | -1.6 | -2.2 | -4.6 | -5.2 |
| Missouri | | | | | | | | | | | | |
| 2014 | 5,592 | 92.2 | 18,483 | 304.8 | 176,436 | 2,909.6 | 35,293 | 582.0 | 124,769 | 2,057.6 | 16,374 | 270.0 |
| 2015 | 6,376 | 104.8 | 20,830 | 342.4 | 173,642 | 2,854.2 | 34,006 | 559.0 | 122,637 | 2,015.8 | 16,999 | 279.4 |
| Percent change | +14.0 | +13.6 | +12.7 | +12.3 | -1.6 | -1.9 | -3.6 | -4.0 | -1.7 | -2.0 | +3.8 | +3.5 |
| Nebraska[6] | | | | | | | | | | | | |
| 2014 | 1,044 | 55.4 | 3,226 | 171.3 | 47,526 | 2,524.0 | 7,936 | 421.5 | 35,063 | 1,862.1 | 4,527 | 240.4 |
| 2015 | 994 | 52.4 | 3,283 | 173.1 | 42,495 | 2,241.1 | 6,422 | 338.7 | 32,072 | 1,691.4 | 4,001 | 211.0 |
| Percent change | -4.8 | -5.5 | +1.8 | +1.1 | -10.6 | -11.2 | -19.1 | -19.6 | -8.5 | -9.2 | -11.6 | -12.2 |
| North Dakota | | | | | | | | | | | | |
| 2014 | 175 | 23.6 | 1,421 | 192.0 | 15,857 | 2,142.7 | 2,751 | 371.7 | 11,559 | 1,561.9 | 1,547 | 209.0 |
| 2015 | 148 | 19.6 | 1,298 | 171.5 | 16,020 | 2,116.5 | 2,997 | 395.9 | 11,440 | 1,511.4 | 1,583 | 209.1 |
| Percent change | -15.4 | -17.3 | -8.7 | -10.7 | +1.0 | -1.2 | +8.9 | +6.5 | -1.0 | -3.2 | +2.3 | * |
| South Dakota | | | | | | | | | | | | |
| 2014 | 199 | 23.3 | 2,101 | 246.2 | 16,036 | 1,879.3 | 2,817 | 330.1 | 12,209 | 1,430.8 | 1,010 | 118.4 |
| 2015 | 216 | 25.2 | 2,546 | 296.6 | 16,680 | 1,943.0 | 2,960 | 344.8 | 12,532 | 1,459.8 | 1,188 | 138.4 |
| Percent change | +8.5 | +7.9 | +21.2 | +20.5 | +4.0 | +3.4 | +5.1 | +4.4 | +2.6 | +2.0 | +17.6 | +16.9 |
| **South[6,7,8,9]** | | | | | | | | | | | | |
| 2014 | 125,692 | 104.9 | 315,021 | 263.0 | 3,522,765 | 2,940.7 | 781,030 | 652.0 | 2,495,515 | 2,083.2 | 246,220 | 205.5 |
| 2015 | 126,454 | 104.3 | 326,825 | 269.7 | 3,369,856 | 2,780.8 | 714,080 | 589.3 | 2,405,604 | 1,985.1 | 250,172 | 206.4 |
| Percent change | +0.6 | -0.5 | +3.7 | +2.6 | -4.3 | -5.4 | -8.6 | -9.6 | -3.6 | -4.7 | +1.6 | +0.4 |
| **South Atlantic[7,8,9]** | | | | | | | | | | | | |
| 2014 | 66,118 | 105.8 | 159,084 | 254.5 | 1,789,367 | 2,862.1 | 385,780 | 617.0 | 1,285,216 | 2,055.7 | 118,371 | 189.3 |
| 2015 | 66,181 | 104.6 | 163,946 | 259.1 | 1,706,080 | 2,696.2 | 348,966 | 551.5 | 1,235,620 | 1,952.7 | 121,494 | 192.0 |
| Percent change | +0.1 | -1.1 | +3.1 | +1.8 | -4.7 | -5.8 | -9.5 | -10.6 | -3.9 | -5.0 | +2.6 | +1.4 |
| Delaware | | | | | | | | | | | | |
| 2014 | 1,271 | 135.8 | 2,857 | 305.2 | 27,915 | 2,982.5 | 5,765 | 615.9 | 20,885 | 2,231.4 | 1,265 | 135.2 |
| 2015 | 1,235 | 130.6 | 3,081 | 325.7 | 25,455 | 2,691.0 | 4,773 | 504.6 | 19,501 | 2,061.6 | 1,181 | 124.9 |
| Percent change | -2.8 | -3.9 | +7.8 | +6.7 | -8.8 | -9.8 | -17.2 | -18.1 | -6.6 | -7.6 | -6.6 | -7.6 |
| District of Columbia[7] | | | | | | | | | | | | |
| 2014 | 3,497 | 530.0 | 4,125 | 625.2 | 34,147 | 5,175.1 | 3,466 | 525.3 | 26,898 | 4,076.5 | 3,783 | 573.3 |
| 2015 | 3,742 | 556.7 | 4,133 | 614.8 | 31,435 | 4,676.2 | 2,971 | 442.0 | 25,200 | 3,748.7 | 3,264 | 485.5 |
| Percent change | +7.0 | +5.0 | +0.2 | -1.7 | -7.9 | -9.6 | -14.3 | -15.9 | -6.3 | -8.0 | -13.7 | -15.3 |
| Florida | | | | | | | | | | | | |
| 2014 | 21,621 | 108.6 | 61,610 | 309.5 | 583,774 | 2,932.7 | 121,379 | 609.8 | 426,197 | 2,141.1 | 36,198 | 181.8 |
| 2015 | 21,137 | 104.3 | 63,895 | 315.2 | 570,270 | 2,813.2 | 109,268 | 539.0 | 420,341 | 2,073.6 | 40,661 | 200.6 |
| Percent change | -2.2 | -4.0 | +3.7 | +1.8 | -2.3 | -4.1 | -10.0 | -11.6 | -1.4 | -3.2 | +12.3 | +10.3 |

## Table 4. Crime,[1] by Region, Geographic Division, and State, 2014–2015—*Continued*

(Number, rate per 100,000 population, percent.)

| Area | Population[2] | Violent crime[3] | | Murder and nonnegligent manslaughter | | Rape (revised definition)[4] | | Rape (legacy definition)[5] | |
|---|---|---|---|---|---|---|---|---|---|
| | | Number | Rate | Number | Rate | Number | Rate | Number | Rate |
| Georgia[8,9] | | | | | | | | | |
| 2014 | 10,097,132 | 38,955 | 385.8 | 607 | 6.0 | 3,147 | 31.2 | 2,209 | 21.9 |
| 2015 | 10,214,860 | 38,643 | 378.3 | 615 | 6.0 | 3,224 | 31.6 | 2,296 | 22.5 |
| Percent change | 1.2 | -0.8 | -1.9 | +1.3 | +0.2 | +2.4 | +1.3 | +3.9 | +2.7 |
| Maryland | | | | | | | | | |
| 2014 | 5,975,346 | 26,767 | 448.0 | 362 | 6.1 | 1,632 | 27.3 | 1,144 | 19.1 |
| 2015 | 6,006,401 | 27,462 | 457.2 | 516 | 8.6 | 1,666 | 27.7 | 1,184 | 19.7 |
| Percent change | 0.5 | +2.6 | +2.1 | +42.5 | +41.8 | +2.1 | +1.6 | +3.5 | +3.0 |
| North Carolina[8] | | | | | | | | | |
| 2014 | 9,940,387 | 32,718 | 329.1 | 498 | 5.0 | 2,432 | 24.5 | 1,738 | 17.5 |
| 2015 | 10,042,802 | 34,852 | 347.0 | 517 | 5.1 | 2,684 | 26.7 | 1,939 | 19.3 |
| Percent change | 1.0 | +6.5 | +5.4 | +3.8 | +2.8 | +10.4 | +9.2 | +11.6 | +10.4 |
| South Carolina | | | | | | | | | |
| 2014 | 4,829,160 | 24,038 | 497.8 | 322 | 6.7 | 2,185 | 45.2 | 1,522 | 31.5 |
| 2015 | 4,896,146 | 24,700 | 504.5 | 399 | 8.1 | 2,297 | 46.9 | 1,707 | 34.9 |
| Percent change | 1.4 | +2.8 | +1.3 | +23.9 | +22.2 | +5.1 | +3.7 | +12.2 | +10.6 |
| Virginia | | | | | | | | | |
| 2014 | 8,328,098 | 16,522 | 198.4 | 350 | 4.2 | 2,416 | 29.0 | 1,687 | 20.3 |
| 2015 | 8,382,993 | 16,399 | 195.6 | 383 | 4.6 | 2,340 | 27.9 | 1,493 | 17.8 |
| Percent change | 0.7 | -0.7 | -1.4 | +9.4 | +8.7 | -3.1 | -3.8 | -11.5 | -12.1 |
| West Virginia | | | | | | | | | |
| 2014 | 1,848,751 | 5,850 | 316.4 | 84 | 4.5 | 594 | 32.1 | 417 | 22.6 |
| 2015 | 1,844,128 | 6,231 | 337.9 | 70 | 3.8 | 672 | 36.4 | 420 | 22.8 |
| Percent change | -0.3 | +6.5 | +6.8 | -16.7 | -16.5 | +13.1 | +13.4 | +0.7 | +1.0 |
| **East South Central[6]** | | | | | | | | | |
| 2014 | 18,800,250 | 78,542 | 417.8 | 1,068 | 5.7 | 7,238 | 38.5 | 5,161 | 27.5 |
| 2015 | 18,876,703 | 81,282 | 430.6 | 1,222 | 6.5 | 7,410 | 39.3 | 5,281 | 28.0 |
| Percent change | 0.4 | +3.5 | +3.1 | +14.4 | +14.0 | +2.4 | +2.0 | +2.3 | +1.9 |
| Alabama | | | | | | | | | |
| 2014 | 4,846,411 | 20,727 | 427.7 | 276 | 5.7 | 2,005 | 41.4 | 1,425 | 29.4 |
| 2015 | 4,858,979 | 22,952 | 472.4 | 348 | 7.2 | 2,039 | 42.0 | 1,456 | 30.0 |
| Percent change | 0.3 | +10.7 | +10.4 | +26.1 | +25.8 | +1.7 | +1.4 | +2.2 | +1.9 |
| Kentucky | | | | | | | | | |
| 2014 | 4,412,617 | 9,495 | 215.2 | 164 | 3.7 | 1,556 | 35.3 | 1,098 | 24.9 |
| 2015 | 4,425,092 | 9,676 | 218.7 | 209 | 4.7 | 1,492 | 33.7 | 997 | 22.5 |
| Percent change | 0.3 | +1.9 | +1.6 | +27.4 | +27.1 | -4.1 | -4.4 | -9.2 | -9.5 |
| Mississippi[6] | | | | | | | | | |
| 2014 | 2,993,443 | 8,331 | 278.3 | 259 | 8.7 | 1,082 | 36.1 | 768 | 25.7 |
| 2015 | 2,992,333 | 8,254 | 275.8 | 259 | 8.7 | 1,203 | 40.2 | 862 | 28.8 |
| Percent change | 0.0 | -0.9 | -0.9 | 0.0 | * | +11.2 | +11.2 | +12.2 | +12.3 |
| Tennessee | | | | | | | | | |
| 2014 | 6,547,779 | 39,989 | 610.7 | 369 | 5.6 | 2,595 | 39.6 | 1,870 | 28.6 |
| 2015 | 6,600,299 | 40,400 | 612.1 | 406 | 6.2 | 2,676 | 40.5 | 1,966 | 29.8 |
| Percent change | 0.8 | +1.0 | +0.2 | +10.0 | +9.2 | +3.1 | +2.3 | +5.1 | +4.3 |
| **West South Central** | | | | | | | | | |
| 2014 | 38,474,513 | 163,994 | 426.2 | 2,023 | 5.3 | 16,696 | 43.4 | 12,033 | 31.3 |
| 2015 | 39,029,380 | 170,467 | 436.8 | 2,212 | 5.7 | 17,753 | 45.5 | 12,837 | 32.9 |
| Percent change | 1.4 | +3.9 | +2.5 | +9.3 | +7.8 | +6.3 | +4.8 | +6.7 | +5.2 |
| Arkansas | | | | | | | | | |
| 2014 | 2,966,835 | 14,248 | 480.2 | 175 | 5.9 | 1,816 | 61.2 | 1,291 | 43.5 |
| 2015 | 2,978,204 | 15,526 | 521.3 | 181 | 6.1 | 1,931 | 64.8 | 1,300 | 43.7 |
| Percent change | 0.4 | +9.0 | +8.6 | +3.4 | +3.0 | +6.3 | +5.9 | +0.7 | +0.3 |
| Louisiana | | | | | | | | | |
| 2014 | 4,648,990 | 23,983 | 515.9 | 476 | 10.2 | 1,382 | 29.7 | 981 | 21.1 |
| 2015 | 4,670,724 | 25,208 | 539.7 | 481 | 10.3 | 1,723 | 36.9 | 1,260 | 27.0 |
| Percent change | 0.5 | +5.1 | +4.6 | +1.1 | +0.6 | +24.7 | +24.1 | +28.4 | +27.8 |
| Oklahoma | | | | | | | | | |
| 2014 | 3,879,610 | 16,052 | 413.8 | 180 | 4.6 | 1,862 | 48.0 | 1,361 | 35.1 |
| 2015 | 3,911,338 | 16,506 | 422.0 | 234 | 6.0 | 1,849 | 47.3 | 1,352 | 34.6 |
| Percent change | 0.8 | +2.8 | +2.0 | +30.0 | +28.9 | -0.7 | -1.5 | -0.7 | -1.5 |
| Texas | | | | | | | | | |
| 2014 | 26,979,078 | 109,711 | 406.7 | 1,192 | 4.4 | 11,636 | 43.1 | 8,400 | 31.1 |
| 2015 | 27,469,114 | 113,227 | 412.2 | 1,316 | 4.8 | 12,250 | 44.6 | 8,925 | 32.5 |
| Percent change | 1.8 | +3.2 | +1.4 | +10.4 | +8.4 | +5.3 | +3.4 | +6.3 | +4.4 |
| **West[6,8]** | | | | | | | | | |
| 2014 | 75,179,041 | 280,111 | 372.6 | 2,907 | 3.9 | 29,420 | 39.1 | 21,243 | 28.3 |
| 2015 | 76,044,679 | 302,216 | 397.4 | 3,167 | 4.2 | 31,355 | 41.2 | 23,105 | 30.4 |
| Percent change | 1.2 | +7.9 | +6.7 | +8.9 | +7.7 | +6.6 | +5.4 | +8.8 | +7.5 |

# Table 4. Crime,[1] by Region, Geographic Division, and State, 2014–2015—*Continued*

(Number, rate per 100,000 population, percent.)

| Area | Robbery Number | Robbery Rate | Aggravated assault Number | Aggravated assault Rate | Property crime Number | Property crime Rate | Burglary Number | Burglary Rate | Larceny-theft Number | Larceny-theft Rate | Motor vehicle theft Number | Motor vehicle theft Rate |
|---|---|---|---|---|---|---|---|---|---|---|---|---|
| **Georgia[8,9]** | | | | | | | | | | | | |
| 2014 | 12,786 | 126.6 | 22,415 | 222.0 | 339,146 | 3,358.8 | 78,029 | 772.8 | 233,359 | 2,311.1 | 27,758 | 274.9 |
| 2015 | 12,247 | 119.9 | 22,557 | 220.8 | 308,723 | 3,022.3 | 66,374 | 649.8 | 215,867 | 2,113.3 | 26,482 | 259.2 |
| Percent change | -4.2 | -5.3 | +0.6 | -0.5 | -9.0 | -10.0 | -14.9 | -15.9 | -7.5 | -8.6 | -4.6 | -5.7 |
| **Maryland** | | | | | | | | | | | | |
| 2014 | 9,565 | 160.1 | 15,208 | 254.5 | 150,390 | 2,516.8 | 28,134 | 470.8 | 109,140 | 1,826.5 | 13,116 | 219.5 |
| 2015 | 9,863 | 164.2 | 15,417 | 256.7 | 139,048 | 2,315.0 | 25,678 | 427.5 | 100,219 | 1,668.5 | 13,151 | 218.9 |
| Percent change | +3.1 | +2.6 | +1.4 | +0.9 | -7.5 | -8.0 | -8.7 | -9.2 | -8.2 | -8.6 | +0.3 | -0.3 |
| **North Carolina[8]** | | | | | | | | | | | | |
| 2014 | 8,411 | 84.6 | 21,377 | 215.1 | 285,498 | 2,872.1 | 79,266 | 797.4 | 192,609 | 1,937.6 | 13,623 | 137.0 |
| 2015 | 8,825 | 87.9 | 22,826 | 227.3 | 276,183 | 2,750.1 | 74,841 | 745.2 | 187,907 | 1,871.1 | 13,435 | 133.8 |
| Percent change | +4.9 | +3.9 | +6.8 | +5.7 | -3.3 | -4.2 | -5.6 | -6.5 | -2.4 | -3.4 | -1.4 | -2.4 |
| **South Carolina** | | | | | | | | | | | | |
| 2014 | 4,018 | 83.2 | 17,513 | 362.7 | 168,281 | 3,484.7 | 37,163 | 769.6 | 118,173 | 2,447.1 | 12,945 | 268.1 |
| 2015 | 3,931 | 80.3 | 18,073 | 369.1 | 161,245 | 3,293.3 | 34,551 | 705.7 | 113,724 | 2,322.7 | 12,970 | 264.9 |
| Percent change | -2.2 | -3.5 | +3.2 | +1.8 | -4.2 | -5.5 | -7.0 | -8.3 | -3.8 | -5.1 | +0.2 | -1.2 |
| **Virginia** | | | | | | | | | | | | |
| 2014 | 4,294 | 51.6 | 9,462 | 113.6 | 161,934 | 1,944.4 | 23,210 | 278.7 | 131,001 | 1,573.0 | 7,723 | 92.7 |
| 2015 | 4,441 | 53.0 | 9,235 | 110.2 | 156,470 | 1,866.5 | 21,340 | 254.6 | 127,019 | 1,515.2 | 8,111 | 96.8 |
| Percent change | +3.4 | +2.7 | -2.4 | -3.0 | -3.4 | -4.0 | -8.1 | -8.7 | -3.0 | -3.7 | +5.0 | +4.3 |
| **West Virginia** | | | | | | | | | | | | |
| 2014 | 655 | 35.4 | 4,517 | 244.3 | 38,282 | 2,070.7 | 9,368 | 506.7 | 26,954 | 1,458.0 | 1,960 | 106.0 |
| 2015 | 760 | 41.2 | 4,729 | 256.4 | 37,251 | 2,020.0 | 9,170 | 497.3 | 25,842 | 1,401.3 | 2,239 | 121.4 |
| Percent change | +16.0 | +16.3 | +4.7 | +5.0 | -2.7 | -2.4 | -2.1 | -1.9 | -4.1 | -3.9 | +14.2 | +14.5 |
| **East South Central[6]** | | | | | | | | | | | | |
| 2014 | 17,718 | 94.2 | 52,518 | 279.3 | 541,794 | 2,881.8 | 133,845 | 711.9 | 374,310 | 1,991.0 | 33,639 | 178.9 |
| 2015 | 17,686 | 93.7 | 54,964 | 291.2 | 519,694 | 2,753.1 | 125,561 | 665.2 | 358,903 | 1,901.3 | 35,230 | 186.6 |
| Percent change | -0.2 | -0.6 | +4.7 | +4.2 | -4.1 | -4.5 | -6.2 | -6.6 | -4.1 | -4.5 | +4.7 | +4.3 |
| **Alabama** | | | | | | | | | | | | |
| 2014 | 4,702 | 97.0 | 13,744 | 283.6 | 154,087 | 3,179.4 | 39,723 | 819.6 | 104,223 | 2,150.5 | 10,141 | 209.2 |
| 2015 | 4,611 | 94.9 | 15,954 | 328.3 | 144,746 | 2,978.9 | 35,255 | 725.6 | 99,156 | 2,040.7 | 10,335 | 212.7 |
| Percent change | -1.9 | -2.2 | +16.1 | +15.8 | -6.1 | -6.3 | -11.2 | -11.5 | -4.9 | -5.1 | +1.9 | +1.6 |
| **Kentucky** | | | | | | | | | | | | |
| 2014 | 3,343 | 75.8 | 4,432 | 100.4 | 99,909 | 2,264.2 | 23,426 | 530.9 | 70,108 | 1,588.8 | 6,375 | 144.5 |
| 2015 | 3,307 | 74.7 | 4,668 | 105.5 | 96,362 | 2,177.6 | 22,260 | 503.0 | 66,320 | 1,498.7 | 7,782 | 175.9 |
| Percent change | -1.1 | -1.4 | +5.3 | +5.0 | -3.6 | -3.8 | -5.0 | -5.2 | -5.4 | -5.7 | +22.1 | +21.7 |
| **Mississippi[6]** | | | | | | | | | | | | |
| 2014 | 2,405 | 80.3 | 4,585 | 153.2 | 86,887 | 2,902.6 | 23,898 | 798.3 | 58,515 | 1,954.8 | 4,474 | 149.5 |
| 2015 | 2,294 | 76.7 | 4,498 | 150.3 | 84,790 | 2,833.6 | 24,799 | 828.8 | 55,748 | 1,863.0 | 4,243 | 141.8 |
| Percent change | -4.6 | -4.6 | -1.9 | -1.9 | -2.4 | -2.4 | +3.8 | +3.8 | -4.7 | -4.7 | -5.2 | -5.1 |
| **Tennessee** | | | | | | | | | | | | |
| 2014 | 7,268 | 111.0 | 29,757 | 454.5 | 200,911 | 3,068.4 | 46,798 | 714.7 | 141,464 | 2,160.5 | 12,649 | 193.2 |
| 2015 | 7,474 | 113.2 | 29,844 | 452.2 | 193,796 | 2,936.2 | 43,247 | 655.2 | 137,679 | 2,086.0 | 12,870 | 195.0 |
| Percent change | +2.8 | +2.0 | +0.3 | -0.5 | -3.5 | -4.3 | -7.6 | -8.3 | -2.7 | -3.5 | +1.7 | +0.9 |
| **West South Central** | | | | | | | | | | | | |
| 2014 | 41,856 | 108.8 | 103,419 | 268.8 | 1,191,604 | 3,097.1 | 261,405 | 679.4 | 835,989 | 2,172.8 | 94,210 | 244.9 |
| 2015 | 42,587 | 109.1 | 107,915 | 276.5 | 1,144,082 | 2,931.3 | 239,553 | 613.8 | 811,081 | 2,078.1 | 93,448 | 239.4 |
| Percent change | +1.7 | +0.3 | +4.3 | +2.9 | -4.0 | -5.4 | -8.4 | -9.7 | -3.0 | -4.4 | -0.8 | -2.2 |
| **Arkansas** | | | | | | | | | | | | |
| 2014 | 2,037 | 68.7 | 10,220 | 344.5 | 99,452 | 3,352.1 | 24,816 | 836.4 | 69,001 | 2,325.7 | 5,635 | 189.9 |
| 2015 | 2,098 | 70.4 | 11,316 | 380.0 | 96,836 | 3,251.5 | 22,640 | 760.2 | 68,424 | 2,297.5 | 5,772 | 193.8 |
| Percent change | +3.0 | +2.6 | +10.7 | +10.3 | -2.6 | -3.0 | -8.8 | -9.1 | -0.8 | -1.2 | +2.4 | +2.0 |
| **Louisiana** | | | | | | | | | | | | |
| 2014 | 5,725 | 123.1 | 16,400 | 352.8 | 161,192 | 3,467.2 | 38,541 | 829.0 | 113,251 | 2,436.0 | 9,400 | 202.2 |
| 2015 | 5,550 | 118.8 | 17,454 | 373.7 | 156,629 | 3,353.4 | 35,453 | 759.0 | 111,435 | 2,385.8 | 9,741 | 208.6 |
| Percent change | -3.1 | -3.5 | +6.4 | +5.9 | -2.8 | -3.3 | -8.0 | -8.4 | -1.6 | -2.1 | +3.6 | +3.1 |
| **Oklahoma** | | | | | | | | | | | | |
| 2014 | 3,073 | 79.2 | 10,937 | 281.9 | 117,445 | 3,027.2 | 29,963 | 772.3 | 76,719 | 1,977.5 | 10,763 | 277.4 |
| 2015 | 3,005 | 76.8 | 11,418 | 291.9 | 112,878 | 2,885.9 | 28,406 | 726.2 | 74,022 | 1,892.5 | 10,450 | 267.2 |
| Percent change | -2.2 | -3.0 | +4.4 | +3.6 | -3.9 | -4.7 | -5.2 | -6.0 | -3.5 | -4.3 | -2.9 | -3.7 |
| **Texas** | | | | | | | | | | | | |
| 2014 | 31,021 | 115.0 | 65,862 | 244.1 | 813,515 | 3,015.4 | 168,085 | 623.0 | 577,018 | 2,138.8 | 68,412 | 253.6 |
| 2015 | 31,934 | 116.3 | 67,727 | 246.6 | 777,739 | 2,831.3 | 153,054 | 557.2 | 557,200 | 2,028.5 | 67,485 | 245.7 |
| Percent change | +2.9 | +1.1 | +2.8 | +1.0 | -4.4 | -6.1 | -8.9 | -10.6 | -3.4 | -5.2 | -1.4 | -3.1 |
| **West[6,8]** | | | | | | | | | | | | |
| 2014 | 77,246 | 102.7 | 170,538 | 226.8 | 2,048,509 | 2,724.8 | 418,153 | 556.2 | 1,372,329 | 1,825.4 | 258,027 | 343.2 |
| 2015 | 82,663 | 108.7 | 185,031 | 243.3 | 2,129,015 | 2,799.7 | 401,849 | 528.4 | 1,444,684 | 1,899.8 | 282,482 | 371.5 |
| Percent change | +7.0 | +5.8 | +8.5 | +7.3 | +3.9 | +2.7 | -3.9 | -5.0 | +5.3 | +4.1 | +9.5 | +8.2 |

# Table 4. Crime,[1] by Region, Geographic Division, and State, 2014–2015—*Continued*

(Number, rate per 100,000 population, percent.)

| Area | Population[2] | Violent crime[3] | | Murder and nonnegligent manslaughter | | Rape (revised definition)[4] | | Rape (legacy definition)[5] | |
|---|---|---|---|---|---|---|---|---|---|
| | | Number | Rate | Number | Rate | Number | Rate | Number | Rate |
| **Mountain[6,8]** ................................. | | | | | | | | | |
| 2014.................................. | 23,195,079 | 87,823 | 378.6 | 884 | 3.8 | 12,123 | 52.3 | 8,749 | 37.7 |
| 2015.................................. | 23,530,498 | 94,878 | 403.2 | 918 | 3.9 | 12,784 | 54.3 | 9,311 | 39.6 |
| Percent change ................... | 1.4 | +8.0 | +6.5 | +3.8 | +2.4 | +5.5 | +3.9 | +6.4 | +4.9 |
| Arizona.................................. | | | | | | | | | |
| 2014.................................. | 6,728,783 | 26,422 | 392.7 | 311 | 4.6 | 3,272 | 48.6 | 2,356 | 35.0 |
| 2015.................................. | 6,828,065 | 28,012 | 410.2 | 309 | 4.5 | 3,108 | 45.5 | 2,294 | 33.6 |
| Percent change ................... | 1.5 | +6.0 | +4.5 | -0.6 | -2.1 | -5.0 | -6.4 | -2.6 | -4.0 |
| Colorado.................................. | | | | | | | | | |
| 2014.................................. | 5,355,588 | 16,487 | 307.8 | 150 | 2.8 | 3,089 | 57.7 | 2,236 | 41.8 |
| 2015.................................. | 5,456,574 | 17,515 | 321.0 | 176 | 3.2 | 3,257 | 59.7 | 2,377 | 43.6 |
| Percent change ................... | 1.9 | +6.2 | +4.3 | +17.3 | +15.2 | +5.4 | +3.5 | +6.3 | +4.3 |
| Idaho.................................. | | | | | | | | | |
| 2014.................................. | 1,634,806 | 3,439 | 210.4 | 32 | 2.0 | 645 | 39.5 | 463 | 28.3 |
| 2015.................................. | 1,654,930 | 3,568 | 215.6 | 32 | 1.9 | 694 | 41.9 | 533 | 32.2 |
| Percent change ................... | 1.2 | +3.8 | +2.5 | 0.0 | -1.2 | +7.6 | +6.3 | +15.1 | +13.7 |
| Montana.................................. | | | | | | | | | |
| 2014.................................. | 1,023,252 | 3,361 | 328.5 | 38 | 3.7 | 558 | 54.5 | 396 | 38.7 |
| 2015.................................. | 1,032,949 | 3,611 | 349.6 | 36 | 3.5 | 547 | 53.0 | 431 | 41.7 |
| Percent change ................... | 0.9 | +7.4 | +6.4 | -5.3 | -6.2 | -2.0 | -2.9 | +8.8 | +7.8 |
| Nevada.................................. | | | | | | | | | |
| 2014.................................. | 2,838,281 | 18,043 | 635.7 | 170 | 6.0 | 1,357 | 47.8 | 987 | 34.8 |
| 2015.................................. | 2,890,845 | 20,118 | 695.9 | 178 | 6.2 | 1,688 | 58.4 | 1,238 | 42.8 |
| Percent change ................... | 1.9 | +11.5 | +9.5 | +4.7 | +2.8 | +24.4 | +22.1 | +25.4 | +23.1 |
| New Mexico[8].................................. | | | | | | | | | |
| 2014.................................. | 2,085,567 | 12,465 | 597.7 | 101 | 4.8 | 1,481 | 71.0 | 1,070 | 51.3 |
| 2015.................................. | 2,085,109 | 13,681 | 656.1 | 117 | 5.6 | 1,672 | 80.2 | 1,215 | 58.3 |
| Percent change ................... | 0.0 | +9.8 | +9.8 | +15.8 | +15.9 | +12.9 | +12.9 | +13.6 | +13.6 |
| Utah[6].................................. | | | | | | | | | |
| 2014.................................. | 2,944,498 | 6,464 | 219.5 | 66 | 2.2 | 1,547 | 52.5 | 1,114 | 37.8 |
| 2015.................................. | 2,995,919 | 7,071 | 236.0 | 54 | 1.8 | 1,645 | 54.9 | 1,098 | 36.6 |
| Percent change ................... | 1.7 | +9.4 | +7.5 | -18.2 | -19.6 | +6.3 | +4.5 | -1.4 | -3.1 |
| Wyoming.................................. | | | | | | | | | |
| 2014.................................. | 584,304 | 1,142 | 195.4 | 16 | 2.7 | 174 | 29.8 | 127 | 21.7 |
| 2015.................................. | 586,107 | 1,302 | 222.1 | 16 | 2.7 | 173 | 29.5 | 125 | 21.3 |
| Percent change ................... | 0.3 | +14.0 | +13.7 | 0.0 | -0.3 | -0.6 | -0.9 | -1.6 | -1.9 |
| **Pacific[6]** ................................. | | | | | | | | | |
| 2014.................................. | 51,983,962 | 192,288 | 369.9 | 2,023 | 3.9 | 17,297 | 33.3 | 12,494 | 24.0 |
| 2015.................................. | 52,514,181 | 207,338 | 394.8 | 2,249 | 4.3 | 18,571 | 35.4 | 13,794 | 26.3 |
| Percent change ................... | 1.0 | +7.8 | +6.7 | +11.2 | +10.0 | +7.4 | +6.3 | +10.4 | +9.3 |
| Alaska.................................. | | | | | | | | | |
| 2014.................................. | 737,046 | 4,684 | 635.5 | 41 | 5.6 | 771 | 104.6 | 553 | 75.0 |
| 2015.................................. | 738,432 | 5,392 | 730.2 | 59 | 8.0 | 901 | 122.0 | 650 | 88.0 |
| Percent change ................... | 0.2 | +15.1 | +14.9 | +43.9 | +43.6 | +16.9 | +16.6 | +17.5 | +17.3 |
| California.................................. | | | | | | | | | |
| 2014.................................. | 38,792,291 | 153,763 | 396.4 | 1,700 | 4.4 | 11,578 | 29.8 | 8,389 | 21.6 |
| 2015.................................. | 39,144,818 | 166,883 | 426.3 | 1,861 | 4.8 | 12,811 | 32.7 | 9,387 | 24.0 |
| Percent change ................... | 0.9 | +8.5 | +7.6 | +9.5 | +8.5 | +10.6 | +9.7 | +11.9 | +10.9 |
| Hawaii.................................. | | | | | | | | | |
| 2014.................................. | 1,420,257 | 3,362 | 236.7 | 20 | 1.4 | 548 | 38.6 | 388 | 27.3 |
| 2015.................................. | 1,431,603 | 4,201 | 293.4 | 19 | 1.3 | 561 | 39.2 | 400 | 27.9 |
| Percent change ................... | 0.8 | +25.0 | +24.0 | -5.0 | -5.8 | +2.4 | +1.6 | +3.1 | +2.3 |
| Oregon[6].................................. | | | | | | | | | |
| 2014.................................. | 3,971,202 | 10,294 | 259.2 | 84 | 2.1 | 1,620 | 40.8 | 1,165 | 29.3 |
| 2015.................................. | 4,028,977 | 10,468 | 259.8 | 99 | 2.5 | 1,593 | 39.5 | 1,164 | 28.9 |
| Percent change ................... | 1.5 | +1.7 | +0.2 | +17.9 | +16.2 | -1.7 | -3.1 | -0.1 | -1.5 |
| Washington[6].................................. | | | | | | | | | |
| 2014.................................. | 7,063,166 | 20,185 | 285.8 | 178 | 2.5 | 2,780 | 39.4 | 1,999 | 28.3 |
| 2015.................................. | 7,170,351 | 20,394 | 284.4 | 211 | 2.9 | 2,705 | 37.7 | 2,193 | 30.6 |
| Percent change ................... | 1.5 | +1.0 | -0.5 | +18.5 | +16.8 | -2.7 | -4.2 | +9.7 | +8.1 |
| **Puerto Rico[10]** ................................. | | | | | | | | | |
| 2014.................................. | 3,534,888 | 8,383 | 237.2 | 681 | 19.3 | 56 | 1.6 | 41 | 1.2 |
| 2015.................................. | 3,474,182 | 7,629 | 219.6 | 584 | 16.8 | 165 | 4.7 | 123 | 3.5 |
| Percent change ................... | -1.7 | -9.0 | -7.4 | -14.2 | -12.7 | +194.6 | +199.8 | +200.0 | +205.2 |

# Table 4. Crime,[1] by Region, Geographic Division, and State, 2014–2015—*Continued*

(Number, rate per 100,000 population, percent.)

| Area | Robbery Number | Robbery Rate | Aggravated assault Number | Aggravated assault Rate | Property crime Number | Property crime Rate | Burglary Number | Burglary Rate | Larceny-theft Number | Larceny-theft Rate | Motor vehicle theft Number | Motor vehicle theft Rate |
|---|---|---|---|---|---|---|---|---|---|---|---|---|
| **Mountain[6,8]** | | | | | | | | | | | | |
| 2014 | 19,073 | 82.2 | 55,743 | 240.3 | 650,561 | 2,804.7 | 130,793 | 563.9 | 461,714 | 1,990.6 | 58,054 | 250.3 |
| 2015 | 20,242 | 86.0 | 60,934 | 259.0 | 661,861 | 2,812.8 | 125,048 | 531.4 | 470,563 | 1,999.8 | 66,250 | 281.5 |
| Percent change | +6.1 | +4.6 | +9.3 | +7.8 | +1.7 | +0.3 | -4.4 | -5.8 | +1.9 | +0.5 | +14.1 | +12.5 |
| Arizona | | | | | | | | | | | | |
| 2014 | 6,225 | 92.5 | 16,614 | 246.9 | 213,406 | 3,171.5 | 43,412 | 645.2 | 152,683 | 2,269.1 | 17,311 | 257.3 |
| 2015 | 6,360 | 93.1 | 18,235 | 267.1 | 207,107 | 3,033.2 | 37,957 | 555.9 | 152,365 | 2,231.5 | 16,785 | 245.8 |
| Percent change | +2.2 | +0.7 | +9.8 | +8.2 | -3.0 | -4.4 | -12.6 | -13.8 | -0.2 | -1.7 | -3.0 | -4.4 |
| Colorado | | | | | | | | | | | | |
| 2014 | 3,037 | 56.7 | 10,211 | 190.7 | 135,789 | 2,535.5 | 23,502 | 438.8 | 99,688 | 1,861.4 | 12,599 | 235.2 |
| 2015 | 3,323 | 60.9 | 10,759 | 197.2 | 144,136 | 2,641.5 | 23,454 | 429.8 | 104,682 | 1,918.5 | 16,000 | 293.2 |
| Percent change | +9.4 | +7.4 | +5.4 | +3.4 | +6.1 | +4.2 | -0.2 | -2.1 | +5.0 | +3.1 | +27.0 | +24.6 |
| Idaho | | | | | | | | | | | | |
| 2014 | 203 | 12.4 | 2,559 | 156.5 | 30,440 | 1,862.0 | 6,466 | 395.5 | 22,297 | 1,363.9 | 1,677 | 102.6 |
| 2015 | 192 | 11.6 | 2,650 | 160.1 | 28,858 | 1,743.8 | 6,124 | 370.0 | 20,863 | 1,260.7 | 1,871 | 113.1 |
| Percent change | -5.4 | -6.6 | +3.6 | +2.3 | -5.2 | -6.3 | -5.3 | -6.4 | -6.4 | -7.6 | +11.6 | +10.2 |
| Montana | | | | | | | | | | | | |
| 2014 | 202 | 19.7 | 2,563 | 250.5 | 25,525 | 2,494.5 | 3,639 | 355.6 | 19,826 | 1,937.5 | 2,060 | 201.3 |
| 2015 | 210 | 20.3 | 2,818 | 272.8 | 27,100 | 2,623.6 | 3,838 | 371.6 | 20,844 | 2,017.9 | 2,418 | 234.1 |
| Percent change | +4.0 | +3.0 | +9.9 | +8.9 | +6.2 | +5.2 | +5.5 | +4.5 | +5.1 | +4.1 | +17.4 | +16.3 |
| Nevada | | | | | | | | | | | | |
| 2014 | 5,954 | 209.8 | 10,562 | 372.1 | 74,574 | 2,627.4 | 21,924 | 772.4 | 42,466 | 1,496.2 | 10,184 | 358.8 |
| 2015 | 6,287 | 217.5 | 11,965 | 413.9 | 77,137 | 2,668.3 | 22,360 | 773.5 | 43,426 | 1,502.2 | 11,351 | 392.7 |
| Percent change | +5.6 | +3.7 | +13.3 | +11.2 | +3.4 | +1.6 | +2.0 | +0.1 | +2.3 | +0.4 | +11.5 | +9.4 |
| New Mexico[8] | | | | | | | | | | | | |
| 2014 | 2,086 | 100.0 | 8,797 | 421.8 | 73,877 | 3,542.3 | 18,505 | 887.3 | 49,082 | 2,353.4 | 6,290 | 301.6 |
| 2015 | 2,485 | 119.2 | 9,407 | 451.2 | 77,094 | 3,697.4 | 17,085 | 819.4 | 51,483 | 2,469.1 | 8,526 | 408.9 |
| Percent change | +19.1 | +19.2 | +6.9 | +7.0 | +4.4 | +4.4 | -7.7 | -7.7 | +4.9 | +4.9 | +35.5 | +35.6 |
| Utah[6] | | | | | | | | | | | | |
| 2014 | 1,313 | 44.6 | 3,538 | 120.2 | 85,473 | 2,902.8 | 11,656 | 395.9 | 66,487 | 2,258.0 | 7,330 | 248.9 |
| 2015 | 1,326 | 44.3 | 4,046 | 135.1 | 89,278 | 2,980.0 | 12,468 | 416.2 | 68,103 | 2,273.2 | 8,707 | 290.6 |
| Percent change | +1.0 | -0.7 | +14.4 | +12.4 | +4.5 | +2.7 | +7.0 | +5.1 | +2.4 | +0.7 | +18.8 | +16.7 |
| Wyoming | | | | | | | | | | | | |
| 2014 | 53 | 9.1 | 899 | 153.9 | 11,477 | 1,964.2 | 1,689 | 289.1 | 9,185 | 1,572.0 | 603 | 103.2 |
| 2015 | 59 | 10.1 | 1,054 | 179.8 | 11,151 | 1,902.6 | 1,762 | 300.6 | 8,797 | 1,500.9 | 592 | 101.0 |
| Percent change | +11.3 | +11.0 | +17.2 | +16.9 | -2.8 | -3.1 | +4.3 | +4.0 | -4.2 | -4.5 | -1.8 | -2.1 |
| **Pacific[6]** | | | | | | | | | | | | |
| 2014 | 58,173 | 111.9 | 114,795 | 220.8 | 1,397,948 | 2,689.2 | 287,360 | 552.8 | 910,615 | 1,751.7 | 199,973 | 384.7 |
| 2015 | 62,421 | 118.9 | 124,097 | 236.3 | 1,467,154 | 2,793.8 | 276,801 | 527.1 | 974,121 | 1,855.0 | 216,232 | 411.8 |
| Percent change | +7.3 | +6.2 | +8.1 | +7.0 | +5.0 | +3.9 | -3.7 | -4.6 | +7.0 | +5.9 | +8.1 | +7.0 |
| Alaska | | | | | | | | | | | | |
| 2014 | 629 | 85.3 | 3,243 | 440.0 | 20,334 | 2,758.9 | 3,150 | 427.4 | 15,445 | 2,095.5 | 1,739 | 235.9 |
| 2015 | 761 | 103.1 | 3,671 | 497.1 | 20,806 | 2,817.6 | 3,511 | 475.5 | 15,249 | 2,065.1 | 2,046 | 277.1 |
| Percent change | +21.0 | +20.8 | +13.2 | +13.0 | +2.3 | +2.1 | +11.5 | +11.3 | -1.3 | -1.5 | +17.7 | +17.4 |
| California | | | | | | | | | | | | |
| 2014 | 48,681 | 125.5 | 91,804 | 236.7 | 947,193 | 2,441.7 | 202,669 | 522.4 | 592,673 | 1,527.8 | 151,851 | 391.4 |
| 2015 | 52,862 | 135.0 | 99,349 | 253.8 | 1,024,914 | 2,618.3 | 197,404 | 504.3 | 656,517 | 1,677.1 | 170,993 | 436.8 |
| Percent change | +8.6 | +7.6 | +8.2 | +7.2 | +8.2 | +7.2 | -2.6 | -3.5 | +10.8 | +9.8 | +12.6 | +11.6 |
| Hawaii | | | | | | | | | | | | |
| 2014 | 952 | 67.0 | 1,842 | 129.7 | 46,022 | 3,240.4 | 7,470 | 526.0 | 33,003 | 2,323.7 | 5,549 | 390.7 |
| 2015 | 1,203 | 84.0 | 2,418 | 168.9 | 54,346 | 3,796.2 | 6,557 | 458.0 | 42,010 | 2,934.5 | 5,779 | 403.7 |
| Percent change | +26.4 | +25.4 | +31.3 | +30.2 | +18.1 | +17.2 | -12.2 | -12.9 | +27.3 | +26.3 | +4.1 | +3.3 |
| Oregon[6] | | | | | | | | | | | | |
| 2014 | 2,270 | 57.2 | 6,320 | 159.1 | 123,142 | 3,100.9 | 18,690 | 470.6 | 94,177 | 2,371.5 | 10,275 | 258.7 |
| 2015 | 2,146 | 53.3 | 6,630 | 164.6 | 118,719 | 2,946.6 | 18,336 | 455.1 | 89,836 | 2,229.7 | 10,547 | 261.8 |
| Percent change | -5.5 | -6.8 | +4.9 | +3.4 | -3.6 | -5.0 | -1.9 | -3.3 | -4.6 | -6.0 | +2.6 | +1.2 |
| Washington[6] | | | | | | | | | | | | |
| 2014 | 5,641 | 79.9 | 11,586 | 164.0 | 261,257 | 3,698.9 | 55,381 | 784.1 | 175,317 | 2,482.1 | 30,559 | 432.7 |
| 2015 | 5,449 | 76.0 | 12,029 | 167.8 | 248,369 | 3,463.8 | 50,993 | 711.2 | 170,509 | 2,378.0 | 26,867 | 374.7 |
| Percent change | -3.4 | -4.8 | +3.8 | +2.3 | -4.9 | -6.4 | -7.9 | -9.3 | -2.7 | -4.2 | -12.1 | -13.4 |
| **Puerto Rico[10]** | | | | | | | | | | | | |
| 2014 | 5,171 | 146.3 | 2,475 | 70.0 | 45,622 | 1,290.6 | 12,035 | 340.5 | 28,948 | 818.9 | 4,639 | 131.2 |
| 2015 | 4,070 | 117.1 | 2,810 | 80.9 | 37,717 | 1,085.6 | 9,150 | 263.4 | 24,493 | 705.0 | 4,074 | 117.3 |
| Percent change | -21.3 | -19.9 | +13.5 | +15.5 | -17.3 | -15.9 | -24.0 | -22.6 | -15.4 | -13.9 | -12.2 | -10.6 |

*Note:* Although arson data are included in the trend and clearance tables, sufficient data are not available to estimate totals for this offense. Therefore, no arson data are published in this table.
X = Not applicable.
* = Less than one-tenth of 1 percent.
[1] The previous year's crime figures have been adjusted.
[2] Population figures are U.S. Census Bureau provisional estimates as of July 1, 2015.
[3] The violent crime figures include the offenses of murder, rape (revised definition), robbery, and aggravated assault.
[4] The figures shown in this column for the offense of rape were estimated using the revised Uniform Crime Reporting (UCR) definition of rape. See chapter notes for more detail.
[5] The figures shown in this column for the offense of rape were estimated using the legacy Uniform Crime Reporting (UCR) definition of rape. See chapter notes for more detail.
[6] Agencies within this state submitted rape data according to both the revised UCR definition of rape and the legacy UCR definition of rape.
[7] Includes offenses reported by the Metro Transit Police and the District of Columbia Fire and Emergency Services Fire Investigation Unit.
[8] This state's agencies submitted rape data according to the legacy UCR definition of rape.
[9] Because of changes in the state/local agency's reporting practices, figures are not comparable to previous years' data.
[10] The figures submitted by Puerto Rico for rape were not verified and may not be comparable to previous years' data.

# Table 5. Crime, by State and Area, 2015

(Number, percent, rate per 100,000 population.)

| Area | Population | Violent crime[1] | Murder and nonnegligent manslaughter | Rape (revised definition)[2] | Rape (legacy definition)[3] | Robbery | Aggra- vated assault | Property crime | Burglary | Larceny- theft | Motor vehicle theft |
|---|---|---|---|---|---|---|---|---|---|---|---|
| **Alabama** | | | | | | | | | | | |
| Metropolitan statistical area | 3,708,033 | | | | | | | | | | |
|   Area actually reporting | 97.1% | 18,122 | 283 | 1,496 | 1,080 | 4,080 | 12,263 | 113,447 | 27,208 | 78,141 | 8,098 |
|   Estimated total | 100.0% | 18,500 | 287 | 1,537 | 1,111 | 4,138 | 12,538 | 115,920 | 27,852 | 79,799 | 8,269 |
| Cities outside metropolitan areas | 522,241 | | | | | | | | | | |
|   Area actually reporting | 97.4% | 3,178 | 32 | 311 | 218 | 354 | 2,481 | 20,873 | 4,438 | 15,106 | 1,329 |
|   Estimated total | 100.0% | 3,240 | 33 | 315 | 222 | 360 | 2,532 | 21,203 | 4,518 | 15,329 | 1,356 |
| Nonmetropolitan counties | 628,705 | | | | | | | | | | |
|   Area actually reporting | 99.4% | 1,205 | 28 | 186 | 122 | 112 | 879 | 7,578 | 2,868 | 4,004 | 706 |
|   Estimated total | 100.0% | 1,212 | 28 | 187 | 123 | 113 | 884 | 7,623 | 2,885 | 4,028 | 710 |
| State total | 4,858,979 | 22,952 | 348 | 2,039 | 1,456 | 4,611 | 15,954 | 144,746 | 35,255 | 99,156 | 10,335 |
|   Rate per 100,000 inhabitants | | 472.4 | 7.2 | 42.0 | 30.0 | 94.9 | 328.3 | 2,978.9 | 725.6 | 2,040.7 | 212.7 |
| **Alaska** | | | | | | | | | | | |
| Metropolitan statistical area | 351,857 | | | | | | | | | | |
|   Area actually reporting | 100.0% | 3,464 | 27 | 541 | 401 | 658 | 2,238 | 14,151 | 1,919 | 10,884 | 1,348 |
| Cities outside metropolitan areas | 127,499 | | | | | | | | | | |
|   Area actually reporting | 97.2% | 886 | 10 | 178 | 128 | 60 | 638 | 3,523 | 530 | 2,737 | 256 |
|   Estimated total | 100.0% | 913 | 10 | 184 | 133 | 62 | 657 | 3,625 | 545 | 2,817 | 263 |
| Nonmetropolitan counties | 259,076 | | | | | | | | | | |
|   Area actually reporting | 100.0% | 1,015 | 22 | 176 | 116 | 41 | 776 | 3,030 | 1,047 | 1,548 | 435 |
| State total | 738,432 | 5,392 | 59 | 901 | 650 | 761 | 3,671 | 20,806 | 3,511 | 15,249 | 2,046 |
|   Rate per 100,000 inhabitants | | 730.2 | 8.0 | 122.0 | 88.0 | 103.1 | 497.1 | 2,817.6 | 475.5 | 2,065.1 | 277.1 |
| **Arizona** | | | | | | | | | | | |
| Metropolitan statistical area | 6,479,810 | | | | | | | | | | |
|   Area actually reporting | 99.7% | 24,725 | 280 | 2,805 | 2,072 | 6,239 | 15,401 | 198,411 | 35,919 | 146,431 | 16,061 |
|   Estimated total | 100.0% | 24,781 | 280 | 2,811 | 2,077 | 6,251 | 15,439 | 198,994 | 36,015 | 146,882 | 16,097 |
| Cities outside metropolitan areas | 124,240 | | | | | | | | | | |
|   Area actually reporting | 93.9% | 2,678 | 24 | 269 | 199 | 91 | 2,294 | 5,854 | 1,280 | 4,095 | 479 |
|   Estimated total | 100.0% | 2,851 | 26 | 286 | 210 | 97 | 2,442 | 6,233 | 1,363 | 4,360 | 510 |
| Nonmetropolitan counties | 224,015 | | | | | | | | | | |
|   Area actually reporting | 100.0% | 380 | 3 | 11 | 7 | 12 | 354 | 1,880 | 579 | 1,123 | 178 |
| State total | 6,828,065 | 28,012 | 309 | 3,108 | 2,294 | 6,360 | 18,235 | 207,107 | 37,957 | 152,365 | 16,785 |
|   Rate per 100,000 inhabitants | | 410.2 | 4.5 | 45.5 | 33.6 | 93.1 | 267.1 | 3,033.2 | 555.9 | 2,231.5 | 245.8 |
| **Arkansas** | | | | | | | | | | | |
| Metropolitan statistical area | 1,837,196 | | | | | | | | | | |
|   Area actually reporting | 99.9% | 10,724 | 124 | 1,133 | 838 | 1,673 | 7,794 | 67,157 | 14,402 | 48,559 | 4,196 |
|   Estimated total | 100.0% | 10,727 | 124 | 1,134 | 839 | 1,673 | 7,796 | 67,180 | 14,407 | 48,576 | 4,197 |
| Cities outside metropolitan areas | 515,124 | | | | | | | | | | |
|   Area actually reporting | 89.3% | 2,724 | 36 | 406 | 248 | 333 | 1,949 | 17,524 | 4,692 | 12,108 | 724 |
|   Estimated total | 100.0% | 3,057 | 40 | 462 | 289 | 373 | 2,182 | 19,622 | 5,254 | 13,557 | 811 |
| Nonmetropolitan counties | 625,884 | | | | | | | | | | |
|   Area actually reporting | 90.1% | 1,559 | 15 | 292 | 143 | 47 | 1,205 | 9,036 | 2,683 | 5,665 | 688 |
|   Estimated total | 100.0% | 1,742 | 17 | 335 | 172 | 52 | 1,338 | 10,034 | 2,979 | 6,291 | 764 |
| State total | 2,978,204 | 15,526 | 181 | 1,931 | 1,300 | 2,098 | 11,316 | 96,836 | 22,640 | 68,424 | 5,772 |
|   Rate per 100,000 inhabitants | | 521.3 | 6.1 | 64.8 | 43.7 | 70.4 | 380.0 | 3,251.5 | 760.2 | 2,297.5 | 193.8 |
| **California** | | | | | | | | | | | |
| Metropolitan statistical area | 38,317,995 | | | | | | | | | | |
|   Area actually reporting | 99.9% | 163,195 | 1,815 | 12,411 | 9,116 | 52,439 | 96,530 | 1,006,421 | 192,016 | 645,773 | 168,632 |
|   Estimated total | 100.0% | 163,219 | 1,815 | 12,413 | 9,117 | 52,447 | 96,544 | 1,006,607 | 192,051 | 645,895 | 168,661 |
| Cities outside metropolitan areas | 268,497 | | | | | | | | | | |
|   Area actually reporting | 100.0% | 1,630 | 15 | 151 | 106 | 245 | 1,219 | 9,889 | 2,189 | 6,747 | 953 |
| Nonmetropolitan counties | 558,326 | | | | | | | | | | |
|   Area actually reporting | 100.0% | 2,034 | 31 | 247 | 164 | 170 | 1,586 | 8,418 | 3,164 | 3,875 | 1,379 |
| State total | 39,144,818 | 166,883 | 1,861 | 12,811 | 9,387 | 52,862 | 99,349 | 1,024,914 | 197,404 | 656,517 | 170,993 |
|   Rate per 100,000 inhabitants | | 426.3 | 4.8 | 32.7 | 24.0 | 135.0 | 253.8 | 2,618.3 | 504.3 | 1,677.1 | 436.8 |
| **Colorado** | | | | | | | | | | | |
| Metropolitan statistical area | 4,763,884 | | | | | | | | | | |
|   Area actually reporting | 99.9% | 16,306 | 164 | 2,991 | 2,196 | 3,235 | 9,916 | 131,216 | 21,077 | 94,787 | 15,352 |
|   Estimated total | 100.0% | 16,308 | 164 | 2,991 | 2,196 | 3,235 | 9,918 | 131,247 | 21,081 | 94,811 | 15,355 |
| Cities outside metropolitan areas | 335,080 | | | | | | | | | | |
|   Area actually reporting | 96.9% | 750 | 6 | 167 | 119 | 75 | 502 | 9,539 | 1,440 | 7,708 | 391 |
|   Estimated total | 100.0% | 771 | 6 | 170 | 122 | 77 | 518 | 9,842 | 1,486 | 7,953 | 403 |
| Nonmetropolitan counties | 357,610 | | | | | | | | | | |
|   Area actually reporting | 98.4% | 430 | 6 | 95 | 58 | 11 | 318 | 2,999 | 873 | 1,888 | 238 |
|   Estimated total | 100.0% | 436 | 6 | 96 | 59 | 11 | 323 | 3,047 | 887 | 1,918 | 242 |
| State total | 5,456,574 | 17,515 | 176 | 3,257 | 2,377 | 3,323 | 10,759 | 144,136 | 23,454 | 104,682 | 16,000 |
|   Rate per 100,000 inhabitants | | 321.0 | 3.2 | 59.7 | 43.6 | 60.9 | 197.2 | 2,641.5 | 429.8 | 1,918.5 | 293.2 |

Table 5. Crime, by State and Area, 2015—*Continued*

(Number, percent, rate per 100,000 population.)

| Area | Population | Violent crime[1] | Murder and nonnegligent manslaughter | Rape (revised definition)[2] | Rape (legacy definition)[3] | Robbery | Aggravated assault | Property crime | Burglary | Larceny-theft | Motor vehicle theft |
|---|---|---|---|---|---|---|---|---|---|---|---|
| **Connecticut** | | | | | | | | | | | |
| Metropolitan statistical area | 2,951,843 | | | | | | | | | | |
| Area actually reporting | 100.0% | 7,441 | 102 | 694 | 521 | 2,819 | 3,826 | 59,961 | 9,050 | 44,991 | 5,920 |
| Cities outside metropolitan areas | 114,485 | | | | | | | | | | |
| Area actually reporting | 100.0% | 110 | 1 | 23 | 20 | 27 | 59 | 1,968 | 269 | 1,606 | 93 |
| Nonmetropolitan counties | 524,558 | | | | | | | | | | |
| Area actually reporting | 100.0% | 294 | 14 | 56 | 41 | 46 | 178 | 3,137 | 734 | 2,078 | 325 |
| State total | 3,590,886 | 7,845 | 117 | 773 | 582 | 2,892 | 4,063 | 65,066 | 10,053 | 48,675 | 6,338 |
| Rate per 100,000 inhabitants | | 218.5 | 3.3 | 21.5 | 16.2 | 80.5 | 113.1 | 1,812.0 | 280.0 | 1,355.5 | 176.5 |
| **Delaware** | | | | | | | | | | | |
| Metropolitan statistical area | 945,934 | | | | | | | | | | |
| Area actually reporting | 100.0% | 4,720 | 63 | 341 | 243 | 1,235 | 3,081 | 25,454 | 4,772 | 19,501 | 1,181 |
| Cities outside metropolitan areas | None | | | | | | | | | | |
| Area actually reporting | None | | | | | | | | | | |
| Nonmetropolitan counties | None | | | | | | | | | | |
| Area actually reporting | None | | | | | | | | | | |
| State total | 672,228 | 8,531 | 162 | 494 | 366 | 3,742 | 4,133 | 31,435 | 2,971 | 25,200 | 3,264 |
| Rate per 100,000 inhabitants | | 1,269.1 | 24.1 | 73.5 | 54.4 | 556.7 | 614.8 | 4,676.2 | 442.0 | 3,748.7 | 485.5 |
| **District of Columbia[4]** | | | | | | | | | | | |
| Metropolitan statistical area | 672,228 | | | | | | | | | | |
| Area actually reporting | 100.0% | 8,531 | 162 | 494 | 366 | 3,742 | 4,133 | 31,435 | 2,971 | 25,200 | 3,264 |
| Cities outside metropolitan areas | None | 8,531 | 162 | 494 | 366 | 3,742 | 4,133 | 31,435 | 2,971 | 25,200 | 3,264 |
| Area actually reporting | None | | | | | | | | | | |
| Nonmetropolitan counties | None | | | | | | | | | | |
| Area actually reporting | None | | | | | | | | | | |
| District total | 672,228 | 8,531 | 162 | 494 | 366 | 3,742 | 4,133 | 31,435 | 2,971 | 25,200 | 3,264 |
| Rate per 100,000 inhabitants | | 1,269.1 | 24.1 | 73.5 | 54.4 | 556.7 | 614.8 | 4,676.2 | 442.0 | 3,748.7 | 485.5 |
| **Florida** | | | | | | | | | | | |
| Metropolitan statistical area | 19,564,380 | | | | | | | | | | |
| Area actually reporting | 99.8% | 89,825 | 999 | 7,321 | 5,273 | 20,811 | 60,694 | 553,343 | 104,601 | 408,936 | 39,806 |
| Estimated total | 100.0% | 89,966 | 1,000 | 7,334 | 5,283 | 20,843 | 60,789 | 554,303 | 104,776 | 409,655 | 39,872 |
| Cities outside metropolitan areas | 147,871 | | | | | | | | | | |
| Area actually reporting | 96.6% | 1,032 | 12 | 54 | 37 | 160 | 806 | 5,799 | 1,224 | 4,299 | 276 |
| Estimated total | 100.0% | 1,067 | 12 | 55 | 38 | 166 | 834 | 6,001 | 1,267 | 4,448 | 286 |
| Nonmetropolitan counties | 559,021 | | | | | | | | | | |
| Area actually reporting | 98.5% | 2,555 | 29 | 162 | 108 | 126 | 2,238 | 9,815 | 3,176 | 6,144 | 495 |
| Estimated total | 100.0% | 2,593 | 29 | 164 | 109 | 128 | 2,272 | 9,966 | 3,225 | 6,238 | 503 |
| State total | 20,271,272 | 93,626 | 1,041 | 7,553 | 5,430 | 21,137 | 63,895 | 570,270 | 109,268 | 420,341 | 40,661 |
| Rate per 100,000 inhabitants | | 461.9 | 5.1 | 37.3 | 26.8 | 104.3 | 315.2 | 2,813.2 | 539.0 | 2,073.6 | 200.6 |
| **Georgia[5]** | | | | | | | | | | | |
| Metropolitan statistical area | 8,441,820 | | | | | | | | | | |
| Area actually reporting | 97.2% | 32,186 | 508 | 2,568 | 1,845 | 11,058 | 18,052 | 253,823 | 53,387 | 176,339 | 24,097 |
| Estimated total | 100.0% | 32,948 | 518 | 2,631 | 1,891 | 11,314 | 18,485 | 260,183 | 54,795 | 180,700 | 24,688 |
| Cities outside metropolitan areas | 643,253 | | | | | | | | | | |
| Area actually reporting | 92.6% | 2,910 | 41 | 258 | 191 | 691 | 1,920 | 26,480 | 5,213 | 20,516 | 751 |
| Estimated total | 100.0% | 3,132 | 44 | 269 | 202 | 746 | 2,073 | 28,595 | 5,629 | 22,155 | 811 |
| Nonmetropolitan counties | 1,129,787 | | | | | | | | | | |
| Area actually reporting | 91.1% | 2,334 | 48 | 294 | 186 | 170 | 1,822 | 18,179 | 5,423 | 11,860 | 896 |
| Estimated total | 100.0% | 2,563 | 53 | 324 | 203 | 187 | 1,999 | 19,945 | 5,950 | 13,012 | 983 |
| State total | 10,214,860 | 38,643 | 615 | 3,224 | 2,296 | 12,247 | 22,557 | 308,723 | 66,374 | 215,867 | 26,482 |
| Rate per 100,000 inhabitants | | 378.3 | 6.0 | 31.6 | 22.5 | 119.9 | 220.8 | 3,022.3 | 649.8 | 2,113.3 | 259.2 |
| **Hawaii** | | | | | | | | | | | |
| Metropolitan statistical area | 1,164,233 | | | | | | | | | | |
| Area actually reporting | 100.0% | 2,994 | 19 | 412 | 302 | 1,009 | 1,554 | 37,090 | 5,291 | 27,346 | 4,453 |
| Cities outside metropolitan areas | None | | | | | | | | | | |
| Nonmetropolitan counties | 267,370 | | | | | | | | | | |
| Area actually reporting | 100.0% | 1,207 | 0 | 149 | 98 | 194 | 864 | 17,256 | 1,266 | 14,664 | 1,326 |
| State total | 1,431,603 | 4,201 | 19 | 561 | 400 | 1,203 | 2,418 | 54,346 | 6,557 | 42,010 | 5,779 |
| Rate per 100,000 inhabitants | | 293.4 | 1.3 | 39.2 | 27.9 | 84.0 | 168.9 | 3,796.2 | 458.0 | 2,934.5 | 403.7 |
| **Idaho** | | | | | | | | | | | |
| Metropolitan statistical area | 1,104,754 | | | | | | | | | | |
| Area actually reporting | 99.9% | 2,537 | 19 | 497 | 369 | 150 | 1,871 | 20,974 | 4,039 | 15,529 | 1,406 |
| Estimated total | 100.0% | 2,538 | 19 | 497 | 369 | 150 | 1,872 | 20,984 | 4,041 | 15,536 | 1,407 |
| Cities outside metropolitan areas | 253,084 | | | | | | | | | | |
| Area actually reporting | 100.0% | 598 | 7 | 122 | 104 | 34 | 435 | 4,927 | 1,056 | 3,644 | 227 |
| Nonmetropolitan counties | 297,092 | | | | | | | | | | |
| Area actually reporting | 100.0% | 432 | 6 | 75 | 60 | 8 | 343 | 2,947 | 1,027 | 1,683 | 237 |
| State total | 1,654,930 | 3,568 | 32 | 694 | 533 | 192 | 2,650 | 28,858 | 6,124 | 20,863 | 1,871 |
| Rate per 100,000 inhabitants | | 215.6 | 1.9 | 41.9 | 32.2 | 11.6 | 160.1 | 1,743.8 | 370.0 | 1,260.7 | 113.1 |

# Table 5. Crime, by State and Area, 2015—*Continued*

(Number, percent, rate per 100,000 population.)

| Area | Population | Violent crime[1] | Murder and nonnegligent manslaughter | Rape (revised definition)[2] | Rape (legacy definition)[3] | Robbery | Aggravated assault | Property crime | Burglary | Larceny-theft | Motor vehicle theft |
|---|---|---|---|---|---|---|---|---|---|---|---|
| **Illinois** | | | | | | | | | | | |
| Metropolitan statistical area.................. | 11,374,234 | | | | | | | | | | |
| Area actually reporting ........................ | 96.3% | 44,926 | 690 | 4,050 | 2,989 | 14,460 | 25,726 | 226,018 | 40,306 | 169,148 | 16,564 |
| Estimated total ...................................... | 100.0% | 45,743 | 697 | 4,186 | 3,093 | 14,654 | 26,206 | 232,866 | 41,454 | 174,548 | 16,864 |
| Cities outside metropolitan areas.......... | 829,658 | | | | | | | | | | |
| Area actually reporting ........................ | 83.3% | 2,168 | 18 | 357 | 257 | 182 | 1,611 | 14,824 | 2,931 | 11,494 | 399 |
| Estimated total ...................................... | 100.0% | 2,601 | 22 | 426 | 316 | 218 | 1,935 | 17,801 | 3,520 | 13,802 | 479 |
| Nonmetropolitan counties ...................... | 656,103 | | | | | | | | | | |
| Area actually reporting ........................ | 94.2% | 950 | 24 | 195 | 131 | 36 | 695 | 4,766 | 1,383 | 3,092 | 291 |
| Estimated total ...................................... | 100.0% | 1,010 | 25 | 209 | 140 | 38 | 738 | 5,062 | 1,469 | 3,284 | 309 |
| State total............................................... | 12,859,995 | 49,354 | 744 | 4,821 | 3,549 | 14,910 | 28,879 | 255,729 | 46,443 | 191,634 | 17,652 |
| Rate per 100,000 inhabitants................ | | 383.8 | 5.8 | 37.5 | 27.6 | 115.9 | 224.6 | 1,988.6 | 361.1 | 1,490.2 | 137.3 |
| **Indiana[6]**................................................. | | | | | | | | | | | |
| Metropolitan statistical area.................. | 5,150,613 | | | | | | | | | | |
| Area actually reporting ........................ | 88.2% | 21,779 | 323 | 1,853 | 1,384 | 6,625 | 12,978 | 136,529 | 27,995 | 97,087 | 11,447 |
| Estimated total....................................... | 100.0% | 22,994 | 335 | 1,979 | 1,479 | 6,851 | 13,829 | 148,065 | 29,832 | 105,957 | 12,276 |
| Cities outside metropolitan areas.......... | 522,395 | | | | | | | | | | |
| Area actually reporting........................ | 70.3% | 1,152 | 12 | 158 | 114 | 135 | 847 | 10,471 | 1,470 | 8,505 | 496 |
| Estimated total....................................... | 100.0% | 1,636 | 17 | 223 | 166 | 192 | 1,204 | 14,889 | 2,090 | 12,094 | 705 |
| Nonmetropolitan counties ...................... | 946,672 | | | | | | | | | | |
| Area actually reporting ........................ | 72.2% | 729 | 15 | 137 | 104 | 49 | 528 | 6,417 | 1,795 | 4,234 | 388 |
| Estimated total....................................... | 100.0% | 1,023 | 21 | 202 | 144 | 68 | 732 | 8,893 | 2,488 | 5,867 | 538 |
| State total............................................... | 6,619,680 | 25,653 | 373 | 2,404 | 1,789 | 7,111 | 15,765 | 171,847 | 34,410 | 123,918 | 13,519 |
| Rate per 100,000 inhabitants................ | | 387.5 | 5.6 | 36.3 | 27.0 | 107.4 | 238.2 | 2,596.0 | 519.8 | 1,872.0 | 204.2 |
| **Iowa** | | | | | | | | | | | |
| Metropolitan statistical area.................. | 1,840,338 | | | | | | | | | | |
| Area actually reporting ........................ | 99.3% | 5,986 | 53 | 782 | 581 | 894 | 4,257 | 44,884 | 9,734 | 31,932 | 3,218 |
| Estimated total ...................................... | 100.0% | 6,018 | 53 | 787 | 585 | 896 | 4,282 | 45,107 | 9,777 | 32,102 | 3,228 |
| Cities outside metropolitan areas.......... | 594,976 | | | | | | | | | | |
| Area actually reporting ........................ | 96.6% | 2,110 | 9 | 249 | 192 | 136 | 1,716 | 14,168 | 3,412 | 10,030 | 726 |
| Estimated total ...................................... | 100.0% | 2,184 | 9 | 258 | 199 | 141 | 1,776 | 14,659 | 3,530 | 10,378 | 751 |
| Nonmetropolitan counties ...................... | 688,585 | | | | | | | | | | |
| Area actually reporting ........................ | 100.0% | 734 | 10 | 111 | 67 | 10 | 603 | 4,191 | 1,585 | 2,243 | 363 |
| State total............................................... | 3,123,899 | 8,936 | 72 | 1,156 | 851 | 1,047 | 6,661 | 63,957 | 14,892 | 44,723 | 4,342 |
| Rate per 100,000 inhabitants................ | | 286.1 | 2.3 | 37.0 | 27.2 | 33.5 | 213.2 | 2,047.3 | 476.7 | 1,431.6 | 139.0 |
| **Kansas** | | | | | | | | | | | |
| Metropolitan statistical area.................. | 1,965,292 | | | | | | | | | | |
| Area actually reporting ........................ | 97.6% | 8,382 | 93 | 1,189 | 928 | 1,616 | 5,484 | 57,049 | 10,398 | 40,905 | 5,746 |
| Estimated total ...................................... | 100.0% | 8,473 | 93 | 1,200 | 936 | 1,627 | 5,553 | 57,942 | 10,562 | 41,561 | 5,819 |
| Cities outside metropolitan areas.......... | 607,622 | | | | | | | | | | |
| Area actually reporting ........................ | 94.0% | 2,022 | 24 | 291 | 231 | 165 | 1,542 | 15,954 | 2,972 | 12,236 | 746 |
| Estimated total ...................................... | 100.0% | 2,147 | 26 | 305 | 242 | 176 | 1,640 | 16,973 | 3,162 | 13,017 | 794 |
| Nonmetropolitan counties ...................... | 338,727 | | | | | | | | | | |
| Area actually reporting ........................ | 97.0% | 711 | 9 | 106 | 70 | 15 | 581 | 4,156 | 1,589 | 2,233 | 334 |
| Estimated total ...................................... | 100.0% | 733 | 9 | 110 | 73 | 15 | 599 | 4,284 | 1,638 | 2,302 | 344 |
| State total............................................... | 2,911,641 | 11,353 | 128 | 1,615 | 1,251 | 1,818 | 7,792 | 79,199 | 15,362 | 56,880 | 6,957 |
| Rate per 100,000 inhabitants................ | | 389.9 | 4.4 | 55.5 | 43.0 | 62.4 | 267.6 | 2,720.1 | 527.6 | 1,953.5 | 238.9 |
| **Kentucky** | | | | | | | | | | | |
| Metropolitan statistical area.................. | 2,589,701 | | | | | | | | | | |
| Area actually reporting ........................ | 100.0% | 7,446 | 124 | 852 | 573 | 2,836 | 3,634 | 72,101 | 15,154 | 50,770 | 6,177 |
| Cities outside metropolitan areas.......... | 540,143 | | | | | | | | | | |
| Area actually reporting ........................ | 99.9% | 906 | 13 | 170 | 123 | 312 | 411 | 14,227 | 2,833 | 10,763 | 631 |
| Estimated total....................................... | 100.0% | 906 | 13 | 170 | 123 | 312 | 411 | 14,235 | 2,835 | 10,769 | 631 |
| Nonmetropolitan counties ...................... | 1,295,248 | | | | | | | | | | |
| Area actually reporting ........................ | 100.0% | 1,324 | 72 | 470 | 301 | 159 | 623 | 10,026 | 4,271 | 4,781 | 974 |
| State total............................................... | 4,425,092 | 9,676 | 209 | 1,492 | 997 | 3,307 | 4,668 | 96,362 | 22,260 | 66,320 | 7,782 |
| Rate per 100,000 inhabitants................ | | 218.7 | 4.7 | 33.7 | 22.5 | 74.7 | 105.5 | 2,177.6 | 503.0 | 1,498.7 | 175.9 |
| **Louisiana** | | | | | | | | | | | |
| Metropolitan statistical area.................. | 3,907,874 | | | | | | | | | | |
| Area actually reporting ........................ | 98.0% | 21,722 | 433 | 1,522 | 1,113 | 5,123 | 14,644 | 133,837 | 29,607 | 95,453 | 8,777 |
| Estimated total ...................................... | 100.0% | 22,042 | 436 | 1,544 | 1,130 | 5,173 | 14,889 | 136,310 | 30,124 | 97,285 | 8,901 |
| Cities outside metropolitan areas.......... | 248,611 | | | | | | | | | | |
| Area actually reporting ........................ | 90.5% | 1,603 | 18 | 68 | 49 | 263 | 1,254 | 11,274 | 2,819 | 8,148 | 307 |
| Estimated total ...................................... | 100.0% | 1,774 | 20 | 77 | 57 | 291 | 1,386 | 12,457 | 3,115 | 9,003 | 339 |
| Nonmetropolitan counties ...................... | 514,239 | | | | | | | | | | |
| Area actually reporting........................ | 97.0% | 1,350 | 24 | 99 | 71 | 83 | 1,144 | 7,628 | 2,148 | 4,994 | 486 |
| Estimated total....................................... | 100.0% | 1,392 | 25 | 102 | 73 | 86 | 1,179 | 7,862 | 2,214 | 5,147 | 501 |
| State total............................................... | 4,670,724 | 25,208 | 481 | 1,723 | 1,260 | 5,550 | 17,454 | 156,629 | 35,453 | 111,435 | 9,741 |
| Rate per 100,000 inhabitants................ | | 539.7 | 10.3 | 36.9 | 27.0 | 118.8 | 373.7 | 3,353.4 | 759.0 | 2,385.8 | 208.6 |

# Table 5. Crime, by State and Area, 2015—*Continued*

(Number, percent, rate per 100,000 population.)

| Area | Population | Violent crime[1] | Murder and nonnegligent manslaughter | Rape (revised definition)[2] | Rape (legacy definition)[3] | Robbery | Aggra-vated assault | Property crime | Burglary | Larceny-theft | Motor vehicle theft |
|---|---|---|---|---|---|---|---|---|---|---|---|
| **Maine**[6] | | | | | | | | | | | |
| Metropolitan statistical area | 785,828 | | | | | | | | | | |
| Area actually reporting | 100.0% | 996 | 7 | 222 | 174 | 245 | 522 | 14,577 | 2,607 | 11,513 | 457 |
| Cities outside metropolitan areas | 265,131 | | | | | | | | | | |
| Area actually reporting | 100.0% | 464 | 10 | 169 | 128 | 55 | 230 | 6,636 | 1,061 | 5,393 | 182 |
| Nonmetropolitan counties | 278,369 | | | | | | | | | | |
| Area actually reporting | 100.0% | 269 | 6 | 83 | 52 | 11 | 169 | 3,114 | 1,016 | 1,923 | 175 |
| State total | 1,329,328 | 1,729 | 23 | 474 | 354 | 311 | 921 | 24,327 | 4,684 | 18,829 | 814 |
| Rate per 100,000 inhabitants | | 130.1 | 1.7 | 35.7 | 26.6 | 23.4 | 69.3 | 1,830.0 | 352.4 | 1,416.4 | 61.2 |
| | | | | | | | | | | | |
| **Maryland** | | | | | | | | | | | |
| Metropolitan statistical area | 5,855,016 | | | | | | | | | | |
| Area actually reporting | 100.0% | 26,972 | 515 | 1,623 | 1,152 | 9,757 | 15,077 | 135,770 | 24,899 | 97,815 | 13,056 |
| Cities outside metropolitan areas | 52,865 | | | | | | | | | | |
| Area actually reporting | 100.0% | 324 | 0 | 22 | 17 | 75 | 227 | 1,915 | 341 | 1,538 | 36 |
| Nonmetropolitan counties | 98,520 | | | | | | | | | | |
| Area actually reporting | 100.0% | 166 | 1 | 21 | 15 | 31 | 113 | 1,363 | 438 | 866 | 59 |
| State total | 6,006,401 | 27,462 | 516 | 1,666 | 1,184 | 9,863 | 15,417 | 139,048 | 25,678 | 100,219 | 13,151 |
| Rate per 100,000 inhabitants | | 457.2 | 8.6 | 27.7 | 19.7 | 164.2 | 256.7 | 2,315.0 | 427.5 | 1,668.5 | 218.9 |
| | | | | | | | | | | | |
| **Massachusetts** | | | | | | | | | | | |
| Metropolitan statistical area | 6,695,032 | | | | | | | | | | |
| Area actually reporting | 96.8% | 25,477 | 124 | 1,965 | 1,520 | 5,160 | 18,228 | 109,844 | 20,931 | 81,135 | 7,778 |
| Estimated total | 100.0% | 26,163 | 126 | 2,030 | 1,570 | 5,267 | 18,740 | 113,118 | 21,554 | 83,565 | 7,999 |
| Cities outside metropolitan areas | 91,950 | | | | | | | | | | |
| Area actually reporting | 86.0% | 337 | 2 | 36 | 31 | 18 | 281 | 1,507 | 289 | 1,158 | 60 |
| Estimated total | 100.0% | 393 | 2 | 43 | 37 | 21 | 327 | 1,753 | 336 | 1,347 | 70 |
| Nonmetropolitan counties | 7,440 | | | | | | | | | | |
| Area actually reporting | 100.0% | 6 | 0 | 2 | 1 | 0 | 4 | 0 | 0 | 0 | 0 |
| State total | 6,794,422 | 26,562 | 128 | 2,075 | 1,608 | 5,288 | 19,071 | 114,871 | 21,890 | 84,912 | 8,069 |
| Rate per 100,000 inhabitants | | 390.9 | 1.9 | 30.5 | 23.7 | 77.8 | 280.7 | 1,690.7 | 322.2 | 1,249.7 | 118.8 |
| | | | | | | | | | | | |
| **Michigan** | | | | | | | | | | | |
| Metropolitan statistical area | 8,121,585 | | | | | | | | | | |
| Area actually reporting | 99.5% | 36,719 | 528 | 4,829 | 3,119 | 7,663 | 23,699 | 162,248 | 34,728 | 112,670 | 14,850 |
| Estimated total | 100.0% | 36,839 | 528 | 4,853 | 3,137 | 7,684 | 23,774 | 163,072 | 34,871 | 113,292 | 14,909 |
| Cities outside metropolitan areas | 599,913 | | | | | | | | | | |
| Area actually reporting | 94.4% | 1,443 | 8 | 491 | 331 | 60 | 884 | 11,083 | 1,537 | 9,242 | 304 |
| Estimated total | 100.0% | 1,537 | 8 | 529 | 361 | 64 | 936 | 11,735 | 1,627 | 9,786 | 322 |
| Nonmetropolitan counties | 1,201,078 | | | | | | | | | | |
| Area actually reporting | 98.7% | 2,813 | 35 | 1,049 | 653 | 47 | 1,682 | 12,134 | 3,497 | 8,111 | 526 |
| Estimated total | 100.0% | 2,855 | 35 | 1,068 | 665 | 48 | 1,704 | 12,294 | 3,543 | 8,218 | 533 |
| State total | 9,922,576 | 41,231 | 571 | 6,450 | 4,163 | 7,796 | 26,414 | 187,101 | 40,041 | 131,296 | 15,764 |
| Rate per 100,000 inhabitants | | 415.5 | 5.8 | 65.0 | 42.0 | 78.6 | 266.2 | 1,885.6 | 403.5 | 1,323.2 | 158.9 |
| | | | | | | | | | | | |
| **Minnesota** | | | | | | | | | | | |
| Metropolitan statistical area | 4,254,071 | | | | | | | | | | |
| Area actually reporting | 100.0% | 11,461 | 104 | 1,813 | 1,327 | 3,633 | 5,911 | 101,503 | 15,434 | 79,140 | 6,929 |
| Cities outside metropolitan areas | 533,363 | | | | | | | | | | |
| Area actually reporting | 100.0% | 1,130 | 12 | 292 | 213 | 119 | 707 | 13,502 | 1,787 | 11,186 | 529 |
| Nonmetropolitan counties | 702,160 | | | | | | | | | | |
| Area actually reporting | 100.0% | 728 | 17 | 216 | 146 | 19 | 476 | 6,979 | 2,078 | 4,378 | 523 |
| State total | 5,489,594 | 13,319 | 133 | 2,321 | 1,686 | 3,771 | 7,094 | 121,984 | 19,299 | 94,704 | 7,981 |
| Rate per 100,000 inhabitants | | 242.6 | 2.4 | 42.3 | 30.7 | 68.7 | 129.2 | 2,222.1 | 351.6 | 1,725.2 | 145.4 |
| | | | | | | | | | | | |
| **Mississippi**[6] | | | | | | | | | | | |
| Metropolitan statistical area | 1,372,083 | | | | | | | | | | |
| Area actually reporting | 77.3% | 3,343 | 95 | 431 | 323 | 1,195 | 1,622 | 33,634 | 8,218 | 23,237 | 2,179 |
| Estimated total | 100.0% | 3,834 | 105 | 490 | 366 | 1,280 | 1,959 | 40,232 | 9,762 | 27,966 | 2,504 |
| Cities outside metropolitan areas | 585,231 | | | | | | | | | | |
| Area actually reporting | 48.0% | 1,147 | 43 | 148 | 108 | 371 | 585 | 14,024 | 3,902 | 9,606 | 516 |
| Estimated total | 100.0% | 2,407 | 90 | 327 | 246 | 772 | 1,218 | 29,192 | 8,122 | 19,996 | 1,074 |
| Nonmetropolitan counties | 1,035,019 | | | | | | | | | | |
| Area actually reporting | 41.8% | 834 | 27 | 154 | 101 | 101 | 552 | 6,422 | 2,890 | 3,254 | 278 |
| Estimated total | 100.0% | 2,013 | 64 | 386 | 250 | 242 | 1,321 | 15,366 | 6,915 | 7,786 | 665 |
| State total | 2,992,333 | 8,254 | 259 | 1,203 | 862 | 2,294 | 4,498 | 84,790 | 24,799 | 55,748 | 4,243 |
| Rate per 100,000 inhabitants | | 275.8 | 8.7 | 40.2 | 28.8 | 76.7 | 150.3 | 2,833.6 | 828.8 | 1,863.0 | 141.8 |
| | | | | | | | | | | | |
| **Missouri** | | | | | | | | | | | |
| Metropolitan statistical area | 4,532,929 | | | | | | | | | | |
| Area actually reporting | 99.9% | 25,261 | 441 | 2,105 | 1,531 | 6,029 | 16,686 | 139,741 | 26,437 | 98,339 | 14,965 |
| Cities outside metropolitan areas | 100.0% | 25,264 | 441 | 2,105 | 1,531 | 6,030 | 16,688 | 139,769 | 26,441 | 98,361 | 14,967 |
| Area actually reporting | 664,269 | | | | | | | | | | |
| Estimated total | 99.4% | 2,770 | 28 | 246 | 179 | 292 | 2,204 | 22,566 | 3,780 | 17,819 | 967 |

# Table 5. Crime, by State and Area, 2015—*Continued*

(Number, percent, rate per 100,000 population.)

| Area | Population | Violent crime[1] | Murder and nonnegligent manslaughter | Rape (revised definition)[2] | Rape (legacy definition)[3] | Robbery | Aggravated assault | Property crime | Burglary | Larceny-theft | Motor vehicle theft |
|---|---|---|---|---|---|---|---|---|---|---|---|
| Nonmetropolitan counties ................... | 100.0% | 2,785 | 28 | 246 | 179 | 294 | 2,217 | 22,699 | 3,802 | 17,924 | 973 |
|   Area actually reporting ........................ | 886,474 | | | | | | | | | | |
|   Estimated total....................................... | 100.0% | 2,212 | 33 | 202 | 144 | 52 | 1,925 | 11,174 | 3,763 | 6,352 | 1,059 |
| State total............................................... | 6,083,672 | 30,261 | 502 | 2,553 | 1,854 | 6,376 | 20,830 | 173,642 | 34,006 | 122,637 | 16,999 |
|   Rate per 100,000 inhabitants................. | | 497.4 | 8.3 | 42.0 | 30.5 | 104.8 | 342.4 | 2,854.2 | 559.0 | 2,015.8 | 279.4 |
| **Montana** | | | | | | | | | | | |
| Metropolitan statistical area................. | 365,179 | | | | | | | | | | |
|   Area actually reporting........................ | 99.9% | 1,299 | 20 | 195 | 135 | 134 | 950 | 12,583 | 1,673 | 9,714 | 1,196 |
|   Estimated total....................................... | 100.0% | 1,300 | 20 | 195 | 135 | 134 | 951 | 12,598 | 1,674 | 9,727 | 1,197 |
| Cities outside metropolitan areas.......... | 218,086 | | | | | | | | | | |
|   Area actually reporting ....................... | 99.1% | 1,134 | 6 | 203 | 172 | 52 | 873 | 7,589 | 895 | 6,136 | 558 |
|   Estimated total ...................................... | 100.0% | 1,145 | 6 | 206 | 174 | 52 | 881 | 7,656 | 903 | 6,190 | 563 |
| Nonmetropolitan counties ................... | 449,684 | | | | | | | | | | |
|   Area actually reporting ........................ | 98.5% | 1,147 | 10 | 142 | 120 | 24 | 971 | 6,743 | 1,242 | 4,853 | 648 |
|   Estimated total....................................... | 100.0% | 1,166 | 10 | 146 | 122 | 24 | 986 | 6,846 | 1,261 | 4,927 | 658 |
| State total............................................... | 1,032,949 | 3,611 | 36 | 547 | 431 | 210 | 2,818 | 27,100 | 3,838 | 20,844 | 2,418 |
|   Rate per 100,000 inhabitants................. | | 349.6 | 3.5 | 53.0 | 41.7 | 20.3 | 272.8 | 2,623.6 | 371.6 | 2,017.9 | 234.1 |
| **Nebraska[6]** | | | | | | | | | | | |
| Metropolitan statistical area................. | 1,227,692 | | | | | | | | | | |
|   Area actually reporting........................ | 99.2% | 4,027 | 50 | 594 | 441 | 929 | 2,454 | 32,043 | 4,539 | 24,109 | 3,395 |
|   Estimated total....................................... | 100.0% | 4,036 | 50 | 597 | 444 | 929 | 2,460 | 32,191 | 4,559 | 24,226 | 3,406 |
| Cities outside metropolitan areas.......... | 335,719 | | | | | | | | | | |
|   Area actually reporting........................ | 93.7% | 781 | 6 | 200 | 152 | 50 | 525 | 7,472 | 1,132 | 5,985 | 355 |
|   Estimated total ...................................... | 100.0% | 838 | 6 | 219 | 167 | 53 | 560 | 7,973 | 1,208 | 6,386 | 379 |
| Nonmetropolitan counties ................... | 332,779 | | | | | | | | | | |
|   Area actually reporting........................ | 90.4% | 305 | 5 | 51 | 38 | 11 | 238 | 2,106 | 592 | 1,319 | 195 |
|   Estimated total ...................................... | 100.0% | 338 | 6 | 57 | 41 | 12 | 263 | 2,331 | 655 | 1,460 | 216 |
| State total............................................... | 1,896,190 | 5,212 | 62 | 873 | 652 | 994 | 3,283 | 42,495 | 6,422 | 32,072 | 4,001 |
|   Rate per 100,000 inhabitants................. | | 274.9 | 3.3 | 46.0 | 34.4 | 52.4 | 173.1 | 2,241.1 | 338.7 | 1,691.4 | 211.0 |
| **Nevada** | | | | | | | | | | | |
| Metropolitan statistical area................. | 2,617,805 | | | | | | | | | | |
|   Area actually reporting ........................ | 100.0% | 19,404 | 166 | 1,565 | 1,156 | 6,244 | 11,429 | 72,206 | 20,939 | 40,285 | 10,982 |
| Cities outside metropolitan areas.......... | 48,996 | | | | | | | | | | |
|   Area actually reporting ........................ | 100.0% | 237 | 2 | 41 | 29 | 10 | 184 | 1,688 | 456 | 1,130 | 102 |
| Nonmetropolitan counties ................... | 224,044 | | | | | | | | | | |
|   Area actually reporting ........................ | 100.0% | 477 | 10 | 82 | 53 | 33 | 352 | 3,243 | 965 | 2,011 | 267 |
| State total............................................... | 2,890,845 | 20,118 | 178 | 1,688 | 1,238 | 6,287 | 11,965 | 77,137 | 22,360 | 43,426 | 11,351 |
|   Rate per 100,000 inhabitants................. | | 695.9 | 6.2 | 58.4 | 42.8 | 217.5 | 413.9 | 2,668.3 | 773.5 | 1,502.2 | 392.7 |
| **New Hampshire** | | | | | | | | | | | |
| Metropolitan statistical area................. | 835,158 | | | | | | | | | | |
|   Area actually reporting ........................ | 97.9% | 1,743 | 14 | 360 | 277 | 365 | 1,004 | 13,955 | 1,967 | 11,385 | 603 |
|   Estimated total ...................................... | 100.0% | 1,766 | 14 | 367 | 283 | 368 | 1,017 | 14,201 | 2,000 | 11,588 | 613 |
| Cities outside metropolitan areas.......... | 443,394 | | | | | | | | | | |
|   Area actually reporting........................ | 89.3% | 750 | 0 | 218 | 148 | 87 | 445 | 7,785 | 1,206 | 6,343 | 236 |
|   Estimated total ...................................... | 100.0% | 847 | 0 | 251 | 173 | 97 | 499 | 8,721 | 1,351 | 7,106 | 264 |
| Nonmetropolitan counties ................... | 52,056 | | | | | | | | | | |
|   Area actually reporting)........................ | 100.0% | 39 | 0 | 9 | 5 | 3 | 27 | 307 | 116 | 177 | 14 |
| State total............................................... | 1,330,608 | 2,652 | 14 | 627 | 461 | 468 | 1,543 | 23,229 | 3,467 | 18,871 | 891 |
|   Rate per 100,000 inhabitants................. | | 199.3 | 1.1 | 47.1 | 34.6 | 35.2 | 116.0 | 1,745.7 | 260.6 | 1,418.2 | 67.0 |
| **New Jersey** ................................................. | | | | | | | | | | | |
| Metropolitan statistical area................. | 8,958,013 | | | | | | | | | | |
|   Area actually reporting........................ | 100.0% | 22,879 | 363 | 1,373 | 1,019 | 9,729 | 11,414 | 145,701 | 27,960 | 105,963 | 11,778 |
| Cities outside metropolitan areas.......... | None | | | | | | | | | | |
|   Area actually reporting........................ | None | | | | | | | | | | |
| Nonmetropolitan counties ................... | None | | | | | | | | | | |
|   Area actually reporting........................ | None | | | | | | | | | | |
| State total............................................... | 8,958,013 | 22,879 | 363 | 1,373 | 1,019 | 9,729 | 11,414 | 145,701 | 27,960 | 105,963 | 11,778 |
|   Rate per 100,000 inhabitants................. | | 255.4 | 4.1 | 15.3 | 11.4 | 108.6 | 127.4 | 1,626.5 | 312.1 | 1,182.9 | 131.5 |
| **New Mexico[5]** | | | | | | | | | | | |
| Metropolitan statistical area................. | 1,390,305 | | | | | | | | | | |
|   Area actually reporting ........................ | 94.9% | 9,007 | 68 | 1,115 | 818 | 2,098 | 5,726 | 54,488 | 10,943 | 36,644 | 6,901 |
|   Estimated total....................................... | 100.0% | 9,319 | 70 | 1,159 | 849 | 2,128 | 5,962 | 55,506 | 11,289 | 37,178 | 7,039 |
| Cities outside metropolitan areas.......... | 398,912 | | | | | | | | | | |
|   Area actually reporting........................ | 96.9% | 2,773 | 28 | 333 | 249 | 307 | 2,105 | 17,423 | 4,310 | 12,114 | 999 |
|   Estimated total ...................................... | 100.0% | 2,864 | 29 | 345 | 258 | 317 | 2,173 | 17,983 | 4,449 | 12,503 | 1,031 |
| Nonmetropolitan counties ................... | 295,892 | | | | | | | | | | |
|   Area actually reporting........................ | 92.8% | 1,389 | 17 | 155 | 100 | 37 | 1,180 | 3,345 | 1,250 | 1,672 | 423 |
|   Estimated total ...................................... | 100.0% | 1,498 | 18 | 168 | 108 | 40 | 1,272 | 3,605 | 1,347 | 1,802 | 456 |
| State total............................................... | 2,085,109 | 13,681 | 117 | 1,672 | 1,215 | 2,485 | 9,407 | 77,094 | 17,085 | 51,483 | 8,526 |
|   Rate per 100,000 inhabitants................. | | 656.1 | 5.6 | 80.2 | 58.3 | 119.2 | 451.2 | 3,697.4 | 819.4 | 2,469.1 | 408.9 |

# Table 5. Crime, by State and Area, 2015—*Continued*

(Number, percent, rate per 100,000 population.)

| Area | Population | Violent crime[1] | Murder and nonnegligent manslaughter | Rape (revised definition)[2] | Rape (legacy definition)[3] | Robbery | Aggravated assault | Property crime | Burglary | Larceny-theft | Motor vehicle theft |
|---|---|---|---|---|---|---|---|---|---|---|---|
| **New York[6]** | | | | | | | | | | | |
| **Metropolitan statistical area** | 18,403,124 | | | | | | | | | | |
| Area actually reporting | 99.9% | 72,574 | 589 | 5,099 | 3,721 | 23,682 | 43,204 | 295,464 | 40,021 | 240,693 | 14,750 |
| Estimated total | 100.0% | 72,606 | 589 | 5,099 | 3,721 | 23,694 | 43,224 | 295,805 | 40,066 | 240,978 | 14,761 |
| **Cities outside metropolitan areas** | 513,230 | | | | | | | | | | |
| Area actually reporting | 97.7% | 1,239 | 9 | 298 | 217 | 182 | 750 | 11,824 | 1,968 | 9,600 | 256 |
| Estimated total | 100.0% | 1,271 | 9 | 308 | 225 | 186 | 768 | 12,108 | 2,015 | 9,831 | 262 |
| **Nonmetropolitan counties** | 879,437 | | | | | | | | | | |
| Area actually reporting | 100.0% | 1,288 | 11 | 667 | 443 | 56 | 554 | 9,616 | 2,195 | 7,131 | 290 |
| **State total** | 19,795,791 | 75,165 | 609 | 6,074 | 4,389 | 23,936 | 44,546 | 317,529 | 44,276 | 257,940 | 15,313 |
| Rate per 100,000 inhabitants | | 379.7 | 3.1 | 30.7 | 22.2 | 120.9 | 225.0 | 1,604.0 | 223.7 | 1,303.0 | 77.4 |
| **North Carolina[5]** | | | | | | | | | | | |
| **Metropolitan statistical area** | 7,835,390 | | | | | | | | | | |
| Area actually reporting | 98.9% | 28,126 | 383 | 2,111 | 1,544 | 7,601 | 18,031 | 216,706 | 55,372 | 150,403 | 10,931 |
| Estimated total | 100.0% | 28,310 | 384 | 2,119 | 1,552 | 7,645 | 18,162 | 218,939 | 55,886 | 152,039 | 11,014 |
| **Cities outside metropolitan areas** | 648,044 | | | | | | | | | | |
| Area actually reporting | 90.7% | 3,558 | 73 | 230 | 169 | 777 | 2,478 | 28,612 | 7,228 | 20,402 | 982 |
| Estimated total | 100.0% | 3,909 | 80 | 240 | 179 | 857 | 2,732 | 31,546 | 7,969 | 22,494 | 1,083 |
| **Nonmetropolitan counties** | 1,559,368 | | | | | | | | | | |
| Area actually reporting | 94.7% | 2,490 | 50 | 305 | 196 | 306 | 1,829 | 24,332 | 10,402 | 12,663 | 1,267 |
| Estimated total | 100.0% | 2,633 | 53 | 325 | 208 | 323 | 1,932 | 25,698 | 10,986 | 13,374 | 1,338 |
| **State total** | 10,042,802 | 34,852 | 517 | 2,684 | 1,939 | 8,825 | 22,826 | 276,183 | 74,841 | 187,907 | 13,435 |
| Rate per 100,000 inhabitants | | 347.0 | 5.1 | 26.7 | 19.3 | 87.9 | 227.3 | 2,750.1 | 745.2 | 1,871.1 | 133.8 |
| **North Dakota** | | | | | | | | | | | |
| **Metropolitan statistical area** | 371,616 | | | | | | | | | | |
| Area actually reporting | 100.0% | 973 | 11 | 179 | 141 | 96 | 687 | 8,388 | 1,370 | 6,358 | 660 |
| **Cities outside metropolitan areas** | 191,270 | | | | | | | | | | |
| Area actually reporting | 100.0% | 660 | 5 | 126 | 106 | 44 | 485 | 5,487 | 1,068 | 3,847 | 572 |
| **Nonmetropolitan counties** | 194,041 | | | | | | | | | | |
| Area actually reporting | 100.0% | 179 | 5 | 40 | 29 | 8 | 126 | 2,145 | 559 | 1,235 | 351 |
| **State total** | 756,927 | 1,812 | 21 | 345 | 276 | 148 | 1,298 | 16,020 | 2,997 | 11,440 | 1,583 |
| Rate per 100,000 inhabitants | | 239.4 | 2.8 | 45.6 | 36.5 | 19.6 | 171.5 | 2,116.5 | 395.9 | 1,511.4 | 209.1 |
| **Ohio[6]** | | | | | | | | | | | |
| **Metropolitan statistical area** | 9,246,915 | | | | | | | | | | |
| Area actually reporting | 91.8% | 29,364 | 443 | 4,055 | 3,277 | 11,591 | 13,275 | 235,870 | 55,250 | 165,442 | 15,178 |
| Estimated total | 100.0% | 30,588 | 455 | 4,291 | 3,459 | 11,999 | 13,843 | 252,958 | 58,231 | 178,945 | 15,782 |
| **Cities outside metropolitan areas** | 1,047,288 | | | | | | | | | | |
| Area actually reporting | 84.6% | 1,608 | 21 | 398 | 338 | 342 | 847 | 26,196 | 5,270 | 20,363 | 563 |
| Estimated total | 100.0% | 1,902 | 25 | 472 | 400 | 404 | 1,001 | 30,966 | 6,230 | 24,071 | 665 |
| **Nonmetropolitan counties** | 1,319,220 | | | | | | | | | | |
| Area actually reporting | 91.5% | 1,277 | 18 | 343 | 266 | 138 | 778 | 15,185 | 4,429 | 10,041 | 715 |
| Estimated total | 100.0% | 1,408 | 20 | 386 | 295 | 151 | 851 | 16,601 | 4,842 | 10,977 | 782 |
| **State total** | 11,613,423 | 33,898 | 500 | 5,149 | 4,154 | 12,554 | 15,695 | 300,525 | 69,303 | 213,993 | 17,229 |
| Rate per 100,000 inhabitants | | 291.9 | 4.3 | 44.3 | 35.8 | 108.1 | 135.1 | 2,587.7 | 596.7 | 1,842.6 | 148.4 |
| **Oklahoma** | | | | | | | | | | | |
| **Metropolitan statistical area** | 2,621,143 | | | | | | | | | | |
| Area actually reporting | 99.9% | 12,556 | 185 | 1,409 | 1,027 | 2,666 | 8,296 | 81,302 | 19,938 | 53,076 | 8,288 |
| Estimated total | 100.0% | 12,559 | 185 | 1,409 | 1,027 | 2,666 | 8,299 | 81,350 | 19,948 | 53,110 | 8,292 |
| **Cities outside metropolitan areas** | 679,145 | | | | | | | | | | |
| Area actually reporting | 99.7% | 3,027 | 29 | 325 | 240 | 312 | 2,361 | 24,467 | 5,647 | 17,354 | 1,466 |
| Estimated total | 100.0% | 3,035 | 29 | 325 | 240 | 313 | 2,368 | 24,544 | 5,665 | 17,408 | 1,471 |
| **Nonmetropolitan counties** | 611,050 | | | | | | | | | | |
| Area actually reporting | 98.0% | 894 | 20 | 113 | 84 | 25 | 736 | 6,847 | 2,738 | 3,435 | 674 |
| Estimated total | 100.0% | 912 | 20 | 115 | 85 | 26 | 751 | 6,984 | 2,793 | 3,504 | 687 |
| **State total** | 3,911,338 | 16,506 | 234 | 1,849 | 1,352 | 3,005 | 11,418 | 112,878 | 28,406 | 74,022 | 10,450 |
| Rate per 100,000 inhabitants | | 422.0 | 6.0 | 47.3 | 34.6 | 76.8 | 291.9 | 2,885.9 | 726.2 | 1,892.5 | 267.2 |
| **Oregon[6]** | | | | | | | | | | | |
| **Metropolitan statistical area** | 3,373,232 | | | | | | | | | | |
| Area actually reporting | 89.8% | 8,284 | 70 | 1,185 | 873 | 1,918 | 5,111 | 95,209 | 13,788 | 72,649 | 8,772 |
| Estimated total | 100.0% | 8,982 | 77 | 1,322 | 971 | 2,002 | 5,581 | 101,615 | 14,998 | 77,274 | 9,343 |
| **Cities outside metropolitan areas** | 306,104 | | | | | | | | | | |
| Area actually reporting | 94.2% | 828 | 11 | 163 | 123 | 110 | 544 | 11,293 | 1,779 | 8,868 | 646 |
| Estimated total | 100.0% | 879 | 12 | 173 | 131 | 117 | 577 | 11,986 | 1,888 | 9,412 | 686 |
| **Nonmetropolitan counties** | 349,641 | | | | | | | | | | |
| Area actually reporting | 97.6% | 592 | 10 | 96 | 61 | 26 | 460 | 4,993 | 1,415 | 3,073 | 505 |
| Estimated total | 100.0% | 607 | 10 | 98 | 62 | 27 | 472 | 5,118 | 1,450 | 3,150 | 518 |
| **State total** | 4,028,977 | 10,468 | 99 | 1,593 | 1,164 | 2,146 | 6,630 | 118,719 | 18,336 | 89,836 | 10,547 |
| Rate per 100,000 inhabitants | | 259.8 | 2.5 | 39.5 | 28.9 | 53.3 | 164.6 | 2,946.6 | 455.1 | 2,229.7 | 261.8 |

# Table 5. Crime, by State and Area, 2015—*Continued*

(Number, percent, rate per 100,000 population.)

| Area | Population | Violent crime[1] | Murder and nonnegligent manslaughter | Rape (revised definition)[2] | Rape (legacy definition)[3] | Robbery | Aggravated assault | Property crime | Burglary | Larceny-theft | Motor vehicle theft |
|---|---|---|---|---|---|---|---|---|---|---|---|
| **Pennsylvania** | | | | | | | | | | | |
| Metropolitan statistical area | 11,319,063 | | | | | | | | | | |
| Area actually reporting | 99.2% | 37,198 | 608 | 3,557 | 2,615 | 12,700 | 20,333 | 210,622 | 34,817 | 164,417 | 11,388 |
| Estimated total | 100.0% | 37,344 | 609 | 3,562 | 2,620 | 12,741 | 20,432 | 212,012 | 35,000 | 165,580 | 11,432 |
| Cities outside metropolitan areas | 683,735 | | | | | | | | | | |
| Area actually reporting | 95.7% | 1,657 | 22 | 171 | 122 | 150 | 1,314 | 9,998 | 1,717 | 7,980 | 301 |
| Estimated total | 100.0% | 1,730 | 23 | 177 | 128 | 157 | 1,373 | 10,448 | 1,794 | 8,339 | 315 |
| Nonmetropolitan counties | 799,705 | | | | | | | | | | |
| Area actually reporting | 100.0% | 1,265 | 26 | 566 | 374 | 105 | 568 | 9,625 | 2,870 | 6,368 | 387 |
| State total | 12,802,503 | 40,339 | 658 | 4,305 | 3,122 | 13,003 | 22,373 | 232,085 | 39,664 | 180,287 | 12,134 |
| Rate per 100,000 inhabitants | | 315.1 | 5.1 | 33.6 | 24.4 | 101.6 | 174.8 | 1,812.8 | 309.8 | 1,408.2 | 94.8 |
| **Puerto Rico[7]** | | | | | | | | | | | |
| Metropolitan statistical area | 3,323,005 | | | | | | | | | | |
| Area actually reporting | 100.0% | 7,566 | 565 | 156 | 116 | 4,063 | 2,782 | 37,598 | 9,100 | 24,426 | 4,072 |
| Cities outside metropolitan areas | 151,177 | | | | | | | | | | |
| Area actually reporting | 100.0% | 63 | 19 | 9 | 7 | 7 | 28 | 119 | 50 | 67 | 2 |
| Total | 3,474,182 | 7,629 | 584 | 165 | 123 | 4,070 | 2,810 | 37,717 | 9,150 | 24,493 | 4,074 |
| Rate per 100,000 inhabitants | | 219.6 | 16.8 | 4.7 | 3.5 | 117.1 | 80.9 | 1,085.6 | 263.4 | 705.0 | 117.3 |
| **Rhode Island[6]** | | | | | | | | | | | |
| Metropolitan statistical area | 1,056,298 | | | | | | | | | | |
| Area actually reporting | 100.0% | 2,537 | 28 | 444 | 331 | 555 | 1,510 | 19,976 | 3,944 | 14,659 | 1,373 |
| Cities outside metropolitan areas | None | | | | | | | | | | |
| Area actually reporting | None | | | | | | | | | | |
| Nonmetropolitan counties | None | | | | | | | | | | |
| Area actually reporting | 100.0% | 25 | 1 | 15 | 7 | 1 | 8 | 67 | 3 | 48 | 16 |
| State total | 1,056,298 | 2,562 | 29 | 459 | 338 | 556 | 1,518 | 20,043 | 3,947 | 14,707 | 1,389 |
| Rate per 100,000 inhabitants | | 242.5 | 2.7 | 43.5 | 32.0 | 52.6 | 143.7 | 1,897.5 | 373.7 | 1,392.3 | 131.5 |
| **South Carolina** | | | | | | | | | | | |
| Metropolitan statistical area | 4,145,678 | | | | | | | | | | |
| Area actually reporting | 98.6% | 20,072 | 331 | 1,881 | 1,414 | 3,338 | 14,522 | 133,964 | 27,404 | 95,276 | 11,284 |
| Estimated total | 100.0% | 20,336 | 335 | 1,908 | 1,434 | 3,374 | 14,719 | 135,587 | 27,788 | 96,369 | 11,430 |
| Cities outside metropolitan areas | 207,146 | | | | | | | | | | |
| Area actually reporting | 93.5% | 1,799 | 26 | 135 | 98 | 326 | 1,312 | 10,889 | 2,281 | 8,175 | 433 |
| Estimated total | 100.0% | 1,923 | 28 | 143 | 105 | 349 | 1,403 | 11,643 | 2,439 | 8,741 | 463 |
| Nonmetropolitan counties | 543,322 | | | | | | | | | | |
| Area actually reporting | 99.2% | 2,421 | 36 | 244 | 167 | 206 | 1,935 | 13,898 | 4,288 | 8,542 | 1,068 |
| Estimated total | 100.0% | 2,441 | 36 | 246 | 168 | 208 | 1,951 | 14,015 | 4,324 | 8,614 | 1,077 |
| State total | 4,896,146 | 24,700 | 399 | 2,297 | 1,707 | 3,931 | 18,073 | 161,245 | 34,551 | 113,724 | 12,970 |
| Rate per 100,000 inhabitants | | 504.5 | 8.1 | 46.9 | 34.9 | 80.3 | 369.1 | 3,293.3 | 705.7 | 2,322.7 | 264.9 |
| **South Dakota** | | | | | | | | | | | |
| Metropolitan statistical area | 412,368 | | | | | | | | | | |
| Area actually reporting | 99.5% | 1,626 | 12 | 303 | 275 | 165 | 1,146 | 10,205 | 1,897 | 7,545 | 763 |
| Estimated total | 100.0% | 1,628 | 12 | 303 | 275 | 165 | 1,148 | 10,224 | 1,900 | 7,560 | 764 |
| Cities outside metropolitan areas | 219,563 | | | | | | | | | | |
| Area actually reporting | 95.9% | 1,391 | 7 | 160 | 138 | 40 | 1,184 | 5,239 | 745 | 4,186 | 308 |
| Estimated total | 100.0% | 1,451 | 7 | 167 | 144 | 42 | 1,235 | 5,465 | 777 | 4,367 | 321 |
| Nonmetropolitan counties | 226,538 | | | | | | | | | | |
| Area actually reporting | 75.6% | 158 | 10 | 18 | 18 | 7 | 123 | 750 | 214 | 458 | 78 |
| Estimated total | 100.0% | 210 | 13 | 25 | 22 | 9 | 163 | 991 | 283 | 605 | 103 |
| State total | 858,469 | 3,289 | 32 | 495 | 441 | 216 | 2,546 | 16,680 | 2,960 | 12,532 | 1,188 |
| Rate per 100,000 inhabitants | | 383.1 | 3.7 | 57.7 | 51.4 | 25.2 | 296.6 | 1,943.0 | 344.8 | 1,459.8 | 138.4 |
| **Tennessee** | | | | | | | | | | | |
| Metropolitan statistical area | 5,103,420 | | | | | | | | | | |
| Area actually reporting | 100.0% | 34,397 | 351 | 2,260 | 1,659 | 7,078 | 24,708 | 158,863 | 34,790 | 113,624 | 10,449 |
| Cities outside metropolitan areas | 513,845 | | | | | | | | | | |
| Area actually reporting | 100.0% | 3,364 | 16 | 253 | 183 | 295 | 2,800 | 20,823 | 3,809 | 16,006 | 1,008 |
| Nonmetropolitan counties | 983,034 | | | | | | | | | | |
| Area actually reporting | 100.0% | 2,639 | 39 | 163 | 124 | 101 | 2,336 | 14,110 | 4,648 | 8,049 | 1,413 |
| State total | 6,600,299 | 40,400 | 406 | 2,676 | 1,966 | 7,474 | 29,844 | 193,796 | 43,247 | 137,679 | 12,870 |
| Rate per 100,000 inhabitants | | 612.1 | 6.2 | 40.5 | 29.8 | 113.2 | 452.2 | 2,936.2 | 655.2 | 2,086.0 | 195.0 |
| **Texas** | | | | | | | | | | | |
| Metropolitan statistical area | 24,422,501 | | | | | | | | | | |
| Area actually reporting | 99.8% | 104,453 | 1,207 | 11,040 | 8,068 | 31,163 | 61,043 | 714,288 | 136,056 | 514,139 | 64,093 |
| Estimated total | 100.0% | 104,564 | 1,207 | 11,055 | 8,081 | 31,189 | 61,113 | 715,398 | 136,238 | 514,990 | 64,170 |
| Cities outside metropolitan areas | 1,425,757 | | | | | | | | | | |
| Area actually reporting | 97.1% | 5,528 | 43 | 657 | 472 | 602 | 4,226 | 41,169 | 9,231 | 30,193 | 1,745 |
| Estimated total | 100.0% | 5,687 | 44 | 679 | 492 | 617 | 4,347 | 42,301 | 9,488 | 31,023 | 1,790 |
| Nonmetropolitan counties | 1,620,856 | | | | | | | | | | |
| Area actually reporting | 99.4% | 2,958 | 65 | 512 | 350 | 127 | 2,254 | 19,923 | 7,285 | 11,122 | 1,516 |
| Estimated total | 100.0% | 2,976 | 65 | 516 | 352 | 128 | 2,267 | 20,040 | 7,328 | 11,187 | 1,525 |

# Table 5. Crime, by State and Area, 2015—*Continued*

(Number, percent, rate per 100,000 population.)

| Area | Population | Violent crime[1] | Murder and nonnegligent manslaughter | Rape (revised definition)[2] | Rape (legacy definition)[3] | Robbery | Aggravated assault | Property crime | Burglary | Larceny-theft | Motor vehicle theft |
|---|---|---|---|---|---|---|---|---|---|---|---|
| State total........................ | 27,469,114 | 113,227 | 1,316 | 12,250 | 8,925 | 31,934 | 67,727 | 777,739 | 153,054 | 557,200 | 67,485 |
| Rate per 100,000 inhabitants................. | | 412.2 | 4.8 | 44.6 | 32.5 | 116.3 | 246.6 | 2,831.3 | 557.2 | 2,028.5 | 245.7 |
| **Utah[6]** | | | | | | | | | | | |
| Metropolitan statistical area............... | 2,675,737 | | | | | | | | | | |
| Area actually reporting ......................... | 98.7% | 6,295 | 49 | 1,448 | 969 | 1,292 | 3,506 | 82,075 | 11,283 | 62,574 | 8,218 |
| Estimated total ..................................... | 100.0% | 6,357 | 49 | 1,462 | 980 | 1,303 | 3,543 | 82,969 | 11,414 | 63,248 | 8,307 |
| Cities outside metropolitan areas.......... | 144,887 | | | | | | | | | | |
| Area actually reporting ......................... | 95.5% | 337 | 1 | 95 | 50 | 12 | 229 | 3,411 | 519 | 2,714 | 178 |
| Estimated total ..................................... | 100.0% | 354 | 1 | 100 | 54 | 13 | 240 | 3,573 | 544 | 2,843 | 186 |
| Nonmetropolitan counties .................... | 175,295 | | | | | | | | | | |
| Area actually reporting ......................... | 96.0% | 346 | 4 | 79 | 61 | 10 | 253 | 2,628 | 490 | 1,932 | 206 |
| Estimated total..................................... | 100.0% | 360 | 4 | 83 | 64 | 10 | 263 | 2,736 | 510 | 2,012 | 214 |
| State total............................................. | 2,995,919 | 7,071 | 54 | 1,645 | 1,098 | 1,326 | 4,046 | 89,278 | 12,468 | 68,103 | 8,707 |
| Rate per 100,000 inhabitants................. | | 236.0 | 1.8 | 54.9 | 36.6 | 44.3 | 135.1 | 2,980.0 | 416.2 | 2,273.2 | 290.6 |
| **Vermont** | | | | | | | | | | | |
| Metropolitan statistical area................. | 217,090 | | | | | | | | | | |
| Area actually reporting ......................... | 100.0% | 279 | 2 | 50 | 48 | 47 | 180 | 4,245 | 815 | 3,396 | 34 |
| Cities outside metropolitan areas.......... | 203,524 | | | | | | | | | | |
| Area actually reporting ......................... | 100.0% | 307 | 5 | 48 | 44 | 42 | 212 | 2,873 | 504 | 2,312 | 57 |
| Nonmetropolitan counties .................... | 205,428 | | | | | | | | | | |
| Area actually reporting ......................... | 100.0% | 153 | 3 | 38 | 29 | 12 | 100 | 1,688 | 649 | 952 | 87 |
| State total............................................. | 626,042 | 739 | 10 | 136 | 121 | 101 | 492 | 8,806 | 1,968 | 6,660 | 178 |
| Rate per 100,000 inhabitants................. | | 118.0 | 1.6 | 21.7 | 19.3 | 16.1 | 78.6 | 1,406.6 | 314.4 | 1,063.8 | 28.4 |
| **Virginia** | | | | | | | | | | | |
| Metropolitan statistical area................. | 7,266,550 | | | | | | | | | | |
| Area actually reporting ......................... | 99.9% | 14,412 | 284 | 1,880 | 1,206 | 4,039 | 8,209 | 143,762 | 19,725 | 117,178 | 6,859 |
| Estimated total ..................................... | 100.0% | 14,413 | 284 | 1,880 | 1,206 | 4,039 | 8,210 | 143,779 | 19,727 | 117,192 | 6,860 |
| Cities outside metropolitan areas.......... | 264,412 | | | | | | | | | | |
| Area actually reporting ......................... | 98.7% | 694 | 15 | 113 | 65 | 144 | 422 | 7,385 | 1,130 | 6,060 | 195 |
| Estimated total ..................................... | 100.0% | 702 | 15 | 113 | 65 | 146 | 428 | 7,484 | 1,145 | 6,141 | 198 |
| Nonmetropolitan counties .................... | 795,327 | | | | | | | | | | |
| Area actually reporting ......................... | 100.0% | 1,225 | 39 | 317 | 161 | 107 | 762 | 9,457 | 2,250 | 6,600 | 607 |
| State total............................................. | 8,326,289 | 16,340 | 338 | 2,310 | 1,432 | 4,292 | 9,400 | 160,720 | 23,122 | 129,933 | 7,665 |
| Rate per 100,000 inhabitants................. | | 196.2 | 4.1 | 27.7 | 17.2 | 51.5 | 112.9 | 1,930.3 | 277.7 | 1,560.5 | 92.1 |
| **Washington[6]** | | | | | | | | | | | |
| Metropolitan statistical area................. | 6,452,326 | | | | | | | | | | |
| Area actually reporting ......................... | 99.9% | 18,899 | 197 | 2,438 | 1,965 | 5,234 | 11,030 | 229,294 | 45,974 | 157,899 | 25,421 |
| Estimated total ..................................... | 100.0% | 18,899 | 197 | 2,438 | 1,965 | 5,234 | 11,030 | 229,304 | 45,976 | 157,906 | 25,422 |
| Cities outside metropolitan areas.......... | 296,377 | | | | | | | | | | |
| Area actually reporting......................... | 97.8% | 922 | 6 | 173 | 151 | 165 | 578 | 12,260 | 2,524 | 8,829 | 907 |
| Estimated total ..................................... | 100.0% | 942 | 6 | 176 | 154 | 169 | 591 | 12,541 | 2,582 | 9,031 | 928 |
| Nonmetropolitan counties .................... | 421,648 | | | | | | | | | | |
| Area actually reporting......................... | 100.0% | 553 | 8 | 91 | 74 | 46 | 408 | 6,524 | 2,435 | 3,572 | 517 |
| State total............................................. | 7,170,351 | 20,394 | 211 | 2,705 | 2,193 | 5,449 | 12,029 | 248,369 | 50,993 | 170,509 | 26,867 |
| Rate per 100,000 inhabitants................. | | 284.4 | 2.9 | 37.7 | 30.6 | 76.0 | 167.8 | 3,463.8 | 711.2 | 2,378.0 | 374.7 |
| **West Virginia** | | | | | | | | | | | |
| Metropolitan statistical area................. | 1,136,862 | | | | | | | | | | |
| Area actually reporting ......................... | 89.8% | 3,557 | 45 | 402 | 245 | 625 | 2,485 | 25,404 | 6,476 | 17,423 | 1,505 |
| Estimated total...................................... | 100.0% | 3,887 | 47 | 433 | 269 | 667 | 2,740 | 28,418 | 7,019 | 19,731 | 1,668 |
| Cities outside metropolitan areas.......... | 189,216 | | | | | | | | | | |
| Area actually reporting ......................... | 53.0% | 280 | 4 | 23 | 18 | 28 | 225 | 1,619 | 264 | 1,285 | 70 |
| Estimated total...................................... | 100.0% | 519 | 8 | 33 | 26 | 53 | 425 | 3,056 | 498 | 2,426 | 132 |
| Nonmetropolitan counties .................... | 518,050 | | | | | | | | | | |
| Area actually reporting ......................... | 73.1% | 1,325 | 11 | 142 | 83 | 29 | 1,143 | 4,223 | 1,208 | 2,694 | 321 |
| Estimated total...................................... | 100.0% | 1,825 | 15 | 206 | 125 | 40 | 1,564 | 5,777 | 1,653 | 3,685 | 439 |
| State total............................................. | 1,844,128 | 6,231 | 70 | 672 | 420 | 760 | 4,729 | 37,251 | 9,170 | 25,842 | 2,239 |
| Rate per 100,000 inhabitants................. | | 337.9 | 3.8 | 36.4 | 22.8 | 41.2 | 256.4 | 2,020.0 | 497.3 | 1,401.3 | 121.4 |
| **Wisconsin[6]** | | | | | | | | | | | |
| Metropolitan statistical area................. | 4,268,682 | | | | | | | | | | |
| Area actually reporting......................... | 96.5% | 15,597 | 207 | 1,368 | 923 | 5,087 | 8,935 | 88,714 | 15,012 | 63,592 | 10,110 |
| Estimated total...................................... | 100.0% | 15,770 | 209 | 1,396 | 945 | 5,131 | 9,034 | 91,251 | 15,314 | 65,713 | 10,224 |
| Cities outside metropolitan areas.......... | 639,613 | | | | | | | | | | |
| Area actually reporting ......................... | 93.8% | 1,015 | 9 | 189 | 141 | 79 | 738 | 14,140 | 1,732 | 12,065 | 343 |
| Estimated total...................................... | 100.0% | 1,082 | 10 | 201 | 150 | 84 | 787 | 15,070 | 1,846 | 12,858 | 366 |
| Nonmetropolitan counties .................... | 863,042 | | | | | | | | | | |
| Area actually reporting ......................... | 100.0% | 795 | 21 | 183 | 129 | 17 | 574 | 7,603 | 2,394 | 4,814 | 395 |
| State total............................................. | 5,771,337 | 17,647 | 240 | 1,780 | 1,224 | 5,232 | 10,395 | 113,924 | 19,554 | 83,385 | 10,985 |
| Rate per 100,000 inhabitants................. | | 305.8 | 4.2 | 30.8 | 21.2 | 90.7 | 180.1 | 1,974.0 | 338.8 | 1,444.8 | 190.3 |

# Table 5. Crime, by State and Area, 2015—*Continued*

(Number, percent, rate per 100,000 population.)

| Area | Population | Violent crime[1] | Murder and nonnegligent manslaughter | Rape (revised definition)[2] | Rape (legacy definition)[3] | Robbery | Aggra-vated assault | Property crime | Burglary | Larceny-theft | Motor vehicle theft |
|---|---|---|---|---|---|---|---|---|---|---|---|
| **Wyoming** | | | | | | | | | | | |
| **Metropolitan statistical area**.................. | 179,738 | | | | | | | | | | |
| Area actually reporting............................ | 100.0% | 366 | 8 | 50 | 36 | 31 | 277 | 4,584 | 763 | 3,579 | 242 |
| **Cities outside metropolitan areas**.......... | 245,549 | | | | | | | | | | |
| Area actually reporting............................ | 96.7% | 629 | 5 | 82 | 62 | 24 | 518 | 5,255 | 693 | 4,313 | 249 |
| Estimated total........................................ | 100.0% | 649 | 5 | 83 | 63 | 25 | 536 | 5,434 | 717 | 4,460 | 257 |
| **Nonmetropolitan counties** .................... | 160,820 | | | | | | | | | | |
| Area actually reporting ........................... | 91.6% | 262 | 3 | 35 | 23 | 3 | 221 | 1,038 | 258 | 695 | 85 |
| Estimated total........................................ | 100.0% | 287 | 3 | 40 | 26 | 3 | 241 | 1,133 | 282 | 758 | 93 |
| **State total**............................................. | 586,107 | 1,302 | 16 | 173 | 125 | 59 | 1,054 | 11,151 | 1,762 | 8,797 | 592 |
| Rate per 100,000 inhabitants................. | | 222.1 | 2.7 | 29.5 | 21.3 | 10.1 | 179.8 | 1,902.6 | 300.6 | 1,500.9 | 101.0 |

*Note:* Although arson data are included in the trend and clearance tables, sufficient data are not available to estimate totals for this offense. Therefore, no arson data are published in this table.
[1] The violent crime figures include the offenses of murder, rape (revised definition), robbery, and aggravated assault.
[2] The figures shown in this column for the offense of rape were estimated using the revised Uniform Crime Reporting (UCR) definition of rape. See chapter notes for more detail.
[3] The figures shown in this column for the offense of rape were estimated using the legacy Uniform Crime Reporting (UCR) definition of rape. See chapter notes for more detail.
[4] Includes offenses reported by the Metro Transit Police and the Arson Investigation Unit of the District of Columbia Fire and Emergency Medical Services.
[5] This state's agencies submitted rape data according to the legacy UCR definition of rape.
[6] Agencies within this state submitted rape data according to both the revised UCR definition of rape and the legacy UCR definition of rape.
[7] The figures submitted by Puerto Rico for rape were not verified and may not be comparable to previous years' data.

# Table 6. Crime, by Selected Metropolitan Statistical Area, 2015

(Number, percent, rate per 100,000 population.)

| Area | Population | Violent crime | Murder and nonnegligent manslaughter | Rape[1] | Robbery | Aggravated assault | Property crime | Burglary | Larceny-theft | Motor vehicle theft |
|---|---|---|---|---|---|---|---|---|---|---|
| **Abilene, TX M.S.A.** | 169,713 | | | | | | | | | |
| Includes Callahan, Jones, and Taylor Counties | | | | | | | | | | |
| City of Abilene | 121,764 | 613 | 7 | 84 | 128 | 394 | 5,354 | 1,168 | 3,798 | 388 |
| Total area actually reporting | 100.0% | 700 | 9 | 95 | 133 | 463 | 6,125 | 1,446 | 4,232 | 447 |
| Rate per 100,000 inhabitants | | 412.5 | 5.3 | 56.0 | 78.4 | 272.8 | 3,609.0 | 852.0 | 2,493.6 | 263.4 |
| **Akron, OH M.S.A.** | 704,320 | | | | | | | | | |
| Includes Portage and Summit Counties | | | | | | | | | | |
| City of Akron | 197,587 | 1,168 | 28 | 166 | 402 | 572 | 8,027 | 2,426 | 5,002 | 599 |
| Total area actually reporting | 91.9% | 1,588 | 35 | 253 | 499 | 801 | 16,668 | 3,826 | 12,014 | 828 |
| Estimated total | 100.0% | 1,679 | 36 | 269 | 530 | 844 | 17,977 | 4,052 | 13,051 | 874 |
| Rate per 100,000 inhabitants | | 238.4 | 5.1 | 38.2 | 75.2 | 119.8 | 2,552.4 | 575.3 | 1,853.0 | 124.1 |
| **Albany, GA M.S.A.** | 154,516 | | | | | | | | | |
| Includes Baker, Dougherty, Lee, Terrell, and Worth Counties | | | | | | | | | | |
| City of Albany | 75,357 | 800 | 10 | 35 | 201 | 554 | 3,902 | 1,137 | 2,616 | 149 |
| Total area actually reporting | 96.0% | 1,010 | 12 | 46 | 236 | 716 | 5,812 | 1,661 | 3,948 | 203 |
| Estimated total | 100.0% | 1,032 | 12 | 47 | 244 | 729 | 6,017 | 1,699 | 4,099 | 219 |
| Rate per 100,000 inhabitants | | 667.9 | 7.8 | 30.4 | 157.9 | 471.8 | 3,894.1 | 1,099.6 | 2,652.8 | 141.7 |
| **Albany, OR M.S.A.** | 120,716 | | | | | | | | | |
| Includes Linn County | | | | | | | | | | |
| City of Albany | 52,394 | 41 | 2 | 10 | 16 | 13 | 1,726 | 173 | 1,447 | 106 |
| Total area actually reporting | 100.0% | 138 | 3 | 34 | 25 | 76 | 3,873 | 585 | 2,989 | 299 |
| Rate per 100,000 inhabitants | | 114.3 | 2.5 | 28.2 | 20.7 | 63.0 | 3,208.4 | 484.6 | 2,476.1 | 247.7 |
| **Albuquerque, NM M.S.A.** | 905,803 | | | | | | | | | |
| Includes Bernalillo, Sandoval, Torrance, and Valencia Counties | | | | | | | | | | |
| City of Albuquerque | 559,721 | 5,406 | 43 | 404 | 1,686 | 3,273 | 33,993 | 5,996 | 22,818 | 5,179 |
| Total area actually reporting | 100.0% | 7,179 | 55 | 578 | 1,872 | 4,674 | 41,738 | 8,002 | 27,605 | 6,131 |
| Rate per 100,000 inhabitants | | 792.6 | 6.1 | 63.8 | 206.7 | 516.0 | 4,607.8 | 883.4 | 3,047.6 | 676.9 |
| **Alexandria, LA M.S.A.** | 154,844 | | | | | | | | | |
| Includes Grant and Rapides Parishes | | | | | | | | | | |
| City of Alexandria | 48,305 | 988 | 7 | 11 | 168 | 802 | 4,046 | 1,011 | 2,794 | 241 |
| Total area actually reporting | 99.3% | 1,445 | 7 | 55 | 185 | 1,198 | 7,028 | 1,799 | 4,743 | 486 |
| Estimated total | 100.0% | 1,450 | 7 | 55 | 186 | 1,202 | 7,070 | 1,807 | 4,775 | 488 |
| Rate per 100,000 inhabitants | | 936.4 | 4.5 | 35.5 | 120.1 | 776.3 | 4,565.9 | 1,167.0 | 3,083.7 | 315.2 |
| **Altoona, PA M.S.A.** | 125,646 | | | | | | | | | |
| Includes Blair County | | | | | | | | | | |
| City of Altoona | 45,379 | 137 | 1 | 26 | 26 | 84 | 894 | 182 | 670 | 42 |
| Total area actually reporting | 99.0% | 270 | 1 | 36 | 31 | 202 | 1,777 | 272 | 1,446 | 59 |
| Estimated total | 100.0% | 272 | 1 | 36 | 32 | 203 | 1,797 | 275 | 1,462 | 60 |
| Rate per 100,000 inhabitants | | 216.5 | 0.8 | 28.7 | 25.5 | 161.6 | 1,430.2 | 218.9 | 1,163.6 | 47.8 |
| **Amarillo, TX M.S.A.** | 262,320 | | | | | | | | | |
| Includes Armstrong, Carson, Oldham, Potter, and Randall Counties | | | | | | | | | | |
| City of Amarillo | 198,770 | 1,278 | 7 | 166 | 272 | 833 | 9,269 | 1,815 | 6,671 | 783 |
| Total area actually reporting | 100.0% | 1,413 | 9 | 189 | 281 | 934 | 10,040 | 2,002 | 7,196 | 842 |
| Rate per 100,000 inhabitants | | 538.7 | 3.4 | 72.0 | 107.1 | 356.1 | 3,827.4 | 763.2 | 2,743.2 | 321.0 |
| **Ames, IA M.S.A.** | 95,279 | | | | | | | | | |
| Includes Story County | | | | | | | | | | |
| City of Ames | 64,383 | 98 | 1 | 29 | 16 | 52 | 1,225 | 198 | 983 | 44 |
| Total area actually reporting | 92.9% | 136 | 1 | 43 | 18 | 74 | 1,650 | 276 | 1,308 | 66 |
| Estimated total | 100.0% | 151 | 1 | 45 | 19 | 86 | 1,761 | 297 | 1,393 | 71 |
| Rate per 100,000 inhabitants | | 158.5 | 1.0 | 47.2 | 19.9 | 90.3 | 1,848.3 | 311.7 | 1,462.0 | 74.5 |
| **Anchorage, AK M.S.A.** | 316,990 | | | | | | | | | |
| Includes Anchorage Municipality and Matanuska-Susitna Borough | | | | | | | | | | |
| City of Anchorage | 301,239 | 3,226 | 26 | 517 | 621 | 2,062 | 11,801 | 1,685 | 8,962 | 1,154 |
| Total area actually reporting | 100.0% | 3,295 | 26 | 525 | 631 | 2,113 | 12,775 | 1,759 | 9,787 | 1,229 |
| Rate per 100,000 inhabitants | | 1,039.5 | 8.2 | 165.6 | 199.1 | 666.6 | 4,030.1 | 554.9 | 3,087.5 | 387.7 |
| **Ann Arbor, MI M.S.A.** | 359,888 | | | | | | | | | |
| Includes Washtenaw County | | | | | | | | | | |
| City of Ann Arbor | 118,730 | 228 | 0 | 58 | 42 | 128 | 2,364 | 274 | 2,018 | 72 |
| Total area actually reporting | 100.0% | 1,150 | 7 | 205 | 185 | 753 | 6,449 | 1,045 | 5,101 | 303 |
| Rate per 100,000 inhabitants | | 319.5 | 1.9 | 57.0 | 51.4 | 209.2 | 1,791.9 | 290.4 | 1,417.4 | 84.2 |

# Table 6. Crime, by Selected Metropolitan Statistical Area, 2015—*Continued*

(Number, percent, rate per 100,000 population.)

| Area | Population | Violent crime | Murder and nonnegligent manslaughter | Rape[1] | Robbery | Aggravated assault | Property crime | Burglary | Larceny-theft | Motor vehicle theft |
|---|---|---|---|---|---|---|---|---|---|---|
| **Anniston-Oxford-Jacksonville, AL M.S.A.** ............. | 115,117 | | | | | | | | | |
| Includes Calhoun County.................................. | | | | | | | | | | |
| City of Anniston......................................... | 22,306 | 607 | 8 | 44 | 79 | 476 | 1,645 | 601 | 970 | 74 |
| City of Oxford........................................... | 16,971 | 58 | 1 | 4 | 10 | 43 | 719 | 116 | 579 | 24 |
| City of Jacksonville..................................... | 12,173 | 50 | 1 | 1 | 6 | 42 | 495 | 116 | 366 | 13 |
| Total area actually reporting ......................... | 99.3% | 801 | 10 | 62 | 98 | 631 | 3,768 | 1,161 | 2,468 | 139 |
| Estimated total.......................................... | 100.0% | 805 | 10 | 62 | 99 | 634 | 3,794 | 1,166 | 2,487 | 141 |
| Rate per 100,000 inhabitants......................... | | 699.3 | 8.7 | 53.9 | 86.0 | 550.7 | 3,295.8 | 1,012.9 | 2,160.4 | 122.5 |
| | | | | | | | | | | |
| **Appleton, WI M.S.A.** ....................................... | 232,783 | | | | | | | | | |
| Includes Calumet and Outagamie Counties................ | | | | | | | | | | |
| City of Appleton......................................... | 74,310 | 201 | 0 | 43 | 13 | 145 | 1,242 | 172 | 1,031 | 39 |
| Total area actually reporting ......................... | 100.0% | 323 | 1 | 56 | 20 | 246 | 3,247 | 481 | 2,688 | 78 |
| Rate per 100,000 inhabitants......................... | | 138.8 | 0.4 | 24.1 | 8.6 | 105.7 | 1,394.9 | 206.6 | 1,154.7 | 33.5 |
| | | | | | | | | | | |
| **Asheville, NC M.S.A.** ...................................... | 446,543 | | | | | | | | | |
| Includes Buncombe, Haywood, Henderson, and Madison Counties | | | | | | | | | | |
| City of Asheville........................................ | 89,003 | 447 | 7 | 35 | 147 | 258 | 4,380 | 870 | 3,264 | 246 |
| Total area actually reporting ......................... | 99.5% | 897 | 12 | 87 | 223 | 575 | 9,577 | 2,633 | 6,367 | 577 |
| Estimated total.......................................... | 100.0% | 902 | 12 | 87 | 224 | 579 | 9,640 | 2,646 | 6,415 | 579 |
| Rate per 100,000 inhabitants......................... | | 202.0 | 2.7 | 19.5 | 50.2 | 129.7 | 2,158.8 | 592.6 | 1,436.6 | 129.7 |
| | | | | | | | | | | |
| **Athens-Clarke County, GA M.S.A.** .......................... | 200,776 | | | | | | | | | |
| Includes Clarke, Madison, Oconee, and Oglethorpe Counties | | | | | | | | | | |
| City of Athens-Clarke County ......................... | 120,858 | 504 | 3 | 57 | 116 | 328 | 4,283 | 934 | 3,110 | 239 |
| Total area actually reporting ......................... | 99.9% | 654 | 5 | 83 | 136 | 430 | 6,234 | 1,356 | 4,562 | 316 |
| Estimated total.......................................... | 100.0% | 654 | 5 | 83 | 136 | 430 | 6,235 | 1,356 | 4,563 | 316 |
| Rate per 100,000 inhabitants......................... | | 325.7 | 2.5 | 41.3 | 67.7 | 214.2 | 3,105.5 | 675.4 | 2,272.7 | 157.4 |
| | | | | | | | | | | |
| **Atlanta-Sandy Springs-Roswell, GA M.S.A.** .......... | 5,704,839 | | | | | | | | | |
| Includes Barrow, Bartow, Butts, Carroll, Cherokee, Clayton, Cobb, Coweta, Dawson, DeKalb, Douglas, Fayette, Forsyth, Fulton, Gwinnett, Haralson, Heard, Henry, Jasper, Lamar, Meriwether, Morgan, Newton, Paulding, Pickens, Pike, Rockdale, Spalding, and Walton Counties.............................................. | | | | | | | | | | |
| City of Atlanta.......................................... | 464,710 | 5,203 | 94 | 170 | 1,995 | 2,944 | 25,556 | 4,781 | 16,493 | 4,282 |
| City of Sandy Springs.................................. | 103,898 | 151 | 3 | 9 | 85 | 54 | 2,498 | 500 | 1,859 | 139 |
| City of Roswell.......................................... | 95,455 | 119 | 1 | 10 | 57 | 51 | 1,668 | 261 | 1,335 | 72 |
| City of Alpharetta...................................... | 64,419 | 31 | 1 | 3 | 14 | 13 | 1,243 | 126 | 1,083 | 34 |
| City of Marietta........................................ | 60,830 | 273 | 7 | 11 | 127 | 128 | 2,467 | 359 | 1,943 | 165 |
| Total area actually reporting ......................... | 99.6% | 22,765 | 351 | 1,212 | 8,617 | 12,585 | 174,121 | 35,741 | 119,785 | 18,595 |
| Estimated total.......................................... | 100.0% | 22,874 | 352 | 1,219 | 8,654 | 12,649 | 175,130 | 35,905 | 120,557 | 18,668 |
| Rate per 100,000 inhabitants......................... | | 401.0 | 6.2 | 21.4 | 151.7 | 221.7 | 3,069.8 | 629.4 | 2,113.2 | 327.2 |
| | | | | | | | | | | |
| **Atlantic City-Hammonton, NJ M.S.A.[2]** .................. | 274,876 | | | | | | | | | |
| Includes Atlantic County[2]........................... | | | | | | | | | | |
| City of Atlantic City[2]................................ | 39,372 | 616 | 7 | 17 | 356 | 236 | 2,546 | 305 | 2,166 | 75 |
| City of Hammonton[2].................................. | 14,757 | 15 | 0 | 2 | 2 | 11 | 96 | 14 | 72 | 10 |
| Total area actually reporting ......................... | 100.0% | 1,138 | 19 | 58 | 514 | 547 | 7,744 | 1,443 | 6,075 | 226 |
| Rate per 100,000 inhabitants......................... | | 414.0 | 6.9 | 21.1 | 187.0 | 199.0 | 2,817.3 | 525.0 | 2,210.1 | 82.2 |
| | | | | | | | | | | |
| **Austin-Round Rock, TX M.S.A.[2]** ........................... | 2,005,823 | | | | | | | | | |
| Includes Bastrop, Caldwell, Hays, Travis, and Williamson Counties ....................................... | | | | | | | | | | |
| City of Austin........................................... | 938,728 | 3,497 | 23 | 487 | 929 | 2,058 | 35,399 | 5,000 | 28,068 | 2,331 |
| City of Round Rock..................................... | 115,955 | 153 | 1 | 39 | 34 | 79 | 2,230 | 205 | 1,979 | 46 |
| Total area actually reporting ......................... | 100.0% | 5,770 | 44 | 900 | 1,227 | 3,599 | 53,611 | 8,338 | 42,059 | 3,214 |
| Rate per 100,000 inhabitants......................... | | 287.7 | 2.2 | 44.9 | 61.2 | 179.4 | 2,672.8 | 415.7 | 2,096.8 | 160.2 |
| | | | | | | | | | | |
| **Bakersfield, CA M.S.A.** ...................................... | 882,213 | | | | | | | | | |
| Includes Kern County..................................... | | | | | | | | | | |
| City of Bakersfield...................................... | 373,887 | 1,810 | 22 | 71 | 655 | 1,062 | 15,559 | 3,877 | 9,288 | 2,394 |
| Total area actually reporting ......................... | 100.0% | 4,908 | 64 | 284 | 1,149 | 3,411 | 30,342 | 8,419 | 16,595 | 5,328 |
| Rate per 100,000 inhabitants......................... | | 556.3 | 7.3 | 32.2 | 130.2 | 386.6 | 3,439.3 | 954.3 | 1,881.1 | 603.9 |
| | | | | | | | | | | |
| **Baltimore-Columbia-Towson, MD M.S.A.** .............. | 2,795,298 | | | | | | | | | |
| Includes Anne Arundel, Baltimore, Carroll, Harford, Howard, and Queen Anne's Counties and Baltimore City.......................................................... | | | | | | | | | | |
| City of Baltimore........................................ | 621,252 | 9,542 | 344 | 287 | 4,313 | 4,598 | 30,941 | 7,757 | 17,658 | 5,526 |
| Total area actually reporting ......................... | 100.0% | 17,462 | 367 | 832 | 6,680 | 9,583 | 73,376 | 14,468 | 50,958 | 7,950 |
| Rate per 100,000 inhabitants......................... | | 624.7 | 13.1 | 29.8 | 239.0 | 342.8 | 2,625.0 | 517.6 | 1,823.0 | 284.4 |

# Table 6. Crime, by Selected Metropolitan Statistical Area, 2015—*Continued*

(Number, percent, rate per 100,000 population.)

| Area | Population | Violent crime | Murder and nonnegligent manslaughter | Rape[1] | Robbery | Aggravated assault | Property crime | Burglary | Larceny-theft | Motor vehicle theft |
|---|---|---|---|---|---|---|---|---|---|---|
| **Bangor, ME M.S.A.** ................................... | 153,137 | | | | | | | | | |
| Includes Penobscot County ............................. | | | | | | | | | | |
| City of Bangor .................................................. | 32,455 | 56 | 1 | 5 | 19 | 31 | 1,276 | 173 | 1,086 | 17 |
| Total area actually reporting .......................... | 100.0% | 103 | 3 | 14 | 27 | 59 | 3,039 | 516 | 2,457 | 66 |
| Rate per 100,000 inhabitants.......................... | | 67.3 | 2.0 | 9.1 | 17.6 | 38.5 | 1,984.5 | 337.0 | 1,604.4 | 43.1 |
| | | | | | | | | | | |
| **Barnstable Town, MA M.S.A.** ................... | 214,749 | | | | | | | | | |
| Includes Barnstable County .......................... | | | | | | | | | | |
| City of Barnstable ........................................... | 44,392 | 411 | 2 | 23 | 25 | 361 | 882 | 169 | 667 | 46 |
| Total area actually reporting .......................... | 100.0% | 1,114 | 3 | 106 | 62 | 943 | 3,699 | 1,022 | 2,514 | 163 |
| Rate per 100,000 inhabitants.......................... | | 518.7 | 1.4 | 49.4 | 28.9 | 439.1 | 1,722.5 | 475.9 | 1,170.7 | 75.9 |
| | | | | | | | | | | |
| **Baton Rouge, LA M.S.A.** ........................... | 829,780 | | | | | | | | | |
| Includes Ascension, East Baton Rouge, East Feliciana, Iberville, Livingston, Pointe Coupee, St. Helena, West Baton Rouge, and West Feliciana Parishes ................ | | | | | | | | | | |
| City of Baton Rouge.......................................... | 228,727 | 2,001 | 60 | 102 | 808 | 1,031 | 10,243 | 2,377 | 7,372 | 494 |
| Total area actually reporting .......................... | 98.7% | 3,925 | 92 | 278 | 1,161 | 2,394 | 28,626 | 6,394 | 21,148 | 1,084 |
| Estimated total.................................................. | 100.0% | 3,974 | 92 | 281 | 1,169 | 2,432 | 29,037 | 6,472 | 21,463 | 1,102 |
| Rate per 100,000 inhabitants.......................... | | 478.9 | 11.1 | 33.9 | 140.9 | 293.1 | 3,499.4 | 780.0 | 2,586.6 | 132.8 |
| | | | | | | | | | | |
| **Battle Creek, MI M.S.A.**............................. | 134,644 | | | | | | | | | |
| Includes Calhoun County................................. | | | | | | | | | | |
| City of Battle Creek........................................... | 61,240 | 462 | 4 | 72 | 63 | 323 | 2,235 | 647 | 1,516 | 72 |
| Total area actually reporting .......................... | 100.0% | 753 | 4 | 140 | 82 | 527 | 3,822 | 1,002 | 2,694 | 126 |
| Rate per 100,000 inhabitants.......................... | | 559.3 | 3.0 | 104.0 | 60.9 | 391.4 | 2,838.6 | 744.2 | 2,000.8 | 93.6 |
| | | | | | | | | | | |
| **Bay City, MI M.S.A.** ................................... | 105,839 | | | | | | | | | |
| Includes Bay County......................................... | | | | | | | | | | |
| City of Bay City ................................................ | 33,965 | 206 | 0 | 49 | 29 | 128 | 1,088 | 312 | 737 | 39 |
| Total area actually reporting .......................... | 100.0% | 300 | 0 | 85 | 39 | 176 | 2,223 | 526 | 1,609 | 88 |
| Rate per 100,000 inhabitants.......................... | | 283.4 | 0.0 | 80.3 | 36.8 | 166.3 | 2,100.4 | 497.0 | 1,520.2 | 83.1 |
| | | | | | | | | | | |
| **Beaumont-Port Arthur, TX M.S.A.**........................... | 406,743 | | | | | | | | | |
| Includes Hardin, Jefferson, Newton, and Orange Counties.......................................................... | | | | | | | | | | |
| City of Beaumont.............................................. | 117,635 | 1,088 | 16 | 92 | 298 | 682 | 4,840 | 1,295 | 3,308 | 237 |
| City of Port Arthur............................................ | 54,557 | 328 | 5 | 27 | 85 | 211 | 2,434 | 794 | 1,518 | 122 |
| Total area actually reporting .......................... | 99.9% | 2,123 | 28 | 173 | 492 | 1,430 | 11,449 | 3,185 | 7,579 | 685 |
| Estimated total.................................................. | 100.0% | 2,124 | 28 | 173 | 492 | 1,431 | 11,462 | 3,187 | 7,589 | 686 |
| Rate per 100,000 inhabitants.......................... | | 522.2 | 6.9 | 42.5 | 121.0 | 351.8 | 2,818.0 | 783.5 | 1,865.8 | 168.7 |
| | | | | | | | | | | |
| **Beckley, WV M.S.A.** ................................... | 122,631 | | | | | | | | | |
| Includes Fayette and Raleigh Counties....................... | | | | | | | | | | |
| City of Beckley.................................................. | 17,137 | 234 | 3 | 22 | 57 | 152 | 1,387 | 319 | 1,024 | 44 |
| Total area actually reporting .......................... | 94.6% | 519 | 8 | 48 | 101 | 362 | 3,489 | 983 | 2,344 | 162 |
| Estimated total.................................................. | 100.0% | 540 | 8 | 50 | 104 | 378 | 3,712 | 1,014 | 2,525 | 173 |
| Rate per 100,000 inhabitants.......................... | | 440.3 | 6.5 | 40.8 | 84.8 | 308.2 | 3,027.0 | 826.9 | 2,059.0 | 141.1 |
| | | | | | | | | | | |
| **Bellingham, WA M.S.A.**............................. | 210,855 | | | | | | | | | |
| Includes Whatcom County ............................. | | | | | | | | | | |
| City of Bellingham ........................................... | 83,976 | 214 | 1 | 47 | 45 | 121 | 4,067 | 543 | 3,362 | 162 |
| Total area actually reporting .......................... | 100.0% | 412 | 6 | 90 | 63 | 253 | 6,243 | 1,137 | 4,836 | 270 |
| Rate per 100,000 inhabitants.......................... | | 195.4 | 2.8 | 42.7 | 29.9 | 120.0 | 2,960.8 | 539.2 | 2,293.5 | 128.1 |
| | | | | | | | | | | |
| **Bend-Redmond, OR M.S.A.**...................... | 174,742 | | | | | | | | | |
| Includes Deschutes County ............................. | | | | | | | | | | |
| City of Bend...................................................... | 86,042 | 134 | 2 | 38 | 16 | 78 | 2,350 | 218 | 2,070 | 62 |
| City of Redmond.............................................. | 28,384 | 75 | 1 | 14 | 11 | 49 | 1,038 | 126 | 852 | 60 |
| Total area actually reporting .......................... | 100.0% | 309 | 3 | 67 | 33 | 206 | 4,131 | 523 | 3,438 | 170 |
| Rate per 100,000 inhabitants.......................... | | 176.8 | 1.7 | 38.3 | 18.9 | 117.9 | 2,364.1 | 299.3 | 1,967.5 | 97.3 |
| | | | | | | | | | | |
| **Billings, MT M.S.A.** ................................... | 168,961 | | | | | | | | | |
| Includes Carbon, Golden Valley, and Yellowstone Counties.......................................................... | | | | | | | | | | |
| City of Billings.................................................. | 109,997 | 484 | 9 | 65 | 67 | 343 | 5,176 | 600 | 3,824 | 752 |
| Total area actually reporting .......................... | 99.7% | 609 | 10 | 82 | 75 | 442 | 6,227 | 786 | 4,542 | 899 |
| Estimated total.................................................. | 100.0% | 610 | 10 | 82 | 75 | 443 | 6,242 | 787 | 4,555 | 900 |
| Rate per 100,000 inhabitants.......................... | | 361.0 | 5.9 | 48.5 | 44.4 | 262.2 | 3,694.3 | 465.8 | 2,695.9 | 532.7 |
| | | | | | | | | | | |
| **Binghamton, NY M.S.A.**........................... | 245,686 | | | | | | | | | |
| Includes Broome and Tioga Counties ....................... | | | | | | | | | | |
| City of Binghamton.......................................... | 46,048 | 310 | 4 | 37 | 89 | 180 | 2,092 | 342 | 1,707 | 43 |
| Total area actually reporting .......................... | 100.0% | 675 | 7 | 176 | 154 | 338 | 6,226 | 1,009 | 5,088 | 129 |
| Rate per 100,000 inhabitants.......................... | | 274.7 | 2.8 | 71.6 | 62.7 | 137.6 | 2,534.1 | 410.7 | 2,070.9 | 52.5 |

# Table 6. Crime, by Selected Metropolitan Statistical Area, 2015—*Continued*

(Number, percent, rate per 100,000 population.)

| Area | Population | Violent crime | Murder and nonnegligent manslaughter | Rape[1] | Robbery | Aggravated assault | Property crime | Burglary | Larceny-theft | Motor vehicle theft |
|---|---|---|---|---|---|---|---|---|---|---|
| **Birmingham-Hoover, AL M.S.A.** ............... | 1,145,825 | | | | | | | | | |
| Includes Bibb, Blount, Chilton, Jefferson, St. Clair, Shelby, and Walker Counties..................... | | | | | | | | | | |
| City of Birmingham.................... | 212,291 | 3,707 | 79 | 159 | 1,114 | 2,355 | 13,499 | 3,146 | 8,838 | 1,515 |
| City of Hoover ..................... | 85,163 | 129 | 3 | 23 | 51 | 52 | 2,457 | 302 | 2,082 | 73 |
| Total area actually reporting ............. | 96.8% | 7,636 | 125 | 513 | 1,776 | 5,222 | 37,094 | 9,134 | 25,001 | 2,959 |
| Estimated total..................... | 100.0% | 7,815 | 127 | 529 | 1,807 | 5,352 | 38,327 | 9,368 | 25,919 | 3,040 |
| Rate per 100,000 inhabitants................ | | 682.0 | 11.1 | 46.2 | 157.7 | 467.1 | 3,344.9 | 817.6 | 2,262.0 | 265.3 |
| **Bismarck, ND M.S.A.** ..................... | 129,464 | | | | | | | | | |
| Includes Burleigh, Morton, Oliver, and Sioux Counties | | | | | | | | | | |
| City of Bismarck................... | 70,873 | 104 | 1 | 7 | 10 | 86 | 924 | 87 | 759 | 78 |
| Total area actually reporting ............. | 100.0% | 294 | 4 | 48 | 17 | 225 | 2,159 | 244 | 1,709 | 206 |
| Rate per 100,000 inhabitants................ | | 227.1 | 3.1 | 37.1 | 13.1 | 173.8 | 1,667.6 | 188.5 | 1,320.1 | 159.1 |
| **Bloomington, IL M.S.A.**..................... | 190,884 | | | | | | | | | |
| Includes DeWitt and McLean Counties...................... | | | | | | | | | | |
| City of Bloomington.................... | 79,233 | 305 | 0 | 61 | 42 | 202 | 1,460 | 264 | 1,121 | 75 |
| Total area actually reporting ............. | 97.9% | 473 | 0 | 117 | 59 | 297 | 3,116 | 604 | 2,385 | 127 |
| Estimated total..................... | 100.0% | 481 | 0 | 118 | 61 | 302 | 3,185 | 615 | 2,440 | 130 |
| Rate per 100,000 inhabitants................ | | 252.0 | 0.0 | 61.8 | 32.0 | 158.2 | 1,668.6 | 322.2 | 1,278.3 | 68.1 |
| **Bloomington, IN M.S.A.** ..................... | 165,263 | | | | | | | | | |
| Includes Monroe and Owen Counties ...................... | | | | | | | | | | |
| City of Bloomington.................... | 84,015 | 313 | 2 | 43 | 64 | 204 | 2,680 | 504 | 2,028 | 148 |
| Total area actually reporting ............. | 87.4% | 431 | 3 | 71 | 74 | 283 | 4,002 | 760 | 3,002 | 240 |
| Estimated total..................... | 100.0% | 459 | 3 | 74 | 78 | 304 | 4,226 | 814 | 3,152 | 260 |
| Rate per 100,000 inhabitants................ | | 277.7 | 1.8 | 44.8 | 47.2 | 183.9 | 2,557.1 | 492.5 | 1,907.3 | 157.3 |
| **Bloomsburg-Berwick, PA M.S.A** ............... | 85,762 | | | | | | | | | |
| Includes Columbia and Montour Counties ............... | | | | | | | | | | |
| City of Bloomsburg Town.................... | 14,697 | 31 | 0 | 4 | 1 | 26 | 198 | 28 | 166 | 4 |
| City of Berwick.................... | 10,274 | 25 | 0 | 4 | 2 | 19 | 225 | 45 | 176 | 4 |
| Total area actually reporting ............. | 99.1% | 130 | 1 | 19 | 6 | 104 | 1,125 | 204 | 897 | 24 |
| Estimated total..................... | 100.0% | 131 | 1 | 19 | 6 | 105 | 1,137 | 206 | 907 | 24 |
| Rate per 100,000 inhabitants................ | | 152.7 | 1.2 | 22.2 | 7.0 | 122.4 | 1,325.8 | 240.2 | 1,057.6 | 28.0 |
| **Boise City, ID M.S.A.**..................... | 678,158 | | | | | | | | | |
| Includes Ada, Boise, Canyon, Gem, and Owyhee Counties.......... | | | | | | | | | | |
| City of Boise ..................... | 218,844 | 676 | 1 | 151 | 44 | 480 | 4,980 | 668 | 4,044 | 268 |
| Total area actually reporting ............. | 99.9% | 1,585 | 12 | 334 | 93 | 1,146 | 11,690 | 2,136 | 8,717 | 837 |
| Estimated total..................... | 100.0% | 1,586 | 12 | 334 | 93 | 1,147 | 11,700 | 2,138 | 8,724 | 838 |
| Rate per 100,000 inhabitants................ | | 233.9 | 1.8 | 49.3 | 13.7 | 169.1 | 1,725.3 | 315.3 | 1,286.4 | 123.6 |
| **Boulder, CO M.S.A.**[3] ..................... | 319,003 | | | | | | | | | |
| Includes Boulder County ............... | | | | | | | | | | |
| City of Boulder.................... | 106,823 | 222 | 2 | 47 | 25 | 148 | 2,825 | 474 | 2,214 | 137 |
| Total area actually reporting ............. | 100.0% | | 3 | 215 | 72 | | 6,810 | 1,056 | 5,388 | 366 |
| Rate per 100,000 inhabitants................ | | | 0.9 | 67.4 | 22.6 | | 2,134.8 | 331.0 | 1,689.0 | 114.7 |
| **Bowling Green, KY M.S.A.**..................... | 167,238 | | | | | | | | | |
| Includes Allen, Butler, Edmonson, and Warren Counties.......... | | | | | | | | | | |
| City of Bowling Green.................... | 63,346 | 225 | 0 | 54 | 83 | 88 | 3,137 | 488 | 2,486 | 163 |
| Total area actually reporting ............. | 100.0% | 290 | 1 | 74 | 87 | 128 | 4,023 | 798 | 2,985 | 240 |
| Rate per 100,000 inhabitants................ | | 173.4 | 0.6 | 44.2 | 52.0 | 76.5 | 2,405.6 | 477.2 | 1,784.9 | 143.5 |
| **Bremerton-Silverdale, WA M.S.A.**..................... | 255,747 | | | | | | | | | |
| Includes Kitsap County.................... | | | | | | | | | | |
| City of Bremerton.................... | 38,755 | 207 | 1 | 36 | 37 | 133 | 1,612 | 301 | 1,174 | 137 |
| Total area actually reporting ............. | 100.0% | 654 | 8 | 120 | 95 | 431 | 7,024 | 1,450 | 5,074 | 500 |
| Rate per 100,000 inhabitants................ | | 255.7 | 3.1 | 46.9 | 37.1 | 168.5 | 2,746.5 | 567.0 | 1,984.0 | 195.5 |
| **Bridgeport-Stamford-Norwalk, CT M.S.A.**............... | 934,152 | | | | | | | | | |
| Includes Fairfield County ............... | | | | | | | | | | |
| City of Bridgeport.................... | 148,313 | 996 | 19 | 80 | 441 | 456 | 3,496 | 817 | 2,053 | 626 |
| City of Stamford.................... | 129,682 | 285 | 3 | 19 | 92 | 171 | 1,869 | 200 | 1,509 | 160 |
| City of Norwalk.................... | 88,692 | 239 | 0 | 20 | 41 | 178 | 1,627 | 202 | 1,307 | 118 |
| City of Danbury.................... | 84,404 | 157 | 0 | 45 | 64 | 48 | 1,361 | 178 | 1,070 | 113 |
| City of Stratford.................... | 53,058 | 69 | 0 | 12 | 31 | 26 | 1,175 | 181 | 829 | 165 |
| Total area actually reporting ............. | 100.0% | 1,882 | 23 | 204 | 718 | 937 | 13,762 | 2,210 | 10,191 | 1,361 |
| Rate per 100,000 inhabitants................ | | 201.5 | 2.5 | 21.8 | 76.9 | 100.3 | 1,473.2 | 236.6 | 1,090.9 | 145.7 |

# Table 6. Crime, by Selected Metropolitan Statistical Area, 2015—*Continued*

(Number, percent, rate per 100,000 population.)

| Area | Population | Violent crime | Murder and nonnegligent manslaughter | Rape[1] | Robbery | Aggravated assault | Property crime | Burglary | Larceny-theft | Motor vehicle theft |
|---|---|---|---|---|---|---|---|---|---|---|
| **Brownsville-Harlingen, TX M.S.A.**............................. | 424,559 | | | | | | | | | |
| Includes Cameron County........................................ | | | | | | | | | | |
| City of Brownsville................................................... | 184,941 | 502 | 3 | 53 | 154 | 292 | 7,656 | 1,015 | 6,498 | 143 |
| City of Harlingen..................................................... | 66,122 | 199 | 1 | 31 | 51 | 116 | 2,188 | 531 | 1,605 | 52 |
| Total area actually reporting ............................... | 100.0% | 1,273 | 7 | 188 | 261 | 817 | 13,712 | 2,411 | 10,992 | 309 |
| Rate per 100,000 inhabitants............................... | | 299.8 | 1.6 | 44.3 | 61.5 | 192.4 | 3,229.7 | 567.9 | 2,589.0 | 72.8 |
| | | | | | | | | | | |
| **Brunswick, GA M.S.A.** ............................................ | 115,567 | | | | | | | | | |
| Includes Brantley, Glynn, and McIntosh Counties........ | | | | | | | | | | |
| City of Brunswick..................................................... | 16,026 | 184 | 2 | 10 | 46 | 126 | 952 | 265 | 622 | 65 |
| Total area actually reporting ............................... | 99.1% | 409 | 3 | 30 | 95 | 281 | 3,815 | 949 | 2,651 | 215 |
| Estimated total........................................................ | 100.0% | 414 | 3 | 30 | 97 | 284 | 3,857 | 956 | 2,683 | 218 |
| Rate per 100,000 inhabitants............................... | | 358.2 | 2.6 | 26.0 | 83.9 | 245.7 | 3,337.5 | 827.2 | 2,321.6 | 188.6 |
| | | | | | | | | | | |
| **Buffalo-Cheektowaga-Niagara Falls, NY M.S.A.....** | 1,134,390 | | | | | | | | | |
| Includes Erie and Niagara Counties ........................... | | | | | | | | | | |
| City of Buffalo ......................................................... | 258,096 | 2,887 | 41 | 173 | 1,033 | 1,640 | 11,176 | 2,777 | 7,421 | 978 |
| City of Cheektowaga Town....................................... | 78,438 | 191 | 2 | 15 | 75 | 99 | 2,376 | 274 | 2,025 | 77 |
| City of Niagara Falls ................................................ | 48,989 | 555 | 3 | 32 | 156 | 364 | 2,526 | 615 | 1,781 | 130 |
| Total area actually reporting ............................... | 100.0% | 4,558 | 50 | 376 | 1,506 | 2,626 | 27,378 | 5,381 | 20,484 | 1,513 |
| Rate per 100,000 inhabitants............................... | | 401.8 | 4.4 | 33.1 | 132.8 | 231.5 | 2,413.5 | 474.4 | 1,805.7 | 133.4 |
| | | | | | | | | | | |
| **Burlington, NC M.S.A.** ............................................ | 156,835 | | | | | | | | | |
| Includes Alamance County......................................... | | | | | | | | | | |
| City of Burlington .................................................... | 52,006 | 372 | 6 | 15 | 75 | 276 | 1,884 | 431 | 1,361 | 92 |
| Total area actually reporting ............................... | 100.0% | 620 | 8 | 31 | 101 | 480 | 3,883 | 1,111 | 2,613 | 159 |
| Rate per 100,000 inhabitants............................... | | 395.3 | 5.1 | 19.8 | 64.4 | 306.1 | 2,475.9 | 708.4 | 1,666.1 | 101.4 |
| | | | | | | | | | | |
| **Burlington-South Burlington, VT M.S.A.** .............. | 217,090 | | | | | | | | | |
| Includes Chittenden, Franklin, and Grand Isle Counties........................................................ | | | | | | | | | | |
| City of Burlington .................................................... | 42,160 | 99 | 1 | 15 | 18 | 65 | 1,450 | 228 | 1,222 | 0 |
| City of South Burlington .......................................... | 18,946 | 25 | 0 | 6 | 7 | 12 | 481 | 30 | 451 | 0 |
| Total area actually reporting ............................... | 100.0% | 279 | 2 | 50 | 47 | 180 | 4,245 | 815 | 3,396 | 34 |
| Rate per 100,000 inhabitants............................... | | 128.5 | 0.9 | 23.0 | 21.7 | 82.9 | 1,955.4 | 375.4 | 1,564.3 | 15.7 |
| | | | | | | | | | | |
| **California-Lexington Park, MD M.S.A.**.................... | 111,234 | | | | | | | | | |
| Includes St. Mary's County ....................................... | | | | | | | | | | |
| Total area actually reporting ............................... | 100.0% | 296 | 1 | 20 | 51 | 224 | 2,286 | 545 | 1,672 | 69 |
| Rate per 100,000 inhabitants............................... | | 266.1 | 0.9 | 18.0 | 45.8 | 201.4 | 2,055.1 | 490.0 | 1,503.1 | 62.0 |
| | | | | | | | | | | |
| **Canton-Massillon, OH M.S.A.** ................................. | 404,017 | | | | | | | | | |
| Includes Carroll and Stark Counties.......................... | | | | | | | | | | |
| City of Canton ......................................................... | 72,111 | 814 | 7 | 69 | 242 | 496 | 3,848 | 1,194 | 2,444 | 210 |
| City of Massillon ..................................................... | 32,301 | 84 | 1 | 25 | 21 | 37 | 846 | 195 | 629 | 22 |
| Total area actually reporting ............................... | 85.1% | 1,224 | 12 | 159 | 342 | 711 | 9,178 | 2,395 | 6,358 | 425 |
| Estimated total........................................................ | 100.0% | 1,308 | 13 | 176 | 368 | 751 | 10,376 | 2,636 | 7,270 | 470 |
| Rate per 100,000 inhabitants............................... | | 323.7 | 3.2 | 43.6 | 91.1 | 185.9 | 2,568.2 | 652.4 | 1,799.4 | 116.3 |
| | | | | | | | | | | |
| **Cape Coral-Fort Myers, FL M.S.A.** ......................... | 698,770 | | | | | | | | | |
| Includes Lee County................................................. | | | | | | | | | | |
| City of Cape Coral ................................................... | 173,844 | 203 | 0 | 12 | 46 | 145 | 3,136 | 581 | 2,415 | 140 |
| City of Fort Myers ................................................... | 73,218 | 744 | 14 | 38 | 178 | 514 | 2,208 | 419 | 1,600 | 189 |
| Total area actually reporting ............................... | 100.0% | 2,488 | 31 | 206 | 565 | 1,686 | 12,586 | 2,844 | 8,880 | 862 |
| Rate per 100,000 inhabitants............................... | | 356.1 | 4.4 | 29.5 | 80.9 | 241.3 | 1,801.2 | 407.0 | 1,270.8 | 123.4 |
| | | | | | | | | | | |
| **Cape Girardeau, MO-IL M.S.A.** ............................... | 98,346 | | | | | | | | | |
| Includes Alexander County, IL and Bollinger and Cape Girardeau Counties, MO | | | | | | | | | | |
| City of Cape Girardeau, MO ..................................... | 39,439 | 210 | 2 | 19 | 62 | 127 | 1,949 | 312 | 1,535 | 102 |
| Total area actually reporting ............................... | 100.0% | 440 | 3 | 46 | 68 | 323 | 2,891 | 592 | 2,140 | 159 |
| Rate per 100,000 inhabitants............................... | | 447.4 | 3.1 | 46.8 | 69.1 | 328.4 | 2,939.6 | 602.0 | 2,176.0 | 161.7 |
| | | | | | | | | | | |
| **Carson City, NV M.S.A.**........................................... | 54,654 | | | | | | | | | |
| Includes Carson City ............................................... | | | | | | | | | | |
| Total area actually reporting ............................... | 100.0% | 172 | 1 | 2 | 20 | 149 | 1,000 | 184 | 733 | 83 |
| Rate per 100,000 inhabitants............................... | | 314.7 | 1.8 | 3.7 | 36.6 | 272.6 | 1,829.7 | 336.7 | 1,341.2 | 151.9 |
| | | | | | | | | | | |
| **Casper, WY M.S.A.**................................................. | 82,795 | | | | | | | | | |
| Includes Natrona County .......................................... | | | | | | | | | | |
| City of Casper.......................................................... | 61,355 | 85 | 1 | 8 | 17 | 59 | 1,670 | 212 | 1,396 | 62 |
| Total area actually reporting ............................... | 100.0% | 194 | 1 | 33 | 22 | 138 | 2,081 | 333 | 1,643 | 105 |
| Rate per 100,000 inhabitants............................... | | 234.3 | 1.2 | 39.9 | 26.6 | 166.7 | 2,513.4 | 402.2 | 1,984.4 | 126.8 |

# Table 6. Crime, by Selected Metropolitan Statistical Area, 2015—*Continued*

(Number, percent, rate per 100,000 population.)

| Area | Population | Violent crime | Murder and nonnegligent manslaughter | Rape[1] | Robbery | Aggravated assault | Property crime | Burglary | Larceny-theft | Motor vehicle theft |
|---|---|---|---|---|---|---|---|---|---|---|
| **Cedar Rapids, IA M.S.A.** | 265,439 | | | | | | | | | |
| Includes Benton, Jones, and Linn Counties | | | | | | | | | | |
| City of Cedar Rapids | 129,863 | 361 | 6 | 30 | 106 | 219 | 4,937 | 983 | 3,659 | 295 |
| Total area actually reporting | 99.1% | 497 | 8 | 49 | 116 | 324 | 6,198 | 1,405 | 4,433 | 360 |
| Estimated total | 100.0% | 503 | 8 | 50 | 116 | 329 | 6,239 | 1,413 | 4,464 | 362 |
| Rate per 100,000 inhabitants | | 189.5 | 3.0 | 18.8 | 43.7 | 123.9 | 2,350.4 | 532.3 | 1,681.7 | 136.4 |
| **Chambersburg-Waynesboro, PA M.S.A.** | 153,595 | | | | | | | | | |
| Includes Franklin County | | | | | | | | | | |
| City of Chambersburg | 20,679 | 92 | 0 | 11 | 27 | 54 | 675 | 89 | 553 | 33 |
| City of Waynesboro | 10,805 | 18 | 0 | 5 | 5 | 8 | 276 | 54 | 211 | 11 |
| Total area actually reporting | 100.0% | 245 | 3 | 58 | 66 | 118 | 2,488 | 472 | 1,894 | 122 |
| Rate per 100,000 inhabitants | | 159.5 | 2.0 | 37.8 | 43.0 | 76.8 | 1,619.8 | 307.3 | 1,233.1 | 79.4 |
| **Charleston, WV M.S.A.** | 221,205 | | | | | | | | | |
| Includes Boone, Clay, and Kanawha Counties | | | | | | | | | | |
| City of Charleston | 50,176 | 622 | 8 | 54 | 137 | 423 | 3,312 | 747 | 2,332 | 233 |
| Total area actually reporting | 90.4% | 1,112 | 18 | 111 | 198 | 785 | 7,395 | 1,633 | 5,173 | 589 |
| Estimated total | 100.0% | 1,173 | 18 | 117 | 206 | 832 | 7,957 | 1,733 | 5,605 | 619 |
| Rate per 100,000 inhabitants | | 530.3 | 8.1 | 52.9 | 93.1 | 376.1 | 3,597.1 | 783.4 | 2,533.8 | 279.8 |
| **Charleston-North Charleston, SC M.S.A.** | 745,359 | | | | | | | | | |
| Includes Berkeley, Charleston, and Dorchester Counties | | | | | | | | | | |
| City of Charleston | 132,585 | 342 | 16 | 43 | 91 | 192 | 3,235 | 474 | 2,477 | 284 |
| City of North Charleston | 109,051 | 802 | 19 | 90 | 251 | 442 | 5,779 | 886 | 4,382 | 511 |
| Total area actually reporting | 99.5% | 2,956 | 63 | 289 | 572 | 2,032 | 21,179 | 4,049 | 15,404 | 1,726 |
| Estimated total | 100.0% | 2,974 | 63 | 291 | 575 | 2,045 | 21,318 | 4,070 | 15,514 | 1,734 |
| Rate per 100,000 inhabitants | | 399.0 | 8.5 | 39.0 | 77.1 | 274.4 | 2,860.1 | 546.0 | 2,081.4 | 232.6 |
| **Charlottesville, VA M.S.A.** | 228,394 | | | | | | | | | |
| Includes Albemarle, Buckingham, Fluvanna, Greene, and Nelson Counties and Charlottesville City | | | | | | | | | | |
| City of Charlottesville | 45,997 | 175 | 2 | 18 | 48 | 107 | 1,157 | 187 | 918 | 52 |
| Total area actually reporting | 100.0% | 376 | 3 | 81 | 72 | 220 | 3,459 | 576 | 2,739 | 144 |
| Rate per 100,000 inhabitants | | 164.6 | 1.3 | 35.5 | 31.5 | 96.3 | 1,514.5 | 252.2 | 1,199.2 | 63.0 |
| **Chattanooga, TN-GA M.S.A.** | 548,811 | | | | | | | | | |
| Includes Catoosa, Dade, and Walker Counties, GA and Hamilton, Marion, and Sequatchie Counties, TN | | | | | | | | | | |
| City of Chattanooga, TN | 174,969 | 1,731 | 23 | 94 | 324 | 1,290 | 10,356 | 1,832 | 7,646 | 878 |
| Total area actually reporting | 100.0% | 2,908 | 32 | 198 | 445 | 2,233 | 18,760 | 3,638 | 13,589 | 1,533 |
| Rate per 100,000 inhabitants | | 529.9 | 5.8 | 36.1 | 81.1 | 406.9 | 3,418.3 | 662.9 | 2,476.1 | 279.3 |
| **Cheyenne, WY M.S.A.** | 96,943 | | | | | | | | | |
| Includes Laramie County | | | | | | | | | | |
| City of Cheyenne | 63,619 | 122 | 7 | 13 | 7 | 95 | 2,039 | 289 | 1,650 | 100 |
| Total area actually reporting | 100.0% | 172 | 7 | 17 | 9 | 139 | 2,503 | 430 | 1,936 | 137 |
| Rate per 100,000 inhabitants | | 177.4 | 7.2 | 17.5 | 9.3 | 143.4 | 2,581.9 | 443.6 | 1,997.0 | 141.3 |
| **Chicago-Naperville-Elgin, IL-IN-WI M.S.A.** | 9,554,259 | | | | | | | | | |
| Includes the Metropolitan Divisions of Chicago-Naperville-Arlington Heights, IL; Elgin, IL; Gary, IN; and Lake County-Kenosha County, IL-WI | | | | | | | | | | |
| City of Chicago, IL | 2,728,695 | 24,663 | 478 | 1,432 | 9,649 | 13,104 | 80,395 | 13,151 | 57,022 | 10,222 |
| City of Naperville, IL | 147,101 | 128 | 0 | 14 | 27 | 87 | 1,652 | 161 | 1,458 | 33 |
| City of Elgin, IL | 111,832 | 261 | 3 | 37 | 68 | 153 | 1,488 | 256 | 1,161 | 71 |
| City of Gary, IN | 77,336 | 455 | 50 | 25 | 204 | 176 | 3,397 | 990 | 2,027 | 380 |
| City of Arlington Heights, IL | 76,241 | 42 | 1 | 6 | 15 | 20 | 648 | 78 | 560 | 10 |
| City of Evanston, IL | 75,930 | 131 | 3 | 0 | 51 | 77 | 1,815 | 313 | 1,440 | 62 |
| City of Schaumburg, IL | 75,050 | 55 | 1 | 13 | 18 | 23 | 1,820 | 127 | 1,652 | 41 |
| City of Skokie, IL | 65,184 | 154 | 0 | 15 | 29 | 110 | 1,333 | 229 | 1,055 | 49 |
| City of Des Plaines, IL | 59,078 | 50 | 0 | 5 | 12 | 33 | 635 | 95 | 508 | 32 |
| City of Hoffman Estates, IL | 52,450 | 39 | 0 | 3 | 10 | 26 | 428 | 68 | 340 | 20 |
| Total area actually reporting | 96.4% | 35,368 | 672 | 2,851 | 12,933 | 18,912 | 185,913 | 30,455 | 140,054 | 15,404 |
| Estimated total | 100.0% | 36,079 | 679 | 2,938 | 13,102 | 19,360 | 192,415 | 31,427 | 145,246 | 15,742 |
| Rate per 100,000 inhabitants | | 377.6 | 7.1 | 30.8 | 137.1 | 202.6 | 2,013.9 | 328.9 | 1,520.2 | 164.8 |
| Chicago-Naperville-Arlington Heights, IL M.D. | 7,344,423 | | | | | | | | | |
| Includes Cook, DuPage, Grundy, Kendall, McHenry, and Will Counties | | | | | | | | | | |

# Table 6. Crime, by Selected Metropolitan Statistical Area, 2015—*Continued*

(Number, percent, rate per 100,000 population.)

| Area | Population | Violent crime | Murder and nonnegligent manslaughter | Rape[1] | Robbery | Aggravated assault | Property crime | Burglary | Larceny-theft | Motor vehicle theft |
|---|---|---|---|---|---|---|---|---|---|---|
| Total area actually reporting............................ | 96.8% | 31,138 | 561 | 2,346 | 11,696 | 16,535 | 148,566 | 24,291 | 110,941 | 13,334 |
| Estimated total.............................................. | 100.0% | 31,600 | 566 | 2,412 | 11,812 | 16,810 | 152,564 | 24,914 | 114,140 | 13,510 |
| Rate per 100,000 inhabitants........................ | | 430.3 | 7.7 | 32.8 | 160.8 | 228.9 | 2,077.3 | 339.2 | 1,554.1 | 183.9 |
|     Elgin, IL M.D. ...................................... | 634,175 | | | | | | | | | |
| Includes DeKalb and Kane Counties.................... | | | | | | | | | | |
| Total area actually reporting............................ | 98.3% | 1,180 | 10 | 178 | 231 | 761 | 8,329 | 1,164 | 6,906 | 259 |
| Estimated total.............................................. | 100.0% | 1,201 | 10 | 181 | 236 | 774 | 8,512 | 1,193 | 7,052 | 267 |
| Rate per 100,000 inhabitants........................ | | 189.4 | 1.6 | 28.5 | 37.2 | 122.0 | 1,342.2 | 188.1 | 1,112.0 | 42.1 |
|     Gary, IN M.D. ...................................... | 703,585 | | | | | | | | | |
| Includes Jasper, Lake, Newton, and Porter Counties ... | | | | | | | | | | |
| Total area actually reporting............................ | 86.6% | 1,671 | 82 | 119 | 599 | 871 | 15,751 | 2,786 | 11,680 | 1,285 |
| Estimated total.............................................. | 100.0% | 1,892 | 84 | 136 | 645 | 1,027 | 18,017 | 3,097 | 13,483 | 1,437 |
| Rate per 100,000 inhabitants........................ | | 268.9 | 11.9 | 19.3 | 91.7 | 146.0 | 2,560.7 | 440.2 | 1,916.3 | 204.2 |
|     Lake County-Kenosha County, IL-WI M.D....... | 872,076 | | | | | | | | | |
| Includes Lake County, IL and Kenosha County, WI...... | | | | | | | | | | |
| Total area actually reporting............................ | 99.6% | 1,379 | 19 | 208 | 407 | 745 | 13,267 | 2,214 | 10,527 | 526 |
| Estimated total.............................................. | 100.0% | 1,386 | 19 | 209 | 409 | 749 | 13,322 | 2,223 | 10,571 | 528 |
| Rate per 100,000 inhabitants........................ | | 158.9 | 2.2 | 24.0 | 46.9 | 85.9 | 1,527.6 | 254.9 | 1,212.2 | 60.5 |
| | | | | | | | | | | |
| **Chico, CA M.S.A.**............................................ | 225,135 | | | | | | | | | |
| Includes Butte County...................................... | | | | | | | | | | |
| City of Chico.................................................. | 89,949 | 317 | 2 | 59 | 87 | 169 | 3,634 | 642 | 2,591 | 401 |
| Total area actually reporting............................ | 100.0% | 778 | 7 | 118 | 147 | 506 | 7,543 | 1,899 | 4,697 | 947 |
| Rate per 100,000 inhabitants........................ | | 345.6 | 3.1 | 52.4 | 65.3 | 224.8 | 3,350.4 | 843.5 | 2,086.3 | 420.6 |
| | | | | | | | | | | |
| **Cincinnati, OH-KY-IN M.S.A.** ...................... | 2,157,633 | | | | | | | | | |
| Includes Dearborn, Ohio, and Union Counties, IN; | | | | | | | | | | |
| Boone, Bracken, Campbell, Gallatin, Grant, Kenton, | | | | | | | | | | |
| and Pendleton Counties, KY; and Brown, Butler, | | | | | | | | | | |
| Clermont, Hamilton, and Warren Counties, OH.......... | | | | | | | | | | |
| City of Cincinnati, OH..................................... | 298,478 | 2,761 | 66 | 236 | 1,263 | 1,196 | 16,446 | 4,413 | 10,873 | 1,160 |
| Total area actually reporting............................ | 93.7% | 5,385 | 98 | 772 | 2,194 | 2,321 | 57,449 | 11,974 | 42,867 | 2,608 |
| Estimated total.............................................. | 100.0% | 5,596 | 100 | 803 | 2,252 | 2,441 | 60,004 | 12,444 | 44,831 | 2,729 |
| Rate per 100,000 inhabitants........................ | | 259.4 | 4.6 | 37.2 | 104.4 | 113.1 | 2,781.0 | 576.7 | 2,077.8 | 126.5 |
| | | | | | | | | | | |
| **Clarksville, TN-KY M.S.A.** .......................... | 282,696 | | | | | | | | | |
| Includes Christian and Trigg Counties, KY and | | | | | | | | | | |
| Montgomery County, TN.................................. | | | | | | | | | | |
| City of Clarksville, TN...................................... | 150,319 | 874 | 13 | 59 | 86 | 716 | 4,294 | 733 | 3,397 | 164 |
| Total area actually reporting............................ | 100.0% | 1,144 | 17 | 98 | 138 | 891 | 6,815 | 1,380 | 5,131 | 304 |
| Rate per 100,000 inhabitants........................ | | 404.7 | 6.0 | 34.7 | 48.8 | 315.2 | 2,410.7 | 488.2 | 1,815.0 | 107.5 |
| | | | | | | | | | | |
| **Cleveland, TN M.S.A.** ............................... | 120,673 | | | | | | | | | |
| Includes Bradley and Polk Counties ...................... | | | | | | | | | | |
| City of Cleveland ............................................ | 43,650 | 368 | 4 | 15 | 38 | 311 | 2,649 | 403 | 2,112 | 134 |
| Total area actually reporting............................ | 100.0% | 583 | 8 | 31 | 49 | 495 | 4,011 | 743 | 2,971 | 297 |
| Rate per 100,000 inhabitants........................ | | 483.1 | 6.6 | 25.7 | 40.6 | 410.2 | 3,323.9 | 615.7 | 2,462.0 | 246.1 |
| | | | | | | | | | | |
| **Coeur d'Alene, ID M.S.A.** .......................... | 149,854 | | | | | | | | | |
| Includes Kootenai County ................................. | | | | | | | | | | |
| City of Coeur d'Alene...................................... | 48,871 | 198 | 1 | 40 | 21 | 136 | 1,335 | 214 | 1,037 | 84 |
| Total area actually reporting............................ | 100.0% | 389 | 2 | 68 | 33 | 286 | 3,261 | 698 | 2,387 | 176 |
| Rate per 100,000 inhabitants........................ | | 259.6 | 1.3 | 45.4 | 22.0 | 190.9 | 2,176.1 | 465.8 | 1,592.9 | 117.4 |
| | | | | | | | | | | |
| **College Station-Bryan, TX M.S.A.** ........................ | 246,944 | | | | | | | | | |
| Includes Brazos, Burleson, and Robertson Counties .... | | | | | | | | | | |
| City of College Station..................................... | 105,855 | 234 | 2 | 62 | 38 | 132 | 2,455 | 393 | 1,964 | 98 |
| City of Bryan................................................. | 82,050 | 363 | 5 | 55 | 64 | 239 | 2,573 | 441 | 2,010 | 122 |
| Total area actually reporting............................ | 100.0% | 779 | 11 | 148 | 114 | 506 | 6,284 | 1,116 | 4,896 | 272 |
| Rate per 100,000 inhabitants........................ | | 315.5 | 4.5 | 59.9 | 46.2 | 204.9 | 2,544.7 | 451.9 | 1,982.6 | 110.1 |
| | | | | | | | | | | |
| **Colorado Springs, CO M.S.A.**................................ | 698,942 | | | | | | | | | |
| Includes El Paso and Teller Counties ...................... | | | | | | | | | | |
| City of Colorado Springs................................... | 452,410 | 1,983 | 25 | 341 | 376 | 1,241 | 16,504 | 2,414 | 12,363 | 1,727 |
| Total area actually reporting............................ | 100.0% | 2,511 | 26 | 461 | 406 | 1,618 | 19,919 | 3,026 | 14,924 | 1,969 |
| Rate per 100,000 inhabitants........................ | | 359.3 | 3.7 | 66.0 | 58.1 | 231.5 | 2,849.9 | 432.9 | 2,135.2 | 281.7 |
| | | | | | | | | | | |
| **Columbia, MO M.S.A.** ............................... | 175,261 | | | | | | | | | |
| Includes Boone County ................................... | | | | | | | | | | |
| City of Columbia............................................ | 118,911 | 600 | 1 | 82 | 141 | 376 | 3,635 | 839 | 2,570 | 226 |
| Total area actually reporting............................ | 100.0% | 754 | 6 | 94 | 158 | 496 | 4,705 | 1,021 | 3,389 | 295 |
| Rate per 100,000 inhabitants........................ | | 430.2 | 3.4 | 53.6 | 90.2 | 283.0 | 2,684.6 | 582.6 | 1,933.7 | 168.3 |

**Part 2. Crime in the United States, 2015  45**

(Number, percent, rate per 100,000 population.)

| Area | Population | Violent crime | Murder and nonnegligent manslaughter | Rape[1] | Robbery | Aggravated assault | Property crime | Burglary | Larceny-theft | Motor vehicle theft |
|---|---|---|---|---|---|---|---|---|---|---|
| **Columbia, SC M.S.A.** ................................ | 810,441 | | | | | | | | | |
| Includes Calhoun, Fairfield, Kershaw, Lexington, Richland, and Saluda Counties................................ | | | | | | | | | | |
| City of Columbia.............................................. | 132,495 | 1,058 | 12 | 83 | 258 | 705 | 7,204 | 1,094 | 5,252 | 858 |
| Total area actually reporting ............................. | 99.8% | 5,263 | 56 | 402 | 803 | 4,002 | 28,000 | 5,077 | 19,930 | 2,993 |
| Estimated total................................................. | 100.0% | 5,273 | 56 | 403 | 805 | 4,009 | 28,074 | 5,088 | 19,989 | 2,997 |
| Rate per 100,000 inhabitants........................... | | 650.6 | 6.9 | 49.7 | 99.3 | 494.7 | 3,464.0 | 627.8 | 2,466.4 | 369.8 |
| **Columbus, GA-AL M.S.A.**................................ | 318,981 | | | | | | | | | |
| Includes Russell County, AL and Chattahoochee, Harris, Marion, and Muscogee Counties, GA ........................ | | | | | | | | | | |
| City of Columbus, GA......................................... | 203,778 | 1,132 | 19 | 68 | 547 | 498 | 11,295 | 2,560 | 7,678 | 1,057 |
| Total area actually reporting ............................. | 99.8% | 1,492 | 22 | 119 | 622 | 729 | 13,826 | 3,249 | 9,280 | 1,297 |
| Estimated total................................................. | 100.0% | 1,495 | 22 | 119 | 623 | 731 | 13,846 | 3,253 | 9,295 | 1,298 |
| Rate per 100,000 inhabitants........................... | | 468.7 | 6.9 | 37.3 | 195.3 | 229.2 | 4,340.7 | 1,019.8 | 2,914.0 | 406.9 |
| **Columbus, IN M.S.A.** .................................... | 81,023 | | | | | | | | | |
| Includes Bartholomew County ........................... | | | | | | | | | | |
| City of Columbus............................................... | 46,640 | 41 | 1 | 20 | 17 | 3 | 2,104 | 244 | 1,729 | 131 |
| Total area actually reporting ............................. | 100.0% | 88 | 1 | 27 | 20 | 40 | 2,663 | 372 | 2,092 | 199 |
| Rate per 100,000 inhabitants........................... | | 108.6 | 1.2 | 33.3 | 24.7 | 49.4 | 3,286.7 | 459.1 | 2,582.0 | 245.6 |
| **Columbus, OH M.S.A.**[2] ................................ | 2,018,210 | | | | | | | | | |
| Includes Delaware, Fairfield, Franklin, Hocking, Licking, Madison, Morrow, Perry, Pickaway, and Union Counties .......................................................... | | | | | | | | | | |
| City of Columbus............................................... | 847,745 | 4,631 | 77 | 806 | 2,240 | 1,508 | 33,353 | 7,219 | 23,021 | 3,113 |
| Total area actually reporting ............................. | 94.0% | 5,819 | 92 | 1,114 | 2,652 | 1,961 | 55,124 | 11,399 | 39,830 | 3,895 |
| Estimated total................................................. | 100.0% | 6,015 | 94 | 1,149 | 2,719 | 2,053 | 57,909 | 11,879 | 42,037 | 3,993 |
| Rate per 100,000 inhabitants........................... | | 298.0 | 4.7 | 56.9 | 134.7 | 101.7 | 2,869.3 | 588.6 | 2,082.9 | 197.8 |
| **Corpus Christi, TX M.S.A.**................................ | 454,268 | | | | | | | | | |
| Includes Aransas, Nueces, and San Patricio Counties .. | | | | | | | | | | |
| City of Corpus Christi......................................... | 324,326 | 2,092 | 17 | 282 | 394 | 1,399 | 11,240 | 2,188 | 8,539 | 513 |
| Total area actually reporting ............................. | 98.9% | 2,737 | 23 | 337 | 431 | 1,946 | 15,182 | 3,147 | 11,355 | 680 |
| Estimated total................................................. | 100.0% | 2,750 | 23 | 339 | 434 | 1,954 | 15,311 | 3,168 | 11,454 | 689 |
| Rate per 100,000 inhabitants........................... | | 605.4 | 5.1 | 74.6 | 95.5 | 430.1 | 3,370.5 | 697.4 | 2,521.4 | 151.7 |
| **Corvallis, OR M.S.A.** .................................... | 87,040 | | | | | | | | | |
| Includes Benton County .................................... | | | | | | | | | | |
| City of Corvallis................................................. | 55,100 | 69 | 1 | 25 | 14 | 29 | 1,546 | 201 | 1,297 | 48 |
| Total area actually reporting ............................. | 100.0% | 102 | 2 | 35 | 17 | 48 | 2,301 | 312 | 1,911 | 78 |
| Rate per 100,000 inhabitants........................... | | 117.2 | 2.3 | 40.2 | 19.5 | 55.1 | 2,643.6 | 358.5 | 2,195.5 | 89.6 |
| **Crestview-Fort Walton Beach-Destin, FL M.S.A....** | 265,270 | | | | | | | | | |
| Includes Okaloosa and Walton Counties.................... | | | | | | | | | | |
| City of Crestview .............................................. | 23,468 | 124 | 0 | 16 | 20 | 88 | 847 | 138 | 677 | 32 |
| City of Fort Walton Beach ................................. | 22,107 | 69 | 6 | 10 | 15 | 38 | 693 | 105 | 559 | 29 |
| Total area actually reporting ............................. | 99.7% | 983 | 13 | 92 | 96 | 782 | 6,273 | 1,241 | 4,758 | 274 |
| Estimated total................................................. | 100.0% | 986 | 13 | 92 | 97 | 784 | 6,298 | 1,245 | 4,777 | 276 |
| Rate per 100,000 inhabitants........................... | | 371.7 | 4.9 | 34.7 | 36.6 | 295.5 | 2,374.2 | 469.3 | 1,800.8 | 104.0 |
| **Cumberland, MD-WV M.S.A.** ................................ | 99,562 | | | | | | | | | |
| Includes Allegany County, MD and Mineral County, WV .......................................................... | | | | | | | | | | |
| City of Cumberland, MD....................................... | 20,095 | 144 | 1 | 13 | 40 | 90 | 1,330 | 280 | 1,025 | 25 |
| Total area actually reporting ............................. | 93.3% | 252 | 4 | 31 | 58 | 159 | 2,493 | 557 | 1,875 | 61 |
| Estimated total................................................. | 100.0% | 274 | 4 | 33 | 61 | 176 | 2,720 | 589 | 2,059 | 72 |
| Rate per 100,000 inhabitants........................... | | 275.2 | 4.0 | 33.1 | 61.3 | 176.8 | 2,732.0 | 591.6 | 2,068.1 | 72.3 |
| **Dallas-Fort Worth-Arlington, TX M.S.A.**[2].............. | 7,101,895 | | | | | | | | | |
| Includes the Metropolitan Divisions of Dallas-Plano-Irving and Fort Worth-Arlington ............................ | | | | | | | | | | |
| City of Dallas .................................................... | 1,301,977 | 9,038 | 136 | 782 | 4,177 | 3,943 | 44,791 | 11,121 | 26,076 | 7,594 |
| City of Fort Worth.............................................. | 829,731 | 4,359 | 56 | 516 | 981 | 2,806 | 29,752 | 6,005 | 21,489 | 2,258 |
| City of Arlington................................................. | 387,565 | 1,946 | 8 | 208 | 529 | 1,201 | 13,346 | 2,170 | 10,298 | 878 |
| City of Plano...................................................... | 282,968 | 433 | 4 | 91 | 116 | 222 | 5,091 | 736 | 4,083 | 272 |
| City of Irving...................................................... | 236,465 | 469 | 9 | 32 | 197 | 231 | 6,041 | 1,100 | 4,339 | 602 |
| City of Denton.................................................... | 131,194 | 296 | 2 | 90 | 62 | 142 | 3,144 | 404 | 2,550 | 190 |
| City of Richardson.............................................. | 111,008 | 167 | 1 | 22 | 70 | 74 | 2,225 | 370 | 1,706 | 149 |

## Table 6. Crime, by Selected Metropolitan Statistical Area, 2015—*Continued*

(Number, percent, rate per 100,000 population.)

| Area | Population | Violent crime | Murder and nonnegligent manslaughter | Rape[1] | Robbery | Aggravated assault | Property crime | Burglary | Larceny-theft | Motor vehicle theft |
|---|---|---|---|---|---|---|---|---|---|---|
| Total area actually reporting | 99.9% | 23,957 | 287 | 2,929 | 7,982 | 12,759 | 181,239 | 35,701 | 127,176 | 18,362 |
| Estimated total | 100.0% | 23,973 | 287 | 2,931 | 7,986 | 12,769 | 181,402 | 35,728 | 127,301 | 18,373 |
| Rate per 100,000 inhabitants | | 337.6 | 4.0 | 41.3 | 112.4 | 179.8 | 2,554.3 | 503.1 | 1,792.5 | 258.7 |
|     Dallas-Plano-Irving, TX M.D. | 4,708,444 | | | | | | | | | |
| Includes Collin, Dallas, Denton, Ellis, Hunt, Kaufman, and Rockwall Counties | | | | | | | | | | |
| Total area actually reporting | 99.9% | 15,558 | 206 | 1,810 | 6,103 | 7,439 | 114,513 | 23,320 | 77,521 | 13,672 |
| Estimated total | 100.0% | 15,567 | 206 | 1,811 | 6,105 | 7,445 | 114,603 | 23,335 | 77,590 | 13,678 |
| Rate per 100,000 inhabitants | | 330.6 | 4.4 | 38.5 | 129.7 | 158.1 | 2,434.0 | 495.6 | 1,647.9 | 290.5 |
|     Fort Worth-Arlington, TX M.D.[2] | 2,393,451 | | | | | | | | | |
| Includes Hood, Johnson, Parker,[2] Somervell, Tarrant, and Wise Counties | | | | | | | | | | |
| Total area actually reporting | 99.9% | 8,399 | 81 | 1,119 | 1,879 | 5,320 | 66,726 | 12,381 | 49,655 | 4,690 |
| Estimated total | 100.0% | 8,406 | 81 | 1,120 | 1,881 | 5,324 | 66,799 | 12,393 | 49,711 | 4,695 |
| Rate per 100,000 inhabitants | | 351.2 | 3.4 | 46.8 | 78.6 | 222.4 | 2,790.9 | 517.8 | 2,077.0 | 196.2 |
| **Dalton, GA M.S.A.** | 143,348 | | | | | | | | | |
| Includes Murray and Whitfield Counties | | | | | | | | | | |
| City of Dalton | 33,617 | 96 | 1 | 15 | 12 | 68 | 1,155 | 178 | 923 | 54 |
| Total area actually reporting | 99.6% | 378 | 3 | 46 | 28 | 301 | 3,942 | 883 | 2,828 | 231 |
| Estimated total | 100.0% | 381 | 3 | 46 | 29 | 303 | 3,967 | 887 | 2,847 | 233 |
| Rate per 100,000 inhabitants | | 265.8 | 2.1 | 32.1 | 20.2 | 211.4 | 2,767.4 | 618.8 | 1,986.1 | 162.5 |
| **Danville, IL M.S.A.** | 79,076 | | | | | | | | | |
| Includes Vermilion County | | | | | | | | | | |
| City of Danville | 32,056 | 452 | 0 | 52 | 87 | 313 | 2,037 | 705 | 1,255 | 77 |
| Total area actually reporting | 98.4% | 614 | 0 | 96 | 96 | 422 | 2,877 | 981 | 1,794 | 102 |
| Estimated total | 100.0% | 617 | 0 | 96 | 97 | 424 | 2,898 | 984 | 1,811 | 103 |
| Rate per 100,000 inhabitants | | 780.3 | 0.0 | 121.4 | 122.7 | 536.2 | 3,664.8 | 1,244.4 | 2,290.2 | 130.3 |
| **Daphne-Fairhope-Foley, AL M.S.A.** | 204,261 | | | | | | | | | |
| Includes Baldwin County | | | | | | | | | | |
| City of Daphne | 25,087 | 32 | 2 | 4 | 4 | 22 | 529 | 76 | 437 | 16 |
| City of Fairhope | 18,821 | 39 | 0 | 2 | 4 | 33 | 518 | 85 | 413 | 20 |
| City of Foley | 16,644 | 51 | 0 | 5 | 11 | 35 | 633 | 84 | 538 | 11 |
| Total area actually reporting | 100.0% | 399 | 3 | 44 | 75 | 277 | 4,217 | 730 | 3,324 | 163 |
| Rate per 100,000 inhabitants | | 195.3 | 1.5 | 21.5 | 36.7 | 135.6 | 2,064.5 | 357.4 | 1,627.3 | 79.8 |
| **Davenport-Moline-Rock Island, IA-IL M.S.A.** | 383,347 | | | | | | | | | |
| Includes Henry, Mercer, and Rock Island Counties, IL and Scott County, IA | | | | | | | | | | |
| City of Davenport, IA | 103,082 | 730 | 6 | 111 | 174 | 439 | 4,609 | 945 | 3,296 | 368 |
| City of Moline, IL | 42,482 | 179 | 1 | 28 | 19 | 131 | 1,294 | 174 | 1,105 | 15 |
| City of Rock Island, IL | 38,551 | 170 | 2 | 3 | 22 | 143 | 906 | 168 | 678 | 60 |
| Total area actually reporting | 94.7% | 1,445 | 10 | 219 | 245 | 971 | 9,355 | 1,822 | 7,031 | 502 |
| Estimated total | 100.0% | 1,480 | 10 | 225 | 250 | 995 | 9,623 | 1,889 | 7,221 | 513 |
| Rate per 100,000 inhabitants | | 386.1 | 2.6 | 58.7 | 65.2 | 259.6 | 2,510.3 | 492.8 | 1,883.7 | 133.8 |
| **Dayton, OH M.S.A.** | 801,315 | | | | | | | | | |
| Includes Greene, Miami, and Montgomery Counties | | | | | | | | | | |
| City of Dayton | 140,683 | 1,325 | 26 | 147 | 479 | 673 | 7,089 | 2,412 | 3,994 | 683 |
| Total area actually reporting | 97.8% | 2,418 | 37 | 464 | 904 | 1,013 | 22,980 | 5,618 | 15,926 | 1,436 |
| Estimated total | 100.0% | 2,447 | 37 | 469 | 914 | 1,027 | 23,391 | 5,689 | 16,252 | 1,450 |
| Rate per 100,000 inhabitants | | 305.4 | 4.6 | 58.5 | 114.1 | 128.2 | 2,919.1 | 710.0 | 2,028.2 | 181.0 |
| **Decatur, AL M.S.A.** | 152,660 | | | | | | | | | |
| Includes Lawrence and Morgan Counties | | | | | | | | | | |
| City of Decatur | 55,483 | 162 | 5 | 17 | 48 | 92 | 2,366 | 469 | 1,754 | 143 |
| Total area actually reporting | 99.7% | 336 | 6 | 37 | 57 | 236 | 3,578 | 873 | 2,478 | 227 |
| Estimated total | 100.0% | 338 | 6 | 37 | 57 | 238 | 3,595 | 876 | 2,491 | 228 |
| Rate per 100,000 inhabitants | | 221.4 | 3.9 | 24.2 | 37.3 | 155.9 | 2,354.9 | 573.8 | 1,631.7 | 149.4 |
| **Decatur, IL M.S.A.** | 107,496 | | | | | | | | | |
| Includes Macon County | | | | | | | | | | |
| City of Decatur | 73,499 | 379 | 6 | 38 | 120 | 215 | 2,399 | 649 | 1,680 | 70 |
| Total area actually reporting | 99.0% | 428 | 6 | 41 | 125 | 256 | 2,796 | 719 | 1,995 | 82 |
| Estimated total | 100.0% | 430 | 6 | 41 | 126 | 257 | 2,815 | 722 | 2,010 | 83 |
| Rate per 100,000 inhabitants | | 400.0 | 5.6 | 38.1 | 117.2 | 239.1 | 2,618.7 | 671.7 | 1,869.8 | 77.2 |

(Number, percent, rate per 100,000 population.)

| Area | Population | Violent crime | Murder and nonnegligent manslaughter | Rape[1] | Robbery | Aggravated assault | Property crime | Burglary | Larceny-theft | Motor vehicle theft |
|---|---|---|---|---|---|---|---|---|---|---|
| **Deltona-Daytona Beach-Ormond Beach, FL M.S.A.**........ | 618,105 | | | | | | | | | |
| Includes Flagler and Volusia Counties......... | | | | | | | | | | |
| City of Daytona Beach ......... | 63,505 | 988 | 10 | 52 | 147 | 779 | 4,180 | 556 | 3,226 | 398 |
| City of Ormond Beach ......... | 39,302 | 238 | 2 | 10 | 31 | 195 | 1,538 | 232 | 1,213 | 93 |
| Total area actually reporting ......... | 99.7% | 2,767 | 24 | 178 | 378 | 2,187 | 17,631 | 3,188 | 13,262 | 1,181 |
| Estimated total......... | 100.0% | 2,775 | 24 | 179 | 380 | 2,192 | 17,689 | 3,198 | 13,306 | 1,185 |
| Rate per 100,000 inhabitants......... | | 449.0 | 3.9 | 29.0 | 61.5 | 354.6 | 2,861.8 | 517.4 | 2,152.7 | 191.7 |
| **Denver-Aurora-Lakewood, CO M.S.A.[3,4]** ......... | 2,817,171 | | | | | | | | | |
| Includes Adams, Arapahoe, Broomfield, Clear Creek, Denver, Douglas, Elbert, Gilpin, Jefferson, and Park Counties ......... | | | | | | | | | | |
| City of Denver......... | 682,418 | 4,599 | 53 | 548 | 1,230 | 2,768 | 24,089 | 4,762 | 14,962 | 4,365 |
| City of Aurora......... | 360,237 | 1,660 | 24 | 352 | 447 | 837 | 10,579 | 1,683 | 7,635 | 1,261 |
| City of Lakewood......... | 151,311 | 859 | 6 | 140 | 210 | 503 | 7,583 | 900 | 5,801 | 882 |
| City of Broomfield......... | 63,935 | 37 | 1 | 18 | 7 | 11 | 1,197 | 130 | 989 | 78 |
| Total area actually reporting ......... | 99.9% | 10,206 | 108 | 1,792 | 2,390 | 5,916 | | | | 10,937 |
| Estimated total......... | 100.0% | 10,207 | 108 | 1,792 | 2,390 | 5,917 | | | | 10,939 |
| Rate per 100,000 inhabitants......... | | 362.3 | 3.8 | 63.6 | 84.8 | 210.0 | | | | 388.3 |
| **Des Moines-West Des Moines, IA M.S.A.** ......... | 622,343 | | | | | | | | | |
| Includes Dallas, Guthrie, Madison, Polk, and Warren Counties ......... | | | | | | | | | | |
| City of Des Moines......... | 210,403 | 1,502 | 19 | 120 | 281 | 1,082 | 8,440 | 2,012 | 5,478 | 950 |
| City of West Des Moines......... | 65,006 | 129 | 0 | 21 | 16 | 92 | 1,418 | 170 | 1,188 | 60 |
| Total area actually reporting ......... | 100.0% | 2,287 | 21 | 232 | 336 | 1,698 | 14,624 | 3,269 | 10,017 | 1,338 |
| Rate per 100,000 inhabitants......... | | 367.5 | 3.4 | 37.3 | 54.0 | 272.8 | 2,349.8 | 525.3 | 1,609.6 | 215.0 |
| **Detroit-Warren-Dearborn, MI M.S.A.** ......... | 4,299,857 | | | | | | | | | |
| Includes the Metropolitan Divisions of Detroit-Dearborn-Livonia and Warren-Troy-Farmington Hills... | | | | | | | | | | |
| City of Detroit......... | 673,225 | 11,846 | 295 | 530 | 3,457 | 7,564 | 27,559 | 7,820 | 14,523 | 5,216 |
| City of Warren......... | 135,367 | 743 | 2 | 104 | 139 | 498 | 3,276 | 737 | 2,018 | 521 |
| City of Dearborn......... | 94,962 | 356 | 1 | 33 | 102 | 220 | 2,932 | 398 | 2,162 | 372 |
| City of Livonia......... | 94,521 | 146 | 1 | 19 | 21 | 105 | 1,857 | 190 | 1,481 | 186 |
| City of Troy......... | 83,642 | 55 | 1 | 15 | 9 | 30 | 1,416 | 120 | 1,230 | 66 |
| City of Farmington Hills......... | 81,862 | 75 | 0 | 12 | 13 | 50 | 935 | 135 | 729 | 71 |
| City of Southfield......... | 73,319 | 228 | 1 | 21 | 75 | 131 | 1,863 | 337 | 1,257 | 269 |
| City of Taylor......... | 61,250 | 298 | 3 | 33 | 66 | 196 | 1,736 | 366 | 1,188 | 182 |
| City of Novi......... | 59,233 | 31 | 1 | 4 | 6 | 20 | 762 | 43 | 688 | 31 |
| Total area actually reporting ......... | 99.8% | 21,393 | 381 | 1,950 | 5,188 | 13,874 | 86,187 | 18,257 | 56,908 | 11,022 |
| Estimated total......... | 100.0% | 21,417 | 381 | 1,954 | 5,192 | 13,890 | 86,358 | 18,287 | 57,037 | 11,034 |
| Rate per 100,000 inhabitants......... | | 498.1 | 8.9 | 45.4 | 120.7 | 323.0 | 2,008.4 | 425.3 | 1,326.5 | 256.6 |
| Detroit-Dearborn-Livonia, MI M.D. ......... | 1,752,927 | | | | | | | | | |
| Includes Wayne County......... | | | | | | | | | | |
| Total area actually reporting ......... | 99.5% | 15,778 | 339 | 998 | 4,326 | 10,115 | 51,292 | 12,256 | 30,885 | 8,151 |
| Estimated total......... | 100.0% | 15,802 | 339 | 1,002 | 4,330 | 10,131 | 51,463 | 12,286 | 31,014 | 8,163 |
| Rate per 100,000 inhabitants......... | | 901.5 | 19.3 | 57.2 | 247.0 | 577.9 | 2,935.8 | 700.9 | 1,769.3 | 465.7 |
| Warren-Troy-Farmington Hills, MI M.D. ......... | 2,546,930 | | | | | | | | | |
| Includes Lapeer, Livingston, Macomb, Oakland, and St. Clair Counties ......... | | | | | | | | | | |
| Total area actually reporting ......... | 99.9% | 5,615 | 42 | 952 | 862 | 3,759 | 34,895 | 6,001 | 26,023 | 2,871 |
| Estimated total......... | 100.0% | 5,619 | 42 | 953 | 863 | 3,761 | 34,918 | 6,005 | 26,040 | 2,873 |
| Rate per 100,000 inhabitants......... | | 220.6 | 1.6 | 37.4 | 33.9 | 147.7 | 1,371.0 | 235.8 | 1,022.4 | 112.8 |
| **Dothan, AL M.S.A.**......... | 148,435 | | | | | | | | | |
| Includes Geneva, Henry, and Houston Counties......... | | | | | | | | | | |
| City of Dothan......... | 67,774 | 269 | 1 | 10 | 63 | 195 | 2,132 | 453 | 1,580 | 99 |
| Total area actually reporting ......... | 99.4% | 515 | 5 | 53 | 73 | 384 | 3,763 | 947 | 2,609 | 207 |
| Estimated total......... | 100.0% | 519 | 5 | 53 | 74 | 387 | 3,791 | 952 | 2,630 | 209 |
| Rate per 100,000 inhabitants......... | | 349.6 | 3.4 | 35.7 | 49.9 | 260.7 | 2,554.0 | 641.4 | 1,771.8 | 140.8 |
| **Dover, DE M.S.A.** ......... | 174,523 | | | | | | | | | |
| Includes Kent County......... | | | | | | | | | | |
| City of Dover......... | 37,691 | 284 | 7 | 13 | 50 | 214 | 1,994 | 84 | 1,852 | 58 |
| Total area actually reporting ......... | 100.0% | 822 | 11 | 87 | 118 | 606 | 4,535 | 639 | 3,755 | 141 |
| Rate per 100,000 inhabitants......... | | 471.0 | 6.3 | 49.9 | 67.6 | 347.2 | 2,598.5 | 366.1 | 2,151.6 | 80.8 |

# Table 6. Crime, by Selected Metropolitan Statistical Area, 2015—*Continued*

(Number, percent, rate per 100,000 population.)

| Area | Population | Violent crime | Murder and nonnegligent manslaughter | Rape[1] | Robbery | Aggravated assault | Property crime | Burglary | Larceny-theft | Motor vehicle theft |
|---|---|---|---|---|---|---|---|---|---|---|
| **Dubuque, IA M.S.A.** ................................... | 97,051 | | | | | | | | | |
| Includes Dubuque County........................... | | | | | | | | | | |
| City of Dubuque........................................ | 58,650 | 168 | 5 | 31 | 27 | 105 | 1,945 | 563 | 1,330 | 52 |
| Total area actually reporting..................... | 100.0% | 181 | 5 | 32 | 28 | 116 | 2,227 | 700 | 1,455 | 72 |
| Rate per 100,000 inhabitants..................... | | 186.5 | 5.2 | 33.0 | 28.9 | 119.5 | 2,294.7 | 721.3 | 1,499.2 | 74.2 |
| | | | | | | | | | | |
| **Duluth, MN-WI M.S.A.** ............................. | 280,066 | | | | | | | | | |
| Includes Carlton and St. Louis Counties, MN and Douglas County, WI ...................................... | | | | | | | | | | |
| City of Duluth, MN ................................... | 86,241 | 352 | 2 | 71 | 54 | 225 | 3,611 | 602 | 2,858 | 151 |
| Total area actually reporting..................... | 100.0% | 680 | 4 | 152 | 82 | 442 | 8,881 | 1,565 | 6,869 | 447 |
| Rate per 100,000 inhabitants..................... | | 242.8 | 1.4 | 54.3 | 29.3 | 157.8 | 3,171.0 | 558.8 | 2,452.6 | 159.6 |
| | | | | | | | | | | |
| **East Stroudsburg, PA M.S.A.** ................... | 165,364 | | | | | | | | | |
| Includes Monroe County............................ | | | | | | | | | | |
| Total area actually reporting..................... | 100.0% | 316 | 2 | 61 | 103 | 150 | 3,744 | 845 | 2,805 | 94 |
| Rate per 100,000 inhabitants..................... | | 191.1 | 1.2 | 36.9 | 62.3 | 90.7 | 2,264.1 | 511.0 | 1,696.3 | 56.8 |
| | | | | | | | | | | |
| **Eau Claire, WI M.S.A.** .............................. | 165,778 | | | | | | | | | |
| Includes Chippewa and Eau Claire Counties .............. | | | | | | | | | | |
| City of Eau Claire ..................................... | 68,046 | 115 | 0 | 19 | 17 | 79 | 1,727 | 241 | 1,418 | 68 |
| Total area actually reporting..................... | 100.0% | 214 | 0 | 35 | 20 | 159 | 2,767 | 462 | 2,164 | 141 |
| Rate per 100,000 inhabitants..................... | | 129.1 | 0.0 | 21.1 | 12.1 | 95.9 | 1,669.1 | 278.7 | 1,305.4 | 85.1 |
| | | | | | | | | | | |
| **El Centro, CA M.S.A.** ............................... | 180,028 | | | | | | | | | |
| Includes Imperial County........................... | | | | | | | | | | |
| City of El Centro ....................................... | 44,033 | 164 | 1 | 10 | 56 | 97 | 2,667 | 493 | 1,983 | 191 |
| Total area actually reporting..................... | 95.8% | 723 | 2 | 27 | 123 | 571 | 6,039 | 1,357 | 4,074 | 608 |
| Estimated total.......................................... | 100.0% | 747 | 2 | 29 | 131 | 585 | 6,225 | 1,392 | 4,196 | 637 |
| Rate per 100,000 inhabitants..................... | | 414.9 | 1.1 | 16.1 | 72.8 | 324.9 | 3,457.8 | 773.2 | 2,330.7 | 353.8 |
| | | | | | | | | | | |
| **Elizabethtown-Fort Knox, KY M.S.A.** ..................... | 151,845 | | | | | | | | | |
| Includes Hardin, Larue, and Meade Counties.............. | | | | | | | | | | |
| City of Elizabethtown................................ | 30,241 | 48 | 0 | 8 | 14 | 26 | 883 | 147 | 716 | 20 |
| Total area actually reporting..................... | 100.0% | 159 | 5 | 34 | 32 | 88 | 1,871 | 413 | 1,373 | 85 |
| Rate per 100,000 inhabitants..................... | | 104.7 | 3.3 | 22.4 | 21.1 | 58.0 | 1,232.2 | 272.0 | 904.2 | 56.0 |
| | | | | | | | | | | |
| **Elkhart-Goshen, IN M.S.A.** ....................... | 202,969 | | | | | | | | | |
| Includes Elkhart County ............................ | | | | | | | | | | |
| City of Elkhart.......................................... | 51,566 | 760 | 4 | 30 | 111 | 615 | 2,120 | 502 | 1,391 | 227 |
| City of Goshen.......................................... | 32,441 | 35 | 0 | 16 | 14 | 5 | 1,224 | 196 | 954 | 74 |
| Total area actually reporting..................... | 100.0% | 812 | 4 | 50 | 129 | 629 | 4,044 | 857 | 2,839 | 348 |
| Rate per 100,000 inhabitants..................... | | 400.1 | 2.0 | 24.6 | 63.6 | 309.9 | 1,992.4 | 422.2 | 1,398.7 | 171.5 |
| | | | | | | | | | | |
| **Elmira, NY M.S.A.** ................................... | 87,307 | | | | | | | | | |
| Includes Chemung County.......................... | | | | | | | | | | |
| City of Elmira .......................................... | 28,489 | 84 | 1 | 1 | 38 | 44 | 872 | 179 | 675 | 18 |
| Total area actually reporting..................... | 100.0% | 159 | 2 | 27 | 42 | 88 | 1,743 | 275 | 1,428 | 40 |
| Rate per 100,000 inhabitants..................... | | 182.1 | 2.3 | 30.9 | 48.1 | 100.8 | 1,996.4 | 315.0 | 1,635.6 | 45.8 |
| | | | | | | | | | | |
| **El Paso, TX M.S.A.** ................................... | 846,141 | | | | | | | | | |
| Includes El Paso and Hudspeth Counties ................... | | | | | | | | | | |
| City of El Paso.......................................... | 686,077 | 2,515 | 17 | 322 | 410 | 1,766 | 13,133 | 1,419 | 10,916 | 798 |
| Total area actually reporting..................... | 99.9% | 2,995 | 23 | 370 | 444 | 2,158 | 15,412 | 1,863 | 12,598 | 951 |
| Estimated total.......................................... | 100.0% | 2,998 | 23 | 370 | 445 | 2,160 | 15,443 | 1,868 | 12,622 | 953 |
| Rate per 100,000 inhabitants..................... | | 354.3 | 2.7 | 43.7 | 52.6 | 255.3 | 1,825.1 | 220.8 | 1,491.7 | 112.6 |
| | | | | | | | | | | |
| **Enid, OK M.S.A.** ..................................... | 63,736 | | | | | | | | | |
| Includes Garfield County........................... | | | | | | | | | | |
| City of Enid............................................. | 51,870 | 173 | 1 | 29 | 20 | 123 | 1,867 | 422 | 1,373 | 72 |
| Total area actually reporting..................... | 100.0% | 181 | 1 | 31 | 20 | 129 | 2,016 | 466 | 1,469 | 81 |
| Rate per 100,000 inhabitants..................... | | 284.0 | 1.6 | 48.6 | 31.4 | 202.4 | 3,163.0 | 731.1 | 2,304.8 | 127.1 |
| | | | | | | | | | | |
| **Erie, PA M.S.A.** ....................................... | 277,783 | | | | | | | | | |
| Includes Erie County ................................ | | | | | | | | | | |
| City of Erie.............................................. | 98,887 | 430 | 9 | 56 | 122 | 243 | 2,499 | 665 | 1,719 | 115 |
| Total area actually reporting..................... | 100.0% | 651 | 11 | 94 | 171 | 375 | 5,700 | 1,235 | 4,280 | 185 |
| Rate per 100,000 inhabitants..................... | | 234.4 | 4.0 | 33.8 | 61.6 | 135.0 | 2,052.0 | 444.6 | 1,540.8 | 66.6 |

## Table 6. Crime, by Selected Metropolitan Statistical Area, 2015—*Continued*

(Number, percent, rate per 100,000 population.)

| Area | Population | Violent crime | Murder and nonnegligent manslaughter | Rape[1] | Robbery | Aggravated assault | Property crime | Burglary | Larceny-theft | Motor vehicle theft |
|---|---|---|---|---|---|---|---|---|---|---|
| **Eugene, OR M.S.A.**................................ | 362,167 | | | | | | | | | |
| Includes Lane County............................... | | | | | | | | | | |
| City of Eugene........................................ | 161,608 | 513 | 4 | 87 | 138 | 284 | 6,259 | 1,103 | 4,609 | 547 |
| Total area actually reporting ..................... | 96.4% | 1,166 | 13 | 152 | 198 | 803 | 11,521 | 1,935 | 8,751 | 835 |
| Estimated total........................................ | 100.0% | 1,194 | 13 | 156 | 205 | 820 | 11,900 | 1,987 | 9,050 | 863 |
| Rate per 100,000 inhabitants.................... | | 329.7 | 3.6 | 43.1 | 56.6 | 226.4 | 3,285.8 | 548.6 | 2,498.8 | 238.3 |
| **Evansville, IN-KY M.S.A.**........................ | 315,764 | | | | | | | | | |
| Includes Posey, Vanderburgh, and Warrick Counties, IN and Henderson County, KY........ | | | | | | | | | | |
| City of Evansville.................................... | 120,414 | 708 | 4 | 80 | 199 | 425 | 6,162 | 980 | 4,814 | 368 |
| Total area actually reporting ..................... | 100.0% | 1,063 | 8 | 110 | 254 | 691 | 9,070 | 1,646 | 6,909 | 515 |
| Rate per 100,000 inhabitants.................... | | 336.6 | 2.5 | 34.8 | 80.4 | 218.8 | 2,872.4 | 521.3 | 2,188.0 | 163.1 |
| **Fairbanks, AK M.S.A.** ............................ | 34,867 | | | | | | | | | |
| Includes Fairbanks North Star Borough...................... | | | | | | | | | | |
| City of Fairbanks..................................... | 32,677 | 157 | 1 | 14 | 24 | 118 | 1,192 | 149 | 938 | 105 |
| Total area actually reporting ..................... | 100.0% | 169 | 1 | 16 | 27 | 125 | 1,376 | 160 | 1,097 | 119 |
| Rate per 100,000 inhabitants.................... | | 484.7 | 2.9 | 45.9 | 77.4 | 358.5 | 3,946.4 | 458.9 | 3,146.2 | 341.3 |
| **Fargo, ND-MN M.S.A.**............................ | 233,045 | | | | | | | | | |
| Includes Clay County, MN and Cass County, ND......... | | | | | | | | | | |
| City of Fargo, ND..................................... | 118,490 | 414 | 3 | 79 | 52 | 280 | 3,522 | 666 | 2,594 | 262 |
| Total area actually reporting ..................... | 100.0% | 581 | 6 | 116 | 65 | 394 | 5,601 | 1,053 | 4,116 | 432 |
| Rate per 100,000 inhabitants.................... | | 249.3 | 2.6 | 49.8 | 27.9 | 169.1 | 2,403.4 | 451.8 | 1,766.2 | 185.4 |
| **Farmington, NM M.S.A.** .......................... | 121,898 | | | | | | | | | |
| Includes San Juan County ......................... | | | | | | | | | | |
| City of Farmington................................... | 44,076 | 187 | 3 | 68 | 40 | 76 | 1,688 | 244 | 1,320 | 124 |
| Total area actually reporting ..................... | 100.0% | 540 | 5 | 112 | 55 | 368 | 2,698 | 494 | 1,989 | 215 |
| Rate per 100,000 inhabitants.................... | | 443.0 | 4.1 | 91.9 | 45.1 | 301.9 | 2,213.3 | 405.3 | 1,631.7 | 176.4 |
| **Flagstaff, AZ M.S.A.**............................... | 138,739 | | | | | | | | | |
| Includes Coconino County ........................ | | | | | | | | | | |
| City of Flagstaff ...................................... | 69,471 | 260 | 0 | 35 | 45 | 180 | 2,654 | 180 | 2,418 | 56 |
| Total area actually reporting ..................... | 100.0% | 503 | 3 | 85 | 50 | 365 | 3,874 | 399 | 3,387 | 88 |
| Rate per 100,000 inhabitants.................... | | 362.6 | 2.2 | 61.3 | 36.0 | 263.1 | 2,792.3 | 287.6 | 2,441.3 | 63.4 |
| **Flint, MI M.S.A.**.................................... | 410,063 | | | | | | | | | |
| Includes Genesee County........................... | | | | | | | | | | |
| City of Flint........................................... | 98,221 | 1,451 | 47 | 77 | 272 | 1,055 | 3,538 | 1,391 | 1,880 | 267 |
| Estimated total........................................ | 100.0% | 2,384 | 53 | 265 | 441 | 1,625 | 10,193 | 2,900 | 6,696 | 597 |
| Rate per 100,000 inhabitants.................... | | 581.4 | 12.9 | 64.6 | 107.5 | 396.3 | 2,485.7 | 707.2 | 1,632.9 | 145.6 |
| **Florence-Muscle Shoals, AL M.S.A.** ........................ | 147,517 | | | | | | | | | |
| Includes Colbert and Lauderdale Counties.................. | | | | | | | | | | |
| City of Florence....................................... | 40,433 | 169 | 0 | 21 | 23 | 125 | 1,518 | 295 | 1,147 | 76 |
| City of Muscle Shoals................................ | 13,720 | 45 | 1 | 4 | 14 | 26 | 670 | 136 | 481 | 53 |
| Total area actually reporting ..................... | 99.8% | 449 | 2 | 54 | 59 | 334 | 3,593 | 866 | 2,474 | 253 |
| Estimated total........................................ | 100.0% | 450 | 2 | 54 | 59 | 335 | 3,603 | 868 | 2,481 | 254 |
| Rate per 100,000 inhabitants.................... | | 305.0 | 1.4 | 36.6 | 40.0 | 227.1 | 2,442.4 | 588.4 | 1,681.8 | 172.2 |
| **Fond du Lac, WI M.S.A.**.......................... | 101,722 | | | | | | | | | |
| Includes Fond du Lac County ..................... | | | | | | | | | | |
| City of Fond du Lac.................................. | 42,887 | 164 | 1 | 42 | 11 | 110 | 996 | 107 | 859 | 30 |
| Total area actually reporting ..................... | 100.0% | 218 | 1 | 52 | 13 | 152 | 1,404 | 183 | 1,166 | 55 |
| Rate per 100,000 inhabitants.................... | | 214.3 | 1.0 | 51.1 | 12.8 | 149.4 | 1,380.2 | 179.9 | 1,146.3 | 54.1 |
| **Fort Collins, CO M.S.A.**.......................... | 331,534 | | | | | | | | | |
| Includes Larimer County............................. | | | | | | | | | | |
| City of Fort Collins .................................. | 159,629 | 313 | 2 | 27 | 37 | 247 | 4,015 | 507 | 3,270 | 238 |
| Total area actually reporting ..................... | 100.0% | 660 | 7 | 91 | 70 | 492 | 7,390 | 933 | 6,032 | 425 |
| Rate per 100,000 inhabitants.................... | | 199.1 | 2.1 | 27.4 | 21.1 | 148.4 | 2,229.0 | 281.4 | 1,819.4 | 128.2 |
| **Fort Smith, AR-OK M.S.A.**........................ | 279,361 | | | | | | | | | |
| Includes Crawford and Sebastian Counties, AR and Le Flore and Sequoyah Counties, OK ........................... | | | | | | | | | | |
| City of Fort Smith, AR .............................. | 87,603 | 704 | 5 | 66 | 119 | 514 | 5,162 | 953 | 3,990 | 219 |
| Total area actually reporting ..................... | 99.7% | 1,243 | 9 | 130 | 146 | 958 | 9,411 | 2,031 | 6,901 | 479 |
| Estimated total........................................ | 100.0% | 1,246 | 9 | 131 | 146 | 960 | 9,434 | 2,036 | 6,918 | 480 |
| Rate per 100,000 inhabitants.................... | | 446.0 | 3.2 | 46.9 | 52.3 | 343.6 | 3,377.0 | 728.8 | 2,476.4 | 171.8 |

# Table 6. Crime, by Selected Metropolitan Statistical Area, 2015—*Continued*

(Number, percent, rate per 100,000 population.)

| Area | Population | Violent crime | Murder and nonnegligent manslaughter | Rape[1] | Robbery | Aggravated assault | Property crime | Burglary | Larceny-theft | Motor vehicle theft |
|---|---|---|---|---|---|---|---|---|---|---|
| **Fort Wayne, IN M.S.A.**............................. | 429,490 | | | | | | | | | |
| Includes Allen, Wells, and Whitley Counties .............. | | | | | | | | | | |
| City of Fort Wayne ........................................... | 259,712 | 984 | 25 | 97 | 446 | 416 | 7,943 | 1,480 | 6,131 | 332 |
| Total area actually reporting ......................... | 90.5% | 1,183 | 27 | 126 | 518 | 512 | 9,562 | 1,762 | 7,361 | 439 |
| Estimated total.................................... | 100.0% | 1,237 | 28 | 131 | 525 | 553 | 10,000 | 1,867 | 7,655 | 478 |
| Rate per 100,000 inhabitants.................................... | | 288.0 | 6.5 | 30.5 | 122.2 | 128.8 | 2,328.3 | 434.7 | 1,782.3 | 111.3 |
| | | | | | | | | | | |
| **Fresno, CA M.S.A.**.............................. | 973,630 | | | | | | | | | |
| Includes Fresno County ............................. | | | | | | | | | | |
| City of Fresno .......................................... | 520,837 | 2,871 | 39 | 167 | 1,012 | 1,653 | 21,606 | 4,429 | 14,184 | 2,993 |
| Total area actually reporting ......................... | 100.0% | 5,231 | 59 | 316 | 1,333 | 3,523 | 33,487 | 7,315 | 21,387 | 4,785 |
| Rate per 100,000 inhabitants.................................... | | 537.3 | 6.1 | 32.5 | 136.9 | 361.8 | 3,439.4 | 751.3 | 2,196.6 | 491.5 |
| | | | | | | | | | | |
| **Gadsden, AL M.S.A.** ............................. | 103,133 | | | | | | | | | |
| Includes Etowah County ............................. | | | | | | | | | | |
| City of Gadsden........................................... | 36,148 | 364 | 3 | 32 | 80 | 249 | 2,724 | 499 | 2,048 | 177 |
| Total area actually reporting ......................... | 98.5% | 541 | 4 | 64 | 85 | 388 | 4,072 | 896 | 2,899 | 277 |
| Estimated total.................................... | 100.0% | 549 | 4 | 65 | 86 | 394 | 4,124 | 906 | 2,938 | 280 |
| Rate per 100,000 inhabitants.................................... | | 532.3 | 3.9 | 63.0 | 83.4 | 382.0 | 3,998.7 | 878.5 | 2,848.7 | 271.5 |
| | | | | | | | | | | |
| **Gainesville, FL M.S.A.**.............................. | 277,049 | | | | | | | | | |
| Includes Alachua and Gilchrist Counties .................... | | | | | | | | | | |
| City of Gainesville ........................................... | 129,410 | 930 | 2 | 111 | 231 | 586 | 4,617 | 543 | 3,767 | 307 |
| Total area actually reporting ......................... | 94.2% | 1,555 | 3 | 183 | 313 | 1,056 | 7,379 | 1,238 | 5,729 | 412 |
| Estimated total.................................... | 100.0% | 1,615 | 4 | 188 | 324 | 1,099 | 7,731 | 1,312 | 5,983 | 436 |
| Rate per 100,000 inhabitants.................................... | | 582.9 | 1.4 | 67.9 | 116.9 | 396.7 | 2,790.5 | 473.6 | 2,159.5 | 157.4 |
| | | | | | | | | | | |
| **Gainesville, GA M.S.A.** ............................. | 193,860 | | | | | | | | | |
| Includes Hall County ............................. | | | | | | | | | | |
| City of Gainesville ........................................... | 36,948 | 150 | 3 | 19 | 41 | 87 | 1,345 | 183 | 1,080 | 82 |
| Total area actually reporting ......................... | 100.0% | 366 | 5 | 43 | 69 | 249 | 3,577 | 724 | 2,576 | 277 |
| Rate per 100,000 inhabitants.................................... | | 188.8 | 2.6 | 22.2 | 35.6 | 128.4 | 1,845.1 | 373.5 | 1,328.8 | 142.9 |
| | | | | | | | | | | |
| **Gettysburg, PA M.S.A.** ............................. | 101,741 | | | | | | | | | |
| Includes Adams County ............................. | | | | | | | | | | |
| City of Gettysburg ........................................... | 7,640 | 21 | 0 | 1 | 8 | 12 | 103 | 17 | 84 | 2 |
| Total area actually reporting ......................... | 100.0% | 138 | 0 | 35 | 14 | 89 | 1,001 | 248 | 718 | 35 |
| Rate per 100,000 inhabitants.................................... | | 135.6 | 0.0 | 34.4 | 13.8 | 87.5 | 983.9 | 243.8 | 705.7 | 34.4 |
| | | | | | | | | | | |
| **Glens Falls, NY M.S.A.**[4] ............................. | 126,688 | | | | | | | | | |
| Includes Warren and Washington[4] Counties .............. | | | | | | | | | | |
| City of Glens Falls ........................................... | 14,364 | 36 | 0 | 11 | 3 | 22 | 235 | 26 | 203 | 6 |
| Total area actually reporting ......................... | 100.0% | 216 | 1 | 86 | 12 | 117 | | 220 | | 27 |
| Rate per 100,000 inhabitants.................................... | | 170.5 | 0.8 | 67.9 | 9.5 | 92.4 | | 173.7 | | 21.3 |
| | | | | | | | | | | |
| **Goldsboro, NC M.S.A.** ............................. | 124,823 | | | | | | | | | |
| Includes Wayne County............................. | | | | | | | | | | |
| City of Goldsboro ........................................... | 36,034 | 465 | 9 | 2 | 91 | 363 | 2,244 | 538 | 1,621 | 85 |
| Total area actually reporting ......................... | 97.7% | 610 | 11 | 4 | 131 | 464 | 4,416 | 1,355 | 2,855 | 206 |
| Estimated total.................................... | 100.0% | 617 | 11 | 4 | 133 | 469 | 4,499 | 1,372 | 2,918 | 209 |
| Rate per 100,000 inhabitants.................................... | | 494.3 | 8.8 | 3.2 | 106.6 | 375.7 | 3,604.3 | 1,099.2 | 2,337.7 | 167.4 |
| | | | | | | | | | | |
| **Grand Forks, ND-MN M.S.A.** ............................. | 102,564 | | | | | | | | | |
| Includes Polk County, MN and Grand Forks County, ND............................. | | | | | | | | | | |
| City of Grand Forks, ND ........................................... | 56,861 | 176 | 2 | 36 | 23 | 115 | 1,643 | 226 | 1,302 | 115 |
| Total area actually reporting ......................... | 100.0% | 250 | 3 | 62 | 27 | 158 | 2,162 | 312 | 1,698 | 152 |
| Rate per 100,000 inhabitants.................................... | | 243.8 | 2.9 | 60.5 | 26.3 | 154.1 | 2,108.0 | 304.2 | 1,655.6 | 148.2 |
| | | | | | | | | | | |
| **Grand Island, NE M.S.A.**............................. | 85,507 | | | | | | | | | |
| Includes Hall, Hamilton, Howard, and Merrick Counties............................. | | | | | | | | | | |
| City of Grand Island ........................................... | 51,861 | 121 | 0 | 36 | 11 | 74 | 1,497 | 214 | 1,201 | 82 |
| Total area actually reporting ......................... | 92.5% | 178 | 0 | 49 | 13 | 116 | 1,792 | 300 | 1,394 | 98 |
| Estimated total.................................... | 100.0% | 184 | 0 | 51 | 13 | 120 | 1,869 | 312 | 1,453 | 104 |
| Rate per 100,000 inhabitants.................................... | | 215.2 | 0.0 | 59.6 | 15.2 | 140.3 | 2,185.8 | 364.9 | 1,699.3 | 121.6 |

## Table 6. Crime, by Selected Metropolitan Statistical Area, 2015—*Continued*

(Number, percent, rate per 100,000 population.)

| Area | Population | Violent crime | Murder and nonnegligent manslaughter | Rape[1] | Robbery | Aggravated assault | Property crime | Burglary | Larceny-theft | Motor vehicle theft |
|---|---|---|---|---|---|---|---|---|---|---|
| **Grand Junction, CO M.S.A.** | 149,249 | | | | | | | | | |
| Includes Mesa County | | | | | | | | | | |
| City of Grand Junction | 60,508 | 257 | 0 | 66 | 26 | 165 | 2,673 | 334 | 2,191 | 148 |
| Total area actually reporting | 99.7% | 488 | 2 | 127 | 38 | 321 | 4,209 | 667 | 3,288 | 254 |
| Estimated total | 100.0% | 489 | 2 | 127 | 38 | 322 | 4,222 | 669 | 3,298 | 255 |
| Rate per 100,000 inhabitants | | 327.6 | 1.3 | 85.1 | 25.5 | 215.7 | 2,828.8 | 448.2 | 2,209.7 | 170.9 |
| **Grand Rapids-Wyoming, MI M.S.A.** | 1,037,936 | | | | | | | | | |
| Includes Barry, Kent, Montcalm, and Ottawa Counties | | | | | | | | | | |
| City of Grand Rapids | 195,268 | 1,420 | 10 | 128 | 423 | 859 | 4,604 | 974 | 3,339 | 291 |
| City of Wyoming | 75,518 | 313 | 2 | 64 | 54 | 193 | 1,635 | 274 | 1,213 | 148 |
| Total area actually reporting | 99.5% | 3,403 | 18 | 778 | 619 | 1,988 | 16,706 | 3,112 | 12,765 | 829 |
| Estimated total | 100.0% | 3,415 | 18 | 780 | 621 | 1,996 | 16,796 | 3,128 | 12,833 | 835 |
| Rate per 100,000 inhabitants | | 329.0 | 1.7 | 75.1 | 59.8 | 192.3 | 1,618.2 | 301.4 | 1,236.4 | 80.4 |
| **Grants Pass, OR M.S.A.** | 84,302 | | | | | | | | | |
| Includes Josephine County | | | | | | | | | | |
| City of Grants Pass | 35,411 | 122 | 1 | 15 | 34 | 72 | 1,990 | 285 | 1,517 | 188 |
| Total area actually reporting | 100.0% | 205 | 7 | 26 | 36 | 136 | 2,385 | 424 | 1,652 | 309 |
| Rate per 100,000 inhabitants | | 243.2 | 8.3 | 30.8 | 42.7 | 161.3 | 2,829.1 | 503.0 | 1,959.6 | 366.5 |
| **Great Falls, MT M.S.A.** | 82,618 | | | | | | | | | |
| Includes Cascade County | | | | | | | | | | |
| City of Great Falls | 59,252 | 153 | 4 | 13 | 29 | 107 | 2,666 | 348 | 2,196 | 122 |
| Total area actually reporting | 100.0% | 207 | 6 | 19 | 29 | 153 | 2,881 | 381 | 2,360 | 140 |
| Rate per 100,000 inhabitants | | 250.6 | 7.3 | 23.0 | 35.1 | 185.2 | 3,487.1 | 461.2 | 2,856.5 | 169.5 |
| **Greeley, CO M.S.A.** | 284,922 | | | | | | | | | |
| Includes Weld County | | | | | | | | | | |
| City of Greeley | 99,993 | 455 | 1 | 76 | 58 | 320 | 2,624 | 423 | 2,027 | 174 |
| Total area actually reporting | 100.0% | 771 | 5 | 134 | 72 | 560 | 4,832 | 856 | 3,592 | 384 |
| Rate per 100,000 inhabitants | | 270.6 | 1.8 | 47.0 | 25.3 | 196.5 | 1,695.9 | 300.4 | 1,260.7 | 134.8 |
| **Green Bay, WI M.S.A.** | 316,323 | | | | | | | | | |
| Includes Brown, Kewaunee, and Oconto Counties | | | | | | | | | | |
| City of Green Bay | 105,119 | 456 | 2 | 62 | 58 | 334 | 2,246 | 375 | 1,780 | 91 |
| Total area actually reporting | 77.3% | 550 | 3 | 69 | 62 | 416 | 3,567 | 547 | 2,882 | 138 |
| Estimated total | 100.0% | 622 | 4 | 79 | 78 | 461 | 4,599 | 689 | 3,724 | 186 |
| Rate per 100,000 inhabitants | | 196.6 | 1.3 | 25.0 | 24.7 | 145.7 | 1,453.9 | 217.8 | 1,177.3 | 58.8 |
| **Greensboro-High Point, NC M.S.A.** | 751,976 | | | | | | | | | |
| Includes Guilford, Randolph, and Rockingham Counties | | | | | | | | | | |
| City of Greensboro | 285,950 | 1,707 | 26 | 72 | 530 | 1,079 | 10,204 | 2,369 | 7,296 | 539 |
| City of High Point | 109,669 | 620 | 8 | 37 | 196 | 379 | 3,722 | 724 | 2,782 | 216 |
| Total area actually reporting | 98.9% | 2,974 | 42 | 158 | 859 | 1,915 | 22,071 | 5,663 | 15,387 | 1,021 |
| Estimated total | 100.0% | 2,994 | 42 | 159 | 864 | 1,929 | 22,323 | 5,715 | 15,578 | 1,030 |
| Rate per 100,000 inhabitants | | 398.2 | 5.6 | 21.1 | 114.9 | 256.5 | 2,968.6 | 760.0 | 2,071.6 | 137.0 |
| **Greenville, NC M.S.A.** | 176,985 | | | | | | | | | |
| Includes Pitt County | | | | | | | | | | |
| City of Greenville | 91,114 | 510 | 7 | 37 | 138 | 328 | 3,307 | 739 | 2,480 | 88 |
| Total area actually reporting | 98.3% | 760 | 14 | 54 | 170 | 522 | 4,900 | 1,198 | 3,571 | 131 |
| Estimated total | 100.0% | 768 | 14 | 55 | 172 | 527 | 4,987 | 1,216 | 3,637 | 134 |
| Rate per 100,000 inhabitants | | 433.9 | 7.9 | 31.1 | 97.2 | 297.8 | 2,817.8 | 687.1 | 2,055.0 | 75.7 |
| **Gulfport-Biloxi-Pascagoula, MS M.S.A.** | 388,848 | | | | | | | | | |
| Included Hancock, Harrison, and Jackson Counties | | | | | | | | | | |
| City of Gulfport | 72,736 | 187 | 8 | 15 | 70 | 94 | 3,716 | 645 | 2,915 | 156 |
| City of Biloxi | 45,208 | 254 | 3 | 54 | 92 | 105 | 2,535 | 843 | 1,545 | 147 |
| City of Pascagoula | 22,202 | 105 | 1 | 21 | 39 | 44 | 1,511 | 253 | 1,181 | 77 |
| Total area actually reporting | 80.3% | 799 | 23 | 130 | 244 | 402 | 12,971 | 2,841 | 9,380 | 750 |
| Estimated total | 100.0% | 907 | 26 | 143 | 261 | 477 | 14,416 | 3,220 | 10,366 | 830 |
| Rate per 100,000 inhabitants | | 233.3 | 6.7 | 36.8 | 67.1 | 122.7 | 3,707.4 | 828.1 | 2,665.8 | 213.5 |

# Table 6. Crime, by Selected Metropolitan Statistical Area, 2015—*Continued*

(Number, percent, rate per 100,000 population.)

| Area | Population | Violent crime | Murder and nonnegligent manslaughter | Rape[1] | Robbery | Aggravated assault | Property crime | Burglary | Larceny-theft | Motor vehicle theft |
|---|---|---|---|---|---|---|---|---|---|---|
| **Hagerstown-Martinsburg, MD-WV M.S.A.** ........... | 261,248 | | | | | | | | | |
| Includes Washington County, MD and Berkeley | | | | | | | | | | |
| County, WV .................................................. | | | | | | | | | | |
| City of Hagerstown, MD ................................... | 40,470 | 240 | 5 | 13 | 97 | 125 | 1,088 | 282 | 720 | 86 |
| City of Martinsburg, WV .................................. | 17,861 | 91 | 1 | 5 | 31 | 54 | 945 | 116 | 800 | 29 |
| Total area actually reporting .......................... | 100.0% | 681 | 11 | 54 | 178 | 438 | 5,548 | 1,293 | 3,958 | 297 |
| Rate per 100,000 inhabitants........................ | | 260.7 | 4.2 | 20.7 | 68.1 | 167.7 | 2,123.7 | 494.9 | 1,515.0 | 113.7 |
| | | | | | | | | | | |
| **Hammond, LA M.S.A.** ...................................... | 128,279 | | | | | | | | | |
| Includes Tangipahoa Parish............................. | | | | | | | | | | |
| City of Hammond ............................................ | 20,449 | 208 | 0 | 11 | 53 | 144 | 2,077 | 564 | 1,448 | 65 |
| Total area actually reporting .......................... | 96.6% | 967 | 5 | 55 | 179 | 728 | 5,951 | 1,731 | 3,829 | 391 |
| Estimated total................................................ | 100.0% | 987 | 5 | 56 | 182 | 744 | 6,120 | 1,763 | 3,959 | 398 |
| Rate per 100,000 inhabitants........................ | | 769.4 | 3.9 | 43.7 | 141.9 | 580.0 | 4,770.9 | 1,374.3 | 3,086.2 | 310.3 |
| | | | | | | | | | | |
| **Hanford-Corcoran, CA M.S.A.**.............................. | 149,604 | | | | | | | | | |
| Includes Kings County....................................... | | | | | | | | | | |
| City of Hanford................................................ | 55,299 | 315 | 1 | 23 | 58 | 233 | 2,012 | 275 | 1,504 | 233 |
| City of Corcoran .............................................. | 22,435 | 104 | 0 | 4 | 13 | 87 | 398 | 107 | 212 | 79 |
| Total area actually reporting .......................... | 100.0% | 694 | 5 | 62 | 103 | 524 | 3,901 | 797 | 2,563 | 541 |
| Rate per 100,000 inhabitants........................ | | 463.9 | 3.3 | 41.4 | 68.8 | 350.3 | 2,607.6 | 532.7 | 1,713.2 | 361.6 |
| | | | | | | | | | | |
| **Harrisonburg, VA M.S.A.** ................................. | 131,648 | | | | | | | | | |
| Includes Rockingham County and Harrisonburg City .. | | | | | | | | | | |
| City of Harrisonburg ........................................ | 53,226 | 119 | 1 | 25 | 12 | 81 | 1,238 | 157 | 1,048 | 33 |
| Total area actually reporting .......................... | 100.0% | 192 | 1 | 48 | 15 | 128 | 2,048 | 398 | 1,581 | 69 |
| Rate per 100,000 inhabitants........................ | | 145.8 | 0.8 | 36.5 | 11.4 | 97.2 | 1,555.7 | 302.3 | 1,200.9 | 52.4 |
| | | | | | | | | | | |
| **Hartford-West Hartford-East Hartford, CT M.S.A.**.... | 1,023,389 | | | | | | | | | |
| Includes Hartford, Middlesex, and Tolland Counties.... | | | | | | | | | | |
| City of Hartford .............................................. | 124,553 | 1,421 | 32 | 44 | 510 | 835 | 5,468 | 958 | 3,613 | 897 |
| City of West Hartford........................................ | 63,301 | 55 | 0 | 2 | 45 | 8 | 1,474 | 156 | 1,206 | 112 |
| City of East Hartford ........................................ | 50,977 | 168 | 1 | 24 | 73 | 70 | 1,106 | 196 | 754 | 156 |
| City of Middletown........................................... | 46,894 | 64 | 1 | 7 | 19 | 37 | 726 | 89 | 579 | 58 |
| Total area actually reporting .......................... | 100.0% | 2,587 | 45 | 230 | 969 | 1,343 | 22,263 | 3,330 | 16,753 | 2,180 |
| Rate per 100,000 inhabitants........................ | | 252.8 | 4.4 | 22.5 | 94.7 | 131.2 | 2,175.4 | 325.4 | 1,637.0 | 213.0 |
| | | | | | | | | | | |
| **Hattiesburg, MS M.S.A.** ........................................ | 149,624 | | | | | | | | | |
| Includes Forrest, Lamar, and Perry Counties.............. | | | | | | | | | | |
| City of Hattiesburg........................................... | 47,315 | 105 | 6 | 16 | 34 | 49 | 3,013 | 606 | 2,350 | 57 |
| Total area actually reporting .......................... | 90.3% | 218 | 6 | 33 | 46 | 133 | 4,276 | 1,111 | 3,073 | 92 |
| Estimated total................................................ | 100.0% | 236 | 6 | 35 | 49 | 146 | 4,526 | 1,183 | 3,236 | 107 |
| Rate per 100,000 inhabitants........................ | | 157.7 | 4.0 | 23.4 | 32.7 | 97.6 | 3,024.9 | 790.6 | 2,162.8 | 71.5 |
| | | | | | | | | | | |
| **Hilton Head Island-Bluffton-Beaufort, SC M.S.A.**...... | 207,507 | | | | | | | | | |
| Includes Beaufort and Jasper Counties ..................... | | | | | | | | | | |
| City of Bluffton................................................ | 15,689 | 36 | 1 | 3 | 6 | 26 | 292 | 65 | 211 | 16 |
| City of Beaufort .............................................. | 13,296 | 121 | 6 | 7 | 34 | 74 | 741 | 117 | 606 | 18 |
| Total area actually reporting .......................... | 100.0% | 725 | 28 | 92 | 152 | 453 | 4,988 | 1,033 | 3,674 | 281 |
| Rate per 100,000 inhabitants........................ | | 349.4 | 13.5 | 44.3 | 73.3 | 218.3 | 2,403.8 | 497.8 | 1,770.5 | 135.4 |
| | | | | | | | | | | |
| **Hinesville, GA M.S.A.** ......................................... | 83,777 | | | | | | | | | |
| Includes Liberty and Long Counties ......................... | | | | | | | | | | |
| City of Hinesville ............................................ | 35,271 | 118 | 1 | 2 | 26 | 89 | 1,211 | 205 | 961 | 45 |
| Total area actually reporting .......................... | 97.5% | 246 | 1 | 8 | 48 | 189 | 1,818 | 397 | 1,324 | 97 |
| Estimated total................................................ | 100.0% | 255 | 1 | 9 | 51 | 194 | 1,902 | 411 | 1,388 | 103 |
| Rate per 100,000 inhabitants........................ | | 304.4 | 1.2 | 10.7 | 60.9 | 231.6 | 2,270.3 | 490.6 | 1,656.8 | 122.9 |
| | | | | | | | | | | |
| **Homosassa Springs, FL M.S.A.** ............................. | 139,635 | | | | | | | | | |
| Includes Citrus County....................................... | | | | | | | | | | |
| Total area actually reporting .......................... | 97.8% | 419 | 2 | 49 | 37 | 331 | 1,912 | 405 | 1,400 | 107 |
| Estimated total................................................ | 100.0% | 431 | 2 | 50 | 40 | 339 | 2,009 | 421 | 1,474 | 114 |
| Rate per 100,000 inhabitants........................ | | 308.7 | 1.4 | 35.8 | 28.6 | 242.8 | 1,438.8 | 301.5 | 1,055.6 | 81.6 |
| | | | | | | | | | | |
| **Houma-Thibodaux, LA M.S.A.** ............................... | 211,844 | | | | | | | | | |
| Includes Lafourche and Terrebonne Parishes.............. | | | | | | | | | | |
| City of Houma ................................................ | 34,238 | 212 | 7 | 18 | 44 | 143 | 1,818 | 258 | 1,502 | 58 |
| City of Thibodaux ............................................ | 14,612 | 84 | 1 | 7 | 5 | 71 | 601 | 84 | 502 | 15 |
| Total area actually reporting .......................... | 100.0% | 945 | 17 | 56 | 129 | 743 | 7,295 | 1,381 | 5,601 | 313 |
| Rate per 100,000 inhabitants........................ | | 446.1 | 8.0 | 26.4 | 60.9 | 350.7 | 3,443.6 | 651.9 | 2,643.9 | 147.8 |

**Part 2. Crime in the United States, 2015    53**

## Table 6. Crime, by Selected Metropolitan Statistical Area, 2015—*Continued*

(Number, percent, rate per 100,000 population.)

| Area | Population | Violent crime | Murder and nonnegligent manslaughter | Rape[1] | Robbery | Aggravated assault | Property crime | Burglary | Larceny-theft | Motor vehicle theft |
|---|---|---|---|---|---|---|---|---|---|---|
| **Houston-The Woodlands-Sugar Land, TX M.S.A.[3]** .......................................... | 6,648,114 | | | | | | | | | |
| Includes Austin, Brazoria, Chambers, Fort Bend, Galveston, Harris, Liberty, Montgomery, and Waller Counties.................................. | | | | | | | | | | |
| City of Houston ......................................... | 2,275,221 | 21,994 | 303 | 986 | 10,278 | 10,427 | 100,053 | 19,859 | 66,634 | 13,560 |
| City of Sugar Land ..................................... | 88,810 | 83 | 1 | 11 | 42 | 29 | 1,470 | 206 | 1,239 | 25 |
| City of Baytown......................................... | 77,145 | 233 | 6 | 34 | 81 | 112 | 2,876 | 483 | 1,967 | 426 |
| City of Conroe........................................... | 68,197 | 229 | 1 | 35 | 72 | 121 | 2,437 | 380 | 1,893 | 164 |
| Total area actually reporting .................... | 99.9% | 37,662 | 458 | 2,477 | 15,219 | 19,508 | | 39,668 | | 24,407 |
| Estimated total.......................................... | 100.0% | 37,667 | 458 | 2,478 | 15,220 | 19,511 | | 39,676 | | 24,411 |
| Rate per 100,000 inhabitants..................... | | 566.6 | 6.9 | 37.3 | 228.9 | 293.5 | | 596.8 | | 367.2 |
| **Huntsville, AL M.S.A.** ............................. | 446,021 | | | | | | | | | |
| Includes Limestone and Madison Counties................. | | | | | | | | | | |
| City of Huntsville....................................... | 190,106 | 1,541 | 18 | 132 | 368 | 1,023 | 8,743 | 1,761 | 6,219 | 763 |
| Total area actually reporting .................... | 100.0% | 2,163 | 27 | 215 | 456 | 1,465 | 13,178 | 2,850 | 9,306 | 1,022 |
| Rate per 100,000 inhabitants..................... | | 485.0 | 6.1 | 48.2 | 102.2 | 328.5 | 2,954.6 | 639.0 | 2,086.4 | 229.1 |
| **Idaho Falls, ID M.S.A.** ............................ | 139,733 | | | | | | | | | |
| Includes Bonneville, Butte, and Jefferson Counties..... | | | | | | | | | | |
| City of Idaho Falls ..................................... | 59,109 | 167 | 2 | 29 | 9 | 127 | 1,605 | 291 | 1,222 | 92 |
| Total area actually reporting .................... | 100.0% | 257 | 2 | 44 | 9 | 202 | 2,547 | 478 | 1,908 | 161 |
| Rate per 100,000 inhabitants..................... | | 183.9 | 1.4 | 31.5 | 6.4 | 144.6 | 1,822.8 | 342.1 | 1,365.5 | 115.2 |
| **Indianapolis-Carmel-Anderson, IN M.S.A.** .............. | 1,990,267 | | | | | | | | | |
| Includes Boone, Brown, Hamilton, Hancock, Hendricks, Johnson, Madison, Marion, Morgan, Putnam, and Shelby Counties..................................... | | | | | | | | | | |
| City of Indianapolis ................................... | 863,675 | 11,124 | 148 | 677 | 3,802 | 6,497 | 41,377 | 11,085 | 25,301 | 4,991 |
| City of Carmel .......................................... | 88,511 | 13 | 0 | 4 | 5 | 4 | 874 | 66 | 766 | 42 |
| City of Anderson........................................ | 55,275 | 233 | 1 | 61 | 86 | 85 | 2,159 | 458 | 1,568 | 133 |
| Total area actually reporting .................... | 86.1% | 12,841 | 157 | 831 | 4,098 | 7,755 | 58,107 | 13,138 | 38,766 | 6,203 |
| Estimated total.......................................... | 100.0% | 13,419 | 164 | 878 | 4,212 | 8,165 | 63,844 | 13,998 | 43,241 | 6,605 |
| Rate per 100,000 inhabitants..................... | | 674.2 | 8.2 | 44.1 | 211.6 | 410.2 | 3,207.8 | 703.3 | 2,172.6 | 331.9 |
| **Iowa City, IA M.S.A.** .............................. | 167,439 | | | | | | | | | |
| Includes Johnson and Washington Counties.............. | | | | | | | | | | |
| City of Iowa City ....................................... | 74,834 | 194 | 0 | 39 | 30 | 125 | 1,923 | 373 | 1,476 | 74 |
| Total area actually reporting .................... | 100.0% | 441 | 1 | 90 | 47 | 303 | 3,318 | 602 | 2,594 | 122 |
| Rate per 100,000 inhabitants..................... | | 263.4 | 0.6 | 53.8 | 28.1 | 181.0 | 1,981.6 | 359.5 | 1,549.2 | 72.9 |
| **Jackson, MI M.S.A.** ............................... | 159,692 | | | | | | | | | |
| Includes Jackson County ............................ | | | | | | | | | | |
| City of Jackson.......................................... | 33,126 | 411 | 3 | 55 | 78 | 275 | 1,477 | 258 | 1,155 | 64 |
| Total area actually reporting .................... | 98.0% | 741 | 6 | 144 | 101 | 490 | 3,569 | 582 | 2,855 | 132 |
| Estimated total.......................................... | 100.0% | 748 | 6 | 145 | 102 | 495 | 3,628 | 592 | 2,900 | 136 |
| Rate per 100,000 inhabitants..................... | | 468.4 | 3.8 | 90.8 | 63.9 | 310.0 | 2,271.9 | 370.7 | 1,816.0 | 85.2 |
| **Jackson, MS M.S.A.** .............................. | 578,246 | | | | | | | | | |
| Includes Copiah, Hinds, Madison, Rankin, Simpson, and Yazoo Counties..................................... | | | | | | | | | | |
| City of Jackson.......................................... | 170,508 | 1,571 | 53 | 139 | 781 | 598 | 8,621 | 2,395 | 5,222 | 1,004 |
| Total area actually reporting .................... | 75.5% | 1,836 | 63 | 160 | 836 | 777 | 12,106 | 3,242 | 7,697 | 1,167 |
| Estimated total.......................................... | 100.0% | 2,078 | 67 | 179 | 883 | 949 | 15,540 | 3,945 | 10,281 | 1,314 |
| Rate per 100,000 inhabitants..................... | | 359.4 | 11.6 | 31.0 | 152.7 | 164.1 | 2,687.4 | 682.2 | 1,778.0 | 227.2 |
| **Jackson, TN M.S.A.** .............................. | 130,284 | | | | | | | | | |
| Includes Chester, Crockett, and Madison Counties..... | | | | | | | | | | |
| City of Jackson.......................................... | 67,415 | 724 | 8 | 44 | 136 | 536 | 3,028 | 736 | 2,169 | 123 |
| Total area actually reporting .................... | 100.0% | 957 | 9 | 56 | 147 | 745 | 3,996 | 1,105 | 2,690 | 201 |
| Rate per 100,000 inhabitants..................... | | 734.5 | 6.9 | 43.0 | 112.8 | 571.8 | 3,067.1 | 848.1 | 2,064.7 | 154.3 |
| **Jacksonville, FL M.S.A.** ......................... | 1,444,994 | | | | | | | | | |
| Includes Baker, Clay, Duval, Nassau, and St. Johns Counties.................................. | | | | | | | | | | |
| City of Jacksonville..................................... | 867,258 | 5,622 | 97 | 471 | 1,398 | 3,656 | 31,854 | 6,082 | 23,456 | 2,316 |
| Total area actually reporting .................... | 100.0% | 7,134 | 108 | 642 | 1,591 | 4,793 | 42,649 | 7,997 | 31,841 | 2,811 |
| Rate per 100,000 inhabitants..................... | | 493.7 | 7.5 | 44.4 | 110.1 | 331.7 | 2,951.5 | 553.4 | 2,203.5 | 194.5 |

# Table 6. Crime, by Selected Metropolitan Statistical Area, 2015—*Continued*

(Number, percent, rate per 100,000 population.)

| Area | Population | Violent crime | Murder and nonnegligent manslaughter | Rape[1] | Robbery | Aggravated assault | Property crime | Burglary | Larceny-theft | Motor vehicle theft |
|---|---|---|---|---|---|---|---|---|---|---|
| **Jacksonville, NC M.S.A.** | 189,628 | | | | | | | | | |
| Includes Onslow County | | | | | | | | | | |
| City of Jacksonville | 68,614 | 106 | 2 | 16 | 33 | 55 | 1,706 | 287 | 1,368 | 51 |
| Total area actually reporting | 100.0% | 331 | 8 | 49 | 65 | 209 | 4,815 | 1,259 | 3,413 | 143 |
| Rate per 100,000 inhabitants | | 174.6 | 4.2 | 25.8 | 34.3 | 110.2 | 2,539.2 | 663.9 | 1,799.8 | 75.4 |
| | | | | | | | | | | |
| **Janesville-Beloit, WI M.S.A.** | 161,324 | | | | | | | | | |
| Includes Rock County | | | | | | | | | | |
| City of Janesville | 64,122 | 146 | 0 | 13 | 25 | 108 | 1,913 | 279 | 1,579 | 55 |
| City of Beloit | 36,862 | 178 | 3 | 27 | 45 | 103 | 1,134 | 163 | 925 | 46 |
| Total area actually reporting | 100.0% | 385 | 6 | 47 | 76 | 256 | 3,787 | 633 | 2,991 | 163 |
| Rate per 100,000 inhabitants | | 238.7 | 3.7 | 29.1 | 47.1 | 158.7 | 2,347.4 | 392.4 | 1,854.0 | 101.0 |
| | | | | | | | | | | |
| **Jefferson City, MO M.S.A.** | 151,162 | | | | | | | | | |
| Includes Callaway, Cole, Moniteau, and Osage Counties | | | | | | | | | | |
| City of Jefferson City | 43,127 | 162 | 2 | 14 | 42 | 104 | 1,378 | 178 | 1,153 | 47 |
| Total area actually reporting | 100.0% | 391 | 2 | 48 | 58 | 283 | 2,901 | 523 | 2,222 | 156 |
| Rate per 100,000 inhabitants | | 258.7 | 1.3 | 31.8 | 38.4 | 187.2 | 1,919.1 | 346.0 | 1,469.9 | 103.2 |
| | | | | | | | | | | |
| **Johnson City, TN M.S.A.** | 201,651 | | | | | | | | | |
| Includes Carter, Unicoi, and Washington Counties | | | | | | | | | | |
| City of Johnson City | 66,369 | 230 | 4 | 16 | 45 | 165 | 2,465 | 399 | 1,974 | 92 |
| Total area actually reporting | 100.0% | 609 | 11 | 40 | 61 | 497 | 4,898 | 958 | 3,733 | 207 |
| Rate per 100,000 inhabitants | | 302.0 | 5.5 | 19.8 | 30.3 | 246.5 | 2,428.9 | 475.1 | 1,851.2 | 102.7 |
| | | | | | | | | | | |
| **Johnstown, PA M.S.A.** | 136,296 | | | | | | | | | |
| Includes Cambria County | | | | | | | | | | |
| City of Johnstown | 21,463 | 105 | 3 | 7 | 25 | 70 | 691 | 195 | 472 | 24 |
| Total area actually reporting | 93.9% | 258 | 6 | 25 | 40 | 187 | 2,095 | 381 | 1,665 | 49 |
| Estimated total | 100.0% | 272 | 6 | 26 | 44 | 196 | 2,227 | 398 | 1,776 | 53 |
| Rate per 100,000 inhabitants | | 199.6 | 4.4 | 19.1 | 32.3 | 143.8 | 1,633.9 | 292.0 | 1,303.0 | 38.9 |
| | | | | | | | | | | |
| **Jonesboro, AR M.S.A.** | 128,185 | | | | | | | | | |
| Includes Craighead and Poinsett Counties | | | | | | | | | | |
| City of Jonesboro | 73,404 | 392 | 4 | 56 | 56 | 276 | 2,944 | 671 | 2,182 | 91 |
| Total area actually reporting | 100.0% | 562 | 5 | 100 | 70 | 387 | 4,221 | 990 | 3,085 | 146 |
| Rate per 100,000 inhabitants | | 438.4 | 3.9 | 78.0 | 54.6 | 301.9 | 3,292.9 | 772.3 | 2,406.7 | 113.9 |
| | | | | | | | | | | |
| **Joplin, MO M.S.A.** | 176,281 | | | | | | | | | |
| Includes Jasper and Newton Counties | | | | | | | | | | |
| City of Joplin | 51,412 | 312 | 3 | 43 | 84 | 182 | 3,514 | 510 | 2,679 | 325 |
| Total area actually reporting | 100.0% | 584 | 9 | 93 | 106 | 376 | 6,832 | 1,202 | 5,030 | 600 |
| Rate per 100,000 inhabitants | | 331.3 | 5.1 | 52.8 | 60.1 | 213.3 | 3,875.6 | 681.9 | 2,853.4 | 340.4 |
| | | | | | | | | | | |
| **Kahului-Wailuku-Lahaina, HI M.S.A.** | 164,926 | | | | | | | | | |
| Includes Kalawao and Maui Counties | | | | | | | | | | |
| Total area actually reporting | 100.0% | 557 | 4 | 94 | 113 | 346 | 6,005 | 1,007 | 4,416 | 582 |
| Rate per 100,000 inhabitants | | 337.7 | 2.4 | 57.0 | 68.5 | 209.8 | 3,641.0 | 610.6 | 2,677.6 | 352.9 |
| | | | | | | | | | | |
| **Kalamazoo-Portage, MI M.S.A.** | 335,944 | | | | | | | | | |
| Includes Kalamazoo and Van Buren Counties | | | | | | | | | | |
| City of Kalamazoo | 76,325 | 861 | 2 | 92 | 172 | 595 | 2,686 | 650 | 1,865 | 171 |
| City of Portage | 48,214 | 88 | 1 | 21 | 21 | 45 | 1,392 | 159 | 1,198 | 35 |
| Total area actually reporting | 100.0% | 1,581 | 11 | 293 | 270 | 1,007 | 8,428 | 1,797 | 6,245 | 386 |
| Rate per 100,000 inhabitants | | 470.6 | 3.3 | 87.2 | 80.4 | 299.8 | 2,508.8 | 534.9 | 1,858.9 | 114.9 |
| | | | | | | | | | | |
| **Kansas City, MO-KS M.S.A.** | 2,085,201 | | | | | | | | | |
| Includes Johnson, Leavenworth, Linn, Miami, and Wyandotte Counties, KS and Bates, Caldwell, Cass, Clay, Clinton, Jackson, Lafayette, Platte, and Ray Counties, MO | | | | | | | | | | |
| City of Kansas City, MO | 473,373 | 6,709 | 109 | 366 | 1,703 | 4,531 | 21,024 | 4,871 | 12,249 | 3,904 |
| City of Overland Park, KS | 187,240 | 399 | 5 | 166 | 52 | 176 | 3,447 | 505 | 2,422 | 520 |
| City of Kansas City, KS | 150,370 | 1,163 | 28 | 264 | 304 | 567 | 7,054 | 1,311 | 4,754 | 989 |
| Total area actually reporting | 98.9% | 11,123 | 175 | 1,177 | 2,565 | 7,206 | 60,914 | 11,547 | 40,927 | 8,440 |
| Estimated total | 100.0% | 11,173 | 175 | 1,184 | 2,572 | 7,242 | 61,414 | 11,622 | 41,310 | 8,482 |
| Rate per 100,000 inhabitants | | 535.8 | 8.4 | 56.8 | 123.3 | 347.3 | 2,945.2 | 557.4 | 1,981.1 | 406.8 |

# Table 6. Crime, by Selected Metropolitan Statistical Area, 2015—*Continued*

(Number, percent, rate per 100,000 population.)

| Area | Population | Violent crime | Murder and nonnegligent manslaughter | Rape[1] | Robbery | Aggravated assault | Property crime | Burglary | Larceny-theft | Motor vehicle theft |
|---|---|---|---|---|---|---|---|---|---|---|
| **Kennewick-Richland, WA M.S.A.** .................. | 280,232 | | | | | | | | | |
| Includes Benton and Franklin Counties...................... | | | | | | | | | | |
| City of Kennewick................ | 78,214 | 155 | 3 | 42 | 24 | 86 | 2,223 | 348 | 1,760 | 115 |
| City of Richland ...... | 54,218 | 75 | 0 | 16 | 6 | 53 | 1,368 | 228 | 1,092 | 48 |
| Total area actually reporting .... | 100.0% | 511 | 8 | 101 | 77 | 325 | 5,929 | 1,100 | 4,490 | 339 |
| Rate per 100,000 inhabitants.................... | | 182.3 | 2.9 | 36.0 | 27.5 | 116.0 | 2,115.7 | 392.5 | 1,602.2 | 121.0 |
| **Killeen-Temple, TX M.S.A.** .................... | 430,095 | | | | | | | | | |
| Includes Bell, Coryell, and Lampasas Counties........... | | | | | | | | | | |
| City of Killeen ...... | 140,497 | 868 | 17 | 190 | 148 | 513 | 4,038 | 1,038 | 2,826 | 174 |
| City of Temple..... | 71,780 | 157 | 2 | 16 | 72 | 67 | 2,702 | 585 | 1,961 | 156 |
| Total area actually reporting ...... | 99.3% | 1,452 | 24 | 289 | 271 | 868 | 10,933 | 2,490 | 7,920 | 523 |
| Estimated total.......... | 100.0% | 1,460 | 24 | 290 | 273 | 873 | 11,010 | 2,503 | 7,979 | 528 |
| Rate per 100,000 inhabitants........ | | 339.5 | 5.6 | 67.4 | 63.5 | 203.0 | 2,559.9 | 582.0 | 1,855.2 | 122.8 |
| **Kingsport-Bristol-Bristol, TN-VA M.S.A.** ............... | 307,482 | | | | | | | | | |
| Includes Hawkins and Sullivan Counties, TN and Scott and Washington Counties and Bristol City, VA .......... | | | | | | | | | | |
| City of Kingsport, TN ...... | 53,091 | 346 | 5 | 30 | 50 | 261 | 2,608 | 369 | 2,094 | 145 |
| City of Bristol, TN...... | 26,732 | 154 | 0 | 11 | 6 | 137 | 783 | 125 | 587 | 71 |
| City of Bristol, VA....... | 16,976 | 45 | 0 | 7 | 9 | 29 | 425 | 56 | 347 | 22 |
| Total area actually reporting ....... | 100.0% | 977 | 11 | 112 | 96 | 758 | 7,383 | 1,424 | 5,451 | 508 |
| Rate per 100,000 inhabitants..... | | 317.7 | 3.6 | 36.4 | 31.2 | 246.5 | 2,401.1 | 463.1 | 1,772.8 | 165.2 |
| **Kingston, NY M.S.A.** ..................... | 179,613 | | | | | | | | | |
| Includes Ulster County ................. | | | | | | | | | | |
| City of Kingston.............. | 23,485 | 71 | 0 | 13 | 30 | 28 | 660 | 98 | 549 | 13 |
| Total area actually reporting ....... | 100.0% | 304 | 0 | 96 | 41 | 167 | 2,688 | 409 | 2,209 | 70 |
| Rate per 100,000 inhabitants............... | | 169.3 | 0.0 | 53.4 | 22.8 | 93.0 | 1,496.6 | 227.7 | 1,229.9 | 39.0 |
| **Knoxville, TN M.S.A.** ....................... | 862,511 | | | | | | | | | |
| Includes Anderson, Blount, Campbell, Grainger, Knox, Loudon, Morgan, Roane, and Union Counties........... | | | | | | | | | | |
| City of Knoxville............ | 185,638 | 1,720 | 22 | 174 | 382 | 1,142 | 11,143 | 1,910 | 8,477 | 756 |
| Total area actually reporting ............ | 100.0% | 3,555 | 29 | 282 | 564 | 2,680 | 25,051 | 5,182 | 18,108 | 1,761 |
| Rate per 100,000 inhabitants................. | | 412.2 | 3.4 | 32.7 | 65.4 | 310.7 | 2,904.4 | 600.8 | 2,099.5 | 204.2 |
| **Kokomo, IN M.S.A.**............................. | 82,974 | | | | | | | | | |
| Includes Howard County.......................... | | | | | | | | | | |
| City of Kokomo ....... | 57,143 | 436 | 3 | 21 | 77 | 335 | 1,737 | 452 | 1,209 | 76 |
| Total area actually reporting ................ | 98.7% | 478 | 3 | 25 | 79 | 371 | 1,884 | 503 | 1,300 | 81 |
| Estimated total........... | 100.0% | 481 | 3 | 25 | 80 | 373 | 1,916 | 507 | 1,326 | 83 |
| Rate per 100,000 inhabitants............... | | 579.7 | 3.6 | 30.1 | 96.4 | 449.5 | 2,309.2 | 611.0 | 1,598.1 | 100.0 |
| **La Crosse-Onalaska, WI-MN M.S.A.** ..................... | 137,392 | | | | | | | | | |
| Includes Houston County, MN and La Crosse County, WI ...... | | | | | | | | | | |
| City of La Crosse, WI............... | 52,716 | 101 | 1 | 20 | 15 | 65 | 2,115 | 327 | 1,734 | 54 |
| City of Onalaska, WI...... | 18,529 | 1 | 0 | 0 | 1 | 0 | 399 | 15 | 375 | 9 |
| Total area actually reporting ........... | 100.0% | 160 | 2 | 29 | 19 | 110 | 2,995 | 435 | 2,484 | 76 |
| Rate per 100,000 inhabitants..... | | 116.5 | 1.5 | 21.1 | 13.8 | 80.1 | 2,179.9 | 316.6 | 1,808.0 | 55.3 |
| **Lafayette, LA M.S.A.** ............................. | 488,766 | | | | | | | | | |
| Includes Acadia, Iberia, Lafayette, St. Martin, and Vermilion Parishes................. | | | | | | | | | | |
| City of Lafayette ....... | 127,273 | 712 | 19 | 19 | 167 | 507 | 6,752 | 1,014 | 5,334 | 404 |
| Total area actually reporting ........ | 97.6% | 1,921 | 37 | 86 | 382 | 1,416 | 14,917 | 3,182 | 10,661 | 1,074 |
| Estimated total.......... | 100.0% | 1,977 | 38 | 90 | 390 | 1,459 | 15,377 | 3,269 | 11,014 | 1,094 |
| Rate per 100,000 inhabitants......... | | 404.5 | 7.8 | 18.4 | 79.8 | 298.5 | 3,146.1 | 668.8 | 2,253.4 | 223.8 |
| **Lafayette-West Lafayette, IN M.S.A.** ..................... | 214,040 | | | | | | | | | |
| Includes Benton, Carroll, and Tippecanoe Counties.... | | | | | | | | | | |
| City of Lafayette ....... | 71,100 | 471 | 4 | 52 | 96 | 319 | 3,311 | 679 | 2,404 | 228 |
| City of West Lafayette......... | 32,758 | 40 | 0 | 6 | 15 | 19 | 603 | 68 | 517 | 18 |
| Total area actually reporting ...... | 87.0% | 582 | 4 | 73 | 120 | 385 | 4,987 | 1,002 | 3,677 | 308 |
| Estimated total............ | 100.0% | 625 | 4 | 77 | 127 | 417 | 5,371 | 1,078 | 3,954 | 339 |
| Rate per 100,000 inhabitants....................... | | 292.0 | 1.9 | 36.0 | 59.3 | 194.8 | 2,509.3 | 503.6 | 1,847.3 | 158.4 |

(Number, percent, rate per 100,000 population.)

| Area | Population | Violent crime | Murder and nonnegligent manslaughter | Rape[1] | Robbery | Aggravated assault | Property crime | Burglary | Larceny-theft | Motor vehicle theft |
|---|---|---|---|---|---|---|---|---|---|---|
| **Lake Charles, LA M.S.A.[2]**................................ | 204,568 | | | | | | | | | |
| Includes Calcasieu and Cameron Parishes.................. | | | | | | | | | | |
| City of Lake Charles............................................ | 75,564 | 559 | 3 | 42 | 149 | 365 | 3,057 | 1,588 | 1,299 | 170 |
| Total area actually reporting .............................. | 100.0% | 1,286 | 9 | 129 | 195 | 953 | 8,628 | 3,076 | 5,084 | 468 |
| Rate per 100,000 inhabitants............................. | | 628.6 | 4.4 | 63.1 | 95.3 | 465.9 | 4,217.7 | 1,503.7 | 2,485.2 | 228.8 |
| | | | | | | | | | | |
| **Lake Havasu City-Kingman, AZ M.S.A.**.................. | 204,520 | | | | | | | | | |
| Includes Mohave County...................................... | | | | | | | | | | |
| City of Lake Havasu City .................................... | 53,220 | 93 | 0 | 30 | 6 | 57 | 987 | 216 | 728 | 43 |
| City of Kingman................................................. | 28,651 | 77 | 1 | 9 | 14 | 53 | 1,443 | 207 | 1,167 | 69 |
| Total area actually reporting .............................. | 97.7% | 398 | 4 | 54 | 54 | 286 | 5,751 | 1,367 | 4,044 | 340 |
| Estimated total.................................................. | 100.0% | 411 | 4 | 55 | 57 | 295 | 5,884 | 1,389 | 4,147 | 348 |
| Rate per 100,000 inhabitants............................. | | 201.0 | 2.0 | 26.9 | 27.9 | 144.2 | 2,877.0 | 679.2 | 2,027.7 | 170.2 |
| | | | | | | | | | | |
| **Lakeland-Winter Haven, FL M.S.A.** ...................... | 646,084 | | | | | | | | | |
| Includes Polk County........................................... | | | | | | | | | | |
| City of Lakeland................................................. | 103,498 | 395 | 4 | 91 | 131 | 169 | 5,036 | 901 | 3,839 | 296 |
| City of Winter Haven ......................................... | 37,002 | 228 | 1 | 19 | 41 | 167 | 1,381 | 273 | 1,033 | 75 |
| Total area actually reporting .............................. | 100.0% | 2,195 | 25 | 214 | 382 | 1,574 | 15,972 | 3,670 | 11,198 | 1,104 |
| Rate per 100,000 inhabitants............................. | | 339.7 | 3.9 | 33.1 | 59.1 | 243.6 | 2,472.1 | 568.0 | 1,733.2 | 170.9 |
| | | | | | | | | | | |
| **Lancaster, PA M.S.A.**............................................ | 536,440 | | | | | | | | | |
| Includes Lancaster County.................................... | | | | | | | | | | |
| City of Lancaster ............................................... | 59,295 | 472 | 7 | 80 | 163 | 222 | 2,168 | 255 | 1,827 | 86 |
| Total area actually reporting .............................. | 100.0% | 968 | 16 | 228 | 274 | 450 | 7,628 | 1,138 | 6,246 | 244 |
| Rate per 100,000 inhabitants............................. | | 180.4 | 3.0 | 42.5 | 51.1 | 83.9 | 1,422.0 | 212.1 | 1,164.3 | 45.5 |
| | | | | | | | | | | |
| **Lansing-East Lansing, MI M.S.A.** ........................... | 472,206 | | | | | | | | | |
| Includes Clinton, Eaton, and Ingham Counties ........... | | | | | | | | | | |
| City of Lansing.................................................. | 114,694 | 1,327 | 9 | 118 | 265 | 935 | 3,450 | 959 | 2,140 | 351 |
| City of East Lansing............................................ | 48,668 | 94 | 1 | 38 | 13 | 42 | 728 | 162 | 479 | 87 |
| Total area actually reporting .............................. | 99.7% | 2,003 | 17 | 333 | 332 | 1,321 | 8,822 | 1,996 | 6,212 | 614 |
| Estimated total.................................................. | 100.0% | 2,007 | 17 | 334 | 333 | 1,323 | 8,846 | 2,000 | 6,230 | 616 |
| Rate per 100,000 inhabitants............................. | | 425.0 | 3.6 | 70.7 | 70.5 | 280.2 | 1,873.3 | 423.5 | 1,319.3 | 130.5 |
| | | | | | | | | | | |
| **Laredo, TX M.S.A.**.............................................. | 271,250 | | | | | | | | | |
| Includes Webb County.......................................... | | | | | | | | | | |
| City of Laredo ................................................... | 256,280 | 972 | 8 | 133 | 162 | 669 | 8,639 | 1,040 | 7,288 | 311 |
| Total area actually reporting .............................. | 100.0% | 1,046 | 8 | 147 | 168 | 723 | 8,917 | 1,138 | 7,451 | 328 |
| Rate per 100,000 inhabitants............................. | | 385.6 | 2.9 | 54.2 | 61.9 | 266.5 | 3,287.4 | 419.5 | 2,746.9 | 120.9 |
| | | | | | | | | | | |
| **Las Cruces, NM M.S.A.** ........................................ | 213,936 | | | | | | | | | |
| Includes Dona Ana County.................................... | | | | | | | | | | |
| City of Las Cruces ............................................. | 102,227 | 268 | 3 | 34 | 54 | 177 | 5,065 | 729 | 4,117 | 219 |
| Total area actually reporting .............................. | 100.0% | 559 | 6 | 83 | 68 | 402 | 6,601 | 1,201 | 5,035 | 365 |
| Rate per 100,000 inhabitants............................. | | 261.3 | 2.8 | 38.8 | 31.8 | 187.9 | 3,085.5 | 561.4 | 2,353.5 | 170.6 |
| | | | | | | | | | | |
| **Las Vegas-Henderson-Paradise, NV M.S.A.** ........... | 2,111,967 | | | | | | | | | |
| Includes Clark County.......................................... | | | | | | | | | | |
| City of Las Vegas Metropolitan Police Department ..... | 1,562,134 | 14,383 | 127 | 1,107 | 5,010 | 8,139 | 46,791 | 14,876 | 24,010 | 7,905 |
| City of Henderson............................................... | 282,554 | 476 | 4 | 98 | 180 | 194 | 5,349 | 1,356 | 3,463 | 530 |
| Total area actually reporting .............................. | 100.0% | 17,212 | 145 | 1,337 | 5,766 | 9,964 | 59,510 | 18,351 | 31,661 | 9,498 |
| Rate per 100,000 inhabitants............................. | | 815.0 | 6.9 | 63.3 | 273.0 | 471.8 | 2,817.8 | 868.9 | 1,499.1 | 449.7 |
| | | | | | | | | | | |
| **Lawton, OK M.S.A.**.............................................. | 131,156 | | | | | | | | | |
| Includes Comanche and Cotton Counties .................. | | | | | | | | | | |
| City of Lawton .................................................. | 96,801 | 942 | 9 | 55 | 208 | 670 | 4,420 | 1,218 | 2,964 | 238 |
| Total area actually reporting .............................. | 99.1% | 974 | 10 | 61 | 214 | 689 | 4,742 | 1,317 | 3,157 | 268 |
| Estimated total.................................................. | 100.0% | 976 | 10 | 61 | 214 | 691 | 4,770 | 1,323 | 3,177 | 270 |
| Rate per 100,000 inhabitants............................. | | 744.2 | 7.6 | 46.5 | 163.2 | 526.9 | 3,636.9 | 1,008.7 | 2,422.3 | 205.9 |
| | | | | | | | | | | |
| **Lebanon, PA M.S.A.**............................................ | 136,979 | | | | | | | | | |
| Includes Lebanon County...................................... | | | | | | | | | | |
| City of Lebanon ................................................ | 25,599 | 84 | 3 | 4 | 32 | 45 | 667 | 119 | 488 | 60 |
| Total area actually reporting .............................. | 93.8% | 239 | 4 | 24 | 39 | 172 | 1,987 | 333 | 1,542 | 112 |
| Estimated total.................................................. | 100.0% | 254 | 4 | 25 | 43 | 182 | 2,122 | 351 | 1,655 | 116 |
| Rate per 100,000 inhabitants............................. | | 185.4 | 2.9 | 18.3 | 31.4 | 132.9 | 1,549.1 | 256.2 | 1,208.2 | 84.7 |

# Table 6. Crime, by Selected Metropolitan Statistical Area, 2015—*Continued*

(Number, percent, rate per 100,000 population.)

| Area | Population | Violent crime | Murder and nonnegligent manslaughter | Rape[1] | Robbery | Aggravated assault | Property crime | Burglary | Larceny-theft | Motor vehicle theft |
|---|---|---|---|---|---|---|---|---|---|---|
| **Lewiston, ID-WA M.S.A.** ............................ | 62,667 | | | | | | | | | |
| Includes Nez Perce County, ID and Asotin County, WA .... | | | | | | | | | | |
| City of Lewiston, ID............................ | 32,621 | 75 | 2 | 24 | 8 | 41 | 1,074 | 295 | 686 | 93 |
| Total area actually reporting ............................ | 100.0% | 134 | 4 | 34 | 18 | 78 | 1,892 | 406 | 1,364 | 122 |
| Rate per 100,000 inhabitants............................ | | 213.8 | 6.4 | 54.3 | 28.7 | 124.5 | 3,019.1 | 647.9 | 2,176.6 | 194.7 |
| **Lewiston-Auburn, ME M.S.A.** ............................ | 107,264 | | | | | | | | | |
| Includes Androscoggin County............................ | | | | | | | | | | |
| City of Lewiston............................ | 36,232 | 68 | 0 | 22 | 20 | 26 | 732 | 180 | 511 | 41 |
| City of Auburn............................ | 22,880 | 23 | 0 | 7 | 4 | 12 | 727 | 88 | 620 | 19 |
| Total area actually reporting ............................ | 100.0% | 148 | 0 | 42 | 31 | 75 | 1,903 | 379 | 1,448 | 76 |
| **Lexington-Fayette, KY M.S.A.** ............................ | 499,000 | | | | | | | | | |
| Includes Bourbon, Clark, Fayette, Jessamine, Scott, and Woodford Counties............................ | | | | | | | | | | |
| City of Lexington............................ | 314,077 | 1,044 | 15 | 163 | 511 | 355 | 12,405 | 2,505 | 8,901 | 999 |
| Total area actually reporting ............................ | 100.0% | 1,279 | 20 | 218 | 593 | 448 | 17,402 | 3,484 | 12,669 | 1,249 |
| Rate per 100,000 inhabitants............................ | | 256.3 | 4.0 | 43.7 | 118.8 | 89.8 | 3,487.4 | 698.2 | 2,538.9 | 250.3 |
| **Lima, OH M.S.A.** ............................ | 104,754 | | | | | | | | | |
| Includes Allen County ............................ | | | | | | | | | | |
| City of Lima............................ | 38,154 | 347 | 2 | 48 | 83 | 214 | 2,166 | 603 | 1,474 | 89 |
| Total area actually reporting ............................ | 96.7% | 401 | 3 | 59 | 100 | 239 | 3,450 | 840 | 2,482 | 128 |
| Estimated total............................ | 100.0% | 407 | 3 | 60 | 102 | 242 | 3,530 | 854 | 2,545 | 131 |
| Rate per 100,000 inhabitants............................ | | 388.5 | 2.9 | 57.3 | 97.4 | 231.0 | 3,369.8 | 815.2 | 2,429.5 | 125.1 |
| **Lincoln, NE M.S.A.** ............................ | 323,292 | | | | | | | | | |
| Includes Lancaster and Seward Counties ............................ | | | | | | | | | | |
| City of Lincoln............................ | 276,585 | 1,025 | 1 | 193 | 214 | 617 | 9,033 | 1,328 | 7,344 | 361 |
| Total area actually reporting ............................ | 99.3% | 1,065 | 1 | 210 | 217 | 637 | 9,509 | 1,427 | 7,698 | 384 |
| Estimated total............................ | 100.0% | 1,067 | 1 | 211 | 217 | 638 | 9,551 | 1,432 | 7,732 | 387 |
| Rate per 100,000 inhabitants............................ | | 330.0 | 0.3 | 65.3 | 67.1 | 197.3 | 2,954.3 | 442.9 | 2,391.6 | 119.7 |
| **Little Rock-North Little Rock-Conway, AR M.S.A.** ............................ | 736,010 | | | | | | | | | |
| Includes Faulkner, Grant, Lonoke, Perry, Pulaski, and Saline Counties............................ | | | | | | | | | | |
| City of Little Rock............................ | 198,647 | 2,950 | 32 | 167 | 670 | 2,081 | 12,855 | 2,349 | 9,590 | 916 |
| City of North Little Rock............................ | 67,943 | 526 | 13 | 8 | 128 | 377 | 3,229 | 596 | 2,345 | 288 |
| City of Conway............................ | 65,764 | 312 | 3 | 34 | 83 | 192 | 3,051 | 396 | 2,494 | 161 |
| Total area actually reporting ............................ | 100.0% | 5,334 | 63 | 385 | 1,006 | 3,880 | 30,364 | 5,956 | 22,251 | 2,157 |
| Rate per 100,000 inhabitants............................ | | 724.7 | 8.6 | 52.3 | 136.7 | 527.2 | 4,125.5 | 809.2 | 3,023.2 | 293.1 |
| **Logan, UT-ID M.S.A.** ............................ | 133,112 | | | | | | | | | |
| Includes Franklin County, ID and Cache County, UT.... | | | | | | | | | | |
| City of Logan, UT............................ | 49,145 | 50 | 0 | 29 | 1 | 20 | 899 | 154 | 721 | 24 |
| Total area actually reporting ............................ | 100.0% | 82 | 1 | 44 | 3 | 34 | 1,599 | 277 | 1,265 | 57 |
| Rate per 100,000 inhabitants............................ | | 61.6 | 0.8 | 33.1 | 2.3 | 25.5 | 1,201.2 | 208.1 | 950.3 | 42.8 |
| **Longview, TX M.S.A.** ............................ | 218,667 | | | | | | | | | |
| Includes Gregg, Rusk, and Upshur Counties ............................ | | | | | | | | | | |
| City of Longview............................ | 79,881 | 412 | 15 | 41 | 126 | 230 | 3,965 | 768 | 2,923 | 274 |
| Total area actually reporting ............................ | 99.5% | 939 | 22 | 114 | 156 | 647 | 7,239 | 1,633 | 5,083 | 523 |
| Estimated total............................ | 100.0% | 942 | 22 | 114 | 157 | 649 | 7,269 | 1,638 | 5,106 | 525 |
| Rate per 100,000 inhabitants............................ | | 430.8 | 10.1 | 52.1 | 71.8 | 296.8 | 3,324.2 | 749.1 | 2,335.1 | 240.1 |
| **Longview, WA M.S.A.** ............................ | 102,438 | | | | | | | | | |
| Includes Cowlitz County ............................ | | | | | | | | | | |
| City of Longview............................ | 36,401 | 142 | 1 | 27 | 35 | 79 | 1,896 | 359 | 1,394 | 143 |
| Total area actually reporting ............................ | 100.0% | 309 | 2 | 67 | 54 | 186 | 3,260 | 640 | 2,340 | 280 |
| Rate per 100,000 inhabitants............................ | | 301.6 | 2.0 | 65.4 | 52.7 | 181.6 | 3,182.4 | 624.8 | 2,284.3 | 273.3 |
| **Los Angeles-Long Beach-Anaheim, CA M.S.A.**....... | 13,356,776 | | | | | | | | | |
| Includes the Metropolitan Divisions of Anaheim-Santa Ana-Irvine and Los Angeles-Long Beach-Glendale ..... | | | | | | | | | | |
| City of Los Angeles............................ | 3,962,726 | 25,156 | 282 | 2,209 | 8,952 | 13,713 | 93,503 | 16,160 | 61,191 | 16,152 |
| City of Long Beach............................ | 476,318 | 2,766 | 36 | 177 | 1,054 | 1,499 | 14,337 | 3,094 | 8,413 | 2,830 |
| City of Anaheim............................ | 349,471 | 1,271 | 18 | 129 | 439 | 685 | 10,038 | 1,476 | 6,893 | 1,669 |
| City of Santa Ana............................ | 337,304 | 1,626 | 12 | 154 | 523 | 937 | 7,270 | 909 | 4,494 | 1,867 |
| City of Irvine............................ | 258,198 | 144 | 2 | 27 | 57 | 58 | 3,868 | 523 | 3,144 | 201 |

(Number, percent, rate per 100,000 population.)

| Area | Population | Violent crime | Murder and nonnegligent manslaughter | Rape[1] | Robbery | Aggravated assault | Property crime | Burglary | Larceny-theft | Motor vehicle theft |
|---|---|---|---|---|---|---|---|---|---|---|
| City of Glendale | 202,298 | 195 | 5 | 17 | 75 | 98 | 3,513 | 530 | 2,630 | 353 |
| City of Torrance | 149,243 | 214 | 2 | 34 | 85 | 93 | 2,881 | 540 | 2,024 | 317 |
| City of Pasadena | 141,815 | 428 | 4 | 57 | 131 | 236 | 3,693 | 830 | 2,540 | 323 |
| City of Orange | 140,572 | 172 | 7 | 11 | 62 | 92 | 2,897 | 525 | 2,016 | 356 |
| City of Costa Mesa | 113,477 | 386 | 1 | 53 | 122 | 210 | 4,723 | 698 | 3,558 | 467 |
| City of Burbank | 105,865 | 159 | 1 | 10 | 50 | 98 | 2,656 | 297 | 2,136 | 223 |
| City of Carson | 93,677 | 433 | 7 | 14 | 115 | 297 | 2,146 | 469 | 1,282 | 395 |
| City of Santa Monica | 93,796 | 445 | 1 | 42 | 172 | 230 | 3,834 | 660 | 2,953 | 221 |
| City of Newport Beach | 87,749 | 112 | 2 | 20 | 24 | 66 | 2,181 | 394 | 1,652 | 135 |
| City of Tustin | 81,953 | 130 | 1 | 10 | 38 | 81 | 1,715 | 217 | 1,344 | 154 |
| City of Monterey Park | 61,750 | 103 | 0 | 6 | 57 | 40 | 1,349 | 378 | 728 | 243 |
| City of Gardena | 60,782 | 301 | 6 | 24 | 149 | 122 | 1,519 | 319 | 841 | 359 |
| City of Arcadia | 58,694 | 68 | 1 | 6 | 31 | 30 | 1,272 | 316 | 892 | 64 |
| City of Fountain Valley | 57,392 | 66 | 1 | 2 | 24 | 39 | 1,517 | 268 | 1,120 | 129 |
| Total area actually reporting | 100.0% | 57,686 | 649 | 4,689 | 19,918 | 32,430 | 308,287 | 55,894 | 199,834 | 52,559 |
| Rate per 100,000 inhabitants | | 431.9 | 4.9 | 35.1 | 149.1 | 242.8 | 2,308.1 | 418.5 | 1,496.1 | 393.5 |
| Anaheim-Santa Ana-Irvine, CA M.D. | 3,175,398 | | | | | | | | | |
| Includes Orange County | | | | | | | | | | |
| Total area actually reporting | 100.0% | 7,220 | 57 | 776 | 2,236 | 4,151 | 68,237 | 10,498 | 49,069 | 8,670 |
| Rate per 100,000 inhabitants | | 227.4 | 1.8 | 24.4 | 70.4 | 130.7 | 2,148.9 | 330.6 | 1,545.3 | 273.0 |
| Los Angeles-Long Beach-Glendale, CA M.D. | 10,181,378 | | | | | | | | | |
| Includes Los Angeles County | | | | | | | | | | |
| Total area actually reporting | 100.0% | 50,466 | 592 | 3,913 | 17,682 | 28,279 | 240,050 | 45,396 | 150,765 | 43,889 |
| Rate per 100,000 inhabitants | | 495.7 | 5.8 | 38.4 | 173.7 | 277.8 | 2,357.7 | 445.9 | 1,480.8 | 431.1 |
| **Louisville/Jefferson County, KY-IN M.S.A.** | 1,276,536 | | | | | | | | | |
| Includes Clark, Floyd, Harrison, Scott, and Washington Counties, IN and Bullitt, Henry, Jefferson, Oldham, Shelby, Spencer, and Trimble Counties, KY | | | | | | | | | | |
| City of Louisville Metro, KY | 680,550 | 4,300 | 81 | 205 | 1,545 | 2,469 | 28,352 | 6,277 | 18,850 | 3,225 |
| Total area actually reporting | 97.0% | 5,323 | 95 | 328 | 1,822 | 3,078 | 40,866 | 8,612 | 27,985 | 4,269 |
| Estimated total | 100.0% | 5,399 | 96 | 335 | 1,836 | 3,132 | 41,590 | 8,728 | 28,541 | 4,321 |
| Rate per 100,000 inhabitants | | 422.9 | 7.5 | 26.2 | 143.8 | 245.4 | 3,258.0 | 683.7 | 2,235.8 | 338.5 |
| **Lubbock, TX M.S.A.** | 309,798 | | | | | | | | | |
| Includes Crosby, Lubbock, and Lynn Counties | | | | | | | | | | |
| City of Lubbock | 247,271 | 2,391 | 16 | 187 | 442 | 1,746 | 12,378 | 2,629 | 8,800 | 949 |
| Total area actually reporting | 98.8% | 2,548 | 17 | 218 | 456 | 1,857 | 13,936 | 2,979 | 9,912 | 1,045 |
| Estimated total | 100.0% | 2,557 | 17 | 219 | 458 | 1,863 | 14,032 | 2,995 | 9,985 | 1,052 |
| Rate per 100,000 inhabitants | | 825.4 | 5.5 | 70.7 | 147.8 | 601.4 | 4,529.4 | 966.8 | 3,223.1 | 339.6 |
| **Lynchburg, VA M.S.A.** | 258,380 | | | | | | | | | |
| Includes Amherst, Appomattox, Bedford, and Campbell Counties and Bedford and Lynchburg Cities | | | | | | | | | | |
| City of Lynchburg | 79,675 | 270 | 2 | 35 | 47 | 186 | 1,709 | 232 | 1,400 | 77 |
| Total area actually reporting | 100.0% | 466 | 9 | 75 | 72 | 310 | 3,760 | 595 | 2,986 | 179 |
| Rate per 100,000 inhabitants | | 180.4 | 3.5 | 29.0 | 27.9 | 120.0 | 1,455.2 | 230.3 | 1,155.7 | 69.3 |
| **Macon-Bibb County, GA M.S.A.** | 230,382 | | | | | | | | | |
| Includes Bibb, Crawford, Jones, Monroe, and Twiggs Counties | | | | | | | | | | |
| Total area actually reporting | 99.2% | 728 | 22 | 55 | 270 | 381 | 8,165 | 1,965 | 5,537 | 663 |
| Estimated total | 100.0% | 737 | 22 | 56 | 273 | 386 | 8,243 | 1,978 | 5,596 | 669 |
| Rate per 100,000 inhabitants | | 319.9 | 9.5 | 24.3 | 118.5 | 167.5 | 3,578.0 | 858.6 | 2,429.0 | 290.4 |
| **Madera, CA M.S.A.** | 155,273 | | | | | | | | | |
| Includes Madera County | | | | | | | | | | |
| City of Madera | 64,127 | 450 | 3 | 18 | 94 | 335 | 1,922 | 462 | 1,135 | 325 |
| Total area actually reporting | 100.0% | 858 | 4 | 38 | 124 | 692 | 3,703 | 1,110 | 2,061 | 532 |
| Rate per 100,000 inhabitants | | 552.6 | 2.6 | 24.5 | 79.9 | 445.7 | 2,384.8 | 714.9 | 1,327.3 | 342.6 |
| **Madison, WI M.S.A.** | 640,451 | | | | | | | | | |
| Includes Columbia, Dane, Green, and Iowa Counties | | | | | | | | | | |
| City of Madison | 248,833 | 890 | 7 | 121 | 221 | 541 | 6,908 | 1,198 | 5,461 | 249 |
| Total area actually reporting | 98.4% | 1,344 | 17 | 188 | 296 | 843 | 12,333 | 1,965 | 9,956 | 412 |
| Estimated total | 100.0% | 1,357 | 17 | 190 | 300 | 850 | 12,532 | 1,986 | 10,125 | 421 |
| Rate per 100,000 inhabitants | | 211.9 | 2.7 | 29.7 | 46.8 | 132.7 | 1,956.7 | 310.1 | 1,580.9 | 65.7 |

# Table 6. Crime, by Selected Metropolitan Statistical Area, 2015—*Continued*

(Number, percent, rate per 100,000 population.)

| Area | Population | Violent crime | Murder and nonnegligent manslaughter | Rape[1] | Robbery | Aggravated assault | Property crime | Burglary | Larceny-theft | Motor vehicle theft |
|---|---|---|---|---|---|---|---|---|---|---|
| **Manchester-Nashua, NH M.S.A.** ............................... | 406,602 | | | | | | | | | |
| Includes Hillsborough County.................................... | | | | | | | | | | |
| City of Manchester ................................................. | 110,661 | 742 | 5 | 86 | 221 | 430 | 4,070 | 669 | 3,192 | 209 |
| City of Nashua...................................................... | 87,433 | 202 | 5 | 53 | 41 | 103 | 1,326 | 133 | 1,125 | 68 |
| Total area actually reporting ................................. | 98.7% | 1,137 | 13 | 188 | 285 | 651 | 7,748 | 1,157 | 6,229 | 362 |
| Estimated total..................................................... | 100.0% | 1,144 | 13 | 190 | 286 | 655 | 7,822 | 1,167 | 6,290 | 365 |
| Rate per 100,000 inhabitants................................. | | 281.4 | 3.2 | 46.7 | 70.3 | 161.1 | 1,923.7 | 287.0 | 1,547.0 | 89.8 |
| **Manhattan, KS M.S.A.** .......................................... | 99,189 | | | | | | | | | |
| Includes Pottawatomie and Riley Counties ................ | | | | | | | | | | |
| Total area actually reporting ................................. | 99.9% | 228 | 2 | 36 | 25 | 165 | 1,672 | 375 | 1,205 | 92 |
| Estimated total..................................................... | 100.0% | 228 | 2 | 36 | 25 | 165 | 1,674 | 375 | 1,207 | 92 |
| Rate per 100,000 inhabitants................................. | | 229.9 | 2.0 | 36.3 | 25.2 | 166.3 | 1,687.7 | 378.1 | 1,216.9 | 92.8 |
| **Mankato-North Mankato, MN M.S.A.** ................... | 98,803 | | | | | | | | | |
| Includes Blue Earth and Nicollet Counties.................. | | | | | | | | | | |
| City of Mankato.................................................... | 40,669 | 99 | 0 | 17 | 19 | 63 | 1,649 | 234 | 1,352 | 63 |
| City of North Mankato............................................ | 13,438 | 15 | 0 | 6 | 1 | 8 | 199 | 34 | 157 | 8 |
| Total area actually reporting ................................. | 100.0% | 151 | 0 | 37 | 22 | 92 | 2,297 | 397 | 1,800 | 100 |
| Rate per 100,000 inhabitants................................. | | 152.8 | 0.0 | 37.4 | 22.3 | 93.1 | 2,324.8 | 401.8 | 1,821.8 | 101.2 |
| **Mansfield, OH M.S.A.** ........................................... | 121,438 | | | | | | | | | |
| Includes Richland County ....................................... | | | | | | | | | | |
| City of Mansfield .................................................. | 46,605 | 228 | 3 | 56 | 74 | 95 | 2,670 | 764 | 1,821 | 85 |
| Total area actually reporting ................................. | 95.3% | 308 | 3 | 91 | 94 | 120 | 4,737 | 1,297 | 3,329 | 111 |
| Estimated total..................................................... | 100.0% | 317 | 3 | 93 | 97 | 124 | 4,867 | 1,319 | 3,432 | 116 |
| Rate per 100,000 inhabitants................................. | | 261.0 | 2.5 | 76.6 | 79.9 | 102.1 | 4,007.8 | 1,086.2 | 2,826.1 | 95.5 |
| **McAllen-Edinburg-Mission, TX M.S.A.**[2] ................. | 846,417 | | | | | | | | | |
| Includes Hidalgo County ........................................ | | | | | | | | | | |
| City of McAllen..................................................... | 140,593 | 152 | 2 | 16 | 51 | 83 | 4,637 | 435 | 4,091 | 111 |
| City of Edinburg.................................................... | 85,137 | 365 | 2 | 49 | 53 | 261 | 4,070 | 596 | 3,314 | 160 |
| City of Mission..................................................... | 83,552 | 85 | 1 | 21 | 20 | 43 | 2,025 | 243 | 1,647 | 135 |
| Total area actually reporting ................................. | 100.0% | 2,523 | 32 | 348 | 400 | 1,743 | 24,545 | 4,252 | 19,181 | 1,112 |
| Rate per 100,000 inhabitants................................. | | 298.1 | 3.8 | 41.1 | 47.3 | 205.9 | 2,899.9 | 502.4 | 2,266.1 | 131.4 |
| **Medford, OR M.S.A.** ............................................. | 213,330 | | | | | | | | | |
| Includes Jackson County ........................................ | | | | | | | | | | |
| City of Medford .................................................... | 79,461 | 393 | 1 | 33 | 56 | 303 | 4,859 | 427 | 4,130 | 302 |
| Total area actually reporting ................................. | 100.0% | 691 | 5 | 66 | 83 | 537 | 8,198 | 1,056 | 6,591 | 551 |
| Rate per 100,000 inhabitants................................. | | 323.9 | 2.3 | 30.9 | 38.9 | 251.7 | 3,842.9 | 495.0 | 3,089.6 | 258.3 |
| **Memphis, TN-MS-AR M.S.A.** ................................. | 1,346,893 | | | | | | | | | |
| Includes Crittenden County, AR; Benton, DeSoto, Marshall, Tate, and Tunica Counties, MS; and Fayette, Shelby, and Tipton Counties, TN ............................... | | | | | | | | | | |
| City of Memphis, TN.............................................. | 657,936 | 11,449 | 135 | 530 | 3,131 | 7,653 | 37,047 | 10,272 | 24,049 | 2,726 |
| Total area actually reporting ................................. | 94.1% | 13,870 | 152 | 692 | 3,483 | 9,543 | 51,859 | 13,716 | 34,625 | 3,518 |
| Estimated total..................................................... | 100.0% | 13,981 | 155 | 705 | 3,501 | 9,620 | 53,328 | 14,106 | 35,621 | 3,601 |
| Rate per 100,000 inhabitants................................. | | 1,038.0 | 11.5 | 52.3 | 259.9 | 714.2 | 3,959.3 | 1,047.3 | 2,644.7 | 267.4 |
| **Merced, CA M.S.A.** ............................................... | 268,577 | | | | | | | | | |
| Includes Merced County ........................................ | | | | | | | | | | |
| City of Merced...................................................... | 82,409 | 763 | 11 | 31 | 151 | 570 | 2,760 | 588 | 1,608 | 564 |
| Total area actually reporting ................................. | 100.0% | 1,668 | 27 | 80 | 260 | 1,301 | 7,928 | 1,842 | 4,570 | 1,516 |
| Rate per 100,000 inhabitants................................. | | 621.1 | 10.1 | 29.8 | 96.8 | 484.4 | 2,951.9 | 685.8 | 1,701.6 | 564.5 |
| **Miami-Fort Lauderdale-West Palm Beach, FL M.S.A.**.............................................................. | 6,050,585 | | | | | | | | | |
| Includes the Metropolitan Divisions of Fort Lauderdale-Pompano Beach-Deerfield Beach, Miami-Miami Beach-Kendall, and West Palm Beach-Boca Raton-Delray Beach ................................................................... | | | | | | | | | | |
| City of Miami........................................................ | 437,969 | 4,473 | 75 | 80 | 1,681 | 2,637 | 19,128 | 3,109 | 13,721 | 2,298 |
| City of Fort Lauderdale........................................... | 178,598 | 1,217 | 10 | 92 | 429 | 686 | 9,670 | 1,931 | 6,936 | 803 |
| City of West Palm Beach......................................... | 104,919 | 924 | 22 | 50 | 277 | 575 | 5,093 | 780 | 3,670 | 643 |
| City of Pompano Beach........................................... | 107,656 | 939 | 6 | 73 | 311 | 549 | 4,731 | 829 | 3,379 | 523 |
| City of Miami Beach............................................... | 92,641 | 998 | 2 | 54 | 418 | 524 | 9,002 | 698 | 7,680 | 624 |
| City of Boca Raton................................................. | 92,932 | 203 | 1 | 30 | 77 | 95 | 2,218 | 462 | 1,621 | 135 |

## Table 6. Crime, by Selected Metropolitan Statistical Area, 2015—*Continued*

(Number, percent, rate per 100,000 population.)

| Area | Population | Violent crime | Murder and nonnegligent manslaughter | Rape[1] | Robbery | Aggravated assault | Property crime | Burglary | Larceny-theft | Motor vehicle theft |
|------|-----------|---------------|--------------------------------------|---------|---------|--------------------|----------------|----------|---------------|---------------------|
| City of Deerfield Beach | 79,824 | 335 | 1 | 40 | 102 | 192 | 1,911 | 350 | 1,372 | 189 |
| City of Delray Beach | 66,159 | 426 | 3 | 25 | 127 | 271 | 2,448 | 362 | 1,930 | 156 |
| City of Jupiter | 62,068 | 104 | 1 | 16 | 17 | 70 | 1,194 | 176 | 961 | 57 |
| Total area actually reporting | 100.0% | 30,865 | 399 | 1,871 | 9,490 | 19,105 | 198,813 | 32,436 | 149,452 | 16,925 |
| Rate per 100,000 inhabitants | | 510.1 | 6.6 | 30.9 | 156.8 | 315.8 | 3,285.8 | 536.1 | 2,470.0 | 279.7 |
| Fort Lauderdale-Pompano Beach-Deerfield Beach, FL M.D. | 1,909,298 | | | | | | | | | |
| Includes Broward County | | | | | | | | | | |
| Total area actually reporting | 100.0% | 7,743 | 85 | 592 | 2,474 | 4,592 | 57,849 | 10,258 | 42,665 | 4,926 |
| Rate per 100,000 inhabitants | | 405.5 | 4.5 | 31.0 | 129.6 | 240.5 | 3,029.9 | 537.3 | 2,234.6 | 258.0 |
| Miami-Miami Beach-Kendall, FL M.D. | 2,717,144 | | | | | | | | | |
| Includes Miami-Dade County | | | | | | | | | | |
| Total area actually reporting | 100.0% | 16,583 | 217 | 756 | 5,366 | 10,244 | 99,734 | 14,533 | 76,401 | 8,800 |
| Rate per 100,000 inhabitants | | 610.3 | 8.0 | 27.8 | 197.5 | 377.0 | 3,670.5 | 534.9 | 2,811.8 | 323.9 |
| West Palm Beach-Boca Raton-Delray Beach, FL M.D. | 1,424,143 | | | | | | | | | |
| Includes Palm Beach County | | | | | | | | | | |
| Total area actually reporting | 100.0% | 6,539 | 97 | 523 | 1,650 | 4,269 | 41,230 | 7,645 | 30,386 | 3,199 |
| Rate per 100,000 inhabitants | | 459.2 | 6.8 | 36.7 | 115.9 | 299.8 | 2,895.1 | 536.8 | 2,133.6 | 224.6 |
| **Michigan City-La Porte, IN M.S.A.** | 111,367 | | | | | | | | | |
| Includes La Porte County | | | | | | | | | | |
| City of Michigan City | 31,497 | 81 | 2 | 11 | 32 | 36 | 1,555 | 212 | 1,264 | 79 |
| City of La Porte | 22,000 | 34 | 1 | 4 | 14 | 15 | 773 | 127 | 623 | 23 |
| Total area actually reporting | 90.5% | 145 | 4 | 25 | 51 | 65 | 2,937 | 564 | 2,216 | 157 |
| Estimated total | 100.0% | 174 | 4 | 27 | 58 | 85 | 3,249 | 602 | 2,470 | 177 |
| Rate per 100,000 inhabitants | | 156.2 | 3.6 | 24.2 | 52.1 | 76.3 | 2,917.4 | 540.6 | 2,217.9 | 158.9 |
| **Midland, MI M.S.A.** | 83,395 | | | | | | | | | |
| Includes Midland County | | | | | | | | | | |
| City of Midland | 41,975 | 49 | 1 | 21 | 2 | 25 | 534 | 47 | 483 | 4 |
| Total area actually reporting | 100.0% | 120 | 2 | 55 | 3 | 60 | 924 | 172 | 735 | 17 |
| Rate per 100,000 inhabitants | | 143.9 | 2.4 | 66.0 | 3.6 | 71.9 | 1,108.0 | 206.2 | 881.3 | 20.4 |
| **Midland, TX M.S.A.** | 166,940 | | | | | | | | | |
| Includes Martin and Midland Counties | | | | | | | | | | |
| City of Midland | 132,625 | 419 | 7 | 46 | 61 | 305 | 3,381 | 656 | 2,544 | 181 |
| Total area actually reporting | 100.0% | 538 | 9 | 47 | 79 | 403 | 4,325 | 875 | 3,158 | 292 |
| Rate per 100,000 inhabitants | | 322.3 | 5.4 | 28.2 | 47.3 | 241.4 | 2,590.8 | 524.1 | 1,891.7 | 174.9 |
| **Milwaukee-Waukesha-West Allis, WI M.S.A.** | 1,575,177 | | | | | | | | | |
| Includes Milwaukee, Ozaukee, Washington, and Waukesha Counties | | | | | | | | | | |
| City of Milwaukee | 600,400 | 9,583 | 145 | 436 | 3,749 | 5,253 | 25,602 | 5,481 | 12,741 | 7,380 |
| City of Waukesha | 71,686 | 108 | 3 | 31 | 25 | 49 | 1,135 | 162 | 940 | 33 |
| City of West Allis | 60,633 | 238 | 1 | 16 | 124 | 97 | 2,407 | 390 | 1,798 | 219 |
| Total area actually reporting | 96.0% | 10,636 | 154 | 565 | 4,165 | 5,752 | 42,269 | 7,330 | 26,495 | 8,444 |
| Estimated total | 100.0% | 10,713 | 155 | 576 | 4,187 | 5,795 | 43,459 | 7,457 | 27,506 | 8,496 |
| Rate per 100,000 inhabitants | | 680.1 | 9.8 | 36.6 | 265.8 | 367.9 | 2,759.0 | 473.4 | 1,746.2 | 539.4 |
| **Minneapolis-St. Paul-Bloomington, MN-WI M.S.A.** | 3,527,776 | | | | | | | | | |
| Includes Anoka, Carver, Chisago, Dakota, Hennepin, Isanti, Le Sueur, Mille Lacs, Ramsey, Scott, Sherburne, Sibley, Washington, and Wright Counties, MN and Pierce and St. Croix Counties, WI | | | | | | | | | | |
| City of Minneapolis, MN | 413,479 | 4,395 | 47 | 407 | 1,896 | 2,045 | 17,341 | 3,555 | 12,069 | 1,717 |
| City of St. Paul, MN | 300,721 | 2,115 | 16 | 204 | 714 | 1,181 | 9,870 | 2,125 | 5,997 | 1,748 |
| City of Bloomington, MN | 87,158 | 144 | 0 | 30 | 58 | 56 | 2,903 | 196 | 2,613 | 94 |
| City of Plymouth, MN | 76,192 | 60 | 0 | 16 | 7 | 37 | 1,029 | 168 | 832 | 29 |
| City of Eagan, MN | 66,549 | 52 | 0 | 18 | 18 | 16 | 1,175 | 127 | 1,005 | 43 |
| City of Eden Prairie, MN | 63,835 | 33 | 0 | 6 | 15 | 12 | 955 | 87 | 846 | 22 |
| Total area actually reporting | 99.9% | 10,059 | 97 | 1,440 | 3,423 | 5,099 | 83,470 | 12,470 | 64,954 | 6,046 |
| Estimated total | 100.0% | 10,062 | 97 | 1,440 | 3,424 | 5,101 | 83,520 | 12,475 | 64,997 | 6,048 |
| Rate per 100,000 inhabitants | | 285.2 | 2.7 | 40.8 | 97.1 | 144.6 | 2,367.5 | 353.6 | 1,842.4 | 171.4 |

(Number, percent, rate per 100,000 population.)

| Area | Population | Violent crime | Murder and nonnegligent manslaughter | Rape[1] | Robbery | Aggravated assault | Property crime | Burglary | Larceny-theft | Motor vehicle theft |
|---|---|---|---|---|---|---|---|---|---|---|
| **Missoula, MT M.S.A.** .......................... | 113,600 | | | | | | | | | |
| Includes Missoula County.......................... | | | | | | | | | | |
| City of Missoula.......................... | 70,553 | 372 | 4 | 66 | 29 | 273 | 3,167 | 390 | 2,635 | 142 |
| Total area actually reporting .......................... | 100.0% | 483 | 4 | 94 | 30 | 355 | 3,475 | 506 | 2,812 | 157 |
| Rate per 100,000 inhabitants.......................... | | 425.2 | 3.5 | 82.7 | 26.4 | 312.5 | 3,059.0 | 445.4 | 2,475.4 | 138.2 |
| **Mobile, AL M.S.A.[5]** .......................... | 414,914 | | | | | | | | | |
| Includes Mobile County .......................... | | | | | | | | | | |
| City of Mobile[5].......................... | 250,346 | 1,529 | 24 | 116 | 402 | 987 | 10,794 | 2,208 | 7,977 | 609 |
| Total area actually reporting .......................... | 100.0% | 2,202 | 44 | 182 | 512 | 1,464 | 15,229 | 3,438 | 10,734 | 1,057 |
| Rate per 100,000 inhabitants.......................... | | 530.7 | 10.6 | 43.9 | 123.4 | 352.8 | 3,670.4 | 828.6 | 2,587.0 | 254.8 |
| **Modesto, CA M.S.A.** .......................... | 535,785 | | | | | | | | | |
| Includes Stanislaus County .......................... | | | | | | | | | | |
| City of Modesto.......................... | 210,794 | 2,025 | 25 | 85 | 488 | 1,427 | 10,123 | 1,639 | 6,749 | 1,735 |
| Total area actually reporting .......................... | 100.0% | 3,093 | 39 | 161 | 817 | 2,076 | 19,782 | 3,887 | 12,185 | 3,710 |
| Rate per 100,000 inhabitants.......................... | | 577.3 | 7.3 | 30.0 | 152.5 | 387.5 | 3,692.2 | 725.5 | 2,274.2 | 692.4 |
| **Monroe, LA M.S.A.[2]** .......................... | 179,142 | | | | | | | | | |
| Includes Ouachita and Union Parishes .......................... | | | | | | | | | | |
| City of Monroe.......................... | 49,703 | 1,293 | 18 | 44 | 167 | 1,064 | 4,165 | 895 | 3,144 | 126 |
| Total area actually reporting .......................... | 96.8% | 2,051 | 27 | 72 | 215 | 1,737 | 8,200 | 2,071 | 5,841 | 288 |
| Estimated total.......................... | 100.0% | 2,078 | 27 | 74 | 219 | 1,758 | 8,423 | 2,113 | 6,012 | 298 |
| Rate per 100,000 inhabitants.......................... | | 1,160.0 | 15.1 | 41.3 | 122.2 | 981.3 | 4,701.9 | 1,179.5 | 3,356.0 | 166.3 |
| **Monroe, MI M.S.A.** .......................... | 149,356 | | | | | | | | | |
| Includes Monroe County.......................... | | | | | | | | | | |
| City of Monroe .......................... | 20,074 | 95 | 0 | 17 | 11 | 67 | 498 | 107 | 373 | 18 |
| Total area actually reporting .......................... | 97.4% | 342 | 3 | 102 | 43 | 194 | 2,455 | 656 | 1,669 | 130 |
| Estimated total.......................... | 100.0% | 353 | 3 | 104 | 45 | 201 | 2,528 | 669 | 1,724 | 135 |
| Rate per 100,000 inhabitants.......................... | | 236.3 | 2.0 | 69.6 | 30.1 | 134.6 | 1,692.6 | 447.9 | 1,154.3 | 90.4 |
| **Montgomery, AL M.S.A.** .......................... | 372,085 | | | | | | | | | |
| Includes Autauga, Elmore, Lowndes, and Montgomery Counties.......................... | | | | | | | | | | |
| City of Montgomery .......................... | 199,139 | 1,042 | 33 | 40 | 391 | 578 | 8,363 | 2,342 | 5,280 | 741 |
| Total area actually reporting .......................... | 99.3% | 1,479 | 39 | 119 | 474 | 847 | 12,666 | 3,439 | 8,201 | 1,026 |
| Estimated total.......................... | 100.0% | 1,491 | 39 | 120 | 476 | 856 | 12,751 | 3,455 | 8,264 | 1,032 |
| Rate per 100,000 inhabitants.......................... | | 400.7 | 10.5 | 32.3 | 127.9 | 230.1 | 3,426.9 | 928.6 | 2,221.0 | 277.4 |
| **Morgantown, WV M.S.A.** .......................... | 138,642 | | | | | | | | | |
| Includes Monongalia and Preston Counties .......................... | | | | | | | | | | |
| City of Morgantown .......................... | 31,621 | 81 | 0 | 12 | 22 | 47 | 675 | 155 | 493 | 27 |
| Total area actually reporting .......................... | 89.1% | 322 | 3 | 60 | 46 | 213 | 1,804 | 533 | 1,183 | 88 |
| Estimated total.......................... | 100.0% | 371 | 3 | 64 | 53 | 251 | 2,316 | 605 | 1,599 | 112 |
| Rate per 100,000 inhabitants.......................... | | 267.6 | 2.2 | 46.2 | 38.2 | 181.0 | 1,670.5 | 436.4 | 1,153.3 | 80.8 |
| **Morristown, TN M.S.A.** .......................... | 116,102 | | | | | | | | | |
| Includes Hamblen and Jefferson Counties .......................... | | | | | | | | | | |
| City of Morristown.......................... | 29,377 | 217 | 0 | 13 | 15 | 189 | 1,542 | 203 | 1,244 | 95 |
| Total area actually reporting .......................... | 100.0% | 420 | 3 | 36 | 27 | 354 | 2,986 | 556 | 2,227 | 203 |
| Rate per 100,000 inhabitants.......................... | | 361.8 | 2.6 | 31.0 | 23.3 | 304.9 | 2,571.9 | 478.9 | 1,918.1 | 174.8 |
| **Mount Vernon-Anacortes, WA M.S.A.** .......................... | 121,669 | | | | | | | | | |
| Includes Skagit County.......................... | | | | | | | | | | |
| City of Mount Vernon.......................... | 33,474 | 73 | 1 | 13 | 26 | 33 | 1,394 | 205 | 1,102 | 87 |
| City of Anacortes.......................... | 16,351 | 13 | 0 | 3 | 2 | 8 | 509 | 84 | 403 | 22 |
| Total area actually reporting .......................... | 100.0% | 216 | 3 | 36 | 50 | 127 | 4,718 | 959 | 3,501 | 258 |
| Rate per 100,000 inhabitants.......................... | | 177.5 | 2.5 | 29.6 | 41.1 | 104.4 | 3,877.7 | 788.2 | 2,877.5 | 212.1 |
| **Muskegon, MI M.S.A.** .......................... | 172,514 | | | | | | | | | |
| Includes Muskegon County.......................... | | | | | | | | | | |
| City of Muskegon.......................... | 38,442 | 278 | 1 | 27 | 64 | 186 | 1,613 | 326 | 1,186 | 101 |
| Total area actually reporting .......................... | 100.0% | 716 | 8 | 149 | 115 | 444 | 5,636 | 925 | 4,438 | 273 |
| Rate per 100,000 inhabitants.......................... | | 415.0 | 4.6 | 86.4 | 66.7 | 257.4 | 3,267.0 | 536.2 | 2,572.5 | 158.2 |
| **Myrtle Beach-Conway-North Myrtle Beach, SC-NC M.S.A.** .......................... | 428,773 | | | | | | | | | |
| Includes Brunswick County, NC and Horry County, SC | | | | | | | | | | |
| City of Myrtle Beach, SC .......................... | 30,731 | 484 | 8 | 54 | 139 | 283 | 4,421 | 442 | 3,574 | 405 |
| City of Conway, SC .......................... | 20,938 | 115 | 9 | 13 | 27 | 66 | 976 | 134 | 793 | 49 |

# Table 6. Crime, by Selected Metropolitan Statistical Area, 2015—*Continued*

(Number, percent, rate per 100,000 population.)

| Area | Population | Violent crime | Murder and nonnegligent manslaughter | Rape[1] | Robbery | Aggravated assault | Property crime | Burglary | Larceny-theft | Motor vehicle theft |
|---|---|---|---|---|---|---|---|---|---|---|
| City of North Myrtle Beach, SC | 15,518 | 95 | 3 | 14 | 25 | 53 | 1,402 | 231 | 1,075 | 96 |
| Total area actually reporting | 99.1% | 1,664 | 61 | 268 | 321 | 1,014 | 16,162 | 3,294 | 11,690 | 1,178 |
| Estimated total | 100.0% | 1,673 | 61 | 269 | 323 | 1,020 | 16,271 | 3,316 | 11,773 | 1,182 |
| Rate per 100,000 inhabitants | | 390.2 | 14.2 | 62.7 | 75.3 | 237.9 | 3,794.8 | 773.4 | 2,745.7 | 275.7 |
| | | | | | | | | | | |
| **Napa, CA M.S.A.** | 142,777 | | | | | | | | | |
| Includes Napa County | | | | | | | | | | |
| City of Napa | 80,749 | 298 | 0 | 38 | 30 | 230 | 1,412 | 355 | 905 | 152 |
| Total area actually reporting | 100.0% | 587 | 3 | 62 | 55 | 467 | 2,586 | 598 | 1,752 | 236 |
| Rate per 100,000 inhabitants | | 411.1 | 2.1 | 43.4 | 38.5 | 327.1 | 1,811.2 | 418.8 | 1,227.1 | 165.3 |
| | | | | | | | | | | |
| **Naples-Immokalee-Marco Island, FL M.S.A.** | 357,485 | | | | | | | | | |
| Includes Collier County | | | | | | | | | | |
| City of Naples | 21,325 | 21 | 0 | 2 | 4 | 15 | 534 | 74 | 451 | 9 |
| City of Marco Island | 17,719 | 12 | 0 | 4 | 0 | 8 | 136 | 26 | 105 | 5 |
| Total area actually reporting | 100.0% | 1,025 | 2 | 106 | 167 | 750 | 4,818 | 947 | 3,601 | 270 |
| Rate per 100,000 inhabitants | | 286.7 | 0.6 | 29.7 | 46.7 | 209.8 | 1,347.7 | 264.9 | 1,007.3 | 75.5 |
| | | | | | | | | | | |
| **Nashville-Davidson–Murfreesboro–Franklin, TN M.S.A.** | 1,823,472 | | | | | | | | | |
| Includes Cannon, Cheatham, Davidson, Dickson, Hickman, Macon, Maury, Robertson, Rutherford, Smith, Sumner, Trousdale, Williamson, and Wilson Counties | | | | | | | | | | |
| City of Nashville Metropolitan | 658,029 | 7,245 | 72 | 507 | 1,847 | 4,819 | 25,043 | 5,132 | 18,463 | 1,448 |
| City of Murfreesboro | 123,994 | 673 | 5 | 62 | 146 | 460 | 4,021 | 779 | 3,065 | 177 |
| City of Franklin | 72,696 | 151 | 1 | 24 | 24 | 102 | 1,058 | 95 | 914 | 49 |
| Total area actually reporting | 100.0% | 11,172 | 100 | 878 | 2,349 | 7,845 | 47,049 | 9,240 | 35,183 | 2,626 |
| Rate per 100,000 inhabitants | | 612.7 | 5.5 | 48.1 | 128.8 | 430.2 | 2,580.2 | 506.7 | 1,929.5 | 144.0 |
| | | | | | | | | | | |
| **New Bern, NC M.S.A.** | 127,617 | | | | | | | | | |
| Includes Craven, Jones, and Pamlico Counties | | | | | | | | | | |
| City of New Bern | 30,433 | 116 | 2 | 3 | 28 | 83 | 1,127 | 204 | 894 | 29 |
| Total area actually reporting | 91.1% | 218 | 7 | 15 | 39 | 157 | 2,381 | 699 | 1,606 | 76 |
| Estimated total | 100.0% | 236 | 7 | 16 | 42 | 171 | 2,590 | 766 | 1,739 | 85 |
| Rate per 100,000 inhabitants | | 184.9 | 5.5 | 12.5 | 32.9 | 134.0 | 2,029.5 | 600.2 | 1,362.7 | 66.6 |
| | | | | | | | | | | |
| **New Orleans-Metairie, LA M.S.A.** | 1,265,042 | | | | | | | | | |
| Includes Jefferson, Orleans, Plaquemines, St. Bernard, St. Charles, St. James, St. John the Baptist, and St. Tammany Parishes | | | | | | | | | | |
| City of New Orleans | 393,447 | 3,736 | 164 | 409 | 1,497 | 1,666 | 15,243 | 2,898 | 9,828 | 2,517 |
| Total area actually reporting | 96.6% | 6,604 | 204 | 592 | 2,100 | 3,708 | 37,209 | 6,470 | 26,989 | 3,750 |
| Estimated total | 100.0% | 6,761 | 206 | 603 | 2,125 | 3,827 | 38,333 | 6,732 | 27,786 | 3,815 |
| Rate per 100,000 inhabitants | | 534.4 | 16.3 | 47.7 | 168.0 | 302.5 | 3,030.2 | 532.2 | 2,196.4 | 301.6 |
| | | | | | | | | | | |
| **Niles-Benton Harbor, MI M.S.A.** | 154,894 | | | | | | | | | |
| Includes Berrien County | | | | | | | | | | |
| City of Niles | 11,352 | 51 | 0 | 13 | 7 | 31 | 289 | 50 | 222 | 17 |
| City of Benton Harbor | 10,012 | 226 | 3 | 13 | 64 | 146 | 402 | 121 | 265 | 16 |
| Total area actually reporting | 90.3% | 559 | 8 | 127 | 99 | 325 | 2,385 | 489 | 1,793 | 103 |
| Estimated total | 100.0% | 598 | 8 | 134 | 106 | 350 | 2,663 | 537 | 2,003 | 123 |
| Rate per 100,000 inhabitants | | 386.1 | 5.2 | 86.5 | 68.4 | 226.0 | 1,719.2 | 346.7 | 1,293.1 | 79.4 |
| | | | | | | | | | | |
| **North Port-Sarasota-Bradenton, FL M.S.A.** | 764,515 | | | | | | | | | |
| Includes Manatee and Sarasota Counties | | | | | | | | | | |
| City of North Port | 61,148 | 101 | 1 | 24 | 13 | 63 | 856 | 164 | 664 | 28 |
| City of Sarasota | 54,743 | 357 | 5 | 28 | 112 | 212 | 2,326 | 417 | 1,798 | 111 |
| City of Bradenton | 53,658 | 334 | 6 | 27 | 60 | 241 | 2,035 | 397 | 1,543 | 95 |
| City of Venice | 21,980 | 35 | 0 | 4 | 3 | 28 | 399 | 87 | 301 | 11 |
| Total area actually reporting | 100.0% | 3,185 | 31 | 309 | 491 | 2,354 | 17,845 | 3,689 | 13,390 | 766 |
| Rate per 100,000 inhabitants | | 416.6 | 4.1 | 40.4 | 64.2 | 307.9 | 2,334.2 | 482.5 | 1,751.4 | 100.2 |
| | | | | | | | | | | |
| **Norwich-New London, CT M.S.A.** | 145,491 | | | | | | | | | |
| Includes New London County | | | | | | | | | | |
| City of Norwich | 40,085 | 127 | 2 | 11 | 28 | 86 | 625 | 154 | 432 | 39 |
| City of New London | 27,312 | 154 | 4 | 18 | 26 | 106 | 640 | 138 | 431 | 71 |
| Total area actually reporting | 100.0% | 471 | 6 | 57 | 101 | 307 | 2,968 | 433 | 2,374 | 161 |
| Rate per 100,000 inhabitants | | 323.7 | 4.1 | 39.2 | 69.4 | 211.0 | 2,040.0 | 297.6 | 1,631.7 | 110.7 |

# Table 6. Crime, by Selected Metropolitan Statistical Area, 2015—*Continued*

(Number, percent, rate per 100,000 population.)

| Area | Population | Violent crime | Murder and nonnegligent manslaughter | Rape[1] | Robbery | Aggravated assault | Property crime | Burglary | Larceny-theft | Motor vehicle theft |
|---|---|---|---|---|---|---|---|---|---|---|
| **Ocala, FL M.S.A.**............................ | 342,895 | | | | | | | | | |
| Includes Marion County ........................... | | | | | | | | | | |
| City of Ocala.......................................... | 57,891 | 378 | 3 | 24 | 108 | 243 | 3,034 | 438 | 2,507 | 89 |
| Total area actually reporting .................... | 99.5% | 1,237 | 10 | 113 | 195 | 919 | 7,133 | 1,712 | 5,088 | 333 |
| Estimated total...................................... | 100.0% | 1,245 | 10 | 114 | 197 | 924 | 7,189 | 1,721 | 5,131 | 337 |
| Rate per 100,000 inhabitants................... | | 363.1 | 2.9 | 33.2 | 57.5 | 269.5 | 2,096.6 | 501.9 | 1,496.4 | 98.3 |
| **Ocean City, NJ M.S.A.[2]**....................... | 94,713 | | | | | | | | | |
| Includes Cape May County[2] | | | | | | | | | | |
| City of Ocean City[2] | 11,296 | 10 | 0 | 2 | 4 | 4 | 475 | 64 | 409 | 2 |
| Total area actually reporting .................... | 100.0% | 218 | 1 | 21 | 51 | 145 | 3,115 | 590 | 2,470 | 55 |
| Rate per 100,000 inhabitants................... | | 230.2 | 1.1 | 22.2 | 53.8 | 153.1 | 3,288.9 | 622.9 | 2,607.9 | 58.1 |
| **Odessa, TX M.S.A.** .............................. | 158,766 | | | | | | | | | |
| Includes Ector County .............................. | | | | | | | | | | |
| City of Odessa ........................................ | 118,606 | 1,228 | 10 | 72 | 161 | 985 | 4,541 | 862 | 3,192 | 487 |
| Total area actually reporting .................... | 100.0% | 1,699 | 12 | 88 | 201 | 1,398 | 6,722 | 1,272 | 4,664 | 786 |
| Rate per 100,000 inhabitants................... | | 1,070.1 | 7.6 | 55.4 | 126.6 | 880.5 | 4,233.9 | 801.2 | 2,937.7 | 495.1 |
| **Ogden-Clearfield, UT M.S.A.[2, 3]**.......... | 642,719 | | | | | | | | | |
| Includes Box Elder, Davis, Morgan, and Weber Counties...................................... | | | | | | | | | | |
| City of Ogden........................................ | 84,642 | 388 | 4 | 112 | 85 | 187 | 3,747 | 522 | 2,923 | 302 |
| City of Clearfield.................................... | 30,557 | 41 | 1 | 10 | 8 | 22 | 584 | 100 | 455 | 29 |
| Total area actually reporting .................... | 95.3% | 956 | 15 | 322 | 154 | 465 | 12,983 | 1,921 | 10,208 | 854 |
| Estimated total...................................... | 100.0% | 1,013 | 15 | 335 | 164 | 499 | | | 10,812 | 935 |
| Rate per 100,000 inhabitants................... | | 157.6 | 2.3 | 52.1 | 25.5 | 77.6 | | | 1,682.2 | 145.5 |
| **Oklahoma City, OK M.S.A.**...................... | 1,358,166 | | | | | | | | | |
| Includes Canadian, Cleveland, Grady, Lincoln, Logan, McClain, and Oklahoma Counties........... | | | | | | | | | | |
| City of Oklahoma City.............................. | 630,621 | 4,828 | 73 | 480 | 1,192 | 3,083 | 24,948 | 5,823 | 16,228 | 2,897 |
| Total area actually reporting .................... | 99.9% | 6,274 | 93 | 712 | 1,455 | 4,014 | 41,484 | 9,534 | 27,807 | 4,143 |
| Estimated total...................................... | 100.0% | 6,275 | 93 | 712 | 1,455 | 4,015 | 41,504 | 9,538 | 27,821 | 4,145 |
| Rate per 100,000 inhabitants................... | | 462.0 | 6.8 | 52.4 | 107.1 | 295.6 | 3,055.9 | 702.3 | 2,048.4 | 305.2 |
| **Olympia-Tumwater, WA M.S.A.** ............. | 270,127 | | | | | | | | | |
| Includes Thurston County ......................... | | | | | | | | | | |
| City of Olympia....................................... | 49,875 | 203 | 0 | 26 | 46 | 131 | 2,309 | 406 | 1,692 | 211 |
| City of Tumwater..................................... | 19,193 | 70 | 0 | 9 | 11 | 50 | 789 | 126 | 605 | 58 |
| Total area actually reporting .................... | 100.0% | 655 | 3 | 101 | 118 | 433 | 7,841 | 1,752 | 5,432 | 657 |
| Rate per 100,000 inhabitants................... | | 242.5 | 1.1 | 37.4 | 43.7 | 160.3 | 2,902.7 | 648.6 | 2,010.9 | 243.2 |
| **Omaha-Council Bluffs, NE-IA M.S.A.[2]**.... | 914,414 | | | | | | | | | |
| Includes Harrison, Mills, and Pottawattamie Counties, IA and Cass, Douglas, Sarpy, Saunders,[2] and Washington Counties, NE ........................ | | | | | | | | | | |
| City of Omaha, NE.................................... | 452,252 | 2,329 | 48 | 174 | 655 | 1,452 | 16,261 | 2,160 | 11,558 | 2,543 |
| City of Council Bluffs, IA .......................... | 62,210 | 160 | 1 | 40 | 50 | 69 | 3,535 | 327 | 2,910 | 298 |
| Total area actually reporting .................... | 99.9% | 2,976 | 50 | 304 | 749 | 1,873 | 24,385 | 3,296 | 17,843 | 3,246 |
| Estimated total...................................... | 100.0% | 2,977 | 50 | 304 | 749 | 1,874 | 24,401 | 3,298 | 17,856 | 3,247 |
| Rate per 100,000 inhabitants................... | | 325.6 | 5.5 | 33.2 | 81.9 | 204.9 | 2,668.5 | 360.7 | 1,952.7 | 355.1 |
| **Orlando-Kissimmee-Sanford, FL M.S.A.** ............... | 2,381,954 | | | | | | | | | |
| Includes Lake, Orange, Osceola, and Seminole Counties...................................... | | | | | | | | | | |
| City of Orlando....................................... | 268,438 | 2,525 | 32 | 182 | 522 | 1,789 | 16,148 | 3,401 | 11,567 | 1,180 |
| City of Kissimmee ................................... | 68,583 | 450 | 5 | 33 | 96 | 316 | 2,647 | 605 | 1,907 | 135 |
| City of Sanford ....................................... | 58,514 | 481 | 4 | 41 | 111 | 325 | 2,649 | 551 | 1,939 | 159 |
| Total area actually reporting .................... | 99.9% | 12,609 | 121 | 1,178 | 2,627 | 8,683 | 73,907 | 17,332 | 51,596 | 4,979 |
| Estimated total...................................... | 100.0% | 12,618 | 121 | 1,179 | 2,629 | 8,689 | 73,979 | 17,344 | 51,651 | 4,984 |
| Rate per 100,000 inhabitants................... | | 529.7 | 5.1 | 49.5 | 110.4 | 364.8 | 3,105.8 | 728.1 | 2,168.4 | 209.2 |
| **Oshkosh-Neenah, WI M.S.A.** ................. | 170,034 | | | | | | | | | |
| Includes Winnebago County ...................... | | | | | | | | | | |
| City of Oshkosh...................................... | 66,766 | 157 | 1 | 6 | 30 | 120 | 1,490 | 257 | 1,188 | 45 |
| City of Neenah........................................ | 25,946 | 47 | 0 | 5 | 3 | 39 | 501 | 64 | 423 | 14 |
| Total area actually reporting .................... | 100.0% | 302 | 4 | 29 | 41 | 228 | 2,863 | 481 | 2,287 | 95 |
| Rate per 100,000 inhabitants................... | | 177.6 | 2.4 | 17.1 | 24.1 | 134.1 | 1,683.8 | 282.9 | 1,345.0 | 55.9 |

# Table 6. Crime, by Selected Metropolitan Statistical Area, 2015—*Continued*

(Number, percent, rate per 100,000 population.)

| Area | Population | Violent crime | Murder and nonnegligent manslaughter | Rape[1] | Robbery | Aggravated assault | Property crime | Burglary | Larceny-theft | Motor vehicle theft |
|---|---|---|---|---|---|---|---|---|---|---|
| **Owensboro, KY M.S.A.** .............................................. | 116,809 | | | | | | | | | |
| Includes Daviess, Hancock, and McLean Counties ...... | | | | | | | | | | |
| City of Owensboro.................................................. | 58,608 | 130 | 0 | 38 | 50 | 42 | 2,178 | 319 | 1,749 | 110 |
| Total area actually reporting .................................. | 100.0% | 159 | 0 | 44 | 52 | 63 | 2,631 | 453 | 2,041 | 137 |
| Rate per 100,000 inhabitants................................. | | 136.1 | 0.0 | 37.7 | 44.5 | 53.9 | 2,252.4 | 387.8 | 1,747.3 | 117.3 |
| **Oxnard-Thousand Oaks-Ventura, CA M.S.A.** ........ | 850,712 | | | | | | | | | |
| Includes Ventura County .......................................... | | | | | | | | | | |
| City of Oxnard........................................................ | 207,221 | 920 | 12 | 21 | 385 | 502 | 6,696 | 1,103 | 4,758 | 835 |
| City of Thousand Oaks............................................ | 129,976 | 136 | 0 | 26 | 23 | 87 | 1,577 | 234 | 1,241 | 102 |
| City of Ventura........................................................ | 110,077 | 374 | 2 | 53 | 124 | 195 | 3,900 | 598 | 3,042 | 260 |
| City of Camarillo..................................................... | 67,325 | 114 | 2 | 16 | 30 | 66 | 1,116 | 217 | 840 | 59 |
| Total area actually reporting .................................. | 100.0% | 2,175 | 24 | 208 | 679 | 1,264 | 17,253 | 3,004 | 12,596 | 1,653 |
| Rate per 100,000 inhabitants................................. | | 255.7 | 2.8 | 24.5 | 79.8 | 148.6 | 2,028.1 | 353.1 | 1,480.6 | 194.3 |
| **Palm Bay-Melbourne-Titusville, FL M.S.A.** | 563,089 | | | | | | | | | |
| Includes Brevard County........................................... | | | | | | | | | | |
| City of Palm Bay..................................................... | 106,469 | 508 | 4 | 51 | 62 | 391 | 2,060 | 441 | 1,483 | 136 |
| City of Melbourne................................................... | 79,032 | 718 | 5 | 62 | 134 | 517 | 3,150 | 512 | 2,488 | 150 |
| City of Titusville..................................................... | 44,752 | 405 | 7 | 46 | 67 | 285 | 1,668 | 385 | 1,096 | 187 |
| Total area actually reporting .................................. | 100.0% | 2,988 | 24 | 338 | 449 | 2,177 | 14,956 | 2,855 | 11,131 | 970 |
| Rate per 100,000 inhabitants................................. | | 530.6 | 4.3 | 60.0 | 79.7 | 386.6 | 2,656.1 | 507.0 | 1,976.8 | 172.3 |
| **Panama City, FL M.S.A.** ......................................... | 198,511 | | | | | | | | | |
| Includes Bay and Gulf Counties................................ | | | | | | | | | | |
| City of Panama City ................................................ | 38,217 | 345 | 2 | 8 | 86 | 249 | 2,339 | 355 | 1,846 | 138 |
| Total area actually reporting .................................. | 100.0% | 1,029 | 10 | 81 | 162 | 776 | 7,160 | 1,309 | 5,466 | 385 |
| Rate per 100,000 inhabitants................................. | | 518.4 | 5.0 | 40.8 | 81.6 | 390.9 | 3,606.9 | 659.4 | 2,753.5 | 193.9 |
| **Parkersburg-Vienna, WV M.S.A.** ......................... | 91,653 | | | | | | | | | |
| Includes Wirt and Wood Counties............................ | | | | | | | | | | |
| City of Parkersburg ................................................. | 30,885 | 71 | 2 | 13 | 10 | 46 | 1,060 | 320 | 676 | 64 |
| City of Vienna......................................................... | 10,515 | 6 | 0 | 0 | 0 | 6 | 207 | 69 | 138 | 0 |
| Total area actually reporting .................................. | 100.0% | 147 | 3 | 29 | 11 | 104 | 1,744 | 541 | 1,110 | 93 |
| Rate per 100,000 inhabitants................................. | | 160.4 | 3.3 | 31.6 | 12.0 | 113.5 | 1,902.8 | 590.3 | 1,211.1 | 101.5 |
| **Pensacola-Ferry Pass-Brent, FL M.S.A.** ................... | 482,571 | | | | | | | | | |
| Includes Escambia and Santa Rosa Counties............... | | | | | | | | | | |
| City of Pensacola.................................................... | 53,331 | 382 | 4 | 26 | 85 | 267 | 2,415 | 423 | 1,873 | 119 |
| Total area actually reporting .................................. | 100.0% | 2,445 | 28 | 237 | 431 | 1,749 | 14,194 | 3,040 | 10,417 | 737 |
| Rate per 100,000 inhabitants................................. | | 506.7 | 5.8 | 49.1 | 89.3 | 362.4 | 2,941.3 | 630.0 | 2,158.6 | 152.7 |
| **Peoria, IL M.S.A.** .................................................. | 379,402 | | | | | | | | | |
| Includes Marshall, Peoria, Stark, Tazewell, and | | | | | | | | | | |
| Woodford Counties .................................................. | | | | | | | | | | |
| City of Peoria.......................................................... | 116,066 | 772 | 14 | 64 | 310 | 384 | 4,448 | 1,084 | 3,224 | 140 |
| Total area actually reporting .................................. | 95.0% | 1,323 | 17 | 165 | 346 | 795 | 8,112 | 1,836 | 6,017 | 259 |
| Estimated total........................................................ | 100.0% | 1,359 | 17 | 170 | 355 | 817 | 8,433 | 1,886 | 6,274 | 273 |
| Rate per 100,000 inhabitants................................. | | 358.2 | 4.5 | 44.8 | 93.6 | 215.3 | 2,222.7 | 497.1 | 1,653.7 | 72.0 |
| **Philadelphia-Camden-Wilmington, PA-NJ-DE-MD M.S.A.**[2] ................................................................... | 6,068,228 | | | | | | | | | |
| Includes the Metropolitan Divisions of Camden, NJ; Montgomery County-Bucks County-Chester County, PA; Philadelphia, PA; and Wilmington, DE-MD-NJ....... | | | | | | | | | | |
| City of Philadelphia, PA .......................................... | 1,567,810 | 16,132 | 280 | 1,322 | 6,765 | 7,765 | 49,345 | 8,083 | 36,228 | 5,034 |
| City of Wilmington, DE ........................................... | 72,078 | 1,231 | 27 | 47 | 424 | 733 | 3,203 | 690 | 2,174 | 339 |
| Total area actually reporting .................................. | 99.9% | 27,896 | 450 | 2,134 | 10,504 | 14,808 | 133,184 | 21,957 | 102,378 | 8,849 |
| Estimated total........................................................ | 100.0% | 27,903 | 450 | 2,134 | 10,506 | 14,813 | 133,244 | 21,965 | 102,428 | 8,851 |
| Rate per 100,000 inhabitants................................. | | 459.8 | 7.4 | 35.2 | 173.1 | 244.1 | 2,195.8 | 362.0 | 1,687.9 | 145.9 |
| Camden, NJ M.D.[2] | 1,249,764 | | | | | | | | | |
| Includes Burlington, Camden, and Gloucester Counties[2]............................................................... | | | | | | | | | | |
| Total area actually reporting .................................. | 100.0% | 3,399 | 45 | 228 | 1,173 | 1,953 | 25,277 | 5,332 | 18,788 | 1,157 |
| Rate per 100,000 inhabitants................................. | | 272.0 | 3.6 | 18.2 | 93.9 | 156.3 | 2,022.5 | 426.6 | 1,503.3 | 92.6 |
| Montgomery County-Bucks County-Chester County, PA M.D. | 1,963,276 | | | | | | | | | |
| Includes Bucks, Chester, and Montgomery Counties... | | | | | | | | | | |
| Total area actually reporting .................................. | 99.9% | 2,513 | 30 | 257 | 726 | 1,500 | 28,390 | 3,431 | 23,925 | 1,034 |
| Estimated total........................................................ | 100.0% | 2,516 | 30 | 257 | 727 | 1,502 | 28,413 | 3,434 | 23,944 | 1,035 |

# Table 6. Crime, by Selected Metropolitan Statistical Area, 2015—*Continued*

(Number, percent, rate per 100,000 population.)

| Area | Population | Violent crime | Murder and nonnegligent manslaughter | Rape[1] | Robbery | Aggravated assault | Property crime | Burglary | Larceny-theft | Motor vehicle theft |
|---|---|---|---|---|---|---|---|---|---|---|
| Rate per 100,000 inhabitants................................... | | 128.2 | 1.5 | 13.1 | 37.0 | 76.5 | 1,447.2 | 174.9 | 1,219.6 | 52.7 |
| Philadelphia, PA M.D.................................. | 2,131,568 | | | | | | | | | |
| Includes Delaware and Philadelphia Counties............ | | | | | | | | | | |
| Total area actually reporting .............................. | 99.9% | 18,351 | 316 | 1,417 | 7,500 | 9,118 | 60,223 | 9,597 | 45,013 | 5,613 |
| Estimated total.................................................. | 100.0% | 18,355 | 316 | 1,417 | 7,501 | 9,121 | 60,260 | 9,602 | 45,044 | 5,614 |
| Rate per 100,000 inhabitants.............................. | | 861.1 | 14.8 | 66.5 | 351.9 | 427.9 | 2,827.0 | 450.5 | 2,113.2 | 263.4 |
| Wilmington, DE-MD-NJ M.D.[2]...................... | 723,620 | | | | | | | | | |
| Includes New Castle County, DE; Cecil County, MD; and Salem County, NJ[2] | | | | | | | | | | |
| Total area actually reporting .............................. | 100.0% | 3,633 | 59 | 232 | 1,105 | 2,237 | 19,294 | 3,597 | 14,652 | 1,045 |
| Rate per 100,000 inhabitants.............................. | | 502.1 | 8.2 | 32.1 | 152.7 | 309.1 | 2,666.3 | 497.1 | 2,024.8 | 144.4 |
| **Phoenix-Mesa-Scottsdale, AZ M.S.A.....................** | 4,571,032 | | | | | | | | | |
| Includes Maricopa and Pinal Counties ...................... | | | | | | | | | | |
| City of Phoenix ................................................ | 1,559,744 | 9,261 | 112 | 1,016 | 3,020 | 5,113 | 54,456 | 12,798 | 34,288 | 7,370 |
| City of Mesa ..................................................... | 471,034 | 1,972 | 16 | 241 | 408 | 1,307 | 11,905 | 2,219 | 8,861 | 825 |
| City of Scottsdale............................................. | 233,872 | 434 | 6 | 106 | 100 | 222 | 5,332 | 829 | 4,311 | 192 |
| City of Tempe ................................................... | 175,556 | 721 | 7 | 101 | 183 | 430 | 7,642 | 1,108 | 6,175 | 359 |
| Total area actually reporting .............................. | 99.9% | 17,748 | 205 | 1,966 | 4,731 | 10,846 | 129,014 | 26,116 | 90,636 | 12,262 |
| Estimated total.................................................. | 100.0% | 17,756 | 205 | 1,967 | 4,733 | 10,851 | 129,095 | 26,129 | 90,699 | 12,267 |
| Rate per 100,000 inhabitants.............................. | | 388.4 | 4.5 | 43.0 | 103.5 | 237.4 | 2,824.2 | 571.6 | 1,984.2 | 268.4 |
| **Pine Bluff, AR M.S.A ...........................................** | 93,426 | | | | | | | | | |
| Includes Cleveland, Jefferson, and Lincoln Counties ... | | | | | | | | | | |
| City of Pine Bluff .............................................. | 44,466 | 569 | 10 | 32 | 104 | 423 | 2,767 | 921 | 1,679 | 167 |
| Total area actually reporting .............................. | 100.0% | 695 | 12 | 50 | 109 | 524 | 3,539 | 1,176 | 2,147 | 216 |
| Rate per 100,000 inhabitants.............................. | | 743.9 | 12.8 | 53.5 | 116.7 | 560.9 | 3,788.0 | 1,258.8 | 2,298.1 | 231.2 |
| **Pittsburgh, PA M.S.A...........................................** | 2,355,032 | | | | | | | | | |
| Includes Allegheny, Armstrong, Beaver, Butler, Fayette, Washington, and Westmoreland Counties ................ | | | | | | | | | | |
| City of Pittsburgh ............................................. | 306,870 | 2,167 | 57 | 82 | 858 | 1,170 | 9,895 | 2,197 | 7,097 | 601 |
| Total area actually reporting .............................. | 98.5% | 6,210 | 109 | 409 | 1,783 | 3,909 | 41,434 | 7,500 | 32,249 | 1,685 |
| Estimated total.................................................. | 100.0% | 6,271 | 110 | 414 | 1,799 | 3,948 | 41,988 | 7,573 | 32,712 | 1,703 |
| Rate per 100,000 inhabitants.............................. | | 266.3 | 4.7 | 17.6 | 76.4 | 167.6 | 1,782.9 | 321.6 | 1,389.0 | 72.3 |
| **Pittsfield, MA M.S.A............................................** | 128,122 | | | | | | | | | |
| Includes Berkshire County ..................................... | | | | | | | | | | |
| City of Pittsfield .............................................. | 43,450 | 284 | 4 | 38 | 34 | 208 | 1,270 | 414 | 807 | 49 |
| Total area actually reporting .............................. | 89.5% | 546 | 4 | 67 | 48 | 427 | 2,362 | 690 | 1,589 | 83 |
| Estimated total.................................................. | 100.0% | 589 | 4 | 71 | 55 | 459 | 2,567 | 729 | 1,741 | 97 |
| Rate per 100,000 inhabitants.............................. | | 459.7 | 3.1 | 55.4 | 42.9 | 358.3 | 2,003.6 | 569.0 | 1,358.9 | 75.7 |
| **Pocatello, ID M.S.A.............................................** | 83,624 | | | | | | | | | |
| Includes Bannock County ...................................... | | | | | | | | | | |
| City of Pocatello .............................................. | 54,272 | 197 | 1 | 21 | 6 | 169 | 1,630 | 344 | 1,183 | 103 |
| Total area actually reporting .............................. | 100.0% | 221 | 1 | 26 | 7 | 187 | 2,229 | 389 | 1,716 | 124 |
| Rate per 100,000 inhabitants.............................. | | 264.3 | 1.2 | 31.1 | 8.4 | 223.6 | 2,665.5 | 465.2 | 2,052.0 | 148.3 |
| **Portland-South Portland, ME M.S.A. ....................** | 525,427 | | | | | | | | | |
| Includes Cumberland, Sagadahoc, and York Counties | | | | | | | | | | |
| City of Portland................................................ | 66,816 | 215 | 2 | 33 | 99 | 81 | 2,022 | 266 | 1,687 | 69 |
| City of South Portland....................................... | 25,540 | 24 | 0 | 9 | 4 | 11 | 602 | 57 | 528 | 17 |
| Total area actually reporting .............................. | 100.0% | 707 | 4 | 128 | 187 | 388 | 9,635 | 1,712 | 7,608 | 315 |
| Rate per 100,000 inhabitants.............................. | | 134.6 | 0.8 | 24.4 | 35.6 | 73.8 | 1,833.7 | 325.8 | 1,448.0 | 60.0 |
| **Port St. Lucie, FL M.S.A. ......................................** | 451,710 | | | | | | | | | |
| Includes Martin and St. Lucie Counties...................... | | | | | | | | | | |
| City of Port St. Lucie ......................................... | 176,364 | 260 | 2 | 18 | 29 | 211 | 2,406 | 392 | 1,929 | 85 |
| Total area actually reporting .............................. | 100.0% | 1,293 | 14 | 129 | 245 | 905 | 8,315 | 1,531 | 6,385 | 399 |
| Rate per 100,000 inhabitants.............................. | | 286.2 | 3.1 | 28.6 | 54.2 | 200.3 | 1,840.8 | 338.9 | 1,413.5 | 88.3 |
| **Prescott, AZ M.S.A. .............................................** | 221,418 | | | | | | | | | |
| Includes Yavapai County ....................................... | | | | | | | | | | |
| City of Prescott ................................................ | 41,393 | 137 | 4 | 11 | 13 | 109 | 1,061 | 140 | 884 | 37 |
| Total area actually reporting .............................. | 100.0% | 651 | 9 | 57 | 27 | 558 | 4,508 | 796 | 3,460 | 252 |
| Rate per 100,000 inhabitants.............................. | | 294.0 | 4.1 | 25.7 | 12.2 | 252.0 | 2,036.0 | 359.5 | 1,562.7 | 113.8 |

# Table 6. Crime, by Selected Metropolitan Statistical Area, 2015—*Continued*

(Number, percent, rate per 100,000 population.)

| Area | Population | Violent crime | Murder and nonnegligent manslaughter | Rape[1] | Robbery | Aggravated assault | Property crime | Burglary | Larceny-theft | Motor vehicle theft |
|---|---|---|---|---|---|---|---|---|---|---|
| **Providence-Warwick, RI-MA M.S.A.** | 1,611,989 | | | | | | | | | |
| Includes Bristol County, MA and Bristol, Kent, Newport, Providence, and Washington Counties RI | | | | | | | | | | |
| City of Providence, RI | 179,522 | 1,018 | 15 | 109 | 282 | 612 | 6,084 | 1,282 | 4,256 | 546 |
| City of Warwick, RI | 81,854 | 66 | 2 | 21 | 11 | 32 | 1,568 | 174 | 1,327 | 67 |
| Total area actually reporting | 100.0% | 5,380 | 35 | 630 | 1,052 | 3,663 | 30,254 | 6,211 | 21,989 | 2,054 |
| Rate per 100,000 inhabitants | | 333.7 | 2.2 | 39.1 | 65.3 | 227.2 | 1,876.8 | 385.3 | 1,364.1 | 127.4 |
| **Provo-Orem, UT M.S.A.** | 584,130 | | | | | | | | | |
| Includes Juab and Utah Counties | | | | | | | | | | |
| City of Provo | 115,294 | 153 | 0 | 60 | 16 | 77 | 2,351 | 245 | 1,959 | 147 |
| City of Orem | 92,577 | 40 | 1 | 8 | 14 | 17 | 2,103 | 196 | 1,784 | 123 |
| Total area actually reporting | 100.0% | 419 | 2 | 147 | 46 | 224 | 9,063 | 1,099 | 7,450 | 514 |
| Rate per 100,000 inhabitants | | 71.7 | 0.3 | 25.2 | 7.9 | 38.3 | 1,551.5 | 188.1 | 1,275.4 | 88.0 |
| **Pueblo, CO M.S.A.** | 163,063 | | | | | | | | | |
| Includes Pueblo County | | | | | | | | | | |
| City of Pueblo | 108,810 | 986 | 12 | 170 | 186 | 618 | 7,274 | 2,060 | 4,318 | 896 |
| Total area actually reporting | 100.0% | 1,004 | 13 | 171 | 187 | 633 | 8,464 | 2,270 | 5,177 | 1,017 |
| Rate per 100,000 inhabitants | | 615.7 | 8.0 | 104.9 | 114.7 | 388.2 | 5,190.6 | 1,392.1 | 3,174.8 | 623.7 |
| **Punta Gorda, FL M.S.A.** | 171,584 | | | | | | | | | |
| Includes Charlotte County | | | | | | | | | | |
| City of Punta Gorda | 17,841 | 22 | 1 | 1 | 5 | 15 | 230 | 16 | 200 | 14 |
| Total area actually reporting | 100.0% | 347 | 1 | 31 | 30 | 285 | 2,590 | 416 | 2,064 | 110 |
| Rate per 100,000 inhabitants | | 202.2 | 0.6 | 18.1 | 17.5 | 166.1 | 1,509.5 | 242.4 | 1,202.9 | 64.1 |
| **Racine, WI M.S.A.** | 194,966 | | | | | | | | | |
| Includes Racine County | | | | | | | | | | |
| City of Racine | 77,887 | 364 | 4 | 16 | 154 | 190 | 2,398 | 774 | 1,528 | 96 |
| Total area actually reporting | 100.0% | 452 | 4 | 36 | 176 | 236 | 3,993 | 999 | 2,859 | 135 |
| Rate per 100,000 inhabitants | | 231.8 | 2.1 | 18.5 | 90.3 | 121.0 | 2,048.0 | 512.4 | 1,466.4 | 69.2 |
| **Rapid City, SD M.S.A.** | 145,125 | | | | | | | | | |
| Includes Custer, Meade, and Pennington Counties | | | | | | | | | | |
| City of Rapid City | 73,801 | 495 | 7 | 92 | 68 | 328 | 2,869 | 451 | 2,191 | 227 |
| Total area actually reporting | 100.0% | 690 | 9 | 152 | 73 | 456 | 3,765 | 647 | 2,828 | 290 |
| Rate per 100,000 inhabitants | | 475.5 | 6.2 | 104.7 | 50.3 | 314.2 | 2,594.3 | 445.8 | 1,948.7 | 199.8 |
| **Reading, PA M.S.A.** | 413,999 | | | | | | | | | |
| Includes Berks County | | | | | | | | | | |
| City of Reading | 87,744 | 700 | 13 | 37 | 291 | 359 | 2,551 | 728 | 1,572 | 251 |
| Total area actually reporting | 99.8% | 1,279 | 15 | 94 | 354 | 816 | 6,947 | 1,445 | 5,087 | 415 |
| Estimated total | 100.0% | 1,280 | 15 | 94 | 354 | 817 | 6,962 | 1,447 | 5,100 | 415 |
| Rate per 100,000 inhabitants | | 309.2 | 3.6 | 22.7 | 85.5 | 197.3 | 1,681.6 | 349.5 | 1,231.9 | 100.2 |
| **Redding, CA M.S.A.** | 180,279 | | | | | | | | | |
| Includes Shasta County | | | | | | | | | | |
| City of Redding | 92,020 | 614 | 2 | 50 | 145 | 417 | 4,169 | 769 | 2,888 | 512 |
| Total area actually reporting | 100.0% | 1,400 | 5 | 123 | 181 | 1,091 | 5,851 | 1,252 | 3,780 | 819 |
| Rate per 100,000 inhabitants | | 776.6 | 2.8 | 68.2 | 100.4 | 605.2 | 3,245.5 | 694.5 | 2,096.8 | 454.3 |
| **Reno, NV M.S.A.** | 451,184 | | | | | | | | | |
| Includes Storey and Washoe Counties | | | | | | | | | | |
| City of Reno | 239,721 | 1,419 | 15 | 136 | 345 | 923 | 7,531 | 1,440 | 5,070 | 1,021 |
| Total area actually reporting | 100.0% | 2,020 | 20 | 226 | 458 | 1,316 | 11,696 | 2,404 | 7,891 | 1,401 |
| Rate per 100,000 inhabitants | | 447.7 | 4.4 | 50.1 | 101.5 | 291.7 | 2,592.3 | 532.8 | 1,749.0 | 310.5 |
| **Richmond, VA M.S.A.** | 1,269,543 | | | | | | | | | |
| Includes Amelia, Caroline, Charles City, Chesterfield, Dinwiddie, Goochland, Hanover, Henrico, King William, New Kent, Powhatan, Prince George, and Sussex Counties and Colonial Heights, Hopewell, Petersburg, and Richmond Cities | | | | | | | | | | |
| City of Richmond | 220,802 | 1,139 | 43 | 60 | 489 | 547 | 8,648 | 1,605 | 6,171 | 872 |
| Total area actually reporting | 100.0% | 3,003 | 95 | 320 | 985 | 1,603 | 29,856 | 4,916 | 23,146 | 1,794 |
| Rate per 100,000 inhabitants | | 236.5 | 7.5 | 25.2 | 77.6 | 126.3 | 2,351.7 | 387.2 | 1,823.2 | 141.3 |

## Table 6. Crime, by Selected Metropolitan Statistical Area, 2015—*Continued*

(Number, percent, rate per 100,000 population.)

| Area | Population | Violent crime | Murder and nonnegligent manslaughter | Rape[1] | Robbery | Aggravated assault | Property crime | Burglary | Larceny-theft | Motor vehicle theft |
|---|---|---|---|---|---|---|---|---|---|---|
| **Riverside-San Bernardino-Ontario, CA M.S.A.** | 4,488,836 | | | | | | | | | |
| Includes Riverside and San Bernardino Counties | | | | | | | | | | |
| City of Riverside | 323,064 | 1,441 | 10 | 137 | 520 | 774 | 10,531 | 1,633 | 7,144 | 1,754 |
| City of San Bernardino | 216,477 | 2,697 | 44 | 98 | 968 | 1,587 | 10,390 | 3,164 | 4,210 | 3,016 |
| City of Ontario | 170,274 | 547 | 3 | 31 | 217 | 296 | 5,169 | 897 | 3,206 | 1,066 |
| City of Corona | 163,633 | 212 | 5 | 30 | 98 | 79 | 3,727 | 615 | 2,646 | 466 |
| City of Victorville | 123,332 | 777 | 6 | 49 | 229 | 493 | 4,008 | 1,095 | 2,285 | 628 |
| City of Temecula | 111,673 | 114 | 1 | 8 | 47 | 58 | 2,917 | 459 | 2,116 | 342 |
| City of Chino | 86,344 | 221 | 0 | 21 | 53 | 147 | 2,138 | 375 | 1,501 | 262 |
| City of Redlands | 71,078 | 212 | 2 | 34 | 74 | 102 | 3,211 | 514 | 2,264 | 433 |
| Total area actually reporting | 100.0% | 16,967 | 196 | 1,097 | 5,076 | 10,598 | 125,208 | 28,023 | 74,268 | 22,917 |
| Rate per 100,000 inhabitants | | 378.0 | 4.4 | 24.4 | 113.1 | 236.1 | 2,789.3 | 624.3 | 1,654.5 | 510.5 |
| **Roanoke, VA M.S.A.** | 313,720 | | | | | | | | | |
| Includes Botetourt, Craig, Franklin, and Roanoke Counties and Roanoke and Salem Cities | | | | | | | | | | |
| City of Roanoke | 99,827 | 337 | 11 | 37 | 67 | 222 | 3,816 | 464 | 3,163 | 189 |
| Total area actually reporting | 100.0% | 671 | 20 | 104 | 89 | 458 | 6,678 | 841 | 5,522 | 315 |
| Rate per 100,000 inhabitants | | 213.9 | 6.4 | 33.2 | 28.4 | 146.0 | 2,128.6 | 268.1 | 1,760.2 | 100.4 |
| **Rochester, MN M.S.A.** | 214,015 | | | | | | | | | |
| Includes Dodge, Fillmore, Olmsted, and Wabasha Counties | | | | | | | | | | |
| City of Rochester | 112,542 | 198 | 1 | 47 | 50 | 100 | 2,546 | 468 | 1,987 | 91 |
| Total area actually reporting | 100.0% | 273 | 1 | 62 | 55 | 155 | 3,241 | 659 | 2,444 | 138 |
| Rate per 100,000 inhabitants | | 127.6 | 0.5 | 29.0 | 25.7 | 72.4 | 1,514.4 | 307.9 | 1,142.0 | 64.5 |
| **Rochester, NY M.S.A.** | 1,082,109 | | | | | | | | | |
| Includes Livingston, Monroe, Ontario, Orleans, Wayne, and Yates Counties | | | | | | | | | | |
| City of Rochester | 209,922 | 1,839 | 33 | 148 | 640 | 1,018 | 8,266 | 1,753 | 5,779 | 734 |
| Total area actually reporting | 99.6% | 3,030 | 41 | 479 | 886 | 1,624 | 22,743 | 4,194 | 17,362 | 1,187 |
| Estimated total | 100.0% | 3,037 | 41 | 480 | 888 | 1,628 | 22,806 | 4,202 | 17,415 | 1,189 |
| Rate per 100,000 inhabitants | | 280.7 | 3.8 | 44.4 | 82.1 | 150.4 | 2,107.6 | 388.3 | 1,609.4 | 109.9 |
| **Rockford, IL M.S.A.** | 339,889 | | | | | | | | | |
| Includes Boone and Winnebago Counties | | | | | | | | | | |
| City of Rockford | 148,176 | 2,349 | 19 | 148 | 504 | 1,678 | 5,856 | 1,440 | 3,928 | 488 |
| Total area actually reporting | 84.4% | 2,694 | 22 | 198 | 563 | 1,911 | 8,277 | 1,962 | 5,697 | 618 |
| Estimated total | 100.0% | 2,783 | 23 | 214 | 581 | 1,965 | 9,010 | 2,126 | 6,234 | 650 |
| Rate per 100,000 inhabitants | | 818.8 | 6.8 | 63.0 | 170.9 | 578.1 | 2,650.9 | 625.5 | 1,834.1 | 191.2 |
| **Rocky Mount, NC M.S.A.** | 148,469 | | | | | | | | | |
| Includes Edgecombe and Nash Counties | | | | | | | | | | |
| City of Rocky Mount | 55,978 | 442 | 12 | 14 | 106 | 310 | 2,326 | 640 | 1,610 | 76 |
| Total area actually reporting | 93.5% | 604 | 20 | 27 | 134 | 423 | 3,737 | 1,215 | 2,384 | 138 |
| Estimated total | 100.0% | 628 | 20 | 29 | 140 | 439 | 4,020 | 1,273 | 2,599 | 148 |
| Rate per 100,000 inhabitants | | 423.0 | 13.5 | 19.5 | 94.3 | 295.7 | 2,707.6 | 857.4 | 1,750.5 | 99.7 |
| **Rome, GA M.S.A.** | 96,139 | | | | | | | | | |
| Includes Floyd County | | | | | | | | | | |
| City of Rome | 35,921 | 210 | 4 | 18 | 49 | 139 | 1,775 | 267 | 1,410 | 98 |
| Total area actually reporting | 100.0% | 337 | 11 | 37 | 74 | 215 | 3,128 | 624 | 2,303 | 201 |
| Rate per 100,000 inhabitants | | 350.5 | 11.4 | 38.5 | 77.0 | 223.6 | 3,253.6 | 649.1 | 2,395.5 | 209.1 |
| **Sacramento–Roseville–Arden-Arcade, CA M.S.A.** | 2,265,532 | | | | | | | | | |
| Includes El Dorado, Placer, Sacramento, and Yolo Counties | | | | | | | | | | |
| City of Sacramento | 489,717 | 3,611 | 43 | 105 | 1,174 | 2,289 | 16,501 | 3,713 | 9,865 | 2,923 |
| City of Roseville | 131,039 | 239 | 0 | 23 | 84 | 132 | 3,295 | 521 | 2,469 | 305 |
| City of Folsom | 76,183 | 71 | 1 | 15 | 15 | 40 | 1,185 | 210 | 899 | 76 |
| Total area actually reporting | 100.0% | 10,081 | 111 | 584 | 2,960 | 6,426 | 58,446 | 12,230 | 37,695 | 8,521 |
| Rate per 100,000 inhabitants | | 445.0 | 4.9 | 25.8 | 130.7 | 283.6 | 2,579.8 | 539.8 | 1,663.8 | 376.1 |
| **Saginaw, MI M.S.A.** | 193,878 | | | | | | | | | |
| Includes Saginaw County | | | | | | | | | | |
| City of Saginaw | 49,459 | 692 | 7 | 58 | 87 | 540 | 1,090 | 460 | 553 | 77 |
| Total area actually reporting | 100.0% | 1,172 | 8 | 162 | 138 | 864 | 3,826 | 1,057 | 2,569 | 200 |
| Rate per 100,000 inhabitants | | 604.5 | 4.1 | 83.6 | 71.2 | 445.6 | 1,973.4 | 545.2 | 1,325.1 | 103.2 |

# Table 6. Crime, by Selected Metropolitan Statistical Area, 2015—*Continued*

(Number, percent, rate per 100,000 population.)

| Area | Population | Violent crime | Murder and nonnegligent manslaughter | Rape[1] | Robbery | Aggravated assault | Property crime | Burglary | Larceny-theft | Motor vehicle theft |
|------|-----------|--------------|-------------------------------------|---------|---------|-------------------|---------------|----------|--------------|---------------------|
| **Salem, OR M.S.A.** ........................... | 409,703 | | | | | | | | | |
| Includes Marion and Polk Counties ........................... | | | | | | | | | | |
| City of Salem ........................... | 163,320 | 537 | 5 | 44 | 127 | 361 | 6,667 | 734 | 5,222 | 711 |
| Total area actually reporting ........................... | 100.0% | 985 | 7 | 93 | 176 | 709 | 12,084 | 1,641 | 9,175 | 1,268 |
| Rate per 100,000 inhabitants........................... | | 240.4 | 1.7 | 22.7 | 43.0 | 173.1 | 2,949.5 | 400.5 | 2,239.4 | 309.5 |
| | | | | | | | | | | |
| **Salinas, CA M.S.A.** ........................... | 434,790 | | | | | | | | | |
| Includes Monterey County ........................... | | | | | | | | | | |
| City of Salinas ........................... | 158,185 | 1,098 | 40 | 76 | 369 | 613 | 4,145 | 679 | 1,534 | 1,932 |
| Total area actually reporting ........................... | 100.0% | 1,927 | 60 | 160 | 557 | 1,150 | 9,535 | 1,812 | 4,892 | 2,831 |
| Rate per 100,000 inhabitants........................... | | 443.2 | 13.8 | 36.8 | 128.1 | 264.5 | 2,193.0 | 416.8 | 1,125.1 | 651.1 |
| | | | | | | | | | | |
| **Salisbury, MD-DE M.S.A.** ........................... | 393,552 | | | | | | | | | |
| Includes Sussex County, DE and Somerset, Wicomico, and Worcester Counties, MD ........................... | | | | | | | | | | |
| City of Salisbury, MD ........................... | 33,125 | 311 | 3 | 23 | 105 | 180 | 1,802 | 262 | 1,493 | 47 |
| Total area actually reporting ........................... | 100.0% | 1,529 | 13 | 153 | 305 | 1,058 | 11,298 | 2,586 | 8,421 | 291 |
| Rate per 100,000 inhabitants........................... | | 388.5 | 3.3 | 38.9 | 77.5 | 268.8 | 2,870.8 | 657.1 | 2,139.7 | 73.9 |
| | | | | | | | | | | |
| **Salt Lake City, UT M.S.A.** ........................... | 1,172,884 | | | | | | | | | |
| Includes Salt Lake and Tooele Counties ........................... | | | | | | | | | | |
| City of Salt Lake City ........................... | 191,992 | 1,642 | 8 | 291 | 469 | 874 | 17,914 | 2,036 | 13,679 | 2,199 |
| Total area actually reporting ........................... | 99.9% | 4,600 | 31 | 840 | 1,073 | 2,656 | | | 41,921 | 6,628 |
| Estimated total........................... | 100.0% | 4,600 | 31 | 840 | 1,073 | 2,656 | | | 41,929 | 6,629 |
| Rate per 100,000 inhabitants........................... | | 392.2 | 2.6 | 71.6 | 91.5 | 226.5 | | | 3,574.9 | 565.2 |
| | | | | | | | | | | |
| **San Angelo, TX M.S.A.** ........................... | 119,966 | | | | | | | | | |
| Includes Irion and Tom Green Counties ........................... | | | | | | | | | | |
| City of San Angelo........................... | 100,356 | 354 | 3 | 56 | 30 | 265 | 4,089 | 737 | 3,101 | 251 |
| Total area actually reporting ........................... | 100.0% | 395 | 4 | 81 | 30 | 280 | 4,499 | 877 | 3,340 | 282 |
| Rate per 100,000 inhabitants........................... | | 329.3 | 3.3 | 67.5 | 25.0 | 233.4 | 3,750.2 | 731.0 | 2,784.1 | 235.1 |
| | | | | | | | | | | |
| **San Antonio-New Braunfels, TX M.S.A.** ........... | 2,379,984 | | | | | | | | | |
| Includes Atascosa, Bandera, Bexar, Comal, Guadalupe, Kendall, Medina, and Wilson Counties ........................... | | | | | | | | | | |
| City of San Antonio........................... | 1,463,586 | 8,594 | 94 | 1,049 | 1,986 | 5,465 | 73,611 | 11,632 | 55,803 | 6,176 |
| City of New Braunfels ........................... | 68,641 | 175 | 2 | 21 | 31 | 121 | 2,058 | 270 | 1,624 | 164 |
| Total area actually reporting ........................... | 99.9% | 10,395 | 128 | 1,405 | 2,241 | 6,621 | 94,042 | 15,640 | 70,970 | 7,432 |
| Estimated total........................... | 100.0% | 10,398 | 128 | 1,405 | 2,242 | 6,623 | 94,072 | 15,645 | 70,993 | 7,434 |
| Rate per 100,000 inhabitants........................... | | 436.9 | 5.4 | 59.0 | 94.2 | 278.3 | 3,952.6 | 657.4 | 2,982.9 | 312.4 |
| | | | | | | | | | | |
| **San Diego-Carlsbad, CA M.S.A.** ........................... | 3,301,484 | | | | | | | | | |
| Includes San Diego County ........................... | | | | | | | | | | |
| City of San Diego........................... | 1,400,467 | 5,582 | 37 | 566 | 1,378 | 3,601 | 29,158 | 5,129 | 18,933 | 5,096 |
| City of Carlsbad........................... | 113,972 | 172 | 0 | 33 | 38 | 101 | 2,134 | 366 | 1,627 | 141 |
| Total area actually reporting ........................... | 100.0% | 10,955 | 84 | 1,100 | 2,802 | 6,969 | 63,458 | 10,744 | 42,808 | 9,906 |
| Rate per 100,000 inhabitants........................... | | 331.8 | 2.5 | 33.3 | 84.9 | 211.1 | 1,922.1 | 325.4 | 1,296.6 | 300.0 |
| | | | | | | | | | | |
| **San Francisco-Oakland-Hayward, CA M.S.A.** ........ | 4,654,400 | | | | | | | | | |
| Includes the Metropolitan Divisions of Oakland-Hayward-Berkeley, San Francisco-Redwood City-South San Francisco, and San Rafael ........................... | | | | | | | | | | |
| City of San Francisco........................... | 863,782 | 6,710 | 53 | 344 | 3,610 | 2,703 | 53,019 | 5,186 | 40,918 | 6,915 |
| City of Oakland........................... | 419,481 | 6,051 | 85 | 285 | 3,290 | 2,391 | 24,568 | 3,333 | 14,846 | 6,389 |
| City of Hayward........................... | 157,157 | 556 | 10 | 71 | 298 | 177 | 4,483 | 729 | 2,366 | 1,388 |
| City of Berkeley........................... | 120,387 | 530 | 1 | 44 | 330 | 155 | 5,906 | 1,090 | 4,099 | 717 |
| City of San Leandro ........................... | 90,438 | 412 | 1 | 23 | 220 | 168 | 3,432 | 501 | 2,028 | 903 |
| City of Redwood City........................... | 84,415 | 190 | 1 | 28 | 88 | 73 | 1,842 | 362 | 1,274 | 206 |
| City of San Ramon........................... | 76,081 | 27 | 0 | 4 | 13 | 10 | 895 | 146 | 654 | 95 |
| City of Pleasanton........................... | 79,611 | 86 | 0 | 13 | 40 | 33 | 1,644 | 232 | 1,253 | 159 |
| City of Walnut Creek........................... | 68,530 | 91 | 1 | 2 | 28 | 60 | 2,540 | 342 | 1,960 | 238 |
| City of South San Francisco........................... | 67,843 | 157 | 1 | 28 | 44 | 84 | 1,421 | 314 | 916 | 191 |
| City of San Rafael ........................... | 59,598 | 236 | 0 | 27 | 85 | 124 | 1,887 | 267 | 1,268 | 352 |
| Total area actually reporting ........................... | 100.0% | 22,570 | 249 | 1,438 | 10,948 | 9,935 | 167,582 | 24,089 | 114,093 | 29,400 |
| Rate per 100,000 inhabitants........................... | | 484.9 | 5.3 | 30.9 | 235.2 | 213.5 | 3,600.5 | 517.6 | 2,451.3 | 631.7 |
| Oakland-Hayward-Berkeley, CA M.D. ........... | 2,760,216 | | | | | | | | | |
| Includes Alameda and Contra Costa Counties........... | | | | | | | | | | |
| Total area actually reporting ........................... | 100.0% | 13,556 | 176 | 814 | 6,617 | 5,949 | 92,793 | 14,446 | 58,513 | 19,834 |
| Rate per 100,000 inhabitants........................... | | 491.1 | 6.4 | 29.5 | 239.7 | 215.5 | 3,361.8 | 523.4 | 2,119.9 | 718.6 |

# Table 6. Crime, by Selected Metropolitan Statistical Area, 2015—*Continued*

(Number, percent, rate per 100,000 population.)

| Area | Population | Violent crime | Murder and nonnegligent manslaughter | Rape[1] | Robbery | Aggravated assault | Property crime | Burglary | Larceny-theft | Motor vehicle theft |
|---|---|---|---|---|---|---|---|---|---|---|
| San Francisco-Redwood City-South San Francisco, CA M.D. ........... | 1,631,661 | | | | | | | | | |
| Includes San Francisco and San Mateo Counties......... | | | | | | | | | | |
| Total area actually reporting ..................... | 100.0% | 8,496 | 67 | 567 | 4,183 | 3,679 | 69,503 | 8,556 | 52,056 | 8,891 |
| Rate per 100,000 inhabitants...................... | | 520.7 | 4.1 | 34.7 | 256.4 | 225.5 | 4,259.6 | 524.4 | 3,190.4 | 544.9 |
| San Rafael, CA M.D. ......... | 262,523 | | | | | | | | | |
| Includes Marin County .......... | | | | | | | | | | |
| Total area actually reporting ..................... | 100.0% | 518 | 6 | 57 | 148 | 307 | 5,286 | 1,087 | 3,524 | 675 |
| Rate per 100,000 inhabitants...................... | | 197.3 | 2.3 | 21.7 | 56.4 | 116.9 | 2,013.5 | 414.1 | 1,342.4 | 257.1 |
| **San Jose-Sunnyvale-Santa Clara, CA M.S.A. .........** | 1,979,743 | | | | | | | | | |
| Includes San Benito and Santa Clara Counties........... | | | | | | | | | | |
| City of San Jose.......................... | 1,031,458 | 3,400 | 30 | 375 | 1,140 | 1,855 | 25,035 | 4,896 | 13,138 | 7,001 |
| City of Sunnyvale...................... | 152,443 | 158 | 1 | 29 | 61 | 67 | 2,355 | 545 | 1,514 | 296 |
| City of Santa Clara...................... | 123,562 | 156 | 1 | 20 | 71 | 64 | 3,579 | 583 | 2,598 | 398 |
| City of Mountain View...................... | 80,705 | 164 | 0 | 10 | 31 | 123 | 2,030 | 327 | 1,561 | 142 |
| City of Milpitas...................... | 75,520 | 77 | 1 | 9 | 37 | 30 | 1,966 | 277 | 1,424 | 265 |
| City of Palo Alto...................... | 67,560 | 68 | 2 | 13 | 26 | 27 | 1,704 | 213 | 1,405 | 86 |
| City of Cupertino...................... | 61,162 | 63 | 0 | 8 | 27 | 28 | 935 | 293 | 583 | 59 |
| Total area actually reporting ..................... | 100.0% | 4,980 | 45 | 586 | 1,585 | 2,764 | 45,865 | 8,690 | 27,842 | 9,333 |
| Rate per 100,000 inhabitants...................... | | 251.5 | 2.3 | 29.6 | 80.1 | 139.6 | 2,316.7 | 438.9 | 1,406.3 | 471.4 |
| **San Luis Obispo-Paso Robles-Arroyo Grande, CA M.S.A...........** | 281,190 | | | | | | | | | |
| Includes San Luis Obispo County...................... | | | | | | | | | | |
| City of San Luis Obispo ...................... | 47,116 | 193 | 0 | 34 | 13 | 146 | 1,844 | 245 | 1,501 | 98 |
| City of Paso Robles...................... | 31,659 | 62 | 0 | 4 | 12 | 46 | 1,106 | 169 | 848 | 89 |
| City of Arroyo Grande...................... | 18,071 | 35 | 0 | 2 | 6 | 27 | 418 | 83 | 299 | 36 |
| Total area actually reporting ..................... | 100.0% | 1,134 | 3 | 82 | 77 | 972 | 6,786 | 1,352 | 4,905 | 529 |
| Rate per 100,000 inhabitants...................... | | 403.3 | 1.1 | 29.2 | 27.4 | 345.7 | 2,413.3 | 480.8 | 1,744.4 | 188.1 |
| **Santa Cruz-Watsonville, CA M.S.A.......................** | 273,754 | | | | | | | | | |
| Includes Santa Cruz County ...................... | | | | | | | | | | |
| City of Santa Cruz...................... | 64,076 | 499 | 2 | 44 | 116 | 337 | 3,561 | 431 | 2,831 | 299 |
| City of Watsonville...................... | 53,581 | 303 | 4 | 33 | 104 | 162 | 1,930 | 254 | 1,261 | 415 |
| Total area actually reporting ..................... | 100.0% | 1,171 | 6 | 118 | 279 | 768 | 9,282 | 1,463 | 6,655 | 1,164 |
| Rate per 100,000 inhabitants...................... | | 427.8 | 2.2 | 43.1 | 101.9 | 280.5 | 3,390.6 | 534.4 | 2,431.0 | 425.2 |
| **Santa Maria-Santa Barbara, CA M.S.A. .................** | 444,458 | | | | | | | | | |
| Includes Santa Barbara County...................... | | | | | | | | | | |
| City of Santa Maria...................... | 104,355 | 463 | 13 | 50 | 133 | 267 | 2,975 | 595 | 1,727 | 653 |
| City of Santa Barbara...................... | 91,877 | 363 | 1 | 62 | 76 | 224 | 2,717 | 374 | 2,209 | 134 |
| Total area actually reporting ..................... | 100.0% | 1,432 | 18 | 194 | 285 | 935 | 9,356 | 1,829 | 6,471 | 1,056 |
| Rate per 100,000 inhabitants...................... | | 322.2 | 4.0 | 43.6 | 64.1 | 210.4 | 2,105.0 | 411.5 | 1,455.9 | 237.6 |
| **Santa Rosa, CA M.S.A. ............................** | 503,831 | | | | | | | | | |
| Includes Sonoma County ...................... | | | | | | | | | | |
| City of Santa Rosa...................... | 175,738 | 606 | 4 | 89 | 131 | 382 | 4,311 | 639 | 3,223 | 449 |
| Total area actually reporting ..................... | 100.0% | 1,898 | 9 | 256 | 300 | 1,333 | 9,943 | 1,750 | 7,162 | 1,031 |
| Rate per 100,000 inhabitants...................... | | 376.7 | 1.8 | 50.8 | 59.5 | 264.6 | 1,973.5 | 347.3 | 1,421.5 | 204.6 |
| **Savannah, GA M.S.A.............................** | 379,567 | | | | | | | | | |
| Includes Bryan, Chatham, and Effingham Counties .... | | | | | | | | | | |
| City of Savannah-Chatham Metropolitan ................... | 240,178 | 1,168 | 54 | 59 | 519 | 536 | 9,236 | 1,872 | 6,241 | 1,123 |
| Total area actually reporting ..................... | 100.0% | 1,520 | 57 | 85 | 599 | 779 | 12,578 | 2,597 | 8,669 | 1,312 |
| Rate per 100,000 inhabitants...................... | | 400.5 | 15.0 | 22.4 | 157.8 | 205.2 | 3,313.8 | 684.2 | 2,283.9 | 345.7 |
| **Seattle-Tacoma-Bellevue, WA M.S.A.[2] ...................** | 3,743,076 | | | | | | | | | |
| Includes the Metropolitan Divisions of Seattle-Bellevue-Everett and Tacoma-Lakewood...................... | | | | | | | | | | |
| City of Seattle...................... | 683,700 | 4,093 | 23 | 144 | 1,532 | 2,394 | 37,754 | 7,677 | 26,199 | 3,878 |
| City of Tacoma...................... | 206,884 | 1,694 | 12 | 147 | 485 | 1,050 | 13,065 | 2,552 | 8,492 | 2,021 |
| City of Bellevue...................... | 138,532 | 152 | 2 | 19 | 61 | 70 | 4,331 | 789 | 3,321 | 221 |
| City of Everett...................... | 107,633 | 422 | 5 | 44 | 148 | 225 | 6,198 | 974 | 4,316 | 908 |
| City of Kent...................... | 127,259 | 338 | 5 | 61 | 144 | 128 | 6,169 | 905 | 4,257 | 1,007 |
| City of Renton...................... | 100,015 | 300 | 4 | 41 | 100 | 155 | 5,795 | 1,175 | 3,715 | 905 |
| City of Auburn...................... | 77,914 | 318 | 7 | 31 | 92 | 188 | 4,235 | 952 | 2,659 | 624 |
| City of Lakewood...................... | 59,958 | 414 | 0 | 43 | 90 | 281 | 2,656 | 537 | 1,865 | 254 |
| City of Redmond...................... | 60,542 | 64 | 0 | 9 | 18 | 37 | 1,796 | 233 | 1,495 | 68 |
| Total area actually reporting ..................... | 100.0% | 12,130 | 112 | 1,181 | 3,885 | 6,952 | 144,190 | 28,751 | 97,879 | 17,560 |

# Table 6. Crime, by Selected Metropolitan Statistical Area, 2015—*Continued*

(Number, percent, rate per 100,000 population.)

| Area | Population | Violent crime | Murder and nonnegligent manslaughter | Rape[1] | Robbery | Aggravated assault | Property crime | Burglary | Larceny-theft | Motor vehicle theft |
|---|---|---|---|---|---|---|---|---|---|---|
| Rate per 100,000 inhabitants | | 324.1 | 3.0 | 31.6 | 103.8 | 185.7 | 3,852.2 | 768.1 | 2,614.9 | 469.1 |
| **Seattle-Bellevue-Everett, WA M.D.[2]** | 2,898,725 | | | | | | | | | |
| Includes King and Snohomish Counties | | | | | | | | | | |
| Total area actually reporting | 100.0% | 8,406 | 78 | 806 | 2,930 | 4,592 | 112,048 | 21,227 | 77,439 | 13,382 |
| Rate per 100,000 inhabitants | | 290.0 | 2.7 | 27.8 | 101.1 | 158.4 | 3,865.4 | 732.3 | 2,671.5 | 461.7 |
| Tacoma-Lakewood, WA M.D. | 844,351 | | | | | | | | | |
| Includes Pierce County | | | | | | | | | | |
| Total area actually reporting | 100.0% | 3,724 | 34 | 375 | 955 | 2,360 | 32,142 | 7,524 | 20,440 | 4,178 |
| Rate per 100,000 inhabitants | | 441.0 | 4.0 | 44.4 | 113.1 | 279.5 | 3,806.7 | 891.1 | 2,420.8 | 494.8 |
| **Sebastian-Vero Beach, FL M.S.A.** | 147,202 | | | | | | | | | |
| Includes Indian River County | | | | | | | | | | |
| City of Sebastian | 23,706 | 56 | 0 | 9 | 9 | 38 | 504 | 89 | 399 | 16 |
| City of Vero Beach | 16,215 | 81 | 0 | 10 | 7 | 64 | 554 | 121 | 413 | 20 |
| Total area actually reporting | 100.0% | 391 | 2 | 36 | 40 | 313 | 3,549 | 707 | 2,692 | 150 |
| Rate per 100,000 inhabitants | | 265.6 | 1.4 | 24.5 | 27.2 | 212.6 | 2,411.0 | 480.3 | 1,828.8 | 101.9 |
| **Sebring, FL M.S.A.** | 98,635 | | | | | | | | | |
| Includes Highlands County | | | | | | | | | | |
| City of Sebring | 10,363 | 34 | 1 | 5 | 15 | 13 | 532 | 104 | 416 | 12 |
| Total area actually reporting | 91.0% | 300 | 5 | 35 | 46 | 214 | 2,421 | 578 | 1,752 | 91 |
| Estimated total | 100.0% | 337 | 5 | 38 | 56 | 238 | 2,702 | 625 | 1,967 | 110 |
| Rate per 100,000 inhabitants | | 341.7 | 5.1 | 38.5 | 56.8 | 241.3 | 2,739.4 | 633.6 | 1,994.2 | 111.5 |
| **Sheboygan, WI M.S.A.** | 115,183 | | | | | | | | | |
| Includes Sheboygan County | | | | | | | | | | |
| City of Sheboygan | 48,667 | 159 | 0 | 21 | 14 | 124 | 1,150 | 128 | 991 | 31 |
| Total area actually reporting | 100.0% | 201 | 3 | 30 | 19 | 149 | 1,808 | 184 | 1,571 | 53 |
| Rate per 100,000 inhabitants | | 174.5 | 2.6 | 26.0 | 16.5 | 129.4 | 1,569.7 | 159.7 | 1,363.9 | 46.0 |
| **Sherman-Denison, TX M.S.A.** | 124,424 | | | | | | | | | |
| Includes Grayson County | | | | | | | | | | |
| City of Sherman | 40,338 | 170 | 2 | 42 | 33 | 93 | 1,199 | 261 | 854 | 84 |
| City of Denison | 22,952 | 138 | 2 | 27 | 25 | 84 | 664 | 151 | 448 | 65 |
| Total area actually reporting | 98.4% | 402 | 8 | 72 | 61 | 261 | 2,590 | 610 | 1,745 | 235 |
| Estimated total | 100.0% | 407 | 8 | 73 | 62 | 264 | 2,642 | 618 | 1,785 | 239 |
| Rate per 100,000 inhabitants | | 327.1 | 6.4 | 58.7 | 49.8 | 212.2 | 2,123.4 | 496.7 | 1,434.6 | 192.1 |
| **Shreveport-Bossier City, LA M.S.A.** | 445,609 | | | | | | | | | |
| Includes Bossier, Caddo, De Soto, and Webster Parishes | | | | | | | | | | |
| City of Shreveport | 197,592 | 1,619 | 22 | 128 | 460 | 1,009 | 10,148 | 2,234 | 7,339 | 575 |
| City of Bossier City | 68,918 | 514 | 5 | 43 | 79 | 387 | 2,984 | 491 | 2,321 | 172 |
| Total area actually reporting | 99.7% | 2,578 | 35 | 199 | 577 | 1,767 | 15,983 | 3,503 | 11,557 | 923 |
| Estimated total | 100.0% | 2,583 | 35 | 199 | 578 | 1,771 | 16,027 | 3,511 | 11,591 | 925 |
| Rate per 100,000 inhabitants | | 579.7 | 7.9 | 44.7 | 129.7 | 397.4 | 3,596.7 | 787.9 | 2,601.2 | 207.6 |
| **Sioux City, IA-NE-SD M.S.A.[2]** | 168,822 | | | | | | | | | |
| Includes Plymouth and Woodbury Counties, IA; Dakota and Dixon Counties, NE; and Union County, SD | | | | | | | | | | |
| City of Sioux City, IA | 82,445 | 346 | 2 | 40 | 54 | 250 | 3,496 | 648 | 2,557 | 291 |
| Total area actually reporting | 98.4% | 453 | 3 | 63 | 59 | 328 | 4,586 | 805 | 3,412 | 369 |
| Estimated total | 100.0% | 455 | 3 | 63 | 59 | 330 | 4,618 | 809 | 3,438 | 371 |
| Rate per 100,000 inhabitants | | 269.5 | 1.8 | 37.3 | 34.9 | 195.5 | 2,735.4 | 479.2 | 2,036.5 | 219.8 |
| **Sioux Falls, SD M.S.A.** | 252,151 | | | | | | | | | |
| Includes Lincoln, McCook, Minnehaha, and Turner Counties | | | | | | | | | | |
| City of Sioux Falls | 172,313 | 819 | 2 | 134 | 87 | 596 | 5,685 | 1,089 | 4,177 | 419 |
| Total area actually reporting | 100.0% | 917 | 3 | 146 | 89 | 679 | 6,312 | 1,241 | 4,606 | 465 |
| Rate per 100,000 inhabitants | | 363.7 | 1.2 | 57.9 | 35.3 | 269.3 | 2,503.3 | 492.2 | 1,826.7 | 184.4 |
| **South Bend-Mishawaka, IN-MI M.S.A.** | 319,106 | | | | | | | | | |
| Includes St. Joseph County, IN and Cass County, MI | | | | | | | | | | |
| City of South Bend, IN | 101,240 | 720 | 17 | 88 | 350 | 265 | 5,410 | 1,430 | 3,612 | 368 |
| City of Mishawaka, IN | 48,164 | 121 | 2 | 21 | 45 | 53 | 2,312 | 302 | 1,878 | 132 |
| Total area actually reporting | 98.0% | 1,114 | 23 | 164 | 427 | 500 | 9,749 | 2,370 | 6,793 | 586 |
| Estimated total | 100.0% | 1,131 | 23 | 167 | 430 | 511 | 9,873 | 2,390 | 6,888 | 595 |
| Rate per 100,000 inhabitants | | 354.4 | 7.2 | 52.3 | 134.8 | 160.1 | 3,094.0 | 749.0 | 2,158.5 | 186.5 |

# Table 6. Crime, by Selected Metropolitan Statistical Area, 2015—*Continued*

(Number, percent, rate per 100,000 population.)

| Area | Population | Violent crime | Murder and nonnegligent manslaughter | Rape[1] | Robbery | Aggravated assault | Property crime | Burglary | Larceny-theft | Motor vehicle theft |
|---|---|---|---|---|---|---|---|---|---|---|
| **Spartanburg, SC M.S.A.** ............................. | 324,202 | | | | | | | | | |
| Includes Spartanburg and Union Counties................. | | | | | | | | | | |
| City of Spartanburg ...................................... | 37,707 | 380 | 6 | 26 | 95 | 253 | 2,383 | 338 | 1,916 | 129 |
| Total area actually reporting ............................. | 100.0% | 1,317 | 25 | 151 | 285 | 856 | 8,988 | 1,963 | 6,478 | 547 |
| Rate per 100,000 inhabitants............................. | | 406.2 | 7.7 | 46.6 | 87.9 | 264.0 | 2,772.3 | 605.5 | 1,998.1 | 168.7 |
| | | | | | | | | | | |
| **Spokane-Spokane Valley, WA M.S.A.** ................. | 546,088 | | | | | | | | | |
| Includes Pend Oreille, Spokane, and Stevens Counties | | | | | | | | | | |
| City of Spokane ........................................... | 212,698 | 1,111 | 12 | 119 | 333 | 647 | 15,971 | 2,817 | 11,408 | 1,746 |
| City of Spokane Valley .................................... | 92,157 | 235 | 0 | 38 | 73 | 124 | 4,779 | 849 | 3,501 | 429 |
| Total area actually reporting ............................. | 99.9% | 1,665 | 21 | 245 | 467 | 932 | 25,902 | 5,037 | 18,287 | 2,578 |
| Estimated total............................................ | 100.0% | 1,665 | 21 | 245 | 467 | 932 | 25,912 | 5,039 | 18,294 | 2,579 |
| Rate per 100,000 inhabitants............................. | | 304.9 | 3.8 | 44.9 | 85.5 | 170.7 | 4,745.0 | 922.7 | 3,350.0 | 472.3 |
| | | | | | | | | | | |
| **Springfield, IL M.S.A.** ............................... | 211,317 | | | | | | | | | |
| Includes Menard and Sangamon Counties ............... | | | | | | | | | | |
| City of Springfield ........................................ | 116,875 | 1,251 | 11 | 103 | 257 | 880 | 5,321 | 1,131 | 3,997 | 193 |
| Total area actually reporting ............................. | 98.8% | 1,517 | 11 | 147 | 276 | 1,083 | 6,455 | 1,407 | 4,797 | 251 |
| Estimated total............................................ | 100.0% | 1,522 | 11 | 148 | 277 | 1,086 | 6,499 | 1,414 | 4,832 | 253 |
| Rate per 100,000 inhabitants............................. | | 720.2 | 5.2 | 70.0 | 131.1 | 513.9 | 3,075.5 | 669.1 | 2,286.6 | 119.7 |
| | | | | | | | | | | |
| **Springfield, MA M.S.A.** .............................. | 630,765 | | | | | | | | | |
| Includes Hampden and Hampshire Counties ............. | | | | | | | | | | |
| City of Springfield ........................................ | 154,090 | 1,654 | 18 | 95 | 510 | 1,031 | 5,168 | 1,303 | 3,261 | 604 |
| Total area actually reporting ............................. | 95.4% | 3,248 | 22 | 319 | 748 | 2,159 | 14,489 | 3,255 | 10,121 | 1,113 |
| Estimated total............................................ | 100.0% | 3,340 | 22 | 328 | 762 | 2,228 | 14,929 | 3,339 | 10,447 | 1,143 |
| Rate per 100,000 inhabitants............................. | | 529.5 | 3.5 | 52.0 | 120.8 | 353.2 | 2,366.8 | 529.4 | 1,656.2 | 181.2 |
| | | | | | | | | | | |
| **Springfield, MO M.S.A.** .............................. | 456,305 | | | | | | | | | |
| Includes Christian, Dallas, Greene, Polk, and Webster Counties.................. | | | | | | | | | | |
| City of Springfield ........................................ | 166,860 | 2,262 | 10 | 298 | 448 | 1,506 | 13,007 | 1,956 | 9,799 | 1,252 |
| Total area actually reporting ............................. | 100.0% | 2,835 | 15 | 368 | 502 | 1,950 | 18,355 | 3,172 | 13,554 | 1,629 |
| Rate per 100,000 inhabitants............................. | | 621.3 | 3.3 | 80.6 | 110.0 | 427.3 | 4,022.5 | 695.1 | 2,970.4 | 357.0 |
| | | | | | | | | | | |
| **Springfield, OH M.S.A.** .............................. | 136,193 | | | | | | | | | |
| Includes Clark County.................................... | | | | | | | | | | |
| City of Springfield ........................................ | 59,804 | 355 | 12 | 31 | 163 | 149 | 3,699 | 1,045 | 2,449 | 205 |
| Total area actually reporting ............................. | 99.5% | 405 | 12 | 41 | 178 | 174 | 4,882 | 1,381 | 3,246 | 255 |
| Estimated total............................................ | 100.0% | 406 | 12 | 41 | 178 | 175 | 4,898 | 1,384 | 3,258 | 256 |
| Rate per 100,000 inhabitants............................. | | 298.1 | 8.8 | 30.1 | 130.7 | 128.5 | 3,596.4 | 1,016.2 | 2,392.2 | 188.0 |
| | | | | | | | | | | |
| **State College, PA M.S.A.** ............................ | 159,850 | | | | | | | | | |
| Includes Centre County................................... | | | | | | | | | | |
| City of State College ...................................... | 57,710 | 27 | 2 | 4 | 5 | 16 | 640 | 77 | 556 | 7 |
| Total area actually reporting ............................. | 100.0% | 164 | 2 | 63 | 13 | 86 | 1,882 | 280 | 1,568 | 34 |
| Rate per 100,000 inhabitants............................. | | 102.6 | 1.3 | 39.4 | 8.1 | 53.8 | 1,177.4 | 175.2 | 980.9 | 21.3 |
| | | | | | | | | | | |
| **Staunton-Waynesboro, VA M.S.A.** ................... | 119,798 | | | | | | | | | |
| Includes Augusta County and Staunton and Waynesboro Cities ....................... | | | | | | | | | | |
| City of Staunton .......................................... | 24,654 | 36 | 0 | 8 | 10 | 18 | 488 | 32 | 440 | 16 |
| City of Waynesboro ....................................... | 21,384 | 43 | 0 | 8 | 12 | 23 | 570 | 26 | 530 | 14 |
| Total area actually reporting ............................. | 100.0% | 167 | 4 | 34 | 29 | 100 | 1,777 | 236 | 1,466 | 75 |
| Rate per 100,000 inhabitants............................. | | 139.4 | 3.3 | 28.4 | 24.2 | 83.5 | 1,483.3 | 197.0 | 1,223.7 | 62.6 |
| | | | | | | | | | | |
| **St. Cloud, MN M.S.A.** ............................... | 193,045 | | | | | | | | | |
| Includes Benton and Stearns Counties..................... | | | | | | | | | | |
| City of St. Cloud .......................................... | 66,498 | 248 | 4 | 55 | 57 | 132 | 3,259 | 399 | 2,736 | 124 |
| Total area actually reporting ............................. | 100.0% | 334 | 4 | 95 | 59 | 176 | 5,126 | 641 | 4,293 | 192 |
| Rate per 100,000 inhabitants............................. | | 173.0 | 2.1 | 49.2 | 30.6 | 91.2 | 2,655.3 | 332.0 | 2,223.8 | 99.5 |
| | | | | | | | | | | |
| **St. George, UT M.S.A.** .............................. | 156,005 | | | | | | | | | |
| Includes Washington County............................... | | | | | | | | | | |
| City of St. George ......................................... | 79,984 | 116 | 0 | 25 | 12 | 79 | 1,398 | 326 | 962 | 110 |
| Total area actually reporting ............................. | 98.1% | 203 | 0 | 58 | 16 | 129 | 2,534 | 569 | 1,792 | 173 |
| Estimated total............................................ | 100.0% | 208 | 0 | 59 | 17 | 132 | 2,615 | 581 | 1,854 | 180 |
| Rate per 100,000 inhabitants............................. | | 133.3 | 0.0 | 37.8 | 10.9 | 84.6 | 1,676.2 | 372.4 | 1,188.4 | 115.4 |

## Table 6. Crime, by Selected Metropolitan Statistical Area, 2015—*Continued*

(Number, percent, rate per 100,000 population.)

| Area | Population | Violent crime | Murder and nonnegligent manslaughter | Rape[1] | Robbery | Aggravated assault | Property crime | Burglary | Larceny-theft | Motor vehicle theft |
|---|---|---|---|---|---|---|---|---|---|---|
| **St. Joseph, MO-KS M.S.A.** ........................... | 127,510 | | | | | | | | | |
| Includes Doniphan County, KS and Andrew, Buchanan, | | | | | | | | | | |
| and DeKalb Counties, MO ......... | | | | | | | | | | |
| City of St. Joseph, MO........................... | 77,035 | 397 | 7 | 61 | 86 | 243 | 4,534 | 847 | 3,235 | 452 |
| Total area actually reporting ......................... | 100.0% | 490 | 12 | 75 | 89 | 314 | 5,146 | 1,021 | 3,612 | 513 |
| Rate per 100,000 inhabitants.......................... | | 384.3 | 9.4 | 58.8 | 69.8 | 246.3 | 4,035.8 | 800.7 | 2,832.7 | 402.3 |
| **St. Louis, MO-IL M.S.A.**[2] ........................... | 2,811,161 | | | | | | | | | |
| Includes Bond, Calhoun, Clinton, Jersey, Macoupin, | | | | | | | | | | |
| Madison, Monroe, and St. Clair Counties, IL and | | | | | | | | | | |
| Franklin, Jefferson, Lincoln, St. Charles,[2] St. Louis, and | | | | | | | | | | |
| Warren Counties and St. Louis City, MO.................... | | | | | | | | | | |
| City of St. Louis, MO........................... | 317,095 | 5,762 | 188 | 263 | 1,790 | 3,521 | 20,028 | 4,202 | 12,680 | 3,146 |
| City of St. Charles, MO........................... | 68,624 | 124 | 1 | 19 | 31 | 73 | 1,716 | 193 | 1,444 | 79 |
| Total area actually reporting ......................... | 98.1% | 13,560 | 294 | 1,066 | 3,383 | 8,817 | 70,316 | 13,207 | 50,833 | 6,276 |
| Estimated total.......................... | 100.0% | 13,663 | 295 | 1,081 | 3,408 | 8,879 | 71,198 | 13,352 | 51,531 | 6,315 |
| Rate per 100,000 inhabitants.......................... | | 486.0 | 10.5 | 38.5 | 121.2 | 315.8 | 2,532.7 | 475.0 | 1,833.1 | 224.6 |
| **Stockton-Lodi, CA M.S.A.** ........................... | 722,160 | | | | | | | | | |
| Includes San Joaquin County........................... | | | | | | | | | | |
| City of Stockton........................... | 304,890 | 4,122 | 49 | 135 | 1,144 | 2,794 | 12,998 | 2,891 | 8,119 | 1,988 |
| City of Lodi........................... | 64,369 | 377 | 4 | 12 | 94 | 267 | 2,093 | 410 | 1,243 | 440 |
| Total area actually reporting ......................... | 100.0% | 5,756 | 64 | 198 | 1,540 | 3,954 | 25,031 | 5,251 | 15,743 | 4,037 |
| Rate per 100,000 inhabitants.......................... | | 797.1 | 8.9 | 27.4 | 213.2 | 547.5 | 3,466.1 | 727.1 | 2,180.0 | 559.0 |
| **Sumter, SC M.S.A.** ........................... | 108,271 | | | | | | | | | |
| Includes Sumter County........................... | | | | | | | | | | |
| City of Sumter........................... | 41,017 | 290 | 4 | 1 | 64 | 221 | 1,872 | 532 | 1,250 | 90 |
| Total area actually reporting ......................... | 100.0% | 673 | 7 | 34 | 96 | 536 | 3,756 | 1,247 | 2,262 | 247 |
| Rate per 100,000 inhabitants.......................... | | 621.6 | 6.5 | 31.4 | 88.7 | 495.1 | 3,469.1 | 1,151.7 | 2,089.2 | 228.1 |
| **Syracuse, NY M.S.A.** ........................... | 659,811 | | | | | | | | | |
| Includes Madison, Onondaga, and Oswego Counties. | | | | | | | | | | |
| City of Syracuse........................... | 144,027 | 1,142 | 22 | 77 | 359 | 684 | 5,087 | 1,194 | 3,577 | 316 |
| Total area actually reporting ......................... | 99.6% | 1,872 | 27 | 317 | 481 | 1,047 | 13,549 | 2,525 | 10,511 | 513 |
| Estimated total.......................... | 100.0% | 1,875 | 27 | 317 | 482 | 1,049 | 13,586 | 2,530 | 10,542 | 514 |
| Rate per 100,000 inhabitants.......................... | | 284.2 | 4.1 | 48.0 | 73.1 | 159.0 | 2,059.1 | 383.4 | 1,597.7 | 77.9 |
| **Tallahassee, FL M.S.A.** ........................... | 379,364 | | | | | | | | | |
| Includes Gadsden, Jefferson, Leon, and Wakulla | | | | | | | | | | |
| Counties........................... | | | | | | | | | | |
| City of Tallahassee........................... | 189,709 | 2,019 | 16 | 235 | 399 | 1,369 | 9,658 | 2,073 | 6,617 | 968 |
| Total area actually reporting ......................... | 99.8% | 2,907 | 25 | 307 | 463 | 2,112 | 14,231 | 3,156 | 9,857 | 1,218 |
| Estimated total.......................... | 100.0% | 2,910 | 25 | 307 | 464 | 2,114 | 14,250 | 3,159 | 9,872 | 1,219 |
| Rate per 100,000 inhabitants.......................... | | 767.1 | 6.6 | 80.9 | 122.3 | 557.2 | 3,756.3 | 832.7 | 2,602.3 | 321.3 |
| **Tampa-St. Petersburg-Clearwater, FL M.S.A.**.......... | 2,963,741 | | | | | | | | | |
| Includes Hernando, Hillsborough, Pasco, and Pinellas | | | | | | | | | | |
| Counties........................... | | | | | | | | | | |
| City of Tampa ........................... | 364,383 | 2,298 | 34 | 77 | 671 | 1,516 | 8,366 | 1,833 | 5,937 | 596 |
| City of St. Petersburg........................... | 255,821 | 1,898 | 14 | 136 | 573 | 1,175 | 14,384 | 2,319 | 10,542 | 1,523 |
| City of Clearwater........................... | 111,316 | 679 | 7 | 82 | 181 | 409 | 4,356 | 638 | 3,420 | 298 |
| City of Largo........................... | 79,263 | 411 | 2 | 67 | 117 | 225 | 3,306 | 506 | 2,580 | 220 |
| Total area actually reporting ......................... | 100.0% | 11,383 | 120 | 968 | 2,593 | 7,702 | 77,874 | 13,999 | 58,214 | 5,661 |
| Rate per 100,000 inhabitants.......................... | | 384.1 | 4.0 | 32.7 | 87.5 | 259.9 | 2,627.6 | 472.3 | 1,964.2 | 191.0 |
| **Texarkana, TX-AR M.S.A.** ........................... | 149,421 | | | | | | | | | |
| Includes Little River and Miller Counties, AR and Bowie | | | | | | | | | | |
| County, TX........................... | | | | | | | | | | |
| City of Texarkana, TX ........................... | 37,415 | 284 | 3 | 20 | 51 | 210 | 1,904 | 320 | 1,464 | 120 |
| Total area actually reporting ......................... | 100.0% | 700 | 8 | 76 | 108 | 508 | 5,179 | 1,112 | 3,721 | 346 |
| Rate per 100,000 inhabitants.......................... | | 468.5 | 5.4 | 50.9 | 72.3 | 340.0 | 3,466.0 | 744.2 | 2,490.3 | 231.6 |
| **The Villages, FL M.S.A.**........................... | 120,632 | | | | | | | | | |
| Includes Sumter County........................... | | | | | | | | | | |
| Total area actually reporting ......................... | 100.0% | 280 | 1 | 18 | 20 | 241 | 1,135 | 311 | 763 | 61 |
| Rate per 100,000 inhabitants.......................... | | 232.1 | 0.8 | 14.9 | 16.6 | 199.8 | 940.9 | 257.8 | 632.5 | 50.6 |

## Table 6. Crime, by Selected Metropolitan Statistical Area, 2015—*Continued*

(Number, percent, rate per 100,000 population.)

| Area | Population | Violent crime | Murder and nonnegligent manslaughter | Rape[1] | Robbery | Aggravated assault | Property crime | Burglary | Larceny-theft | Motor vehicle theft |
|---|---|---|---|---|---|---|---|---|---|---|
| **Toledo, OH M.S.A.[2]** | 607,043 | | | | | | | | | |
| Includes Fulton, Lucas, and Wood Counties | | | | | | | | | | |
| City of Toledo | 279,552 | 3,156 | 24 | 228 | 902 | 2,002 | 12,510 | 4,127 | 7,483 | 900 |
| Total area actually reporting | 91.7% | 3,462 | 26 | 300 | 965 | 2,171 | 17,059 | 5,074 | 10,906 | 1,079 |
| Estimated total | 100.0% | 3,543 | 27 | 314 | 993 | 2,209 | 18,209 | 5,272 | 11,818 | 1,119 |
| Rate per 100,000 inhabitants | | 583.6 | 4.4 | 51.7 | 163.6 | 363.9 | 2,999.6 | 868.5 | 1,946.8 | 184.3 |
| **Topeka, KS M.S.A.** | 233,316 | | | | | | | | | |
| Includes Jackson, Jefferson, Osage, Shawnee, and Wabaunsee Counties | | | | | | | | | | |
| City of Topeka | 127,096 | 720 | 11 | 93 | 228 | 388 | 6,601 | 1,176 | 4,876 | 549 |
| Total area actually reporting | 98.2% | 906 | 14 | 112 | 234 | 546 | 8,385 | 1,808 | 5,933 | 644 |
| Estimated total | 100.0% | 914 | 14 | 113 | 235 | 552 | 8,473 | 1,821 | 6,001 | 651 |
| Rate per 100,000 inhabitants | | 391.7 | 6.0 | 48.4 | 100.7 | 236.6 | 3,631.6 | 780.5 | 2,572.0 | 279.0 |
| **Trenton, NJ M.S.A.[2]** | 371,812 | | | | | | | | | |
| Includes Mercer County[2] | | | | | | | | | | |
| City of Trenton[2] | 83,662 | 1,018 | 17 | 48 | 402 | 551 | 2,030 | 771 | 784 | 475 |
| Total area actually reporting | 100.0% | 1,391 | 20 | 93 | 538 | 740 | 6,637 | 1,507 | 4,419 | 711 |
| Rate per 100,000 inhabitants | | 374.1 | 5.4 | 25.0 | 144.7 | 199.0 | 1,785.0 | 405.3 | 1,188.5 | 191.2 |
| **Tucson, AZ M.S.A.** | 1,012,244 | | | | | | | | | |
| Includes Pima County | | | | | | | | | | |
| City of Tucson | 529,675 | 3,472 | 31 | 422 | 1,059 | 1,960 | 35,185 | 3,664 | 29,592 | 1,929 |
| Total area actually reporting | 100.0% | 4,266 | 46 | 531 | 1,252 | 2,437 | 48,066 | 5,623 | 39,846 | 2,597 |
| Rate per 100,000 inhabitants | | 421.4 | 4.5 | 52.5 | 123.7 | 240.8 | 4,748.5 | 555.5 | 3,936.4 | 256.6 |
| **Tulsa, OK M.S.A.[2]** | 977,354 | | | | | | | | | |
| Includes Creek, Okmulgee, Osage, Pawnee, Rogers, Tulsa, and Wagoner Counties | | | | | | | | | | |
| City of Tulsa | 401,520 | 3,628 | 55 | 365 | 854 | 2,354 | 20,892 | 5,512 | 12,729 | 2,651 |
| Total area actually reporting | 100.0% | 4,895 | 79 | 582 | 964 | 3,270 | 30,890 | 8,058 | 19,185 | 3,647 |
| Rate per 100,000 inhabitants | | 500.8 | 8.1 | 59.5 | 98.6 | 334.6 | 3,160.6 | 824.5 | 1,963.0 | 373.2 |
| **Tuscaloosa, AL M.S.A.** | 239,269 | | | | | | | | | |
| Includes Hale, Pickens, and Tuscaloosa Counties | | | | | | | | | | |
| City of Tuscaloosa | 97,511 | 560 | 7 | 45 | 200 | 308 | 4,210 | 1,132 | 2,892 | 186 |
| Total area actually reporting | 99.0% | 929 | 10 | 85 | 256 | 578 | 6,936 | 1,750 | 4,823 | 363 |
| Estimated total | 100.0% | 940 | 10 | 86 | 258 | 586 | 7,015 | 1,765 | 4,882 | 368 |
| Rate per 100,000 inhabitants | | 392.9 | 4.2 | 35.9 | 107.8 | 244.9 | 2,931.8 | 737.7 | 2,040.4 | 153.8 |
| **Tyler, TX M.S.A.** | 221,472 | | | | | | | | | |
| Includes Smith County | | | | | | | | | | |
| City of Tyler | 102,481 | 395 | 5 | 54 | 66 | 270 | 4,086 | 673 | 3,210 | 203 |
| Total area actually reporting | 99.1% | 650 | 12 | 61 | 105 | 472 | 6,475 | 1,350 | 4,660 | 465 |
| Estimated total | 100.0% | 655 | 12 | 62 | 106 | 475 | 6,523 | 1,358 | 4,697 | 468 |
| Rate per 100,000 inhabitants | | 295.7 | 5.4 | 28.0 | 47.9 | 214.5 | 2,945.3 | 613.2 | 2,120.8 | 211.3 |
| **Urban Honolulu, HI M.S.A.** | 999,307 | | | | | | | | | |
| Includes Honolulu County | | | | | | | | | | |
| Total area actually reporting | 100.0% | 2,437 | 15 | 318 | 896 | 1,208 | 31,085 | 4,284 | 22,930 | 3,871 |
| Rate per 100,000 inhabitants | | 243.9 | 1.5 | 31.8 | 89.7 | 120.9 | 3,110.7 | 428.7 | 2,294.6 | 387.4 |
| **Utica-Rome, NY M.S.A.** | 295,366 | | | | | | | | | |
| Includes Herkimer and Oneida Counties | | | | | | | | | | |
| City of Utica | 61,109 | 349 | 6 | 44 | 86 | 213 | 2,196 | 443 | 1,660 | 93 |
| City of Rome | 32,376 | 40 | 0 | 12 | 11 | 17 | 618 | 122 | 482 | 14 |
| Total area actually reporting | 98.2% | 681 | 8 | 165 | 112 | 396 | 5,774 | 1,039 | 4,533 | 202 |
| Estimated total | 100.0% | 690 | 8 | 166 | 115 | 401 | 5,858 | 1,050 | 4,603 | 205 |
| Rate per 100,000 inhabitants | | 233.6 | 2.7 | 56.2 | 38.9 | 135.8 | 1,983.3 | 355.5 | 1,558.4 | 69.4 |
| **Vallejo-Fairfield, CA M.S.A.** | 435,113 | | | | | | | | | |
| Includes Solano County | | | | | | | | | | |
| City of Vallejo | 121,257 | 1,031 | 18 | 102 | 351 | 560 | 4,986 | 2,352 | 1,536 | 1,098 |
| City of Fairfield | 112,582 | 486 | 8 | 46 | 167 | 265 | 3,429 | 456 | 2,406 | 567 |
| Total area actually reporting | 100.0% | 2,063 | 31 | 192 | 671 | 1,169 | 13,012 | 3,571 | 7,243 | 2,198 |
| Rate per 100,000 inhabitants | | 474.1 | 7.1 | 44.1 | 154.2 | 268.7 | 2,990.5 | 820.7 | 1,664.6 | 505.2 |

# Table 6. Crime, by Selected Metropolitan Statistical Area, 2015—*Continued*

(Number, percent, rate per 100,000 population.)

| Area | Population | Violent crime | Murder and nonnegligent manslaughter | Rape[1] | Robbery | Aggravated assault | Property crime | Burglary | Larceny-theft | Motor vehicle theft |
|---|---|---|---|---|---|---|---|---|---|---|
| **Victoria, TX M.S.A.** ........................................... | 100,024 | | | | | | | | | |
| Includes Goliad and Victoria Counties ........................ | | | | | | | | | | |
| City of Victoria........................................................... | 66,988 | 334 | 3 | 47 | 50 | 234 | 2,252 | 440 | 1,711 | 101 |
| Total area actually reporting ....................................... | 100.0% | 452 | 3 | 78 | 53 | 318 | 2,825 | 618 | 2,066 | 141 |
| Rate per 100,000 inhabitants....................................... | | 451.9 | 3.0 | 78.0 | 53.0 | 317.9 | 2,824.3 | 617.9 | 2,065.5 | 141.0 |
| **Vineland-Bridgeton, NJ M.S.A.[2]** ........................... | 157,182 | | | | | | | | | |
| Includes Cumberland County[2]...................................... | | | | | | | | | | |
| City of Vineland[2]......................................................... | 61,265 | 336 | 7 | 32 | 108 | 189 | 2,559 | 525 | 1,966 | 68 |
| City of Bridgeton[2]....................................................... | 25,363 | 292 | 5 | 7 | 126 | 154 | 1,141 | 353 | 757 | 31 |
| Total area actually reporting ....................................... | 100.0% | 917 | 16 | 77 | 345 | 479 | 6,463 | 1,446 | 4,852 | 165 |
| Rate per 100,000 inhabitants....................................... | | 583.4 | 10.2 | 49.0 | 219.5 | 304.7 | 4,111.8 | 920.0 | 3,086.9 | 105.0 |
| **Virginia Beach-Norfolk-Newport News, VA-NC M.S.A.**........................................................... | 1,721,471 | | | | | | | | | |
| Includes Currituck and Gates Counties, NC and Gloucester, Isle of Wight, James City, Mathews, and York Counties and Chesapeake, Hampton, Newport News, Norfolk, Poquoson, Portsmouth, Suffolk, Virginia Beach, and Williamsburg Cities, VA ............... | | | | | | | | | | |
| City of Virginia Beach, VA .......................................... | 452,797 | 626 | 19 | 103 | 270 | 234 | 9,987 | 956 | 8,596 | 435 |
| City of Norfolk, VA...................................................... | 245,400 | 1,329 | 28 | 108 | 454 | 739 | 9,002 | 1,097 | 7,518 | 387 |
| City of Newport News, VA .......................................... | 182,975 | 793 | 26 | 87 | 244 | 436 | 5,585 | 927 | 4,255 | 403 |
| City of Hampton, VA.................................................... | 136,381 | 382 | 16 | 35 | 186 | 145 | 4,474 | 650 | 3,476 | 348 |
| City of Portsmouth, VA ............................................... | 95,877 | 670 | 27 | 44 | 231 | 368 | 4,838 | 1,191 | 3,332 | 315 |
| Total area actually reporting ....................................... | 99.3% | 5,309 | 137 | 537 | 1,688 | 2,947 | 46,768 | 6,614 | 37,680 | 2,474 |
| Estimated total............................................................ | 100.0% | 5,325 | 137 | 538 | 1,690 | 2,960 | 46,947 | 6,681 | 37,783 | 2,483 |
| Rate per 100,000 inhabitants....................................... | | 309.3 | 8.0 | 31.3 | 98.2 | 171.9 | 2,727.1 | 388.1 | 2,194.8 | 144.2 |
| **Visalia-Porterville, CA M.S.A.** ................................ | 461,593 | | | | | | | | | |
| Includes Tulare County ................................................ | | | | | | | | | | |
| City of Visalia ............................................................. | 130,405 | 608 | 6 | 106 | 130 | 366 | 3,995 | 814 | 2,621 | 560 |
| City of Porterville ........................................................ | 55,760 | 186 | 2 | 12 | 41 | 131 | 1,384 | 314 | 844 | 226 |
| Total area actually reporting ....................................... | 100.0% | 1,827 | 45 | 175 | 331 | 1,276 | 11,806 | 2,715 | 7,252 | 1,839 |
| Rate per 100,000 inhabitants....................................... | | 395.8 | 9.7 | 37.9 | 71.7 | 276.4 | 2,557.7 | 588.2 | 1,571.1 | 398.4 |
| **Waco, TX M.S.A.** .................................................... | 262,694 | | | | | | | | | |
| Includes Falls and McLennan Counties ...................... | | | | | | | | | | |
| City of Waco............................................................... | 131,413 | 695 | 22 | 78 | 142 | 453 | 4,913 | 1,143 | 3,614 | 156 |
| Total area actually reporting ....................................... | 97.9% | 1,067 | 23 | 144 | 179 | 721 | 7,791 | 1,710 | 5,779 | 302 |
| Estimated total............................................................ | 100.0% | 1,081 | 23 | 146 | 182 | 730 | 7,931 | 1,733 | 5,886 | 312 |
| Rate per 100,000 inhabitants....................................... | | 411.5 | 8.8 | 55.6 | 69.3 | 277.9 | 3,019.1 | 659.7 | 2,240.6 | 118.8 |
| **Walla Walla, WA M.S.A.**.......................................... | 64,264 | | | | | | | | | |
| Includes Columbia and Walla Walla Counties ............. | | | | | | | | | | |
| City of Walla Walla ..................................................... | 31,940 | 175 | 4 | 18 | 23 | 130 | 1,526 | 249 | 1,182 | 95 |
| Total area actually reporting ....................................... | 100.0% | 200 | 4 | 28 | 24 | 144 | 2,155 | 398 | 1,615 | 142 |
| Rate per 100,000 inhabitants....................................... | | 311.2 | 6.2 | 43.6 | 37.3 | 224.1 | 3,353.4 | 619.3 | 2,513.1 | 221.0 |
| **Warner Robins, GA M.S.A.** ..................................... | 189,693 | | | | | | | | | |
| Includes Houston, Peach, and Pulaski Counties .......... | | | | | | | | | | |
| City of Warner Robins................................................. | 74,363 | 398 | 2 | 28 | 117 | 251 | 3,973 | 784 | 3,014 | 175 |
| Total area actually reporting ....................................... | 100.0% | 680 | 5 | 43 | 191 | 441 | 6,527 | 1,396 | 4,843 | 288 |
| Rate per 100,000 inhabitants....................................... | | 358.5 | 2.6 | 22.7 | 100.7 | 232.5 | 3,440.8 | 735.9 | 2,553.1 | 151.8 |
| **Washington-Arlington-Alexandria, DC-VA-MD-WV M.S.A.** ........................................ | 6,113,776 | | | | | | | | | |
| Includes the Metropolitan Divisions of Silver Spring-Frederick-Rockville, MD and Washington-Arlington-Alexandria, DC-VA-MD-WV ...................................... | | | | | | | | | | |
| City of Washington, D.C. ............................................ | 672,228 | 8,084 | 162 | 494 | 3,404 | 4,024 | 30,359 | 2,971 | 24,194 | 3,194 |
| City of Alexandria, VA................................................. | 152,710 | 312 | 4 | 18 | 142 | 148 | 2,854 | 227 | 2,372 | 255 |
| City of Frederick, MD.................................................. | 69,162 | 341 | 3 | 22 | 66 | 250 | 1,406 | 143 | 1,211 | 52 |
| Total area actually reporting ....................................... | 99.9% | 19,799 | 327 | 1,662 | 7,529 | 10,281 | 117,814 | 13,159 | 94,789 | 9,866 |
| Estimated total............................................................ | 100.0% | 19,812 | 327 | 1,663 | 7,531 | 10,291 | 117,946 | 13,177 | 94,897 | 9,872 |
| Rate per 100,000 inhabitants....................................... | | 324.1 | 5.3 | 27.2 | 123.2 | 168.3 | 1,929.2 | 215.5 | 1,552.2 | 161.5 |
| **Silver Spring-Frederick-Rockville, MD M.D.** ................ | 1,286,701 | | | | | | | | | |
| Includes Frederick and Montgomery Counties ........... | | | | | | | | | | |
| Total area actually reporting ....................................... | 100.0% | 2,627 | 36 | 308 | 747 | 1,536 | 20,060 | 2,543 | 16,637 | 880 |
| Rate per 100,000 inhabitants....................................... | | 204.2 | 2.8 | 23.9 | 58.1 | 119.4 | 1,559.0 | 197.6 | 1,293.0 | 68.4 |

## Table 6. Crime, by Selected Metropolitan Statistical Area, 2015—*Continued*

(Number, percent, rate per 100,000 population.)

| Area | Population | Violent crime | Murder and nonnegligent manslaughter | Rape[1] | Robbery | Aggravated assault | Property crime | Burglary | Larceny-theft | Motor vehicle theft |
|---|---|---|---|---|---|---|---|---|---|---|
| Washington-Arlington-Alexandria, DC-VA-MD-WV M.D. | 4,827,075 | | | | | | | | | |
| Includes District of Columbia; Calvert, Charles, and Prince George's Counties, MD; Arlington, Clarke, Culpeper, Fairfax, Fauquier, Loudoun, Prince William, Rappahannock, Spotsylvania, Stafford, and Warren Counties and Alexandria, Fairfax, Falls Church, Fredericksburg, Manassas, and Manassas Park Cities, VA; and Jefferson County, WV | | | | | | | | | | |
| Total area actually reporting | 99.9% | 17,172 | 291 | 1,354 | 6,782 | 8,745 | 97,754 | 10,616 | 78,152 | 8,986 |
| Estimated total | 100.0% | 17,185 | 291 | 1,355 | 6,784 | 8,755 | 97,886 | 10,634 | 78,260 | 8,992 |
| Rate per 100,000 inhabitants | | 356.0 | 6.0 | 28.1 | 140.5 | 181.4 | 2,027.9 | 220.3 | 1,621.3 | 186.3 |
| **Waterloo-Cedar Falls, IA M.S.A.** | 170,617 | | | | | | | | | |
| Includes Black Hawk, Bremer, and Grundy Counties | | | | | | | | | | |
| City of Waterloo | 68,355 | 660 | 4 | 60 | 54 | 542 | 2,303 | 779 | 1,396 | 128 |
| City of Cedar Falls | 41,252 | 44 | 0 | 13 | 4 | 27 | 671 | 114 | 533 | 24 |
| Total area actually reporting | 100.0% | 848 | 4 | 84 | 60 | 700 | 3,541 | 1,065 | 2,307 | 169 |
| Rate per 100,000 inhabitants | | 497.0 | 2.3 | 49.2 | 35.2 | 410.3 | 2,075.4 | 624.2 | 1,352.2 | 99.1 |
| **Watertown-Fort Drum, NY M.S.A.** | 119,514 | | | | | | | | | |
| Includes Jefferson County | | | | | | | | | | |
| City of Watertown | 27,717 | 145 | 3 | 48 | 15 | 79 | 1,326 | 229 | 1,067 | 30 |
| Total area actually reporting | 97.6% | 220 | 3 | 82 | 17 | 118 | 2,300 | 391 | 1,859 | 50 |
| Estimated total | 100.0% | 226 | 3 | 83 | 19 | 121 | 2,344 | 397 | 1,896 | 51 |
| Rate per 100,000 inhabitants | | 189.1 | 2.5 | 69.4 | 15.9 | 101.2 | 1,961.3 | 332.2 | 1,586.4 | 42.7 |
| **Wausau, WI M.S.A.** | 136,124 | | | | | | | | | |
| Includes Marathon County | | | | | | | | | | |
| City of Wausau | 39,351 | 105 | 2 | 14 | 23 | 66 | 766 | 111 | 626 | 29 |
| Total area actually reporting | 97.5% | 147 | 2 | 24 | 25 | 96 | 1,579 | 248 | 1,285 | 46 |
| Estimated total | 100.0% | 151 | 2 | 25 | 26 | 98 | 1,645 | 255 | 1,341 | 49 |
| Rate per 100,000 inhabitants | | 110.9 | 1.5 | 18.4 | 19.1 | 72.0 | 1,208.5 | 187.3 | 985.1 | 36.0 |
| **Wenatchee, WA M.S.A.** | 115,605 | | | | | | | | | |
| Includes Chelan and Douglas Counties | | | | | | | | | | |
| City of Wenatchee | 33,525 | 52 | 0 | 15 | 7 | 30 | 1,154 | 179 | 912 | 63 |
| Total area actually reporting | 100.0% | 116 | 1 | 20 | 12 | 83 | 2,440 | 537 | 1,740 | 163 |
| Rate per 100,000 inhabitants | | 100.3 | 0.9 | 17.3 | 10.4 | 71.8 | 2,110.6 | 464.5 | 1,505.1 | 141.0 |
| **Wheeling, WV-OH M.S.A.** | 144,361 | | | | | | | | | |
| Includes Belmont County, OH and Marshall and Ohio Counties, WV | | | | | | | | | | |
| City of Wheeling, WV | 27,617 | 247 | 1 | 13 | 30 | 203 | 575 | 158 | 381 | 36 |
| Total area actually reporting | 90.9% | 457 | 5 | 44 | 50 | 358 | 1,839 | 429 | 1,318 | 92 |
| Estimated total | 100.0% | 482 | 5 | 48 | 57 | 372 | 2,165 | 483 | 1,577 | 105 |
| Rate per 100,000 inhabitants | | 333.9 | 3.5 | 33.2 | 39.5 | 257.7 | 1,499.7 | 334.6 | 1,092.4 | 72.7 |
| **Wichita, KS M.S.A.[6]** | 642,476 | | | | | | | | | |
| Includes Butler, Harvey, Kingman, Sedgwick, and Sumner Counties | | | | | | | | | | |
| City of Wichita | 389,824 | 3,839 | 27 | 349 | 733 | 2,730 | 19,652 | 3,480 | 14,127 | 2,045 |
| Total area actually reporting | 99.6% | 4,319 | 30 | 427 | 762 | 3,100 | | | 17,380 | 2,312 |
| Estimated total | 100.0% | 4,325 | 30 | 428 | 763 | 3,104 | | | 17,425 | 2,317 |
| Rate per 100,000 inhabitants | | 673.2 | 4.7 | 66.6 | 118.8 | 483.1 | | | 2,712.2 | 360.6 |
| **Wichita Falls, TX M.S.A.** | 151,849 | | | | | | | | | |
| Includes Archer, Clay, and Wichita Counties | | | | | | | | | | |
| City of Wichita Falls | 105,186 | 406 | 1 | 85 | 109 | 211 | 3,821 | 899 | 2,751 | 171 |
| Total area actually reporting | 93.5% | 482 | 2 | 98 | 118 | 264 | 4,700 | 1,156 | 3,287 | 257 |
| Estimated total | 100.0% | 508 | 2 | 102 | 124 | 280 | 4,950 | 1,197 | 3,479 | 274 |
| Rate per 100,000 inhabitants | | 334.5 | 1.3 | 67.2 | 81.7 | 184.4 | 3,259.8 | 788.3 | 2,291.1 | 180.4 |
| **Williamsport, PA M.S.A.** | 116,554 | | | | | | | | | |
| Includes Lycoming County | | | | | | | | | | |
| City of Williamsport | 29,150 | 120 | 7 | 19 | 38 | 56 | 908 | 138 | 749 | 21 |
| Total area actually reporting | 100.0% | 244 | 7 | 56 | 55 | 126 | 2,087 | 342 | 1,695 | 50 |
| Rate per 100,000 inhabitants | | 209.3 | 6.0 | 48.0 | 47.2 | 108.1 | 1,790.6 | 293.4 | 1,454.3 | 42.9 |

# Table 6. Crime, by Selected Metropolitan Statistical Area, 2015—*Continued*

(Number, percent, rate per 100,000 population.)

| Area | Population | Violent crime | Murder and nonnegligent manslaughter | Rape[1] | Robbery | Aggravated assault | Property crime | Burglary | Larceny-theft | Motor vehicle theft |
|---|---|---|---|---|---|---|---|---|---|---|
| **Wilmington, NC M.S.A.** | 276,859 | | | | | | | | | |
| Includes New Hanover and Pender Counties | | | | | | | | | | |
| City of Wilmington | 115,434 | 880 | 14 | 62 | 274 | 530 | 5,170 | 1,405 | 3,471 | 294 |
| Total area actually reporting | 99.1% | 1,167 | 20 | 94 | 335 | 718 | 9,040 | 2,434 | 6,181 | 425 |
| Estimated total | 100.0% | 1,173 | 20 | 94 | 337 | 722 | 9,114 | 2,449 | 6,237 | 428 |
| Rate per 100,000 inhabitants | | 423.7 | 7.2 | 34.0 | 121.7 | 260.8 | 3,291.9 | 884.6 | 2,252.8 | 154.6 |
| **Winchester, VA-WV M.S.A.** | 134,250 | | | | | | | | | |
| Includes Frederick County and Winchester City, VA and Hampshire County, WV | | | | | | | | | | |
| City of Winchester, VA | 27,821 | 72 | 0 | 23 | 21 | 28 | 1,035 | 118 | 889 | 28 |
| Total area actually reporting | 84.0% | 181 | 1 | 69 | 33 | 78 | 2,364 | 332 | 1,928 | 104 |
| Estimated total | 100.0% | 233 | 2 | 76 | 38 | 117 | 2,713 | 431 | 2,153 | 129 |
| Rate per 100,000 inhabitants | | 173.6 | 1.5 | 56.6 | 28.3 | 87.2 | 2,020.9 | 321.0 | 1,603.7 | 96.1 |
| **Worcester, MA-CT M.S.A.** | 859,394 | | | | | | | | | |
| Includes Windham County, CT and Worcester County, MA | | | | | | | | | | |
| City of Worcester, MA | 183,377 | 1,627 | 8 | 26 | 407 | 1,186 | 5,375 | 1,214 | 3,765 | 396 |
| Total area actually reporting | 93.0% | 3,545 | 13 | 255 | 597 | 2,680 | 14,094 | 3,029 | 10,250 | 815 |
| Estimated total | 100.0% | 3,737 | 14 | 273 | 627 | 2,823 | 15,007 | 3,203 | 10,928 | 876 |
| Rate per 100,000 inhabitants | | 434.8 | 1.6 | 31.8 | 73.0 | 328.5 | 1,746.2 | 372.7 | 1,271.6 | 101.9 |
| **Yakima, WA M.S.A.** | 249,480 | | | | | | | | | |
| Includes Yakima County | | | | | | | | | | |
| City of Yakima | 93,798 | 514 | 7 | 51 | 126 | 330 | 5,091 | 1,307 | 3,110 | 674 |
| Total area actually reporting | 100.0% | 732 | 21 | 78 | 192 | 441 | 8,825 | 2,265 | 5,428 | 1,132 |
| Rate per 100,000 inhabitants | | 293.4 | 8.4 | 31.3 | 77.0 | 176.8 | 3,537.4 | 907.9 | 2,175.7 | 453.7 |
| **York-Hanover, PA M.S.A.** | 441,919 | | | | | | | | | |
| Includes York County | | | | | | | | | | |
| City of York | 43,864 | 325 | 10 | 19 | 178 | 118 | 1,399 | 336 | 939 | 124 |
| City of Hanover | 15,494 | 24 | 0 | 3 | 6 | 15 | 453 | 27 | 419 | 7 |
| Total area actually reporting | 100.0% | 961 | 19 | 103 | 284 | 555 | 6,856 | 1,028 | 5,547 | 281 |
| Rate per 100,000 inhabitants | | 217.5 | 4.3 | 23.3 | 64.3 | 125.6 | 1,551.4 | 232.6 | 1,255.2 | 63.6 |
| **Yuba City, CA M.S.A.** | 170,322 | | | | | | | | | |
| Includes Sutter and Yuba Counties | | | | | | | | | | |
| City of Yuba City | 65,974 | 216 | 0 | 28 | 66 | 122 | 1,792 | 429 | 1,160 | 203 |
| Total area actually reporting | 100.0% | 633 | 6 | 63 | 139 | 425 | 4,409 | 1,123 | 2,650 | 636 |
| Rate per 100,000 inhabitants | | 371.6 | 3.5 | 37.0 | 81.6 | 249.5 | 2,588.6 | 659.3 | 1,555.9 | 373.4 |
| **Yuma, AZ M.S.A.** | 205,233 | | | | | | | | | |
| Includes Yuma County | | | | | | | | | | |
| City of Yuma | 93,923 | 453 | 5 | 46 | 74 | 328 | 2,925 | 682 | 1,984 | 259 |
| Total area actually reporting | 100.0% | 672 | 10 | 71 | 92 | 499 | 4,617 | 1,287 | 2,920 | 410 |
| Rate per 100,000 inhabitants | | 327.4 | 4.9 | 34.6 | 44.8 | 243.1 | 2,249.6 | 627.1 | 1,422.8 | 199.8 |
| **Aguadilla-Isabela, Puerto Rico M.S.A.** | 315,685 | | | | | | | | | |
| Includes Aguada, Aguadilla, Anasco, Isabela, Lares, Moca, Rincon, San Sebastian, and Utuado Municipios | | | | | | | | | | |
| Total area actually reporting | 100.0% | 343 | 15 | 11 | 128 | 189 | 2,242 | 898 | 1,273 | 71 |
| Rate per 100,000 inhabitants | | 108.7 | 4.8 | 3.5 | 40.5 | 59.9 | 710.2 | 284.5 | 403.3 | 22.5 |
| **Arecibo, Puerto Rico M.S.A.** | 188,295 | | | | | | | | | |
| Includes Arecibo, Camuy, Hatillo, and Quebradillas Municipios | | | | | | | | | | |
| Total area actually reporting | 100.0% | 187 | 13 | 5 | 100 | 69 | 1,943 | 541 | 1,263 | 139 |
| Rate per 100,000 inhabitants | | 99.3 | 6.9 | 2.7 | 53.1 | 36.6 | 1,031.9 | 287.3 | 670.8 | 73.8 |
| **Guayama, Puerto Rico M.S.A.** | 79,086 | | | | | | | | | |
| Includes Arroyo, Guayama, and Patillas Municipios | | | | | | | | | | |
| Total area actually reporting | 100.0% | 199 | 9 | 5 | 59 | 126 | 651 | 210 | 420 | 21 |
| Rate per 100,000 inhabitants | | 251.6 | 11.4 | 6.3 | 74.6 | 159.3 | 823.2 | 265.5 | 531.1 | 26.6 |
| **Mayaguez, Puerto Rico M.S.A.** | 95,988 | | | | | | | | | |
| Includes Hormigueros and Mayaguez Municipios | | | | | | | | | | |
| Total area actually reporting | 100.0% | 228 | 11 | 5 | 79 | 133 | 1,267 | 362 | 827 | 78 |
| Rate per 100,000 inhabitants | | 237.5 | 11.5 | 5.2 | 82.3 | 138.6 | 1,320.0 | 377.1 | 861.6 | 81.3 |

# Table 6. Crime, by Selected Metropolitan Statistical Area, 2015—*Continued*

(Number, percent, rate per 100,000 population.)

| Area | Population | Violent crime | Murder and nonnegligent manslaughter | Rape[1] | Robbery | Aggravated assault | Property crime | Burglary | Larceny-theft | Motor vehicle theft |
|---|---|---|---|---|---|---|---|---|---|---|
| **Ponce, Puerto Rico M.S.A.** ..................................... | 317,185 | | | | | | | | | |
| Includes Guanica, Guyanilla, Juana Diaz, Penuelas, Ponce, Villalba, and Yauco Municipios........................ | | | | | | | | | | |
| Total area actually reporting ..................................... | 100.0% | 734 | 57 | 16 | 210 | 451 | 2,807 | 680 | 2,006 | 121 |
| Rate per 100,000 inhabitants...................................... | | 231.4 | 18.0 | 5.0 | 66.2 | 142.2 | 885.0 | 214.4 | 632.4 | 38.1 |
| **San German, Puerto Rico M.S.A.** ........................... | 130,228 | | | | | | | | | |
| Includes Cabo Rojo, Lajas, Sabana Grande, and San German Municipios.................................................. | | | | | | | | | | |
| Total area actually reporting ..................................... | 100.0% | 120 | 7 | 6 | 21 | 86 | 547 | 220 | 295 | 32 |
| Rate per 100,000 inhabitants...................................... | | 92.1 | 5.4 | 4.6 | 16.1 | 66.0 | 420.0 | 168.9 | 226.5 | 24.6 |
| **San Juan-Carolina-Caguas, Puerto Rico M.S.A.** ..... | 2,196,538 | | | | | | | | | |
| Includes Aguas Buenas, Aibonito, Barceloneta, Barranquitas, Bayamon, Caguas, Canovanas, Carolina, Catano, Cayey, Ceiba, Ciales, Cidra, Comerio, Corozal, Dorado, Fajardo, Florida, Guaynabo, Gurabo, Humacao, Juncos, Las Piedras, Loiza, Luquillo, Manati, Maunabo, Morovis, Naguabo, Naranjito, Orocovis, Rio Grande, San Juan, San Lorenzo, Toa Alta, Toa Baja, Trujillo Alto, Vega Alta, Vega Baja, and Yabucoa Municipios................................................................ | | | | | | | | | | |
| Total area actually reporting ..................................... | 100.0% | 5,755 | 453 | 108 | 3,466 | 1,728 | 28,141 | 6,189 | 18,342 | 3,610 |
| Rate per 100,000 inhabitants...................................... | | 262.0 | 20.6 | 4.9 | 157.8 | 78.7 | 1,281.2 | 281.8 | 835.0 | 164.3 |

[1] The rape figures in this table are an aggregate total of the data submitted using both the revised and legacy Uniform Crime Reporting (UCR) definitions.  See data declaration for further explanation.
[2] Because of changes in the state/local agency's reporting practices, figures are not comparable to previous years' data.
[3] The FBI determined that the agency's data were overreported. Consequently, those data are not included in this table.
[4] The FBI determined that the agency's data were underreported. Consequently, those data are not included in this table.
[5] The population for the city of Mobile, Alabama, includes 55,819 inhabitants from the jurisdiction of the Mobile County Sheriff's Department.
[6] The FBI determined that the agency did not follow national UCR Program guidelines for reporting an offense. Consequently, this figure is not included in this table.

# Table 7. Offense Analysis, United States, 2011–2015

(Number.)

| Classification | 2011 | 2012 | 2013[1] | 2014 | 2015 |
|---|---|---|---|---|---|
| **Murder** | 14,661 | 14,856 | 14,319 | 14,164 | 15,696 |
| **Rape (revised definition)[2]** | X | X | 113,695 | 118,027 | 124,047 |
| **Rape (legacy definition)[3]** | 84,175 | 85,141 | 82,109 | 84,868 | 90,185 |
| **Robbery[4]** | 354,746 | 355,051 | 345,093 | 322,905 | 327,374 |
| By location | | | | | |
| Street/highway | 155,218 | 154,289 | 146,499 | 132,269 | 130,431 |
| Commercial house | 46,156 | 47,151 | 45,760 | 45,273 | 47,123 |
| Gas or service station | 8,539 | 8,660 | 8,354 | 8,072 | 8,896 |
| Convenience store | 18,108 | 18,180 | 17,103 | 17,380 | 18,619 |
| Residence | 60,138 | 59,979 | 57,372 | 54,120 | 54,021 |
| Bank | 7,038 | 6,666 | 6,512 | 5,939 | 5,678 |
| Miscellaneous | 59,549 | 60,126 | 63,495 | 59,853 | 62,606 |
| **Burglary[4]** | 2,185,140 | 2,109,932 | 1,932,139 | 1,713,153 | 1,579,527 |
| By location | | | | | |
| Residence (dwelling) | 1,628,656 | 1,571,635 | 1,428,448 | 1,253,915 | 1,130,910 |
| Residence, night | 442,390 | 429,662 | 395,604 | 349,441 | 327,072 |
| Residence, day | 859,299 | 832,944 | 756,617 | 669,364 | 591,658 |
| Residence, unknown | 326,967 | 309,028 | 276,227 | 235,111 | 212,180 |
| Nonresidence (store, office, etc.) | 556,484 | 538,297 | 503,691 | 459,238 | 448,617 |
| Nonresidence, night | 227,446 | 220,784 | 206,031 | 188,010 | 188,210 |
| Nonresidence, day | 196,461 | 192,963 | 183,380 | 167,749 | 158,371 |
| Nonresidence, unknown | 132,577 | 124,550 | 114,280 | 103,480 | 102,036 |
| **Larceny-theft (except motor vehicle theft)[4]** | 6,151,095 | 6,168,874 | 6,019,465 | 5,809,054 | 5,706,346 |
| By type | | | | | |
| Pocket-picking | 26,518 | 29,550 | 32,426 | 31,213 | 31,115 |
| Purse-snatching | 27,082 | 26,407 | 25,867 | 23,479 | 23,075 |
| Shoplifting | 1,077,791 | 1,147,679 | 1,199,157 | 1,247,199 | 1,272,752 |
| From motor vehicles (except accessories) | 1,523,950 | 1,480,790 | 1,405,858 | 1,332,924 | 1,369,605 |
| Motor vehicle accessories | 497,980 | 467,369 | 439,151 | 408,545 | 398,255 |
| Bicycles | 216,987 | 223,786 | 212,889 | 209,762 | 204,984 |
| From buildings | 728,050 | 745,238 | 740,092 | 712,073 | 662,391 |
| From coin-operated machines | 19,536 | 17,240 | 15,906 | 13,328 | 12,981 |
| All others | 2,033,200 | 2,030,815 | 1,948,120 | 1,830,531 | 1,731,188 |
| By value | | | | | |
| Under $50 | 2,850,302 | 2,872,445 | 2,819,518 | 2,687,591 | 2,605,506 |
| $50 to $200 | 1,399,484 | 1,398,870 | 1,342,473 | 1,306,350 | 1,274,199 |
| Over $200 | 1,901,309 | 1,897,560 | 1,857,474 | 1,815,113 | 1,826,641 |
| **Motor vehicle theft** | 716,508 | 723,186 | 700,288 | 686,803 | 707,758 |

X = Not applicable.
[1] The crime figures have been adjusted.
[2] The figures shown in this column for the offense of rape were estimated using the revised Uniform Crime Reporting (UCR) definition of rape. See chapter notes for more detail.
[3] The figures shown in this column for the offense of rape were estimated using the legacy Uniform Crime Reporting (UCR) definition of rape. See chapter notes for more detail.
[4] Because of rounding, the number of offenses may not add to the total.

# Table 8. Crime Trends, by Population Group, 2014–2015

(Number, percent change.)

| Population group | Violent crime | Murder and nonnegligent manslaughter | Rape (revised definition)[1] | Rape (legacy definition)[2] | Robbery | Aggravated assault | Property crime | Burglary | Larceny-theft | Motor vehicle theft | Arson | Number of agencies | Estimated population, 2015 |
|---|---|---|---|---|---|---|---|---|---|---|---|---|---|
| **Total, All Agencies** | | | | | | | | | | | | | |
| 2014 | 1,118,918 | 13,594 | 89,098 | 7,115 | 310,511 | 698,600 | 7,730,805 | 1,613,258 | 5,464,398 | 653,149 | 42,914 | | |
| 2015 | 1,160,664 | 15,192 | 94,717 | 7,586 | 315,660 | 727,509 | 7,549,676 | 1,489,820 | 5,383,743 | 676,113 | 41,376 | 15,545 | 305,159,115 |
| Percent change | +3.7 | +11.8 | +6.3 | +6.6 | +1.7 | +4.1 | -2.3 | -7.7 | -1.5 | +3.5 | -3.6 | | |
| **Total, Cities** | | | | | | | | | | | | | |
| 2014 | 894,588 | 10,513 | 66,134 | 4,782 | 272,092 | 541,067 | 6,103,377 | 1,176,651 | 4,404,971 | 521,755 | 32,603 | | |
| 2015 | 929,348 | 11,862 | 70,759 | 5,123 | 276,831 | 564,773 | 5,998,043 | 1,092,856 | 4,362,498 | 542,689 | 31,557 | 11,122 | 206,728,529 |
| Percent change | +3.9 | +12.8 | +7.0 | +7.1 | +1.7 | +4.4 | -1.7 | -7.1 | -1.0 | +4.0 | -3.2 | | |
| **Group I (250,000 and over)** | | | | | | | | | | | | | |
| 2014 | 420,517 | 5,370 | 24,607 | 1,040 | 150,505 | 238,995 | 2,006,899 | 404,912 | 1,361,161 | 240,826 | 11,730 | | |
| 2015 | 437,895 | 6,146 | 26,947 | 1,129 | 154,760 | 248,913 | 1,987,100 | 378,045 | 1,365,521 | 243,534 | 11,931 | 80 | 59,097,749 |
| Percent change | +4.1 | +14.5 | +9.5 | +8.6 | +2.8 | +4.1 | -1.0 | -6.6 | +0.3 | +1.1 | +1.7 | | |
| **1,000,000 and over (Group I subset)** | | | | | | | | | | | | | |
| 2014 | 177,366 | 2,017 | 10,367 | - | 67,346 | 97,636 | 737,431 | 139,640 | 504,988 | 92,803 | 4,149 | | |
| 2015 | 187,350 | 2,231 | 12,147 | - | 69,301 | 103,671 | 726,998 | 131,803 | 501,699 | 93,496 | 3,921 | 11 | 27,404,679 |
| Percent change | +5.6 | +10.6 | +17.2 | - | +2.9 | +6.2 | -1.4 | -5.6 | -0.7 | +0.7 | -5.5 | | |
| **500,000 to 999,999 (Group I subset)** | | | | | | | | | | | | | |
| 2014 | 132,955 | 1,719 | 7,755 | 612 | 43,570 | 79,299 | 675,699 | 138,006 | 460,506 | 77,187 | 3,184 | | |
| 2015 | 135,732 | 2,066 | 7,919 | 620 | 46,025 | 79,102 | 668,848 | 129,169 | 463,493 | 76,186 | 3,480 | 22 | 15,610,663 |
| Percent change | +2.1 | +20.2 | +2.1 | +1.3 | +5.6 | -0.2 | -1.0 | -6.4 | +0.6 | -1.3 | +9.3 | | |
| **250,000 to 499,999 (Group I subset)** | | | | | | | | | | | | | |
| 2014 | 110,196 | 1,634 | 6,485 | 428 | 39,589 | 62,060 | 593,769 | 127,266 | 395,667 | 70,836 | 4,397 | | |
| 2015 | 114,813 | 1,849 | 6,881 | 509 | 39,434 | 66,140 | 591,254 | 117,073 | 400,329 | 73,852 | 4,530 | 47 | 16,082,407 |
| Percent change | +4.2 | +13.2 | +6.1 | +18.9 | -0.4 | +6.6 | -0.4 | -8.0 | +1.2 | +4.3 | +3.0 | | |
| **Group II (100,000 to 249,999)** | | | | | | | | | | | | | |
| 2014 | 143,201 | 1,797 | 11,010 | 678 | 44,227 | 85,489 | 1,056,023 | 213,004 | 741,802 | 101,217 | 5,356 | | |
| 2015 | 150,861 | 1,999 | 11,875 | 789 | 44,821 | 91,377 | 1,054,055 | 198,842 | 746,268 | 108,945 | 4,999 | 216 | 32,227,725 |
| Percent change | +5.3 | +11.2 | +7.9 | +16.4 | +1.3 | +6.9 | -0.2 | -6.6 | +0.6 | +7.6 | -6.7 | | |
| **Group III (50,000 to 99,999)** | | | | | | | | | | | | | |
| 2014 | 108,643 | 1,116 | 8,527 | 641 | 30,670 | 67,689 | 896,590 | 169,982 | 656,450 | 70,158 | 4,358 | | |
| 2015 | 111,117 | 1,243 | 8,772 | 729 | 30,638 | 69,735 | 891,484 | 157,891 | 657,274 | 76,319 | 4,142 | 481 | 33,490,047 |
| Percent change | +2.3 | +11.4 | +2.9 | +13.7 | -0.1 | +3.0 | -0.6 | -7.1 | +0.1 | +8.8 | -5.0 | | |
| **Group IV (25,000 to 49,999)** | | | | | | | | | | | | | |
| 2014 | 83,487 | 915 | 7,803 | 763 | 21,487 | 52,519 | 772,777 | 141,808 | 585,795 | 45,174 | 3,728 | | |
| 2015 | 86,591 | 1,013 | 8,325 | 841 | 21,376 | 55,036 | 753,094 | 131,479 | 574,041 | 47,574 | 3,476 | 861 | 29,777,604 |
| Percent change | +3.7 | +10.7 | +6.7 | +10.2 | -0.5 | +4.8 | -2.5 | -7.3 | -2.0 | +5.3 | -6.8 | | |
| **Group V (10,000 to 24,999)** | | | | | | | | | | | | | |
| 2014 | 74,277 | 731 | 7,206 | 793 | 15,606 | 49,941 | 731,328 | 134,348 | 560,627 | 36,353 | 3,183 | | |
| 2015 | 76,808 | 834 | 7,693 | 767 | 15,685 | 51,829 | 704,558 | 122,779 | 544,020 | 37,759 | 3,044 | 1,805 | 28,863,408 |
| Percent change | +3.4 | +14.1 | +6.8 | -3.3 | +0.5 | +3.8 | -3.7 | -8.6 | -3.0 | +3.9 | -4.4 | | |
| **Group VI (under 10,000)** | | | | | | | | | | | | | |
| 2014 | 64,463 | 584 | 6,981 | 867 | 9,597 | 46,434 | 639,760 | 112,597 | 499,136 | 28,027 | 4,248 | | |
| 2015 | 66,076 | 627 | 7,147 | 868 | 9,551 | 47,883 | 607,752 | 103,820 | 475,374 | 28,558 | 3,965 | 7,679 | 23,271,996 |
| Percent change | +2.5 | +7.4 | +2.4 | +0.1 | -0.5 | +3.1 | -5.0 | -7.8 | -4.8 | +1.9 | -6.7 | | |

# Table 8. Crime Trends, by Population Group, 2014–2015—*Continued*

(Number, percent change.)

| Population group | Violent crime | Murder and nonnegligent manslaughter | Rape (revised definition)[1] | Rape (legacy definition)[2] | Robbery | Aggravated assault | Property crime | Burglary | Larceny-theft | Motor vehicle theft | Arson | Number of agencies | Estimated population, 2015 |
|---|---|---|---|---|---|---|---|---|---|---|---|---|---|
| **Metropolitan Counties......................** | | | | | | | | | | | | | |
| 2014...................... | 179,958 | 2,340 | 16,116 | 1,802 | 35,727 | 123,973 | 1,300,465 | 329,479 | 861,902 | 109,084 | 7,564 | | |
| 2015...................... | 185,888 | 2,476 | 17,206 | 1,842 | 36,195 | 128,169 | 1,247,681 | 298,050 | 838,438 | 111,193 | 7,379 | 1,946 | 73,347,881 |
| Percent change....... | +3.3 | +5.8 | +6.8 | +2.2 | +1.3 | +3.4 | -4.1 | -9.5 | -2.7 | +1.9 | -2.4 | | |
| **Nonmetropolitan Counties[3]......................** | | | | | | | | | | | | | |
| 2014...................... | 44,372 | 741 | 6,848 | 531 | 2,692 | 33,560 | 326,963 | 107,128 | 197,525 | 22,310 | 2,747 | | |
| 2015...................... | 45,428 | 854 | 6,752 | 621 | 2,634 | 34,567 | 303,952 | 98,914 | 182,807 | 22,231 | 2,440 | 2,477 | 25,082,705 |
| Percent change....... | +2.4 | +15.2 | -1.4 | +16.9 | -2.2 | +3.0 | -7.0 | -7.7 | -7.5 | -0.4 | -11.2 | | |
| **Suburban Areas[4] ........** | | | | | | | | | | | | | |
| 2014...................... | 313,352 | 3,670 | 28,816 | 3,001 | 67,667 | 210,198 | 2,680,468 | 566,379 | 1,928,061 | 186,028 | 14,074 | | |
| 2015...................... | 323,844 | 3,900 | 30,758 | 3,048 | 68,209 | 217,929 | 2,582,715 | 514,887 | 1,875,964 | 191,864 | 13,388 | 8,480 | 132,726,573 |
| Percent change....... | +3.3 | +6.3 | +6.7 | +1.6 | +0.8 | +3.7 | -3.6 | -9.1 | -2.7 | +3.1 | -4.9 | | |

NOTE: No agencies over 1,000,000 in population submitted rape data using the legacy UCR definition in 2015; therefore, the UCR Program could not provide a 2-year comparison for this agency group size.
[1] The figures shown in the rape (revised definition) column include only those reported by law enforcement agencies that used the revised Uniform Crime Reporting (UCR) definition of rape.
[2] The figures shown in the rape (legacy definition) column include only those reported by law enforcement agencies that used the legacy UCR definition of rape.
[3] Includes state police agencies that report aggregately for the entire state.
[4] Suburban areas include law enforcement agencies in cities with less than 50,000 inhabitants and county law enforcement agencies that are within a Metropolitan Statistical Area. Suburban areas exclude all metropolitan agencies associated with a principal city. The agencies associated with suburban areas also appear in other groups within this table.

# Table 9. Rate: Number of Crimes Per 100,000 Population, by Population Group, 2015

(Number, rate.)

| Population group | Violent crime Number of offenses known | Rate | Murder and nonnegligent manslaughter Number of offenses known | Rate | Rape (revised definition)[1] Number of offenses known | Rate | Rape (legacy definition)[2] Number of offenses known | Rate | Robbery Number of offenses known | Rate |
|---|---|---|---|---|---|---|---|---|---|---|
| Total, All Agencies.............................................. | 1,154,081 | 385.9 | 14,856 | 5.0 | 105,626 | 39.3 | 7,340 | 24.0 | 308,504 | 103.1 |
| Total, Cities ...................................................... | 922,794 | 454.1 | 11,571 | 5.7 | 79,075 | 42.2 | 4,940 | 31.0 | 270,386 | 133.1 |
| Group I  (250,000 and over)................................. | 436,315 | 734.2 | 5,990 | 10.1 | 29,951 | 52.8 | 1,129 | 41.5 | 151,664 | 255.2 |
| 1,000,000 and over (Group I subset).............. | 188,291 | 687.1 | 2,231 | 8.1 | 13,088 | 47.8 | 0 | 0.0 | 69,301 | 252.9 |
| 500,000 to 999,999 (Group I subset)............. | 138,863 | 836.0 | 2,081 | 12.5 | 8,931 | 58.9 | 620 | 43.1 | 46,921 | 282.5 |
| 250,000 to 499,999 (Group I subset)............. | 109,161 | 708.2 | 1,678 | 10.9 | 7,932 | 56.1 | 509 | 39.6 | 35,442 | 229.9 |
| Group II (100,000 to 249,999).......................... | 147,363 | 471.0 | 1,934 | 6.2 | 13,530 | 45.6 | 638 | 38.9 | 43,121 | 137.8 |
| Group III (50,000 to 99,999) ............................ | 111,334 | 337.9 | 1,231 | 3.7 | 10,342 | 34.0 | 742 | 29.4 | 30,289 | 91.9 |
| Group IV (25,000 to 49,999)............................. | 85,566 | 293.8 | 980 | 3.4 | 9,151 | 34.7 | 834 | 30.4 | 20,643 | 70.9 |
| Group V (10,000 to 24,999) ............................. | 75,676 | 269.8 | 820 | 2.9 | 8,188 | 33.1 | 757 | 23.0 | 15,374 | 54.8 |
| Group VI (under 10,000)................................... | 66,540 | 297.5 | 616 | 2.8 | 7,913 | 40.8 | 840 | 28.0 | 9,295 | 41.6 |
| Metropolitan Counties ...................................... | 185,490 | 258.4 | 2,424 | 3.4 | 19,156 | 31.3 | 1,774 | 16.7 | 35,544 | 49.5 |
| Nonmetropolitan Counties[3] ........................... | 45,797 | 190.1 | 861 | 3.6 | 7,395 | 37.0 | 626 | 15.2 | 2,574 | 10.7 |
| Suburban Areas[4] .............................................. | 323,651 | 249.2 | 3,822 | 2.9 | 34,560 | 30.4 | 2,963 | 18.3 | 66,964 | 51.6 |

[1] The figures shown in the rape (revised definition) column include only those reported by law enforcement agencies that used the revised Uniform Crime Reporting (UCR) definition of rape.
[2] The figures shown in the rape (legacy definition) column include only those reported by law enforcement agencies that used the legacy UCR definition of rape.
[3] Includes state police agencies that report aggregately for the entire state.
[4] Suburban areas include law enforcement agencies in cities with less than 50,000 inhabitants and county law enforcement agencies that are within a Metropolitan Statistical Area.  Suburban areas exclude all metropolitan agencies associated with a principal city.  The agencies associated with suburban areas also appear in other groups within this table.

(Number, rate.)

| Population group | Aggravated assault | | Property crime | | Burglary | | Larceny-theft | | Motor vehicle theft | | Number of agencies | Estimated population, 2015 |
|---|---|---|---|---|---|---|---|---|---|---|---|---|
| | Number of offenses known | Rate | Number of offenses known | Rate | Number of offenses known | Rate | Number of offenses known | Rate | Number of offenses known | Rate | | |
| Total, All Agencies............................... | 717,755 | 240.0 | 7,448,474 | 2,490.4 | 1,463,001 | 489.1 | 5,317,451 | 1,777.9 | 668,022 | 223.4 | 15,010 | 299,091,598 |
| Total, Cities ............................................ | 556,822 | 274.0 | 5,922,526 | 2,914.5 | 1,072,772 | 527.9 | 4,313,452 | 2,122.7 | 536,302 | 263.9 | 10,645 | 203,209,630 |
| Group I  (250,000 and over)...................... | 247,581 | 416.6 | 1,996,197 | 3,359.0 | 376,442 | 633.4 | 1,377,365 | 2,317.7 | 242,390 | 407.9 | 79 | 59,428,247 |
| 1,000,000 and over (Group I subset)..... | 103,671 | 378.3 | 726,998 | 2,652.8 | 131,803 | 481.0 | 501,699 | 1,830.7 | 93,496 | 341.2 | 11 | 27,404,679 |
| 500,000 to 999,999 (Group I subset).... | 80,310 | 483.5 | 699,933 | 4,213.9 | 133,453 | 803.5 | 486,423 | 2,928.5 | 80,057 | 482.0 | 23 | 16,609,970 |
| 250,000 to 499,999 (Group I subset).... | 63,600 | 412.6 | 569,266 | 3,693.3 | 111,186 | 721.4 | 389,243 | 2,525.3 | 68,837 | 446.6 | 45 | 15,413,598 |
| Group II (100,000 to 249,999)................. | 88,140 | 281.7 | 1,023,012 | 3,269.9 | 191,758 | 612.9 | 724,775 | 2,316.6 | 106,479 | 340.3 | 210 | 31,285,733 |
| Group III (50,000 to 99,999) ..................... | 68,730 | 208.6 | 881,376 | 2,674.6 | 155,964 | 473.3 | 649,674 | 1,971.5 | 75,738 | 229.8 | 474 | 32,952,951 |
| Group IV (25,000 to 49,999)...................... | 53,958 | 185.3 | 734,604 | 2,522.3 | 127,488 | 437.7 | 560,385 | 1,924.1 | 46,731 | 160.5 | 841 | 29,124,007 |
| Group V (10,000 to 24,999) ..................... | 50,537 | 180.2 | 690,297 | 2,461.0 | 120,047 | 428.0 | 533,415 | 1,901.7 | 36,835 | 131.3 | 1,752 | 28,049,861 |
| Group VI (under 10,000)............................ | 47,876 | 214.0 | 597,040 | 2,669.1 | 101,073 | 451.8 | 467,838 | 2,091.5 | 28,129 | 125.8 | 7,289 | 22,368,831 |
| Metropolitan Counties .......................... | 126,592 | 176.3 | 1,229,840 | 1,713.0 | 294,084 | 409.6 | 825,786 | 1,150.2 | 109,970 | 153.2 | 1,954 | 71,792,662 |
| Nonmetropolitan Counties³ .................. | 34,341 | 142.6 | 296,108 | 1,229.2 | 96,145 | 399.1 | 178,213 | 739.8 | 21,750 | 90.3 | 2,411 | 24,089,306 |
| Suburban Areas⁴ ...................................... | 215,342 | 165.8 | 2,545,775 | 1,960.3 | 507,213 | 390.6 | 1,849,006 | 1,423.8 | 189,556 | 146.0 | 8,263 | 129,863,798 |

¹ The figures shown in the rape (revised definition) column include only those reported by law enforcement agencies that used the revised Uniform Crime Reporting (UCR) definition of rape.
² The figures shown in the rape (legacy definition) column include only those reported by law enforcement agencies that used the legacy UCR definition of rape.
³ Includes state police agencies that report aggregately for the entire state.
⁴ Suburban areas include law enforcement agencies in cities with less than 50,000 inhabitants and county law enforcement agencies that are within a Metropolitan Statistical Area.  Suburban areas exclude all metropolitan agencies associated with a principal city.  The agencies associated with suburban areas also appear in other groups within this table.

# Table 10. Rate: Number of Crimes Per 100,000 Inhabitants, by Suburban and Nonsuburban Cities,[1] by Population Group, 2015

(Number, rate.)

| Population group | Violent crime | | Murder and nonnegligent manslaughter | | Rape (revised definition)[2] | | Rape (legacy definition)[3] | | Robbery | | Aggravated assault | |
|---|---|---|---|---|---|---|---|---|---|---|---|---|
| | Number of offenses known | Rate | Number of offenses known | Rate | Number of offenses known | Rate | Number of offenses known | Rate | Number of offenses known | Rate | Number of offenses known | Rate |
| **Total, Suburban Cities**............... | 138,161 | 237.9 | 1,398 | 2.4 | 15,404 | 29.4 | 1,189 | 21.2 | 31,420 | 54.1 | 88,750 | 152.8 |
| Group IV (25,000 to 49,999).......... | 52,740 | 233.2 | 592 | 2.6 | 5,965 | 28.5 | 314 | 19.0 | 13,968 | 61.8 | 31,901 | 141.1 |
| Group V (10,000 to 24,999) ......... | 47,731 | 223.4 | 498 | 2.3 | 4,986 | 26.2 | 419 | 18.0 | 10,917 | 51.1 | 30,911 | 144.7 |
| Group VI (under 10,000)............... | 37,690 | 267.4 | 308 | 2.2 | 4,453 | 35.7 | 456 | 27.9 | 6,535 | 46.4 | 25,938 | 184.0 |
| **Total, Nonsuburban Cities** ......... | 89,621 | 417.4 | 1,018 | 4.7 | 9,848 | 54.6 | 1,242 | 36.3 | 13,892 | 64.7 | 63,621 | 296.3 |
| Group IV (25,000 to 49,999).......... | 32,826 | 504.2 | 388 | 6.0 | 3,186 | 58.8 | 520 | 47.7 | 6,675 | 102.5 | 22,057 | 338.8 |
| Group V (10,000 to 24,999) ......... | 27,945 | 417.9 | 322 | 4.8 | 3,202 | 56.0 | 338 | 34.9 | 4,457 | 66.6 | 19,626 | 293.5 |
| Group VI (under 10,000)............... | 28,850 | 348.7 | 308 | 3.7 | 3,460 | 50.1 | 384 | 28.2 | 2,760 | 33.4 | 21,938 | 265.2 |

| Population group | Property crime | | Burglary | | Larceny-theft | | Motor vehicle theft | | Number of agencies | Estimated population, 2015 |
|---|---|---|---|---|---|---|---|---|---|---|
| | Number of offenses known | Rate | Number of offenses known | Rate | Number of offenses known | Rate | Number of offenses known | Rate | | |
| **Total, Suburban Cities**........................ | 1,315,935 | 2,266.1 | 213,129 | 367.0 | 1,023,220 | 1,762.0 | 79,586 | 137.0 | 6,309 | 58,071,136 |
| Group IV (25,000 to 49,999).................. | 489,051 | 2,162.7 | 81,257 | 359.3 | 373,859 | 1,653.3 | 33,935 | 150.1 | 659 | 22,613,365 |
| Group V (10,000 to 24,999) ................... | 451,327 | 2,112.7 | 74,825 | 350.3 | 349,196 | 1,634.6 | 27,306 | 127.8 | 1,325 | 21,362,471 |
| Group VI (under 10,000)........................ | 375,557 | 2,664.4 | 57,047 | 404.7 | 300,165 | 2,129.5 | 18,345 | 130.1 | 4,325 | 14,095,300 |
| **Total, Nonsuburban Cities** ................... | 706,006 | 3,288.1 | 135,479 | 631.0 | 538,418 | 2,507.6 | 32,109 | 149.5 | 3,573 | 21,471,563 |
| Group IV (25,000 to 49,999).................. | 245,553 | 3,771.6 | 46,231 | 710.1 | 186,526 | 2,864.9 | 12,796 | 196.5 | 182 | 6,510,642 |
| Group V (10,000 to 24,999) ................... | 238,970 | 3,573.4 | 45,222 | 676.2 | 184,219 | 2,754.7 | 9,529 | 142.5 | 427 | 6,687,390 |
| Group VI (under 10,000)........................ | 221,483 | 2,677.0 | 44,026 | 532.1 | 167,673 | 2,026.6 | 9,784 | 118.3 | 2,964 | 8,273,531 |

[1] Suburban cities include law enforcement agencies in cities with less than 50,000 inhabitants that are within a Metropolitan Statistical Area. Suburban cities exclude all metropolitan agencies associated with a principal city. Nonsuburban cities include law enforcement agencies in cities with less than 50,000 inhabitants that are not associated with a Metropolitan Statistical Area.
[2] The figures shown in the rape (revised definition) column include only those reported by law enforcement agencies that used the revised Uniform Crime Reporting (UCR) definition of rape.
[3] The figures shown in the rape (legacy definition) column include only those reported by law enforcement agencies that used the legacy UCR definition of rape.

## Table 11. Offense Analysis, Number and Percent Change, 2014–2015

(Number, percent, dollars; 14,137 agencies; 2015 estimated population 283,415,007.)

| Classification | Number of offenses, 2015 | Percent change from 2014 | Percent distribution[1] | Average value (dollars) |
|---|---|---|---|---|
| Murder.................................... | 13,452 | +11.7 | NA | X |
| Rape[2] ....................................... | 94,175 | NA | NA | X |
| Robbery ..................................... | 284,772 | +2.0 | 100.0 | $1,190 |
| By location...................... | | | | |
| Street/highway.................... | 113,458 | -0.3 | 39.8 | 1,023 |
| Commercial house ................ | 40,991 | +4.9 | 14.4 | 1,416 |
| Gas or service station ........... | 7,738 | +10.1 | 2.7 | 938 |
| Convenience store ............... | 16,196 | +6.7 | 5.7 | 623 |
| Residence ........................... | 46,991 | * | 16.5 | 1,545 |
| Bank ................................... | 4,939 | -2.5 | 1.7 | 3,884 |
| Miscellaneous ...................... | 54,459 | +4.5 | 19.1 | 1,023 |
| Burglary ..................................... | 1,395,913 | -9.0 | 100.0 | 2,316 |
| By location...................... | | | | |
| Residence (dwelling) ............ | 999,446 | -10.8 | 71.6 | 2,296 |
| Residence, night .............. | 289,051 | -7.3 | 20.7 | 1,904 |
| Residence, day................. | 522,880 | -12.1 | 37.5 | 2,316 |
| Residence, unknown.......... | 187,515 | -12.3 | 13.4 | 2,844 |
| Nonresidence (store, office, etc.) ...... | 396,467 | -4.1 | 28.4 | 2,366 |
| Nonresidence, night........... | 166,331 | -0.7 | 11.9 | 2,154 |
| Nonresidence, day ............. | 139,961 | -6.1 | 10.0 | 2,244 |
| Nonresidence, unknown ...... | 90,175 | -6.8 | 6.5 | 2,946 |
| Larceny-theft (except motor vehicle theft)...... | 5,014,269 | -2.1 | 100.0 | 929 |
| By type ........................... | | | | |
| Pocket-picking.................... | 27,341 | +2.8 | 0.5 | 652 |
| Purse-snatching .................. | 20,276 | -2.2 | 0.4 | 563 |
| Shoplifting.......................... | 1,118,390 | +1.3 | 22.3 | 262 |
| From motor vehicles (except accessories)......... | 1,203,497 | +3.7 | 24.0 | 782 |
| Motor vehicle accessories............... | 349,954 | -1.7 | 7.0 | 573 |
| Bicycles............................... | 180,123 | -0.2 | 3.6 | 444 |
| From buildings.................... | 582,055 | -7.4 | 11.6 | 1,394 |
| From coin-operated machines........ | 11,407 | -4.5 | 0.2 | 497 |
| All others............................. | 1,521,226 | -7.0 | 30.3 | 1,512 |
| By value........................... | | | | |
| Over $200 ............................ | 2,289,505 | -3.3 | 45.7 | 1,969 |
| $50 to $200 ......................... | 1,119,662 | -3.0 | 22.3 | 106 |
| Under $50 ............................ | 1,605,102 | +0.1 | 32.0 | 20 |
| Motor Vehicle Theft........................... | 637,965 | +5.2 | NA | 7,001 |

NA = Not available.
X = Not applicable.
* = Less than one-tenth of one percent.
[1]Because of rounding, the percentages may not add to 100.0.
[2] The rape figure in this table is an aggregate total of the data submitted using both the revised and legacy Uniform Crime Reporting definitions.

## Table 12. Property Stolen and Recovered, by Type and Value, 2015

(Dollars, percent; 13,563 agencies; 2015 estimated population 274,504,582.)

| Type of property | Value of property (dollars) | | Percent recovered |
| --- | --- | --- | --- |
| | Stolen | Recovered | |
| **Total** | $12,420,364,454 | $3,242,537,763 | 26.1 |
| Currency, notes, etc. | 1,134,705,216 | 35,597,500 | 3.1 |
| Jewelry and precious metals | 1,408,801,054 | 70,292,897 | 5.0 |
| Clothing and furs | 335,822,063 | 60,416,228 | 18.0 |
| Locally stolen motor vehicles | 4,550,267,741 | 2,646,912,427 | 58.2 |
| Office equipment | 525,327,094 | 28,697,932 | 5.5 |
| Televisions, radios, stereos, etc. | 512,934,655 | 25,130,139 | 4.9 |
| Firearms | 164,428,081 | 14,190,402 | 8.6 |
| Household goods | 261,072,326 | 10,374,714 | 4.0 |
| Consumable goods | 121,698,954 | 15,541,571 | 12.8 |
| Livestock | 19,735,289 | 2,291,803 | 11.6 |
| Miscellaneous | 3,385,571,981 | 333,092,150 | 9.8 |

# Table 13. Number and Percent of Offenses Cleared by Arrest or Exceptional Means, by Population Group, 2015

(Number, percent.)

| Population group | Violent crime | Murder and nonnegligent manslaughter | Rape (revised definition)[1] | Rape (legacy definition)[2] | Robbery | Aggravated assault | Property crime | Burglary | Larceny-theft | Motor vehicle theft | Arson[3] | Number of agencies | Estimated population, 2015 |
|---|---|---|---|---|---|---|---|---|---|---|---|---|---|
| **Total, All Agencies** | | | | | | | | | | | | | |
| Offenses known | 1,131,223 | 14,392 | 103,064 | 7,518 | 299,232 | 707,017 | 7,332,702 | 1,450,074 | 5,225,538 | 657,090 | 40,260 | 15,239 | 294,548,721 |
| Percent cleared by arrest | 46.0 | 61.5 | 37.8 | 36.2 | 29.3 | 54.0 | 19.4 | 12.9 | 21.9 | 13.1 | 20.4 | | |
| **Total Cities** | | | | | | | | | | | | | |
| Offenses known | 898,247 | 11,088 | 76,863 | 4,984 | 260,582 | 544,730 | 5,794,921 | 1,056,498 | 4,210,946 | 527,477 | 30,534 | 10,912 | 197,774,675 |
| Percent cleared by arrest | 44.3 | 60.2 | 36.2 | 36.6 | 29.0 | 52.5 | 19.5 | 12.3 | 22.3 | 12.0 | 19.7 | | |
| Group I (250,000 and over) | | | | | | | | | | | | | |
| Offenses known | 414,444 | 5,607 | 28,613 | 1,129 | 143,631 | 235,464 | 1,922,569 | 364,724 | 1,323,342 | 234,503 | 11,825 | 79 | 56,980,440 |
| Percent cleared by arrest | 39.6 | 57.0 | 38.5 | 32.6 | 26.3 | 47.5 | 14.1 | 9.7 | 16.2 | 8.8 | 15.4 | | |
| 1,000,000 and over (Group I subset) | | | | | | | | | | | | | |
| Offenses known | 163,628 | 1,753 | 11,656 | 0 | 59,652 | 90,567 | 646,603 | 118,652 | 444,677 | 83,274 | 3,387 | 10 | 24,675,984 |
| Percent cleared by arrest | 45.1 | 66.5 | 40.8 | 0.0 | 30.9 | 54.6 | 13.9 | 9.6 | 16.2 | 7.7 | 14.4 | | |
| 500,000 to 999,999 (Group I subset) | | | | | | | | | | | | | |
| Offenses known | 138,863 | 2,081 | 8,931 | 620 | 46,921 | 80,310 | 699,933 | 133,453 | 486,423 | 80,057 | 4,120 | 23 | 16,609,970 |
| Percent cleared by arrest | 34.1 | 50.2 | 36.3 | 31.6 | 20.7 | 41.2 | 12.3 | 8.6 | 14.0 | 8.7 | 14.7 | | |
| 250,000 to 499,999 (Group I subset) | | | | | | | | | | | | | |
| Offenses known | 111,953 | 1,773 | 8,026 | 509 | 37,058 | 64,587 | 576,033 | 112,619 | 392,242 | 71,172 | 4,318 | 46 | 15,694,486 |
| Percent cleared by arrest | 38.4 | 55.5 | 37.7 | 33.8 | 25.8 | 45.3 | 16.4 | 11.3 | 19.0 | 10.2 | 17.0 | | |
| Group II (100,000 to 249,999) | | | | | | | | | | | | | |
| Offenses known | 144,680 | 1,896 | 13,356 | 638 | 42,393 | 86,397 | 1,007,676 | 189,128 | 712,125 | 106,423 | 4,688 | 206 | 30,700,345 |
| Percent cleared by arrest | 42.4 | 61.5 | 34.5 | 27.3 | 28.4 | 50.2 | 17.6 | 11.1 | 20.2 | 12.0 | 20.5 | | |
| Group III (50,000 to 99,999) | | | | | | | | | | | | | |
| Offenses known | 110,778 | 1,185 | 10,380 | 727 | 29,879 | 68,607 | 874,080 | 155,071 | 644,078 | 74,931 | 4,240 | 467 | 32,486,967 |
| Percent cleared by arrest | 49.6 | 64.9 | 36.5 | 42.5 | 33.7 | 58.3 | 21.5 | 12.9 | 24.5 | 12.5 | 20.0 | | |
| Group IV (25,000 to 49,999) | | | | | | | | | | | | | |
| Offenses known | 83,010 | 950 | 8,727 | 835 | 20,130 | 52,368 | 717,148 | 125,511 | 545,356 | 46,281 | 3,164 | 805 | 27,955,655 |
| Percent cleared by arrest | 48.6 | 64.4 | 33.8 | 34.9 | 33.2 | 56.9 | 23.8 | 13.6 | 27.0 | 14.8 | 23.3 | | |
| Group V (10,000 to 24,999) | | | | | | | | | | | | | |
| Offenses known | 74,653 | 800 | 7,873 | 763 | 14,951 | 50,266 | 675,532 | 118,369 | 520,633 | 36,530 | 2,894 | 1,698 | 27,053,854 |
| Percent cleared by arrest | 52.8 | 62.9 | 36.0 | 42.2 | 36.2 | 60.4 | 26.5 | 15.3 | 29.6 | 18.5 | 24.9 | | |
| Group VI (under 10,000) | | | | | | | | | | | | | |
| Offenses known | 70,682 | 650 | 7,914 | 892 | 9,598 | 51,628 | 597,916 | 103,695 | 465,412 | 28,809 | 3,723 | 7,657 | 22,597,414 |
| Percent cleared by arrest | 53.1 | 66.5 | 33.3 | 40.4 | 37.7 | 59.1 | 24.4 | 17.2 | 26.0 | 23.8 | 24.9 | | |
| **Metropolitan Counties** | | | | | | | | | | | | | |
| Offenses known | 186,909 | 2,454 | 18,904 | 1,873 | 36,015 | 127,663 | 1,239,486 | 296,527 | 835,410 | 107,549 | 7,321 | 1,965 | 72,455,105 |
| Percent cleared by arrest | 51.5 | 64.3 | 42.5 | 34.4 | 30.8 | 58.7 | 18.8 | 14.2 | 20.7 | 16.1 | 20.9 | | |
| **Nonmetropolitan Counties** | | | | | | | | | | | | | |
| Offenses known | 46,067 | 850 | 7,297 | 661 | 2,635 | 34,624 | 298,295 | 97,049 | 179,182 | 22,064 | 2,405 | 2,362 | 24,318,941 |
| Percent cleared by arrest | 56.7 | 70.8 | 43.0 | 38.4 | 40.9 | 60.8 | 18.7 | 15.9 | 19.6 | 24.0 | 27.1 | | |
| **Suburban Areas[4]** | | | | | | | | | | | | | |
| Offenses known | 321,368 | 3,808 | 33,502 | 3,091 | 66,347 | 214,620 | 2,514,382 | 505,533 | 1,822,792 | 186,057 | 12,968 | 8,257 | 128,133,525 |
| Percent cleared by arrest | 51.8 | 63.5 | 39.3 | 38.1 | 33.0 | 59.5 | 21.4 | 14.5 | 23.9 | 16.1 | 22.1 | | |

[1] The figures shown in this column for the offense of rape were reported using the revised Uniform Crime Reporting (UCR) definition of rape. See chapter notes for more detail.
[2] The figures shown in this column for the offense of rape were reported using the legacy Uniform Crime Reporting (UCR) definition of rape. See chapter notes for more detail.
[3] Not all agencies submit reports for arson to the FBI. As a result, the number of reports the FBI uses to compute the percent of offenses cleared for arson is less than the number it uses to compute the percent of offenses cleared for all other offenses.
[4] Suburban area includes law enforcement agencies in cities with less than 50,000 inhabitants and county law enforcement agencies that are within a Metropolitan Statistical Area. Suburban area excludes all metropolitan agencies associated with a principal city. The agencies associated with suburban areas also appear in other groups within this table.

# Table 14. Number of Offenses Cleared by Arrest or Exceptional Means and Percent Involving Persons Under 18 Years of Age, by Population Group, 2015

(Number, percent.)

| Population group | Violent crime | Murder and non-negligent manslaughter | Rape (revised definition)[1] | Rape (legacy definition)[2] | Robbery | Aggravated assault | Property crime | Burglary | Larceny-theft | Motor vehicle theft | Arson[3] | Number of agencies | Estimated population, 2015 |
|---|---|---|---|---|---|---|---|---|---|---|---|---|---|
| **Total, All Agencies** | | | | | | | | | | | | | |
| Offenses known.............. | 473,793 | 8,232 | 35,521 | 2,723 | 80,641 | 346,676 | 1,296,532 | 168,516 | 1,050,449 | 77,567 | 7,847 | 14,592 | 274,604,622 |
| Percent under 18 years .... | 8.5 | 4.1 | 14.6 | 11.1 | 12.5 | 7.0 | 10.1 | 10.0 | 9.9 | 11.8 | 24.9 | | |
| **Total Cities** | | | | | | | | | | | | | |
| Offenses known.............. | 373,044 | 6,309 | 26,213 | 1,824 | 71,253 | 267,445 | 1,059,235 | 120,141 | 880,450 | 58,644 | 5,845 | 10,595 | 188,057,806 |
| Percent under 18 years .... | 8.7 | 4.4 | 13.9 | 10.9 | 12.8 | 7.1 | 10.4 | 10.8 | 10.2 | 12.4 | 26.3 | | |
| Group I (250,000 and over) | | | | | | | | | | | | | |
| Offenses known.............. | 157,297 | 3,057 | 10,478 | 368 | 36,569 | 106,825 | 256,304 | 33,198 | 203,623 | 19,483 | 1,777 | 74 | 54,786,571 |
| Percent under 18 years .... | 8.5 | 4.6 | 12.9 | 7.9 | 14.7 | 6.1 | 10.8 | 11.8 | 10.3 | 13.7 | 23.5 | | |
| 1,000,000 and over (Group I subset) | | | | | | | | | | | | | |
| Offenses known.............. | 73,768 | 1,165 | 4,751 | 0 | 18,425 | 49,427 | 89,891 | 11,349 | 72,147 | 6,395 | 487 | 10 | 24,675,984 |
| Percent under 18 years .... | 8.4 | 4.1 | 13.0 | 0.0 | 15.8 | 5.4 | 9.7 | 9.1 | 9.6 | 11.9 | 18.9 | | |
| 500,000 to 999,999 (Group I subset) | | | | | | | | | | | | | |
| Offenses known.............. | 44,997 | 1,000 | 2,941 | 196 | 9,390 | 31,470 | 81,320 | 10,578 | 64,170 | 6,572 | 594 | 22 | 15,742,712 |
| Percent under 18 years .... | 8.6 | 5.4 | 12.4 | 11.2 | 14.1 | 6.7 | 11.5 | 14.0 | 10.6 | 16.4 | 27.4 | | |
| 250,000 to 499,999 (Group I subset) | | | | | | | | | | | | | |
| Offenses known.............. | 38,532 | 892 | 2,786 | 172 | 8,754 | 25,928 | 85,093 | 11,271 | 67,306 | 6,516 | 696 | 42 | 14,367,875 |
| Percent under 18 years .... | 8.6 | 4.4 | 13.2 | 4.1 | 13.0 | 6.8 | 11.3 | 12.6 | 10.9 | 12.9 | 23.3 | | |
| Group II (100,000 to 249,999) | | | | | | | | | | | | | |
| Offenses known.............. | 56,565 | 1,101 | 4,271 | 174 | 11,184 | 39,835 | 162,451 | 19,323 | 131,579 | 11,549 | 916 | 189 | 28,281,300 |
| Percent under 18 years .... | 8.5 | 4.5 | 15.8 | 9.8 | 11.2 | 7.1 | 11.3 | 11.9 | 11.0 | 12.9 | 22.2 | | |
| Group III (50,000 to 99,999) | | | | | | | | | | | | | |
| Offenses known.............. | 49,353 | 696 | 3,486 | 309 | 8,950 | 35,912 | 171,173 | 18,073 | 144,621 | 8,479 | 820 | 435 | 30,343,562 |
| Percent under 18 years .... | 8.9 | 4.5 | 13.5 | 12.6 | 11.7 | 7.8 | 11.5 | 10.4 | 11.6 | 11.3 | 27.7 | | |
| Group IV (25,000 to 49,999) | | | | | | | | | | | | | |
| Offenses known.............. | 36,994 | 573 | 2,752 | 291 | 6,095 | 27,283 | 159,435 | 15,630 | 137,548 | 6,257 | 716 | 769 | 26,625,101 |
| Percent under 18 years .... | 8.9 | 3.8 | 14.4 | 13.7 | 10.3 | 8.1 | 9.9 | 9.9 | 9.8 | 11.9 | 33.7 | | |
| Group V (10,000 to 24,999) | | | | | | | | | | | | | |
| Offenses known.............. | 36,678 | 467 | 2,679 | 322 | 5,010 | 28,200 | 168,427 | 16,887 | 145,213 | 6,327 | 705 | 1,630 | 25,941,688 |
| Percent under 18 years .... | 8.9 | 3.2 | 15.0 | 11.2 | 10.0 | 8.2 | 9.5 | 10.1 | 9.4 | 11.1 | 31.2 | | |
| Group VI (under 10,000) | | | | | | | | | | | | | |
| Offenses known.............. | 36,157 | 415 | 2,547 | 360 | 3,445 | 29,390 | 141,445 | 17,030 | 117,866 | 6,549 | 911 | 7,498 | 22,079,584 |
| Percent under 18 years .... | 9.0 | 4.6 | 13.6 | 10.3 | 10.5 | 8.4 | 8.7 | 9.8 | 8.4 | 10.9 | 25.0 | | |
| **Metropolitan Counties** | | | | | | | | | | | | | |
| Offenses known.............. | 76,409 | 1,346 | 6,272 | 645 | 8,381 | 59,765 | 184,115 | 33,808 | 136,484 | 13,823 | 1,370 | 1,726 | 62,778,487 |
| Percent under 18 years .... | 8.1 | 3.3 | 16.9 | 13.3 | 10.8 | 6.8 | 9.4 | 8.7 | 9.5 | 10.1 | 23.2 | | |
| **Nonmetropolitan Counties** | | | | | | | | | | | | | |
| Offenses known.............. | 24,340 | 577 | 3,036 | 254 | 1,007 | 19,466 | 53,182 | 14,567 | 33,515 | 5,100 | 632 | 2,271 | 23,768,329 |
| Percent under 18 years .... | 6.8 | 2.8 | 16.1 | 7.1 | 4.3 | 5.6 | 6.6 | 6.3 | 6.5 | 8.5 | 15.5 | | |
| **Suburban Areas[4]** | | | | | | | | | | | | | |
| Offenses known.............. | 140,676 | 2,111 | 11,070 | 1,178 | 18,229 | 108,088 | 470,020 | 62,506 | 382,135 | 25,379 | 2,673 | 7,799 | 115,973,258 |
| Percent under 18 years .... | 8.8 | 3.4 | 16.0 | 12.7 | 10.9 | 7.7 | 9.3 | 9.3 | 9.2 | 10.3 | 27.2 | | |

[1] The figures shown in this column for the offense of rape were reported using the revised Uniform Crime Reporting (UCR) definition of rape. See chapter notes for more detail.
[2] The figures shown in this column for the offense of rape were reported using the legacy Uniform Crime Reporting (UCR) definition of rape. See chapter notes for more detail.
[3] Not all agencies submit reports for arson to the FBI. As a result, the number of reports the FBI uses to compute the percent of offenses cleared for arson is less than the number it uses to compute the percent of offenses cleared for all other offenses.
[4] Suburban area includes law enforcement agencies in cities with less than 50,000 inhabitants and county law enforcement agencies that are within a Metropolitan Statistical Area. Suburban area excludes all metropolitan agencies associated with a principal city. The agencies associated with suburban areas also appear in other groups within this table.

# Table 15. Estimated Number of Arrests, 2015

(Number.)

| Offense | Arrests |
|---|---|
| Total[1] ......................................................................................... | 10,797,088 |
| | |
| **Violent crime[2]** ............................................................................ | 505,681 |
| Murder and nonnegligent manslaughter ..................................... | 11,092 |
| Rape[3] ............................................................................................. | 22,863 |
| Robbery .......................................................................................... | 95,572 |
| Aggravated assault ........................................................................ | 376,154 |
| | |
| **Property crime[2]** .......................................................................... | 1,463,213 |
| Burglary .......................................................................................... | 216,010 |
| Larceny-theft .................................................................................. | 1,160,390 |
| Motor vehicle theft ........................................................................ | 77,979 |
| Arson.............................................................................................. | 8,834 |
| | |
| Other assaults................................................................................ | 1,081,019 |
| Forgery and counterfeiting............................................................ | 55,333 |
| Fraud............................................................................................... | 133,138 |
| Embezzlement ................................................................................ | 15,909 |
| Stolen property; buying, receiving, possessing ............................ | 88,576 |
| Vandalism........................................................................................ | 191,015 |
| | |
| Weapons; carrying, possessing, etc. ............................................. | 145,358 |
| Prostitution and commercialized vice............................................ | 41,877 |
| Sex offenses (except forcible rape and prostitution)..................... | 51,388 |
| Drug abuse violations..................................................................... | 1,488,707 |
| Gambling......................................................................................... | 4,825 |
| | |
| Offenses against the family and children ...................................... | 94,837 |
| Driving under the influence............................................................ | 1,089,171 |
| Liquor laws ..................................................................................... | 266,250 |
| Drunkenness................................................................................... | 405,880 |
| Disorderly conduct ........................................................................ | 386,078 |
| | |
| Vagrancy......................................................................................... | 25,151 |
| All other offenses........................................................................... | 3,218,880 |
| Suspicion ........................................................................................ | 1,389 |
| Curfew and loitering law violations ............................................... | 44,802 |

[1] Does not include suspicion.
[2] Violent crimes are offenses of murder and nonnegligent manslaughter, rape, robbery, and aggravated assault. Property crimes are offenses of burglary, larceny-theft, motor vehicle theft, and arson.
[3] The rape figures in this table are an aggregate total of the data submitted using both the revised and legacy Uniform Crime Reporting definitions.

# Table 16. Number and Rate of Arrests, by Geographic Region, 2015

(Number, rate per 100,000 inhabitants.)

| Offense charged | United States total (12,706 agencies; population 246,947,242) | | Northeast (3,093 agencies; population 44,262,090) | | Midwest (3,149 agencies; population 48,363,834) | | South (4,578 agencies; population 84,603,838) | | West (1,886 agencies; population 69,717,480) | |
|---|---|---|---|---|---|---|---|---|---|---|
| | Total | Rate | Total | Rate | Total | Rate | Total | Rate | Total | Rate |
| Total[1] ............................ | 8,304,874 | 3,363.0 | 1,242,395 | 2,806.9 | 1,624,037 | 3,358.0 | 3,070,944 | 3,629.8 | 2,367,498 | 3,395.8 |
| Violent crime[2] ........................ | 388,082 | 157.2 | 56,942 | 128.6 | 60,167 | 124.4 | 118,884 | 140.5 | 152,089 | 218.2 |
| Murder and nonnegligent manslaughter............................ | 8,533 | 3.5 | 1,073 | 2.4 | 1,543 | 3.2 | 3,665 | 4.3 | 2,252 | 3.2 |
| Rape[3]................................. | 17,504 | 7.1 | 3,209 | 7.2 | 3,819 | 7.9 | 5,565 | 6.6 | 4,911 | 7.0 |
| Robbery.............................. | 73,230 | 29.7 | 13,998 | 31.6 | 11,562 | 23.9 | 23,928 | 28.3 | 23,742 | 34.1 |
| Aggravated assault ................... | 288,815 | 117.0 | 38,662 | 87.3 | 43,243 | 89.4 | 85,726 | 101.3 | 121,184 | 173.8 |
| Property crime[2]........................ | 1,133,319 | 458.9 | 178,153 | 402.5 | 220,642 | 456.2 | 434,986 | 514.1 | 299,538 | 429.6 |
| Burglary............................. | 166,609 | 67.5 | 23,132 | 52.3 | 22,653 | 46.8 | 58,250 | 68.9 | 62,574 | 89.8 |
| Larceny-theft ......................... | 900,077 | 364.5 | 147,661 | 333.6 | 185,039 | 382.6 | 358,706 | 424.0 | 208,671 | 299.3 |
| Motor vehicle theft ................... | 59,831 | 24.2 | 6,269 | 14.2 | 11,788 | 24.4 | 16,034 | 19.0 | 25,740 | 36.9 |
| Arson................................. | 6,802 | 2.8 | 1,091 | 2.5 | 1,162 | 2.4 | 1,996 | 2.4 | 2,553 | 3.7 |
| Other assaults.......................... | 831,684 | 336.8 | 139,741 | 315.7 | 159,716 | 330.2 | 329,328 | 389.3 | 202,899 | 291.0 |
| Forgery and counterfeiting........ | 42,681 | 17.3 | 7,688 | 17.4 | 6,929 | 14.3 | 18,794 | 22.2 | 9,270 | 13.3 |
| Fraud................................. | 102,339 | 41.4 | 20,238 | 45.7 | 18,538 | 38.3 | 46,872 | 55.4 | 16,691 | 23.9 |
| Embezzlement ......................... | 12,247 | 5.0 | 1,386 | 3.1 | 2,006 | 4.1 | 6,813 | 8.1 | 2,042 | 2.9 |
| Stolen property; buying, receiving, possessing................. | 68,341 | 27.7 | 10,276 | 23.2 | 12,420 | 25.7 | 20,213 | 23.9 | 25,432 | 36.5 |
| Vandalism............................. | 147,191 | 59.6 | 32,315 | 73.0 | 28,900 | 59.8 | 38,820 | 45.9 | 47,156 | 67.6 |
| Weapons; carrying, possessing, etc..................................... | 111,316 | 45.1 | 13,967 | 31.6 | 22,930 | 47.4 | 37,283 | 44.1 | 37,136 | 53.3 |
| Prostitution and commercialized vice.................................. | 31,534 | 12.8 | 4,196 | 9.5 | 4,176 | 8.6 | 9,954 | 11.8 | 13,208 | 18.9 |
| Sex offenses (except forcible rape and prostitution) ............... | 39,393 | 16.0 | 6,291 | 14.2 | 7,565 | 15.6 | 11,024 | 13.0 | 14,513 | 20.8 |
| Drug abuse violations................ | 1,144,021 | 463.3 | 193,773 | 437.8 | 220,858 | 456.7 | 412,432 | 487.5 | 316,958 | 454.6 |
| Gambling.............................. | 3,607 | 1.5 | 534 | 1.2 | 1,191 | 2.5 | 1,524 | 1.8 | 358 | 0.5 |
| Offenses against the family and children ............................... | 72,418 | 29.3 | 13,445 | 30.4 | 15,769 | 32.6 | 30,445 | 36.0 | 12,759 | 18.3 |
| Driving under the influence........ | 833,833 | 337.7 | 127,447 | 287.9 | 179,271 | 370.7 | 258,027 | 305.0 | 269,088 | 386.0 |
| Liquor laws ............................. | 204,665 | 82.9 | 25,234 | 57.0 | 70,045 | 144.8 | 49,906 | 59.0 | 59,480 | 85.3 |
| Drunkenness............................ | 314,856 | 127.5 | 29,672 | 67.0 | 20,363 | 42.1 | 165,031 | 195.1 | 99,790 | 143.1 |
| Disorderly conduct.................... | 298,253 | 120.8 | 72,771 | 164.4 | 98,520 | 203.7 | 74,894 | 88.5 | 52,068 | 74.7 |
| Vagrancy............................... | 19,414 | 7.9 | 1,581 | 3.6 | 3,427 | 7.1 | 4,253 | 5.0 | 10,153 | 14.6 |
| All other offenses (except traffic) | 2,471,772 | 1,000.9 | 294,195 | 664.7 | 463,999 | 959.4 | 993,954 | 1,174.8 | 719,624 | 1,032.2 |
| Suspicion ............................... | 1,045 | 0.4 | 99 | 0.2 | 171 | 0.4 | 435 | 0.5 | 340 | 0.5 |
| Curfew and loitering law violations ............................... | 33,908 | 13.7 | 12,550 | 28.4 | 6,605 | 13.7 | 7,507 | 8.9 | 7,246 | 10.4 |

[1] Does not include suspicion.
[2] Violent crimes are offenses of murder and nonnegligent manslaughter, rape, robbery, and aggravated assault. Property crimes are offenses of burglary, larceny-theft, motor vehicle theft, and arson.
[3] The rape figures in this table are an aggregate total of the data submitted using both the revised and legacy Uniform Crime Reporting definitions.

# Table 17. Number and Rate of Arrests, by Population Group, 2015

(Number, rate per 100,000 inhabitants.)

| Offense charged | Total (12,706 agencies; population 246,947,242) | | Total cities (9,115 cities; population 168,734,653) | | Group I (66 cities, 250,000 and over; population 44,563,106) | | Group II (180 cities, 100,000 to 249,999; population 27,033,841) | | Group III (404 cities, 50,000 to 99,999; population 28,217,031) | | Group IV (726 cities, 25,000 to 49,999; population 25,112,170) | |
|---|---|---|---|---|---|---|---|---|---|---|---|---|
| | Total | Rate | Total | Rate | Total | Rate | Total | Rate | Total | Rate | Total | Rate |
| Total[2] ............................................ | 8,304,874 | 3,363.0 | 6,034,206 | 3,576.2 | 1,449,692 | 3,253.1 | 933,850 | 3,454.4 | 949,975 | 3,366.7 | 839,653 | 3,343.6 |
| Violent crime[3] ................................ | 388,082 | 157.2 | 299,984 | 177.8 | 108,478 | 243.4 | 53,861 | 199.2 | 46,308 | 164.1 | 32,819 | 130.7 |
| Murder and nonnegligent manslaughter ...................... | 8,533 | 3.5 | 6,258 | 3.7 | 2,771 | 6.2 | 1,169 | 4.3 | 767 | 2.7 | 632 | 2.5 |
| Rape[4] ............................................. | 17,504 | 7.1 | 12,521 | 7.4 | 4,128 | 9.3 | 1,879 | 7.0 | 1,863 | 6.6 | 1,536 | 6.1 |
| Robbery ........................................... | 73,230 | 29.7 | 62,265 | 36.9 | 27,161 | 60.9 | 10,792 | 39.9 | 9,219 | 32.7 | 6,407 | 25.5 |
| Aggravated assault ........................... | 288,815 | 117.0 | 218,940 | 129.8 | 74,418 | 167.0 | 40,021 | 148.0 | 34,459 | 122.1 | 24,244 | 96.5 |
| Property crime[3] .............................. | 1,133,319 | 458.9 | 929,358 | 550.8 | 207,416 | 465.4 | 152,576 | 564.4 | 158,016 | 560.0 | 143,723 | 572.3 |
| Burglary ........................................... | 166,609 | 67.5 | 123,383 | 73.1 | 32,908 | 73.8 | 23,084 | 85.4 | 21,426 | 75.9 | 16,311 | 65.0 |
| Larceny-theft .................................... | 900,077 | 364.5 | 756,295 | 448.2 | 157,390 | 353.2 | 119,421 | 441.7 | 129,062 | 457.4 | 122,330 | 487.1 |
| Motor vehicle theft ........................... | 59,831 | 24.2 | 44,572 | 26.4 | 15,895 | 35.7 | 9,028 | 33.4 | 6,828 | 24.2 | 4,455 | 17.7 |
| Arson ............................................... | 6,802 | 2.8 | 5,108 | 3.0 | 1,223 | 2.7 | 1,043 | 3.9 | 700 | 2.5 | 627 | 2.5 |
| Other assaults .................................. | 831,684 | 336.8 | 624,009 | 369.8 | 171,099 | 383.9 | 99,791 | 369.1 | 99,999 | 354.4 | 85,694 | 341.2 |
| Forgery and counterfeiting ................. | 42,681 | 17.3 | 31,437 | 18.6 | 6,200 | 13.9 | 5,015 | 18.6 | 5,248 | 18.6 | 4,790 | 19.1 |
| Fraud ............................................... | 102,339 | 41.4 | 70,891 | 42.0 | 13,350 | 30.0 | 9,435 | 34.9 | 11,223 | 39.8 | 11,324 | 45.1 |
| Embezzlement .................................. | 12,247 | 5.0 | 9,562 | 5.7 | 2,358 | 5.3 | 1,408 | 5.2 | 1,708 | 6.1 | 1,477 | 5.9 |
| Stolen property; buying, receiving, possessing ............... | 68,341 | 27.7 | 50,592 | 30.0 | 12,910 | 29.0 | 8,704 | 32.2 | 9,691 | 34.3 | 7,352 | 29.3 |
| Vandalism ......................................... | 147,191 | 59.6 | 113,543 | 67.3 | 27,794 | 62.4 | 17,112 | 63.3 | 18,762 | 66.5 | 17,244 | 68.7 |
| Weapons; carrying, possessing, etc. ..... | 111,316 | 45.1 | 85,618 | 50.7 | 31,535 | 70.8 | 14,199 | 52.5 | 12,194 | 43.2 | 9,027 | 35.9 |
| Prostitution and commercialized vice ............................. | 31,534 | 12.8 | 28,450 | 16.9 | 19,017 | 42.7 | 4,138 | 15.3 | 2,353 | 8.3 | 1,246 | 5.0 |
| Sex offenses (except forcible rape and prostitution) ........ | 39,393 | 16.0 | 27,417 | 16.2 | 7,777 | 17.5 | 4,282 | 15.8 | 4,460 | 15.8 | 3,586 | 14.3 |
| Drug abuse violations ......................... | 1,144,021 | 463.3 | 810,262 | 480.2 | 204,753 | 459.5 | 129,009 | 477.2 | 131,689 | 466.7 | 108,677 | 432.8 |
| Gambling .......................................... | 3,607 | 1.5 | 2,848 | 1.7 | 1,645 | 3.7 | 216 | 0.8 | 295 | 1.0 | 97 | 0.4 |
| Offenses against the family and children ....................... | 72,418 | 29.3 | 37,512 | 22.2 | 5,975 | 13.4 | 6,420 | 23.7 | 5,585 | 19.8 | 5,576 | 22.2 |
| Driving under the influence ................. | 833,833 | 337.7 | 468,701 | 277.8 | 94,408 | 211.9 | 62,531 | 231.3 | 70,006 | 248.1 | 68,851 | 274.2 |
| Liquor laws ....................................... | 204,665 | 82.9 | 160,696 | 95.2 | 25,348 | 56.9 | 19,435 | 71.9 | 20,421 | 72.4 | 21,446 | 85.4 |
| Drunkenness ..................................... | 314,856 | 127.5 | 271,597 | 161.0 | 44,198 | 99.2 | 43,997 | 162.7 | 46,923 | 166.3 | 35,479 | 141.3 |
| Disorderly conduct ............................ | 298,253 | 120.8 | 247,467 | 146.7 | 41,893 | 94.0 | 30,411 | 112.5 | 36,229 | 128.4 | 36,844 | 146.7 |
| Vagrancy .......................................... | 19,414 | 7.9 | 16,892 | 10.0 | 5,574 | 12.5 | 3,400 | 12.6 | 3,861 | 13.7 | 1,549 | 6.2 |
| All other offenses (except traffic) ....................... | 2,471,772 | 1,000.9 | 1,715,484 | 1,016.7 | 400,810 | 899.4 | 265,232 | 981.1 | 261,665 | 927.3 | 240,097 | 956.1 |
| Suspicion ......................................... | 1,045 | 0.4 | 842 | 0.5 | 4 | * | 0 | 0.0 | 139 | 0.5 | 56 | 0.2 |
| Curfew and loitering law violations ............................. | 33,908 | 13.7 | 31,886 | 18.9 | 17,154 | 38.5 | 2,678 | 9.9 | 3,339 | 11.8 | 2,755 | 11.0 |

* = Less than one-tenth of one percent.
[1] Suburban areas include law enforcement agencies in cities with less than 50,000 inhabitants and county law enforcement agencies that are within a Metropolitan Statistical Area. Suburban areas exclude all metropolitan agencies associated with a principal city. The agencies associated with suburban areas also appear in other groups within this table.
[2] Does not include suspicion.
[3] Violent crimes are offenses of murder and nonnegligent manslaughter, forcible rape, robbery, and aggravated assault. Property crimes are offenses of burglary, larceny-theft, motor vehicle theft, and arson.
[4] The rape figures in this table are an aggregate total of the data submitted using both the revised and legacy Uniform Crime Reporting definitions.

# Table 17. Number and Rate of Arrests, by Population Group, 2015—*Continued*

(Number, rate per 100,000 inhabitants.)

| Offense charged | Group V (1,501 cities, 10,000 to 24,999; population 23,998,482) | | Group VI (6,238 cities, under 10,000; population 19,810,023) | | Metropolitan counties (1,536 agencies; population 56,900,141) | | Nonmetropolitan counties (2,055 agencies; population 21,312,448) | | Suburban areas[1] (7,022 agencies; population 111,227,944) | |
|---|---|---|---|---|---|---|---|---|---|---|
| | Total | Rate | Total | Rate | Total | Rate | Total | Rate | Total | Rate |
| Total[2] ........... | 887,804 | 3,699.4 | 973,232 | 4,912.8 | 1,593,867 | 2,801.2 | 676,801 | 3,175.6 | 3,484,480 | 3,132.7 |
| Violent crime[3] ........... | 30,874 | 128.6 | 27,644 | 139.5 | 67,337 | 118.3 | 20,761 | 97.4 | 133,451 | 120.0 |
| Murder and nonnegligent manslaughter ........... | 538 | 2.2 | 381 | 1.9 | 1,675 | 2.9 | 600 | 2.8 | 2,713 | 2.4 |
| Rape[4] ........... | 1,589 | 6.6 | 1,526 | 7.7 | 3,427 | 6.0 | 1,556 | 7.3 | 6,639 | 6.0 |
| Robbery ........... | 5,297 | 22.1 | 3,389 | 17.1 | 9,667 | 17.0 | 1,298 | 6.1 | 21,909 | 19.7 |
| Aggravated assault ........... | 23,450 | 97.7 | 22,348 | 112.8 | 52,568 | 92.4 | 17,307 | 81.2 | 102,190 | 91.9 |
| Property crime[3] ........... | 150,713 | 628.0 | 116,914 | 590.2 | 159,526 | 280.4 | 44,435 | 208.5 | 458,610 | 412.3 |
| Burglary ........... | 15,604 | 65.0 | 14,050 | 70.9 | 30,602 | 53.8 | 12,624 | 59.2 | 63,491 | 57.1 |
| Larceny-theft ........... | 130,263 | 542.8 | 97,829 | 493.8 | 116,364 | 204.5 | 27,418 | 128.6 | 371,823 | 334.3 |
| Motor vehicle theft ........... | 4,127 | 17.2 | 4,239 | 21.4 | 11,442 | 20.1 | 3,817 | 17.9 | 20,720 | 18.6 |
| Arson ........... | 719 | 3.0 | 796 | 4.0 | 1,118 | 2.0 | 576 | 2.7 | 2,576 | 2.3 |
| Other assaults ........... | 84,879 | 353.7 | 82,547 | 416.7 | 151,543 | 266.3 | 56,132 | 263.4 | 327,735 | 294.7 |
| Forgery and counterfeiting ........... | 5,139 | 21.4 | 5,045 | 25.5 | 8,719 | 15.3 | 2,525 | 11.8 | 19,346 | 17.4 |
| Fraud ........... | 11,027 | 45.9 | 14,532 | 73.4 | 21,816 | 38.3 | 9,632 | 45.2 | 47,639 | 42.8 |
| Embezzlement ........... | 1,445 | 6.0 | 1,166 | 5.9 | 2,154 | 3.8 | 531 | 2.5 | 5,050 | 4.5 |
| Stolen property; buying, receiving, possessing ........... | 6,675 | 27.8 | 5,260 | 26.6 | 13,606 | 23.9 | 4,143 | 19.4 | 28,868 | 26.0 |
| Vandalism ........... | 16,088 | 67.0 | 16,543 | 83.5 | 25,194 | 44.3 | 8,454 | 39.7 | 59,966 | 53.9 |
| Weapons; carrying, possessing, etc. ........... | 8,673 | 36.1 | 9,990 | 50.4 | 18,786 | 33.0 | 6,912 | 32.4 | 39,175 | 35.2 |
| Prostitution and commercialized vice ........... | 1,082 | 4.5 | 614 | 3.1 | 2,860 | 5.0 | 224 | 1.1 | 5,413 | 4.9 |
| Sex offenses (except forcible rape and prostitution) ........... | 3,637 | 15.2 | 3,675 | 18.6 | 8,775 | 15.4 | 3,201 | 15.0 | 16,661 | 15.0 |
| Drug abuse violations ........... | 111,099 | 462.9 | 125,035 | 631.2 | 234,082 | 411.4 | 99,677 | 467.7 | 488,748 | 439.4 |
| Gambling ........... | 266 | 1.1 | 329 | 1.7 | 601 | 1.1 | 158 | 0.7 | 982 | 0.9 |
| Offenses against the family and children ........... | 5,822 | 24.3 | 8,134 | 41.1 | 25,945 | 45.6 | 8,961 | 42.0 | 37,718 | 33.9 |
| Driving under the influence ........... | 79,161 | 329.9 | 93,744 | 473.2 | 213,047 | 374.4 | 152,085 | 713.6 | 387,181 | 348.1 |
| Liquor laws ........... | 26,020 | 108.4 | 48,026 | 242.4 | 28,369 | 49.9 | 15,600 | 73.2 | 90,670 | 81.5 |
| Drunkenness ........... | 39,409 | 164.2 | 61,591 | 310.9 | 29,836 | 52.4 | 13,423 | 63.0 | 109,959 | 98.9 |
| Disorderly conduct ........... | 45,801 | 190.8 | 56,289 | 284.1 | 34,508 | 60.6 | 16,278 | 76.4 | 127,083 | 114.3 |
| Vagrancy ........... | 964 | 4.0 | 1,544 | 7.8 | 2,191 | 3.9 | 331 | 1.6 | 5,324 | 4.8 |
| All other offenses (except traffic) ........... | 255,954 | 1,066.5 | 291,726 | 1,472.6 | 543,199 | 954.7 | 213,089 | 999.8 | 1,086,779 | 977.1 |
| Suspicion ........... | 30 | 0.1 | 613 | 3.1 | 42 | 0.1 | 161 | 0.8 | 277 | 0.2 |
| Curfew and loitering law violations ........... | 3,076 | 12.8 | 2,884 | 14.6 | 1,773 | 3.1 | 249 | 1.2 | 8,122 | 7.3 |

\* = Less than one-tenth of one percent.
[1] Suburban areas include law enforcement agencies in cities with less than 50,000 inhabitants and county law enforcement agencies that are within a Metropolitan Statistical Area. Suburban areas exclude all metropolitan agencies associated with a principal city. The agencies associated with suburban areas also appear in other groups within this table.
[2] Does not include suspicion.
[3] Violent crimes are offenses of murder and nonnegligent manslaughter, forcible rape, robbery, and aggravated assault. Property crimes are offenses of burglary, larceny-theft, motor vehicle theft, and arson.
[4] The rape figures in this table are an aggregate total of the data submitted using both the revised and legacy Uniform Crime Reporting definitions.

# Table 18. Ten-Year Arrest Trends, 2006 and 2015

(Number, percent change; 9,581 agencies; 2015 estimated population 199,921,204; 2006 estimated population 186,371,331.)

| Offense charged | Total, all ages | | | Under 18 years of age | | | 18 years of age and over | | |
|---|---|---|---|---|---|---|---|---|---|
| | 2006 | 2015 | Percent change | 2006 | 2015 | Percent change | 2006 | 2015 | Percent change |
| Total[1] | 8,676,456 | 6,739,363 | -22.3 | 1,280,195 | 578,538 | -54.8 | 7,396,261 | 6,160,825 | -16.7 |
| Violent crime[2] | 361,401 | 305,977 | -15.3 | 56,938 | 30,130 | -47.1 | 304,463 | 275,847 | -9.4 |
| Murder and nonnegligent manslaughter | 7,104 | 6,201 | -12.7 | 642 | 421 | -34.4 | 6,462 | 5,780 | -10.6 |
| Rape[3] | 14,120 | 13,945 | NA | 2,111 | 2,239 | NA | 12,009 | 11,706 | NA |
| Robbery | 68,437 | 54,003 | -21.1 | 18,201 | 9,753 | -46.4 | 50,236 | 44,250 | -11.9 |
| Aggravated assault | 271,740 | 231,828 | -14.7 | 35,984 | 17,717 | -50.8 | 235,756 | 214,111 | -9.2 |
| Property crime[2] | 950,507 | 942,330 | -0.9 | 255,450 | 133,312 | -47.8 | 695,057 | 809,018 | +16.4 |
| Burglary | 188,122 | 136,465 | -27.5 | 51,953 | 22,056 | -57.5 | 136,169 | 114,409 | -16.0 |
| Larceny-theft | 679,290 | 753,665 | +10.9 | 180,623 | 101,898 | -43.6 | 498,667 | 651,767 | +30.7 |
| Motor vehicle theft | 72,650 | 46,463 | -36.0 | 17,651 | 7,547 | -57.2 | 54,999 | 38,916 | -29.2 |
| Arson | 10,445 | 5,737 | -45.1 | 5,223 | 1,811 | -65.3 | 5,222 | 3,926 | -24.8 |
| Other assaults | 792,178 | 678,537 | -14.3 | 152,396 | 83,689 | -45.1 | 639,782 | 594,848 | -7.0 |
| Forgery and counterfeiting | 68,319 | 34,911 | -48.9 | 2,288 | 632 | -72.4 | 66,031 | 34,279 | -48.1 |
| Fraud | 181,863 | 86,484 | -52.4 | 5,090 | 2,776 | -45.5 | 176,773 | 83,708 | -52.6 |
| Embezzlement | 13,008 | 9,923 | -23.7 | 949 | 391 | -58.8 | 12,059 | 9,532 | -21.0 |
| Stolen property; buying, receiving, possessing | 79,077 | 57,918 | -26.8 | 14,032 | 6,600 | -53.0 | 65,045 | 51,318 | -21.1 |
| Vandalism | 189,867 | 124,058 | -34.7 | 76,202 | 27,793 | -63.5 | 113,665 | 96,265 | -15.3 |
| Weapons; carrying, possessing, etc. | 114,104 | 86,443 | -24.2 | 27,707 | 11,614 | -58.1 | 86,397 | 74,829 | -13.4 |
| Prostitution and commercialized vice | 33,402 | 17,663 | -47.1 | 733 | 269 | -63.3 | 32,669 | 17,394 | -46.8 |
| Sex offenses (except forcible rape and prostitution) | 50,656 | 32,356 | -36.1 | 9,948 | 5,643 | -43.3 | 40,708 | 26,713 | -34.4 |
| Drug abuse violations | 1,078,156 | 928,122 | -13.9 | 113,132 | 63,035 | -44.3 | 965,024 | 865,087 | -10.4 |
| Gambling | 2,807 | 1,657 | -41.0 | 292 | 133 | -54.5 | 2,515 | 1,524 | -39.4 |
| Offenses against the family and children | 79,568 | 58,377 | -26.6 | 3,348 | 2,208 | -34.1 | 76,220 | 56,169 | -26.3 |
| Driving under the influence | 925,818 | 675,960 | -27.0 | 12,947 | 4,294 | -66.8 | 912,871 | 671,666 | -26.4 |
| Liquor laws | 408,511 | 174,230 | -57.3 | 94,729 | 29,530 | -68.8 | 313,782 | 144,700 | -53.9 |
| Drunkenness | 368,271 | 251,424 | -31.7 | 11,093 | 3,528 | -68.2 | 357,178 | 247,896 | -30.6 |
| Disorderly conduct | 422,187 | 240,723 | -43.0 | 129,948 | 45,659 | -64.9 | 292,239 | 195,064 | -33.3 |
| Vagrancy | 18,106 | 15,017 | -17.1 | 3,475 | 598 | -82.8 | 14,631 | 14,419 | -1.4 |
| All other offenses (except traffic) | 2,477,981 | 1,997,799 | -19.4 | 248,829 | 107,250 | -56.9 | 2,229,152 | 1,890,549 | -15.2 |
| Suspicion | 1,125 | 480 | -57.3 | 203 | 127 | -37.4 | 922 | 353 | -61.7 |
| Curfew and loitering law violations | 60,669 | 19,454 | -67.9 | 60,669 | 19,454 | -67.9 | NA | NA | NA |

NA = Not available.
[1] Does not include suspicion.
[2] Violent crimes are offenses of murder and nonnegligent manslaughter, rape, robbery, and aggravated assault. Property crimes are offenses of burglary, larceny-theft, motor vehicle theft, and arson.
[3] The 2006 rape figures are based on the legacy definition, and the 2015 rape figures are aggregate totals based on both the legacy and revised Uniform Crime Reporting definitions. For this reason, a percent change is not provided.

# Table 19. Current Year Over Previous Year Arrest Trends, 2014–2015

(Number, percent change; 11,437 agencies; 2015 estimated population 229,446,072; 2014 estimated population 228,153,502.)

| Offense charged | Number of persons arrested | | | | | | | | | | | |
|---|---|---|---|---|---|---|---|---|---|---|---|---|
| | Total, all ages | | | Under 15 years of age | | | Under 18 years of age | | | 18 years of age and over | | |
| | 2014 | 2015 | Percent change | 2014 | 2015 | Percent change | 2014 | 2015 | Percent change | 2014 | 2015 | Percent change |
| Total[1] ............................ | 7,967,934 | 7,689,755 | -3.5 | 197,475 | 180,987 | -8.3 | 709,317 | 649,970 | -8.4 | 7,258,617 | 7,039,785 | -3.0 |
| Violent crime[2] ...................... | 355,761 | 361,241 | +1.5 | 10,546 | 10,053 | -4.7 | 37,020 | 35,886 | -3.1 | 318,741 | 325,355 | +2.1 |
| Murder and nonnegligent manslaughter ..... | 7,044 | 7,519 | +6.7 | 41 | 47 | +14.6 | 488 | 521 | +6.8 | 6,556 | 6,998 | +6.7 |
| Rape[3] ................................. | 14,991 | 15,934 | +6.3 | 939 | 991 | +5.5 | 2,356 | 2,515 | +6.7 | 12,635 | 13,419 | +6.2 |
| Robbery ............................... | 64,612 | 66,138 | +2.4 | 2,533 | 2,348 | -7.3 | 12,597 | 12,347 | -2.0 | 52,015 | 53,791 | +3.4 |
| Aggravated assault ................... | 269,114 | 271,650 | +0.9 | 7,033 | 6,667 | -5.2 | 21,579 | 20,503 | -5.0 | 247,535 | 251,147 | +1.5 |
| Property crime[2] ..................... | 1,116,807 | 1,054,672 | -5.6 | 47,057 | 41,747 | -11.3 | 165,739 | 149,774 | -9.6 | 951,068 | 904,898 | -4.9 |
| Burglary .............................. | 171,437 | 156,419 | -8.8 | 8,052 | 7,543 | -6.3 | 28,386 | 25,527 | -10.1 | 143,051 | 130,892 | -8.5 |
| Larceny-theft ........................ | 891,541 | 838,874 | -5.9 | 35,758 | 31,006 | -13.3 | 126,889 | 113,114 | -10.9 | 764,652 | 725,760 | -5.1 |
| Motor vehicle theft ................... | 47,027 | 53,315 | +13.4 | 1,917 | 2,055 | +7.2 | 8,182 | 9,236 | +12.9 | 38,845 | 44,079 | +13.5 |
| Arson ................................. | 6,802 | 6,064 | -10.8 | 1,330 | 1,143 | -14.1 | 2,282 | 1,897 | -16.9 | 4,520 | 4,167 | -7.8 |
| Other assaults ........................ | 775,729 | 768,114 | -1.0 | 37,723 | 35,954 | -4.7 | 97,993 | 94,079 | -4.0 | 677,736 | 674,035 | -0.5 |
| Forgery and counterfeiting ............ | 40,838 | 39,918 | -2.3 | 111 | 92 | -17.1 | 844 | 752 | -10.9 | 39,994 | 39,166 | -2.1 |
| Fraud ................................. | 101,126 | 94,201 | -6.8 | 606 | 583 | -3.8 | 3,138 | 2,977 | -5.1 | 97,988 | 91,224 | -6.9 |
| Embezzlement ........................ | 11,837 | 11,657 | -1.5 | 21 | 25 | +19.0 | 330 | 436 | +32.1 | 11,507 | 11,221 | -2.5 |
| Stolen property; buying, receiving, possessing | 64,555 | 63,702 | -1.3 | 1,663 | 1,628 | -2.1 | 7,333 | 7,407 | +1.0 | 57,222 | 56,295 | -1.6 |
| Vandalism ............................ | 140,863 | 138,415 | -1.7 | 12,765 | 11,870 | -7.0 | 32,429 | 30,534 | -5.8 | 108,434 | 107,881 | -0.5 |
| Weapons; carrying, possessing, etc. ... | 97,809 | 101,895 | +4.2 | 4,685 | 4,262 | -9.0 | 13,994 | 13,317 | -4.8 | 83,815 | 88,578 | +5.7 |
| Prostitution and commercialized vice ... | 32,767 | 29,274 | -10.7 | 68 | 48 | -29.4 | 533 | 426 | -20.1 | 32,234 | 28,848 | -10.5 |
| Sex offenses (except forcible rape and prostitution) ..... | 38,930 | 37,123 | -4.6 | 3,303 | 3,038 | -8.0 | 6,786 | 6,390 | -5.8 | 32,144 | 30,733 | -4.4 |
| Drug abuse violations ................. | 1,102,280 | 1,058,297 | -4.0 | 13,510 | 11,222 | -16.9 | 79,504 | 69,964 | -12.0 | 1,022,776 | 988,333 | -3.4 |
| Gambling ............................. | 2,686 | 2,580 | -3.9 | 44 | 33 | -25.0 | 244 | 224 | -8.2 | 2,442 | 2,356 | -3.5 |
| Offenses against the family and children ..... | 70,042 | 68,628 | -2.0 | 914 | 877 | -4.0 | 2,513 | 2,384 | -5.1 | 67,529 | 66,244 | -1.9 |
| Driving under the influence ........... | 819,396 | 783,473 | -4.4 | 121 | 108 | -10.7 | 4,999 | 4,753 | -4.9 | 814,397 | 778,720 | -4.4 |
| Liquor laws ........................... | 231,142 | 193,643 | -16.2 | 3,641 | 3,316 | -8.9 | 38,408 | 31,549 | -17.9 | 192,734 | 162,094 | -15.9 |
| Drunkenness ......................... | 314,519 | 289,734 | -7.9 | 586 | 499 | -14.8 | 4,949 | 4,026 | -18.7 | 309,570 | 285,708 | -7.7 |
| Disorderly conduct ................... | 298,631 | 272,809 | -8.6 | 21,239 | 20,005 | -5.8 | 55,145 | 50,888 | -7.7 | 243,486 | 221,921 | -8.9 |
| Vagrancy ............................. | 20,254 | 18,856 | -6.9 | 165 | 205 | +24.2 | 707 | 792 | +12.0 | 19,547 | 18,064 | -7.6 |
| All other offenses (except traffic) ..... | 2,306,755 | 2,278,685 | -1.2 | 32,180 | 29,528 | -8.2 | 131,502 | 120,574 | -8.3 | 2,175,253 | 2,158,111 | -0.8 |
| Suspicion ............................. | 750 | 836 | +11.5 | 58 | 48 | -17.2 | 164 | 135 | -17.7 | 586 | 701 | +19.6 |
| Curfew and loitering law violations ..... | 25,207 | 22,838 | -9.4 | 6,527 | 5,894 | -9.7 | 25,207 | 22,838 | -9.4 | NA | NA | NA |

NA = Not available.
* = Less than one-tenth of 1 percent.
[1] Does not include suspicion.
[2] Violent crimes are offenses of murder and nonnegligent manslaughter, rape, robbery, and aggravated assault. Property crimes are offenses of burglary, larceny-theft, motor vehicle theft, and arson.
[3] The rape figures in this table are aggregate totals of the data submitted based on both the legacy and revised Uniform Crime Reporting definitions.

# Table 20. Full-Time Law Enforcement Employees,[1] by Region and Geographic Division and Population Group, 2015

(Number, rate per 1,000 inhabitants.)

| Region/geographic division | Total (10,075 cities; population 187,551,939) | Group I (76 cities, 250,000 and over; population 56,116,904) | Group II (195 cities, 100,000 to 249,999; population 28,956,838) | Group III (419 cities, 50,000 to 99,999; population 29,206,031) | Group IV (764 cities, 25,000 to 49,999; population 26,443,466) | Group V (1,612 cities, 10,000 to 24,999; population 25,662,681) | Group VI (7,009 cities, under 10,000; population 21,166,019) |
|---|---|---|---|---|---|---|---|
| **Total** | | | | | | | |
| Number of employees.................................................. | 519,134 | 183,302 | 63,094 | 59,540 | 56,074 | 57,693 | 99,431 |
| Average number of employees per 1,000 inhabitants............ | 2.8 | 3.3 | 2.2 | 2.0 | 2.1 | 2.2 | 4.7 |
| **Northeast** | | | | | | | |
| Number of employees.................................................. | 148,043 | 64,281 | 8,340 | 15,341 | 18,188 | 18,863 | 23,030 |
| Average number of employees per 1,000 inhabitants............ | 3.3 | 5.4 | 3.0 | 2.3 | 2.2 | 2.1 | 3.5 |
| New England | | | | | | | |
| Number of employees.................................................. | 34,360 | 2,689 | 4,449 | 6,262 | 6,987 | 7,250 | 6,723 |
| Average number of employees per 1,000 inhabitants............ | 2.6 | 4.0 | 3.0 | 2.3 | 2.1 | 2.2 | 3.6 |
| Middle Atlantic | | | | | | | |
| Number of employees.................................................. | 113,683 | 61,592 | 3,891 | 9,079 | 11,201 | 11,613 | 16,307 |
| Average number of employees per 1,000 inhabitants............ | 3.5 | 5.5 | 3.1 | 2.3 | 2.2 | 2.0 | 3.4 |
| **Midwest** | | | | | | | |
| Number of employees.................................................. | 83,685 | 17,741 | 8,053 | 12,302 | 12,391 | 13,914 | 19,284 |
| Average number of employees per 1,000 inhabitants............ | 2.3 | 2.9 | 2.0 | 1.8 | 1.9 | 2.0 | 3.4 |
| East North Central | | | | | | | |
| Number of employees.................................................. | 51,330 | 10,132 | 4,815 | 7,965 | 9,342 | 8,654 | 10,422 |
| Average number of employees per 1,000 inhabitants............ | 2.3 | 2.9 | 2.2 | 1.9 | 1.9 | 2.0 | 3.2 |
| West North Central | | | | | | | |
| Number of employees.................................................. | 32,355 | 7,609 | 3,238 | 4,337 | 3,049 | 5,260 | 8,862 |
| Average number of employees per 1,000 inhabitants............ | 2.4 | 2.9 | 1.9 | 1.7 | 1.8 | 2.1 | 3.6 |
| **South** | | | | | | | |
| Number of employees.................................................. | 176,675 | 53,548 | 26,676 | 16,871 | 17,053 | 18,730 | 43,797 |
| Average number of employees per 1,000 inhabitants............ | 3.2 | 2.9 | 2.6 | 2.5 | 2.6 | 2.9 | 6.6 |
| South Atlantic | | | | | | | |
| Number of employees.................................................. | 85,018 | 23,727 | 13,074 | 9,189 | 8,106 | 8,821 | 22,101 |
| Average number of employees per 1,000 inhabitants............ | 3.7 | 3.8 | 2.7 | 2.6 | 2.8 | 3.1 | 8.1 |
| East South Central | | | | | | | |
| Number of employees.................................................. | 29,747 | 6,893 | 3,962 | 2,360 | 3,765 | 3,928 | 8,839 |
| Average number of employees per 1,000 inhabitants............ | 3.4 | 2.7 | 3.2 | 2.7 | 2.7 | 3.1 | 6.1 |
| West South Central | | | | | | | |
| Number of employees.................................................. | 61,910 | 22,928 | 9,640 | 5,322 | 5,182 | 5,981 | 12,857 |
| Average number of employees per 1,000 inhabitants............ | 2.7 | 2.4 | 2.2 | 2.2 | 2.4 | 2.6 | 5.3 |
| **West** | | | | | | | |
| Number of employees.................................................. | 110,731 | 47,732 | 20,025 | 15,026 | 8,442 | 6,186 | 13,320 |
| Average number of employees per 1,000 inhabitants............ | 2.2 | 2.4 | 1.7 | 1.7 | 1.7 | 1.9 | 6.1 |
| Mountain | | | | | | | |
| Number of employees.................................................. | 39,725 | 15,480 | 6,940 | 4,760 | 3,280 | 2,232 | 7,033 |
| Average number of employees per 1,000 inhabitants............ | 2.5 | 2.5 | 2.0 | 2.0 | 1.8 | 2.1 | 6.4 |
| Pacific | | | | | | | |
| Number of employees.................................................. | 71,006 | 32,252 | 13,085 | 10,266 | 5,162 | 3,954 | 6,287 |
| Average number of employees per 1,000 inhabitants............ | 2.0 | 2.4 | 1.6 | 1.5 | 1.6 | 1.8 | 5.8 |

[1] Full-time law enforcement employees include civilians.
[2] The designation county is a combination of both metropolitan and nonmetropolitan counties.
[3] Suburban areas include law enforcement agencies in cities with less than 50,000 inhabitants and county law enforcement agencies that are within a Metropolitan Statistical Area (see Data Declaration). Suburban areas exclude all metropolitan agencies associated with a principal city. The agencies associated with suburban areas also appear in other groups within this table.

# Table 20. Full-Time Law Enforcement Employees,[1] by Region and Geographic Division and Population Group, 2015—Continued

(Number, rate per 1,000 inhabitants.)

| Region/geographic division | Total city agencies | 2015 estimated city population | County[2] (3,085 agencies; population 85,548,031) | Total city and county agencies | 2015 estimated total agency population | Suburban areas[3] (7,034 agencies; population 116,427,469) |
|---|---|---|---|---|---|---|
| **Total** | | | | | | |
| Number of employees | 10,075 | 187,551,939 | 394,027 | 13,160 | 273,099,970 | 429,617 |
| Average number of employees per 1,000 inhabitants | | | 4.6 | | | 3.7 |
| **Northeast** | | | | | | |
| Number of employees | 2,676 | 45,371,564 | | | | |
| Average number of employees per 1,000 inhabitants | | | | | | |
| New England | | | | | | |
| Number of employees | 832 | 13,220,257 | | | | |
| Average number of employees per 1,000 inhabitants | | | | | | |
| Middle Atlantic | | | | | | |
| Number of employees | 1,844 | 32,151,307 | | | | |
| Average number of employees per 1,000 inhabitants | | | | | | |
| **Midwest** | | | | | | |
| Number of employees | 2,611 | 36,148,697 | | | | |
| Average number of employees per 1,000 inhabitants | | | | | | |
| East North Central | | | | | | |
| Number of employees | 1,448 | 22,615,127 | | | | |
| Average number of employees per 1,000 inhabitants | | | | | | |
| West North Central | | | | | | |
| Number of employees | 1,163 | 13,533,570 | | | | |
| Average number of employees per 1,000 inhabitants | | | | | | |
| **South** | | | | | | |
| Number of employees | 3,452 | 54,978,984 | | | | |
| Average number of employees per 1,000 inhabitants | | | | | | |
| South Atlantic | | | | | | |
| Number of employees | 1,544 | 23,116,445 | | | | |
| Average number of employees per 1,000 inhabitants | | | | | | |
| East South Central | | | | | | |
| Number of employees | 757 | 8,809,884 | | | | |
| Average number of employees per 1,000 inhabitants | | | | | | |
| West South Central | | | | | | |
| Number of employees | 1,151 | 23,052,655 | | | | |
| Average number of employees per 1,000 inhabitants | | | | | | |
| **West** | | | | | | |
| Number of employees | 1,336 | 51,052,694 | | | | |
| Average number of employees per 1,000 inhabitants | | | | | | |
| Mountain | | | | | | |
| Number of employees | 602 | 16,040,517 | | | | |
| Average number of employees per 1,000 inhabitants | | | | | | |
| Pacific | | | | | | |
| Number of employees | 734 | 35,012,177 | | | | |
| Average number of employees per 1,000 inhabitants | | | | | | |

[1] Full-time law enforcement employees include civilians.
[2] The designation county is a combination of both metropolitan and nonmetropolitan counties.
[3] Suburban areas include law enforcement agencies in cities with less than 50,000 inhabitants and county law enforcement agencies that are within a Metropolitan Statistical Area (see Data Declaration). Suburban areas exclude all metropolitan agencies associated with a principal city. The agencies associated with suburban areas also appear in other groups within this table.

# Table 21. Full-Time Law Enforcement Officers, by Region and Geographic Division, and Population Group, 2015

(Number, rate per 1,000 inhabitants.)

| Region/geographic division | Total (10,075 cities; population 187,551,939) | Group I (76 cities, 250,000 and over; population 56,116,904) | Group II (195 cities, 100,000 to 249,999; population 28,956,838) | Group III (419 cities, 50,000 to 99,999; population 29,206,031) | Group IV (764 cities, 25,000 to 49,999; population 26,443,466) | Group V (1,612 cities, 10,000 to 24,999; population 25,662,681) | Group VI (7,009 cities, under 10,000; population 21,166,019) |
|---|---|---|---|---|---|---|---|
| **Total** | | | | | | | |
| Number of officers........................................... | 402,978 | 139,335 | 48,159 | 46,318 | 44,803 | 47,085 | 77,278 |
| Average number of officers per 1,000 inhabitants............... | 2.1 | 2.5 | 1.7 | 1.6 | 1.7 | 1.8 | 3.7 |
| **Northeast** | | | | | | | |
| Number of officers........................................... | 117,556 | 47,390 | 6,956 | 12,747 | 15,369 | 16,048 | 19,046 |
| Average number of officers per 1,000 inhabitants............... | 2.6 | 4.0 | 2.5 | 1.9 | 1.8 | 1.8 | 2.9 |
| New England | | | | | | | |
| Number of officers........................................... | 28,274 | 2,139 | 3,787 | 5,333 | 5,849 | 5,871 | 5,295 |
| Average number of officers per 1,000 inhabitants............... | 2.1 | 3.2 | 2.5 | 2.0 | 1.8 | 1.8 | 2.8 |
| Middle Atlantic | | | | | | | |
| Number of officers........................................... | 89,282 | 45,251 | 3,169 | 7,414 | 9,520 | 10,177 | 13,751 |
| Average number of officers per 1,000 inhabitants............... | 2.8 | 4.0 | 2.5 | 1.9 | 1.8 | 1.7 | 2.9 |
| **Midwest** | | | | | | | |
| Number of officers........................................... | 68,546 | 14,420 | 6,714 | 9,916 | 9,964 | 11,494 | 16,038 |
| Average number of officers per 1,000 inhabitants............... | 1.9 | 2.3 | 1.7 | 1.5 | 1.5 | 1.7 | 2.8 |
| East North Central | | | | | | | |
| Number of officers........................................... | 42,634 | 8,654 | 4,084 | 6,457 | 7,528 | 7,211 | 8,700 |
| Average number of officers per 1,000 inhabitants............... | 1.9 | 2.5 | 1.8 | 1.5 | 1.5 | 1.6 | 2.7 |
| West North Central | | | | | | | |
| Number of officers........................................... | 25,912 | 5,766 | 2,630 | 3,459 | 2,436 | 4,283 | 7,338 |
| Average number of officers per 1,000 inhabitants............... | 1.9 | 2.2 | 1.5 | 1.4 | 1.5 | 1.7 | 3.0 |
| **South** | | | | | | | |
| Number of officers........................................... | 136,482 | 42,000 | 20,339 | 13,106 | 13,309 | 14,780 | 32,948 |
| Average number of officers per 1,000 inhabitants............... | 2.5 | 2.3 | 2.0 | 1.9 | 2.1 | 2.3 | 5.0 |
| South Atlantic | | | | | | | |
| Number of officers........................................... | 65,624 | 18,026 | 10,040 | 7,228 | 6,407 | 7,082 | 16,841 |
| Average number of officers per 1,000 inhabitants............... | 2.8 | 2.9 | 2.1 | 2.0 | 2.2 | 2.5 | 6.2 |
| East South Central | | | | | | | |
| Number of officers........................................... | 23,496 | 5,701 | 3,073 | 1,859 | 2,975 | 3,138 | 6,750 |
| Average number of officers per 1,000 inhabitants............... | 2.7 | 2.2 | 2.5 | 2.1 | 2.1 | 2.4 | 4.6 |
| West South Central | | | | | | | |
| Number of officers........................................... | 47,362 | 18,273 | 7,226 | 4,019 | 3,927 | 4,560 | 9,357 |
| Average number of officers per 1,000 inhabitants............... | 2.1 | 1.9 | 1.7 | 1.7 | 1.8 | 2.0 | 3.9 |
| **West** | | | | | | | |
| Number of officers........................................... | 80,394 | 35,525 | 14,150 | 10,549 | 6,161 | 4,763 | 9,246 |
| Average number of officers per 1,000 inhabitants............... | 1.6 | 1.8 | 1.2 | 1.2 | 1.2 | 1.5 | 4.2 |
| Mountain | | | | | | | |
| Number of officers........................................... | 28,564 | 11,228 | 4,984 | 3,295 | 2,468 | 1,733 | 4,856 |
| Average number of officers per 1,000 inhabitants............... | 1.8 | 1.8 | 1.4 | 1.4 | 1.4 | 1.7 | 4.4 |
| Pacific | | | | | | | |
| Number of officers........................................... | 51,830 | 24,297 | 9,166 | 7,254 | 3,693 | 3,030 | 4,390 |
| Average number of officers per 1,000 inhabitants............... | 1.5 | 1.8 | 1.1 | 1.1 | 1.2 | 1.4 | 4.1 |

[1] The designation county is a combination of both metropolitan and nonmetropolitan counties.
[2] Suburban areas include law enforcement agencies in cities with less than 50,000 inhabitants and county law enforcement agencies that are within a Metropolitan Statistical Area. Suburban areas exclude all metropolitan agencies associated with a principal city. The agencies associated with suburban areas also appear in other groups within this table.

# Table 21. Full-Time Law Enforcement Officers, by Region and Geographic Division, and Population Group, 2015—Continued

(Number, rate per 1,000 inhabitants.)

| Region/geographic division | Total city agencies | 2015 estimated city population | County[1] (3,085 agencies; population 85,548,031) | Total city and county agencies | 2015 estimated total agency population | Suburban areas[2] (7,034 agencies; population 116,427,469) |
|---|---|---|---|---|---|---|
| **Total** | | | | | | |
| Number of officers.................................................. | 10,075 | 187,551,939 | 232,803 | 13,160 | 273,099,970 | 283,285 |
| Average number of officers per 1,000 inhabitants....... | | | 2.7 | | | 2.4 |
| | | | | | | |
| **Northeast** | | | | | | |
| Number of officers.................................................. | 2,676 | 45,371,564 | | | | |
| Average number of officers per 1,000 inhabitants....... | | | | | | |
| New England | | | | | | |
| Number of officers.................................................. | 832 | 13,220,257 | | | | |
| Average number of officers per 1,000 inhabitants....... | | | | | | |
| Middle Atlantic | | | | | | |
| Number of officers.................................................. | 1,844 | 32,151,307 | | | | |
| Average number of officers per 1,000 inhabitants....... | | | | | | |
| | | | | | | |
| **Midwest** | | | | | | |
| Number of officers.................................................. | 2,611 | 36,148,697 | | | | |
| Average number of officers per 1,000 inhabitants....... | | | | | | |
| East North Central | | | | | | |
| Number of officers.................................................. | 1,448 | 22,615,127 | | | | |
| Average number of officers per 1,000 inhabitants....... | | | | | | |
| West North Central | | | | | | |
| Number of officers.................................................. | 1,163 | 13,533,570 | | | | |
| Average number of officers per 1,000 inhabitants....... | | | | | | |
| | | | | | | |
| **South** | | | | | | |
| Number of officers.................................................. | 3,452 | 54,978,984 | | | | |
| Average number of officers per 1,000 inhabitants....... | | | | | | |
| South Atlantic | | | | | | |
| Number of officers.................................................. | 1,544 | 23,116,445 | | | | |
| Average number of officers per 1,000 inhabitants....... | | | | | | |
| East South Central | | | | | | |
| Number of officers.................................................. | 757 | 8,809,884 | | | | |
| Average number of officers per 1,000 inhabitants....... | | | | | | |
| West South Central | | | | | | |
| Number of officers.................................................. | 1,151 | 23,052,655 | | | | |
| Average number of officers per 1,000 inhabitants....... | | | | | | |
| | | | | | | |
| **West** | | | | | | |
| Number of officers.................................................. | 1,336 | 51,052,694 | | | | |
| Average number of officers per 1,000 inhabitants....... | | | | | | |
| Mountain | | | | | | |
| Number of officers.................................................. | 602 | 16,040,517 | | | | |
| Average number of officers per 1,000 inhabitants....... | | | | | | |
| Pacific | | | | | | |
| Number of officers.................................................. | 734 | 35,012,177 | | | | |
| Average number of officers per 1,000 inhabitants....... | | | | | | |

[1] The designation county is a combination of both metropolitan and nonmetropolitan counties.
[2] Suburban areas include law enforcement agencies in cities with less than 50,000 inhabitants and county law enforcement agencies that are within a Metropolitan Statistical Area. Suburban areas exclude all metropolitan agencies associated with a principal city. The agencies associated with suburban areas also appear in other groups within this table.

# Table 22. Full-Time State Law Enforcement Employees, by Selected State, 2015

(Number.)

| State/agency | Law enforcement employees | Officers | | Civilians | |
|---|---|---|---|---|---|
| | | Male | Female | Male | Female |
| **Alabama**[1] | | | | | |
| Highway Patrol ............................................. | 1,364 | 751 | 19 | 167 | 427 |
| Other state agencies ..................................... | 35 | 28 | 0 | 1 | 6 |
| **Arizona** | | | | | |
| Department of Public Safety........................... | 1,907 | 1,074 | 50 | 318 | 465 |
| **Arkansas**[1] | | | | | |
| Other state agencies ..................................... | 34 | 28 | 0 | 1 | 5 |
| **California** | | | | | |
| Highway Patrol ............................................. | 10,414 | 6,747 | 479 | 1,344 | 1,844 |
| Other state agencies[2] ................................... | 1,228 | 937 | 188 | 29 | 74 |
| **Colorado** | | | | | |
| State Police ................................................... | 1,162 | 717 | 46 | 157 | 242 |
| Other state agencies ..................................... | 263 | 50 | 6 | 48 | 159 |
| **Connecticut** | | | | | |
| State Police ................................................... | 1,658 | 1,038 | 96 | 225 | 299 |
| Other state agencies ..................................... | 43 | 31 | 1 | 8 | 3 |
| **Delaware** | | | | | |
| State Police ................................................... | 961 | 631 | 90 | 99 | 141 |
| Other state agencies ..................................... | 687 | 210 | 20 | 140 | 317 |
| **Florida** | | | | | |
| Highway Patrol ............................................. | 2,297 | 1,649 | 202 | 133 | 313 |
| Other state agencies ..................................... | 2,296 | 628 | 157 | 520 | 991 |
| **Georgia**[1] | | | | | |
| Other state agencies ..................................... | 355 | 135 | 22 | 91 | 107 |
| **Idaho** | | | | | |
| State Police ................................................... | 491 | 260 | 12 | 59 | 160 |
| **Illinois** | | | | | |
| State Police ................................................... | 2,839 | 1,570 | 176 | 423 | 670 |
| Other state agencies ..................................... | 234 | 123 | 8 | 65 | 38 |
| **Indiana** | | | | | |
| State Police ................................................... | 1,714 | 1,184 | 61 | 175 | 294 |
| Other state agencies ..................................... | 84 | 63 | 14 | 0 | 7 |
| **Iowa** | | | | | |
| Department of Public Safety........................... | 872 | 545 | 35 | 134 | 158 |
| **Kansas** | | | | | |
| Highway Patrol ............................................. | 753 | 448 | 17 | 113 | 175 |
| Other state agencies ..................................... | 515 | 282 | 22 | 83 | 128 |
| **Kentucky**[1] | | | | | |
| Other state agencies ..................................... | 236 | 205 | 6 | 15 | 10 |
| **Maine** | | | | | |
| State Police ................................................... | 424 | 278 | 24 | 52 | 70 |
| Other state agencies[2] ................................... | 56 | 26 | 2 | 18 | 10 |
| **Maryland** | | | | | |
| State Police ................................................... | 2,148 | 1,350 | 107 | 356 | 335 |
| Other state agencies ..................................... | 1,719 | 897 | 135 | 351 | 336 |
| **Massachusetts** | | | | | |
| State Police ................................................... | 2,618 | 1,983 | 129 | 205 | 301 |
| Other state agencies ..................................... | 394 | 317 | 33 | 19 | 25 |
| **Michigan** | | | | | |
| State Police ................................................... | 2,757 | 1,621 | 179 | 412 | 545 |

## Table 22. Full-Time State Law Enforcement Employees, by Selected State, 2015—*Continued*

(Number.)

| State/agency | Law enforcement employees | Officers | | Civilians | |
|---|---|---|---|---|---|
| | | Male | Female | Male | Female |
| **Minnesota** | | | | | |
| State Patrol............................................ | 598 | 459 | 41 | 52 | 46 |
| Other state agencies ............................. | 75 | 16 | 3 | 46 | 10 |
| **Mississippi**[1] | | | | | |
| Other state agencies ............................. | 41 | 34 | 2 | 1 | 4 |
| **Missouri** | | | | | |
| State Highway Patrol............................. | 2,304 | 1,132 | 64 | 506 | 602 |
| Other state agencies ............................. | 465 | 397 | 35 | 0 | 33 |
| **Montana** | | | | | |
| Highway Patrol ...................................... | 292 | 222 | 17 | 17 | 36 |
| **Nebraska** | | | | | |
| State Patrol............................................ | 705 | 434 | 29 | 82 | 160 |
| **Nevada** | | | | | |
| Highway Patrol ...................................... | 525 | 397 | 41 | 39 | 48 |
| Other state agencies ............................. | 67 | 32 | 4 | 11 | 20 |
| **New Hampshire** | | | | | |
| State Police............................................ | 511 | 299 | 29 | 66 | 117 |
| Other state agencies ............................. | 29 | 14 | 4 | 3 | 8 |
| **New Jersey** | | | | | |
| State Police............................................ | 3,828 | 2,487 | 119 | 574 | 648 |
| Other state agencies ............................. | 461 | 359 | 31 | 39 | 32 |
| Port Authority of New York and New Jersey[3]............... | 1,753 | 1,422 | 188 | 67 | 76 |
| **New York** | | | | | |
| State Police............................................ | 5,528 | 4,381 | 426 | 264 | 457 |
| Other state agencies ............................. | 271 | 222 | 32 | 6 | 11 |
| **North Carolina** | | | | | |
| Highway Patrol ...................................... | 2,178 | 1,595 | 56 | 304 | 223 |
| Other state agencies ............................. | 1,088 | 700 | 122 | 102 | 164 |
| **North Dakota** | | | | | |
| Highway Patrol ...................................... | 205 | 154 | 8 | 31 | 12 |
| **Ohio** | | | | | |
| Highway Patrol ...................................... | 2,556 | 1,488 | 137 | 482 | 449 |
| **Oklahoma**[1] | | | | | |
| Other state agencies ............................. | 70 | 16 | 4 | 38 | 12 |
| **Oregon** | | | | | |
| State Police............................................ | 1,266 | 647 | 63 | 197 | 359 |
| Other state agencies ............................. | 53 | 35 | 10 | 0 | 8 |
| **Pennsylvania** | | | | | |
| State Police............................................ | 6,407 | 4,131 | 248 | 1,007 | 1,021 |
| Other state agencies ............................. | 440 | 306 | 24 | 82 | 28 |
| **Rhode Island** | | | | | |
| State Police............................................ | 280 | 202 | 20 | 30 | 28 |
| Other state agencies ............................. | 76 | 57 | 4 | 10 | 5 |
| **South Carolina** | | | | | |
| Highway Patrol ...................................... | 1,237 | 885 | 52 | 101 | 199 |
| Other state agencies[2]........................... | 1,289 | 754 | 130 | 136 | 269 |
| **South Dakota** | | | | | |
| Highway Patrol ...................................... | 248 | 167 | 5 | 43 | 33 |
| Other state agencies ............................. | 171 | 49 | 2 | 43 | 77 |

## Table 22. Full-Time State Law Enforcement Employees, by Selected State, 2015—*Continued*

(Number.)

| State/agency | Law enforcement employees | Officers | | Civilians | |
|---|---|---|---|---|---|
| | | Male | Female | Male | Female |
| **Tennessee** | | | | | |
| Department of Safety | 1,672 | 784 | 40 | 585 | 263 |
| Other state agencies | 1,234 | 676 | 86 | 179 | 293 |
| **Utah** | | | | | |
| Highway Patrol | 593 | 432 | 21 | 26 | 114 |
| Other state agencies | 134 | 123 | 8 | 1 | 2 |
| **Vermont** | | | | | |
| State Police | 311 | 234 | 32 | 18 | 27 |
| Other state agencies | 120 | 87 | 6 | 12 | 15 |
| **Virginia** | | | | | |
| State Police | 2,702 | 1,848 | 111 | 256 | 487 |
| Other state agencies | 725 | 455 | 55 | 86 | 129 |
| **Washington** | | | | | |
| State Patrol | 2,127 | 909 | 86 | 581 | 551 |
| Other state agencies | 111 | 48 | 19 | 11 | 33 |
| **West Virginia** | | | | | |
| State Patrol | 1,160 | 733 | 134 | 39 | 254 |
| Other state agencies | 225 | 179 | 5 | 15 | 26 |
| **Wisconsin** | | | | | |
| State Patrol | 581 | 383 | 39 | 80 | 79 |
| Other state agencies | 456 | 358 | 58 | 15 | 25 |

*Note:* Caution should be used when comparing data from one state to that of another. The responsibilities of the various state police, highway patrol, and department of public safety agencies range from full law enforcement duties to only traffic patrol, which can impact both the level of employment for agencies as well as the ratio of sworn officers to civilians employed. Any valid comparison must take these factors and the other identified variables affecting crime into consideration.

[1] Police employee data were not received from the State Police/Highway Patrol/Department of Public Safety for the state.
[2] The total employee count includes employees from agencies that are not represented in other law enforcement employee tables.
[3] Data reported are the number of law enforcement employees for the state of New Jersey.


## Table 23. Murder Victims, by Race, Ethnicity, and Sex, 2015

(Number.)

| Race | Total | Sex | | |
|---|---|---|---|---|
| | | Male | Female | Unknown |
| **Total** | 13,455 | 10,608 | 2,818 | 29 |
| White | 5,854 | 4,117 | 1,734 | 3 |
| Black | 7,039 | 6,115 | 923 | 1 |
| Other race | 366 | 251 | 115 | 0 |
| Unknown race | 196 | 125 | 46 | 25 |
| Hispanic or Latino[1] | 2,028 | 1,669 | 359 | 0 |
| Not Hispanic or Latino[1] | 7,971 | 6,192 | 1,777 | 2 |
| Unknown[1] | 2,224 | 1,731 | 468 | 25 |

[1] Not all agencies provide ethnicity data, therefore the race and ethnicity totals will not equal.

## Table 24. Murder Victims, by Age, Sex, Race, and Ethnicity, 2015

(Number; percent; single victim/single offender.)

| Age | Total | Sex | | | Race | | | | Ethnicity | | |
|---|---|---|---|---|---|---|---|---|---|---|---|
| | | Male | Female | Unknown | White | Black or African American | Other[1] | Unknown | Hispanic/ Latino | Not Hispanic/ Latino | Unknown |
| Total ............................ | 13,455 | 10,608 | 2,818 | 29 | 5,854 | 7,039 | 366 | 196 | 2,028 | 7,971 | 2,224 |
| Percent distribution[2]................ | 100.0 | 78.8 | 20.9 | 0.2 | 43.5 | 52.3 | 2.7 | 1.5 | 16.6 | 65.2 | 18.2 |
| Under 18[3]........................................ | 1,093 | 761 | 329 | 3 | 504 | 544 | 26 | 19 | 193 | 611 | 189 |
| Under 22[3]........................................ | 2,624 | 2,135 | 487 | 2 | 954 | 1,598 | 44 | 28 | 488 | 1,484 | 443 |
| 18 and over[3]................................... | 12,228 | 9,773 | 2,448 | 7 | 5,296 | 6,451 | 339 | 142 | 1,823 | 7,305 | 1,974 |
| Infant (under 1)........................... | 168 | 104 | 63 | 1 | 89 | 65 | 8 | 6 | 24 | 104 | 28 |
| 1 to 4 ............................................. | 260 | 153 | 106 | 1 | 130 | 117 | 6 | 7 | 32 | 160 | 58 |
| 5 to 8 ............................................. | 91 | 49 | 42 | 0 | 58 | 30 | 1 | 2 | 12 | 57 | 16 |
| 9 to 12 ........................................... | 56 | 35 | 20 | 1 | 30 | 22 | 3 | 1 | 9 | 30 | 6 |
| 13 to 16 ......................................... | 282 | 218 | 64 | 0 | 110 | 167 | 4 | 1 | 62 | 141 | 49 |
| 17 to 19 ......................................... | 996 | 870 | 126 | 0 | 325 | 647 | 16 | 8 | 191 | 546 | 159 |
| 20 to 24 ......................................... | 2,431 | 2,102 | 329 | 0 | 764 | 1,596 | 45 | 26 | 414 | 1,398 | 368 |
| 25 to 29 ......................................... | 2,071 | 1,733 | 338 | 0 | 717 | 1,290 | 48 | 16 | 321 | 1,201 | 331 |
| 30 to 34 ......................................... | 1,647 | 1,340 | 307 | 0 | 650 | 927 | 49 | 21 | 266 | 974 | 254 |
| 35 to 39 ......................................... | 1,263 | 1,021 | 241 | 1 | 539 | 666 | 45 | 13 | 200 | 728 | 223 |
| 40 to 44 ......................................... | 925 | 701 | 222 | 2 | 467 | 428 | 23 | 7 | 150 | 545 | 158 |
| 45 to 49 ......................................... | 781 | 586 | 194 | 1 | 399 | 330 | 33 | 19 | 118 | 485 | 115 |
| 50 to 54 ......................................... | 737 | 568 | 169 | 0 | 428 | 282 | 17 | 10 | 84 | 468 | 120 |
| 55 to 59 ......................................... | 580 | 425 | 154 | 1 | 363 | 183 | 27 | 7 | 57 | 389 | 102 |
| 60 to 64 ......................................... | 360 | 250 | 109 | 1 | 226 | 114 | 12 | 8 | 36 | 231 | 54 |
| 65 to 69 ......................................... | 235 | 168 | 67 | 0 | 166 | 59 | 6 | 4 | 14 | 168 | 41 |
| 70 to 74 ......................................... | 159 | 93 | 65 | 1 | 113 | 33 | 9 | 4 | 11 | 100 | 33 |
| 75 and over ................................... | 279 | 118 | 161 | 0 | 226 | 39 | 13 | 1 | 15 | 191 | 48 |
| Unknown........................................ | 134 | 74 | 41 | 19 | 54 | 44 | 1 | 35 | 12 | 55 | 61 |

[1] Includes American Indian or Alaska Native; Asian; Native Hawaiian or Other Pacific Islander.
[2] Because of rounding, the percentages may not add to 100.0.
[3] Does not include unknown ages.

# Table 25. Murder Offenders, by Age, Sex, Race, and Ethnicity, 2015

(Number; percent; single victim/single offender.)

| Age | Total | Sex | | | Race | | | | Ethnicity[1] | | |
|---|---|---|---|---|---|---|---|---|---|---|---|
| | | Male | Female | Unknown | White | Black or African American | Other[2] | Unknown | Hispanic/ Latino | Not Hispanic/ Latino | Unknown |
| Total ................... | 15,326 | 9,553 | 1,180 | 4,593 | 4,636 | 5,620 | 283 | 4,787 | 1,312 | 4,598 | 4,408 |
| Percent distribution[3]......... | 100.0 | 62.3 | 7.7 | 30.0 | 30.2 | 36.7 | 1.8 | 31.2 | 12.7 | 44.6 | 42.7 |
| Under 18[4] ........................ | 667 | 616 | 51 | 0 | 236 | 412 | 14 | 5 | 104 | 269 | 91 |
| Under 22[4] ........................ | 2,648 | 2,403 | 239 | 6 | 916 | 1,638 | 69 | 25 | 404 | 1,108 | 322 |
| 18 and over[4] ...................... | 9,456 | 8,327 | 1,109 | 20 | 4,324 | 4,755 | 268 | 109 | 1,183 | 4,125 | 1,169 |
| Infant (under 1).................... | 0 | 0 | 0 | 0 | 0 | 0 | 0 | 0 | 0 | 0 | 0 |
| 1 to 4 .............................. | 1 | 1 | 0 | 0 | 0 | 1 | 0 | 0 | 0 | 0 | 0 |
| 5 to 8 .............................. | 2 | 1 | 1 | 0 | 1 | 1 | 0 | 0 | 0 | 0 | 1 |
| 9 to 12 ............................ | 9 | 8 | 1 | 0 | 4 | 5 | 0 | 0 | 2 | 2 | 2 |
| 13 to 16 ............................ | 341 | 320 | 21 | 0 | 119 | 210 | 9 | 3 | 54 | 147 | 44 |
| 17 to 19 ............................ | 1,263 | 1,143 | 119 | 1 | 442 | 784 | 28 | 9 | 193 | 527 | 156 |
| 20 to 24 ............................ | 2,448 | 2,180 | 262 | 6 | 844 | 1,513 | 66 | 25 | 330 | 1,030 | 273 |
| 25 to 29 ............................ | 1,814 | 1,607 | 204 | 3 | 739 | 997 | 52 | 26 | 214 | 756 | 244 |
| 30 to 34 ............................ | 1,251 | 1,082 | 165 | 4 | 610 | 584 | 40 | 17 | 175 | 509 | 173 |
| 35 to 39 ............................ | 840 | 733 | 107 | 0 | 449 | 368 | 17 | 6 | 104 | 382 | 115 |
| 40 to 44 ............................ | 594 | 506 | 88 | 0 | 350 | 223 | 17 | 4 | 79 | 269 | 69 |
| 45 to 49 ............................ | 449 | 384 | 63 | 2 | 251 | 175 | 20 | 3 | 47 | 200 | 56 |
| 50 to 54 ............................ | 453 | 390 | 60 | 3 | 295 | 128 | 16 | 14 | 46 | 225 | 46 |
| 55 to 59 ............................ | 278 | 248 | 29 | 1 | 174 | 94 | 9 | 1 | 23 | 148 | 30 |
| 60 to 64 ............................ | 149 | 136 | 13 | 0 | 103 | 41 | 1 | 4 | 5 | 74 | 23 |
| 65 to 69 ............................ | 88 | 77 | 11 | 0 | 60 | 27 | 0 | 1 | 7 | 44 | 12 |
| 70 to 74 ............................ | 52 | 42 | 10 | 0 | 37 | 10 | 4 | 1 | 3 | 32 | 7 |
| 75 and over ........................ | 91 | 85 | 6 | 0 | 82 | 6 | 3 | 0 | 5 | 49 | 9 |
| Unknown.............................. | 5,203 | 610 | 20 | 4,573 | 76 | 453 | 1 | 4,673 | 25 | 204 | 3,148 |

[1] Not all agencies provide ethnicity data, therefore the race and ethnicity totals will not equal.
[2] Includes American Indian or Alaska Native; Asian; Native Hawaiian or Other Pacific Islander.
[3] Because of rounding, the percentages may not add to 100.0.
[4] Does not include unknown ages.

# Table 26. Murder, by Victim/Offender Situations, 2015

(Number; percent; single victim/single offender.)

| Situation | Total | Percent distribution (may not add to 100.0 due to rounding) |
|---|---|---|
| Total ........................................... | 13,455 | 100.0 |
| Single victim/single offender ......................................... | 6,137 | 45.6 |
| Single victim/unknown offender or offenders............................. | 4,239 | 31.5 |
| Single victim/multiple offenders ...................................... | 1,551 | 11.5 |
| Multiple victims/single offender........................................ | 835 | 6.2 |
| Multiple victims/unknown offender or offenders .......................... | 246 | 1.8 |
| Multiple victims/multiple offenders.................................... | 447 | 3.3 |

## Table 27. Murder Age of Victim, by Age of Offender, 2015

(Number; single victim/single offender.)

| Age of victim | Total | Age of offender | | |
| --- | --- | --- | --- | --- |
| | | Under 18 years | 18 years and over | Unknown |
| **Total** .............................................................. | 6,137 | 257 | 5,625 | 255 |
| Under 18 ........................................................... | 520 | 86 | 419 | 15 |
| 18 and over ...................................................... | 5,573 | 171 | 5,166 | 236 |
| Unknown........................................................... | 44 | 0 | 40 | 4 |

*Note:* This table is based on incidents where some information about the offender is known by law enforcement; therefore, when the offender age, sex, and race are all reported as unknown, these data are excluded from the table.


## Table 28. Murder, Race, Ethnicity, and Sex of Victim by Race, Ethnicity, and Sex of Offender, 2015

(Number; single victim/single offender.)

| Victim characteristic | Total | Sex | | | Race | | | | Ethnicity | | |
| --- | --- | --- | --- | --- | --- | --- | --- | --- | --- | --- | --- |
| | | Male | Female | Unknown | White | Black or African American | Other[1] | Unknown | Hispanic/ Latino | Not Hispanic/ Latino | Unknown |
| **Race** | | | | | | | | | | | |
| White ............................................. | 3,167 | 2,574 | 500 | 49 | 44 | 2,817 | 306 | 44 | 633 | 1,086 | 1,448 |
| Black or African American....................... | 2,664 | 229 | 2,380 | 13 | 42 | 2,391 | 231 | 42 | 99 | 1,135 | 1,430 |
| Other race[1] ................................... | 222 | 60 | 34 | 126 | 2 | 192 | 28 | 2 | 15 | 108 | 99 |
| Unknown ...................................... | 84 | 34 | 20 | 6 | 24 | 49 | 11 | 24 | 4 | 19 | 61 |
| **Sex** | | | | | | | | | | | |
| Male ............................................. | 4,333 | 1,834 | 2,299 | 126 | 74 | 3,845 | 414 | 74 | 558 | 1,682 | 2,093 |
| Female........................................... | 1,719 | 1,029 | 614 | 62 | 14 | 1,554 | 151 | 14 | 189 | 647 | 883 |
| Unknown......................................... | 85 | 34 | 21 | 6 | 24 | 50 | 11 | 24 | 4 | 19 | 62 |
| **Ethnicity** | | | | | | | | | | | |
| Hispanic or Latino ............................. | 757 | 600 | 138 | 9 | 10 | 703 | 44 | 10 | 535 | 180 | 42 |
| Not Hispanic or Latino........................ | 2,360 | 1,000 | 1,249 | 96 | 15 | 2,111 | 234 | 15 | 189 | 2,116 | 55 |
| Unknown......................................... | 3,020 | 1,297 | 1,547 | 89 | 87 | 2,635 | 298 | 87 | 27 | 52 | 2,941 |

*Note:* This table is based on incidents where some information about the offender is known by law enforcement; therefore, when the offender age, sex, and race are all reported as unknown, these data are excluded from the table.
[1] Includes American Indian or Alaska Native; Asian; Native Hawaiian or Other Pacific Islander.

## Table 29. Murder, Types of Weapons Used, Percent Distribution by Region, 2015[1]

(Percent.)

| Region | Total, all weapons[2] | Firearms | Knives or cutting instruments | Unknown or other dangerous weapons | Personal weapons (hands, fists, feet, etc.)[3] |
|---|---|---|---|---|---|
| Total ............................................. | 100.0 | 71.5 | 11.5 | 12.4 | 4.7 |
| Northeast............................................. | 100.0 | 69.3 | 14.0 | 12.5 | 4.3 |
| Midwest ............................................. | 100.0 | 74.4 | 8.9 | 12.6 | 4.1 |
| South............................................. | 100.0 | 73.7 | 10.5 | 11.2 | 4.6 |
| West............................................. | 100.0 | 66.0 | 14.1 | 14.3 | 5.6 |

[1] Guam and Virgin Islands totals are not included in this table.
[2] Because of rounding, the percentages may not add to 100.0.
[3] Pushed is included in personal weapons.

## Table 30. Murder Victims, by Weapons, 2011–2015

(Number.)

| Weapons | 2011 | 2012 | 2013 | 2014 | 2015 |
|---|---|---|---|---|---|
| Total ............................................. | 12,795 | 12,888 | 12,253 | 12,270 | 13,455 |
| Total firearms............................................. | 8,653 | 8,897 | 8,454 | 8,312 | 9,616 |
| Handguns............................................. | 6,251 | 6,404 | 5,782 | 5,673 | 6,447 |
| Rifles............................................. | 332 | 298 | 285 | 258 | 252 |
| Shotguns............................................. | 362 | 310 | 308 | 264 | 269 |
| Other guns............................................. | 97 | 116 | 123 | 93 | 171 |
| Firearms, type not stated............................................. | 1,611 | 1,769 | 1,956 | 2,024 | 2,477 |
| Knives or cutting instruments............................................. | 1,716 | 1,604 | 1,490 | 1,595 | 1,544 |
| Blunt objects (clubs, hammers, etc.) ............................................. | 502 | 522 | 428 | 446 | 437 |
| Personal weapons (hands, fists, feet, etc.)[1] ............................................. | 751 | 707 | 687 | 682 | 624 |
| Poison............................................. | 5 | 13 | 11 | 10 | 7 |
| Explosives ............................................. | 6 | 8 | 2 | 7 | 1 |
| Fire............................................. | 76 | 87 | 94 | 71 | 82 |
| Narcotics............................................. | 33 | 38 | 53 | 70 | 70 |
| Drowning............................................. | 15 | 14 | 4 | 14 | 14 |
| Strangulation............................................. | 88 | 90 | 85 | 89 | 96 |
| Asphyxiation............................................. | 92 | 106 | 95 | 102 | 120 |
| Other weapons or weapons not stated ............................................. | 858 | 802 | 850 | 872 | 844 |

[1] Pushed is included in personal weapons.

## Table 31. Murder Victims by Age, by Weapon, 2015

(Number.)

| Age | Total murder victims | Weapons | | | | | | | | | | |
|---|---|---|---|---|---|---|---|---|---|---|---|---|
| | | Firearms | Knives or cutting instruments | Blunt objects (clubs, hammers, etc.) | Personal weapons (hands, fists, feet, etc.)[1] | Poison | Explosives | Fire | Narcotics | Strangulation | Asphyxiation | Other weapon or weapon not stated[2] |
| **Total** ..................................... | 13,455 | 9,616 | 1,544 | 437 | 624 | 7 | 1 | 82 | 70 | 96 | 120 | 858 |
| Percent distribution[3].......... | 100.0 | 71.5 | 11.5 | 3.2 | 4.6 | 0.1 | 0.0 | 0.6 | 0.5 | 0.7 | 0.9 | 6.4 |
| Under 18[4] ........................... | 1,093 | 553 | 76 | 42 | 205 | 2 | 0 | 16 | 13 | 9 | 42 | 135 |
| Under 22[4] ........................... | 2,624 | 2,011 | 195 | 43 | 150 | 2 | 0 | 18 | 16 | 11 | 29 | 149 |
| 18 and over[4] ........................ | 12,227 | 9,014 | 1,460 | 388 | 404 | 5 | 1 | 61 | 53 | 85 | 77 | 679 |
| Infant (under 1)....................... | 168 | 8 | 5 | 15 | 77 | 1 | 0 | 3 | 2 | 3 | 17 | 37 |
| 1 to 4 ................................. | 260 | 42 | 9 | 20 | 107 | 1 | 0 | 3 | 5 | 2 | 15 | 56 |
| 5 to 8 ................................. | 91 | 42 | 10 | 2 | 8 | 0 | 0 | 2 | 3 | 2 | 6 | 16 |
| 9 to 12 ................................ | 56 | 30 | 8 | 2 | 3 | 0 | 0 | 6 | 0 | 0 | 3 | 4 |
| 13 to 16 ............................... | 282 | 235 | 21 | 2 | 5 | 0 | 0 | 1 | 2 | 1 | 1 | 14 |
| 17 to 19 ............................... | 996 | 854 | 72 | 7 | 17 | 1 | 0 | 4 | 5 | 3 | 1 | 32 |
| 20 to 24 ............................... | 2,431 | 2,060 | 211 | 18 | 25 | 0 | 0 | 6 | 10 | 9 | 8 | 84 |
| 25 to 29 ............................... | 2,071 | 1,704 | 187 | 27 | 39 | 0 | 0 | 6 | 15 | 7 | 13 | 73 |
| 30 to 34 ............................... | 1,647 | 1,308 | 164 | 34 | 38 | 2 | 0 | 4 | 4 | 10 | 5 | 78 |
| 35 to 39 ............................... | 1,263 | 938 | 164 | 32 | 39 | 0 | 0 | 5 | 4 | 6 | 5 | 70 |
| 40 to 44 ............................... | 925 | 679 | 107 | 24 | 27 | 1 | 0 | 4 | 7 | 8 | 6 | 62 |
| 45 to 49 ............................... | 781 | 499 | 121 | 41 | 34 | 1 | 0 | 7 | 2 | 11 | 7 | 58 |
| 50 to 54 ............................... | 737 | 399 | 156 | 48 | 50 | 0 | 0 | 7 | 4 | 6 | 10 | 57 |
| 55 to 59 ............................... | 580 | 293 | 107 | 58 | 47 | 0 | 0 | 4 | 1 | 8 | 4 | 58 |
| 60 to 64 ............................... | 360 | 174 | 68 | 34 | 34 | 0 | 1 | 6 | 1 | 5 | 3 | 34 |
| 65 to 69 ............................... | 235 | 113 | 57 | 17 | 16 | 0 | 0 | 0 | 0 | 3 | 3 | 26 |
| 70 to 74 ............................... | 159 | 70 | 27 | 13 | 14 | 0 | 0 | 2 | 0 | 4 | 5 | 24 |
| 75 and over ........................... | 279 | 119 | 43 | 36 | 29 | 0 | 0 | 7 | 1 | 6 | 7 | 31 |
| Unknown................................ | 134 | 49 | 7 | 7 | 15 | 0 | 0 | 5 | 4 | 2 | 1 | 44 |

[1] Pushed is included in personal weapons.
[2] Includes drowning.
[3] Because of rounding, the percentages may not add to 100.0.
[4] Does not include unknown ages.

# Table 32. Murder Circumstances, by Relationship, 2015[1]

(Number.)

| Circumstances | Total murder victims | Husband | Wife | Mother | Father | Son | Daughter | Brother | Sister | Other family |
|---|---|---|---|---|---|---|---|---|---|---|
| **Total** | 13,455 | 113 | 509 | 125 | 131 | 255 | 162 | 108 | 32 | 286 |
| Felony type total | 2,014 | 3 | 37 | 8 | 12 | 28 | 18 | 7 | 9 | 36 |
| Rape | 12 | 0 | 0 | 0 | 0 | 1 | 0 | 0 | 0 | 0 |
| Robbery | 595 | 0 | 0 | 1 | 0 | 0 | 0 | 0 | 0 | 3 |
| Burglary | 102 | 0 | 0 | 0 | 1 | 1 | 0 | 0 | 0 | 7 |
| Larceny-theft | 16 | 0 | 0 | 0 | 0 | 0 | 0 | 0 | 0 | 0 |
| Motor vehicle theft | 41 | 0 | 0 | 0 | 1 | 0 | 0 | 0 | 0 | 4 |
| Arson | 19 | 0 | 2 | 0 | 0 | 1 | 0 | 0 | 1 | 1 |
| Prostitution and commercialized vice | 6 | 0 | 0 | 0 | 0 | 0 | 0 | 0 | 0 | 0 |
| Other sex offenses | 15 | 0 | 1 | 0 | 0 | 0 | 0 | 0 | 0 | 0 |
| Narcotic drug laws | 468 | 0 | 0 | 0 | 0 | 1 | 1 | 0 | 0 | 4 |
| Gambling | 5 | 0 | 0 | 0 | 0 | 0 | 0 | 0 | 0 | 0 |
| Other-not specified | 735 | 3 | 34 | 7 | 10 | 24 | 17 | 7 | 8 | 17 |
| Suspected felony type | 117 | 4 | 7 | 1 | 0 | 7 | 3 | 0 | 1 | 4 |
| Other than felony type total: | 5,958 | 84 | 367 | 80 | 92 | 171 | 110 | 88 | 19 | 176 |
| Romantic triangle | 106 | 3 | 14 | 2 | 0 | 0 | 0 | 0 | 0 | 1 |
| Child killed by babysitter | 36 | 0 | 0 | 0 | 0 | 0 | 0 | 0 | 0 | 3 |
| Brawl due to influence of alcohol | 112 | 0 | 2 | 0 | 2 | 1 | 1 | 11 | 0 | 4 |
| Brawl due to influence of narcotics | 75 | 0 | 2 | 2 | 1 | 5 | 2 | 1 | 0 | 1 |
| Argument over money or property | 184 | 2 | 5 | 3 | 2 | 4 | 0 | 4 | 1 | 10 |
| Other arguments | 2,941 | 64 | 242 | 45 | 64 | 35 | 20 | 62 | 5 | 100 |
| Gangland killings | 188 | 1 | 0 | 0 | 0 | 1 | 0 | 0 | 0 | 1 |
| Juvenile gang killings | 604 | 0 | 0 | 0 | 0 | 0 | 0 | 0 | 0 | 0 |
| Institutional killings | 24 | 0 | 1 | 0 | 0 | 0 | 0 | 0 | 0 | 0 |
| Sniper attack | 5 | 0 | 1 | 0 | 0 | 0 | 0 | 0 | 0 | 0 |
| Other-not specified | 1,683 | 14 | 100 | 28 | 23 | 125 | 87 | 10 | 13 | 56 |
| Unknown | 5,366 | 22 | 98 | 36 | 27 | 49 | 31 | 13 | 3 | 70 |

*Note:* The relationship categories of husband and wife include both common-law and ex-spouses. The categories of mother, father, sister, brother, son, and daughter include stepparents, stepchildren, and stepsiblings. The category of acquaintance includes homosexual relationships and the composite category of other known to victim.
[1] Relationship is that of victim to offender.

## Table 32. Murder Circumstances, by Relationship, 2015[1]—*Continued*

(Number.)

| Circumstances | Acquaintance | Friend | Boyfriend | Girlfriend | Neighbor | Employee | Employer | Stranger | Unknown |
|---|---|---|---|---|---|---|---|---|---|
| **Total** .................... | 2,801 | 365 | 152 | 496 | 95 | 8 | 10 | 1,375 | 6,432 |
| Felony type total .................... | 533 | 68 | 9 | 34 | 18 | 5 | 1 | 388 | 800 |
| Rape .................... | 6 | 0 | 0 | 2 | 1 | 0 | 0 | 0 | 2 |
| Robbery .................... | 128 | 20 | 1 | 0 | 2 | 3 | 1 | 211 | 225 |
| Burglary .................... | 30 | 1 | 0 | 2 | 4 | 1 | 0 | 24 | 31 |
| Larceny-theft .................... | 6 | 2 | 0 | 1 | 0 | 0 | 0 | 5 | 2 |
| Motor vehicle theft .................... | 11 | 0 | 0 | 3 | 0 | 0 | 0 | 13 | 9 |
| Arson .................... | 2 | 0 | 0 | 0 | 0 | 0 | 0 | 6 | 6 |
| Prostitution and commercialized vice .................... | 1 | 0 | 1 | 0 | 0 | 0 | 0 | 1 | 3 |
| Other sex offenses .................... | 5 | 0 | 1 | 1 | 1 | 0 | 0 | 3 | 3 |
| Narcotic drug laws .................... | 174 | 22 | 0 | 4 | 0 | 0 | 0 | 28 | 234 |
| Gambling .................... | 5 | 0 | 0 | 0 | 0 | 0 | 0 | 0 | 0 |
| Other-not specified .................... | 165 | 23 | 6 | 21 | 10 | 1 | 0 | 97 | 285 |
| Suspected felony type .................... | 19 | 2 | 0 | 6 | 0 | 0 | 0 | 8 | 55 |
| Other than felony type total: .................... | 1,714 | 229 | 120 | 355 | 59 | 2 | 7 | 588 | 1,697 |
| Romantic triangle .................... | 52 | 4 | 3 | 9 | 0 | 0 | 0 | 8 | 10 |
| Child killed by babysitter .................... | 30 | 1 | 0 | 0 | 1 | 0 | 0 | 0 | 1 |
| Brawl due to influence of alcohol .................... | 37 | 8 | 1 | 1 | 4 | 1 | 0 | 20 | 19 |
| Brawl due to influence of narcotics .................... | 28 | 8 | 1 | 3 | 0 | 0 | 0 | 7 | 14 |
| Argument over money or property .................... | 100 | 9 | 3 | 3 | 5 | 0 | 0 | 11 | 22 |
| Other arguments .................... | 940 | 150 | 97 | 276 | 34 | 1 | 4 | 281 | 521 |
| Gangland killings .................... | 36 | 6 | 0 | 0 | 0 | 0 | 0 | 28 | 115 |
| Juvenile gang killings .................... | 105 | 3 | 0 | 0 | 0 | 0 | 0 | 56 | 440 |
| Institutional killings .................... | 18 | 0 | 0 | 0 | 0 | 0 | 0 | 3 | 2 |
| Sniper attack .................... | 1 | 0 | 0 | 0 | 0 | 0 | 0 | 0 | 3 |
| Other-not specified .................... | 367 | 40 | 15 | 63 | 15 | 0 | 3 | 174 | 550 |
| Unknown .................... | 535 | 66 | 23 | 101 | 18 | 1 | 2 | 391 | 3,880 |

*Note:* The relationship categories of husband and wife include both common-law and ex-spouses. The categories of mother, father, sister, brother, son, and daughter include stepparents, stepchildren, and stepsiblings. The category of acquaintance includes homosexual relationships and the composite category of other known to victim.
[1] Relationship is that of victim to offender.

# Table 33. Murder Circumstances, by Weapon, 2015

(Number.)

| Circumstances | Total murder victims | Total firearms | Handguns | Rifles | Shotguns | Other guns or type not stated | Knives or cutting instruments | Blunt objects (clubs, hammers, etc.) | Personal weapons (hands, fists, feet, etc.) |
|---|---|---|---|---|---|---|---|---|---|
| Total ............................................................ | 13,455 | 9,616 | 6,447 | 252 | 269 | 2,648 | 1,544 | 437 | 623 |
| Felony type total .......................................... | 2,014 | 1,458 | 1,042 | 36 | 40 | 340 | 178 | 84 | 72 |
| Rape ......................................................... | 12 | 2 | 2 | 0 | 0 | 0 | 1 | 2 | 4 |
| Robbery .................................................... | 595 | 467 | 366 | 5 | 15 | 81 | 42 | 27 | 26 |
| Burglary .................................................... | 102 | 66 | 33 | 7 | 4 | 22 | 13 | 8 | 2 |
| Larceny-theft ............................................ | 16 | 12 | 8 | 0 | 0 | 4 | 1 | 0 | 1 |
| Motor vehicle theft ................................... | 41 | 19 | 9 | 1 | 1 | 8 | 10 | 2 | 2 |
| Arson......................................................... | 19 | 0 | 0 | 0 | 0 | 0 | 1 | 0 | 0 |
| Prostitution and commercialized vice...... | 6 | 3 | 3 | 0 | 0 | 0 | 1 | 1 | 0 |
| Other sex offenses ................................... | 15 | 6 | 5 | 0 | 1 | 0 | 1 | 1 | 2 |
| Narcotic drug laws ................................... | 468 | 389 | 306 | 7 | 2 | 74 | 19 | 7 | 4 |
| Gambling.................................................. | 5 | 4 | 3 | 0 | 0 | 1 | 1 | 0 | 0 |
| Other-not specified ................................. | 735 | 490 | 307 | 16 | 17 | 150 | 88 | 36 | 31 |
| Suspected felony type .................................. | 117 | 84 | 56 | 1 | 4 | 23 | 9 | 3 | 2 |
| Other than felony type total:......................... | 5,958 | 3,941 | 2,884 | 140 | 162 | 755 | 913 | 203 | 410 |
| Romantic triangle ..................................... | 106 | 76 | 54 | 3 | 7 | 12 | 19 | 4 | 4 |
| Child killed by babysitter ......................... | 36 | 1 | 0 | 0 | 0 | 1 | 0 | 4 | 19 |
| Brawl due to influence of alcohol............ | 112 | 41 | 27 | 2 | 2 | 10 | 31 | 9 | 14 |
| Brawl due to influence of narcotics ......... | 75 | 41 | 26 | 2 | 1 | 12 | 8 | 1 | 6 |
| Argument over money or property ........... | 184 | 127 | 95 | 10 | 5 | 17 | 31 | 12 | 3 |
| Other arguments ...................................... | 2,941 | 1,822 | 1,325 | 50 | 99 | 348 | 633 | 111 | 186 |
| Gangland killings ...................................... | 188 | 175 | 146 | 5 | 0 | 24 | 8 | 1 | 1 |
| Juvenile gang killings ............................... | 604 | 578 | 465 | 6 | 3 | 104 | 20 | 1 | 2 |
| Institutional killings ................................. | 24 | 1 | 0 | 0 | 0 | 1 | 2 | 2 | 13 |
| Sniper attack............................................ | 5 | 4 | 1 | 2 | 1 | 0 | 0 | 1 | 0 |
| Other-not specified ................................. | 1,683 | 1,075 | 745 | 60 | 44 | 226 | 161 | 57 | 162 |
| Unknown....................................................... | 5,366 | 4,133 | 2,465 | 75 | 63 | 1,530 | 444 | 147 | 139 |

# Table 33. Murder Circumstances, by Weapon, 2015—*Continued*

(Number.)

| Circumstances | Poison | Pushed or thrown out window | Explosives | Fire | Narcotics | Drowning | Strangulation | Asphyxiation | Other |
|---|---|---|---|---|---|---|---|---|---|
| Total ............................................. | 7 | 1 | 1 | 82 | 70 | 14 | 96 | 120 | 844 |
| Felony type total ................................ | 1 | 0 | 0 | 34 | 40 | 2 | 16 | 14 | 115 |
| Rape......................................... | 0 | 0 | 0 | 0 | 0 | 0 | 1 | 0 | 2 |
| Robbery..................................... | 0 | 0 | 0 | 0 | 0 | 0 | 7 | 5 | 21 |
| Burglary..................................... | 0 | 0 | 0 | 3 | 0 | 0 | 0 | 2 | 8 |
| Larceny-theft............................... | 0 | 0 | 0 | 0 | 0 | 0 | 0 | 1 | 1 |
| Motor vehicle theft ....................... | 0 | 0 | 0 | 0 | 0 | 0 | 0 | 1 | 7 |
| Arson........................................ | 0 | 0 | 0 | 14 | 0 | 0 | 0 | 0 | 4 |
| Prostitution and commercialized vice....... | 0 | 0 | 0 | 0 | 0 | 0 | 0 | 0 | 1 |
| Other sex offenses ......................... | 0 | 0 | 0 | 0 | 0 | 0 | 2 | 0 | 3 |
| Narcotic drug laws......................... | 1 | 0 | 0 | 0 | 35 | 0 | 0 | 0 | 13 |
| Gambling.................................... | 0 | 0 | 0 | 0 | 0 | 0 | 0 | 0 | 0 |
| Other-not specified ....................... | 0 | 0 | 0 | 17 | 5 | 2 | 6 | 5 | 55 |
| Suspected felony type ......................... | 0 | 0 | 0 | 0 | 0 | 0 | 2 | 4 | 13 |
| Other than felony type total:................... | 4 | 0 | 0 | 11 | 20 | 9 | 47 | 72 | 328 |
| Romantic triangle.......................... | 0 | 0 | 0 | 0 | 0 | 0 | 1 | 1 | 1 |
| Child killed by babysitter ................. | 0 | 0 | 0 | 0 | 0 | 1 | 0 | 1 | 10 |
| Brawl due to influence of alcohol.......... | 0 | 0 | 0 | 1 | 0 | 0 | 0 | 1 | 15 |
| Brawl due to influence of narcotics ....... | 0 | 0 | 0 | 0 | 9 | 0 | 0 | 1 | 9 |
| Argument over money or property.......... | 0 | 0 | 0 | 0 | 0 | 0 | 5 | 1 | 5 |
| Other arguments .......................... | 2 | 0 | 0 | 7 | 1 | 5 | 29 | 29 | 116 |
| Gangland killings .......................... | 0 | 0 | 0 | 1 | 0 | 0 | 0 | 1 | 1 |
| Juvenile gang killings ..................... | 0 | 0 | 0 | 0 | 0 | 0 | 0 | 0 | 3 |
| Institutional killings....................... | 0 | 0 | 0 | 0 | 0 | 0 | 2 | 3 | 1 |
| Sniper attack............................... | 0 | 0 | 0 | 0 | 0 | 0 | 0 | 0 | 0 |
| Other-not specified ....................... | 2 | 0 | 0 | 2 | 10 | 3 | 10 | 34 | 167 |
| Unknown......................................... | 2 | 1 | 1 | 37 | 10 | 3 | 31 | 30 | 388 |

# Table 34. Murder Circumstances, 2011–2015

(Number.)

| Circumstances | 2011 | 2012 | 2013 [1] | 2014 [1] | 2015 [1] |
|---|---|---|---|---|---|
| **Total** .............................................. | 12,795 | 12,888 | 12,253 | 12,270 | 13,455 |
| Felony type total ............................................. | 1,842 | 1,842 | 1,909 | 1,862 | 2,014 |
| Rape.......................................................... | 16 | 16 | 20 | 26 | 12 |
| Robbery..................................................... | 750 | 656 | 686 | 586 | 595 |
| Burglary..................................................... | 95 | 91 | 94 | 82 | 102 |
| Larceny-theft ............................................ | 12 | 15 | 16 | 24 | 16 |
| Motor vehicle theft .................................. | 23 | 22 | 27 | 25 | 41 |
| Arson......................................................... | 38 | 32 | 37 | 23 | 19 |
| Prostitution and commercialized vice......... | 3 | 6 | 13 | 19 | 6 |
| Other sex offenses .................................... | 10 | 13 | 9 | 3 | 15 |
| Narcotic drug laws .................................... | 397 | 375 | 386 | 386 | 468 |
| Gambling................................................... | 8 | 7 | 7 | 11 | 5 |
| Other-not specified ................................... | 490 | 609 | 614 | 677 | 735 |
| Suspected felony type ................................... | 62 | 137 | 122 | 84 | 117 |
| Other than felony type total:.......................... | 6,056 | 6,320 | 5,782 | 5,771 | 5,958 |
| Romantic triangle...................................... | 88 | 98 | 69 | 85 | 106 |
| Child killed by babysitter ......................... | 38 | 26 | 30 | 39 | 36 |
| Brawl due to influence of alcohol............. | 113 | 84 | 93 | 100 | 112 |
| Brawl due to influence of narcotics ......... | 121 | 65 | 59 | 50 | 75 |
| Argument over money or property........... | 156 | 152 | 133 | 151 | 184 |
| Other arguments ...................................... | 3,163 | 3,147 | 2,889 | 2,863 | 2,941 |
| Gangland killings ...................................... | 149 | 152 | 138 | 144 | 188 |
| Juvenile gang killings ............................... | 526 | 722 | 584 | 578 | 604 |
| Institutional killings ................................. | 22 | 13 | 15 | 18 | 24 |
| Sniper attack............................................. | 1 | 1 | 6 | 3 | 5 |
| Other-not specified ................................... | 1,679 | 1,860 | 1,766 | 1,740 | 1,683 |
| Unknown...................................................... | 4,835 | 4,589 | 4,440 | 4,553 | 5,366 |

[1] The rape figures in this table are an aggregate total of the data submitted using both the revised and legacy Uniform Crime Reporting definitions.

## Table 35. Murder Circumstances, by Sex of Victim, 2015

(Number.)

| Circumstances | Total murder victims | Male | Female | Unknown |
|---|---|---|---|---|
| **Total** | 13,455 | 10,608 | 2,818 | 29 |
| Felony type total | 2,014 | 1,641 | 370 | 3 |
| Rape | 12 | 2 | 10 | 0 |
| Robbery | 595 | 541 | 54 | 0 |
| Burglary | 102 | 71 | 31 | 0 |
| Larceny-theft | 16 | 15 | 1 | 0 |
| Motor vehicle theft | 41 | 25 | 15 | 1 |
| Arson | 19 | 10 | 9 | 0 |
| Prostitution and commercialized vice | 6 | 2 | 4 | 0 |
| Other sex offenses | 15 | 8 | 7 | 0 |
| Narcotic drug laws | 468 | 426 | 42 | 0 |
| Gambling | 5 | 5 | 0 | 0 |
| Other-not specified | 735 | 536 | 197 | 2 |
| Suspected felony type | 117 | 85 | 32 | 0 |
| Other than felony type total: | 5,958 | 4,474 | 1,476 | 8 |
| Romantic triangle | 106 | 73 | 33 | 0 |
| Child killed by babysitter | 36 | 26 | 10 | 0 |
| Brawl due to influence of alcohol | 112 | 99 | 13 | 0 |
| Brawl due to influence of narcotics | 75 | 53 | 22 | 0 |
| Argument over money or property | 184 | 153 | 31 | 0 |
| Other arguments | 2,941 | 2,118 | 822 | 1 |
| Gangland killings | 188 | 178 | 10 | 0 |
| Juvenile gang killings | 604 | 584 | 20 | 0 |
| Institutional killings | 24 | 23 | 1 | 0 |
| Sniper attack | 5 | 4 | 1 | 0 |
| Other-not specified | 1,683 | 1,163 | 513 | 7 |
| Unknown | 5,366 | 4,408 | 940 | 18 |

## Table 36. Justifiable Homicide by Weapon, Law Enforcement,[1] 2011–2015

(Number.)

| Year | Total | Total firearms | Handguns | Rifles | Shotguns | Firearms, type not stated | Knives or cutting instruments | Other dangerous weapons | Personal weapons |
|---|---|---|---|---|---|---|---|---|---|
| 2011 | 404 | 401 | 305 | 36 | 11 | 49 | 2 | 0 | 1 |
| 2012 | 426 | 423 | 339 | 38 | 7 | 39 | 0 | 3 | 0 |
| 2013 | 471 | 467 | 334 | 46 | 9 | 78 | 0 | 3 | 1 |
| 2014 | 453 | 451 | 331 | 45 | 4 | 71 | 1 | 1 | 0 |
| 2015 | 442 | 441 | 302 | 42 | 7 | 90 | 0 | 1 | 0 |

[1] The killing of a felon by a law enforcement officer in the line of duty.

## Table 37. Justifiable Homicide by Weapon, Private Citizen,[1] 2011–2015

(Number.)

| Year | Total | Total firearms | Handguns | Rifles | Shotguns | Firearms, type not stated | Knives or cutting instruments | Other dangerous weapons | Personal weapons |
|---|---|---|---|---|---|---|---|---|---|
| 2011............................ | 270 | 209 | 156 | 13 | 11 | 29 | 49 | 9 | 3 |
| 2012............................ | 315 | 263 | 198 | 20 | 15 | 30 | 35 | 6 | 11 |
| 2013............................ | 286 | 227 | 174 | 6 | 11 | 36 | 35 | 13 | 11 |
| 2014............................ | 277 | 231 | 181 | 10 | 11 | 29 | 35 | 2 | 9 |
| 2015............................ | 328 | 268 | 215 | 8 | 13 | 32 | 37 | 9 | 14 |

[1] The killing of a felon, during the commission of a felony, by a private citizen.


## Table 38. Robbery, Location, Percent Distribution Within Region, 2015

(Percent.)

| Region | Total[1] | Street/ highway | Commercial house | Gas or service station | Convenience store | Residence | Bank | Miscellaneous |
|---|---|---|---|---|---|---|---|---|
| Total ......................... | 100.0 | 39.8 | 14.4 | 2.7 | 5.7 | 16.5 | 1.7 | 19.1 |
| Northeast............................. | 100.0 | 48.5 | 8.4 | 2.1 | 5.4 | 12.6 | 2.2 | 20.8 |
| Midwest .............................. | 100.0 | 44.2 | 13.1 | 3.7 | 3.9 | 16.9 | 1.9 | 16.3 |
| South................................. | 100.0 | 35.1 | 13.8 | 2.9 | 6.1 | 22.0 | 1.5 | 18.5 |
| West.................................. | 100.0 | 38.7 | 19.8 | 2.4 | 6.2 | 10.8 | 1.6 | 20.4 |

[1] Because of rounding, the percentages may not add to 100.0.


## Table 39. Robbery, Location, Percent Distribution Within Population Group, 2015

(Percent.)

| Type | Group I (76 cities, 250,000 and over; population 54,888,080) | Group II (198 cities, 100,000 to 249,999; population 29,178,656) | Group III (448 cities, 50,000 to 99,999; population 31,108,306) | Group IV (772 cities, 25,000 to 49,999; population 26,762,807) | Group V (1,663 cities, 10,000 to 24,999; population 26,528,553) | Group VI (7,249 cities, under 10,000; population 21,879,557) | County agencies (4,014 agencies; population 93,069,048) |
|---|---|---|---|---|---|---|---|
| Total[1] ........................ | 100.0 | 100.0 | 100.0 | 100.0 | 100.0 | 100.0 | 100.0 |
| Street/highway......................... | 48.2 | 36.8 | 35.5 | 32.9 | 26.9 | 22.0 | 28.9 |
| Commercial house ................... | 12.9 | 16.6 | 15.8 | 15.6 | 16.1 | 12.8 | 15.5 |
| Gas or service station ............... | 2.0 | 3.0 | 2.9 | 3.8 | 4.0 | 4.0 | 3.6 |
| Convenience store ................... | 4.1 | 7.0 | 7.2 | 6.7 | 7.6 | 8.4 | 6.9 |
| Residence ................................ | 15.1 | 14.8 | 13.9 | 16.2 | 18.3 | 18.1 | 24.2 |
| Bank.......................................... | 1.2 | 1.8 | 2.3 | 2.6 | 3.2 | 2.7 | 2.2 |
| Miscellaneous .......................... | 16.5 | 20.0 | 22.5 | 22.2 | 23.8 | 32.1 | 18.7 |

[1] Because of rounding, the percentages may not add to 100.0.

## Table 40. Robbery, Types of Weapons Used, Percent Distribution Within Region, 2015

(Percent.)

| Region | Total all weapons[1] | Armed | | | Strong arm |
|---|---|---|---|---|---|
| | | Firearms | Knives or cutting instruments | Other weapons | |
| Total ................................................................. | 100.0 | 40.8 | 7.9 | 9.1 | 42.2 |
| Northeast................................................. | 100.0 | 29.2 | 10.3 | 8.8 | 51.7 |
| Midwest ................................................... | 100.0 | 46.5 | 5.6 | 8.7 | 39.2 |
| South........................................................ | 100.0 | 51.4 | 6.4 | 8.2 | 33.9 |
| West.......................................................... | 100.0 | 29.6 | 9.8 | 10.7 | 49.9 |

[1] Because of rounding, the percentages may not add to 100.0.

## Table 41. Aggravated Assault, Types of Weapons Used, Percent Distribution by Region, 2015

(Percent.)

| Region | Total all weapons[1] | Firearms | Knives or cutting instruments | Other weapons (clubs, blunt objects, etc.) | Personal weapons (hands, feet, fists, etc.) |
|---|---|---|---|---|---|
| Total ................................................................. | 100.0 | 24.2 | 18.1 | 31.4 | 26.3 |
| Northeast................................................. | 100.0 | 14.4 | 22.0 | 31.2 | 32.4 |
| Midwest ................................................... | 100.0 | 27.0 | 15.8 | 27.6 | 29.6 |
| South........................................................ | 100.0 | 29.1 | 17.8 | 32.0 | 21.1 |
| West.......................................................... | 100.0 | 19.5 | 17.7 | 32.9 | 29.9 |

[1] Because of rounding, the percentages may not add to 100.0.

## Table 42. Larceny-Theft, Percent Distribution Within Region, 2015

(Percent.)

| Region | Total[1] | Pocket-picking | Purse snatching | Shoplifting | From motor vehicles (except accessories) | Motor vehicle accessories | Bicycles | From buildings | From coin-operated machines | All others |
|---|---|---|---|---|---|---|---|---|---|---|
| Total ........................................ | 100.0 | 0.5 | 0.4 | 22.3 | 24.0 | 7.0 | 3.6 | 11.6 | 0.2 | 30.3 |
| Northeast.................................... | 100.0 | 1.0 | 0.5 | 23.5 | 19.1 | 5.1 | 4.4 | 18.0 | 0.2 | 28.1 |
| Midwest ...................................... | 100.0 | 0.6 | 0.4 | 23.1 | 19.1 | 7.2 | 3.0 | 14.7 | 0.2 | 31.7 |
| South........................................... | 100.0 | 0.4 | 0.4 | 22.1 | 23.9 | 7.2 | 2.6 | 9.3 | 0.2 | 34.0 |
| West............................................. | 100.0 | 0.5 | 0.4 | 21.5 | 29.7 | 7.4 | 5.2 | 10.5 | 0.2 | 24.6 |

[1] Because of rounding, the percentages may not add to 100.0.

## Table 43. Motor Vehicle Theft, Percent Distribution Within Region, 2015

(Percent.)

| Region | Total[1] | Autos | Trucks and buses | Other vehicles |
|---|---|---|---|---|
| Total ........................................................ | 100.0 | 74.7 | 14.8 | 10.5 |
| Northeast............................................. | 100.0 | 83.9 | 4.4 | 11.7 |
| Midwest............................................... | 100.0 | 75.9 | 14.0 | 10.1 |
| South................................................... | 100.0 | 68.0 | 18.8 | 13.2 |
| West.................................................... | 100.0 | 78.3 | 13.5 | 8.1 |

[1] Because of rounding, the percentages may not add to 100.0.


## Table 44. Arson Rates, by Population Group, 2015

(13,443 agencies; 2015 estimated population 271,729,739; rate per 100,000 inhabitants.)

| Population group | Rate per 100,000 inhabitants |
|---|---|
| Total, All Agencies........................................................... | 14.3 |
| Total Cities ...................................................................... | 16.4 |
| Group I (250,000 and over)............................................... | 25.4 |
| 1,000,000 and over (Group I subset) .............................. | 21.3 |
| 500,000 to 999,999 (Group I subset) .............................. | 27.6 |
| 250,000 to 499,999 (Group I subset) .............................. | 28.5 |
| Group II (100,000 to 249,999)........................................... | 15.4 |
| Group III (50,000 to 99,999) ............................................. | 13.1 |
| Group IV (25,000 to 49,999)............................................. | 11.4 |
| Group V (10,000 to 24,999) .............................................. | 10.6 |
| Group VI (under 10,000) ................................................... | 17.3 |
| Metropolitan counties....................................................... | 10.3 |
| Nonmetropolitan counties................................................. | 10.1 |
| Suburban areas[1]............................................................... | 10.1 |

[1] Suburban areas include law enforcement agencies in cities with less than 50,000 inhabitants and county law enforcement agencies that are within a Metropolitan Statistical Area. Suburban areas exclude all metropolitan agencies associated with a principal city. The agencies associated with suburban areas also appear in other groups within this table.


## Table 45. Arson, by Type of Property, 2015

(Number; percent; dollars. 114,986 agencies; 2015 estimated population 267,682,525.)

| Property classification | Number of arson offenses | Percent distribution[1] | Percent not in use | Average damage (dollars) | Total clearances | Percent of arsons cleared[2] | Percent of clearances under 18 |
|---|---|---|---|---|---|---|---|
| Total ........................................ | 36,757 | 100.0 | X | $14,182 | 7,631 | 20.8 | 25.1 |
| Total structure.............................. | 16,809 | 45.7 | 15.2 | $25,716 | 4,325 | 25.7 | 24.7 |
| Single occupancy residential................ | 8,157 | 22.2 | 15.4 | $23,900 | 1,984 | 24.3 | 18.3 |
| Other residential ................................. | 2,758 | 7.5 | 10.4 | $25,382 | 840 | 30.5 | 16.8 |
| Storage................................................ | 1,006 | 2.7 | 20.3 | $12,377 | 221 | 22.0 | 39.4 |
| Industrial/manufacturing..................... | 158 | 0.4 | 25.9 | $270,462 | 43 | 27.2 | 14.0 |
| Other commercial ............................... | 1,583 | 4.3 | 19.3 | $51,231 | 380 | 24.0 | 16.8 |
| Community/public ............................... | 1,550 | 4.2 | 16.3 | $10,168 | 505 | 32.6 | 59.6 |
| Other structure ................................... | 1,597 | 4.3 | 12.8 | $9,553 | 352 | 22.0 | 30.4 |
| Total mobile.................................. | 8,895 | 24.2 | X | $7,482 | 877 | 9.9 | 12.5 |
| Motor vehicles .................................... | 8,330 | 22.7 | X | $7,309 | 771 | 9.3 | 10.9 |
| Other mobile ....................................... | 565 | 1.5 | X | $10,038 | 106 | 18.8 | 24.5 |
| Other................................................... | 11,053 | 30.1 | X | $2,033 | 2,429 | 22.0 | 30.4 |

X = Not applicable.
[1] Because of rounding, the percentages may not add to 100.0.
[2] Includes arsons cleared by arrest or exceptional means.

# METHODOLOGY

Submitting Uniform Crime Reporting (UCR) program data to the Federal Bureau of Investigation (FBI) is a collective effort on the part of city, county, state, tribal, and federal law enforcement agencies to present a nationwide view of crime. Law enforcement agencies in 46 states and the District of Columbia voluntarily contribute crime data to the UCR program through their respective state UCR programs. For those states that do not have a state program, local agencies submit crime statistics directly to the FBI. The state UCR programs function as liaisons between local agencies and the FBI. Many states have mandatory reporting requirements, and many state programs collect data beyond the scope of the UCR program to address crime problems specific to their particular jurisdictions. In most cases, state programs also provide direct and frequent service to participating law enforcement agencies, make information readily available for statewide use, and help streamline the national program's operations.

## A Note Regarding Rape

In 2013, the FBI UCR Program initiated collection of rape data under a revised definition within the Summary Reporting System. Previously, offense data for forcible rape was collected under the legacy UCR definition: the carnal knowledge of a female forcibly and against her will. Beginning with the 2013 data year, the term "forcible" was removed from the offense title, and the definition was changed. The revised UCR definition of rape is: Penetration, no matter how slight, of the vagina or anus with any body part or object, or oral penetration by a sex organ of another person, without the consent of the victim. Attempts or assaults to commit rape are also included; however, statutory rape and incest are excluded. For more information, please see https://www.fbi.gov/about-us/cjis/ucr/crime-in-the-u.s/2013/crime-in-the-u.s.-2013/rape-addendum/rape_addendum_final.

All rape data submitted in 2013—whether collected under the revised definition or the legacy definition—are presented in this publication. However, because only one year of rape data has been collected under the revised definition, the overview presented here discusses only legacy definition rape data.

## Criteria for State UCR programs

The criteria established for state programs ensure consistency and comparability in the data submitted to the national program, as well as regular and timely reporting. These criteria are:

A UCR Program must conform to the FBI UCR Program's submission standards, definitions, specifications, and required deadlines.

A UCR Program must establish data integrity procedures and have personnel assigned to assist contributing agencies in quality assurance practices and crime reporting procedures. Data integrity procedures should include crime trend assessments, offense classification verification, and technical specification validation.

A UCR Program's submissions must cover more than 50 percent of the law enforcement agencies within its established reporting domain and be willing to cover any and all UCR-contributing agencies that wish to use the UCR Program from within its domain. (An agency wishing to become a UCR Program must be willing to report for all of the agencies within the state.)

A UCR Program must furnish the FBI UCR Program with all of the UCR data collected by the law enforcement agencies within its domain.

These requirements do not prohibit the state from gathering other statistical data beyond the national collection.

## Data Completeness and Quality

National program staff members contact the state UCR program in connection with crime-reporting matters and, when necessary and approved by the state, they contact individual contributors within the state. To fulfill its responsibilities in connection with the UCR program, the FBI reviews and edits individual agency reports for completeness and quality. Upon request, they conduct training programs within the state on law enforcement record-keeping and crime-reporting procedures. The FBI conducts an audit of each state's UCR data collection procedures once every three years, in accordance with audit standards established by the federal government. Should circumstances develop in which the state program does not comply with the aforementioned requirements, the national program may institute a direct collection of data from law enforcement agencies within the state.

## Reporting Procedures

**Offenses known and value of property**–Law enforcement agencies tabulate the number of Part I offenses reported based on records of all reports of crime received from victims, officers who discover infractions, or other sources, and submit these reports each month to the FBI directly or through their state UCR programs. Part I offenses include murder and non-negligent manslaughter, forcible rape, robbery, aggravated assault, burglary, larceny-theft, motor vehicle theft, and arson. Each month, law enforcement agencies also submit to the FBI the value of property stolen and recovered in connection with the offenses and detailed information pertaining to criminal homicide.

**Unfounded offenses and clearances**—When, through investigation, an agency determines that complaints of crimes are unfounded or false, the agency eliminates that offense from its crime tally through an entry on the monthly report. The report also provides the total number of actual Part I offenses, the number of offenses cleared, and the number of clearances that involve only offenders under the age of 18. (Law enforcement can clear crimes in one of two ways: by the arrest of at least one person who is charged and turned over to the court for prosecution or by exceptional means—when some element beyond law enforcement's control precludes the arrest of a known offender.)

**Persons arrested**—In addition to reporting Part I offenses each month, law enforcement agencies also provide data on the age, sex, and race of persons arrested for Part I and Part II offenses. Part II offenses encompass all crimes, except traffic violations, that are not classified as Part I offenses.

**Officers killed or assaulted**—Each month, law enforcement agencies also report information to the UCR program regarding law enforcement officers killed or assaulted, and each year they report the number of full-time sworn and civilian law enforcement personnel employed as of October 31.

## Editing Procedures

The UCR program thoroughly examines each report it receives for arithmetical accuracy and for deviations in crime data from month to month and from present to past years that may indicate errors. UCR staff members compare an agency's monthly reports with its previous submissions and with reports from similar agencies to identify any unusual fluctuations in the agency's crime count. Considerable variations in crime levels may indicate modified records procedures, incomplete reporting, or changes in the jurisdiction's geopolitical structure.

**Evaluation of trends**—Data reliability is a high priority of the FBI, which brings any deviations or arithmetical adjustments to the attention of state UCR programs or the submitting agencies. Typically, FBI staff members study the monthly reports to evaluate periodic trends prepared for individual reporting units. Any significant increase or decrease becomes the subject of a special inquiry. Changes in crime reporting procedures or annexations that affect an agency's jurisdiction can influence the level of reported crime. When this occurs, the FBI excludes the figures for specific crime categories or totals, if necessary, from the trend tabulations.

**Training for contributors**—In addition to the evaluation of trends, the FBI provides training seminars and instructional materials on crime reporting procedures to assist contributors in complying with UCR standards. Throughout the country, representatives from the national program coordinate with representatives of state programs and law enforcement personnel and hold training sessions to explain the purpose of the program, the rules of uniform classification and scoring, and the methods of assembling the information for reporting. When an individual agency has specific problems with compiling its crime statistics and its remedial efforts are unsuccessful, personnel from the FBI's Criminal Justice Information Services Division may visit the contributor to aid in resolving the problems.

*UCR Handbook*—The national UCR program publishes the *Uniform Crime Reporting (UCR) Handbook* (revised 2004), which details procedures for classifying and scoring offenses and serves as the contributing agencies' basic resource for preparing reports. The national staff also produces letters to UCR contributors, state program bulletins, and UCR newsletters as needed. These publications provide policy updates and new information, as well as clarification of reporting issues.

The final responsibility for data submissions rests with the individual contributing law enforcement agency. Although the FBI makes every effort through its editing procedures, training practices, and correspondence to ensure the validity of the data it receives, the accuracy of the statistics depends primarily on the adherence of each contributor to the established standards of reporting. Deviations from these established standards that cannot be resolved by the national UCR program may be brought to the attention of the Criminal Justice Information Systems Committees of the International Association of Chiefs of Police and the National Sheriffs' Association.

## NIBRS Conversion

Thirty-three state programs are certified to provide their UCR data in the expanded National Incident-Based Reporting System (NIBRS) format. For presentation in this book, the NIBRS data were converted to the historical Summary Reporting System data. The UCR program staff constructed the NIBRS database to allow for such conversion so that UCR's long-running time series could continue.

## Crime Trends

By showing fluctuations from year to year, trend statistics offer the data user an added perspective from which to study crime.

Percent change tabulations in this publication are computed only for reporting agencies that provided comparable data for the periods under consideration. The FBI excludes from the trend calculations all figures except those received for common months from common agencies. Also excluded are unusual fluctuations of data that the FBI determines are the result of such variables as improved records procedures, annexations, and so on.

## Caution to Users

Data users should exercise care in making any direct comparison between data in this publication and those in prior issues of *Crime in the United States*. Because of differing levels of participation from year to year and reporting problems that require the FBI to estimate crime counts for certain contributors, some data may not be comparable. In addition, this publication may contain updates to data provided in prior years' publications.

For information about the FBI's caution against ranking, including warnings about variables affecting crime and characteristics of jurisdictions, please see http://www.fbi.gov/about-us/cjis/ucr/ucr-statistics-their-proper-use.

## Offense Estimation

Some tables in this publication contain statistics for the entire United States. Because not all law enforcement agencies provide data for complete reporting periods, the FBI includes estimated crime numbers in these presentations. The FBI estimates data for three areas: Metropolitan Statistical Areas (MSAs), cities outside MSAs, and nonmetropolitan counties; and computes estimates for participating agencies that do not provide 12 months of complete data. For agencies supplying 3 to 11 months of data, the national UCR program estimates for the missing data by following a standard estimation procedure using the data provided by the agency. If an agency has supplied less than 3 months of data, the FBI computes estimates

by using the known crime figures of similar areas within a state and assigning the same proportion of crime volumes to nonreporting agencies. The estimation process considers the following: population size covered by the agency; type of jurisdiction; for example, police department versus sheriff's office; and geographic location.

## Estimation of State-Level Data

In response to various circumstances, the FBI calculates estimated offense totals for certain states. For example, some states do not provide forcible rape figures in accordance with UCR guidelines. In addition, problems at the state level have, at times, resulted in no useable data. Also, the conversion of the National Incident-Based Reporting System (NIBRS) data to summary data has contributed to the need for unique estimation procedures.

## Expanded Offense Tables

Expanded offense data are the details of the various offenses that the Uniform Crime Reporting Program collects beyond the count of how many crimes law enforcement agencies report. These details may include the type of weapon used in a crime, the type or value of items stolen, and so forth. Expanded homicide data provide supplemental details about murders such as the age, sex, and race of both the victim and the offender, the weapon used in the homicide, the circumstances surrounding the offense, and the relationship of the victim to the offender. In addition, expanded data includes trends (for example, 2-year comparisons) and rates per 100,000 inhabitants.

Expanded offense data, including expanded homicide data, are information collected in addition to the reports of the number of crimes known. As a result, law enforcement agencies can report an offense without providing the supplemental data about that offense.

# PART 3

# Crimes Against Persons with Disabilities, 2010–2014

# HIGHLIGHTS

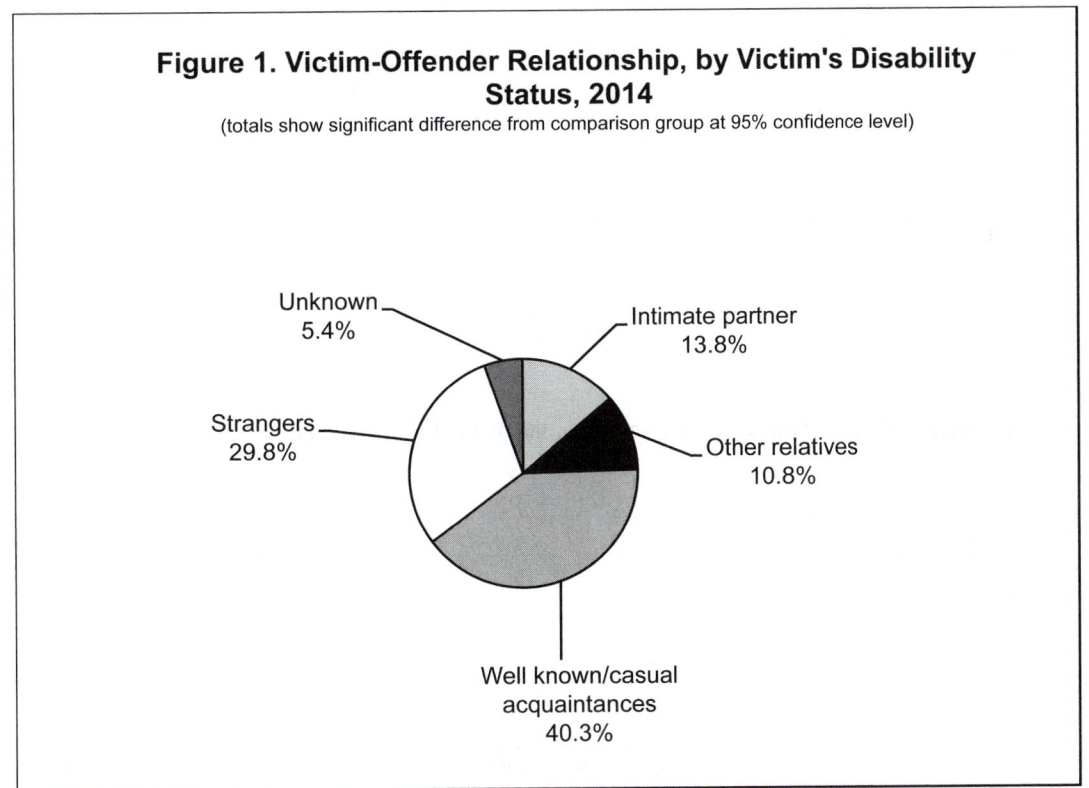

**Figure 1. Victim-Offender Relationship, by Victim's Disability Status, 2014**

(totals show significant difference from comparison group at 95% confidence level)

Unknown
5.4%

Intimate partner
13.8%

Strangers
29.8%

Other relatives
10.8%

Well known/casual acquaintances
40.3%

- The rate of violent victimization against persons with disabilities (31.7 per 1,000 persons 12 years of age or older) was 2.5 times more than the age-adjusted rate for persons without disabilities (12.5 per 1,000 population) in 2014. Persons with disabilities experienced 1.3 million violent victimizations, accounting for 21 percent of all violent victimizations. Nonfatal violent crimes include rape, sexual assault, robbery, aggravated assault, and simple assault.

- Persons with and without disabilities experienced an increase in violent victimization rates from 2011 to 2012 and remained steady in 2014.

- In 2010–2014, for each age group measured (except for persons age 65 or older), the rate of violent victimization against persons with disabilities was at least double the rate for those without disabilities. Among persons age 65

or older, there was no statistically significant difference in the rate of violent victimization by disability status. This is consistent with the data from the last report (2009–2013).

- In 2014, as in 2013, the rate of serious violent victimization for persons with disabilities (12.7 per 1,000 population) was more than three times higher than the age-adjusted rate for persons without disabilities (3.9 per 1,000 population).

- In 2014, for both males and females, the rate of violent victimization was higher for persons with disabilities than the age-adjusted rate for those without disabilities.

- In 2014, approximately 20 percent of violent crime victims with disabilities believed they were targeted due to their disability, an increase from 2009 (13 percent).

## Table 1. Rate of Violent Victimization and Average Annual Number of Persons, by Victim's Disability Status and Age, 2010–2014

(Rate per 1,000 persons.)

| Age of victim | Persons with disabilities | | Persons without disabilities | |
|---|---|---|---|---|
| | Average annual number | Rate per 1,000 persons with disabilities[1] | Average annual number | Rate per 1,000 persons without disabilities* |
| Total ........................................ | 36,441,380 | 30.7 | 224,942,560 | 20.9 |
| 12–15................................. | 925,630 | 129.1 | 15,715,390 | 37.5 |
| 16–19................................. | 955,730 | 106.1 | 16,245,700 | 32.8 |
| 20–24................................. | 1,233,610 | 94.6 | 20,828,730 | 30.3 |
| 25–34................................. | 2,398,500 | 58.7 | 38,873,530 | 28.6 |
| 35–49................................. | 5,425,330 | 50.1 | 56,426,000 | 19.5 |
| 50–64................................. | 10,309,830 | 30.0 | 50,181,060 | 12.5 |
| 65 or older......................... | 15,192,760 | 3.9 | 26,672,150 | 3.8 |

Note: Based on the noninstitutionalized U.S. residential population age 12 or older.
* = Comparison group.
[1] Significant difference from comparison group at 95% confidence level for all of the values in this column.


## Table 2. Rates of Violent Victimization Against Persons With and Without Disabilities, by Type of Crime, 2010–2014

(Rate per 1,000 persons.)

| Type of crime | Persons with disabilities[1] | Persons without disabilities* |
|---|---|---|
| Total crime ........................................ | 30.7 | 12.8 |
| Serious violent crime........................... | 12.7 | 3.9 |
| Rape/sexual assault ...................... | 1.7 | 0.5 |
| Robbery....................................... | 4.9 | 1.4 |
| Aggravated assault ...................... | 6.1 | 2.0 |
| Simple assault ............................. | 18.0 | 8.8 |

Note: Based on the noninstitutionalized U.S. residential population age 12 or older. Rates for persons without disabilities were adjusted using direct standardization with the population with disabilities as the standard population.
* = Comparison group.
[1] Significant difference from comparison group at 95% confidence level for values in this column.


## Table 3. Rates of Violent Victimization Against Persons With and Without Disabilities, by Victim Characteristics, 2010–2014

(Rate per 1,000 persons.)

| Victim characteristic | Persons with disabilities | Persons without disabilities[1] |
|---|---|---|
| Total crime ........................................ | 30.7 | 12.8 |
| Sex ..................................................... | | |
| Male* ........................................... | 31.2 | 14.8 |
| Female.......................................... | 30.3 | 11.0 [A] |
| Race/Hispanic origin............................ | | |
| White[2,*] ...................................... | 29.7 | 12.1 |
| Black[2] ......................................... | 28.8 | 18.8 [A] |
| Hispanic....................................... | 28.6 | 13.0 |
| Other [2,3] .................................... | 28.0 | 7.1 [A] |
| Two or more races[2] ...................... | 101.4 [A] | 30.4 [A] |

Note: Based on the noninstitutionalized U.S. residential population age 12 or older.
* = Comparison group.
A = Significant difference from comparison group at 95% confidence level.
[1] Rates for persons without disabilities were adjusted using direct standardization with the population with disabilities as the standard population.
[2] Excludes persons of Hispanic or Latino origin.
[3] Includes persons identified as American Indian or Alaska Native and Asian, Native Hawaiian, or Other Pacific Islander.

## Table 4. Rate of Violent Victimization Against Persons With Disabilities, by Disability Type and Type of Crime, 2010–2014

(Rate per 1,000 persons age 12 or older, except for independent living disabilities, which is per 1,000 persons age 15 or older.)

| Disability type | Total violent crime | Serious violent crime | Simple assault |
|---|---|---|---|
| Hearing* | 15.5 | 7.6 | 7.9 |
| Vision | 27.8 A | 11.1 B | 16.7 A |
| Ambulatory | 26.9 A | 12.7 A | 14.2 A |
| Cognitive | 56.6 A | 24.0 A | 32.6 A |
| Self-care | 24.5 A | 10.4 B | 14.1 A |
| Independent living | 29.4 A | 13.1 A | 16.3 A |

Note: Based on the noninstitutionalized U.S. residential population age 12 or older. Includes persons with multiple disability types. Serious violent crime includes rape, sexual assault, robbery, and aggravated assault.
A = Significant difference from comparison group at 95% confidence level.
B = Significant difference from comparison group at 90% confidence level.


## Table 5. Rate of Violent Victimization, by Victim's Sex and Disability Type, 2010–2014

(Rate per 1,000 persons age 12 or older, except for independent living disability, which is per 1,000 persons age 15 or older.)

| Disability type | Male* | Female |
|---|---|---|
| Hearing | 15.0 | 16.1 |
| Vision | 22.8 | 31.9 A |
| Ambulatory | 30.0 | 24.9 |
| Cognitive | 55.1 | 58.0 |
| Self-care | 25.4 | 23.8 |
| Independent living | 26.7 | 31.2 |

Note: Based on the noninstitutionalized U.S. residential population age 12 or older. Includes persons with multiple disability types.
* = Comparison group.
A = Significant difference from comparison group at 95% confidence level.


## Table 6. Percent of Violence Against Persons with Disabilities, by Type of Crime and Number of Disability Types, 2010–2014

(Percent.)

| Type of crime | Total | Single disability type | Multiple disability types |
|---|---|---|---|
| **Total** | 100.0 | 47.2 | 52.8 A |
| Serious violent crime | 100.0 | 44.3 | 55.7 A |
| Rape/sexual assault | 100.0 | 31.0 | 69.0 |
| Robbery | 100.0 | 48.1 | 51.9 |
| Aggravated assault | 100.0 | 45.0 | 55.0 B |
| Simple assault | 100.0 | 49.3 | 50.7 |

Note: Based on the noninstitutionalized U.S. residential population age 12 or older. For persons age 12 to 14, independent living disabilities is not included as a disability type.
A = Significant difference from comparison group at 95% confidence level.
B = Significant difference from comparison group at 90% confidence level.

## Table 7. Rate of Violent Victimization, by Number of Disability Types and Type of Crime, 2010–2014

(Rate per 1,000 persons.)

| Type of crime | Single disability type* | Multiple disability types |
|---|---|---|
| Total | 28.6 | 32.8 |
| Serious violent crime | 11.1 | 14.4 A |
|     Rape/sexual assault | 1.1 | 2.4 A |
|     Robbery | 4.6 | 5.1 |
|     Aggravated assault | 5.4 | 6.8 |
|     Simple assault | 17.5 | 18.5 |

Note: Based on the noninstitutionalized U.S. residential population age 12 or older. For persons age 12 to 14, independent living disabilities is not included as a disability type.
* = Comparison group.
A = Significant difference from comparison group at 95% confidence level.

## Table 8. Victim-Offender Relationship, by Victim's Disability Status, 2010–2014

(Percent.)

| Type of crime | Persons with disabilities | Persons without disabilities* |
|---|---|---|
| Total | 100.0 | 100.0 |
| Intimate partner | 13.8 | 13.0 |
| Other relatives | 10.8 A | 6.6 |
| Well known/casual acquaintances | 40.3 A | 32.0 |
| Strangers | 29.8 A | 39.5 |
| Unknown | 5.4 A | 8.9 |

Note: Based on the noninstitutionalized U.S. residential population age 12 or older.
* = Comparison group.
A = Significant difference from comparison group at 95% confidence level.

## Table 9. Time Violent Crime Occurred, by Victim's Disability Status, 2010–2014

(Percent.)

| Type of crime | Persons with disabilities | Persons without disabilities* |
|---|---|---|
| Total | 100.0 | 100.0 |
| Daytime (6 a.m.–6 p.m.) | 58.9 A | 53.2 |
| Nighttime (6 p.m.–6 a.m.) | 36.5 A | 43.4 |
| Unknown | 4.7 B | 3.4 |

Note: Based on the noninstitutionalized U.S. residential population age 12 or older.
* = Comparison group.
A = Significant difference from comparison group at 95% confidence level.
B = Significant difference from comparison group at 90% confidence level.

## Table 10. Percent of Violent Crime Reported to Police, by Victim's Disability Status and Disability Type, 2010–2014

(Percent.)

| Disability status and type | Reported to police |
|---|---|
| Persons without disabilities* | 46.9 |
| Persons with disabilities[1] | 47.0 |
|     Single disability type | 46.6 |
|     Multiple disability types | 47.4 |
| Disability type[2] | |
|     Hearing | 49.3 |
|     Vision | 39.4 A |
|     Ambulatory | 51.4 |
|     Cognitive | 46.2 |
|     Self-care | 43.7 |
|     Independent living | 48.0 |

Note: Based on the noninstitutionalized U.S. residential population age 12 or older.
* = Comparison group.
A = Significant difference from comparison group at 95% confidence level.
[1] For persons ages 12 to 14, independent living disabilities are not included as a disability type.
[2] Includes persons with multiple disability types.


## Table 11. Person Who Notified Police of Violent Crime, by Victim's Disability Status, 2010–2014

(Percent.)

| Person who contacted police | Persons with disabilities | Persons without disabilities |
|---|---|---|
| **Total** | 100.0 | 100.0 |
| Victim | 62.2 | 60.7 |
| Other household member | 5.6 A | 10.5 |
| Someone official | 5.7 A | 8.9 |
| Someone else | 20.7 A | 10.6 |
| Police were at the scene | 3.2 A | 6.3 |
| Offender was a police officer | 0.2 A | 0.7 |
| Some other way | 2.3 A | 2.1 |
| Unknown | -- | 0.3 |

Note: Based on the noninstitutionalized U.S. residential population age 12 or older. Someone official includes a guard, apartment manager, school official, and other officials.
-- = Less than 0.05%.
* = Comparison group.
A = Significant difference from comparison group at 95% confidence level.

## Table 12. Reasons for Not Reporting Violent Crime to Police, by Victim's Disability Status, 2010–2014

(Percent.)

| Reason for not reporting crime to police | Persons with disabilities | Persons without disabilities* |
|---|---|---|
| Dealt with another way[1] | 38.9 | 41.0 |
| Not important enough to victim[2] | 20.3 | 23.3 |
| Insurance would not cover | 0.1 ! | 0.2 ! |
| Police could not do anything[3] | 2.5 | 3.6 |
| Police would not help[4] | 21.9 | 18.6 |
| Other[5] | 37.8 | 35.0 |

Note: Based on the noninstitutionalized U.S. residential population age 12 or older. Detail may sum to more than 100% because more than one response was allowed.
! = Interpret with caution. Estimate is based on 10 or fewer sample cases, or coefficient of variation is greater than 50%.
* = Comparison group.
[1] Includes reported to another official and private or personal matter.
[2] Includes minor or unsuccessful crime, child offender, and not clear if a crime occurred.
[3] Includes did not find out until too late, could not recover or identify property, and could not find or identify offender.
[4] Includes police would not think it was important enough, police would be inefficient, police would be biased, and offender was a police officer.
[5] Includes did not want to get offender in trouble with the law, was advised not to report to police, afraid of reprisal, too inconvenient, did not know why it was not reported, and other reasons.

## Table 13. Percent of Violent Crime Victims in Which Assistance from Nonpolice Victim Services Agency Was Received, by Victim's Disability Status, 2010–2014

(Percent.)

| Disability status of victim | Percent of violent victimizations |
|---|---|
| Persons with disabilities | 12.6 A |
| Persons without disabilities* | 8.2 |

Note: Based on the noninstitutionalized U.S. residential population age 12 or older.
* = Comparison group.
A = Significant difference from comparison group at 95% confidence level.

# METHODOLOGY

## About the Data

**The use of age-adjusted rates:** The differences in age distributions between the two populations must be taken into account when making direct comparisons of the violent victimization rate between persons with and without disabilities. The age distribution of persons with disabilities differs considerably from that of persons without disabilities, and violent crime victimization rates vary significantly with age. According to the U.S. Census Bureau's American Community Survey (ACS), persons with disabilities are generally older than persons without disabilities. The age adjustment standardizes the rate of violence to show what the rate would be if persons without disabilities had the same age distribution as persons with disabilities.

## Survey Coverage

The National Crime Victimization Survey (NCVS) is an ongoing data collection conducted by the U.S. Census Bureau for the Bureau of Justice Statistics (BJS). The NCVS is a self-report survey in which interviewed persons are asked about the number and characteristics of victimizations they experienced during the prior 6 months. The NCVS collects information on nonfatal personal crimes (rape or sexual assault, robbery, aggravated and simple assault, and personal larceny) and household property crimes (burglary, motor vehicle theft, and other theft) both reported and not reported to police. In addition to providing annual level and change estimates on criminal victimization, the NCVS is the primary source of information on the nature of criminal victimization incidents. Survey respondents provide information about themselves (e.g., age, sex, race and Hispanic origin, marital status, education level, and income) and whether they experienced a victimization.

The NCVS collects information for each victimization incident about the offender (e.g., age, race and Hispanic origin, sex, and victim–offender relationship), characteristics of the crime (including time and place of occurrence, use of weapons, nature of injury, and economic consequences), whether the crime was reported to police, reasons the crime was or was not reported, and victims' experiences with the criminal justice system. The NCVS is administered to persons age 12 or older from a nationally representative sample of households in the United States. The NCVS defines a household as a group of members who all reside at a sampled address. Persons are considered household members when the sampled address is their usual place of residence at the time of the interview and when they have no usual place of residence elsewhere. Once selected, households remain in the sample for 3 years, and eligible persons in these households are interviewed every 6 months either in person or over the phone, for a total of seven interviews. All first interviews are conducted in person with subsequent interviews conducted either in person or by phone. New households rotate into the sample on an ongoing basis to replace outgoing households that have been in the sample for the 3-year period. The sample includes persons living in group quarters (such as dormitories, rooming houses, and religious group dwellings) and excludes persons living in military barracks and institutional settings (such as correctional or hospital facilities) and persons who are homeless.

In 2007, the NCVS adopted questions from the U.S. Census Bureau's American Community Survey (ACS) to measure the rate of victimization against people with disabilities. The NCVS does not identify persons in the general population with disabilities. The ACS Subcommittee on Disability Questions developed the disability questions based on questions used in the 2000 Decennial Census and earlier versions of the ACS. The questions identify persons who may require assistance to maintain their independence, be at risk for discrimination, or lack opportunities available to the general population because of limitations related to a prolonged (i.e., 6 months or longer) sensory, physical, mental, or emotional condition. More information about the ACS and the disability questions is available on the U.S. Census Bureau website at http://www.census.gov/acs/www/.

## Definitions of Disability Type

Disabilities are classified according to six limitations: hearing, vision, cognitive, ambulatory, self-care, and independent living.

Hearing limitation entails deafness or serious difficulty hearing.

Vision limitation is blindness or serious difficulty seeing, even when wearing glasses.

Cognitive limitation includes serious difficulty in concentrating, remembering, or making decisions because of a physical, mental, or emotional condition.

Ambulatory limitation is difficulty walking or climbing stairs.

Self-care limitation is a condition that causes difficulty dressing or bathing.

Independent living limitation is a physical, mental, or emotional condition that impedes doing errands alone, such as visiting a doctor or shopping.

# PART 4.
# Criminal Victimization, 2015

## Prevalence of Violent Crime, by Victim Demographic Characteristics, 2014 and 2015

(e per 1,000 persons age 12 years or older.)

| Victim demographic characteristic | Number of persons victimized[1] | | Prevalence rate[2] | |
|---|---|---|---|---|
| | 2014* | 2015 | 2014* | 2015 |
| | 2,948,540 | 2,650,670 ^A | 1.1 | 1.0 ^B |
| | | | | |
| | 1,497,430 | 1,227,870 ^B | 1.2 | 0.9 ^B |
| | 1,451,110 | 1,422,800 | 1.1 | 1.0 |
| nic Origin | | | | |
| | 1,848,860 | 1,667,090 | 1.1 | 1.0 |
| | 453,650 | 394,770 | 1.4 | 1.2 |
| | 457,320 | 400,720 | 1.1 | 0.9 |
| | 188,710 | 188,090 | 1.0 | 0.9 |
| | | | | |
| | 422,460 | 407,850 | 1.7 | 1.6 |
| | 478,740 | 445,760 | 1.6 | 1.5 |
| | 650,560 | 476,630 ^B | 1.5 | 1.1 ^B |
| | 703,980 | 686,380 | 1.2 | 1.1 |
| | 579,770 | 497,800 | 0.9 | 0.8 |
| over | 113,030 | 136,250 | 0.3 | 0.3 |
| tus | | | | |
| d | 1,482,570 | 1,343,010 | 1.6 | 1.4 |
| | 806,200 | 692,470 ^A | 0.6 | 0.5 ^A |
| | 77,420 | 92,330 | 0.5 | 0.6 |
| | 410,540 | 428,830 | 1.6 | 1.6 |
| | 151,630 | 84,370 ^B | 3.0 | 1.7 ^B |

ay not sum to total due to rounding.
n year.
idifference from comparison year at the 90% confidence level.
idifference from comparison year at the 95% confidence level.
rsons age 12 or older who experienced at least one victimization during the year for violent crime.
rsons age 12 or older who experienced at least one victimization during the year for violent crime.
ons of Hispanic or Latino origin.
tican Indians and Alaska Natives; Asians, Native Hawaiians, and other Pacific Islanders; and persons of two or more races.

# HIGHLIGHTS

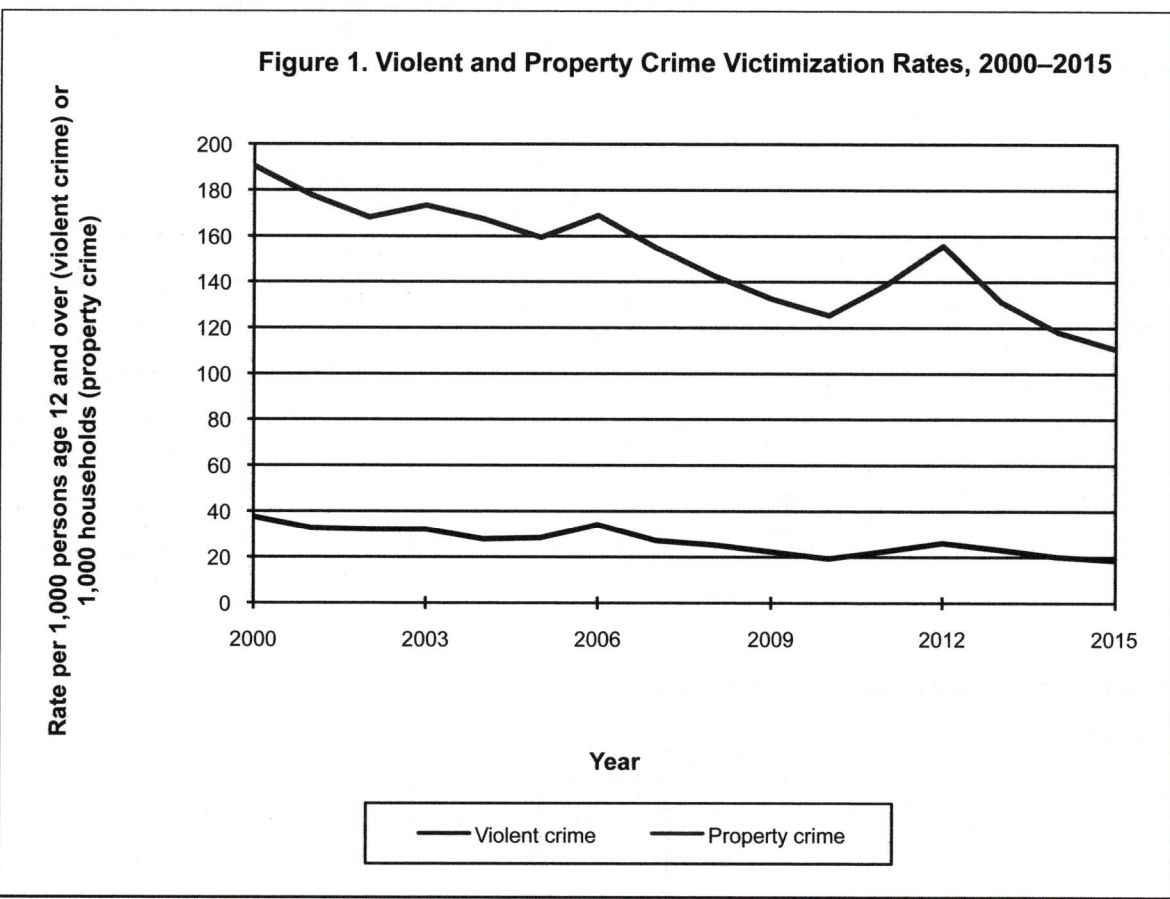

Figure 1. Violent and Property Crime Victimization Rates, 2000–2015

- In 2015, U.S. residents age 12 years or older experienced approximately 5.0 million violent victimizations and 14.6 million property victimizations.

- No significant change was noted in the violent crime victimization rate from 2014 to 2015 (20.1 to 18.6 incidents per 1,000 inhabitants age 12 years or over, respectively). The percentage of violent victimizations reported to police also remained steady (46 percent in 2014 and 47 percent in 2015).

- The rate of property crime (per 1,000 households) decreased from 118.1 victimizations per 1,000 households in 2014 to 110.7 per 1,000 in 2015.

- Approximately 0.7 percent of all persons age years 12 or older (2.7 million persons) experienced at least one violent victimization in 2015, while approximately 7.6 percent of all households (10.0 million households) experienced one or more property victimizations.

- Victim service agencies assisted an estimated 14.4 percent of those who suffered serious violent crimes and 18.3 percent of intimate partner violence victims.

## Table 1. Violent Victimization, by Type of Violent Crime, 2014 and 2015

(Number; rate per 1,000 persons age 12 years or older.)

| Type of crime | Number | | Rate per 1,000 persons age 12 or older | |
|---|---|---|---|---|
| | 2014* | 2015 | 2014* | 2015 |
| Violent Crime[1] | 5,359,570 | 5,006,620 | 20.1 | 18.6 |
| Rape/sexual assault[2] | 284,350 | 431,840 A | 1.1 | 1.6 A |
| Robbery | 664,210 | 578,580 | 2.5 | 2.1 |
| Assault | 4,411,010 | 3,996,200 | 16.5 | 14.8 |
| Aggravated assault | 1,092,090 | 816,760 A | 4.1 | 3.0 A |
| Simple assault | 3,318,920 | 3,179,440 | 12.4 | 11.8 |
| Domestic violence[3] | 1,109,880 | 1,094,660 | 4.2 | 4.1 |
| Intimate partner violence[4] | 634,610 | 806,050 A | 2.4 | 3.0 |
| Stranger violence | 2,166,130 | 1,821,310 | 8.1 | 6.8 |
| Violent crime involving injury | 1,375,950 | 1,303,290 | 5.2 | 4.8 |
| Serious Violent Crime[5] | 2,040,650 | 1,827,170 | 7.7 | 6.8 |
| Serious domestic violence[3] | 400,030 | 460,450 | 1.5 | 1.7 |
| Serious intimate partner violence[4] | 265,890 | 333,210 | 1.0 | 1.2 |
| Serious stranger violence | 930,690 | 690,550 A | 3.5 | 2.6 |
| Serious violent crime involving weapons | 1,306,900 | 977,840 B | 4.9 | 3.6 A |
| Serious violent crime involving injury | 692,470 | 658,040 | 2.6 | 2.4 |

Note: Detail may not sum to total due to rounding. Detail may not sum to total due to rounding. Total population age 12 or older was 266,665,160 in 2014 and 269,526,470 in 2015.
* = Comparison year.
A = Significant difference from comparison year at the 90% confidence level.
B = Significant difference from comparison year at the 95% confidence level.
[1] Excludes homicide because the NCVS is based on interviews with victims and therefore cannot measure murder.
[2] BJS has initiated projects examining collection methods for self-report data on rape and sexual assault.
[3] Includes victimization committed by intimate partners and family members.
[4] Includes victimization committed by current or former spouses, boyfriends, or girlfriends.
[5] In the NCVS, serious violent crime includes rape or sexual assault, robbery, and aggravated assault.

## Table 2. Nonfatal Firearm Victimizations, 2014 and 2015

(Number; rate per 1,000 persons age 12 years or older; percent.)

| Characteristic | Estimates | | Standard errors | | 95 percent confidence interval | | | |
|---|---|---|---|---|---|---|---|---|
| | | | | | 2014 | | 2015 | |
| | 2014* | 2015 | 2014 | 2015 | Lower bound | Upper bound | Lower bound | Upper bound |
| Firearm incidents | 414,700 | 260,200 A | 67,207 | 51,588 | 282,970 | 546,422 | 159,091 | 361,315 |
| Firearm victimizations | 466,100 | 284,910 A | 72,678 | 54,750 | 323,663 | 608,563 | 177,600 | 392,220 |
| Rate of firearm victimizations | 1.7 | 1.0 A | 0.27 | 0.2 | 1.21 | 2.28 | 0.66 | 1.46 |
| Percent of firearms victimizations reported to police | 81.9 | 77.0 | 4.8 | 6.64 | 72.46 | 91.3 | 63.45 | 89.48 |

* = Comparison year.
A = Significant difference from comparison year at the 90% confidence level.

## Table 3. Property Victimization, by Type of Property Crime, 2014 and 2015

(Number; rate per 1,000 households.)

| Type of property crime | Number | | Rate per 1,000 persons a |
|---|---|---|---|
| | 2014* | 2015 | 2014* |
| Total | 15,288,470 | 14,611,040 A | 118.1 |
| Burglary | 2,993,480 | 2,904,570 | 23.1 |
| Motor vehicle theft | 534,370 | 564,160 | 4.1 |
| Theft | 11,760,620 | 11,142,310 B | 90.8 |

Note: Detail may not sum to total due to rounding. Total number of households was 129,492,740 in 2014 and 131,962,260 in 2015.
* = Comparison year.
A = Significant difference from comparison year at the 90% confidence level.
B = Significant difference from comparison year at the 95% confidence level.

## Table 4. Number of Victims and Prevalence Rate, by Type of Crime, 2014 and 2015

(Number; rate per 1,000 persons age 12 years or older.)

| Type of crime | Number of persons victimized[1] | | Prevalence ra |
|---|---|---|---|
| | 2014* | 2015 | 2014* |
| Violent Crime[3] | 2,948,540 | 2,650,670 A | 1.1 |
| Rape/sexual assault[4] | 150,420 | 204,000 | 0.1 |
| Robbery | 435,830 | 375,280 | 0.2 |
| Assault | 2,449,820 | 2,175,520 B | 0.9 |
| Aggravated assault | 681,280 | 560,720 A | 0.3 |
| Simple assault | 1,842,100 | 1,690,190 | 0.7 |
| Domestic violence[5] | 596,270 | 493,310 | 0.2 |
| Intimate partner violence[6] | 319,950 | 310,090 | 0.1 |
| Stranger violence | 1,274,100 | 1,117,340 | 0.5 |
| Violent crime involving injury | 856,760 | 778,300 | 0.3 |
| Serious Violent Crime[7] | 1,235,290 | 1,099,400 | 0.5 |
| Serious domestic violence[5] | 239,330 | 212,690 | 0.1 |
| Serious intimate partner violence[6] | 128,090 | 141,530 | 0.1 |
| Serious stranger violence | 600,650 | 479,870 B | 0.2 |
| Serious violent crime involving weapons | 815,380 | 644,370 B | 0.3 |
| Serious violent crime involving injury | 440,690 | 399,360 | 0.2 |
| Property Crime | 10,352,520 | 10,030,500 | 8.0 |
| Burglary | 2,166,890 | 2,175,380 | 1.7 |
| Motor vehicle theft | 429,840 | 465,650 | 0.3 |
| Theft | 8,297,290 | 7,941,030 | 6.4 |

Note: Detail may not sum to total because a person or household may experience multiple types of crime.
* = Comparison year.
A = Significant difference from comparison year at the 90% confidence level.
B = Significant difference from comparison year at the 95% confidence level.
[1] Number of persons age 12 or older who experienced at least one victimization during the year for violent crime, and number of households that experienced at least one victimization during the year for property c
[2] Percent of persons age 12 or older who experienced at least one victimization during the year for violent crime, and percent of households that experienced at least one victimization during the year for property cri
[3] Excludes homicide because the NCVS is based on interviews with victims and therefore cannot measure murder.
[4] BJS has initiated projects examining collection methods for self-report data on rape and sexual assault.
[5] Includes victimization committed by intimate partners and family members.
[6] Includes victimization committed by current or former spouses, boyfriends, or girlfriends.
[7] In the NCVS, serious violent crime includes rape or sexual assault, robbery, and aggravated assault.

# Table 6. Percent of Victimizations Reported to Police, by Type of Crime, 2014 and 2015

(Percent.)

| Type of crime | 2014* | 2015 |
|---|---|---|
| **Violent Crime**[1] | 46.0 | 46.5 |
| Rape/sexual assault[2] | 33.6 | 32.5 |
| Robbery | 60.9 | 61.9 |
| Assault | 44.6 | 45.8 |
|    Aggravated assault | 58.4 | 61.9 |
|    Simple assault | 40.0 | 41.7 |
| Domestic violence[3] | 56.1 | 57.7 |
|    Intimate partner violence[4] | 57.9 | 54.1 |
| Stranger violence | 48.8 | 42.1 |
| Violent crime involving injury | 54.9 | 57.0 |
| **Serious Violent Crime**[5] | 55.8 | 54.9 |
| Serious domestic violence[3] | 60.0 | 60.8 |
|    Serious intimate partner violence[4] | 56.7 | 49.6 |
| Serious stranger violence | 65.4 | 54.3 |
| Serious violent crime involving weapons | 57.6 | 56.3 |
| Serious violent crime involving injury | 61.0 | 59.0 |
| **Property Crime** | 37.0 | 34.6 A |
| Burglary | 60.0 | 50.8 A |
| Motor vehicle theft | 83.3 | 69.0 A |
| Theft | 29.0 | 28.6 |

\* = Comparison year.
A = Significant difference from comparison year at the 95% confidence level.
[1] Excludes homicide because the NCVS is based on interviews with victims and therefore cannot measure murder.
[2] BJS has initiated projects examining collection methods for self-report data on rape and sexual assault.
[3] Includes victimization committed by intimate partners and family members.
[4] Includes victimization committed by current or former spouses, boyfriends, or girlfriends.
[5] In the NCVS, serious violent crime includes rape or sexual assault, robbery, and aggravated assault.

## Table 7. Rate of Victimization Reported and Not Reported to the Police, by Type of Crime, 2014 and 2015

(Rates per 1,000 persons age 12 or older for violent crime and per 1,000 households for property crime.)

| Type of violent crime | Reported to police | | Not reported to police | |
|---|---|---|---|---|
| | 2014* | 2015 | 2014* | 2015 |
| **Violent Crime[1]** .................................................. | 9.2 | 8.6 | 10.5 | 9.5 |
| Rape/sexual assault[2] .......................................... | 0.4 | 0.5 | 0.7 | 1.1 |
| Robbery................................................................ | 1.5 | 1.3 | 1.0 | 0.8 |
| Assault.................................................................. | 7.4 | 6.8 | 8.9 | 7.6 |
|    Aggravated assault ........................................ | 2.4 | 1.9 | 1.7 | 1.1 |
|    Simple assault .............................................. | 5.0 | 4.9 | 7.2 | 6.5 |
| Domestic violence[3]............................................. | 2.3 | 2.3 | 1.7 | 1.7 |
|    Intimate partner violence[4] ............................ | 1.4 | 1.6 | 0.9 | 1.4 |
| Stranger violence................................................. | 4.0 | 2.8 A | 4.1 | 3.6 |
| Violent crime involving injury ............................. | 2.8 | 2.8 | 2.3 | 2.0 |
| **Serious Violent Crime[5]** ................................... | 4.3 | 3.7 | 3.3 | 3.0 |
| Serious domestic violence[3] ................................ | 0.9 | 1.0 | 0.6 | 0.7 |
|    Serious intimate partner violence[4] ............... | 0.6 | 0.6 | 0.4 | 0.6 |
| Serious stranger violence.................................... | 2.3 | 1.4 B | 1.2 | 1.1 |
| Serious violent crime involving weapons............ | 2.8 | 2.0 | 2.0 | 1.5 |
| Serious violent crime involving injury ................ | 1.6 | 1.4 | 1.0 | 1.0 |
| **Property Crime** .................................................. | 43.7 | 38.3 B | 72.8 | 71.3 |
| Burglary............................................................... | 13.9 | 11.2 B | 8.8 | 10.5 B |
| Motor vehicle theft ............................................ | 3.4 | 3.0 | 0.7 | 1.3 B |
| Theft.................................................................... | 26.4 | 24.1 A | 63.3 | 59.5 A |

*Note:* Victimization rates are per 1,000 persons age 12 or older for violent crime or per 1,000 households for property crime. Excludes victimizations in which it was unknown whether the victimization was reported to police.
\* = Comparison year.
A = Significant difference from comparison year at the 90% confidence level.
B = Significant difference from comparison year at the 95% confidence level.
[1] Excludes homicide because the NCVS is based on interviews with victims and therefore cannot measure murder.
[2] BJS has initiated projects examining collection methods for self-report data on rape and sexual assault.
[3] Includes victimization committed by intimate partners and family members.
[4] Includes victimization committed by current or former spouses, boyfriends, or girlfriends.
[5] In the NCVS, serious violent crime includes rape or sexual assault, robbery, and aggravated assault.


## Table 8. Percent of Violent Victimizations in Which Assistance from a Victim Service Agency was Received, by Type of Crime, 2014 and 2015

(Percent.)

| Type of crime | 2014* | 2015 |
|---|---|---|
| **Violent Crime[1]** .................................................. | 10.5 | 9.1 |
|    Serious violent crime[2].......................................... | 12.3 | 14.4 |
|    Simple assault.......................................................... | 9.5 | 6.0 A |
| Intimate partner violence[3] ...................................... | 28.2 | 18.3 A |
| Violent crime involving injury ................................... | 14.9 | 16.9 |
| Violent crime involving weapon ............................... | 7.2 | 15.0 B |

\* = Comparison year.
A = Significant difference from comparison year at the 90% confidence level.
B = Significant difference from comparison year at the 95% confidence level.
[1] Includes rape or sexual assault, robbery, aggravated assault, and simple assault. Excludes homicide because the NCVS is based on interviews with victims and therefore cannot measure murder.
[2] In the NCVS, serious violent crime includes rape or sexual assault, robbery, and aggravated assault.
[3] Includes victimization committed by current or former spouses, boyfriends, or girlfriends.

# Table 9. Rate of Violent Victimization, by Victim Demographic Characteristics, 2014 and 2015

(Rate per 1,000 persons age 12 years or older.)

| Victim demographic characteristic | Violent crime[1] | | Serious violent crime[2] | |
|---|---|---|---|---|
| | 2014* | 2015 | 2014* | 2015 |
| **Total** ............................................ | 20.1 | 18.6 | 7.7 | 6.8 |
| **Sex**................................................ | | | | |
| Male................................................ | 21.1 | 15.9 [A] | 8.3 | 5.4 [A] |
| Female.............................................. | 19.1 | 21.1 | 7.0 | 8.1 |
| **Race/Hispanic Origin**........................ | | | | |
| White[3] ............................................ | 20.3 | 17.4 | 7.0 | 6.0 |
| Black[3] ............................................. | 22.5 | 22.6 | 10.1 | 8.4 |
| Hispanic............................................ | 16.2 | 16.8 | 8.3 | 7.1 |
| Other[3,4]............................................ | 23.0 | 25.7 | 7.7 | 10.4 |
| **Age**................................................ | | | | |
| 12–17 years...................................... | 30.1 | 31.3 | 8.8 | 7.8 |
| 18–24 years...................................... | 26.8 | 25.1 | 13.6 | 10.7 |
| 25–34 years...................................... | 28.5 | 21.8 [B] | 8.6 | 9.3 |
| 35–49 years...................................... | 21.6 | 22.6 | 8.9 | 7.8 |
| 50–64 years...................................... | 17.9 | 14.2 | 7.0 | 5.7 |
| 65 years and over .............................. | 3.1 | 5.2 [B] | 1.3 | 1.5 |
| **Marital Status**.................................. | | | | |
| Never married .................................... | 27.9 | 26.2 | 10.7 | 9.4 |
| Married............................................. | 12.4 | 9.9 | 4.0 | 3.5 |
| Widowed........................................... | 8.7 | 8.5 | 2.9 | 2.9 |
| Divorced ........................................... | 30.3 | 35.3 | 14.2 | 13.0 |
| Separated .......................................... | 52.8 | 39.5 | 27.7 | 20.6 |
| **Household Income[5]** ........................... | | | | |
| $9,999 or less.................................... | 39.7 | 39.2 | 18.7 | 17.7 |
| $10,000–$14,999................................ | 36.0 | 27.7 | 16.8 | 12.0 |
| $15,000–$24,999................................ | 25.3 | 25.9 | 8.4 | 8.2 |
| $25,000–$34,999................................ | 19.7 | 16.3 | 8.3 | 5.5 |
| $35,000–$49,999................................ | 19.0 | 20.5 | 8.1 | 7.1 |
| $50,000–$74,999................................ | 16.4 | 16.3 | 5.4 | 5.9 |
| $75,000 or more................................. | 15.1 | 12.8 | 4.7 | 4.5 |

\* = Comparison year.
A = Significant difference from comparison year at the 95% confidence level.
B = Significant difference from comparison year at the 90% confidence level.
[1] Includes rape or sexual assault, robbery, aggravated assault, and simple assault. Excludes homicide because the NCVS is based on interviews with victims and therefore cannot measure murder.
[2] In the NCVS, serious violent crime includes rape or sexual assault, robbery, and aggravated assault.
[3] Excludes persons of Hispanic or Latino origin.
[4] Includes American Indians and Alaska Natives; Asians, Native Hawaiians, and other Pacific Islanders; and persons of two or more races.
[5] Household income was imputed for 2014 and 2015.

## Table 10. Rate of Violent and Property Victimization, by Household Location, 2014 and 2015

(Rate per 1,000 persons age 12 years or older for violent crime; rate per 1,000 households for property crime.)

| Household location | Violent crime[1] | | Serious violent crime[2] | | Property crime[3] | |
|---|---|---|---|---|---|---|
| | 2014* | 2015 | 2014* | 2015 | 2014* | 2015 |
| Total ................................................... | 20.1 | 18.6 | 7.7 | 6.8 | 118.1 | 110.7 A |
| **Region**................................................ | | | | | | |
| Northeast.............................................. | 18.9 | 17.1 | 6.2 | 5.1 | 85.8 | 81.6 |
| Midwest ................................................ | 20.6 | 19.6 | 7.5 | 7.5 | 111.8 | 105.0 |
| South.................................................... | 20.2 | 16.9 | 7.6 | 5.8 | 116.2 | 107.6 A |
| West..................................................... | 20.3 | 21.3 | 8.9 | 8.8 | 153.0 | 144.7 |
| **Location of Residence**........................... | | | | | | |
| Urban ................................................... | 22.2 | 22.7 | 9.3 | 8.6 | 148.8 | 135.4 A |
| Suburban............................................... | 19.3 | 17.3 | 6.9 | 6.3 | 101.7 | 98.4 |
| Rural..................................................... | 18.3 | 14.0 | 6.5 | 4.2 | 103.2 | 95.7 |

\* = Comparison year.
A = Significant difference from comparison year at the 95% confidence level.
[1] Includes rape or sexual assault, robbery, aggravated assault, and simple assault. Excludes homicide because the NCVS is based on interviews with victims and therefore cannot measure murder.
[2] In the NCVS, serious violent crime includes rape or sexual assault, robbery, and aggravated assault.
[3] Includes household burglary, motor vehicle theft, and theft.


## Table 11. Rape and Sexual Assault Victimizations, 2014 and 2015

(Number; rate.)

| Rape/sexual assault | 2014* | 2015 |
|---|---|---|
| **Number**................................................................... | 284,350 | 431,840 A |
| 95% confidence interval................................................ | 189,088 | 305,393 |
| Lower bound .......................................................... | 379,612 | 558,287 |
| Upper bound .......................................................... | 48,603 | 64,514 |
| **Rate Per 1,000 Persons Age 12 or Older**........................ | 1.1 | 1.6 A |
| 95% confidence interval................................................ | 1 | 1 |
| Lower bound .......................................................... | 1 | 2 |
| Upper bound .......................................................... | 0 | 0 |
| Unweighted cases....................................................... | 69 | 103 |

\* = Comparison year.
A = Significant difference from comparison year at the 90% confidence level.

# Table 12. Distribution of Types of Rape and Sexual Assault Victimizations, 2006–2015

(Percent.)

| Type of rape/sexual assault | Percent |
|---|---:|
| **Total** | 100 |
| Completed rape | 28 |
| Attempted rape | 21 |
| Sexual assault | 27 |
| Unwanted sexual contact without force | 6 |
| Verbal threats of rape and sexual assault | 17 |

# METHODOLOGY

The National Crime Victimization Survey (NCVS) is an annual data collection conducted by the U.S. Census Bureau for the Bureau of Justice Statistics (BJS). The NCVS is a self-report survey in which interviewed persons are asked about the number and characteristics of victimizations experienced during the prior 6 months. The NCVS collects information on nonfatal personal crimes (rape or sexual assault, robbery, aggravated and simple assault, and personal larceny) and household property crimes (burglary, motor vehicle theft, and other theft) both reported and not reported to police. In addition to providing annual level and change estimates on criminal victimization, the NCVS is the primary source of information on the nature of criminal victimization incidents. *Criminal Victimization* can be found here: http://www.bjs.gov/index.cfm?ty=pbdetail&iid=5804.

Survey respondents provide information about themselves (e.g., age, sex, race and Hispanic origin, marital status, education level, and income) and whether they experienced a victimization. The NCVS collects information for each victimization incident about the offender (e.g., age, race and Hispanic origin, sex, and victim–offender relationship), characteristics of the crime (including time and place of occurrence, use of weapons, nature of injury, and economic consequences), whether the crime was reported to police, reasons the crime was or was not reported, and victim experiences with the criminal justice system.

The NCVS is administered to persons age 12 or older from a nationally representative sample of households in the United States. The NCVS defines a household as a group of persons who all reside at a sampled address. Persons are considered household members when the sampled address is their usual place of residence at the time of the interview and when they have no usual place of residence elsewhere. Once selected, households remain in the sample for 3 years, and eligible persons in these households are interviewed every 6 months either in person or over the phone for a total of 7 interviews.

All first interviews are conducted in person with subsequent interviews conducted either in person or by phone. New households rotate into the sample on an ongoing basis to replace outgoing households that have been in the sample for the 3-year period. The sample includes persons living in group quarters, such as dormitories, rooming houses, and religious group dwellings, and excludes persons living in military barracks and institutional settings such as correctional or hospital facilities, and persons who are homeless.

## Nonresponse and Weighting Adjustments

In 2015, 95,760 households and 163,880 persons age 12 or older were interviewed for the NCVS. Each household was interviewed twice during the year. The response rate was 82 percent for households and 86 percent for eligible persons. Victimizations that occurred outside of the United States were excluded from this report. In 2015, less than 1 percent of the unweighted victimizations occurred outside of the United States and were excluded from the analyses.

Estimates in this report use data from the 1993 to 2015 NCVS data files, weighted to produce annual estimates of victimization for persons age 12 or older living in U.S. households. Because the NCVS relies on a sample rather than a census of the entire U.S. population, weights are designed to inflate sample point estimates to known population totals and to compensate for survey nonresponse and other aspects of the sample design.

The NCVS data files include both person and household weights. Person weights provide an estimate of the population represented by each person in the sample. Household weights provide an estimate of the U.S. household population represented by each household in the sample. After proper adjustment, both household and person weights are also typically used to form the denominator in calculations of crime rates.

Victimization weights used in this analysis account for the number of persons present during an incident and for high frequency repeat victimizations (i.e., series victimizations). Series victimizations are similar in type but occur with such frequency that a victim is unable to recall each individual event or describe each event in detail. Survey procedures allow NCVS interviewers to identify and classify these similar victimizations as series victimizations and to collect detailed information on only the most recent incident in the series.

The weight counts series incidents as the actual number of incidents reported by the victim, up to a maximum of 10 incidents. Including series victimizations in national rates results in large increases in the level of violent victimization; however, trends in violent crime are generally similar, regardless of whether series victimizations are included.

In 2015, series incidents accounted for about 1 percent of all victimizations and 4 percent of all violent victimizations. Weighting series incidents as the number of incidents up to a maximum of 10 incidents produces more reliable estimates of crime levels, while the cap at 10 minimizes the effect of extreme outliers on rates. Additional information on the series enumeration is detailed in the report *Methods for Counting High-Frequency Repeat Victimizations in the National Crime Victimization Survey* (NCJ 237308, BJS web, April 2012).

## Standard Error Computations

When national estimates are derived from a sample, as with the NCVS, caution must be used when comparing one estimate to another estimate or when comparing estimates over time.

Although one estimate may be larger than another, estimates based on a sample have some degree of sampling error. The sampling error of an estimate depends on several factors, including the amount of variation in the responses and the size of the sample. When the sampling error around an estimate is taken into account, the estimates that appear different may not be statistically different.

One measure of the sampling error associated with an estimate is the standard error. The standard error can vary from one estimate to the next. Generally, an estimate with a small standard error provides a more reliable approximation of the true value than an estimate with a large standard error. Estimates with relatively large standard errors are associated with less precision and reliability and should be interpreted with caution.

To generate standard errors around numbers and estimates from the NCVS, the Census Bureau produced generalized variance function (GVF) parameters for BJS. The GVFs take into account aspects of the NCVS complex sample design and represent the curve fitted to a selection of individual standard errors based on the Jackknife Repeated Replication technique. The GVF parameters were used to generate standard errors for each point estimate (e.g., counts, percentages, and rates).

BJS conducted tests to determine whether differences in estimated numbers, percentages, and rates in this report were statistically significant once sampling error was taken into account. Using statistical programs developed specifically for the NCVS, all comparisons in the text were tested for significance. The primary test procedure was the Student's t-statistic, which tests the difference between two sample estimates. Differences described as higher, lower, or different passed a test at the 0.05 level of statistical significance (95 percent confidence level). Differences described as somewhat, slightly, or marginally different, or with some indication of difference, passed a test at the 0.10 level of statistical significance (90 percent confidence level). Caution is required when comparing estimates not explicitly discussed in this report.

Data users can use the estimates and the standard errors of the estimates provided in this report to generate a confidence interval around the estimate as a measure of the margin of error.

In this report, BJS also calculated a coefficient of variation (CV) for all estimates, representing the ratio of the standard error to the estimate. CVs provide a measure of reliability and a means for comparing the precision of estimates across measures with differing levels or metrics.

## NCVS Measurement of Rape and Sexual Assault

### Definition of rape and sexual assault

The measurement of rape and sexual assault presents many challenges. Victims may not be willing to reveal or share their experiences with an interviewer. The level and type of sexual violence reported by victims is sensitive a variety of factors related to the interview process, including how items are worded, definitions are used, and the data collection mode. In addition, the legal definitions of rape and sexual assault vary across jurisdictions.

For the NCVS, survey respondents are asked to respond to a series of questions about the nature and characteristics of their victimization. The NCVS classifies victimizations as rape or sexual assault even if other crimes, such as robbery or assault, occurred at the same time. Then, the NCVS uses the following rape and sexual assault definitions:

**Rape** is the unlawful penetration of a person against the will of the victim, with use or threatened use of force, or attempting such an act. Rape includes psychological coercion and physical force, and forced sexual intercourse means vaginal, anal, or oral penetration by the offender. Rape also includes incidents where penetration is from a foreign object (e.g., a bottle), victimizations against male and female victims, and both heterosexual and homosexual rape. Attempted rape includes verbal threats of rape.

**Sexual assault** is defined across a wide range of victimizations, separate from rape or attempted rape. These crimes include attacks or attempted attacks generally involving unwanted sexual contact between a victim and offender. Sexual assault may or may not involve force and includes grabbing or fondling.

From 2005 to 2014, 30 percent of NCVS rape and sexual assault victimizations were classified as completed rape. Attempted rape or other sexual assault accounted for nearly 50 percent of rape or sexual assault victimizations. About 1 in 5 (18 percent) were verbal threats of rape or sexual assault.

## Comparison of NCVS Estimates to Other Survey Estimates

Over the past several decades, a number of other surveys have also been used to study rape and sexual assault in the general population. BJS estimates of rape and sexual assault from the NCVS have typically been lower than estimates derived from other federal and private surveys. However, the NCVS methodology and definitions of rape and sexual assault differ from many of these surveys in important ways that contribute to the variation in estimates of the prevalence and incidence of these victimization. Additional information about differences in self-report estimates of rape and sexual assault is available on the BJS website. BJS continues an active research program on the collection of rape and sexual assault data in an effort to improve the quality and accuracy of these estimates.

PART 5.

# Hate Crime Statistics, 2015

# HIGHLIGHTS

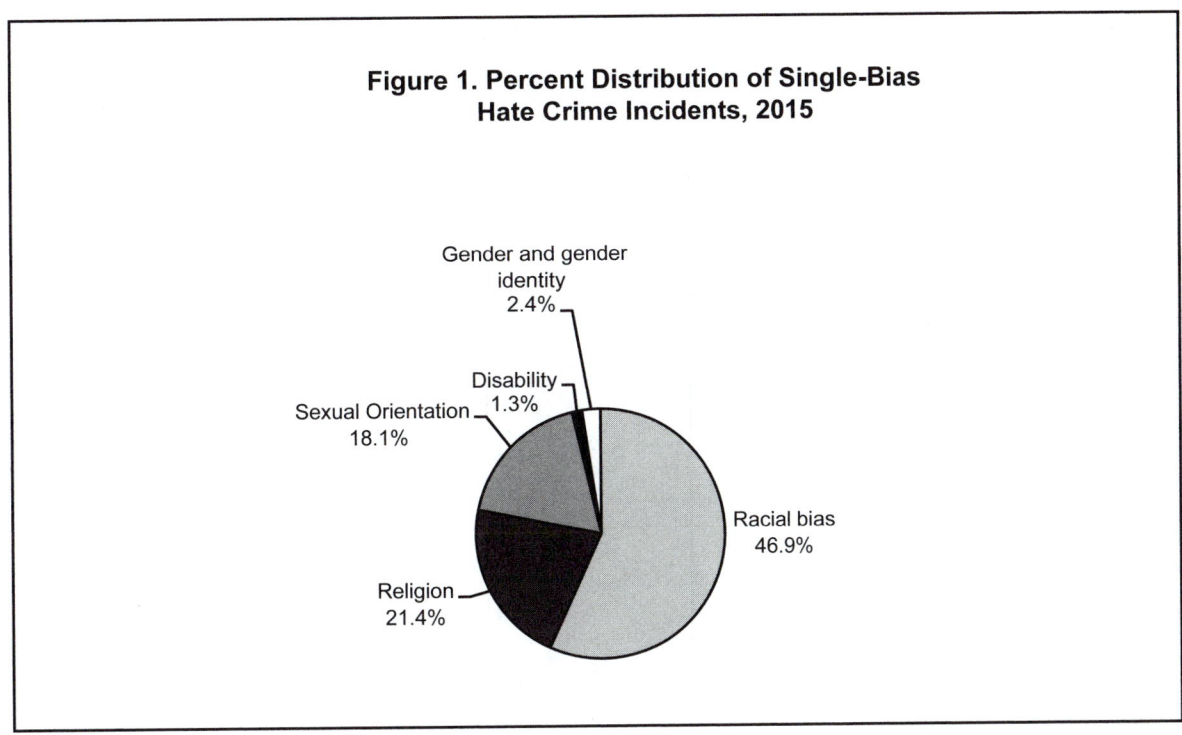

**Figure 1. Percent Distribution of Single-Bias Hate Crime Incidents, 2015**

Gender and gender identity 2.4%

Disability 1.3%

Sexual Orientation 18.1%

Racial bias 46.9%

Religion 21.4%

- In 2015, 14,997 law enforcement agencies participated in the Hate Crime Statistics Program. Of these agencies, 1,742 reported 5,850 hate crime incidents involving 6,885 offenses.

- There were 5,818 single-bias incidents that involved 6,837 offenses, 7,121 victims, and 5,475 known offenders. Among the 6,837 offenses, approximately 58.9 percent were racially/ethnically/ancestrally motivated, 17.8 percent resulted from sexual-orientation bias, 19.8 percent were motivated by religious bias, 1.7 percent were motivated by gender-identity bias, 1.3 percent were prompted by disability bias, and 0.4 (29 offenses) percent resulted from gender bias.

- The 32 multiple-bias incidents reported in 2015 involved 48 offenses, 52 victims, and 18 known offenders.

- The majority of the 2,338 hate crime offenses that were crimes against property (72.6 percent) were acts of destruction/damage/vandalism; the remaining crimes against property (27.4 percent) consisted of robbery, burglary, larceny-theft, motor vehicle theft, arson, and other crime.

- There were 65 offenses defined as crimes against society (e.g., drug or narcotic offenses or prostitution).

## Table 1. Incidents, Offenses, Victims, and Known Offenders, by Bias Motivation, 2015

(Number.)

| Bias motivation | Incidents | Offenses | Victims[1] | Known offenders[2] |
|---|---|---|---|---|
| **Total** | 5,850 | 6,885 | 7,173 | 5,493 |
| **Single-Bias Incidents** | 5,818 | 6,837 | 7,121 | 5,475 |
| Race | 3,310 | 4,029 | 4,216 | 3,196 |
| Anti-White | 613 | 734 | 789 | 681 |
| Anti-Black or African American | 1,745 | 2,125 | 2,201 | 1,605 |
| Anti-American Indian or Alaska Native | 131 | 137 | 141 | 113 |
| Anti-Asian | 111 | 132 | 136 | 108 |
| Anti-Native Hawaiian or Other Pacific Islander | 4 | 6 | 6 | 3 |
| Anti-Multiple races, group | 113 | 138 | 160 | 83 |
| Anti-Arab | 37 | 47 | 48 | 35 |
| Anti-Hispanic or Latino | 299 | 379 | 392 | 325 |
| Anti-Other Race/Ethnicity/Ancestry | 257 | 331 | 343 | 243 |
| Religion | 1,244 | 1,354 | 1,402 | 809 |
| Anti-Jewish | 664 | 695 | 731 | 387 |
| Anti-Catholic | 53 | 59 | 60 | 29 |
| Anti-Protestant | 37 | 47 | 48 | 18 |
| Anti-Islamic (Muslim) | 257 | 301 | 307 | 228 |
| Anti-other religion | 96 | 104 | 107 | 53 |
| Anti-multiple religions, group | 51 | 57 | 58 | 30 |
| Anti-Mormon | 8 | 8 | 8 | 6 |
| Anti-Jehovah's Witness | 1 | 1 | 1 | 0 |
| Anti-Eastern Orthodox (Russian, Greek, Other) | 48 | 50 | 50 | 36 |
| Anti-Other Christian | 15 | 18 | 18 | 15 |
| Anti-Buddhist | 1 | 1 | 1 | 1 |
| Anti-Hindu | 5 | 5 | 5 | 2 |
| Anti-Sikh | 6 | 6 | 6 | 4 |
| Anti-atheism/agnosticism/etc. | 2 | 2 | 2 | 0 |
| Sexual orientation | 1,053 | 1,219 | 1,263 | 1,221 |
| Anti-gay (male) | 664 | 758 | 786 | 803 |
| Anti-lesbian | 136 | 168 | 170 | 142 |
| Anti-lesbian, gay, bisexual, or transgender (mixed group) | 203 | 235 | 248 | 218 |
| Anti-heterosexual | 19 | 23 | 24 | 19 |
| Anti-bisexual | 31 | 35 | 35 | 39 |
| Disability | 74 | 88 | 88 | 73 |
| Anti-physical | 43 | 52 | 52 | 40 |
| Anti-mental | 31 | 36 | 36 | 33 |
| Gender | 23 | 29 | 30 | 19 |
| Anti-male | 7 | 8 | 8 | 6 |
| Anti-female | 16 | 21 | 22 | 13 |
| Gender Identity | 114 | 118 | 122 | 157 |
| Anti-transgender | 73 | 75 | 76 | 114 |
| Anti-gender nonconforming | 41 | 43 | 46 | 43 |
| **Multiple-Bias Incidents[3]** | 32 | 48 | 52 | 18 |

[1] The term victim may refer to a person, business, institution, or society as a whole.
[2] The term known offender does not imply that the identity of the suspect is known, but only that an attribute of the suspect has been identified, which distinguishes him/her from an unknown offender.
[3] A multiple-bias incident is an incident in which one or more offense types are motivated by two or more biases.

## Table 2. Incidents, Offenses, Victims, and Known Offenders, by Offense Type, 2015

(Number.)

| Offense type | Incidents[1] | Offenses | Victims[2] | Known offenders[3] |
|---|---|---|---|---|
| **Total** | 5,850 | 6,885 | 7,173 | 5,493 |
| **Crimes against persons** | 3,646 | 4,482 | 4,482 | 4,230 |
| Murder and nonnegligent manslaughter | 8 | 18 | 18 | 9 |
| Rape (revised definition)[4] | 12 | 12 | 12 | 10 |
| Rape (legacy definition)[5] | 1 | 1 | 1 | 1 |
| Aggravated assault | 681 | 882 | 882 | 968 |
| Simple assault | 1,436 | 1,696 | 1,696 | 1,797 |
| Intimidation | 1,495 | 1,853 | 1,853 | 1,433 |
| Other[6] | 13 | 20 | 20 | 12 |
| **Crimes against property** | 2,338 | 2,338 | 2,626 | 1,440 |
| Robbery | 120 | 120 | 148 | 227 |
| Burglary | 147 | 147 | 173 | 115 |
| Larceny-theft | 255 | 255 | 274 | 177 |
| Motor vehicle theft | 22 | 22 | 24 | 16 |
| Arson | 30 | 30 | 36 | 21 |
| Destruction/damage/vandalism | 1,698 | 1,698 | 1,897 | 836 |
| Other[6] | 66 | 66 | 74 | 48 |
| **Crimes against society[6]** | 65 | 65 | 65 | 74 |

[1] The actual number of incidents is 5,850. However, the column figures will not add to the total because incidents may include more than one offense type, and these are counted in each appropriate offense type category.
[2] The term victim may refer to a person, business, institution, or society as a whole.
[3] The term known offender does not imply that the identity of the suspect is known, but only that an attribute of the suspect has been identified, which distinguishes him/her from an unknown offender. The actual number of known offenders is 5,814. However, the column figures will not add to the total because some offenders are responsible for more than one offense type, and are, therefore, counted more than once in this table.
[4] The figures shown in this row for the offense of rape include only those reported by law enforcement agencies that used the revised Uniform Crime Reporting (UCR) definition of rape.
[5] The figures shown in this row for the offense of rape include only those reported by law enforcement agencies that used the legacy UCR definition of rape.
[6] Includes additional offenses collected in the National Incident-Based Reporting System.

## Table 3. Offenses, Known Offender's Race and Ethnicity, by Offense Type, 2015

(Number.)

| Bias motivation | Total offenses | Known offender's race | | | | | | | Known offender's ethnicity[1] | | | | Unknown offender |
|---|---|---|---|---|---|---|---|---|---|---|---|---|---|
| | | White | Black or African American | American Indian or Alaska Native | Asian | Native Hawaiian or Other Pacific Islander | Group of multiple races | Unknown race | Hispanic or Latino | Not Hispanic or Latino | Group of multiple ethnicities | Unknown ethnicity | |
| **Total** .................................. | 6,885 | 2,761 | 1,129 | 65 | 60 | 7 | 304 | 842 | 182 | 875 | 27 | 2,158 | 1,717 |
| Crimes against persons ...................... | 4,482 | 2,295 | 942 | 58 | 52 | 6 | 262 | 415 | 160 | 735 | 17 | 1,583 | 452 |
| Murder and nonnegligent manslaughter........................................ | 18 | 12 | 1 | 0 | 0 | 0 | 1 | 4 | 1 | 3 | 0 | 11 | 0 |
| Rape (revised definition)[2]................. | 12 | 6 | 4 | 0 | 0 | 0 | 0 | 0 | 2 | 4 | 0 | 4 | 2 |
| Rape (legacy definition)[3]................. | 1 | 0 | 1 | 0 | 0 | 0 | 0 | 0 | 0 | 1 | 0 | 0 | 0 |
| Aggravated assault ......................... | 882 | 444 | 230 | 15 | 9 | 3 | 79 | 61 | 55 | 162 | 2 | 298 | 41 |
| Simple assault ................................. | 1,696 | 795 | 439 | 26 | 29 | 2 | 135 | 185 | 54 | 299 | 12 | 582 | 85 |
| Intimidation ..................................... | 1,853 | 1,026 | 262 | 17 | 14 | 1 | 47 | 164 | 48 | 260 | 3 | 676 | 322 |
| Other[4]............................................ | 20 | 12 | 5 | 0 | 0 | 0 | 0 | 1 | 0 | 6 | 0 | 12 | 2 |
| Crimes against property ...................... | 2,338 | 425 | 173 | 5 | 8 | 1 | 39 | 425 | 21 | 116 | 7 | 541 | 1,262 |
| Robbery.............................................. | 120 | 38 | 60 | 1 | 0 | 0 | 7 | 11 | 3 | 30 | 4 | 50 | 3 |
| Burglary............................................. | 147 | 31 | 15 | 0 | 1 | 0 | 10 | 21 | 3 | 6 | 0 | 38 | 69 |
| Larceny-theft .................................... | 255 | 67 | 27 | 1 | 1 | 0 | 4 | 36 | 1 | 12 | 0 | 110 | 119 |
| Motor vehicle theft .......................... | 22 | 8 | 0 | 1 | 0 | 0 | 0 | 5 | 0 | 1 | 0 | 13 | 8 |
| Arson.................................................. | 30 | 11 | 3 | 0 | 0 | 0 | 0 | 5 | 0 | 3 | 0 | 6 | 11 |
| Destruction/damage/ vandalism ...... | 1,698 | 248 | 62 | 2 | 6 | 1 | 17 | 338 | 12 | 60 | 3 | 292 | 1,024 |
| Other[4]............................................ | 66 | 22 | 6 | 0 | 0 | 0 | 1 | 9 | 2 | 4 | 0 | 32 | 28 |
| Crimes against society[4] ...................... | 65 | 41 | 14 | 2 | 0 | 0 | 3 | 2 | 1 | 24 | 3 | 34 | 3 |

[1] The sum of offenses by the known offender's ethnicity does not equal the sum of offenses by the known offender's race because not all law enforcement agencies that report offender race data also report offender ethnicity data.
[2] The figures shown in the rape (revised definition) row include only those reported by law enforcement agencies that used the revised Uniform Crime Reporting (UCR) definition of rape.
[3] The figures shown in the rape (legacy definition) row include only those reported by law enforcement agencies that used the legacy UCR definition of rape.
[4] Includes additional offenses collected in the National Incident-Based Reporting System.

# Table 4. Offenses, Offense Type, by Bias Motivation, 2015

(Number.)

| Bias motivation | Total offenses | Crimes against persons | | | | | | |
|---|---|---|---|---|---|---|---|---|
| | | Murder and nonnegligent manslaughter | Rape (revised definition)[1] | Rape (legacy definition)[2] | Aggravated assault | Simple assault | Intimidation | Other[3] |
| **Total** | 6,885 | 18 | 12 | 1 | 882 | 1,696 | 1,853 | 20 |
| **Single-Bias Incidents** | 6,837 | 17 | 12 | 1 | 876 | 1,690 | 1,834 | 20 |
| Race/Ethnicity/Ancestry | 4,029 | 11 | 4 | 1 | 557 | 967 | 1,258 | 13 |
| Anti-White | 734 | 1 | 2 | 1 | 101 | 206 | 165 | 3 |
| Anti-Black or African American | 2,125 | 10 | 2 | 0 | 279 | 488 | 764 | 3 |
| Anti-American Indian or Alaska Native | 137 | 0 | 0 | 0 | 8 | 18 | 27 | 1 |
| Anti-Asian | 132 | 0 | 0 | 0 | 21 | 32 | 41 | 0 |
| Anti-Native Hawaiian or Other Pacific Islander | 6 | 0 | 0 | 0 | 3 | 1 | 1 | 0 |
| Anti-Multiple Races, Group | 138 | 0 | 0 | 0 | 12 | 15 | 34 | 0 |
| Anti-Arab | 47 | 0 | 0 | 0 | 2 | 22 | 11 | 0 |
| Anti-Hispanic or Latino | 379 | 0 | 0 | 0 | 82 | 98 | 116 | 3 |
| Anti-Other Race/Ethnicity/Ancestry | 331 | 0 | 0 | 0 | 49 | 87 | 99 | 3 |
| Religion | 1,354 | 4 | 1 | 0 | 68 | 188 | 280 | 1 |
| Anti-Jewish | 695 | 0 | 0 | 0 | 22 | 78 | 114 | 1 |
| Anti-Catholic | 59 | 0 | 0 | 0 | 1 | 10 | 2 | 0 |
| Anti-Protestant | 47 | 0 | 0 | 0 | 8 | 3 | 4 | 0 |
| Anti-Islamic (Muslim) | 301 | 4 | 0 | 0 | 27 | 64 | 120 | 0 |
| Anti-Other Religion | 104 | 0 | 1 | 0 | 2 | 8 | 28 | 0 |
| Anti-Multiple Religions, Group | 57 | 0 | 0 | 0 | 3 | 7 | 8 | 0 |
| Anti-Mormon | 8 | 0 | 0 | 0 | 0 | 2 | 0 | 0 |
| Anti-Jehovah's Witness | 1 | 0 | 0 | 0 | 0 | 0 | 0 | 0 |
| Anti-Eastern Orthodox (Russian, Greek, Other) | 50 | 0 | 0 | 0 | 3 | 10 | 0 | 0 |
| Anti-Other Christian | 18 | 0 | 0 | 0 | 1 | 4 | 1 | 0 |
| Anti-Buddhist | 1 | 0 | 0 | 0 | 0 | 0 | 0 | 0 |
| Anti-Hindu | 5 | 0 | 0 | 0 | 1 | 0 | 2 | 0 |
| Anti-Sikh | 6 | 0 | 0 | 0 | 0 | 1 | 1 | 0 |
| Anti-Atheism/Agnosticism/etc. | 2 | 0 | 0 | 0 | 0 | 1 | 0 | 0 |
| Sexual Orientation | 1,219 | 1 | 5 | 0 | 214 | 461 | 253 | 4 |
| Anti-Gay (Male) | 758 | 1 | 2 | 0 | 140 | 297 | 144 | 2 |
| Anti-Lesbian | 168 | 0 | 2 | 0 | 31 | 66 | 38 | 0 |
| Anti-Lesbian, Gay, Bisexual, or Transgender (Mixed Group) | 235 | 0 | 1 | 0 | 39 | 75 | 58 | 0 |
| Anti-Heterosexual | 23 | 0 | 0 | 0 | 1 | 8 | 5 | 1 |
| Anti-Bisexual | 35 | 0 | 0 | 0 | 3 | 15 | 8 | 1 |
| Disability | 88 | 0 | 0 | 0 | 11 | 27 | 16 | 1 |
| Anti-Physical | 52 | 0 | 0 | 0 | 6 | 17 | 10 | 0 |
| Anti-Mental | 36 | 0 | 0 | 0 | 5 | 10 | 6 | 1 |
| Gender | 29 | 0 | 1 | 0 | 4 | 11 | 8 | 0 |
| Anti-Male | 8 | 0 | 0 | 0 | 0 | 3 | 3 | 0 |
| Anti-Female | 21 | 0 | 1 | 0 | 4 | 8 | 5 | 0 |
| Gender Identity | 118 | 1 | 1 | 0 | 22 | 36 | 19 | 1 |
| Anti-Transgender | 75 | 1 | 1 | 0 | 15 | 27 | 15 | 1 |
| Anti-Gender Non-Conforming | 43 | 0 | 0 | 0 | 7 | 9 | 4 | 0 |
| **Multiple-Bias Incidents[4]** | 48 | 1 | 0 | 0 | 6 | 6 | 19 | 0 |

# Table 4. Offenses, Offense Type, by Bias Motivation, 2015—*Continued*

(Number.)

| Bias motivation | Crimes against property | | | | | | | Crimes against society[3] |
|---|---|---|---|---|---|---|---|---|
| | Robbery | Burglary | Larceny-theft | Motor vehicle theft | Arson | Destruction/ damage/ vandalism | Other[3] | |
| **Total** | 120 | 147 | 255 | 22 | 30 | 1,698 | 66 | 65 |
| **Single-Bias Incidents** | 120 | 146 | 253 | 22 | 29 | 1,686 | 66 | 65 |
| Race/Ethnicity/Ancestry | 58 | 81 | 153 | 16 | 14 | 809 | 44 | 43 |
| Anti-White | 20 | 25 | 70 | 6 | 3 | 86 | 28 | 17 |
| Anti-Black or African American | 12 | 20 | 27 | 4 | 9 | 489 | 5 | 13 |
| Anti-American Indian or Alaska Native | 5 | 14 | 28 | 4 | 0 | 22 | 6 | 4 |
| Anti-Asian | 2 | 7 | 4 | 2 | 1 | 22 | 0 | 0 |
| Anti-Native Hawaiian or Other Pacific Islander | 0 | 0 | 0 | 0 | 0 | 1 | 0 | 0 |
| Anti-Multiple Races, Group | 1 | 3 | 4 | 0 | 0 | 64 | 2 | 3 |
| Anti-Arab | 2 | 0 | 0 | 0 | 0 | 10 | 0 | 0 |
| Anti-Hispanic or Latino | 15 | 5 | 8 | 0 | 1 | 50 | 1 | 0 |
| Anti-Other Race/Ethnicity/Ancestry | 1 | 7 | 12 | 0 | 0 | 65 | 2 | 6 |
| Religion | 7 | 35 | 60 | 2 | 12 | 678 | 10 | 8 |
| Anti-Jewish | 1 | 12 | 14 | 0 | 4 | 447 | 2 | 0 |
| Anti-Catholic | 1 | 4 | 5 | 1 | 2 | 30 | 1 | 2 |
| Anti-Protestant | 0 | 2 | 8 | 0 | 1 | 18 | 2 | 1 |
| Anti-Islamic (Muslim) | 4 | 4 | 4 | 0 | 1 | 70 | 0 | 3 |
| Anti-Other Religion | 1 | 6 | 1 | 0 | 3 | 54 | 0 | 0 |
| Anti-Multiple Religions, Group | 0 | 1 | 3 | 0 | 1 | 33 | 0 | 1 |
| Anti-Mormon | 0 | 1 | 3 | 0 | 0 | 1 | 0 | 1 |
| Anti-Jehovah's Witness | 0 | 0 | 0 | 0 | 0 | 1 | 0 | 0 |
| Anti-Eastern Orthodox (Russian, Greek, Other) | 0 | 5 | 17 | 1 | 0 | 11 | 3 | 0 |
| Anti-Other Christian | 0 | 0 | 3 | 0 | 0 | 7 | 2 | 0 |
| Anti-Buddhist | 0 | 0 | 0 | 0 | 0 | 1 | 0 | 0 |
| Anti-Hindu | 0 | 0 | 0 | 0 | 0 | 2 | 0 | 0 |
| Anti-Sikh | 0 | 0 | 2 | 0 | 0 | 2 | 0 | 0 |
| Anti-Atheism/Agnosticism/etc. | 0 | 0 | 0 | 0 | 0 | 1 | 0 | 0 |
| Sexual Orientation | 47 | 22 | 23 | 1 | 3 | 178 | 5 | 2 |
| Anti-Gay (Male) | 29 | 18 | 8 | 1 | 1 | 112 | 3 | 0 |
| Anti-Lesbian | 3 | 3 | 2 | 0 | 0 | 23 | 0 | 0 |
| Anti-Lesbian, Gay, Bisexual, or Transgender (Mixed Group) | 12 | 1 | 8 | 0 | 2 | 38 | 1 | 0 |
| Anti-Heterosexual | 1 | 0 | 1 | 0 | 0 | 3 | 1 | 2 |
| Anti-Bisexual | 2 | 0 | 4 | 0 | 0 | 2 | 0 | 0 |
| Disability | 2 | 1 | 6 | 1 | 0 | 14 | 4 | 5 |
| Anti-Physical | 2 | 1 | 2 | 1 | 0 | 9 | 0 | 4 |
| Anti-Mental | 0 | 0 | 4 | 0 | 0 | 5 | 4 | 1 |
| Gender | 0 | 0 | 2 | 1 | 0 | 2 | 0 | 0 |
| Anti-Male | 0 | 0 | 2 | 0 | 0 | 0 | 0 | 0 |
| Anti-Female | 0 | 0 | 0 | 1 | 0 | 2 | 0 | 0 |
| Gender Identity | 6 | 7 | 9 | 1 | 0 | 5 | 3 | 7 |
| Anti-Transgender | 5 | 1 | 4 | 0 | 0 | 4 | 0 | 1 |
| Anti-Gender Non-Conforming | 1 | 6 | 5 | 1 | 0 | 1 | 3 | 6 |
| **Multiple-Bias Incidents[4]** | 0 | 1 | 2 | 0 | 1 | 12 | 0 | 0 |

[1] The figures shown in this column for the offense of rape include only those reported by law enforcement agencies that used the revised Uniform Crime Reporting (UCR) definition of rape.
[2] The figures shown in this column for the offense of rape include only those reported by law enforcement agencies that used the legacy UCR definition of rape.
[3] Includes additional offenses collected in the National Incident-Based Reporting System.
[4] A multiple-bias incident is an incident in which one or more offense types are motivated by two or more biases.

# Table 5. Offenses, Known Offender's Race and Ethnicity, by Bias Motivation, 2015

(Number.)

| Bias motivation | Total offenses | Known offender's race | | | | | | | Known offender's ethnicity[1] | | | | Unknown offender |
|---|---|---|---|---|---|---|---|---|---|---|---|---|---|
| | | White | Black or African American | American Indian or Alaska Native | Asian | Native Hawaiian or Other Pacific Islander | Group of multiple races | Unknown race | Hispanic or Latino | Not Hispanic or Latino | Group of multiple ethnicities | Unknown ethnicity | |
| **Total** .................... | 6,885 | 2,761 | 1,129 | 65 | 60 | 7 | 304 | 842 | 182 | 875 | 27 | 2,158 | 1,717 |
| **Single-Bias Incidents** ........................ | 6,837 | 2,744 | 1,126 | 63 | 60 | 7 | 304 | 840 | 182 | 866 | 27 | 2,151 | 1,693 |
| Race/Ethnicity/Ancestry ................. | 4,029 | 1,833 | 646 | 58 | 41 | 5 | 175 | 391 | 102 | 563 | 5 | 1,463 | 880 |
| Anti-White ............................. | 734 | 144 | 339 | 17 | 5 | 0 | 26 | 67 | 8 | 114 | 1 | 334 | 136 |
| Anti-Black or African American ......................... | 2,125 | 1,227 | 72 | 23 | 22 | 0 | 97 | 202 | 69 | 259 | 4 | 756 | 482 |
| Anti-American Indian or Alaska Native ......................... | 137 | 37 | 33 | 11 | 1 | 0 | 1 | 9 | 1 | 3 | 0 | 79 | 45 |
| Anti-Asian .............................. | 132 | 50 | 32 | 0 | 4 | 0 | 7 | 11 | 0 | 26 | 0 | 26 | 28 |
| Anti-Native Hawaiian or Other Pacific Islander ..................... | 6 | 0 | 1 | 0 | 0 | 3 | 0 | 1 | 0 | 3 | 0 | 1 | 1 |
| Anti-Multiple Races, Group ...... | 138 | 50 | 11 | 0 | 0 | 0 | 13 | 15 | 9 | 12 | 0 | 45 | 49 |
| Anti-Arab ............................... | 47 | 25 | 6 | 0 | 0 | 0 | 0 | 6 | 4 | 8 | 0 | 15 | 10 |
| Anti-Hispanic or Latino ............. | 379 | 191 | 84 | 6 | 1 | 1 | 13 | 28 | 4 | 68 | 0 | 98 | 55 |
| Anti-Other Race/Ethnicity/Ancestry ......................... | 331 | 109 | 68 | 1 | 8 | 1 | 18 | 52 | 7 | 70 | 0 | 109 | 74 |
| Religion ......................... | 1,354 | 346 | 89 | 1 | 7 | 2 | 28 | 316 | 8 | 86 | 5 | 267 | 565 |
| Anti-Jewish ............................ | 695 | 121 | 31 | 0 | 2 | 0 | 8 | 211 | 0 | 13 | 1 | 68 | 322 |
| Anti-Catholic ......................... | 59 | 12 | 5 | 1 | 0 | 0 | 1 | 10 | 0 | 2 | 0 | 13 | 30 |
| Anti-Protestant ....................... | 47 | 9 | 5 | 0 | 0 | 0 | 1 | 8 | 0 | 7 | 0 | 14 | 24 |
| Anti-Islamic (Muslim) .............. | 301 | 134 | 28 | 0 | 1 | 0 | 10 | 53 | 5 | 39 | 1 | 93 | 75 |
| Anti-Other Religion ................. | 104 | 23 | 5 | 0 | 0 | 2 | 3 | 20 | 2 | 3 | 3 | 26 | 51 |
| Anti-Multiple Religions, Group ......................... | 57 | 11 | 5 | 0 | 2 | 0 | 2 | 6 | 0 | 5 | 0 | 17 | 31 |
| Anti-Mormon ......................... | 8 | 3 | 2 | 0 | 0 | 0 | 0 | 1 | 0 | 5 | 0 | 1 | 2 |
| Anti-Jehovah's Witness ............. | 1 | 0 | 0 | 0 | 0 | 0 | 0 | 0 | 0 | 0 | 0 | 0 | 1 |
| Anti-Eastern Orthodox (Russian, Greek, Other) ................... | 50 | 24 | 5 | 0 | 0 | 0 | 2 | 1 | 0 | 5 | 0 | 26 | 18 |
| Anti-Other Christian ................ | 18 | 6 | 3 | 0 | 0 | 0 | 0 | 6 | 0 | 2 | 0 | 9 | 3 |
| Anti-Buddhist ......................... | 1 | 0 | 0 | 0 | 1 | 0 | 0 | 0 | 0 | 1 | 0 | 0 | 0 |
| Anti-Hindu ............................. | 5 | 1 | 0 | 0 | 1 | 0 | 0 | 0 | 0 | 2 | 0 | 0 | 3 |
| Anti-Sikh ............................... | 6 | 2 | 0 | 0 | 0 | 0 | 1 | 0 | 1 | 2 | 0 | 0 | 3 |
| Anti-Atheism/Agnosticism/etc. . | 2 | 0 | 0 | 0 | 0 | 0 | 0 | 0 | 0 | 0 | 0 | 0 | 2 |
| Sexual Orientation ..................... | 1,219 | 481 | 332 | 3 | 10 | 0 | 83 | 109 | 58 | 171 | 7 | 340 | 201 |
| Anti-Gay (Male) ...................... | 758 | 296 | 210 | 2 | 6 | 0 | 59 | 72 | 36 | 113 | 2 | 188 | 113 |
| Anti-Lesbian ........................... | 168 | 56 | 52 | 1 | 1 | 0 | 13 | 14 | 11 | 17 | 2 | 46 | 31 |
| Anti-Lesbian, Gay, Bisexual, or Transgender (Mixed Group) ................. | 235 | 105 | 52 | 0 | 3 | 0 | 9 | 18 | 11 | 31 | 1 | 82 | 48 |
| Anti-Heterosexual ................... | 23 | 10 | 5 | 0 | 0 | 0 | 2 | 1 | 0 | 2 | 2 | 9 | 5 |
| Anti-Bisexual .......................... | 35 | 14 | 13 | 0 | 0 | 0 | 0 | 4 | 0 | 8 | 0 | 15 | 4 |
| Disability ..................... | 88 | 38 | 15 | 1 | 1 | 0 | 8 | 9 | 1 | 14 | 5 | 44 | 16 |
| Anti-Physical .......................... | 52 | 22 | 5 | 1 | 0 | 0 | 8 | 2 | 1 | 5 | 5 | 22 | 14 |
| Anti-Mental ........................... | 36 | 16 | 10 | 0 | 1 | 0 | 0 | 7 | 0 | 9 | 0 | 22 | 2 |
| Gender ..................... | 29 | 12 | 6 | 0 | 0 | 0 | 0 | 4 | 5 | 6 | 0 | 10 | 7 |
| Anti-Male ............................... | 8 | 5 | 1 | 0 | 0 | 0 | 0 | 0 | 0 | 0 | 0 | 6 | 2 |
| Anti-Female ........................... | 21 | 7 | 5 | 0 | 0 | 0 | 0 | 4 | 5 | 6 | 0 | 4 | 5 |
| Gender Identity ........................... | 118 | 34 | 38 | 0 | 1 | 0 | 10 | 11 | 8 | 26 | 5 | 27 | 24 |
| Anti-Transgender ................... | 75 | 19 | 32 | 0 | 1 | 0 | 6 | 8 | 5 | 18 | 2 | 15 | 9 |
| Anti-Gender Non-Conforming . | 43 | 15 | 6 | 0 | 0 | 0 | 4 | 3 | 3 | 8 | 3 | 12 | 15 |
| **Multiple-Bias Incidents[2]** .................... | 48 | 17 | 3 | 2 | 0 | 0 | 0 | 2 | 0 | 9 | 0 | 7 | 24 |

[1] The total number of offenses by the known offender's ethnicity do not equal the total number of offenses by the known offender's race because not all law enforcement agencies that report offender race data also report offender ethnicity data.

[2] A multiple-bias incident is an incident in which one or more offense types are motivated by two or more biases.

## Table 6. Offenses, Victim Type, by Offense Type, 2015

(Number.)

| Offense type | Total offenses | Victim type | | | | | |
|---|---|---|---|---|---|---|---|
| | | Individual | Business/ financial institution | Government | Religious organization | Society/ public[1] | Other/ unknown/ multiple |
| **Total** .................................. | 6,885 | 5,725 | 310 | 144 | 188 | 65 | 453 |
| Crimes against persons[2] ................ | 4,482 | 4,482 | NA | NA | NA | NA | NA |
| Crimes against property ................ | 2,338 | 1,243 | 310 | 144 | 188 | 0 | 453 |
| Robbery .................................... | 120 | 119 | 1 | 0 | 0 | 0 | 0 |
| Burglary .................................... | 147 | 95 | 16 | 1 | 14 | 0 | 21 |
| Larceny-theft ........................... | 255 | 166 | 57 | 2 | 8 | 0 | 22 |
| Motor vehicle theft ................. | 22 | 21 | 1 | 0 | 0 | 0 | 0 |
| Arson........................................ | 30 | 16 | 1 | 1 | 7 | 0 | 5 |
| Destruction/damage/ vandalism .................................... | 1,698 | 777 | 222 | 139 | 159 | 0 | 401 |
| Other[2]...................................... | 66 | 49 | 12 | 1 | 0 | 0 | 4 |
| Crimes against society[2] ................. | 65 | NA | NA | NA | NA | 65 | NA |

NA = Not available.
[1] The victim type *society/public* is collected only in the National Incident-Based Reporting System (NIBRS).
[2] Includes additional offenses collected in the NIBRS.

# Table 7. Victims, Offense Type, by Bias Motivation, 2015

(Number.)

| Bias motivation | Total victims[1] | Total number of adult victims[2] | Total number of juvenile victims[2] | Crimes against persons | | | | | | |
|---|---|---|---|---|---|---|---|---|---|---|
| | | | | Murder and nonnegligent manslaughter | Rape (revised definition)[3] | Rape (legacy definition)[4] | Aggravated assault | Simple assault | Intimidation | Other[5] |
| **Total** .................................. | 7,173 | 3,702 | 496 | 18 | 12 | 1 | 882 | 1,696 | 1,853 | 20 |
| **Single-Bias Incidents** .......................... | 7,121 | 3,673 | 493 | 17 | 12 | 1 | 876 | 1,690 | 1,834 | 20 |
| Race/Ethnicity/Ancestry .................... | 4,216 | 2,357 | 346 | 11 | 4 | 1 | 557 | 967 | 1,258 | 13 |
| Anti-White.................................. | 789 | 479 | 54 | 1 | 2 | 1 | 101 | 206 | 165 | 3 |
| Anti-Black or African American ... | 2,201 | 1,172 | 203 | 10 | 2 | 0 | 279 | 488 | 764 | 3 |
| Anti-American Indian or Alaska Native | 141 | 106 | 6 | 0 | 0 | 0 | 8 | 18 | 27 | 1 |
| Anti-Asian.................................. | 136 | 69 | 8 | 0 | 0 | 0 | 21 | 32 | 41 | 0 |
| Anti-Native Hawaiian or Other Pacific Islander ................................. | 6 | 6 | 0 | 0 | 0 | 0 | 3 | 1 | 1 | 0 |
| Anti-Multiple Races, Group ........ | 160 | 81 | 14 | 0 | 0 | 0 | 12 | 15 | 34 | 0 |
| Anti-Arab.................................. | 48 | 33 | 4 | 0 | 0 | 0 | 2 | 22 | 11 | 0 |
| Anti-Hispanic or Latino.............. | 392 | 219 | 26 | 0 | 0 | 0 | 82 | 98 | 116 | 3 |
| Anti-Other Race/Ethnicity/Ancestry ................................. | 343 | 192 | 31 | 0 | 0 | 0 | 49 | 87 | 99 | 3 |
| Religion ................................. | 1,402 | 454 | 44 | 4 | 1 | 0 | 68 | 188 | 280 | 1 |
| Anti-Jewish ................................. | 731 | 156 | 9 | 0 | 0 | 0 | 22 | 78 | 114 | 1 |
| Anti-Catholic ................................. | 60 | 13 | 1 | 0 | 0 | 0 | 1 | 10 | 2 | 0 |
| Anti-Protestant ........................ | 48 | 20 | 2 | 0 | 0 | 0 | 8 | 3 | 4 | 0 |
| Anti-Islamic (Muslim)................... | 307 | 139 | 16 | 4 | 0 | 0 | 27 | 64 | 120 | 0 |
| Anti-Other Religion .................... | 107 | 40 | 3 | 0 | 1 | 0 | 2 | 8 | 28 | 0 |
| Anti-Multiple Religions, Group .... | 58 | 26 | 4 | 0 | 0 | 0 | 3 | 7 | 8 | 0 |
| Anti-Mormon........................ | 8 | 4 | 0 | 0 | 0 | 0 | 0 | 2 | 0 | 0 |
| Anti-Jehovah's Witness............... | 1 | 0 | 0 | 0 | 0 | 0 | 0 | 0 | 0 | 0 |
| Anti-Eastern Orthodox (Russian, Greek, Other)........................ | 50 | 38 | 5 | 0 | 0 | 0 | 3 | 10 | 0 | 0 |
| Anti-Other Christian................... | 18 | 10 | 2 | 0 | 0 | 0 | 1 | 4 | 1 | 0 |
| Anti-Buddhist......................... | 1 | 0 | 0 | 0 | 0 | 0 | 0 | 0 | 0 | 0 |
| Anti-Hindu........................ | 5 | 4 | 0 | 0 | 0 | 0 | 1 | 0 | 2 | 0 |
| Anti-Sikh........................ | 6 | 4 | 1 | 0 | 0 | 0 | 0 | 1 | 1 | 0 |
| Anti-Atheism/Agnosticism/etc. .... | 2 | 0 | 1 | 0 | 0 | 0 | 0 | 1 | 0 | 0 |
| Sexual Orientation .................... | 1,263 | 710 | 79 | 1 | 5 | 0 | 214 | 461 | 253 | 4 |
| Anti-Gay (Male) ........................ | 786 | 428 | 40 | 1 | 2 | 0 | 140 | 297 | 144 | 2 |
| Anti-Lesbian................................. | 170 | 90 | 9 | 0 | 2 | 0 | 31 | 66 | 38 | 0 |
| Anti-Lesbian, Gay, Bisexual, or Transgender (Mixed Group)...................... | 248 | 160 | 18 | 0 | 1 | 0 | 39 | 75 | 58 | 0 |
| Anti-Heterosexual ...................... | 24 | 18 | 0 | 0 | 0 | 0 | 1 | 8 | 5 | 1 |
| Anti-Bisexual............................ | 35 | 14 | 12 | 0 | 0 | 0 | 3 | 15 | 8 | 1 |
| Disability ................................. | 88 | 52 | 14 | 0 | 0 | 0 | 11 | 27 | 16 | 1 |
| Anti-Physical ............................ | 52 | 34 | 6 | 0 | 0 | 0 | 6 | 17 | 10 | 0 |
| Anti-Mental ............................ | 36 | 18 | 8 | 0 | 0 | 0 | 5 | 10 | 6 | 1 |
| Gender ................................. | 30 | 25 | 2 | 0 | 1 | 0 | 4 | 11 | 8 | 0 |
| Anti-Male ................................. | 8 | 6 | 0 | 0 | 0 | 0 | 0 | 3 | 3 | 0 |
| Anti-Female ............................ | 22 | 19 | 2 | 0 | 1 | 0 | 4 | 8 | 5 | 0 |
| Gender Identity........................ | 122 | 75 | 8 | 1 | 1 | 0 | 22 | 36 | 19 | 1 |
| Anti-Transgender ...................... | 76 | 49 | 3 | 1 | 1 | 0 | 15 | 27 | 15 | 1 |
| Anti-Gender Non-Conforming .... | 46 | 26 | 5 | 0 | 0 | 0 | 7 | 9 | 4 | 0 |
| **Multiple-Bias Incidents**[6] ...................... | 52 | 29 | 3 | 1 | 0 | 0 | 6 | 6 | 19 | 0 |

# Table 7. Victims, Offense Type, by Bias Motivation, 2015—*Continued*

(Number.)

| Bias motivation | Crimes against property | | | | | | | Crimes against society[5] |
|---|---|---|---|---|---|---|---|---|
| | Robbery | Burglary | Larceny-theft | Motor vehicle theft | Arson | Destruction/ damage/ vandalism | Other[5] | |
| **Total** ................................. | 148 | 173 | 274 | 24 | 36 | 1,897 | 74 | 65 |
| **Single-Bias Incidents** .......................... | 148 | 172 | 272 | 24 | 35 | 1,881 | 74 | 65 |
| Race/Ethnicity/Ancestry ..................... | 76 | 98 | 168 | 17 | 17 | 937 | 49 | 43 |
| Anti-White............................ | 34 | 29 | 78 | 7 | 4 | 109 | 32 | 17 |
| Anti-Black or African American ... | 12 | 27 | 28 | 4 | 11 | 555 | 5 | 13 |
| Anti-American Indian or Alaska Native ................................. | 6 | 14 | 31 | 4 | 0 | 22 | 6 | 4 |
| Anti-Asian............................ | 2 | 7 | 5 | 2 | 1 | 25 | 0 | 0 |
| Anti-Native Hawaiian or Other Pacific Islander ......................... | 0 | 0 | 0 | 0 | 0 | 1 | 0 | 0 |
| Anti-Multiple Races, Group ......... | 1 | 4 | 5 | 0 | 0 | 83 | 3 | 3 |
| Anti-Arab............................ | 2 | 0 | 0 | 0 | 0 | 11 | 0 | 0 |
| Anti-Hispanic or Latino............... | 18 | 6 | 8 | 0 | 1 | 59 | 1 | 0 |
| Anti-Other Race/Ethnicity/ Ancestry ................................. | 1 | 11 | 13 | 0 | 0 | 72 | 2 | 6 |
| Religion ................................. | 7 | 35 | 61 | 2 | 14 | 722 | 11 | 8 |
| Anti-Jewish ........................... | 1 | 12 | 14 | 0 | 6 | 481 | 2 | 0 |
| Anti-Catholic ......................... | 1 | 4 | 6 | 1 | 2 | 30 | 1 | 2 |
| Anti-Protestant ...................... | 0 | 2 | 8 | 0 | 1 | 18 | 3 | 1 |
| Anti-Islamic (Muslim)................. | 4 | 4 | 4 | 0 | 1 | 76 | 0 | 3 |
| Anti-Other Religion ................... | 1 | 6 | 1 | 0 | 3 | 57 | 0 | 0 |
| Anti-Multiple Religions, Group .... | 0 | 1 | 3 | 0 | 1 | 34 | 0 | 1 |
| Anti-Mormon.......................... | 0 | 1 | 3 | 0 | 0 | 1 | 0 | 1 |
| Anti-Jehovah's Witness............... | 0 | 0 | 0 | 0 | 0 | 1 | 0 | 0 |
| Anti-Eastern Orthodox (Russian, Greek, Other)......................... | 0 | 5 | 17 | 1 | 0 | 11 | 3 | 0 |
| Anti-Other Christian................... | 0 | 0 | 3 | 0 | 0 | 7 | 2 | 0 |
| Anti-Buddhist............................ | 0 | 0 | 0 | 0 | 0 | 1 | 0 | 0 |
| Anti-Hindu............................ | 0 | 0 | 0 | 0 | 0 | 2 | 0 | 0 |
| Anti-Sikh............................ | 0 | 0 | 2 | 0 | 0 | 2 | 0 | 0 |
| Anti-Atheism/Agnosticism/etc. .... | 0 | 0 | 0 | 0 | 0 | 1 | 0 | 0 |
| Sexual Orientation .......................... | 56 | 29 | 26 | 1 | 4 | 200 | 7 | 2 |
| Anti-Gay (Male) ...................... | 35 | 24 | 8 | 1 | 2 | 126 | 4 | 0 |
| Anti-Lesbian........................... | 3 | 3 | 2 | 0 | 0 | 25 | 0 | 0 |
| Anti-Lesbian, Gay, Bisexual, or Transgender (Mixed Group)................... | 15 | 2 | 11 | 0 | 2 | 44 | 1 | 0 |
| Anti-Heterosexual ..................... | 1 | 0 | 1 | 0 | 0 | 3 | 2 | 2 |
| Anti-Bisexual............................ | 2 | 0 | 4 | 0 | 0 | 2 | 0 | 0 |
| Disability................................. | 2 | 1 | 6 | 1 | 0 | 14 | 4 | 5 |
| Anti-Physical ......................... | 2 | 1 | 2 | 1 | 0 | 9 | 0 | 4 |
| Anti-Mental.......................... | 0 | 0 | 4 | 0 | 0 | 5 | 4 | 1 |
| Gender ................................. | 0 | 0 | 2 | 2 | 0 | 2 | 0 | 0 |
| Anti-Male ................................. | 0 | 0 | 2 | 0 | 0 | 0 | 0 | 0 |
| Anti-Female .............................. | 0 | 0 | 0 | 2 | 0 | 2 | 0 | 0 |
| Gender Identity.............................. | 7 | 9 | 9 | 1 | 0 | 6 | 3 | 7 |
| Anti-Transgender ...................... | 5 | 1 | 4 | 0 | 0 | 5 | 0 | 1 |
| Anti-Gender Non-Conforming .... | 2 | 8 | 5 | 1 | 0 | 1 | 3 | 6 |
| **Multiple-Bias Incidents[6]** ...................... | 0 | 1 | 2 | 0 | 1 | 16 | 0 | 0 |

NOTE: The aggregate of adult and juvenile individual victims does not equal the total number of victims because total victims include individuals, businesses, institutions, and society as a whole. In addition, the aggregate of adult and juvenile individual victims does not equal the aggregate of victims of crimes against persons because not all law enforcement agencies report the ages of individual victims.

[1] A victim can be an individual, a business, an institution, or society as a whole.
[2] The figures shown in this column are individual victims only.
[3] The figures shown in this column for the offense of rape include only those reported by law enforcement agencies that used the revised Uniform Crime Reporting (UCR) definition of rape.
[4] The figures shown in this column for the offense of rape include only those reported by law enforcement agencies that used the legacy UCR definition of rape.
[5] Includes additional offenses collected in the National Incident-Based Reporting System.
[6] A multiple-bias incident is an incident in which one or more offense types are motivated by two or more biases.

## Table 8. Incidents, Victim Type, by Bias Motivation, 2015

(Number.)

| Bias motivation | Total incidents | Victim type | | | | | |
|---|---|---|---|---|---|---|---|
| | | Individual | Business/ financial institution | Government | Religious organization | Society/ public[1] | Other/ unknown/ multiple |
| **Total** ............................................ | 5,850 | 4,714 | 295 | 140 | 178 | 49 | 474 |
| **Single-Bias Incidents** ........................... | 5,818 | 4,689 | 295 | 138 | 176 | 49 | 471 |
| Race/Ethnicity/Ancestry ............................. | 3,310 | 2,861 | 160 | 72 | 19 | 30 | 168 |
| Religion ............................................ | 1,244 | 667 | 107 | 53 | 150 | 7 | 260 |
| Sexual Orientation ................................. | 1,053 | 976 | 20 | 11 | 5 | 1 | 40 |
| Disability ........................................... | 74 | 64 | 2 | 2 | 0 | 4 | 2 |
| Gender ............................................. | 23 | 21 | 2 | 0 | 0 | 0 | 0 |
| Gender Identity ................................... | 114 | 100 | 4 | 0 | 2 | 7 | 1 |
| **Multiple-Bias Incidents[2]** ................................. | 32 | 25 | 0 | 2 | 2 | 0 | 3 |

[1] The victim type society/public is collected only in the National Incident-Based Reporting System.
[2] A multiple-bias incident is an incident in which one or more offense types are motivated by two or more biases.

## Table 9. Known Offenders,[1] by Known Offender's Race, Ethnicity, and Age, 2015

(Number.)

| Race/ethnicity/age | Total |
|---|---|
| **Race**.......................................................................................... | 5,493 |
| White ........................................................................................ | 2,657 |
| Black or African American........................................................... | 1,336 |
| American Indian or Alaska Native................................................ | 52 |
| Asian ........................................................................................ | 53 |
| Native Hawaiian or Other Pacific Islander .................................. | 4 |
| Group of multiple races[2] ............................................................ | 499 |
| Unknown race ........................................................................... | 892 |
| **Ethnicity[3]** .................................................................................. | 3,421 |
| Hispanic or Latino ..................................................................... | 209 |
| Not Hispanic or Latino................................................................ | 880 |
| Group of multiple ethnicities[4] ................................................... | 54 |
| Unknown ethnicity...................................................................... | 2,278 |
| **Age[3]**.......................................................................................... | 3,331 |
| Total known offenders 18 and over............................................ | 2,823 |
| Total known offenders under 18 ................................................ | 508 |

[1] The term known offender does not imply that the identity of the suspect is known, but only that an attribute of the suspect has been identified, which distinguishes him/her from an unknown offender.
[2] The term group of multiple races is used to describe a group of offenders of varying races.
[3] The total number of known offenders by age and the total number of known offenders by ethnicity do not equal the total number of known offenders by race because not all law enforcement agencies report the age and/or ethnicity of the known offenders.
[4] The term group of multiple ethnicities is used to describe a group of offenders of varying ethnicities.

## Table 10. Incidents, Bias Motivation, by Location, 2015

(Number.)

| Location | Total incidents | Bias motivation | | | | | | Multiple-bias incidents[1] |
|---|---|---|---|---|---|---|---|---|
| | | Race | Religion | Sexual orientation | Disability | Gender | Gender Identity | |
| Total ......................................................... | 5,850 | 3,310 | 1,244 | 1,053 | 74 | 23 | 114 | 32 |
| Abandoned/condemned structure................................. | 5 | 2 | 3 | 0 | 0 | 0 | 0 | 0 |
| Air/bus/train terminal ............................................ | 82 | 57 | 9 | 15 | 0 | 0 | 0 | 1 |
| Amusement park .................................................. | 1 | 1 | 0 | 0 | 0 | 0 | 0 | 0 |
| Arena/stadium/fairgrounds/coliseum .......................... | 7 | 4 | 1 | 1 | 0 | 0 | 1 | 0 |
| ATM separate from bank ......................................... | 1 | 1 | 0 | 0 | 0 | 0 | 0 | 0 |
| Auto dealership new/used........................................ | 4 | 1 | 2 | 1 | 0 | 0 | 0 | 0 |
| Bank/savings and loan............................................ | 12 | 7 | 1 | 1 | 0 | 0 | 2 | 1 |
| Bar/nightclub ..................................................... | 99 | 55 | 9 | 32 | 0 | 0 | 3 | 0 |
| Camp/campground................................................ | 3 | 1 | 2 | 0 | 0 | 0 | 0 | 0 |
| Church/synagogue/temple/mosque ........................... | 259 | 45 | 199 | 8 | 0 | 0 | 5 | 2 |
| Commercial office building ...................................... | 111 | 56 | 32 | 15 | 3 | 0 | 4 | 1 |
| Community center................................................. | 15 | 5 | 10 | 0 | 0 | 0 | 0 | 0 |
| Construction site.................................................. | 11 | 9 | 2 | 0 | 0 | 0 | 0 | 0 |
| Convenience store ................................................ | 94 | 67 | 14 | 11 | 1 | 0 | 1 | 0 |
| Daycare facility.................................................... | 2 | 1 | 0 | 0 | 1 | 0 | 0 | 0 |
| Department/discount store....................................... | 68 | 48 | 12 | 5 | 0 | 2 | 1 | 0 |
| Dock/wharf/freight/modal terminal ........................... | 3 | 3 | 0 | 0 | 0 | 0 | 0 | 0 |
| Drug store/doctor's office/hospital............................. | 66 | 50 | 10 | 4 | 0 | 1 | 1 | 0 |
| Farm facility ...................................................... | 3 | 3 | 0 | 0 | 0 | 0 | 0 | 0 |
| Field/woods ....................................................... | 31 | 21 | 4 | 3 | 1 | 0 | 1 | 1 |
| Gambling facility/casino/race track ............................ | 3 | 3 | 0 | 0 | 0 | 0 | 0 | 0 |
| Government/public building...................................... | 104 | 74 | 13 | 12 | 1 | 0 | 3 | 1 |
| Grocery/supermarket............................................. | 48 | 35 | 5 | 6 | 1 | 0 | 1 | 0 |
| Highway/road/alley/street/sidewalk............................ | 1,018 | 588 | 99 | 266 | 16 | 2 | 38 | 9 |
| Hotel/motel/etc................................................... | 49 | 28 | 9 | 9 | 1 | 1 | 1 | 0 |
| Industrial site ..................................................... | 14 | 11 | 0 | 2 | 0 | 0 | 1 | 0 |
| Jail/prison/penitentiary/corrections facility.................... | 58 | 38 | 6 | 11 | 2 | 1 | 0 | 0 |
| Lake/waterway/beach ............................................ | 9 | 5 | 0 | 4 | 0 | 0 | 0 | 0 |
| Liquor store ....................................................... | 14 | 8 | 3 | 3 | 0 | 0 | 0 | 0 |
| Military installation............................................... | 2 | 1 | 1 | 0 | 0 | 0 | 0 | 0 |
| Park/playground.................................................. | 88 | 53 | 18 | 13 | 1 | 0 | 3 | 0 |
| Parking/drop lot/garage ......................................... | 328 | 212 | 51 | 53 | 3 | 1 | 7 | 1 |
| Rental storage facility............................................ | 4 | 2 | 1 | 0 | 0 | 1 | 0 | 0 |
| Residence/home................................................... | 1,843 | 1,109 | 318 | 345 | 28 | 10 | 27 | 6 |
| Rest area........................................................... | 4 | 3 | 1 | 0 | 0 | 0 | 0 | 0 |
| Restaurant ........................................................ | 125 | 83 | 13 | 25 | 1 | 0 | 1 | 2 |
| School/college[2] .................................................. | 149 | 73 | 57 | 19 | 0 | 0 | 0 | 0 |
| School—college/university....................................... | 152 | 85 | 41 | 19 | 2 | 0 | 3 | 2 |
| School—elementary/secondary ................................. | 184 | 103 | 44 | 25 | 4 | 2 | 4 | 2 |
| Service/gas station ............................................... | 65 | 46 | 11 | 7 | 0 | 0 | 0 | 1 |
| Shelter—mission/homeless....................................... | 8 | 7 | 0 | 0 | 1 | 0 | 0 | 0 |
| Shopping mall..................................................... | 11 | 7 | 0 | 2 | 0 | 0 | 1 | 1 |
| Specialty store (TV, fur, etc.) ................................... | 43 | 25 | 8 | 8 | 2 | 0 | 0 | 0 |
| Other/unknown ................................................... | 642 | 269 | 235 | 125 | 5 | 2 | 5 | 1 |
| Multiple locations ................................................ | 8 | 5 | 0 | 3 | 0 | 0 | 0 | 0 |

[1] A multiple-bias incident is an incident in which one or more offense types are motivated by two or more biases.
[2] The location designation School/college has been retained for agencies that have not updated their records management systems to include the new location designations of School—college/university and School—elementary/secondary, which allow for more specificity in reporting.

# Table 11. Offenses, Offense Type, by Participating State, 2015

(Number.)

| State | Total offenses | Crimes against persons | | | | | | |
|---|---|---|---|---|---|---|---|---|
| | | Murder and nonnegligent manslaughter | Rape (revised definition)[1] | Rape (legacy definition)[2] | Aggravated assault | Simple assault | Intimidation | Other[3] |
| Total | 6,885 | 18 | 12 | 1 | 882 | 1,696 | 1,853 | 20 |
| Alabama | 12 | 0 | 0 | | 2 | 4 | 4 | 0 |
| Alaska | 19 | 0 | 0 | | 2 | 2 | 13 | 0 |
| Arizona | 322 | 1 | 0 | | 59 | 89 | 77 | 0 |
| Arkansas | 8 | 0 | 0 | | 1 | 0 | 5 | 0 |
| California | 1,017 | 3 | 0 | | 211 | 237 | 247 | 0 |
| Colorado | 143 | 0 | 3 | | 28 | 32 | 49 | 0 |
| Connecticut | 107 | 0 | 0 | | 5 | 15 | 42 | 0 |
| Delaware | 11 | 0 | 0 | | 0 | 2 | 4 | 0 |
| District of Columbia | 74 | 0 | 1 | | 16 | 29 | 12 | 0 |
| Florida | 83 | 0 | 0 | | 15 | 22 | 18 | 0 |
| Georgia | 49 | 0 | | 0 | 1 | 11 | 29 | 0 |
| Idaho | 46 | 0 | 0 | | 5 | 19 | 4 | 0 |
| Illinois | 101 | 0 | 1 | | 23 | 20 | 24 | 0 |
| Indiana | 76 | 0 | 0 | 0 | 10 | 19 | 21 | 1 |
| Iowa | 6 | 0 | 0 | | 3 | 0 | 1 | 0 |
| Kansas | 81 | 0 | 1 | | 14 | 24 | 16 | 0 |
| Kentucky | 218 | 0 | 0 | | 13 | 60 | 46 | 0 |
| Louisiana | 45 | 0 | 1 | | 10 | 15 | 1 | 0 |
| Maine | 45 | 0 | 0 | 0 | 2 | 3 | 29 | 0 |
| Maryland | 43 | 0 | 0 | | 6 | 12 | 0 | 0 |
| Massachusetts | 483 | 0 | 1 | | 59 | 114 | 163 | 0 |
| Michigan | 373 | 1 | 0 | | 50 | 99 | 109 | 2 |
| Minnesota | 132 | 0 | 0 | | 15 | 38 | 44 | 0 |
| Mississippi | 0 | 0 | 0 | 0 | 0 | 0 | 0 | 0 |
| Missouri | 137 | 0 | 0 | | 10 | 51 | 47 | 0 |
| Montana | 47 | 0 | 0 | | 8 | 5 | 1 | 0 |
| Nebraska | 19 | 0 | 0 | 0 | 2 | 7 | 2 | 0 |
| Nevada | 70 | 0 | 0 | | 20 | 10 | 19 | 0 |
| New Hampshire | 15 | 0 | 0 | | 1 | 3 | 7 | 0 |
| New Jersey | 349 | 0 | 0 | | 2 | 13 | 195 | 0 |
| New Mexico | 14 | 0 | | 0 | 2 | 5 | 1 | 0 |
| New York | 515 | 0 | 0 | 0 | 45 | 230 | 0 | 0 |
| North Carolina | 208 | 0 | 0 | 1 | 36 | 40 | 72 | 0 |
| North Dakota | 54 | 0 | 0 | | 3 | 17 | 17 | 0 |
| Ohio | 470 | 0 | 1 | 0 | 16 | 49 | 205 | 2 |
| Oklahoma | 47 | 0 | 0 | | 9 | 6 | 18 | 0 |
| Oregon | 79 | 0 | 1 | 0 | 8 | 16 | 19 | 0 |
| Pennsylvania | 71 | 0 | 0 | | 7 | 13 | 35 | 0 |
| Rhode Island | 19 | 0 | 0 | 0 | 3 | 6 | 0 | 0 |
| South Carolina | 69 | 9 | 0 | | 9 | 13 | 10 | 0 |
| South Dakota | 20 | 0 | 0 | | 4 | 9 | 4 | 0 |
| Tennessee | 294 | 3 | 0 | | 39 | 95 | 66 | 6 |
| Texas | 219 | 1 | 0 | | 35 | 70 | 45 | 0 |
| Utah | 56 | 0 | 0 | 0 | 4 | 14 | 5 | 0 |
| Vermont | 8 | 0 | 0 | | 0 | 4 | 1 | 0 |
| Virginia | 184 | 0 | 1 | | 19 | 48 | 33 | 1 |
| Washington | 326 | 0 | 0 | 0 | 36 | 84 | 83 | 4 |
| West Virginia | 49 | 0 | 1 | | 3 | 14 | 2 | 4 |
| Wisconsin | 47 | 0 | 0 | 0 | 8 | 6 | 8 | 0 |
| Wyoming | 2 | 0 | 0 | | 0 | 2 | 0 | 0 |
| Guam | 3 | 0 | 0 | | 3 | 0 | 0 | 0 |

[1] The figures shown in this column for the offense of rape include only those reported by law enforcement agencies that used the revised Uniform Crime Reporting (UCR) definition of rape.
[2] The figures shown in this column for the offense of rape include only those reported by law enforcement agencies that used the legacy UCR definition of rape.
[3] Includes additional offenses collected in the National Incident-Based Reporting System.

## Table 11. Offenses, Offense Type, by Participating State, 2015—*Continued*

(Number.)

| State | Crimes against property | | | | | | | Crimes against society[3] |
|---|---|---|---|---|---|---|---|---|
| | Robbery | Burglary | Larceny-theft | Motor vehicle theft | Arson | Destruction/ damage/ vandalism | Other[3] | |
| Total ........................................ | 120 | 147 | 255 | 22 | 30 | 1,698 | 66 | 65 |
| Alabama.................................. | 0 | 0 | 0 | 0 | 0 | 2 | 0 | 0 |
| Alaska...................................... | 0 | 0 | 0 | 0 | 1 | 1 | 0 | 0 |
| Arizona.................................... | 7 | 4 | 3 | 0 | 0 | 82 | 0 | 0 |
| Arkansas.................................. | 0 | 0 | 0 | 0 | 0 | 2 | 0 | 0 |
| California................................. | 26 | 11 | 3 | 0 | 5 | 274 | 0 | 0 |
| Colorado ................................. | 5 | 3 | 0 | 0 | 1 | 21 | 1 | 0 |
| Connecticut............................. | 2 | 0 | 5 | 2 | 0 | 33 | 2 | 1 |
| Delaware.................................. | 1 | 0 | 0 | 0 | 0 | 4 | 0 | 0 |
| District of Columbia................. | 8 | 0 | 0 | 0 | 0 | 8 | 0 | 0 |
| Florida ..................................... | 0 | 1 | 1 | 0 | 1 | 25 | 0 | 0 |
| Georgia ................................... | 0 | 0 | 0 | 0 | 0 | 8 | 0 | 0 |
| Idaho....................................... | 0 | 3 | 4 | 0 | 3 | 7 | 1 | 0 |
| Illinois..................................... | 1 | 0 | 3 | 0 | 0 | 29 | 0 | 0 |
| Indiana.................................... | 1 | 1 | 3 | 0 | 1 | 16 | 0 | 3 |
| Iowa........................................ | 0 | 1 | 1 | 0 | 0 | 0 | 0 | 0 |
| Kansas..................................... | 1 | 5 | 4 | 1 | 0 | 14 | 0 | 1 |
| Kentucky ................................. | 4 | 14 | 25 | 2 | 1 | 44 | 8 | 1 |
| Louisiana ................................ | 2 | 2 | 6 | 0 | 0 | 5 | 2 | 1 |
| Maine ...................................... | 0 | 0 | 0 | 0 | 0 | 11 | 0 | 0 |
| Maryland ................................. | 1 | 0 | 0 | 0 | 0 | 24 | 0 | 0 |
| Massachusetts ......................... | 2 | 8 | 15 | 3 | 0 | 110 | 3 | 5 |
| Michigan ................................. | 5 | 6 | 14 | 2 | 0 | 71 | 10 | 4 |
| Minnesota ............................... | 4 | 1 | 1 | 0 | 1 | 28 | 0 | 0 |
| Mississippi .............................. | 0 | 0 | 0 | 0 | 0 | 0 | 0 | 0 |
| Missouri .................................. | 1 | 2 | 3 | 1 | 1 | 18 | 0 | 3 |
| Montana.................................. | 1 | 1 | 13 | 1 | 0 | 10 | 3 | 4 |
| Nebraska ................................. | 0 | 1 | 1 | 0 | 0 | 6 | 0 | 0 |
| Nevada .................................... | 6 | 1 | 0 | 0 | 2 | 12 | 0 | 0 |
| New Hampshire ....................... | 0 | 0 | 1 | 0 | 0 | 3 | 0 | 0 |
| New Jersey............................... | 0 | 0 | 8 | 0 | 0 | 131 | 0 | 0 |
| New Mexico.............................. | 1 | 2 | 0 | 0 | 0 | 3 | 0 | 0 |
| New York.................................. | 0 | 21 | 9 | 0 | 3 | 207 | 0 | 0 |
| North Carolina......................... | 5 | 1 | 2 | 0 | 2 | 49 | 0 | 0 |
| North Dakota........................... | 0 | 1 | 10 | 0 | 1 | 2 | 3 | 0 |
| Ohio ........................................ | 10 | 27 | 44 | 3 | 2 | 97 | 9 | 5 |
| Oklahoma................................ | 0 | 4 | 3 | 1 | 0 | 5 | 1 | 0 |
| Oregon .................................... | 1 | 1 | 1 | 0 | 0 | 29 | 0 | 3 |
| Pennsylvania ........................... | 0 | 0 | 3 | 0 | 0 | 13 | 0 | 0 |
| Rhode Island ........................... | 0 | 0 | 0 | 0 | 0 | 10 | 0 | 0 |
| South Carolina......................... | 3 | 2 | 4 | 0 | 2 | 15 | 1 | 1 |
| South Dakota........................... | 0 | 0 | 0 | 0 | 0 | 3 | 0 | 0 |
| Tennessee ................................ | 5 | 2 | 9 | 0 | 1 | 50 | 3 | 15 |
| Texas....................................... | 4 | 5 | 4 | 0 | 1 | 50 | 1 | 3 |
| Utah ........................................ | 1 | 3 | 7 | 0 | 0 | 17 | 3 | 2 |
| Vermont .................................. | 0 | 0 | 0 | 0 | 0 | 3 | 0 | 0 |
| Virginia.................................... | 0 | 4 | 14 | 0 | 0 | 58 | 3 | 3 |
| Washington ............................. | 10 | 6 | 18 | 4 | 0 | 69 | 8 | 4 |
| West Virginia ........................... | 1 | 1 | 9 | 2 | 0 | 5 | 2 | 5 |
| Wisconsin ................................ | 1 | 2 | 4 | 0 | 1 | 14 | 2 | 1 |
| Wyoming.................................. | 0 | 0 | 0 | 0 | 0 | 0 | 0 | 0 |
| Guam....................................... | 0 | 0 | 0 | 0 | 0 | 0 | 0 | 0 |

[1] The figures shown in this column for the offense of rape include only those reported by law enforcement agencies that used the revised Uniform Crime Reporting (UCR) definition of rape.
[2] The figures shown in this column for the offense of rape include only those reported by law enforcement agencies that used the legacy UCR definition of rape.
[3] Includes additional offenses collected in the National Incident-Based Reporting System.

## Table 12. Agency Hate Crime Reporting, by Participating State and Territory, 2015

(Number.)

| State | Number of participating agencies | Population covered | Agencies submitting incident reports | Total number of incidents reported |
|---|---|---|---|---|
| Total | 14,997 | 283,884,034 | 1,742 | 5,850 |
| Alabama | 34 | 1,252,146 | 3 | 10 |
| Alaska | 33 | 734,820 | 4 | 8 |
| Arizona | 101 | 6,622,880 | 21 | 276 |
| Arkansas | 279 | 2,754,543 | 4 | 5 |
| California | 730 | 39,137,326 | 213 | 837 |
| Colorado | 234 | 5,445,853 | 42 | 107 |
| Connecticut | 95 | 3,399,068 | 44 | 93 |
| Delaware | 60 | 945,934 | 7 | 11 |
| District of Columbia | 2 | 672,228 | 2 | 65 |
| Florida | 38 | 5,356,877 | 36 | 72 |
| Georgia | 473 | 7,991,234 | 7 | 44 |
| Idaho | 112 | 1,654,475 | 19 | 34 |
| Illinois | 741 | 12,501,008 | 43 | 90 |
| Indiana | 168 | 3,224,755 | 18 | 63 |
| Iowa | 237 | 3,105,094 | 5 | 6 |
| Kansas | 345 | 2,741,323 | 34 | 62 |
| Kentucky | 403 | 4,402,368 | 83 | 188 |
| Louisiana | 148 | 3,711,824 | 15 | 38 |
| Maine | 184 | 1,329,328 | 14 | 38 |
| Maryland | 154 | 6,006,401 | 11 | 41 |
| Massachusetts | 342 | 6,566,279 | 85 | 411 |
| Michigan | 617 | 9,834,270 | 127 | 309 |
| Minnesota | 319 | 5,218,435 | 27 | 109 |
| Mississippi | 43 | 763,830 | 0 | 0 |
| Missouri | 628 | 6,079,483 | 28 | 100 |
| Montana | 101 | 1,023,807 | 13 | 45 |
| Nebraska | 227 | 1,821,196 | 3 | 19 |
| Nevada | 53 | 2,890,845 | 6 | 58 |
| New Hampshire | 168 | 1,267,715 | 9 | 13 |
| New Jersey | 508 | 8,956,395 | 123 | 330 |
| New Mexico | 18 | 574,972 | 2 | 13 |
| New York | 575 | 19,766,342 | 60 | 500 |
| North Carolina | 532 | 10,041,690 | 52 | 161 |
| North Dakota | 112 | 756,927 | 19 | 36 |
| Ohio | 595 | 9,781,677 | 109 | 416 |
| Oklahoma | 351 | 3,896,985 | 29 | 37 |
| Oregon | 130 | 1,671,416 | 16 | 65 |
| Pennsylvania | 1,436 | 12,550,581 | 26 | 64 |
| Rhode Island | 49 | 1,056,298 | 8 | 18 |
| South Carolina | 436 | 4,826,241 | 40 | 55 |
| South Dakota | 121 | 782,152 | 9 | 16 |
| Tennessee | 463 | 6,600,299 | 61 | 221 |
| Texas | 1,026 | 27,390,337 | 62 | 191 |
| Utah | 133 | 2,966,781 | 22 | 47 |
| Vermont | 90 | 626,042 | 5 | 8 |
| Virginia | 414 | 8,380,278 | 58 | 158 |
| Washington | 256 | 7,163,444 | 79 | 275 |
| West Virginia | 229 | 1,494,503 | 12 | 41 |
| Wisconsin | 395 | 5,580,752 | 25 | 43 |
| Wyoming | 57 | 564,577 | 1 | 2 |
| Guam[1] | 1 | | 1 | 1 |
| U.S. Virgin Islands[1] | 1 | | 0 | 0 |

[1] The 2015 population estimates were not available at the time of publication.

# Table 13. Hate Crime Incidents Per Bias Motivation and Quarter, by Selected State and Agency, 2015

(Number.)

| State/agency | Number of incidents per bias motivation | | | | | | Number of incidents per quarter | | | | Population[1] |
|---|---|---|---|---|---|---|---|---|---|---|---|
| | Race/ Ethnicity/ Ancestry | Religion | Sexual orientation | Disability | Gender | Gender Identity | 1st quarter | 2nd quarter | 3rd quarter | 4th quarter | |
| **ALABAMA** | | | | | | | | | | | |
| Total ........................... | 8 | 0 | 2 | 0 | 0 | 0 | | | | | |
| | | | | | | | | | | | |
| Cities ............................... | 7 | 1 | 0 | 0 | 0 | 0 | | | | | |
| Birmingham............................ | 3 | 0 | 2 | 0 | 0 | 0 | 1 | 1 | 1 | 2 | 212,291 |
| Hoover.................................... | 4 | 0 | 0 | 0 | 0 | 0 | 0 | 3 | 1 | 0 | 85,163 |
| Prattville................................ | 1 | 0 | 0 | 0 | 0 | 0 | 0 | 1 | | 0 | 35,637 |
| | | | | | | | | | | | |
| **ALASKA** | | | | | | | | | | | |
| Total ........................... | 7 | 0 | 1 | 0 | 0 | 0 | | | | | |
| | | | | | | | | | | | |
| Cities ............................... | 7 | 0 | 1 | 0 | 0 | 0 | | | | | |
| Anchorage............................. | 4 | 0 | 1 | 0 | 0 | 0 | 1 | 1 | 2 | 1 | 301,239 |
| | | | | | | | | | | | |
| **ARIZONA** | | | | | | | | | | | |
| Total ........................... | 162 | 52 | 57 | 5 | 0 | 0 | | | | | |
| | | | | | | | | | | | |
| Cities ............................... | 157 | 49 | 57 | 5 | 0 | 0 | | | | | |
| Apache Junction ......................... | 2 | 0 | 0 | 0 | 0 | 0 | 1 | 1 | 0 | 0 | 38,519 |
| Avondale ................................ | 1 | 1 | 0 | 0 | 0 | 0 | 0 | 0 | 0 | 2 | 80,533 |
| Chandler................................. | 1 | 0 | 0 | 0 | 0 | 0 | 0 | 0 | 1 | 0 | 258,875 |
| El Mirage ................................ | 0 | 1 | 0 | 0 | 0 | 0 | 0 | 1 | 0 | 0 | 33,985 |
| Gilbert .................................... | 3 | 1 | 0 | 0 | 0 | 0 | 2 | 1 | 1 | 0 | 247,324 |
| Glendale ................................. | 5 | 2 | 1 | 0 | 0 | 0 | 2 | 2 | 2 | 2 | 240,374 |
| Holbrook ................................ | 0 | 0 | 1 | 0 | 0 | 0 | 0 | 1 | 0 | 0 | 5,007 |
| Mesa ...................................... | 2 | 2 | 0 | 0 | 0 | 0 | 1 | 0 | 1 | 2 | 471,034 |
| Nogales .................................. | 0 | 1 | 0 | 0 | 0 | 0 | 0 | 0 | 0 | 1 | 20,312 |
| Phoenix................................... | 137 | 40 | 49 | 5 | 0 | 0 | 76 | 77 | 44 | 34 | 1,559,744 |
| Prescott.................................. | 1 | 0 | 0 | 0 | 0 | 0 | 1 | | 0 | 0 | 41,393 |
| Scottsdale............................... | 1 | 1 | 1 | 0 | 0 | 0 | 2 | 0 | 1 | 0 | 233,872 |
| Tucson.................................... | 1 | 0 | 3 | 0 | 0 | 0 | 2 | 0 | 1 | 1 | 529,675 |
| Williams.................................. | 0 | 0 | 1 | 0 | 0 | 0 | 0 | 1 | | | 3,110 |
| Yuma...................................... | 3 | 0 | 1 | 0 | 0 | 0 | 0 | 2 | 1 | 1 | 93,923 |
| | | | | | | | | | | | |
| **Universities and Colleges ........** | 2 | 0 | 0 | 0 | 0 | 0 | | | | | |
| Arizona State University, Main | | | | | | | | | | | |
| Campus.................................... | 2 | 0 | 0 | 0 | 0 | 0 | 1 | 1 | 0 | 0 | 83,260 |
| | | | | | | | | | | | |
| **Metropolitan Counties ............** | 3 | 2 | 0 | 0 | 0 | 0 | | | | | |
| Maricopa................................. | 1 | 0 | 0 | 0 | 0 | 0 | 1 | 0 | 0 | 0 | |
| Pima....................................... | 1 | 1 | 0 | 0 | 0 | 0 | 0 | 2 | 0 | 0 | |
| Pinal ...................................... | 1 | 0 | 0 | 0 | 0 | 0 | | 1 | | | |
| Yavapai................................... | 0 | 1 | 0 | 0 | 0 | 0 | 1 | 0 | 0 | 0 | |
| | | | | | | | | | | | |
| **Nonmetropolitan Counties......** | | | | | | | | | | | |
| Graham................................... | 0 | 1 | 0 | 0 | 0 | 0 | 1 | 0 | 0 | 0 | |
| | | | | | | | | | | | |
| **ARKANSAS** | | | | | | | | | | | |
| Total ........................... | 3 | 0 | 2 | 0 | 0 | 0 | | | | | |
| | | | | | | | | | | | |
| Cities ............................... | 1 | 0 | 2 | 0 | 0 | 0 | | | | | |
| Bryant..................................... | 1 | 0 | 0 | 0 | 0 | 0 | 1 | 0 | 0 | 0 | 20,404 |
| Fort Smith............................... | 0 | 0 | 2 | 0 | 0 | 0 | 1 | 0 | 0 | 1 | 87,603 |
| | | | | | | | | | | | |
| **Metropolitan Counties ............** | 1 | 0 | 0 | 0 | 0 | 0 | | | | | |
| Sebastian................................. | 1 | 0 | 0 | 0 | 0 | 0 | 0 | 1 | 0 | 0 | |
| | | | | | | | | | | | |
| **Nonmetropolitan Counties......** | 1 | 0 | 0 | 0 | 0 | 0 | | | | | |
| Boone..................................... | 1 | 0 | 0 | 0 | 0 | 0 | 1 | 0 | 0 | 0 | |
| | | | | | | | | | | | |
| **CALIFORNIA** | | | | | | | | | | | |
| Total ........................... | 427 | 191 | 188 | 4 | 1 | 26 | | | | | |
| | | | | | | | | | | | |
| Cities ............................... | 291 | 117 | 166 | 1 | 0 | 6 | | | | | |
| Alameda.................................. | 1 | 1 | 0 | 0 | 0 | 0 | 1 | 0 | 1 | 0 | 78,613 |
| Alhambra................................. | 0 | 1 | 0 | 0 | 0 | 0 | 0 | 0 | 1 | 0 | 86,175 |
| Antioch................................... | 5 | 2 | 1 | 0 | 0 | 0 | 2 | 1 | 2 | 3 | 110,537 |
| Azusa ..................................... | 2 | 1 | 0 | 0 | 0 | 0 | 0 | 2 | 1 | 0 | 49,431 |

# Table 13. Hate Crime Incidents Per Bias Motivation and Quarter, by Selected State and Agency, 2015

(Number.)

| State/agency | Race/ Ethnicity/ Ancestry | Religion | Sexual orientation | Disability | Gender | Gender Identity | 1st quarter | 2nd quarter | 3rd quarter | 4th quarter | Population[1] |
|---|---|---|---|---|---|---|---|---|---|---|---|
| Bakersfield | 1 | 0 | 3 | 0 | 0 | 0 | 3 | 0 | 0 | 1 | 373,887 |
| Banning | 1 | 1 | 0 | 0 | 0 | 0 | 0 | 1 | 1 | 0 | 31,030 |
| Bellflower | 1 | 1 | 0 | 0 | 0 | 0 | 0 | 1 | 0 | 1 | 78,635 |
| Bell Gardens | 2 | 0 | 0 | 0 | 0 | 0 | 0 | 1 | 0 | 1 | 43,411 |
| Berkeley | 2 | 1 | 1 | 0 | 0 | 0 | 0 | 1 | 0 | 3 | 120,387 |
| Beverly Hills | 0 | 2 | 0 | 0 | 0 | 0 | 0 | 2 | 0 | 0 | 35,054 |
| Brisbane | 1 | 0 | 1 | 0 | 0 | 0 | 0 | 1 | 0 | 1 | 4,696 |
| Buena Park | 0 | 1 | 0 | 0 | 0 | 0 | 0 | 0 | 0 | 1 | 83,684 |
| Burbank | 1 | 0 | 0 | 0 | 0 | 0 | 0 | 1 | 0 | 0 | 105,865 |
| Calabasas | 1 | 0 | 0 | 0 | 0 | 0 | 0 | 0 | 1 | 0 | 24,505 |
| Camarillo | 1 | 0 | 0 | 0 | 0 | 0 | 0 | 1 | 0 | 0 | 67,325 |
| Carmel | 0 | 1 | 0 | 0 | 0 | 0 | 0 | 0 | 1 | 0 | 3,913 |
| Carson | 3 | 0 | 0 | 0 | 0 | 0 | 1 | 1 | 1 | 0 | 93,677 |
| Chino Hills | 0 | 1 | 0 | 0 | 0 | 0 | 0 | 0 | 0 | 1 | 77,515 |
| Chula Vista | 1 | 0 | 2 | 0 | 0 | 0 | 0 | 1 | 1 | 1 | 265,215 |
| Citrus Heights | 1 | 1 | 0 | 0 | 0 | 0 | 0 | 0 | 0 | 2 | 86,853 |
| Claremont | 1 | 2 | 1 | 0 | 0 | 0 | 0 | 2 | 0 | 2 | 36,331 |
| Clearlake | 5 | 2 | 0 | 0 | 0 | 0 | 2 | 0 | 3 | 2 | 15,044 |
| Clovis | 1 | 1 | 0 | 0 | 0 | 0 | 0 | 0 | 1 | 1 | 103,769 |
| Coachella | 0 | 1 | 0 | 0 | 0 | 0 | 0 | 0 | 0 | 1 | 44,953 |
| Colton | 0 | 1 | 0 | 0 | 0 | 0 | 0 | 1 | 0 | 0 | 54,503 |
| Commerce | 0 | 0 | 1 | 0 | 0 | 0 | 0 | 0 | 1 | 0 | 13,137 |
| Compton | 1 | 0 | 1 | 0 | 0 | 0 | 0 | 1 | 1 | 0 | 99,125 |
| Concord | 3 | 1 | 1 | 0 | 0 | 0 | 2 | 0 | 0 | 3 | 128,767 |
| Covina | 1 | 0 | 0 | 0 | 0 | 0 | 1 | 0 | 0 | 0 | 49,300 |
| Cypress | 1 | 1 | 0 | 0 | 0 | 0 | 1 | 1 | 0 | 0 | 49,560 |
| Daly City | 1 | 0 | 1 | 0 | 0 | 0 | 1 | 0 | 1 | 0 | 107,320 |
| Davis | 2 | 2 | 2 | 0 | 0 | 0 | 5 | 0 | 1 | 0 | 67,034 |
| Diamond Bar | 2 | 0 | 0 | 0 | 0 | 0 | 1 | 0 | 1 | 0 | 57,085 |
| East Palo Alto | 0 | 1 | 1 | 0 | 0 | 0 | 0 | 0 | 1 | 1 | 29,864 |
| El Cajon | 0 | 0 | 1 | 0 | 0 | 0 | 1 | 0 | 0 | 0 | 103,942 |
| El Cerrito | 2 | 0 | 0 | 0 | 0 | 0 | 0 | 1 | 1 | 0 | 24,842 |
| Elk Grove | 2 | 0 | 0 | 0 | 0 | 0 | 1 | 0 | 1 | 0 | 166,183 |
| El Monte | 2 | 0 | 1 | 0 | 0 | 0 | 2 | 0 | 0 | 1 | 117,376 |
| El Segundo | 1 | 0 | 0 | 0 | 0 | 0 | 0 | 0 | 1 | 0 | 17,164 |
| Escondido | 6 | 0 | 0 | 0 | 0 | 0 | 2 | 1 | 1 | 2 | 151,732 |
| Eureka | 2 | 0 | 0 | 0 | 0 | 0 | 1 | 0 | 1 | 0 | 26,858 |
| Fairfield | 0 | 0 | 1 | 0 | 0 | 0 | 0 | 0 | 1 | 0 | 112,582 |
| Firebaugh | 1 | 0 | 0 | 0 | 0 | 0 | 1 | 0 | 0 | 0 | 8,484 |
| Folsom | 2 | 0 | 0 | 0 | 0 | 0 | 0 | 0 | 1 | 1 | 76,183 |
| Fort Bragg | 0 | 1 | 0 | 0 | 0 | 0 | 0 | 0 | 1 | 0 | 7,310 |
| Foster City | 0 | 0 | 1 | 0 | 0 | 0 | 0 | 0 | 1 | 0 | 33,313 |
| Fremont | 2 | 1 | 0 | 0 | 0 | 0 | 2 | 1 | 0 | 0 | 232,427 |
| Fresno | 7 | 0 | 1 | 0 | 0 | 2 | 3 | 1 | 5 | 1 | 520,837 |
| Fullerton | 1 | 0 | 0 | 0 | 0 | 1 | 1 | 0 | 0 | 1 | 140,771 |
| Galt | 2 | 0 | 0 | 0 | 0 | 0 | 2 | 0 | 0 | 0 | 25,106 |
| Garden Grove | 1 | 1 | 0 | 0 | 0 | 0 | 2 | 0 | 0 | 0 | 176,041 |
| Glendale | 1 | 0 | 0 | 0 | 0 | 1 | 0 | 0 | 2 | 0 | 202,298 |
| Glendora | 1 | 0 | 0 | 0 | 0 | 0 | 0 | 0 | 1 | 0 | 51,753 |
| Goleta | 1 | 0 | 0 | 0 | 0 | 0 | 1 | 0 | 0 | 0 | 31,011 |
| Greenfield | 0 | 0 | 1 | 0 | 0 | 0 | 0 | 0 | 1 | 0 | 17,061 |
| Gridley | 1 | 0 | 0 | 0 | 0 | 0 | 0 | 0 | 0 | 1 | 6,580 |
| Hanford | 1 | 2 | 0 | 0 | 0 | 0 | 0 | 1 | 0 | 2 | 55,299 |
| Hawaiian Gardens | 2 | 0 | 0 | 0 | 0 | 0 | 1 | 0 | 0 | 1 | 14,629 |
| Hawthorne | 3 | 0 | 1 | 0 | 0 | 0 | 1 | 0 | 2 | 1 | 88,410 |
| Hayward | 3 | 1 | 0 | 0 | 0 | 0 | 0 | 1 | 3 | 0 | 157,157 |
| Hemet | 2 | 0 | 0 | 0 | 0 | 0 | 1 | 0 | 0 | 1 | 84,030 |
| Hermosa Beach | 1 | 0 | 0 | 0 | 0 | 0 | 1 | 0 | 0 | 0 | 19,986 |
| Hesperia | 0 | 0 | 2 | 0 | 0 | 0 | 1 | 0 | 0 | 1 | 93,348 |
| Hollister | 0 | 0 | 1 | 0 | 0 | 0 | 0 | 0 | 0 | 1 | 37,604 |
| Huntington Beach | 0 | 2 | 1 | 0 | 0 | 1 | 0 | 1 | 1 | 2 | 203,233 |
| Huntington Park | 3 | 0 | 1 | 0 | 0 | 0 | 3 | 0 | 1 | 0 | 59,668 |
| Imperial | 1 | 0 | 0 | 0 | 0 | 0 | 0 | 1 | 0 | 0 | 17,338 |
| Imperial Beach | 1 | 0 | 0 | 0 | 0 | 0 | 0 | 1 | 0 | 0 | 27,341 |
| Indio | 1 | 0 | 0 | 0 | 0 | 0 | 0 | 0 | 1 | 0 | 87,195 |
| Industry | 1 | 0 | 0 | 0 | 0 | 0 | 0 | 1 | 0 | 0 | 206 |
| Irvine | 1 | 1 | 1 | 0 | 0 | 0 | 0 | 1 | 1 | 1 | 258,198 |
| Jurupa Valley | 1 | 0 | 0 | 0 | 0 | 0 | 0 | 0 | 1 | 0 | 99,706 |
| Kerman | 0 | 0 | 1 | 0 | 0 | 0 | 0 | 0 | 1 | 0 | 14,595 |

| State/agency | Race/ Ethnicity/ Ancestry | Religion | Sexual orientation | Disability | Gender | Gender Identity | 1st quarter | 2nd quarter | 3rd quarter | 4th quarter | Population[1] |
|---|---|---|---|---|---|---|---|---|---|---|---|
| | Number of incidents per bias motivation | | | | | | Number of incidents per quarter | | | | |
| Laguna Beach | 1 | 0 | 1 | 0 | 0 | 0 | 0 | 0 | 2 | 0 | 23,485 |
| Lake Elsinore | 0 | 0 | 1 | 0 | 0 | 0 | 1 | 0 | 0 | 0 | 61,871 |
| Lake Forest | 4 | 0 | 0 | 0 | 0 | 0 | 0 | 0 | 1 | 3 | 80,798 |
| Lakewood | 2 | 0 | 0 | 0 | 0 | 0 | 0 | 0 | 0 | 2 | 82,047 |
| La Mirada | 1 | 1 | 0 | 0 | 0 | 0 | 1 | 0 | 0 | 1 | 49,685 |
| Lancaster | 3 | 2 | 2 | 0 | 0 | 0 | 0 | 2 | 2 | 3 | 162,095 |
| Lawndale | 0 | 0 | 1 | 0 | 0 | 0 | 1 | 0 | 0 | 0 | 33,605 |
| Lemoore | 1 | 0 | 0 | 0 | 0 | 0 | 0 | 0 | 0 | 1 | 25,348 |
| Livermore | 0 | 4 | 1 | 0 | 0 | 0 | 3 | 1 | 1 | 0 | 88,316 |
| Lodi | 1 | 1 | 0 | 0 | 0 | 0 | 0 | 1 | 0 | 1 | 64,369 |
| Lomita | 1 | 0 | 0 | 0 | 0 | 0 | 0 | 0 | 1 | 0 | 20,893 |
| Long Beach | 6 | 0 | 6 | 0 | 0 | 0 | 3 | 3 | 4 | 2 | 476,318 |
| Los Alamitos | 1 | 0 | 0 | 0 | 0 | 0 | 1 | 0 | 0 | 0 | 11,789 |
| Los Angeles | 92 | 50 | 45 | 0 | 0 | 5 | 45 | 53 | 41 | 53 | 3,962,726 |
| Los Gatos | 1 | 0 | 0 | 0 | 0 | 0 | 0 | 0 | 1 | 0 | 31,044 |
| Malibu | 0 | 1 | 0 | 0 | 0 | 0 | 0 | 0 | 1 | 0 | 13,033 |
| Manhattan Beach | 1 | 0 | 0 | 0 | 0 | 0 | 0 | 0 | 0 | 1 | 36,065 |
| Manteca | 0 | 2 | 0 | 0 | 0 | 0 | 1 | 0 | 1 | 0 | 75,019 |
| Marina | 0 | 0 | 1 | 0 | 0 | 0 | 1 | 0 | 0 | 0 | 21,094 |
| Marysville | 1 | 0 | 0 | 0 | 0 | 0 | 1 | 0 | 0 | 0 | 12,264 |
| Menifee | 1 | 0 | 0 | 0 | 0 | 0 | 0 | 1 | 0 | 0 | 87,051 |
| Merced | 1 | 0 | 0 | 0 | 0 | 0 | 0 | 0 | 0 | 1 | 82,409 |
| Mission Viejo | 1 | 0 | 0 | 0 | 0 | 0 | 0 | 0 | 0 | 1 | 98,217 |
| Modesto | 4 | 0 | 0 | 0 | 0 | 0 | 0 | 2 | 0 | 2 | 210,794 |
| Montebello | 0 | 1 | 0 | 0 | 0 | 0 | 1 | 0 | 0 | 0 | 64,280 |
| Monterey Park | 2 | 1 | 1 | 0 | 0 | 0 | 3 | 0 | 1 | 0 | 61,750 |
| Moorpark | 0 | 1 | 0 | 0 | 0 | 0 | 0 | 0 | 0 | 1 | 35,804 |
| Moreno Valley | 0 | 0 | 1 | 0 | 0 | 0 | 0 | 0 | 0 | 1 | 205,182 |
| Napa | 1 | 0 | 0 | 0 | 0 | 0 | 0 | 1 | 0 | 0 | 80,749 |
| National City | 1 | 0 | 0 | 0 | 0 | 0 | 0 | 1 | 0 | 0 | 60,768 |
| Newark | 0 | 1 | 0 | 0 | 0 | 0 | 0 | 0 | 0 | 1 | 45,258 |
| Newport Beach | 1 | 1 | 0 | 0 | 0 | 0 | 2 | 0 | 0 | 0 | 87,749 |
| Norwalk | 3 | 0 | 0 | 0 | 0 | 0 | 2 | 0 | 1 | 0 | 107,470 |
| Oakland | 6 | 3 | 8 | 0 | 0 | 1 | 2 | 9 | 6 | 1 | 419,481 |
| Oceanside | 1 | 1 | 0 | 0 | 0 | 0 | 0 | 0 | 1 | 1 | 176,319 |
| Ontario | 0 | 1 | 1 | 0 | 0 | 0 | 0 | 0 | 0 | 2 | 170,274 |
| Orange | 1 | 2 | 0 | 0 | 0 | 0 | 0 | 1 | 2 | 0 | 140,572 |
| Oxnard | 7 | 0 | 0 | 0 | 0 | 0 | 0 | 4 | 3 | 0 | 207,221 |
| Palmdale | 2 | 0 | 0 | 0 | 0 | 0 | 1 | 0 | 1 | 0 | 159,613 |
| Palm Desert | 0 | 1 | 0 | 0 | 0 | 0 | 1 | 0 | 0 | 0 | 51,847 |
| Palm Springs | 0 | 0 | 3 | 0 | 0 | 0 | 0 | 2 | 0 | 1 | 47,388 |
| Palo Alto | 3 | 0 | 0 | 0 | 0 | 0 | 0 | 1 | 1 | 1 | 67,560 |
| Paramount | 2 | 0 | 0 | 0 | 0 | 0 | 1 | 1 | 0 | 0 | 55,727 |
| Pasadena | 0 | 0 | 2 | 0 | 0 | 0 | 0 | 0 | 1 | 1 | 141,815 |
| Placentia | 1 | 0 | 0 | 1 | 0 | 0 | 0 | 2 | 0 | 0 | 52,753 |
| Pleasant Hill | 1 | 0 | 0 | 0 | 0 | 0 | 0 | 1 | 0 | 0 | 34,829 |
| Port Hueneme | 1 | 0 | 0 | 0 | 0 | 0 | 1 | 0 | 0 | 0 | 22,249 |
| Rancho Cucamonga | 4 | 0 | 0 | 0 | 0 | 0 | 2 | 1 | 0 | 1 | 176,376 |
| Rancho Palos Verdes | 1 | 1 | 0 | 0 | 0 | 0 | 0 | 0 | 2 | 0 | 42,993 |
| Redding | 6 | 3 | 2 | 0 | 0 | 0 | 1 | 4 | 2 | 4 | 92,020 |
| Redlands | 2 | 0 | 0 | 0 | 0 | 0 | 0 | 1 | 0 | 1 | 71,078 |
| Redondo Beach | 1 | 0 | 0 | 0 | 0 | 0 | 0 | 1 | 0 | 0 | 68,492 |
| Rialto | 1 | 0 | 0 | 0 | 0 | 0 | 0 | 1 | 0 | 0 | 103,590 |
| Richmond | 1 | 0 | 0 | 0 | 0 | 0 | 0 | 0 | 0 | 1 | 109,716 |
| Riverside | 3 | 4 | 0 | 0 | 0 | 0 | 0 | 0 | 5 | 2 | 323,064 |
| Roseville | 1 | 1 | 0 | 0 | 0 | 0 | 0 | 2 | 0 | 0 | 131,039 |
| Sacramento | 3 | 0 | 4 | 0 | 0 | 1 | 1 | 4 | 2 | 1 | 489,717 |
| Salinas | 1 | 0 | 1 | 0 | 0 | 1 | 0 | 0 | 2 | 1 | 158,185 |
| San Bernardino | 3 | 0 | 1 | 0 | 0 | 0 | 1 | 2 | 1 | 0 | 216,477 |
| San Diego | 14 | 7 | 12 | 0 | 0 | 3 | 10 | 9 | 6 | 11 | 1,400,467 |
| San Dimas | 1 | 0 | 0 | 0 | 0 | 0 | 0 | 1 | 0 | 0 | 34,955 |
| San Francisco | 10 | 6 | 9 | 0 | 0 | 3 | 8 | 11 | 7 | 2 | 863,782 |
| San Jacinto | 1 | 0 | 0 | 0 | 0 | 0 | 0 | 1 | 0 | 0 | 47,022 |
| San Jose | 3 | 2 | 1 | 0 | 0 | 0 | 2 | 1 | 0 | 3 | 1,031,458 |
| San Juan Capistrano | 0 | 1 | 0 | 0 | 0 | 0 | 0 | 1 | 0 | 0 | 36,666 |
| San Leandro | 2 | 1 | 0 | 0 | 0 | 0 | 1 | 0 | 1 | 1 | 90,438 |
| San Marino | 1 | 0 | 0 | 0 | 0 | 0 | 0 | 0 | 1 | 0 | 13,491 |
| San Mateo | 0 | 1 | 1 | 0 | 0 | 0 | 0 | 0 | 0 | 2 | 104,306 |
| Santa Ana | 2 | 5 | 2 | 0 | 0 | 1 | 2 | 3 | 5 | 0 | 337,304 |

(Number.)

| State/agency | Number of incidents per bias motivation | | | | | | Number of incidents per quarter | | | | Population[1] |
| --- | --- | --- | --- | --- | --- | --- | --- | --- | --- | --- | --- |
| | Race/ Ethnicity/ Ancestry | Religion | Sexual orientation | Disability | Gender | Gender Identity | 1st quarter | 2nd quarter | 3rd quarter | 4th quarter | |
| Santa Barbara | 0 | 0 | 1 | 0 | 0 | 0 | 0 | 1 | 0 | 0 | 91,877 |
| Santa Clarita | 2 | 1 | 1 | 0 | 0 | 0 | 2 | 1 | 0 | 1 | 211,132 |
| Santa Cruz | 4 | 1 | 0 | 0 | 0 | 1 | 2 | 1 | 1 | 2 | 64,076 |
| Santa Monica | 0 | 0 | 1 | 0 | 0 | 1 | 0 | | 2 | 0 | 93,796 |
| Santa Rosa | 1 | 0 | 1 | 0 | 0 | 0 | 1 | 0 | 0 | 1 | 175,738 |
| Santee | 0 | 0 | 1 | 0 | 0 | 0 | 0 | 0 | 1 | 0 | 57,934 |
| Scotts Valley | 1 | 0 | 0 | 0 | 0 | 0 | 0 | 0 | 1 | 0 | 11,926 |
| Seaside | 1 | 0 | 0 | 0 | 0 | 0 | 0 | 1 | 0 | 0 | 34,459 |
| Selma | 0 | 1 | 0 | 0 | 0 | 0 | 0 | 0 | 1 | 0 | 24,532 |
| Simi Valley | 4 | 1 | 0 | 0 | 0 | 0 | 1 | 1 | 1 | 2 | 127,472 |
| Sonoma | 1 | 1 | 0 | 0 | 0 | 0 | 0 | 1 | 1 | 0 | 11,107 |
| Sonora | 0 | 0 | 1 | 0 | 0 | 0 | 0 | 1 | 0 | 0 | 4,779 |
| South Gate | 0 | 2 | 0 | 0 | 0 | 0 | 0 | 0 | 0 | 2 | 96,775 |
| Stockton | 1 | 1 | 1 | 0 | 0 | 1 | 1 | 0 | 1 | 2 | 304,890 |
| Temecula | 1 | 0 | 0 | 0 | 0 | 0 | 0 | 0 | 1 | 0 | 111,673 |
| Thousand Oaks | 0 | 2 | 0 | 0 | 0 | 0 | 0 | 1 | 1 | 0 | 129,976 |
| Torrance | 0 | 1 | 0 | 0 | 0 | 0 | 0 | 1 | 0 | 0 | 149,243 |
| Tracy | 2 | 1 | 0 | 0 | 0 | 0 | 0 | 1 | 2 | 0 | 86,477 |
| Turlock | 3 | 2 | 1 | 0 | 0 | 0 | 1 | 1 | 1 | 3 | 71,895 |
| Upland | 1 | 0 | 0 | 0 | 0 | 0 | 0 | 0 | 1 | 0 | 76,581 |
| Ventura | 2 | 0 | 2 | 0 | 0 | 0 | 1 | 1 | 2 | 0 | 110,077 |
| Victorville | 0 | 0 | 1 | 0 | 0 | 1 | 1 | 1 | 0 | 0 | 123,332 |
| Visalia | 2 | 0 | 1 | 0 | 0 | 0 | 1 | 1 | 0 | 1 | 130,405 |
| Vista | 2 | 0 | 1 | 0 | 0 | 0 | 0 | 0 | 3 | 0 | 99,097 |
| Walnut Creek | 1 | 2 | 1 | 0 | 0 | 0 | 2 | 0 | 1 | 1 | 68,530 |
| West Covina | 2 | 0 | 0 | 0 | 0 | 0 | 2 | 0 | 0 | 0 | 109,030 |
| West Hollywood | 3 | 0 | 3 | 0 | 0 | 0 | 2 | 1 | 2 | 1 | 36,256 |
| Westminster | 0 | 1 | 1 | 0 | 0 | 0 | 0 | 1 | 1 | 0 | 92,640 |
| **Universities and Colleges** | 14 | 8 | 4 | 0 | 0 | 2 | | | | | |
| California State Polytechnic University, San Luis Obispo | 1 | 1 | 0 | 0 | 0 | 0 | 0 | 0 | 0 | 2 | 20,186 |
| California State University | | | | | | | | | | | |
| Dominguez Hills | 1 | 0 | 0 | 0 | 0 | 0 | 0 | 0 | 0 | 1 | 14,687 |
| Fullerton | 0 | 0 | 0 | 0 | 0 | 1 | 1 | 0 | 0 | 0 | 38,128 |
| Northridge | 1 | 0 | 0 | 0 | 0 | 0 | 0 | 0 | 1 | 0 | 40,131 |
| San Jose | 1 | 0 | 0 | 0 | 0 | 1 | 1 | 0 | 0 | 1 | 32,713 |
| Humboldt State University | 1 | 1 | 1 | 0 | 0 | 0 | 0 | 1 | 1 | 1 | 8,485 |
| San Diego State University | 1 | 1 | 0 | 0 | 0 | 0 | 0 | 0 | 1 | 1 | 33,483 |
| University of California | | | | | | | | | | | |
| Berkeley | 0 | 2 | 0 | 0 | 0 | 0 | 1 | 0 | 1 | 0 | 37,565 |
| Davis | 2 | 3 | 0 | 0 | 0 | 0 | 0 | 1 | 3 | 1 | 34,508 |
| Los Angeles | 5 | 0 | 2 | 0 | 0 | 0 | 3 | 1 | 2 | 1 | 41,845 |
| Santa Cruz | 0 | 0 | 1 | 0 | 0 | 0 | 1 | 0 | 0 | 0 | 17,866 |
| Ventura County Community College District | 1 | 0 | 0 | 0 | 0 | 0 | 0 | 0 | 1 | 0 | 33,956 |
| **Metropolitan Counties** | 43 | 18 | 22 | 2 | 0 | 0 | | | | | |
| Kern | 2 | 0 | 2 | 0 | 0 | 0 | 0 | 2 | 1 | 1 | |
| Kings | 0 | 0 | 1 | 0 | 0 | 0 | 0 | 0 | 0 | 1 | |
| Los Angeles | 16 | 2 | 9 | 1 | 0 | 0 | 4 | 12 | 8 | 4 | |
| Marin | 0 | 1 | 0 | 0 | 0 | 0 | 1 | 0 | 0 | 0 | |
| Orange | 1 | 1 | 0 | 0 | 0 | 0 | 1 | 0 | 0 | 1 | |
| Placer | 0 | 3 | 0 | 0 | 0 | 0 | 0 | 0 | 3 | 0 | |
| Riverside | 1 | 1 | 1 | 0 | 0 | 0 | 0 | 2 | 0 | 1 | |
| Sacramento | 6 | 2 | 0 | 0 | 0 | 0 | 2 | 2 | 3 | 1 | |
| San Bernardino | 5 | 0 | 1 | 0 | 0 | 0 | 2 | 0 | 2 | 2 | |
| San Diego | 8 | 4 | 3 | 0 | 0 | 0 | 4 | 4 | 3 | 4 | |
| San Joaquin | 0 | 2 | 1 | 0 | 0 | 0 | 0 | 0 | 1 | 2 | |
| San Luis Obispo | 1 | 0 | 1 | 0 | 0 | 0 | 1 | 0 | 1 | 0 | |
| San Mateo | 2 | 0 | 1 | 0 | 0 | 0 | 0 | 0 | 1 | 2 | |
| Santa Clara | 0 | 1 | 0 | 1 | 0 | 0 | 0 | 1 | 1 | 0 | |
| Sonoma | 1 | 1 | 0 | 0 | 0 | 0 | 0 | 0 | 0 | 2 | |
| Stanislaus | 0 | 0 | 1 | 0 | 0 | 0 | 1 | 0 | 0 | 0 | |
| Ventura | 0 | 0 | 1 | 0 | 0 | 0 | 0 | 1 | 0 | 0 | |
| **Nonmetropolitan Counties** | | | | | | | | | | | |
| Amador | 1 | 1 | 0 | 0 | 0 | 0 | 0 | 2 | 0 | 0 | |
| Calaveras | 0 | 0 | 1 | 0 | 0 | 0 | 0 | 0 | 0 | 1 | |
| Colusa | 1 | 0 | 0 | 0 | 0 | 0 | 0 | 1 | 0 | 0 | |

| State/agency | Number of incidents per bias motivation | | | | | | Number of incidents per quarter | | | | Population[1] |
|---|---|---|---|---|---|---|---|---|---|---|---|
| | Race/ Ethnicity/ Ancestry | Religion | Sexual orientation | Disability | Gender | Gender Identity | 1st quarter | 2nd quarter | 3rd quarter | 4th quarter | |
| Del Norte | 0 | 0 | 0 | 1 | 0 | 0 | 0 | 0 | 0 | 1 | |
| Lake | 1 | 0 | 1 | 0 | 0 | 0 | 0 | 1 | 1 | 0 | |
| Mendocino | 1 | 0 | 0 | 0 | 0 | 0 | 1 | 0 | 0 | 0 | |
| Nevada | 2 | 0 | 0 | 0 | 0 | 0 | 0 | 0 | 2 | 0 | |
| **Other Agencies** | 14 | 1 | 11 | 0 | 0 | 0 | | | | | |
| East Bay Regional Parks, Alameda County | 0 | 1 | 0 | 0 | 0 | 0 | 0 | 0 | 0 | 1 | |
| Los Angeles Transportation Services Bureau | 10 | 1 | 5 | 0 | 1 | 0 | 7 | 7 | 2 | 1 | |
| Port of San Diego Harbor | 0 | 1 | 0 | 0 | 0 | 0 | 0 | 0 | 0 | 1 | |
| San Francisco Bay Area Rapid Transit | | | | | | | | | | | |
| Alameda County | 2 | 1 | 0 | 0 | 0 | 0 | 1 | 2 | 0 | 0 | |
| Contra Costa County | 1 | 1 | 0 | 0 | 0 | 0 | 1 | 0 | 1 | 0 | |
| San Francisco County | 1 | 0 | 0 | 0 | 0 | 0 | 0 | 1 | 0 | 0 | |
| San Mateo County | 1 | 1 | 0 | 0 | 0 | 0 | 1 | 0 | 0 | 1 | |
| **COLORADO** | | | | | | | | | | | |
| **Total** | 65 | 16 | 20 | 3 | 0 | 3 | | | | | |
| **Cities** | 47 | 9 | 19 | 2 | 0 | 1 | | | | | |
| Arvada | 1 | 0 | 1 | 0 | 0 | 0 | 1 | 0 | 1 | 0 | 113,008 |
| Aspen | 1 | 0 | 0 | 0 | 0 | 0 | 0 | 0 | 0 | 1 | 350,948 |
| Aurora | 4 | 1 | 1 | 0 | 0 | 0 | 0 | 2 | 2 | 2 | 36,185 |
| Basalt | 1 | 0 | 0 | 0 | 0 | 0 | 0 | 0 | 1 | 0 | 16,291 |
| Boulder | 1 | 0 | 0 | 0 | 0 | 0 | 1 | 0 | 0 | 0 | 54,253 |
| Breckenridge | 1 | 0 | 0 | 0 | 0 | 0 | 0 | 1 | 0 | 0 | 107,485 |
| Castle Rock | 1 | 0 | 0 | 0 | 0 | 0 | 0 | 0 | 1 | 0 | 444,949 |
| Centennial | 1 | 0 | 0 | 0 | 0 | 0 | 0 | 1 | 0 | 0 | 50,754 |
| Colorado Springs | 5 | 1 | 2 | 0 | 0 | 0 | 2 | 2 | 3 | 1 | 665,353 |
| Craig | 1 | 0 | 0 | 0 | 0 | 0 | 0 | 1 | 0 | 0 | 17,710 |
| Denver | 8 | 2 | 9 | 1 | 0 | 0 | 3 | 8 | 6 | 3 | 154,015 |
| Durango | 1 | 0 | 1 | 0 | 0 | 0 | 0 | 2 | 0 | 0 | 11,422 |
| Englewood | 0 | 0 | 1 | 0 | 0 | 0 | 0 | 0 | 1 | 0 | 4,558 |
| Fort Collins | 3 | 0 | 1 | 0 | 0 | 0 | 1 | 1 | 2 | 0 | 9,909 |
| Glenwood Springs | 2 | 0 | 0 | 0 | 0 | 0 | 0 | 1 | 0 | 1 | 19,556 |
| Golden | 1 | 0 | 0 | 0 | 0 | 0 | 1 | 0 | 0 | 0 | 59,972 |
| Grand Junction | 1 | 0 | 1 | 0 | 0 | 0 | 0 | 1 | 1 | 0 | 14,824 |
| Greeley | 1 | 0 | 0 | 0 | 0 | 0 | 0 | 0 | 1 | 0 | 5,865 |
| Greenwood Village | 2 | 1 | 0 | 0 | 0 | 0 | 1 | 1 | 0 | 1 | 1,677 |
| La Junta | 1 | 0 | 0 | 0 | 0 | 0 | 0 | 1 | 0 | 0 | 148,236 |
| Littleton | 0 | 1 | 0 | 0 | 0 | 0 | 0 | 1 | 0 | 0 | 13,824 |
| Longmont | 2 | 0 | 0 | 0 | 0 | 0 | 1 | 0 | 1 | 0 | 90,813 |
| Loveland | 0 | 1 | 0 | 0 | 0 | 1 | 0 | 0 | 1 | 1 | 72,465 |
| Pueblo | 5 | 2 | 2 | 0 | 0 | 0 | 3 | 2 | 0 | 4 | 4,595 |
| Sterling | 1 | 0 | 0 | 0 | 0 | 0 | 1 | 0 | 0 | 0 | 1,100 |
| Trinidad | 0 | 0 | 0 | 1 | 0 | 0 | 0 | 1 | 0 | 0 | 108,591 |
| Walsenburg | 2 | 0 | 0 | 0 | 0 | 0 | 0 | 1 | 1 | 0 | 12,114 |
| **Universities and Colleges** | 2 | 1 | 0 | 0 | 0 | 0 | | | | | |
| Auraria Higher Education Center[2] | 0 | 1 | 0 | 0 | 0 | 0 | 1 | 0 | 0 | 0 | |
| University of Colorado | | | | | | | | | | | |
| Boulder | 1 | 0 | 0 | 0 | 0 | 0 | 0 | 1 | 0 | 0 | 32,432 |
| Colorado Springs | 1 | 0 | 0 | 0 | 0 | 0 | 0 | 0 | 0 | 1 | 11,761 |
| **Metropolitan Counties** | 14 | 4 | 1 | 1 | 0 | 2 | | | | | |
| Adams | 1 | 0 | 0 | 0 | 0 | 0 | 0 | 0 | 1 | 0 | |
| Arapahoe | 5 | 3 | 0 | 1 | 0 | 0 | 1 | 1 | 3 | 4 | |
| Boulder | 2 | 1 | 0 | 0 | 0 | 1 | 0 | 1 | 3 | 0 | |
| El Paso | 1 | 0 | 0 | 0 | 0 | 0 | 0 | 1 | 0 | 0 | |
| Jefferson | 0 | 0 | 0 | 0 | 0 | 1 | 0 | 1 | 0 | 0 | |
| Larimer | 1 | 0 | 1 | 0 | 0 | 0 | 1 | 1 | 0 | 0 | |
| Mesa | 1 | 0 | 0 | 0 | 0 | 0 | 0 | 1 | 0 | 0 | |
| Pueblo | 1 | 0 | 0 | 0 | 0 | 0 | 0 | 1 | 0 | 0 | |
| Weld | 2 | 0 | 0 | 0 | 0 | 0 | 0 | 0 | 2 | 0 | |

## Table 13. Hate Crime Incidents Per Bias Motivation and Quarter, by Selected State and Agency, 2015—*Continued*

(Number.)

| State/agency | Number of incidents per bias motivation | | | | | | Number of incidents per quarter | | | | Population[1] |
|---|---|---|---|---|---|---|---|---|---|---|---|
| | Race/ Ethnicity/ Ancestry | Religion | Sexual orientation | Disability | Gender | Gender Identity | 1st quarter | 2nd quarter | 3rd quarter | 4th quarter | |
| **Nonmetropolitan Counties......** | | | | | | | | | | | |
| La Plata................................. | Garfield | 1 | 1 | 0 | 0 | 0 | 0 | 0 | 2 | 0 | 0 |
| Montezuma............................ | La Plata | 0 | 1 | 0 | 0 | 0 | 0 | 1 | 0 | 0 | 0 |
| Summit.................................. | Pitkin | 1 | 0 | 0 | 0 | 0 | 0 | 1 | 0 | 0 | 0 |
| **CONNECTICUT** | | | | | | | | | | | |
| **Total** ..................... | 62 | 19 | 9 | 4 | 0 | 0 | | | | | |
| **Cities** ......................... | 56 | 26 | 22 | 1 | 0 | 0 | | | | | |
| Bethel................................... | 1 | 0 | 0 | 0 | 0 | 0 | 0 | 0 | 0 | 1 | 19,560 |
| Bloomfield............................ | 0 | 2 | 0 | 0 | 0 | 0 | 0 | 0 | 2 | 0 | 20,901 |
| Bridgeport............................ | 5 | 0 | 1 | 0 | 0 | 0 | 1 | 3 | 1 | 1 | 148,313 |
| Bristol................................... | 1 | 0 | 1 | 0 | 0 | 0 | 0 | 1 | 0 | 1 | 60,593 |
| Cheshire................................ | 1 | 0 | 0 | 0 | 0 | 0 | 0 | 1 | 0 | 0 | 29,245 |
| Danbury................................ | 2 | 1 | 0 | 1 | 0 | 0 | 1 | 1 | 1 | 1 | 84,404 |
| Derby.................................... | 1 | 0 | 0 | 0 | 0 | 0 | 0 | 0 | 1 | 0 | 12,735 |
| Groton Town ........................ | 0 | 1 | 0 | 0 | 0 | 0 | 0 | 1 | 0 | 0 | 30,387 |
| Guilford................................ | 2 | 0 | 0 | 0 | 0 | 0 | | | | 2 | 22,421 |
| Hartford[3] ............................. | 1 | 1 | 1 | 0 | 0 | 0 | | 1 | 1 | | 124,553 |
| Manchester........................... | 1 | 1 | 1 | 0 | 0 | 0 | | 1 | | 2 | 58,070 |
| Meriden................................ | 1 | 0 | 0 | 1 | 0 | 0 | | 1 | 1 | | 60,149 |
| Middletown.......................... | 3 | 0 | 1 | 0 | 0 | 0 | 0 | 1 | 1 | 2 | 46,894 |
| New Britain........................... | 1 | 0 | 0 | 0 | 0 | 0 | | | 1 | | 72,788 |
| New Haven............................ | 7 | 0 | 1 | 0 | 0 | 0 | 1 | 4 | 2 | 1 | 130,403 |
| Newington............................ | 1 | 0 | 0 | 0 | 0 | 0 | | | | 1 | 30,714 |
| New London ......................... | 1 | 0 | 0 | 0 | 0 | 0 | 0 | 0 | 0 | 1 | 27,312 |
| New Milford .......................... | 1 | 0 | 0 | 0 | 0 | 0 | 1 | 0 | 0 | 0 | 27,317 |
| North Branford ..................... | 0 | 1 | 0 | 0 | 0 | 0 | 1 | 0 | 0 | 0 | 14,300 |
| North Haven ......................... | 1 | 0 | 0 | 0 | 0 | 0 | 0 | 0 | 1 | 0 | 23,865 |
| Norwalk................................ | 1 | 0 | 0 | 0 | 0 | 0 | 1 | 0 | 0 | 0 | 88,692 |
| Old Saybrook ........................ | 1 | 0 | 0 | 0 | 0 | 0 | 1 | 0 | 0 | 0 | 10,213 |
| Plainfield.............................. | 1 | 0 | 0 | 0 | 0 | 0 | 0 | 1 | 0 | 0 | 15,071 |
| Redding................................ | 0 | 1 | 0 | 0 | 0 | 0 | 0 | 0 | 1 | 0 | 9,344 |
| Simsbury.............................. | 0 | 1 | 0 | 0 | 0 | 0 | 0 | 0 | 0 | 1 | 24,093 |
| Southington.......................... | 1 | 0 | 0 | 0 | 0 | 0 | 0 | 0 | 1 | 0 | 43,979 |
| Stamford .............................. | 7 | 2 | 0 | 1 | 0 | 0 | 2 | 1 | 2 | 5 | 129,682 |
| Stonington............................ | 1 | 0 | 0 | 0 | 0 | 0 | 1 | 0 | 0 | 0 | 18,505 |
| Stratford ............................... | 2 | 0 | 0 | 0 | 0 | 0 | 1 | 0 | 1 | 0 | 53,058 |
| Suffield................................. | 1 | 0 | 0 | 0 | 0 | 0 | 0 | 0 | 1 | 0 | 15,823 |
| Torrington............................ | 3 | 1 | 0 | 0 | 0 | 0 | 0 | 1 | 0 | 3 | 34,910 |
| Trumbull .............................. | 1 | 1 | 1 | 0 | 0 | 0 | 0 | 0 | 1 | 2 | 36,708 |
| Vernon.................................. | 1 | 0 | 0 | 0 | 0 | 0 | 1 | 0 | 0 | 0 | 29,079 |
| Wallingford........................... | 1 | 0 | 0 | 0 | 0 | 0 | 0 | 0 | 1 | 0 | 45,054 |
| Waterford.............................. | 1 | 1 | 0 | 0 | 0 | 0 | 0 | 0 | 0 | 2 | 19,407 |
| West Hartford........................ | 1 | 0 | 0 | 0 | 0 | 0 | 1 | 0 | 0 | 0 | 63,301 |
| West Haven .......................... | 1 | 0 | 1 | 0 | 0 | 0 | 0 | 1 | 0 | 1 | 54,741 |
| Westport............................... | 0 | 1 | 0 | 1 | 0 | 0 | 1 | 1 | 0 | 0 | 27,848 |
| Winchester ........................... | 1 | 2 | 0 | 0 | 0 | 0 | 2 | 0 | 0 | 1 | 10,855 |
| Windsor................................. | 1 | 0 | 0 | 0 | 0 | 0 | 1 | 0 | 0 | 0 | 29,063 |
| **Universities and Colleges .......** | | | | | | | | | | | |
| Central Connecticut State University.............................. | 2 | 0 | 0 | 0 | 0 | 0 | 1 | 0 | 1 | 0 | 12,037 |
| University of Connecticut, Storrs, Avery Point and Hartford[2] .......... | 1 | 0 | 0 | 0 | 0 | 0 | 0 | 0 | 1 | 0 | |
| Western Connecticut State University.............................. | 2 | 0 | 0 | 0 | 0 | 0 | 1 | 0 | 0 | 1 | 5,952 |
| **State Police Agencies..............** | | | | | | | | | | | |
| Connecticut State Police ............ | 0 | 2 | 1 | 0 | 0 | 0 | 1 | 0 | 1 | 1 | 524,558 |
| **DELAWARE** | | | | | | | | | | | |
| **Total** ........................... | 9 | 2 | 0 | 0 | 0 | 0 | | | | | |
| **Cities** ......................... | 5 | 0 | 0 | 0 | 0 | 0 | | | | | |
| Laurel................................... | 1 | 0 | 0 | 0 | 0 | 0 | 0 | 0 | 1 | 0 | 4,051 |
| Milford ................................. | 1 | 0 | 0 | 0 | 0 | 0 | 0 | 0 | 0 | 1 | 10,331 |
| Milton................................... | 1 | 0 | 0 | 0 | 0 | 0 | 1 | 0 | 0 | 0 | 2,805 |
| Wilmington ........................... | 2 | 0 | 0 | 0 | 0 | 0 | 1 | 0 | 0 | 1 | 72,078 |

| State/agency | Number of incidents per bias motivation | | | | | | Number of incidents per quarter | | | | Population[1] |
|---|---|---|---|---|---|---|---|---|---|---|---|
| | Race/ Ethnicity/ Ancestry | Religion | Sexual orientation | Disability | Gender | Gender Identity | 1st quarter | 2nd quarter | 3rd quarter | 4th quarter | |
| **Metropolitan Counties** ........... | 3 | 0 | 0 | 0 | 0 | 0 | | | | | |
| New Castle County Police Department .............................. | 3 | 0 | 0 | 0 | 0 | 0 | 1 | 1 | 0 | 1 | |
| **State Police Agencies** .............. | 0 | 2 | 0 | 0 | 0 | 0 | | | | | |
| Sussex County ........................... | 0 | 2 | 0 | 0 | 0 | 0 | 0 | 2 | 0 | 0 | |
| **Other Agencies** ....................... | 1 | 0 | 0 | 0 | 0 | 0 | | | | | |
| State Fire Marshal ..................... | 1 | 0 | 0 | 0 | 0 | 0 | 0 | 1 | 0 | 0 | |
| **DISTRICT OF COLUMBIA** | | | | | | | | | | | |
| Total ....................................... | 23 | 5 | 27 | 0 | 0 | 10 | | | | | |
| **Cities** ..................................... | 22 | 5 | 27 | 0 | 0 | 10 | | | | | |
| Washington .............................. | 22 | 5 | 27 | 0 | 0 | 10 | 13 | 13 | 18 | 20 | 672,228 |
| **Other Agencies** ....................... | 1 | 0 | 0 | 0 | 0 | 0 | | | | | |
| Metro Transit Police ................... | 1 | 0 | 0 | 0 | 0 | 0 | 0 | 1 | 0 | 0 | |
| **FLORIDA** | | | | | | | | | | | |
| Total ....................................... | 44 | 13 | 14 | 0 | 0 | 1 | | | | | |
| **Cities** ..................................... | 21 | 13 | 10 | 0 | 0 | 1 | | | | | |
| Clearwater ................................ | 2 | 0 | 0 | 0 | 0 | 0 | | 2 | | | 111,316 |
| Coral Springs ............................ | 0 | 1 | 0 | 0 | 0 | 0 | | | 1 | | 129,631 |
| Daytona Beach Shores ................ | 1 | 0 | 0 | 0 | 0 | 0 | | | 1 | | 4,336 |
| Deland ...................................... | 0 | 1 | 0 | 0 | 0 | 0 | | | 1 | | 29,773 |
| Fort Myers ................................ | 0 | 0 | 1 | 0 | 0 | 0 | | | 1 | | 73,218 |
| Gainesville ................................ | 2 | 0 | 1 | 0 | 0 | 0 | | | 2 | 1 | 129,410 |
| Melbourne ................................ | 0 | 1 | 0 | 0 | 0 | 0 | | 1 | | | 79,032 |
| Miami Beach .............................. | 2 | 6 | 3 | 0 | 0 | 1 | 6 | 1 | 1 | 4 | 92,641 |
| Miami Gardens .......................... | 6 | 0 | 0 | 0 | 0 | 0 | 4 | 1 | | 1 | 113,469 |
| New Port Richey ........................ | 0 | 0 | 1 | 0 | 0 | 0 | | 1 | | | 15,688 |
| North Miami ............................. | 0 | 0 | 1 | 0 | 0 | 0 | | 1 | | | 62,010 |
| North Palm Beach ...................... | 0 | 1 | 0 | 0 | 0 | 0 | | | | 1 | 12,597 |
| North Port ................................. | 1 | 0 | 0 | 0 | 0 | 0 | 1 | | | | 61,148 |
| Ocala ........................................ | 1 | 0 | 0 | 0 | 0 | 0 | 1 | | | | 57,891 |
| Palm Bay ................................... | 3 | 0 | 1 | 0 | 0 | 0 | 1 | 2 | 1 | | 106,469 |
| Pembroke Pines ......................... | 0 | 2 | 0 | 0 | 0 | 0 | | | 1 | 1 | 167,266 |
| Port St. Lucie ............................. | 1 | 0 | 0 | 0 | 0 | 0 | | 1 | | | 176,364 |
| South Daytona ........................... | 1 | 0 | 0 | 0 | 0 | 0 | | | 1 | | 12,435 |
| Tallahassee ................................ | 0 | 0 | 1 | 0 | 0 | 0 | | 1 | | | 189,709 |
| Venice ....................................... | 1 | 0 | 0 | 0 | 0 | 0 | | | 1 | | 21,980 |
| West Palm Beach ....................... | 0 | 1 | 0 | 0 | 0 | 0 | 1 | | | | 104,919 |
| Winter Garden ........................... | 0 | 0 | 1 | 0 | 0 | 0 | | | | 1 | 39,783 |
| **Universities and Colleges** ........ | 1 | 0 | 0 | 0 | 0 | 0 | | | | | |
| University of South Florida, Tampa ........................................ | 1 | 0 | 0 | 0 | 0 | 0 | 1 | | | | 41,938 |
| **Metropolitan Counties** ............ | 22 | 0 | 4 | 0 | 0 | 0 | | | | | |
| Charlotte ................................... | 1 | 0 | 0 | 0 | 0 | 0 | | | | 1 | |
| Clay .......................................... | 3 | 0 | 0 | 0 | 0 | 0 | | 1 | 1 | 1 | |
| Collier ....................................... | 1 | 0 | 1 | 0 | 0 | 0 | | 1 | 1 | | |
| Escambia ................................... | 2 | 0 | 0 | 0 | 0 | 0 | 1 | | | 1 | |
| Lake .......................................... | 1 | 0 | 0 | 0 | 0 | 0 | | | 1 | | |
| Orange ...................................... | 2 | 0 | 1 | 0 | 0 | 0 | | 1 | | 2 | |
| Osceola ..................................... | 1 | 0 | 0 | 0 | 0 | 0 | | | | 1 | |
| Pasco ........................................ | 1 | 0 | 1 | 0 | 0 | 0 | | 2 | | | |
| Pinellas ..................................... | 0 | 0 | 1 | 0 | 0 | 0 | | | | 1 | |
| Seminole ................................... | 1 | 0 | 0 | 0 | 0 | 0 | | 1 | | | |
| St. Johns ................................... | 2 | 0 | 0 | 0 | 0 | 0 | | 2 | | | |
| Volusia ...................................... | 6 | 0 | 0 | 0 | 0 | 0 | 1 | 2 | 2 | 1 | |
| Walton ...................................... | 1 | 0 | 0 | 0 | 0 | 0 | | 1 | | | |

# Table 13. Hate Crime Incidents Per Bias Motivation and Quarter, by Selected State and Agency, 2015—*Continued*

(Number.)

| State/agency | Number of incidents per bias motivation | | | | | | Number of incidents per quarter | | | | Population[1] |
|---|---|---|---|---|---|---|---|---|---|---|---|
| | Race/ Ethnicity/ Ancestry | Religion | Sexual orientation | Disability | Gender | Gender Identity | 1st quarter | 2nd quarter | 3rd quarter | 4th quarter | |
| **GEORGIA** | | | | | | | | | | | |
| Total ......................... | 32 | 5 | 7 | 0 | 0 | 0 | | | | | |
| **Cities** ..................... | 2 | 0 | 3 | 0 | 0 | 0 | | | | | |
| Athens-Clarke County................ | 0 | 0 | 1 | 0 | 0 | 0 | 1 | 0 | 0 | 0 | 120,858 |
| Atlanta ............................ | 2 | 0 | 2 | 0 | 0 | 0 | 0 | 4 | 0 | 0 | 464,710 |
| **Universities and Colleges** ........ | | | | | | | | | | | |
| Georgia Institute of Technology... | 1 | 1 | 0 | 0 | 0 | 0 | 0 | 0 | 1 | 1 | 23,109 |
| University of Georgia ................. | 2 | 0 | 1 | 0 | 0 | 0 | 2 | 1 | 0 | 0 | 35,197 |
| **Metropolitan Counties** ........... | 27 | 4 | 3 | 0 | 0 | 0 | | | | | |
| Cobb County Police Department. | 23 | 4 | 3 | 0 | 0 | 0 | 5 | 8 | 13 | 4 | |
| Gwinnett County Police Department ................................ | 1 | 0 | 0 | 0 | 0 | 0 | 0 | 0 | 1 | 0 | |
| Henry County Police Department | 3 | 0 | 0 | 0 | 0 | 0 | 0 | 1 | 1 | 1 | |
| **IDAHO** | | | | | | | | | | | |
| Total ......................... | 14 | 12 | 6 | 2 | 0 | 0 | | | | | |
| **Cities** ..................... | 9 | 5 | 6 | 2 | 0 | 0 | | | | | |
| Boise.............................. | 1 | 2 | 2 | 0 | 0 | 0 | 1 | 1 | 2 | 1 | 218,844 |
| Caldwell .......................... | 1 | 0 | 0 | 0 | 0 | 0 | 1 | 0 | 0 | 0 | 51,206 |
| Coeur d'Alene ........................ | 1 | 0 | 0 | 0 | 0 | 0 | 1 | 0 | 0 | 0 | 48,871 |
| Garden City ....................... | 0 | 0 | 1 | 0 | 0 | 0 | 0 | 1 | 0 | 0 | 11,533 |
| Grangeville ....................... | 0 | 0 | 1 | 0 | 0 | 0 | 0 | 0 | 1 | 0 | 3,139 |
| Kimberly .......................... | 1 | 0 | 0 | 1 | 0 | 0 | 1 | 0 | 1 | 0 | 3,570 |
| Nampa............................. | 1 | 0 | 0 | 0 | 0 | 0 | 1 | 0 | 0 | 0 | 89,875 |
| Osburn ............................ | 1 | 0 | 0 | 0 | 0 | 0 | 0 | 1 | 0 | 0 | 1,493 |
| Pocatello........................... | 1 | 1 | 0 | 0 | 0 | 0 | 0 | 0 | 1 | 1 | 54,286 |
| Post Falls.......................... | 1 | 0 | 0 | 0 | 0 | 0 | 0 | 0 | 0 | 1 | 30,461 |
| Rexburg ........................... | 0 | 1 | 0 | 0 | 0 | 0 | 0 | 1 | 0 | 0 | 27,499 |
| Shoshone.......................... | 0 | 0 | 1 | 0 | 0 | 0 | 1 | 0 | 0 | 0 | 1,500 |
| Spirit Lake......................... | 0 | 0 | 1 | 0 | 0 | 0 | 1 | 0 | 0 | 0 | 2,067 |
| St. Maries.......................... | 1 | 0 | 0 | 0 | 0 | 0 | 0 | 1 | 0 | 0 | 2,334 |
| Twin Falls.......................... | 0 | 1 | 0 | 1 | 0 | 0 | 0 | 0 | 0 | 2 | 47,048 |
| **Metropolitan Counties** ........... | 3 | 1 | 0 | 0 | 0 | 0 | | | | | |
| Canyon............................ | 0 | 1 | 0 | 0 | 0 | 0 | 0 | 1 | 0 | 0 | |
| Kootenai........................... | 3 | 0 | 0 | 0 | 0 | 0 | 2 | 1 | 0 | 0 | |
| **Nonmetropolitan Counties**...... | | | | | | | | | | | |
| Cassia.............................. | 1 | 0 | 0 | 0 | 0 | 0 | 0 | 0 | 0 | 1 | |
| Elmore ............................ | 1 | 6 | 0 | 0 | 0 | 0 | 0 | 7 | 0 | 0 | |
| **ILLINOIS** | | | | | | | | | | | |
| Total ......................... | 59 | 12 | 16 | 0 | 1 | 2 | | | | | |
| **Cities** ..................... | 57 | 11 | 15 | 0 | 1 | 2 | | | | | |
| Addison........................... | 0 | 0 | 1 | 0 | 0 | 0 | 0 | 1 | 0 | 0 | 37,370 |
| Aurora............................. | 1 | 0 | 0 | 0 | 0 | 0 | 1 | 0 | 0 | 0 | 201,034 |
| Beecher............................ | 1 | 0 | 0 | 0 | 0 | 0 | 1 | 0 | 0 | 0 | 4,483 |
| Belleville........................... | 1 | 0 | 0 | 0 | 0 | 0 | 0 | 0 | 1 | 0 | 42,150 |
| Berwyn............................ | 1 | 0 | 1 | 0 | 0 | 0 | 0 | 0 | 2 | 0 | 56,697 |
| Bloomington....................... | 1 | 0 | 0 | 0 | 0 | 0 | 0 | 1 | 0 | 0 | 79,233 |
| Centralia........................... | 1 | 0 | 0 | 0 | 0 | 0 | 0 | 0 | 1 | 0 | 12,669 |
| Champaign......................... | 1 | 0 | 0 | 0 | 0 | 0 | 0 | 1 | 0 | 0 | 85,362 |
| Chicago............................ | 19 | 8 | 10 | 0 | 0 | 1 | 6 | 10 | 14 | 8 | 2,728,695 |
| Chicago Ridge ..................... | 1 | 0 | 0 | 0 | 0 | 0 | 1 | 0 | 0 | 0 | 14,463 |
| Danville............................ | 1 | 0 | 0 | 0 | 0 | 0 | 0 | 1 | 0 | 0 | 32,056 |
| De Kalb............................ | 1 | 0 | 1 | 0 | 0 | 0 | 1 | 0 | 1 | 0 | 44,046 |
| Des Plaines........................ | 0 | 0 | 0 | 0 | 0 | 1 | 0 | 0 | 1 | 0 | 59,078 |
| Elgin .............................. | 1 | 0 | 0 | 0 | 0 | 0 | 0 | 1 | 0 | | 111,832 |
| Evanston........................... | 0 | 1 | 0 | 0 | 0 | 0 | 1 | 0 | 0 | 0 | 75,930 |
| Geneseo ........................... | 1 | 0 | 0 | 0 | 0 | 0 | 0 | 1 | 0 | 0 | 6,517 |
| Glenview .......................... | 1 | 0 | 0 | 0 | 0 | 0 | 0 | 1 | 0 | 0 | 47,292 |
| Grayslake.......................... | 0 | 1 | 0 | 0 | 0 | 0 | 1 | 0 | 0 | 0 | 21,048 |
| Lombard ........................... | 1 | 0 | 0 | 0 | 0 | 0 | 0 | 0 | 0 | 1 | 44,008 |
| Macomb............................ | 1 | 0 | 0 | 0 | 0 | 0 | 0 | 1 | 0 | 0 | 18,859 |

# Table 13. Hate Crime Incidents Per Bias Motivation and Quarter, by Selected State and Agency, 2015—*Continued*

(Number.)

| State/agency | Race/ Ethnicity/ Ancestry | Religion | Sexual orientation | Disability | Gender | Gender Identity | 1st quarter | 2nd quarter | 3rd quarter | 4th quarter | Population[1] |
|---|---|---|---|---|---|---|---|---|---|---|---|
| | Number of incidents per bias motivation | | | | | | Number of incidents per quarter | | | | |
| Marissa | 1 | 0 | 0 | 0 | 0 | 0 | 0 | 0 | 1 | 0 | 1,859 |
| Monmouth | 2 | 0 | 0 | 0 | 0 | 0 | 0 | 0 | 1 | 1 | 9,548 |
| Moweaqua | 1 | 0 | 0 | 0 | 0 | 0 | 1 | 0 | 0 | 0 | 1,764 |
| Normal | 2 | 0 | 1 | 0 | 0 | 0 | 1 | 0 | 1 | 1 | 55,096 |
| North Chicago | 3 | 0 | 0 | 0 | 0 | 0 | 0 | 0 | 1 | 2 | 29,898 |
| North Riverside | 1 | 0 | 0 | 0 | 0 | 0 | 0 | 1 | 0 | 0 | 6,703 |
| Oak Forest | 1 | 0 | 0 | 0 | 0 | 0 | 0 | 1 | 0 | 0 | 28,222 |
| Orland Park | 1 | 0 | 0 | 0 | 0 | 0 | 0 | 0 | 1 | 0 | 59,161 |
| Rantoul | 1 | 0 | 0 | 0 | 0 | 0 | 0 | 1 | 0 | 0 | 13,138 |
| Rockford | 2 | 0 | 0 | 0 | 0 | 0 | 1 | 0 | 1 | 0 | 148,178 |
| Rolling Meadows | 1 | 0 | 0 | 0 | 0 | 0 | 1 | 0 | 0 | 0 | 24,321 |
| Round Lake Park | 1 | 0 | 0 | 0 | 0 | 0 | 0 | 1 | 0 | 0 | 7,350 |
| Schaumburg | 0 | 1 | 0 | 0 | 0 | 0 | 1 | 0 | 0 | 0 | 75,050 |
| Silvis | 1 | 0 | 0 | 0 | 0 | 0 | 0 | 1 | 0 | 0 | 7,529 |
| Skokie | 1 | 0 | 0 | 0 | 0 | 0 | 0 | 0 | 0 | 1 | 65,184 |
| Springfield | 2 | 0 | 0 | 0 | 0 | 0 | 2 | 0 | 0 | 0 | 116,875 |
| Tuscola | 0 | 0 | 1 | 0 | 0 | 0 | 0 | 1 | 0 | 0 | 4,458 |
| Urbana | 1 | 0 | 0 | 0 | 1 | 0 | 2 | 0 | 0 | 0 | 42,169 |
| Wheeling | 1 | 0 | 0 | 0 | 0 | 0 | 0 | 0 | 1 | 0 | 38,092 |
| **Universities and Colleges** | 0 | 0 | 1 | 0 | 0 | 0 | | | | | |
| Northern Illinois University | 0 | 0 | 1 | 0 | 0 | 0 | 0 | 0 | 0 | 1 | 20,611 |
| **Metropolitan Counties** | 2 | 1 | 0 | 0 | 0 | 0 | | | | | |
| Champaign | 1 | 0 | 0 | 0 | 0 | 0 | 0 | 1 | 0 | 0 | |
| DuPage | 1 | 0 | 0 | 0 | 0 | 0 | 0 | 1 | 0 | 0 | |
| Sangamon | 0 | 1 | 0 | 0 | 0 | 0 | 0 | 0 | 1 | 0 | |
| **INDIANA** | | | | | | | | | | | |
| **Total** | 43 | 9 | 14 | 0 | 1 | 0 | | | | | |
| **Cities** | 32 | 7 | 12 | 0 | 0 | 0 | | | | | |
| Bloomington[3] | 6 | 2 | 3 | 0 | 0 | 0 | 2 | 1 | 6 | 1 | 84,015 |
| Fort Wayne | 1 | 0 | 0 | 0 | 0 | 0 | 0 | 0 | 1 | 0 | 259,712 |
| Hammond | 2 | 0 | 0 | 0 | 0 | 0 | 0 | 2 | 0 | 0 | 77,803 |
| Indianapolis | 15 | 4 | 7 | 0 | 0 | 0 | 7 | 5 | 6 | 8 | 863,675 |
| Muncie | 1 | 1 | 1 | 0 | 0 | 0 | 1 | 1 | 0 | 1 | 70,217 |
| Plainfield | 1 | 0 | 0 | 0 | 0 | 0 | 0 | 0 | 0 | 1 | 31,123 |
| Shelbyville | 0 | 0 | 1 | 0 | 0 | 0 | 0 | 1 | 0 | 0 | 19,176 |
| South Bend | 6 | 0 | 0 | 0 | 0 | 0 | 2 | 3 | | 1 | 101,240 |
| **Universities and Colleges** | 1 | 0 | 0 | 0 | 0 | 0 | | | | | |
| Bloomington[3] | 2 | 0 | 1 | 0 | 0 | 0 | | | 2 | | 46,416 |
| Indianapolis | 1 | 0 | 0 | 0 | 0 | 0 | | | | 1 | 30,690 |
| **Metropolitan Counties** | 1 | 2 | 0 | 0 | 1 | 0 | | | | | |
| Clark[3] | 0 | 1 | 0 | 0 | 1 | 0 | | | 1 | | |
| Morgan[3] | 1 | 1 | 0 | 0 | 0 | 0 | | | | 1 | |
| **State Police Agencies** | 7 | 0 | 1 | 0 | 0 | 0 | | | | | |
| Decatur County | 1 | 0 | 1 | 0 | 0 | 0 | 1 | 0 | 0 | 1 | |
| Miami County | 1 | 0 | 0 | 0 | 0 | 0 | 1 | 0 | 0 | 0 | |
| Ripley County | 1 | 0 | 0 | 0 | 0 | 0 | 0 | 1 | 0 | 0 | |
| Rush County | 2 | 0 | 0 | 0 | 0 | 0 | 1 | 1 | 0 | 0 | |
| Scott County | 1 | 0 | 0 | 0 | 0 | 0 | 1 | 0 | 0 | 0 | |
| Wayne County | 1 | 0 | 0 | 0 | 0 | 0 | 0 | 0 | 0 | 1 | |
| **IOWA** | | | | | | | | | | | |
| **Total** | 3 | 1 | 1 | 1 | 0 | 0 | | | | | |
| **Cities** | 2 | 1 | 0 | 1 | 0 | 0 | | | | | |
| Ames | 0 | 1 | 0 | 0 | 0 | 0 | 0 | 1 | 0 | 0 | 129,863 |
| Atlantic | 1 | 0 | 0 | 0 | 0 | 0 | 0 | 0 | 0 | 1 | 210,403 |
| Bettendorf | 1 | 0 | 0 | 1 | 0 | 0 | 0 | 1 | 1 | 0 | 5,236 |
| **Universities and Colleges** | 1 | 0 | 0 | 1 | 0 | 0 | | | | | |
| Iowa State University | 1 | 0 | 0 | 0 | 0 | 0 | 0 | 0 | 0 | 1 | 34,435 |
| **Metropolitan Counties** | 0 | 0 | 1 | 0 | 0 | 0 | | | | | |
| Scott | 0 | 0 | 1 | 0 | 0 | 0 | 0 | 0 | 1 | 0 | |

# Table 13. Hate Crime Incidents Per Bias Motivation and Quarter, by Selected State and Agency, 2015—*Continued*

(Number.)

| State/agency | Number of incidents per bias motivation | | | | | | Number of incidents per quarter | | | | Population[1] |
|---|---|---|---|---|---|---|---|---|---|---|---|
| | Race/ Ethnicity/ Ancestry | Religion | Sexual orientation | Disability | Gender | Gender Identity | 1st quarter | 2nd quarter | 3rd quarter | 4th quarter | |
| **KANSAS** | | | | | | | | | | | |
| Total ........................ | 46 | 8 | 8 | 0 | 1 | 0 | | | | | |
| | | | | | | | | | | | |
| **Cities ........................** | 36 | 7 | 5 | 0 | 1 | 0 | | | | | |
| Baxter Springs.................... | 1 | 0 | 0 | 0 | 0 | 0 | 0 | 1 | 0 | 0 | 4,035 |
| Clay Center...................... | 1 | 0 | 0 | 0 | 0 | 0 | 0 | 0 | 0 | 1 | 4,136 |
| Colby............................ | 1 | 0 | 0 | 0 | 0 | 0 | 0 | 0 | 1 | 0 | 5,381 |
| Derby............................ | 1 | 0 | 0 | 0 | 0 | 0 | 0 | 0 | 1 | 0 | 23,430 |
| Dodge City ...................... | 2 | 1 | 1 | 0 | 0 | 0 | 0 | 2 | 0 | 2 | 28,271 |
| Elwood.......................... | 1 | 0 | 0 | 0 | 0 | 0 | 0 | 0 | 1 | 0 | 1,199 |
| Garden City ..................... | 1 | 0 | 0 | 0 | 0 | 0 | 0 | 0 | 0 | 1 | 27,059 |
| Great Bend ...................... | 1 | 0 | 0 | 0 | 0 | 0 | 0 | 0 | 0 | 1 | 15,800 |
| Hoisington....................... | 1 | 0 | 0 | 0 | 0 | 0 | 0 | 0 | 1 | 0 | 2,654 |
| Hutchinson ...................... | 2 | 1 | 0 | 0 | 0 | 0 | 1 | 2 | 0 | 0 | 41,499 |
| Iola............................. | 1 | 0 | 0 | 0 | 0 | 0 | 1 | 0 | 0 | 0 | 5,515 |
| Leavenworth..................... | 1 | 0 | 0 | 0 | 0 | 0 | 0 | 0 | 0 | 1 | 36,154 |
| Liberal........................... | 1 | 0 | 0 | 0 | 0 | 0 | 0 | 0 | 1 | 0 | 21,128 |
| Newton .......................... | 2 | 1 | 0 | 0 | 0 | 0 | 0 | 1 | 2 | 0 | 19,103 |
| Overland Park[3]................. | 4 | 0 | 2 | 0 | 1 | 0 | 3 | 2 | 0 | 1 | 187,240 |
| Salina........................... | 3 | 0 | 0 | 0 | 0 | 0 | 0 | 0 | 1 | 2 | 47,874 |
| Topeka........................... | 1 | 0 | 0 | 0 | 0 | 0 | 0 | 0 | 0 | 1 | 127,096 |
| Valley Center .................... | 0 | 1 | 0 | 0 | 0 | 0 | 0 | 1 | 0 | 0 | 7,113 |
| Wichita.......................... | 10 | 3 | 2 | 0 | 0 | 0 | 2 | 1 | 10 | 2 | 389,824 |
| Winfield......................... | 1 | 0 | 0 | 0 | 0 | 0 | 0 | 0 | 1 | 0 | 12,235 |
| | | | | | | | | | | | |
| **Universities and Colleges ........** | 1 | 0 | 1 | 0 | 0 | 0 | | | | | |
| Kansas State University .............. | 0 | 0 | 1 | 0 | 0 | 0 | 1 | 0 | 0 | 0 | 24,766 |
| University of Kansas, Medical Center[2] ......... | 1 | 0 | 0 | 0 | 0 | 0 | 0 | 0 | 0 | 1 | |
| | | | | | | | | | | | |
| **Metropolitan Counties ...........** | 3 | 0 | 2 | 0 | 0 | 0 | | | | | |
| Riley County Police Department .. | 0 | 0 | 1 | 0 | 0 | 0 | 0 | 1 | 0 | 0 | |
| Sedgwick........................ | 1 | 0 | 0 | 0 | 0 | 0 | 0 | 1 | 0 | 0 | |
| Shawnee......................... | 0 | 0 | 1 | 0 | 0 | 0 | 0 | 1 | 0 | 0 | |
| Sumner.......................... | 1 | 0 | 0 | 0 | 0 | 0 | 0 | 0 | 1 | 0 | |
| Wyandotte....................... | 1 | 0 | 0 | 0 | 0 | 0 | 0 | 0 | 0 | 1 | |
| | | | | | | | | | | | |
| **Nonmetropolitan Counties......** | 4 | 1 | 0 | 0 | 0 | 0 | | | | | |
| Cowley........................... | 1 | 0 | 0 | 0 | 0 | 0 | 0 | 0 | 0 | 1 | |
| Crawford......................... | 1 | 0 | 0 | 0 | 0 | 0 | 1 | 0 | 0 | 0 | |
| Ellis............................. | 0 | 1 | 0 | 0 | 0 | 0 | 0 | 0 | 1 | 0 | |
| Ford............................. | 1 | 0 | 0 | 0 | 0 | 0 | 1 | 0 | 0 | 0 | |
| Gray ............................. | 1 | 0 | 0 | 0 | 0 | 0 | 0 | 0 | 1 | 0 | |
| | | | | | | | | | | | |
| **State Police Agencies..............** | 1 | 0 | 0 | 0 | 0 | 0 | | | | | |
| Kansas Highway Patrol.............. | 1 | 0 | 0 | 0 | 0 | 0 | 1 | 0 | 0 | 0 | |
| | | | | | | | | | | | |
| **Other Agencies.......................** | 1 | 0 | 0 | 0 | 0 | 0 | | | | | |
| Blue Valley School District .......... | 1 | 0 | 0 | 0 | 0 | 0 | 0 | 1 | 0 | 0 | |
| | | | | | | | | | | | |
| **KENTUCKY** | | | | | | | | | | | |
| Total ........................ | 113 | 53 | 19 | 2 | 0 | 1 | | | | | |
| | | | | | | | | | | | |
| **Cities ........................** | 80 | 44 | 17 | 2 | 0 | 0 | | | | | |
| Alexandria ..................... | 0 | 1 | 0 | 0 | 0 | 0 | 0 | 1 | 0 | 0 | 8,860 |
| Anchorage ..................... | 0 | 0 | 0 | 1 | 0 | 0 | 0 | 0 | 1 | 0 | 2,422 |
| Ashland ........................ | 3 | 2 | 0 | 0 | 0 | 0 | 0 | 4 | 1 | 0 | 21,232 |
| Bardstown ...................... | 2 | 0 | 0 | 0 | 0 | 0 | 0 | 0 | 0 | 2 | 13,087 |
| Benton.......................... | 0 | 1 | 0 | 0 | 0 | 0 | 0 | 1 | 0 | 0 | 4,309 |
| Bowling Green................... | 5 | 4 | 0 | 0 | 0 | 0 | 1 | 4 | 2 | 2 | 63,346 |
| Brownsville ..................... | 0 | 0 | 1 | 0 | 0 | 0 | 0 | 0 | 0 | 1 | 824 |
| Carrollton ...................... | 1 | 0 | 0 | 0 | 0 | 0 | 0 | 0 | 1 | 0 | 3,930 |
| Corbin .......................... | 1 | 0 | 0 | 0 | 0 | 0 | 0 | 0 | 1 | 0 | 7,305 |
| Covington....................... | 2 | 2 | 1 | 0 | 0 | 0 | 2 | 3 | 0 | 0 | 41,056 |
| Dawson Springs................. | 0 | 0 | 2 | 0 | 0 | 0 | 0 | 2 | 0 | 0 | 2,740 |
| Dayton.......................... | 2 | 0 | 0 | 0 | 0 | 0 | 0 | 1 | 1 | 0 | 5,446 |
| Erlanger........................ | 3 | 0 | 0 | 0 | 0 | 0 | 1 | 1 | 0 | 1 | 22,774 |
| Flemingsburg................... | 0 | 1 | 0 | 0 | 0 | 0 | 0 | 1 | 0 | 0 | 2,709 |
| Florence........................ | 1 | 0 | 1 | 0 | 0 | 0 | 0 | 2 | 0 | 0 | 32,357 |

(Number.)

| State/agency | Number of incidents per bias motivation | | | | | | Number of incidents per quarter | | | | Population[1] |
|---|---|---|---|---|---|---|---|---|---|---|---|
| | Race/ Ethnicity/ Ancestry | Religion | Sexual orientation | Disability | Gender | Gender Identity | 1st quarter | 2nd quarter | 3rd quarter | 4th quarter | |
| Frankfort.................... | 2 | 3 | 0 | 0 | 0 | 0 | 2 | 1 | 2 | 0 | 27,603 |
| Franklin.................... | 1 | 0 | 0 | 0 | 0 | 0 | 1 | 0 | 0 | 0 | 8,755 |
| Georgetown.............. | 5 | 0 | 0 | 0 | 0 | 0 | 0 | 3 | 0 | 2 | 32,273 |
| Glasgow................... | 2 | 1 | 0 | 0 | 0 | 0 | 1 | 0 | 0 | 2 | 14,413 |
| Henderson................ | 2 | 1 | 1 | 0 | 0 | 0 | 0 | 0 | 2 | 2 | 28,928 |
| Independence............ | 0 | 2 | 0 | 0 | 0 | 0 | 0 | 2 | 0 | 0 | 26,773 |
| Indian Hills.............. | 0 | 1 | 0 | 0 | 0 | 0 | 0 | 0 | 1 | 0 | 2,965 |
| La Grange................ | 0 | 0 | 0 | 1 | 0 | 0 | 0 | 0 | 1 | 0 | 8,625 |
| Lexington................. | 10 | 11 | 4 | 0 | 0 | 0 | 4 | 7 | 5 | 9 | 314,077 |
| Louisville Metro......... | 9 | 1 | 3 | 0 | 0 | 0 | 4 | 1 | 4 | 4 | 680,550 |
| Lynnview.................. | 1 | 0 | 0 | 0 | 0 | 0 | 0 | 0 | 1 | 0 | 943 |
| Mayfield................... | 5 | 0 | 0 | 0 | 0 | 0 | 3 | 1 | 1 | 0 | 10,141 |
| Monticello................ | 1 | 0 | 0 | 0 | 0 | 0 | 1 | 0 | 0 | 0 | 6,072 |
| Murray.................... | 0 | 2 | 0 | 0 | 0 | 0 | 0 | 1 | 0 | 1 | 18,810 |
| Newport................... | 2 | 1 | 0 | 0 | 0 | 0 | 0 | 1 | 1 | 1 | 15,413 |
| Nicholasville............. | 1 | 0 | 0 | 0 | 0 | 0 | 0 | 0 | 0 | 1 | 29,351 |
| Oak Grove................ | 1 | 0 | 0 | 0 | 0 | 0 | 0 | 1 | 0 | 0 | 7,515 |
| Owensboro............... | 3 | 1 | 1 | 0 | 0 | 0 | 1 | 1 | 1 | 2 | 58,608 |
| Owingsville............... | 1 | 0 | 0 | 0 | 0 | 0 | 0 | 0 | 1 | 0 | 1,597 |
| Paducah................... | 1 | 3 | 1 | 0 | 0 | 0 | 2 | 2 | 1 | 0 | 24,968 |
| Paris....................... | 1 | 0 | 0 | 0 | 0 | 0 | 0 | 0 | 1 | 0 | 9,747 |
| Pembroke................. | 1 | 0 | 0 | 0 | 0 | 0 | 0 | 0 | 1 | 0 | 895 |
| Princeton................. | 2 | 0 | 1 | 0 | 0 | 0 | 0 | 1 | 2 | 0 | 6,166 |
| Scottsville................ | 1 | 0 | 0 | 0 | 0 | 0 | 0 | 0 | 1 | 0 | 4,373 |
| Shepherdsville............ | 2 | 1 | 0 | 0 | 0 | 0 | 0 | 1 | 1 | 1 | 11,990 |
| Shively.................... | 2 | 1 | 0 | 0 | 0 | 0 | 1 | 0 | 0 | 2 | 15,733 |
| Simpsonville.............. | 1 | 0 | 0 | 0 | 0 | 0 | 1 | 0 | 0 | 0 | 2,695 |
| Taylor Mill............... | 2 | 0 | 0 | 0 | 0 | 0 | 0 | 0 | 0 | 2 | 6,748 |
| Taylorsville............... | 0 | 1 | 0 | 0 | 0 | 0 | 0 | 0 | 1 | 0 | 796 |
| Versailles................. | 0 | 2 | 0 | 0 | 0 | 0 | 0 | 2 | 0 | 0 | 9,105 |
| West Buechel............ | 0 | 1 | 0 | 0 | 0 | 0 | 1 | 0 | 0 | 0 | 1,272 |
| Winchester............... | 1 | 0 | 1 | 0 | 0 | 0 | 0 | 0 | 0 | 2 | 18,462 |
| **Universities and Colleges ........** | 6 | 0 | 1 | 0 | 0 | 0 | | | | | |
| Eastern Kentucky University ........ | 1 | 0 | 0 | 0 | 0 | 0 | 0 | 1 | 0 | 0 | 16,305 |
| Murray State University.............. | 1 | 0 | 1 | 0 | 0 | 0 | 1 | 1 | 0 | 0 | 11,207 |
| Northern Kentucky University...... | 1 | 0 | 0 | 0 | 0 | 0 | 1 | 0 | 0 | 0 | 15,090 |
| University of Kentucky ................ | 2 | 0 | 0 | 0 | 0 | 0 | 0 | 0 | 2 | 0 | 29,203 |
| University of Louisville ............... | 1 | 0 | 0 | 0 | 0 | 0 | 0 | 0 | 1 | 0 | 21,561 |
| **Metropolitan Counties ............** | 9 | 1 | 1 | 0 | 0 | 1 | | | | | |
| Boone...................... | 1 | 0 | 0 | 0 | 0 | 1 | 0 | 0 | 2 | 0 | |
| Bracken ................... | 0 | 0 | 1 | 0 | 0 | 0 | 0 | 1 | 0 | 0 | |
| Bullitt...................... | 1 | 0 | 0 | 0 | 0 | 0 | 0 | 0 | 0 | 1 | |
| Campbell County Police Department ................. | 1 | 0 | 0 | 0 | 0 | 0 | 0 | 0 | 0 | 1 | |
| Larue ...................... | 0 | 1 | 0 | 0 | 0 | 0 | 0 | 1 | 0 | 0 | |
| Meade ..................... | 1 | 0 | 0 | 0 | 0 | 0 | 0 | 0 | 0 | 1 | |
| Scott....................... | 1 | 0 | 0 | 0 | 0 | 0 | 1 | 0 | 0 | 0 | |
| Shelby..................... | 1 | 0 | 0 | 0 | 0 | 0 | 0 | 1 | 0 | 0 | |
| Warren .................... | 3 | 0 | 0 | 0 | 0 | 0 | 1 | 0 | 1 | 1 | |
| **Nonmetropolitan Counties......** | 11 | 1 | 0 | 0 | 0 | 0 | | | | | |
| Anderson.................. | 0 | 1 | 0 | 0 | 0 | 0 | 0 | 1 | 0 | 0 | |
| Ballard .................... | 1 | 0 | 0 | 0 | 0 | 0 | 0 | 0 | 0 | 1 | |
| Bell ........................ | 1 | 0 | 0 | 0 | 0 | 0 | 0 | 1 | 0 | 0 | |
| Franklin................... | 1 | 0 | 0 | 0 | 0 | 0 | 0 | 0 | 1 | 0 | |
| Graves..................... | 1 | 0 | 0 | 0 | 0 | 0 | 0 | 0 | 1 | 0 | |
| Grayson ................... | 1 | 0 | 0 | 0 | 0 | 0 | 0 | 0 | 0 | 1 | |
| Jackson.................... | 1 | 0 | 0 | 0 | 0 | 0 | 0 | 1 | 0 | 0 | |
| Laurel ..................... | 1 | 0 | 0 | 0 | 0 | 0 | 0 | 1 | 0 | 0 | |
| Mason ..................... | 1 | 0 | 0 | 0 | 0 | 0 | 0 | 1 | 0 | 0 | |
| Union ...................... | 1 | 0 | 0 | 0 | 0 | 0 | 0 | 0 | 1 | 0 | |
| Webster.................... | 2 | 0 | 0 | 0 | 0 | 0 | 0 | 0 | 1 | 1 | |
| **State Police Agencies..............** | 4 | 7 | 0 | 0 | 0 | 0 | | | | | |
| Ashland .................... | 0 | 2 | 0 | 0 | 0 | 0 | 0 | 0 | 1 | 1 | |
| Bowling Green............ | 1 | 0 | 0 | 0 | 0 | 0 | 1 | 0 | 0 | 0 | |
| Dry Ridge.................. | 0 | 1 | 0 | 0 | 0 | 0 | 0 | 0 | 1 | 0 | |
| Hazard..................... | 1 | 0 | 0 | 0 | 0 | 0 | 0 | 1 | 0 | 0 | |

(Number.)

| State/agency | Number of incidents per bias motivation | | | | | | Number of incidents per quarter | | | | Population[1] |
|---|---|---|---|---|---|---|---|---|---|---|---|
| | Race/ Ethnicity/ Ancestry | Religion | Sexual orientation | Disability | Gender | Gender Identity | 1st quarter | 2nd quarter | 3rd quarter | 4th quarter | |
| London | 0 | 2 | 0 | 0 | 0 | 0 | 1 | 0 | 0 | 1 | |
| Madisonville | 0 | 1 | 0 | 0 | 0 | 0 | 0 | 0 | 0 | 1 | |
| Mayfield | 1 | 0 | 0 | 0 | 0 | 0 | 0 | 0 | 1 | 0 | |
| Morehead | 1 | 0 | 0 | 0 | 0 | 0 | 0 | 1 | 0 | 0 | |
| Pikeville | 0 | 1 | 0 | 0 | 0 | 0 | 0 | 0 | 1 | 0 | |
| **Other Agencies** | 3 | 0 | 0 | 0 | 0 | 0 | | | | | |
| Fayette County Schools | 1 | 0 | 0 | 0 | 0 | 0 | 1 | 0 | 0 | 0 | |
| Jefferson County School District | 2 | 0 | 0 | 0 | 0 | 0 | 1 | 0 | 0 | 1 | |
| **LOUISIANA** | | | | | | | | | | | |
| **Total** | 22 | 11 | 5 | 0 | 0 | 0 | | | | | |
| **Cities** | 7 | 0 | 3 | 0 | 0 | 0 | | | | | |
| Mamou | 1 | 0 | 0 | 0 | 0 | 0 | 0 | 1 | 0 | 0 | 3,173 |
| Natchitoches | 1 | 0 | 0 | 0 | 0 | 0 | 1 | 0 | 0 | 0 | 18,350 |
| New Orleans | 2 | 0 | 3 | 0 | 0 | 0 | 0 | 1 | 2 | 2 | 393,447 |
| Shreveport | 1 | 0 | 0 | 0 | 0 | 0 | 0 | 0 | 0 | 1 | 197,592 |
| Vinton | 1 | 0 | 0 | 0 | 0 | 0 | 0 | 1 | | | 3,353 |
| Westlake | 1 | 0 | 0 | 0 | 0 | 0 | 1 | 0 | 0 | 0 | 4,625 |
| **Metropolitan Counties** | 13 | 11 | 2 | 0 | 0 | 0 | | | | | |
| Bossier | 1 | 1 | 0 | 0 | 0 | 0 | 0 | 0 | 0 | 2 | 9,323 |
| Calcasieu | 0 | 9 | 1 | 0 | 0 | 0 | 3 | 2 | 3 | 2 | |
| East Feliciana | 1 | 0 | 0 | 0 | 0 | 0 | 0 | 0 | 1 | 0 | |
| Jefferson | 1 | 0 | 1 | 0 | 0 | 0 | 0 | 2 | 0 | 0 | |
| Lafourche | 8 | 0 | 0 | 0 | 0 | 0 | 0 | 1 | 0 | 7 | |
| Ouachita | 0 | 1 | 0 | 0 | 0 | 0 | | | 0 | 1 | |
| St. Charles | 1 | 0 | 0 | 0 | 0 | 0 | | | 1 | 0 | |
| St. Helena | 1 | 0 | 0 | 0 | 0 | 0 | 0 | 1 | 0 | 0 | |
| **Nonmetropolitan Counties** | 2 | 0 | 0 | 0 | 0 | 0 | | | | | |
| Madison | 2 | 0 | 0 | 0 | 0 | 0 | 1 | 0 | 0 | 1 | |
| **MAINE** | | | | | | | | | | | |
| **Total** | 16 | 9 | 13 | 0 | 0 | 0 | | | | | |
| **Cities** | 15 | 9 | 11 | 0 | 0 | 0 | | | | | |
| Augusta | 2 | 0 | 2 | 0 | 0 | 0 | 1 | 0 | 1 | 2 | 18,608 |
| Brewer | 1 | 0 | 0 | 0 | 0 | 0 | 0 | 1 | 0 | 0 | 9,279 |
| Islesboro | 0 | 0 | 2 | 0 | 0 | 0 | 0 | 2 | 0 | 0 | 568 |
| Lewiston | 4 | 0 | 0 | 0 | 0 | 0 | 0 | 1 | 2 | 1 | 36,232 |
| Livermore Falls | 1 | 0 | 0 | 0 | 0 | 0 | 0 | 1 | 0 | 0 | 3,134 |
| Old Orchard Beach | 2 | 0 | 1 | 0 | 0 | 0 | 2 | 1 | 0 | 0 | 8,790 |
| Portland | 1 | 5 | 1 | 0 | 0 | 0 | 0 | 1 | 1 | 5 | 66,816 |
| Saco | 1 | 1 | 3 | 0 | 0 | 0 | 2 | 0 | 2 | 1 | 19,146 |
| Sanford | 0 | 1 | 0 | 0 | 0 | 0 | 0 | 0 | 1 | 0 | 20,936 |
| Scarborough | 1 | 1 | 0 | 0 | 0 | 0 | 0 | 1 | 1 | 0 | 19,682 |
| South Portland | 1 | 1 | 2 | 0 | 0 | 0 | 0 | 3 | 1 | 0 | 25,540 |
| Topsham | 1 | 0 | 0 | 0 | 0 | 0 | 0 | 0 | 1 | 0 | 8,703 |
| **Metropolitan Counties** | 0 | 0 | 2 | 0 | 0 | 0 | | | | | |
| Sagadahoc | 0 | 0 | 2 | 0 | 0 | 0 | 0 | 2 | 0 | 0 | |
| **State Police Agencies** | 1 | 0 | 0 | 0 | 0 | 0 | | | | | |
| State Police, Franklin County | 1 | 0 | 0 | 0 | 0 | 0 | 0 | 0 | 0 | 1 | |
| **MARYLAND** | | | | | | | | | | | |
| **Total** | 22 | 14 | 7 | 0 | 0 | 0 | | | | | |
| **Cities** | 7 | 1 | 5 | 0 | 0 | 0 | | | | | 621,252 |
| Baltimore | 1 | 1 | 2 | 0 | 0 | 0 | 2 | 0 | 2 | | |
| Bowie | 0 | 0 | 1 | 0 | 0 | 0 | 1 | 0 | 0 | 0 | 58,304 |
| Frederick | 1 | 0 | 0 | 0 | 0 | 0 | 1 | 0 | 0 | 0 | 69,162 |
| Greenbelt | 1 | 0 | 2 | 0 | 0 | 0 | 0 | 0 | 2 | 1 | 24,385 |
| Laurel | 4 | 0 | 0 | 0 | 0 | 0 | 0 | 0 | 4 | 0 | 26,406 |

## Table 13. Hate Crime Incidents Per Bias Motivation and Quarter, by Selected State and Agency, 2015—*Continued*

(Number.)

| State/agency | Race/ Ethnicity/ Ancestry | Religion | Sexual orientation | Disability | Gender | Gender Identity | 1st quarter | 2nd quarter | 3rd quarter | 4th quarter | Population[1] |
|---|---|---|---|---|---|---|---|---|---|---|---|
| | Number of incidents per bias motivation | | | | | | Number of incidents per quarter | | | | |
| **Universities and Colleges** ........ | 0 | 1 | 0 | 0 | 0 | 0 | | | | | |
| Towson University ...................... | 0 | 1 | 0 | 0 | 0 | 0 | 1 | 0 | 0 | 0 | 22,285 |
| **Metropolitan Counties** ........... | 13 | 12 | 2 | 0 | 0 | 0 | | | | | |
| Baltimore County Police Department ........................... | 1 | 0 | 1 | 0 | 0 | 0 | 1 | 0 | 1 | 0 | |
| Frederick ................................. | 1 | 0 | 1 | 0 | 0 | 0 | 0 | 2 | 0 | 0 | |
| Harford ................................... | 1 | 0 | 0 | 0 | 0 | 0 | 1 | 0 | 0 | 0 | |
| Montgomery County Police Department[3] ............................ | 10 | 12 | 0 | 0 | 0 | 0 | 5 | 6 | 2 | 7 | |
| **State Police Agencies**.............. | 2 | 0 | 0 | 0 | 0 | 0 | | | | | |
| State Police, Carroll County........ | 2 | 0 | 0 | 0 | 0 | 0 | 0 | 0 | 2 | 0 | |
| **MASSACHUSETTS** | | | | | | | | | | | |
| Total ......................................... | 198 | 81 | 81 | 4 | 15 | 45 | | | | | |
| **Cities** ..................................... | 184 | 69 | 77 | 4 | 15 | 45 | | | | | |
| Acton[3] .................................... | 2 | 6 | 0 | 0 | 0 | 1 | 4 | 2 | 2 | 1 | 23,573 |
| Agawam.................................... | 0 | 0 | 2 | 0 | 0 | 0 | 0 | 0 | 2 | 0 | 28,853 |
| Amesbury................................. | 2 | 0 | 0 | 0 | 0 | 0 | 0 | 1 | 0 | 1 | 16,922 |
| Andover.................................... | 1 | 0 | 1 | 0 | 0 | 0 | 0 | 2 | 0 | 0 | 35,562 |
| Arlington ................................. | 1 | 2 | 0 | 0 | 1 | 1 | 0 | 2 | 0 | 3 | 44,873 |
| Attleboro ................................. | 1 | 0 | 1 | 0 | 0 | 0 | 0 | 1 | 1 | 0 | 44,079 |
| Barnstable................................ | 1 | 0 | 0 | 0 | 0 | 0 | 1 | 0 | 0 | 0 | 44,392 |
| Bedford.................................... | 1 | 0 | 0 | 0 | 0 | 0 | 0 | 0 | 1 | 0 | 14,435 |
| Bellingham................................ | 1 | 0 | 0 | 0 | 0 | 0 | 1 | 0 | 0 | 0 | 16,879 |
| Belmont.................................... | 0 | 1 | 0 | 0 | 0 | 0 | 0 | 1 | 0 | 0 | 25,692 |
| Beverly..................................... | 0 | 1 | 0 | 0 | 0 | 0 | 0 | 0 | 0 | 1 | 41,281 |
| Billerica.................................... | 0 | 1 | 0 | 0 | 0 | 0 | 0 | 0 | 1 | 0 | 42,762 |
| Boston[3].................................. | 81 | 14 | 46 | 0 | 1 | 6 | 28 | 40 | 40 | 31 | 665,258 |
| Braintree.................................. | 3 | 0 | 0 | 0 | 0 | 0 | 0 | 1 | 2 | 0 | 37,772 |
| Brockton................................... | 0 | 0 | 0 | 1 | 0 | 0 | 0 | 0 | 0 | 1 | 95,049 |
| Cambridge................................. | 10 | 7 | 2 | 0 | 0 | 0 | 3 | 7 | 4 | 5 | 110,953 |
| Chicopee................................... | 2 | 0 | 1 | 0 | 0 | 0 | 0 | 1 | 2 | 0 | 55,926 |
| Cohasset................................... | 0 | 0 | 0 | 0 | 1 | 0 | 1 | 0 | 0 | 0 | 8,550 |
| Danvers[3] ................................. | 2 | 2 | 1 | 0 | 1 | 0 | 0 | 3 | 1 | 1 | 27,708 |
| Dracut ..................................... | 0 | 1 | 0 | 0 | 0 | 0 | 0 | 0 | 0 | 1 | 31,486 |
| Easthampton ............................ | 0 | 0 | 1 | 0 | 0 | 0 | 0 | 0 | 1 | 0 | 16,033 |
| Everett..................................... | 2 | 0 | 0 | 0 | 0 | 0 | 1 | 0 | 0 | 1 | 44,898 |
| Falmouth.................................. | 1 | 0 | 0 | 0 | 0 | 0 | 0 | 0 | 1 | 0 | 31,666 |
| Granby ..................................... | 1 | 0 | 0 | 0 | 0 | 0 | 0 | 0 | 1 | 0 | 6,357 |
| Haverhill................................... | 2 | 0 | 0 | 0 | 0 | 3 | 0 | 2 | 2 | 1 | 62,895 |
| Hingham................................... | 1 | 0 | 0 | 0 | 0 | 1 | 0 | 0 | 1 | 1 | 23,165 |
| Lowell....................................... | 0 | 1 | 0 | 0 | 0 | 1 | 0 | 1 | 0 | 1 | 110,819 |
| Ludlow...................................... | 1 | 0 | 0 | 0 | 0 | 0 | 0 | 0 | 1 | 0 | 21,510 |
| Lynn ........................................ | 7 | 2 | 1 | 1 | 1 | 7 | 1 | 7 | 9 | 2 | 92,584 |
| Malden..................................... | 1 | 1 | 1 | 0 | 0 | 5 | 2 | 1 | 3 | 2 | 61,211 |
| Mansfield.................................. | 0 | 3 | 0 | 0 | 0 | 0 | 0 | 2 | 1 | 0 | 23,705 |
| Marblehead .............................. | 0 | 1 | 0 | 0 | 0 | 0 | 0 | 0 | 1 | 0 | 20,616 |
| Medford.................................... | 5 | 1 | 1 | 0 | 2 | 0 | 1 | 3 | 4 | 1 | 57,742 |
| Mendon.................................... | 0 | 1 | 0 | 0 | 0 | 0 | 0 | 0 | 0 | 1 | 5,991 |
| Methuen................................... | 2 | 0 | 0 | 0 | 0 | 0 | 0 | 1 | 1 | 0 | 49,579 |
| Middleboro[3]............................. | 1 | 0 | 0 | 1 | 0 | 0 | 0 | 0 | 0 | 2 | 24,357 |
| Milford .................................... | 1 | 0 | 0 | 0 | 0 | 0 | 0 | 1 | 0 | 0 | 28,553 |
| Milton...................................... | 0 | 2 | 0 | 0 | 0 | 0 | 0 | 0 | 2 | 0 | 27,449 |
| Montague.................................. | 0 | 1 | 0 | 0 | 0 | 0 | 1 | 0 | 0 | 0 | 8,300 |
| Nahant..................................... | 1 | 0 | 0 | 0 | 0 | 0 | 0 | 1 | 0 | 0 | 3,496 |
| Natick ...................................... | 0 | 0 | 1 | 0 | 0 | 0 | 1 | 0 | 0 | 0 | 36,184 |
| Newton[3] .................................. | 4 | 3 | 1 | 0 | 1 | 2 | 1 | 4 | 3 | 3 | 89,053 |
| Northampton[3]........................... | 1 | 1 | 1 | 0 | 0 | 0 | 0 | 1 | 0 | 1 | 28,534 |
| North Attleboro ........................ | 0 | 0 | 0 | 0 | 1 | 0 | 0 | 0 | 0 | 1 | 28,965 |
| Northbridge.............................. | 0 | 1 | 0 | 0 | 0 | 0 | 0 | 0 | 1 | 0 | 16,587 |
| Northfield ................................ | 0 | 2 | 0 | 0 | 0 | 0 | 0 | 0 | 0 | 2 | 3,008 |
| Norton...................................... | 0 | 0 | 0 | 0 | 0 | 1 | 1 | 0 | 0 | 0 | 19,464 |
| Palmer ..................................... | 1 | 0 | 0 | 0 | 0 | 0 | 0 | 1 | 0 | 0 | 12,183 |
| Plymouth.................................. | 3 | 2 | 0 | 0 | 0 | 0 | 1 | 0 | 1 | 3 | 58,705 |
| Provincetown[3]........................... | 1 | 0 | 2 | 0 | 0 | 0 | 0 | 0 | 3 | 0 | 2,989 |
| Quincy[3].................................... | 16 | 4 | 1 | 0 | 0 | 2 | 5 | 3 | 8 | 5 | 93,671 |

(Number.)

| State/agency | Number of incidents per bias motivation | | | | | | Number of incidents per quarter | | | | Population[1] |
|---|---|---|---|---|---|---|---|---|---|---|---|
| | Race/ Ethnicity/ Ancestry | Religion | Sexual orientation | Disability | Gender | Gender Identity | 1st quarter | 2nd quarter | 3rd quarter | 4th quarter | |
| Randolph | 1 | 0 | 0 | 0 | 0 | 0 | 0 | 0 | 1 | 0 | 33,947 |
| Raynham | 0 | 1 | 1 | 0 | 0 | 0 | 0 | 0 | 1 | 1 | 13,772 |
| Reading | 1 | 0 | 0 | 0 | 0 | 0 | 0 | 0 | 1 | 0 | 25,705 |
| Rockport | 0 | 1 | 0 | 0 | 0 | 0 | 0 | 0 | 0 | 1 | 7,229 |
| Salem | 3 | 1 | 3 | 0 | 0 | 0 | 3 | 1 | 2 | 1 | 43,090 |
| Salisbury | 1 | 0 | 0 | 0 | 0 | 0 | 0 | 0 | 1 | 0 | 8,813 |
| Sherborn | 0 | 1 | 0 | 0 | 0 | 0 | 1 | 0 | 0 | 0 | 4,320 |
| Somerville[3] | 3 | 0 | 1 | 0 | 1 | 1 | 2 | 0 | 2 | 2 | 79,734 |
| Southborough | 1 | 0 | 0 | 0 | 0 | 0 | 0 | 0 | 1 | 0 | 9,989 |
| South Hadley | 0 | 0 | 1 | 0 | 0 | 0 | 0 | 0 | 1 | 0 | 17,684 |
| Springfield | 4 | 0 | 3 | 0 | 0 | 0 | 1 | 2 | 2 | 2 | 154,090 |
| Stoneham | 3 | 1 | 0 | 0 | 0 | 1 | 0 | 0 | 3 | 2 | 22,041 |
| Stoughton | 0 | 0 | 1 | 0 | 0 | 0 | 0 | 0 | 1 | 0 | 28,748 |
| Sutton | 1 | 0 | 0 | 0 | 0 | 0 | 0 | 0 | 0 | 1 | 9,264 |
| Swampscott | 0 | 0 | 0 | 0 | 2 | 0 | 0 | 1 | 1 | 0 | 14,071 |
| Taunton | 0 | 0 | 1 | 0 | 3 | 10 | 6 | 2 | 5 | 1 | 56,731 |
| Tisbury | 1 | 0 | 0 | 0 | 0 | 0 | 0 | 0 | 0 | 1 | 4,173 |
| Wakefield | 0 | 1 | 0 | 0 | 0 | 0 | 0 | 1 | 0 | 0 | 27,206 |
| Waltham | 0 | 0 | 1 | 1 | 0 | 3 | 0 | 0 | 2 | 3 | 63,590 |
| Wareham | 1 | 0 | 0 | 0 | 0 | 0 | 1 | 0 | 0 | 0 | 22,640 |
| Watertown | 0 | 1 | 1 | 0 | 0 | 0 | 2 | 0 | 0 | 0 | 34,701 |
| Woburn | 1 | 0 | 0 | 0 | 0 | 0 | 1 | 0 | 0 | 0 | 39,539 |
| Worcester | 3 | 1 | 0 | 0 | 0 | 0 | 1 | 2 | 1 | 0 | 183,377 |
| **Universities and Colleges** | 13 | 10 | 4 | 0 | 0 | 0 | | | | | |
| Bentley University | 0 | 1 | 0 | 0 | 0 | 0 | 0 | 0 | 1 | 0 | 5,565 |
| Boston University | 3 | 1 | 1 | 0 | 0 | 0 | 1 | 1 | 2 | 1 | 32,112 |
| Bristol Community College | 1 | 0 | 0 | 0 | 0 | 0 | 1 | 0 | 0 | 0 | 9,189 |
| Clark University | 0 | 2 | 0 | 0 | 0 | 0 | 0 | 0 | 1 | 1 | 3,423 |
| Emerson College | 1 | 0 | 0 | 0 | 0 | 0 | 1 | 0 | 0 | 0 | 4,545 |
| Endicott College | 0 | 1 | 0 | 0 | 0 | 0 | 0 | 0 | 0 | 1 | 4,429 |
| Framingham State University | 0 | 1 | 0 | 0 | 0 | 0 | 0 | 0 | 1 | 0 | 6,499 |
| Massachusetts Institute of Technology | 3 | 0 | 0 | 0 | 0 | 0 | 2 | 1 | 0 | 0 | 11,319 |
| Northeastern University | 4 | 4 | 3 | 0 | 0 | 0 | 4 | 0 | 1 | 6 | 19,798 |
| Springfield Technical Community College | 1 | 0 | 0 | 0 | 0 | 0 | 0 | 1 | 0 | 0 | 6,622 |
| **Other Agencies** | 1 | 2 | 0 | 0 | 0 | 0 | | | | | |
| Massachusetts General Hospital | 1 | 2 | 0 | 0 | 0 | 0 | 0 | 1 | 1 | 1 | |
| **MICHIGAN** | | | | | | | | | | | |
| **Total** | 198 | 48 | 51 | 11 | 1 | 0 | | | | | |
| **Cities** | 167 | 35 | 41 | 10 | 1 | 0 | | | | | |
| Adrian | 1 | 0 | 0 | 0 | 0 | 0 | 0 | 0 | 1 | 0 | 20,762 |
| Albion | 0 | 3 | 1 | 0 | 1 | 0 | 1 | 0 | 0 | 4 | 8,184 |
| Ann Arbor | 3 | 3 | 2 | 0 | 0 | 0 | 3 | 1 | 3 | 1 | 118,730 |
| Bangor | 1 | 0 | 0 | 0 | 0 | 0 | 0 | 0 | 1 | 0 | 1,852 |
| Battle Creek | 2 | 0 | 0 | 0 | 0 | 0 | 0 | 1 | 1 | 0 | 61,240 |
| Benton Harbor | 1 | 0 | 0 | 0 | 0 | 0 | 0 | 1 | 0 | 0 | 10,012 |
| Berkley | 2 | 0 | 0 | 0 | 0 | 0 | 0 | 1 | 0 | 1 | 15,349 |
| Blackman Township | 1 | 0 | 0 | 0 | 0 | 0 | 0 | 0 | 0 | 1 | 37,632 |
| Bloomfield Hills | 1 | 0 | 0 | 0 | 0 | 0 | 0 | 0 | 0 | 1 | 4,021 |
| Bloomfield Township | 1 | 0 | 0 | 0 | 0 | 0 | 1 | 0 | 0 | 0 | 42,190 |
| Cadillac | 2 | 1 | 0 | 0 | 0 | 0 | 0 | 1 | 0 | 2 | 10,329 |
| Calumet | 1 | 0 | 0 | 0 | 0 | 0 | 0 | 0 | 1 | 0 | 703 |
| Canton Township | 1 | 0 | 1 | 0 | 0 | 0 | 1 | 0 | 1 | 0 | 89,628 |
| Cassopolis | 1 | 0 | 0 | 0 | 0 | 0 | 0 | 0 | 1 | 0 | 1,730 |
| Cheboygan | 1 | 0 | 0 | 0 | 0 | 0 | 0 | 0 | 0 | 1 | 4,760 |
| Chocolay Township | 0 | 1 | 0 | 0 | 0 | 0 | 0 | 0 | 0 | 1 | 6,003 |
| Clay Township | 0 | 1 | 0 | 0 | 0 | 0 | 0 | 0 | 1 | 0 | 8,861 |
| Clinton Township | 1 | 0 | 1 | 1 | 0 | 0 | 0 | 1 | 1 | 1 | 99,662 |
| Clio | 1 | 0 | 0 | 0 | 0 | 0 | 0 | 1 | 0 | 0 | 2,533 |
| Coleman | 1 | 0 | 0 | 0 | 0 | 0 | 0 | 0 | 1 | 0 | 1,203 |
| Dearborn | 3 | 3 | 0 | 0 | 0 | 0 | 1 | 1 | 3 | 1 | 94,962 |
| Decatur | 1 | 0 | 0 | 0 | 0 | 0 | 1 | 0 | 0 | 0 | 1,764 |
| Detroit | 2 | 0 | 6 | 0 | 0 | 0 | 1 | 2 | 5 | 0 | 673,225 |
| East Lansing | 3 | 0 | 0 | 0 | 0 | 0 | 0 | 0 | 1 | 2 | 48,668 |

# Table 13. Hate Crime Incidents Per Bias Motivation and Quarter, by Selected State and Agency, 2015—*Continued*

(Number.)

| State/agency | Race/Ethnicity/Ancestry | Religion | Sexual orientation | Disability | Gender | Gender Identity | 1st quarter | 2nd quarter | 3rd quarter | 4th quarter | Population[1] |
|---|---|---|---|---|---|---|---|---|---|---|---|
| Elsie | 1 | 0 | 0 | 0 | 0 | 0 | 1 | 0 | 0 | 0 | 981 |
| Ferndale | 1 | 1 | 1 | 0 | 0 | 0 | 1 | 0 | 2 | 0 | 20,345 |
| Flint | 3 | 0 | 1 | 2 | 0 | 0 | 1 | 0 | 4 | 1 | 98,221 |
| Flint Township | 2 | 0 | 0 | 0 | 0 | 0 | 1 | 0 | 1 | 0 | 30,654 |
| Fraser | 1 | 1 | 0 | 0 | 0 | 0 | 0 | 1 | 1 | 0 | 14,658 |
| Galesburg | 13 | 0 | 0 | 0 | 0 | 0 | 4 | 5 | 1 | 3 | 2,046 |
| Gaylord | 1 | 0 | 0 | 0 | 0 | 0 | 0 | 0 | 1 | 0 | 3,648 |
| Genesee Township | 1 | 1 | 0 | 0 | 0 | 0 | 0 | 1 | 1 | 0 | 20,540 |
| Gibraltar | 1 | 0 | 0 | 0 | 0 | 0 | 0 | 0 | 1 | 0 | 4,523 |
| Grand Haven | 1 | 0 | 0 | 0 | 0 | 0 | 0 | 1 | 0 | 0 | 11,108 |
| Grand Rapids | 3 | 0 | 0 | 0 | 0 | 0 | 0 | 0 | 2 | 1 | 195,268 |
| Grandville | 2 | 0 | 0 | 0 | 0 | 0 | 1 | 1 | 0 | 0 | 15,980 |
| Grosse Pointe Woods | 0 | 0 | 1 | 0 | 0 | 0 | 0 | 0 | 0 | 1 | 15,773 |
| Hamtramck | 0 | 3 | 0 | 0 | 0 | 0 | 0 | 2 | 0 | 1 | 22,030 |
| Highland Township | 1 | 0 | 0 | 0 | 0 | 0 | 1 | 0 | 0 | 0 | 19,856 |
| Hillsdale | 3 | 0 | 0 | 0 | 0 | 0 | 2 | 0 | 0 | 1 | 8,116 |
| Holland | 1 | 0 | 1 | 0 | 0 | 0 | 2 | 0 | 0 | 0 | 33,794 |
| Howell | 1 | 0 | 0 | 0 | 0 | 0 | 0 | 1 | 0 | 0 | 9,629 |
| Huron Township | 0 | 0 | 0 | 1 | 0 | 0 | 0 | 0 | 1 | 0 | 15,635 |
| Independence Township | 1 | 1 | 0 | 0 | 0 | 0 | 0 | 1 | 0 | 1 | 36,520 |
| Jackson | 1 | 1 | 3 | 0 | 0 | 0 | 0 | 0 | 0 | 5 | 33,126 |
| Keego Harbor | 1 | 0 | 0 | 0 | 0 | 0 | 0 | 0 | 1 | 0 | 3,040 |
| Kentwood | 1 | 3 | 1 | 0 | 0 | 0 | 0 | 0 | 3 | 2 | 51,287 |
| Kinde | 1 | 0 | 0 | 0 | 0 | 0 | 1 | 0 | 0 | 0 | 432 |
| Lake Linden | 1 | 0 | 0 | 0 | 0 | 0 | 1 | 0 | 0 | 0 | 990 |
| Lansing | 2 | 0 | 3 | 0 | 0 | 0 | 1 | 1 | 1 | 2 | 114,694 |
| Lansing Township | 0 | 0 | 0 | 2 | 0 | 0 | 0 | 1 | 0 | 1 | 8,109 |
| Lapeer | 4 | 0 | 0 | 0 | 0 | 0 | 0 | 1 | 1 | 2 | 8,747 |
| Lincoln Park | 2 | 0 | 0 | 0 | 0 | 0 | 0 | 0 | 1 | 1 | 37,027 |
| Marshall | 0 | 2 | 0 | 0 | 0 | 0 | 2 | 0 | 0 | 0 | 7,024 |
| Mason | 2 | 0 | 0 | 0 | 0 | 0 | 0 | 0 | 2 | 0 | 8,335 |
| Meridian Township | 1 | 1 | 1 | 1 | 0 | 0 | 0 | 2 | 1 | 1 | 42,304 |
| Milan | 1 | 0 | 0 | 0 | 0 | 0 | 1 | 0 | 0 | 0 | 5,978 |
| Milford | 0 | 1 | 0 | 0 | 0 | 0 | 0 | 0 | 1 | 0 | 16,676 |
| Monroe | 5 | 0 | 1 | 0 | 0 | 0 | 1 | 0 | 5 | 0 | 20,074 |
| Muskegon | 3 | 0 | 1 | 0 | 0 | 0 | 0 | 2 | 2 | 0 | 38,442 |
| Muskegon Township | 1 | 0 | 0 | 0 | 0 | 0 | 0 | 1 | 0 | 0 | 17,762 |
| Negaunee | 1 | 0 | 0 | 0 | 0 | 0 | 0 | 0 | 0 | 1 | 4,628 |
| Northfield Township | 1 | 0 | 1 | 0 | 0 | 0 | 0 | 0 | 2 | 0 | 8,675 |
| Northville Township | 1 | 0 | 0 | 0 | 0 | 0 | 0 | 1 | 0 | 0 | 28,897 |
| Oscoda Township | 2 | 0 | 1 | 0 | 0 | 0 | 1 | 2 | 0 | 0 | 6,856 |
| Owosso | 3 | 0 | 0 | 0 | 0 | 0 | 0 | 1 | 0 | 2 | 14,679 |
| Oxford Township | 2 | 0 | 0 | 0 | 0 | 0 | 1 | 1 | 0 | 0 | 17,989 |
| Pittsfield Township | 0 | 0 | 1 | 0 | 0 | 0 | 0 | 0 | 1 | 0 | 38,255 |
| Pleasant Ridge | 0 | 0 | 1 | 0 | 0 | 0 | 0 | 0 | 1 | 0 | 2,574 |
| Port Huron | 6 | 0 | 0 | 0 | 0 | 0 | 0 | 0 | 1 | 5 | 28,946 |
| Redford Township | 1 | 0 | 0 | 0 | 0 | 0 | 0 | 1 | 0 | 0 | 47,244 |
| Rochester | 2 | 0 | 0 | 1 | 0 | 0 | 1 | 1 | 0 | 1 | 13,067 |
| Rochester Hills | 2 | 0 | 1 | 0 | 0 | 0 | 0 | 3 | 0 | 0 | 73,660 |
| Romulus | 1 | 0 | 0 | 0 | 0 | 0 | 0 | 0 | 1 | 0 | 23,386 |
| Roseville | 8 | 0 | 1 | 0 | 0 | 0 | 0 | 5 | 2 | 2 | 47,673 |
| Royal Oak | 2 | 1 | 0 | 0 | 0 | 0 | 1 | 2 | 0 | 0 | 59,535 |
| Saginaw | 1 | 0 | 1 | 0 | 0 | 0 | 0 | 0 | 0 | 2 | 49,459 |
| Saline | 0 | 0 | 1 | 0 | 0 | 0 | 1 | 0 | 0 | 0 | 9,246 |
| Shelby Township | 3 | 0 | 0 | 0 | 0 | 0 | 1 | 0 | 0 | 2 | 77,636 |
| Southfield | 5 | 1 | 1 | 0 | 0 | 0 | 2 | 4 | 1 | 0 | 73,319 |
| St. Clair Shores | 2 | 0 | 0 | 0 | 0 | 0 | 0 | 1 | 0 | 1 | 60,116 |
| St. Joseph | 2 | 0 | 0 | 0 | 0 | 0 | 0 | 0 | 0 | 2 | 8,316 |
| Swartz Creek | 1 | 0 | 0 | 0 | 0 | 0 | 0 | 0 | 0 | 1 | 5,549 |
| Taylor | 0 | 0 | 2 | 0 | 0 | 0 | 0 | 0 | 1 | 1 | 61,250 |
| Traverse City | 1 | 1 | 2 | 0 | 0 | 0 | 0 | 2 | 2 | 0 | 15,137 |
| Trenton | 2 | 0 | 0 | 0 | 0 | 0 | 0 | 1 | 1 | 0 | 18,332 |
| Troy | 3 | 1 | 0 | 0 | 0 | 0 | 0 | 3 | 0 | 1 | 83,642 |
| Van Buren Township | 1 | 0 | 0 | 0 | 0 | 0 | 0 | 0 | 1 | 0 | 28,202 |
| Vassar | 0 | 0 | 1 | 0 | 0 | 0 | 0 | 1 | 0 | 0 | 2,611 |
| Warren[3] | 13 | 2 | 2 | 2 | 0 | 0 | 4 | 5 | 4 | 6 | 135,367 |
| Wayne | 1 | 0 | 0 | 0 | 0 | 0 | 0 | 0 | 1 | 0 | 16,977 |
| West Bloomfield Township | 2 | 1 | 0 | 0 | 0 | 0 | 0 | 0 | 1 | 2 | 66,274 |
| Westland | 0 | 1 | 0 | 0 | 0 | 0 | 1 | 0 | 0 | 0 | 81,917 |

# Table 13. Hate Crime Incidents Per Bias Motivation and Quarter, by Selected State and Agency, 2015—*Continued*

(Number.)

| State/agency | Race/ Ethnicity/ Ancestry | Religion | Sexual orientation | Disability | Gender | Gender Identity | 1st quarter | 2nd quarter | 3rd quarter | 4th quarter | Population[1] |
|---|---|---|---|---|---|---|---|---|---|---|---|
| Wixom | 1 | 0 | 0 | 0 | 0 | 0 | 0 | 0 | 1 | 0 | 13,806 |
| Yale | 1 | 0 | 0 | 0 | 0 | 0 | 0 | 0 | 1 | 0 | 1,909 |
| Ypsilanti | 2 | 0 | 0 | 0 | 0 | 0 | 0 | 2 | 0 | 0 | 20,208 |
| **Universities and Colleges** | 3 | 2 | 2 | 0 | 0 | 0 | | | | | |
| Eastern Michigan University | 0 | 0 | 1 | 0 | 0 | 0 | 0 | 0 | 0 | 1 | 22,401 |
| Ferris State University | 1 | 0 | 0 | 0 | 0 | 0 | 1 | 0 | 0 | 0 | 14,600 |
| Michigan State University | 1 | 1 | 1 | 0 | 0 | 0 | 1 | 2 | 0 | 0 | 50,081 |
| University of Michigan, Ann Arbor | 1 | 1 | 0 | 0 | 0 | 0 | 0 | 1 | 0 | 1 | 43,625 |
| **Metropolitan Counties** | 19 | 7 | 3 | 1 | 0 | 0 | | | | | |
| Calhoun | 1 | 0 | 0 | 0 | 0 | 0 | 0 | 0 | 1 | 0 | |
| Eaton | 2 | 0 | 1 | 0 | 0 | 0 | 0 | 1 | 0 | 2 | |
| Genesee | 0 | 1 | 0 | 0 | 0 | 0 | 0 | 1 | 0 | 0 | |
| Kalamazoo | 1 | 0 | 0 | 0 | 0 | 0 | 0 | 0 | 1 | 0 | |
| Kent | 1 | 1 | 1 | 0 | 0 | 0 | 1 | 1 | 1 | 0 | |
| Lapeer | 1 | 1 | 0 | 0 | 0 | 0 | 0 | 1 | 0 | 1 | |
| Livingston | 1 | 0 | 0 | 1 | 0 | 0 | 0 | 0 | 2 | 0 | |
| Macomb | 2 | 0 | 0 | 0 | 0 | 0 | 0 | 1 | 0 | 1 | |
| Midland | 1 | 0 | 0 | 0 | 0 | 0 | 0 | 0 | 1 | 0 | |
| Monroe | 1 | 1 | 0 | 0 | 0 | 0 | 1 | 1 | 0 | 0 | |
| Montcalm | 0 | 1 | 0 | 0 | 0 | 0 | 0 | 0 | 0 | 1 | |
| Oakland | 1 | 0 | 0 | 0 | 0 | 0 | 0 | 0 | 1 | 0 | |
| Ottawa | 2 | 0 | 0 | 0 | 0 | 0 | 0 | 1 | 1 | 0 | |
| Van Buren | 1 | 1 | 0 | 0 | 0 | 0 | 0 | 0 | 2 | 0 | |
| Washtenaw | 4 | 1 | 1 | 0 | 0 | 0 | 2 | 3 | 0 | 1 | |
| **Nonmetropolitan Counties** | 2 | 4 | 0 | 0 | 0 | 0 | | | | | |
| Allegan | 1 | 0 | 0 | 0 | 0 | 0 | 0 | 0 | 1 | 0 | |
| Cheboygan | 1 | 0 | 0 | 0 | 0 | 0 | 0 | 0 | 0 | 1 | |
| Emmet | 0 | 0 | 2 | 0 | 0 | 0 | 0 | 1 | 1 | 0 | |
| Grand Traverse | 2 | 1 | 1 | 0 | 0 | 0 | 0 | 2 | 2 | 0 | |
| Ionia | 1 | 0 | 0 | 0 | 0 | 0 | 0 | 0 | 0 | 1 | |
| Missaukee | 1 | 1 | 1 | 0 | 0 | 0 | 1 | 0 | 0 | 2 | |
| Oceana | 1 | 0 | 0 | 0 | 0 | 0 | 0 | 1 | 0 | 0 | |
| **State Police Agencies** | 2 | 1 | 1 | 0 | 0 | 0 | | | | | |
| Kent County | 1 | 0 | 0 | 0 | 0 | 0 | 0 | 0 | 0 | 1 | |
| Monroe County | 1 | 0 | 0 | 0 | 0 | 0 | 0 | 0 | 1 | 0 | |
| Montcalm County | 0 | 1 | 0 | 0 | 0 | 0 | 0 | 0 | 0 | 1 | |
| Oakland County | 0 | 0 | 1 | 0 | 0 | 0 | 0 | 0 | 1 | 0 | |
| **Other Agencies** | 0 | 1 | 0 | 0 | 0 | 0 | | | | | |
| Wayne County Airport | 0 | 1 | 0 | 0 | 0 | 0 | 0 | 1 | 0 | 0 | |
| **MINNESOTA** | | | | | | | | | | | |
| **Total** | 58 | 20 | 31 | 0 | 0 | 0 | | | | | |
| **Cities** | 58 | 19 | 30 | 0 | 0 | 0 | | | | | |
| Blaine | 1 | 0 | 0 | 0 | 0 | 0 | 1 | 0 | 0 | 0 | 62,177 |
| Brooklyn Park | 5 | 1 | 2 | 0 | 0 | 0 | 1 | 4 | 0 | 3 | 79,433 |
| Coon Rapids | 2 | 0 | 0 | 0 | 0 | 0 | 0 | 1 | 0 | 1 | 62,256 |
| Duluth | 2 | 0 | 0 | 0 | 0 | 0 | 1 | 0 | 0 | 1 | 86,241 |
| Eagan | 1 | 0 | 0 | 0 | 0 | 0 | 0 | 1 | 0 | 0 | 66,549 |
| Eden Prairie | 1 | 0 | 0 | 0 | 0 | 0 | 1 | 0 | 0 | 0 | 63,835 |
| Hopkins | 2 | 0 | 0 | 0 | 0 | 0 | 0 | 0 | 1 | 1 | 18,167 |
| Inver Grove Heights | 1 | 0 | 0 | 0 | 0 | 0 | 0 | 1 | 0 | 0 | 34,912 |
| Mankato | 10 | 1 | 0 | 0 | 0 | 0 | 0 | 5 | 5 | 1 | 40,669 |
| Maple Grove | 1 | 1 | 1 | 0 | 0 | 0 | 0 | 1 | 1 | 1 | 68,297 |
| Maplewood | 4 | 0 | 0 | 0 | 0 | 0 | 1 | 0 | 3 | 0 | 40,742 |
| Minneapolis | 6 | 8 | 16 | 0 | 0 | 0 | 3 | 10 | 10 | 7 | 413,479 |
| Minnetonka | 0 | 1 | 0 | 0 | 0 | 0 | 0 | 0 | 0 | 1 | 51,921 |
| Moorhead | 0 | 0 | 1 | 0 | 0 | 0 | 0 | 0 | 1 | 0 | 40,283 |
| New Hope | 1 | 0 | 0 | 0 | 0 | 0 | 0 | 0 | 0 | 1 | 20,900 |
| Plymouth | 1 | 1 | 0 | 0 | 0 | 0 | 0 | 1 | 1 | 0 | 76,192 |
| Rochester | 1 | 0 | 1 | 0 | 0 | 0 | 0 | 0 | 2 | 0 | 112,542 |
| Roseville | 2 | 0 | 2 | 0 | 0 | 0 | 0 | 2 | 2 | 0 | 35,729 |
| Sartell | 0 | 1 | 0 | 0 | 0 | 0 | 0 | 0 | 1 | 0 | 16,648 |

(Number.)

| State/agency | Number of incidents per bias motivation | | | | | | Number of incidents per quarter | | | | Population[1] |
|---|---|---|---|---|---|---|---|---|---|---|---|
| | Race/ Ethnicity/ Ancestry | Religion | Sexual orientation | Disability | Gender | Gender Identity | 1st quarter | 2nd quarter | 3rd quarter | 4th quarter | |
| Spring Lake Park | 2 | 0 | 0 | 0 | 0 | 0 | 0 | 0 | 1 | 1 | 6,476 |
| St. Cloud | 1 | 2 | 0 | 0 | 0 | 0 | | | 1 | 2 | 66,498 |
| St. Louis Park | 1 | 2 | 1 | 0 | 0 | 0 | 0 | 3 | 1 | 0 | 48,074 |
| St. Paul | 10 | 1 | 6 | 0 | 0 | 0 | 2 | 5 | 9 | 1 | 300,721 |
| Wadena | 2 | 0 | 0 | 0 | 0 | 0 | 0 | 0 | 2 | 0 | 4,107 |
| Worthington | 1 | 0 | 0 | 0 | 0 | 0 | 0 | 1 | 0 | 0 | 12,969 |
| **Metropolitan Counties** | 0 | 1 | 1 | 0 | 0 | 0 | | | | | |
| Nicollet | 0 | 1 | 0 | 0 | 0 | 0 | 0 | 0 | 1 | 0 | |
| Wright | 0 | 0 | 1 | 0 | 0 | 0 | 0 | 0 | 0 | 1 | |
| **MISSOURI** | | | | | | | | | | | |
| **Total** | 70 | 19 | 8 | 1 | 0 | 2 | | | | | |
| **Cities** | 56 | 15 | 7 | 1 | 0 | 2 | | | | | |
| Columbia | 3 | 1 | 0 | 0 | 0 | 0 | 0 | 1 | 2 | 1 | 118,911 |
| Fredericktown | 0 | 0 | 1 | 0 | 0 | 0 | 0 | 0 | 1 | 0 | 4,078 |
| Gladstone | 0 | 1 | 0 | 0 | 0 | 0 | 0 | 1 | 0 | 0 | 27,141 |
| Independence | 3 | 0 | 0 | 0 | 0 | 0 | 1 | 1 | 1 | 0 | 117,639 |
| Joplin | 1 | 0 | 0 | 0 | 0 | 0 | 0 | 0 | 1 | 0 | 51,412 |
| Kansas City | 28 | 8 | 4 | 1 | 0 | 1 | 6 | 7 | 14 | 15 | 473,373 |
| Kirksville | 1 | 0 | 1 | 0 | 0 | 0 | 0 | 0 | 1 | 1 | 17,662 |
| Lee's Summit | 2 | 0 | 0 | 0 | 0 | 0 | 0 | 1 | 0 | 1 | 94,450 |
| Maryville | 1 | 0 | 0 | 0 | 0 | 0 | 1 | 0 | 0 | 0 | 12,009 |
| Overland | 1 | 0 | 0 | 0 | 0 | 0 | 0 | 0 | 1 | 0 | 15,967 |
| Pagedale | 1 | 0 | 0 | 0 | 0 | 0 | 0 | 0 | 1 | 0 | 3,310 |
| Rolla | 2 | 0 | 0 | 0 | 0 | 0 | 0 | 2 | 0 | 0 | 19,995 |
| Springfield | 2 | 1 | 0 | 0 | 0 | 0 | 1 | 0 | 2 | 0 | 166,860 |
| St. Joseph | 1 | 0 | 1 | 0 | 0 | 0 | 0 | 1 | 0 | 1 | 77,035 |
| St. Louis | 7 | 1 | 0 | 0 | 0 | 0 | 1 | 1 | 3 | 3 | 317,095 |
| St. Peters | 0 | 0 | 0 | 0 | 0 | 1 | 0 | 0 | 0 | 1 | 56,923 |
| University City | 2 | 3 | 0 | 0 | 0 | 0 | 0 | 3 | 0 | 2 | 35,058 |
| Warrenton | 1 | 0 | 0 | 0 | 0 | 0 | 0 | 0 | 1 | 0 | 8,109 |
| **Universities and Colleges** | 4 | 4 | 0 | 0 | 0 | 0 | | | | | |
| Northwest Missouri State University | 1 | 0 | 0 | 0 | 0 | 0 | 0 | 1 | 0 | 0 | 6,720 |
| St. Louis Community College, Meramec | 1 | 0 | 0 | 0 | 0 | 0 | 0 | 1 | 0 | 0 | 21,218 |
| University of Missouri, Columbia | 2 | 4 | 0 | 0 | 0 | 0 | 1 | 1 | 1 | 3 | 35,425 |
| **Metropolitan Counties** | 5 | 0 | 0 | 0 | 0 | 0 | | | | | |
| St. Louis County Police Department | 5 | 0 | 0 | 0 | 0 | 0 | 2 | 1 | 0 | 2 | |
| **Nonmetropolitan Counties** | 4 | 0 | 1 | 0 | 0 | 0 | | | | | |
| Laclede | 1 | 0 | 0 | 0 | 0 | 0 | 0 | 0 | 1 | 0 | |
| Nodaway | 1 | 0 | 0 | 0 | 0 | 0 | 0 | 1 | 0 | 0 | |
| Schuyler | 0 | 0 | 1 | 0 | 0 | 0 | 1 | 0 | 0 | 0 | |
| Taney | 1 | 0 | 0 | 0 | 0 | 0 | 0 | 0 | 1 | 0 | |
| Worth | 1 | 0 | 0 | 0 | 0 | 0 | 0 | 0 | 1 | 0 | |
| **State Police Agencies** | 1 | 0 | 0 | 0 | 0 | 0 | | | | | |
| State Highway Patrol, Jefferson City | 1 | 0 | 0 | 0 | 0 | 0 | 0 | 0 | 0 | 1 | |
| **MONTANA** | | | | | | | | | | | |
| **Total** | 28 | 14 | 2 | 1 | 0 | 0 | | | | | |
| **Cities** | 7 | 6 | 1 | 0 | 0 | 0 | | | | | |
| Billings | 3 | 0 | 0 | 0 | 0 | 0 | 1 | 0 | 2 | 0 | 109,997 |
| Helena | 0 | 5 | 0 | 0 | 0 | 0 | 0 | 3 | 1 | 1 | 30,363 |
| Kalispell | 1 | 1 | 0 | 0 | 0 | 0 | 1 | 1 | 0 | 0 | 21,932 |
| Red Lodge | 0 | 0 | 1 | 0 | 0 | 0 | 0 | 0 | 1 | 0 | 2,237 |
| Ronan City | 1 | 0 | 0 | 0 | 0 | 0 | 0 | 1 | 0 | 0 | 1,942 |
| Sidney | 1 | 0 | 0 | 0 | 0 | 0 | 0 | 0 | 1 | 0 | 6,817 |
| Stevensville | 1 | 0 | 0 | 0 | 0 | 0 | 0 | 0 | 0 | 1 | 1,925 |

| State/agency | Number of incidents per bias motivation | | | | | | Number of incidents per quarter | | | | Population[1] |
|---|---|---|---|---|---|---|---|---|---|---|---|
| | Race/ Ethnicity/ Ancestry | Religion | Sexual orientation | Disability | Gender | Gender Identity | 1st quarter | 2nd quarter | 3rd quarter | 4th quarter | |
| **Metropolitan Counties** ............ | 17 | 0 | 1 | 0 | 0 | 0 | | | | | |
| Yellowstone.................................. | 17 | 0 | 1 | 0 | 0 | 0 | 3 | 3 | 11 | 1 | |
| | | | | | | | | | | | |
| **Nonmetropolitan Counties......** | 4 | 8 | 0 | 1 | 0 | 0 | | | | | |
| Flathead...................................... | 0 | 2 | 0 | 0 | 0 | 0 | 0 | 1 | 1 | 0 | |
| Lewis and Clark ......................... | 3 | 5 | 0 | 0 | 0 | 0 | 2 | 6 | 0 | 0 | |
| McCone....................................... | 0 | 0 | 0 | 1 | 0 | 0 | 0 | 1 | 0 | 0 | |
| Rosebud...................................... | 1 | 0 | 0 | 0 | 0 | 0 | 0 | 0 | 0 | 1 | |
| Stillwater ................................... | 0 | 1 | 0 | 0 | 0 | 0 | 0 | 1 | 0 | 0 | |
| | | | | | | | | | | | |
| **NEBRASKA** | | | | | | | | | | | |
| **Total** ........................................ | 10 | 1 | 7 | 0 | 0 | 1 | | | | | |
| | | | | | | | | | | | |
| **Cities** ...................................... | 30 | 1 | 10 | 0 | 0 | 0 | | | | | |
| Lincoln....................................... | 9 | 1 | 5 | 0 | 0 | 1 | 2 | 4 | 4 | 6 | 276,585 |
| Omaha........................................ | 0 | 0 | 2 | 0 | 0 | 0 | 1 | 0 | 0 | 1 | 452,252 |
| | | | | | | | | | | | |
| **Universities and Colleges ........** | 1 | 0 | 0 | 0 | 0 | 0 | | | | | |
| University of Nebraska, Lincoln.... | 1 | 0 | 0 | 0 | 0 | 0 | 1 | 0 | 0 | 0 | 25,006 |
| | | | | | | | | | | | |
| **NEVADA** | | | | | | | | | | | |
| **Total** ........................................ | 36 | 5 | 17 | 0 | 0 | 0 | | | | | |
| | | | | | | | | | | | |
| **Cities** ...................................... | 34 | 5 | 17 | 0 | 0 | 0 | | | | | |
| Henderson.................................. | 7 | 1 | 0 | 0 | 0 | 0 | 2 | 2 | 3 | 1 | 282,554 |
| Las Vegas Metropolitan Police Department[3] ............................. | 22 | 4 | 15 | 0 | 0 | 0 | 6 | 14 | 12 | 9 | 1,562,134 |
| North Las Vegas ......................... | 4 | 0 | 2 | 0 | 0 | 0 | 2 | 1 | 1 | 2 | 234,386 |
| Reno............................................ | 1 | 0 | 0 | 0 | 0 | 0 | 0 | 0 | 1 | 0 | 239,721 |
| | | | | | | | | | | | |
| **Universities and Colleges ........** | 2 | 0 | 0 | 0 | 0 | 0 | | | | | |
| Truckee Meadows Community College .................................... | 1 | 0 | 0 | 0 | 0 | 0 | 0 | 0 | 1 | 0 | 11,106 |
| University of Nevada, Las Vegas .. | 1 | 0 | 0 | 0 | 0 | 0 | 0 | 0 | 0 | 1 | 28,515 |
| | | | | | | | | | | | |
| **NEW HAMPSHIRE** | | | | | | | | | | | |
| **Total** ........................................ | 8 | 3 | 2 | 0 | 0 | 0 | | | | | |
| | | | | | | | | | | | |
| **Cities** ...................................... | 8 | 3 | 2 | 0 | 0 | 0 | | | | | |
| Antrim........................................ | 1 | 0 | 0 | 0 | 0 | 0 | 0 | 1 | 0 | 0 | 2,659 |
| Barrington ................................. | 1 | 0 | 0 | 0 | 0 | 0 | 0 | 1 | 0 | 0 | 8,814 |
| Concord ..................................... | 3 | 0 | 0 | 0 | 0 | 0 | 0 | 1 | 0 | 2 | 42,389 |
| Dublin......................................... | 1 | 0 | 0 | 0 | 0 | 0 | 0 | 0 | 0 | 1 | 1,560 |
| Epping ....................................... | 0 | 0 | 1 | 0 | 0 | 0 | 0 | 0 | 0 | 1 | 6,880 |
| Exeter ........................................ | 1 | 1 | 0 | 0 | 0 | 0 | 0 | 2 | 0 | 0 | 14,617 |
| Hampton .................................... | 1 | 0 | 1 | 0 | 0 | 0 | 0 | 0 | 1 | 1 | 15,280 |
| Hampton Falls............................ | 0 | 1 | 0 | 0 | 0 | 0 | 1 | 0 | 0 | 0 | 2,314 |
| Manchester................................ | 0 | 1 | 0 | 0 | 0 | 0 | 0 | 0 | 0 | 1 | 110,661 |
| | | | | | | | | | | | |
| **NEW JERSEY** | | | | | | | | | | | |
| **Total** ........................................ | 169 | 125 | 33 | 3 | 0 | 0 | | | | | |
| | | | | | | | | | | | |
| **Cities** ...................................... | 167 | 125 | 33 | 3 | 0 | 0 | | | | | |
| Aberdeen Township ................... | 6 | 0 | 2 | 0 | 0 | 0 | 3 | 1 | 0 | 4 | 18,312 |
| Bayonne ..................................... | 0 | 1 | 0 | 0 | 0 | 0 | 0 | 0 | 0 | 1 | 66,582 |
| Belleville..................................... | 2 | 0 | 0 | 0 | 0 | 0 | 0 | 0 | 1 | 1 | 36,452 |
| Bloomingdale.............................. | 1 | 0 | 0 | 0 | 0 | 0 | 0 | 0 | 1 | 0 | 8,299 |
| Boonton ..................................... | 1 | 0 | 0 | 0 | 0 | 0 | 0 | 0 | 1 | 0 | 8,427 |
| Bordentown Township ................ | 3 | 0 | 0 | 0 | 0 | 0 | 1 | 0 | 2 | 0 | 11,662 |
| Bound Brook............................... | 1 | 0 | 0 | 0 | 0 | 0 | 0 | 0 | 1 | 0 | 11,300 |
| Bridgewater Township................ | 0 | 0 | 1 | 0 | 0 | 0 | 1 | 0 | 0 | 0 | 44,996 |
| Butler......................................... | 0 | 1 | 0 | 0 | 0 | 0 | 1 | 0 | 0 | 0 | 7,719 |
| Chatham .................................... | 1 | 0 | 0 | 0 | 0 | 0 | 1 | 0 | 0 | 0 | 9,039 |
| Chatham Township..................... | 1 | 0 | 0 | 0 | 0 | 0 | 0 | 0 | 0 | 1 | 10,654 |
| Clifton ....................................... | 1 | 0 | 0 | 0 | 0 | 0 | 0 | 0 | 0 | 1 | 86,224 |
| Collingswood.............................. | 1 | 0 | 0 | 0 | 0 | 0 | 0 | 0 | 1 | 0 | 13,948 |
| Colts Neck Township.................. | 0 | 1 | 0 | 0 | 0 | 0 | 0 | 0 | 0 | 1 | 10,045 |
| Delran Township ........................ | 4 | 0 | 0 | 0 | 0 | 0 | 2 | 1 | 0 | 1 | 16,745 |
| Eastampton Township................ | 0 | 1 | 0 | 0 | 0 | 0 | 0 | 0 | 0 | 1 | 6,053 |

| State/agency | Number of incidents per bias motivation | | | | | | Number of incidents per quarter | | | | Population[1] |
|---|---|---|---|---|---|---|---|---|---|---|---|
| | Race/ Ethnicity/ Ancestry | Religion | Sexual orientation | Disability | Gender | Gender Identity | 1st quarter | 2nd quarter | 3rd quarter | 4th quarter | |
| East Brunswick Township | 5 | 3 | 0 | 0 | 0 | 0 | 3 | 3 | 0 | 2 | 48,625 |
| East Hanover Township | 1 | 0 | 0 | 0 | 0 | 0 | 0 | 0 | | 1 | 11,317 |
| East Windsor Township | 2 | 1 | 0 | 0 | 0 | 0 | 1 | 2 | 0 | 0 | 27,569 |
| Edison Township | 1 | 1 | 0 | 0 | 0 | 0 | 1 | 0 | 1 | 0 | 102,281 |
| Egg Harbor Township | 1 | 0 | 0 | 0 | 0 | 0 | 0 | 0 | 1 | | 43,965 |
| Englewood | 1 | 1 | 1 | 0 | 0 | 0 | 1 | 0 | 1 | 1 | 27,752 |
| Evesham Township | 5 | 1 | 1 | 1 | 0 | 0 | 3 | 0 | 2 | 3 | 45,586 |
| Ewing Township | 0 | 1 | 0 | 0 | 0 | 0 | 1 | 0 | 0 | 0 | 36,668 |
| Fairfield Township, Essex County | 0 | 1 | 0 | 0 | 0 | 0 | 0 | 0 | 0 | 1 | 7,559 |
| Florham Park | 0 | 1 | 0 | 0 | 0 | 0 | 0 | 1 | 0 | 0 | 11,852 |
| Franklin Township, Somerset County | 2 | 0 | 0 | 0 | 0 | 0 | 0 | 1 | 1 | 0 | 66,831 |
| Freehold | 1 | 0 | 1 | 0 | 0 | 0 | 0 | 1 | 1 | 0 | 11,950 |
| Freehold Township | 1 | 0 | 0 | 0 | 0 | 0 | 0 | 1 | 0 | 0 | 35,723 |
| Galloway Township | 1 | 0 | 0 | 0 | 0 | 0 | 1 | 0 | 0 | 0 | 37,637 |
| Garwood | 0 | 1 | 0 | 0 | 0 | 0 | 1 | 0 | 0 | 0 | 4,540 |
| Gibbsboro | 1 | 0 | 0 | 0 | 0 | 0 | 0 | 0 | 0 | 1 | 2,229 |
| Glassboro | 2 | 16 | 1 | 0 | 0 | 0 | 1 | 1 | 1 | 16 | 19,087 |
| Glen Rock | 0 | 1 | 0 | 0 | 0 | 0 | 0 | 0 | 1 | 0 | 11,953 |
| Gloucester City | 1 | 0 | 0 | 0 | 0 | 0 | 0 | 1 | 0 | 0 | 11,265 |
| Green Brook Township | 1 | 0 | 0 | 0 | 0 | 0 | 1 | 0 | 0 | 0 | 7,261 |
| Guttenberg | 1 | 0 | 0 | 0 | 0 | 0 | 1 | 0 | 0 | 0 | 11,534 |
| Hackettstown | 1 | 0 | 0 | 0 | 0 | 0 | 0 | 0 | 1 | 0 | 9,506 |
| Hamilton Township, Atlantic County | 1 | 0 | 0 | 0 | 0 | 0 | 0 | 0 | 1 | 0 | 26,671 |
| Hamilton Township, Mercer County | 2 | 0 | 0 | 0 | 0 | 0 | 0 | 1 | 1 | 0 | 89,124 |
| Hanover Township | 0 | 1 | 0 | 0 | 0 | 0 | 0 | 0 | 0 | 1 | 14,905 |
| Harrison Township | 1 | 0 | 1 | 0 | 0 | 0 | 1 | 0 | 1 | 0 | 12,893 |
| Hawthorne | 2 | 0 | 0 | 0 | 0 | 0 | 0 | 2 | 0 | 0 | 19,078 |
| High Bridge | 0 | 1 | 0 | 0 | 0 | 0 | 0 | 0 | 1 | 0 | 3,573 |
| Highland Park | 1 | 2 | 0 | 0 | 0 | 0 | 0 | 0 | 1 | 2 | 14,525 |
| Hightstown | 1 | 0 | 0 | 0 | 0 | 0 | 1 | 0 | 0 | 0 | 5,574 |
| Hillsborough Township | 1 | 0 | 0 | 0 | 0 | 0 | 0 | 1 | 0 | 0 | 39,830 |
| Hoboken | 3 | 1 | 3 | 1 | 0 | 0 | 2 | 1 | 2 | 3 | 54,050 |
| Ho-Ho-Kus | 0 | 1 | 0 | 0 | 0 | 0 | 0 | 1 | 0 | 0 | 4,188 |
| Hopewell Township | 1 | 0 | 0 | 0 | 0 | 0 | 0 | 0 | 0 | 1 | 18,389 |
| Howell Township | 5 | 1 | 1 | 0 | 0 | 0 | 2 | 5 | 0 | 0 | 52,097 |
| Jackson Township | 0 | 1 | 0 | 0 | 0 | 0 | 0 | 0 | 0 | 1 | 56,815 |
| Jersey City | 0 | 0 | 2 | 1 | 0 | 0 | 0 | 0 | 3 | 0 | 265,159 |
| Keansburg | 2 | 0 | 0 | 0 | 0 | 0 | 0 | 1 | 1 | 0 | 9,815 |
| Lacey Township | 2 | 0 | 0 | 0 | 0 | 0 | 2 | 0 | 0 | 0 | 28,340 |
| Lakewood Township | 8 | 17 | 0 | 0 | 0 | 0 | 4 | 11 | 6 | 4 | 95,743 |
| Little Falls Township | 1 | 2 | 1 | 0 | 0 | 0 | 2 | 0 | 0 | 2 | 14,510 |
| Livingston Township | 0 | 2 | 0 | 0 | 0 | 0 | 0 | 2 | 0 | 0 | 30,021 |
| Lodi | 1 | 0 | 0 | 0 | 0 | 0 | 0 | 0 | 0 | 1 | 24,734 |
| Lower Township | 1 | 0 | 1 | 0 | 0 | 0 | 0 | 0 | 2 | 0 | 22,108 |
| Madison | 3 | 3 | 0 | 0 | 0 | 0 | 0 | 3 | 2 | 1 | 16,197 |
| Manalapan Township | 1 | 3 | 0 | 0 | 0 | 0 | 0 | 3 | 1 | 0 | 40,238 |
| Manasquan | 0 | 1 | 0 | 0 | 0 | 0 | 0 | 0 | 1 | 0 | 5,731 |
| Manchester Township | 1 | 0 | 0 | 0 | 0 | 0 | 0 | 0 | 0 | 1 | 43,661 |
| Medford Lakes | 0 | 1 | 0 | 0 | 0 | 0 | 0 | 0 | 0 | 1 | 4,102 |
| Medford Township | 1 | 2 | 0 | 0 | 0 | 0 | 2 | 0 | 1 | 0 | 23,439 |
| Middlesex | 1 | 0 | 0 | 0 | 0 | 0 | 0 | 0 | 0 | 1 | 13,926 |
| Middle Township | 0 | 0 | 1 | 0 | 0 | 0 | 0 | 0 | 0 | 1 | 18,873 |
| Midland Park | 0 | 2 | 0 | 0 | 0 | 0 | 0 | 2 | 0 | 0 | 7,335 |
| Millburn Township | 0 | 1 | 0 | 0 | 0 | 0 | 0 | 1 | 0 | 0 | 20,441 |
| Monroe Township, Gloucester County | 2 | 0 | 0 | 0 | 0 | 0 | 1 | 1 | 0 | 0 | 37,624 |
| Monroe Township, Middlesex County | 7 | 1 | 0 | 0 | 0 | 0 | 2 | 3 | 3 | 0 | 43,654 |
| Montclair | 2 | 1 | 1 | 0 | 0 | 0 | 2 | 1 | 1 | 0 | 38,192 |
| Montville Township | 0 | 1 | 0 | 0 | 0 | 0 | 0 | 1 | 0 | 0 | 21,917 |
| Morris Township | 0 | 2 | 0 | 0 | 0 | 0 | 0 | 0 | 1 | 1 | 22,605 |
| Mount Laurel Township | 2 | 0 | 0 | 0 | 0 | 0 | 0 | 0 | 0 | 2 | 41,705 |
| Neptune Township | 8 | 0 | 2 | 0 | 0 | 0 | 2 | 4 | 1 | 3 | 27,659 |
| New Brunswick | 4 | 7 | 5 | 0 | 0 | 0 | 2 | 8 | 1 | 5 | 57,580 |
| New Milford | 0 | 1 | 1 | 0 | 0 | 0 | 2 | 0 | 0 | 0 | 16,729 |

# Table 13. Hate Crime Incidents Per Bias Motivation and Quarter, by Selected State and Agency, 2015—*Continued*

(Number.)

| State/agency | Number of incidents per bias motivation | | | | | | Number of incidents per quarter | | | | Population[1] |
|---|---|---|---|---|---|---|---|---|---|---|---|
| | Race/ Ethnicity/ Ancestry | Religion | Sexual orientation | Disability | Gender | Gender Identity | 1st quarter | 2nd quarter | 3rd quarter | 4th quarter | |
| North Bergen Township............. | 1 | 0 | 0 | 0 | 0 | 0 | 0 | 1 | 0 | 0 | 62,928 |
| North Brunswick Township......... | 1 | 0 | 0 | 0 | 0 | 0 | 0 | 0 | 1 | 0 | 42,696 |
| Northfield ................................. | 1 | 0 | 0 | 0 | 0 | 0 | 0 | 0 | 0 | 1 | 8,600 |
| North Haledon .......................... | 1 | 0 | 0 | 0 | 0 | 0 | 1 | 0 | 0 | 0 | 8,521 |
| Norwood .................................. | 2 | 1 | 0 | 0 | 0 | 0 | 0 | 1 | 1 | 1 | 5,843 |
| Palmyra.................................... | 1 | 0 | 1 | 0 | 0 | 0 | 1 | 0 | 1 | 0 | 7,318 |
| Paramus................................... | 1 | 1 | 0 | 0 | 0 | 0 | 0 | 0 | 0 | 2 | 26,903 |
| Park Ridge ............................... | 0 | 0 | 1 | 0 | 0 | 0 | 0 | 1 | 0 | 0 | 8,872 |
| Parsippany-Troy Hills Township .... | 0 | 1 | 0 | 0 | 0 | 0 | 1 | 0 | 0 | 0 | 53,790 |
| Passaic..................................... | 0 | 3 | 1 | 0 | 0 | 0 | 0 | 3 | 1 | 0 | 71,807 |
| Piscataway Township................. | 5 | 0 | 0 | 0 | 0 | 0 | 3 | 0 | 1 | 1 | 59,622 |
| Princeton ................................. | 0 | 3 | 0 | 0 | 0 | 0 | 1 | 1 | 0 | 1 | 30,447 |
| Randolph Township................... | 5 | 1 | 0 | 0 | 0 | 0 | 1 | 3 | 2 | 0 | 26,033 |
| Ridgefield Park.......................... | 0 | 0 | 1 | 0 | 0 | 0 | 0 | 0 | 1 | 0 | 13,037 |
| Ridgewood ............................... | 0 | 1 | 0 | 0 | 0 | 0 | 0 | 0 | 0 | 1 | 25,581 |
| River Edge................................ | 0 | 2 | 0 | 0 | 0 | 0 | 0 | 0 | 0 | 2 | 11,615 |
| Roselle ..................................... | 1 | 0 | 0 | 0 | 0 | 0 | 0 | 1 | 0 | 0 | 21,621 |
| Saddle Brook Township.............. | 2 | 0 | 0 | 0 | 0 | 0 | 2 | 0 | 0 | 0 | 14,037 |
| Scotch Plains Township .............. | 0 | 1 | 0 | 0 | 0 | 0 | 0 | 1 | 0 | 0 | 24,179 |
| Sea Girt ................................... | 0 | 1 | 0 | 0 | 0 | 0 | 0 | 1 | 0 | 0 | 1,810 |
| Secaucus.................................. | 1 | 1 | 0 | 0 | 0 | 0 | 0 | 0 | 0 | 2 | 18,959 |
| Somerville................................ | 0 | 1 | 0 | 0 | 0 | 0 | 1 | 0 | 0 | 0 | 12,162 |
| South Amboy............................ | 1 | 0 | 0 | 0 | 0 | 0 | 0 | 0 | 1 | 0 | 8,886 |
| South Brunswick Township......... | 9 | 1 | 0 | 0 | 0 | 0 | 2 | 2 | 5 | 1 | 45,509 |
| South Plainfield........................ | 1 | 1 | 0 | 0 | 0 | 0 | 0 | 0 | 1 | 1 | 24,053 |
| South River .............................. | 1 | 0 | 0 | 0 | 0 | 0 | 0 | 1 | 0 | 0 | 16,382 |
| Springfield ............................... | 0 | 1 | 0 | 0 | 0 | 0 | 0 | 1 | 0 | 0 | 17,518 |
| Stone Harbor ............................ | 1 | 0 | 0 | 0 | 0 | 0 | 0 | 1 | 0 | 0 | 839 |
| Union City ............................... | 1 | 0 | 0 | 0 | 0 | 0 | 0 | 0 | 0 | 1 | 69,077 |
| Verona..................................... | 0 | 6 | 0 | 0 | 0 | 0 | 0 | 1 | 5 | 0 | 13,769 |
| Voorhees Township.................... | 1 | 1 | 0 | 0 | 0 | 0 | 0 | 2 | 0 | 0 | 28,890 |
| Wallington ............................... | 0 | 1 | 0 | 0 | 0 | 0 | 0 | 0 | 1 | 0 | 11,674 |
| Washington Township, Gloucester County.................... | 1 | 0 | 0 | 0 | 0 | 0 | 0 | 1 | 0 | 0 | 47,588 |
| Wayne Township........................ | 2 | 2 | 0 | 0 | 0 | 0 | 3 | 1 | 0 | 0 | 55,036 |
| West Deptford Township............. | 2 | 1 | 1 | 0 | 0 | 0 | 0 | 1 | 1 | 2 | 21,276 |
| West Long Branch...................... | 0 | 5 | 0 | 0 | 0 | 0 | 3 | 1 | 0 | 1 | 8,375 |
| West Milford Township ............... | 2 | 0 | 0 | 0 | 0 | 0 | 1 | 1 | 0 | 0 | 26,678 |
| West Windsor Township.............. | 0 | 1 | 0 | 0 | 0 | 0 | 1 | 0 | 0 | 0 | 28,700 |
| Winfield Township ..................... | 1 | 0 | 0 | 0 | 0 | 0 | 0 | 1 | 0 | 0 | 1,506 |
| Woodbridge Township ............... | 2 | 0 | 0 | 0 | 0 | 0 | 1 | 1 | 0 | 0 | 100,950 |
| Woodbury ................................ | 5 | 0 | 2 | 0 | 0 | 0 | 0 | 5 | 1 | 1 | 9,961 |
| Woodstown............................... | 0 | 1 | 0 | 0 | 0 | 0 | 0 | 0 | 1 | 0 | 3,443 |
| **Metropolitan Counties** ........... | 1 | 0 | 0 | 0 | 0 | 0 | | | | | |
| Camden County Police Department ............................... | 1 | 0 | 0 | 0 | 0 | 0 | 0 | 0 | 1 | 0 | |
| **State Police Agencies**............. | 1 | 0 | 0 | 0 | 0 | 0 | | | | | |
| State Police, Monmouth County ..................................... | 1 | 0 | 0 | 0 | 0 | 0 | 0 | 1 | 0 | 0 | |
| **NEW MEXICO** | | | | | | | | | | | |
| **Total** ........................................ | 8 | 2 | 3 | 0 | 0 | 0 | | | | | |
| **Cities** ........................................ | 8 | 2 | 3 | 0 | 0 | 0 | | | | | |
| Albuquerque.............................. | 7 | 2 | 3 | 0 | 0 | 0 | 6 | 5 | 1 | | 559,721 |
| Los Lunas................................. | 1 | 0 | 0 | 0 | 0 | 0 | 1 | | | | 15,251 |
| **NEW YORK**................................ | | | | | | | | | | | |
| **Total** ........................................ | 136 | 256 | 104 | 1 | 0 | 3 | | | | | |
| **Cities** ........................................ | 99 | 170 | 90 | 1 | 0 | 2 | | | | | |
| Albany..................................... | 3 | 0 | 0 | 0 | 0 | 0 | 1 | 1 | 1 | 0 | 98,772 |
| Amherst Town ........................... | 2 | 0 | 0 | 0 | 0 | 0 | 0 | 0 | 2 | 0 | 120,207 |
| Auburn..................................... | 0 | 0 | 1 | 0 | 0 | 0 | 1 | 0 | 0 | 0 | 26,865 |
| Buffalo..................................... | 3 | 0 | 3 | 0 | 0 | 0 | 1 | 1 | 2 | 2 | 258,096 |
| Cairo Town ............................... | 1 | 0 | 0 | 0 | 0 | 0 | 0 | 1 | 0 | 0 | 6,465 |
| Cheektowaga Town.................... | 1 | 0 | 0 | 0 | 0 | 0 | 0 | 0 | 1 | 0 | 78,438 |

# Table 13. Hate Crime Incidents Per Bias Motivation and Quarter, by Selected State and Agency, 2015—*Continued*

(Number.)

| State/agency | Number of incidents per bias motivation | | | | | | Number of incidents per quarter | | | | Population[1] |
|---|---|---|---|---|---|---|---|---|---|---|---|
| | Race/ Ethnicity/ Ancestry | Religion | Sexual orientation | Disability | Gender | Gender Identity | 1st quarter | 2nd quarter | 3rd quarter | 4th quarter | |
| Clarkstown Town | 0 | 3 | 0 | 0 | 0 | 0 | 1 | 1 | 0 | 1 | 82,156 |
| Cooperstown Village | 1 | 0 | 0 | 0 | 0 | 0 | 0 | 0 | 1 | 0 | 1,802 |
| Crawford Town | 0 | 2 | 0 | 0 | 0 | 0 | 0 | 0 | 1 | 1 | 9,213 |
| Freeport Village | 0 | 2 | 0 | 0 | 0 | 0 | 0 | 1 | 1 | 0 | 43,403 |
| Greenburgh Town | 0 | 1 | 0 | 0 | 0 | 0 | 1 | 0 | 0 | 0 | 45,362 |
| Hamburg Town | 1 | 0 | 0 | 0 | 0 | 0 | 0 | 1 | 0 | 0 | 45,942 |
| Hastings-on-Hudson Village | 0 | 1 | 0 | 0 | 0 | 0 | 0 | 0 | 0 | 1 | 8,005 |
| Ithaca | 0 | 0 | 1 | 0 | 0 | 0 | 0 | 0 | 0 | 1 | 30,892 |
| Jamestown | 1 | 0 | 0 | 0 | 0 | 0 | 0 | 1 | 0 | 0 | 30,263 |
| Lancaster Town | 0 | 1 | 0 | 0 | 0 | 0 | 0 | 0 | 0 | 1 | 37,134 |
| Middletown | 0 | 1 | 0 | 0 | 0 | 0 | 0 | 0 | 0 | 1 | 27,633 |
| Monroe Village | 0 | 2 | 0 | 0 | 0 | 0 | 1 | 0 | 1 | 0 | 8,605 |
| Mount Vernon | 1 | 0 | 0 | 0 | 0 | 0 | 0 | 0 | 1 | 0 | 68,734 |
| New Rochelle | 1 | 0 | 0 | 0 | 0 | 0 | 0 | 0 | 1 | 0 | 80,270 |
| New York | 71 | 154 | 81 | 1 | 0 | 0 | 56 | 96 | 71 | 84 | 8,550,861 |
| North Greenbush Town | 0 | 0 | 1 | 0 | 0 | 0 | 0 | 0 | 1 | 0 | 12,132 |
| Ogdensburg | 0 | 0 | 1 | 0 | 0 | 0 | 0 | 0 | 1 | 0 | 10,844 |
| Oswego City | 1 | 0 | 0 | 0 | 0 | 0 | 0 | 1 | 0 | 0 | 17,941 |
| Port Washington | 0 | 1 | 0 | 0 | 0 | 0 | 0 | 0 | 0 | 1 | 19,215 |
| Poughkeepsie | 3 | 0 | 0 | 0 | 0 | 0 | 1 | 0 | 1 | 1 | 30,416 |
| Rochester | 0 | 0 | 0 | 0 | 0 | 1 | 0 | 0 | 1 | 0 | 209,922 |
| Saratoga Springs | 1 | 0 | 0 | 0 | 0 | 0 | 0 | 0 | 0 | 1 | 27,653 |
| Schenectady | 0 | 1 | 0 | 0 | 0 | 0 | 0 | 0 | 0 | 1 | 65,875 |
| Scotia Village | 1 | 0 | 0 | 0 | 0 | 0 | 0 | 1 | 0 | 0 | 7,822 |
| Solvay Village | 1 | 0 | 0 | 0 | 0 | 0 | 0 | 0 | 1 | 0 | 6,423 |
| Spring Valley Village | 1 | 0 | 0 | 0 | 0 | 0 | 0 | 1 | 0 | 0 | 32,795 |
| Troy | 1 | 0 | 0 | 0 | 0 | 0 | 0 | 1 | 0 | 0 | 49,872 |
| Tupper Lake Village | 1 | 0 | 0 | 0 | 0 | 0 | 0 | 0 | 1 | 0 | 3,609 |
| Webster Town and Village | 1 | 0 | 0 | 0 | 0 | 0 | 0 | 0 | 1 | 0 | 44,211 |
| Yonkers | 2 | 1 | 2 | 0 | 0 | 1 | 0 | 2 | 3 | 1 | 201,753 |
| **Universities and Colleges** | 4 | 6 | 3 | 0 | 0 | 0 | | | | | |
| State University of New York, Binghamton | 1 | 1 | 1 | 0 | 0 | 0 | 1 | 0 | 1 | 1 | 16,695 |
| State University of New York Agricultural and Technical College, Morrisville | 1 | 1 | 0 | 0 | 0 | 0 | 0 | 0 | 0 | 2 | 2,910 |
| State University of New York College | | | | | | | | | | | |
| New Paltz | 0 | 1 | 0 | 0 | 0 | 0 | 1 | 0 | 0 | 0 | 7,692 |
| Oneonta | 0 | 1 | 0 | 0 | 0 | 0 | 0 | 0 | 0 | 1 | 6,101 |
| Potsdam | 1 | 0 | 2 | 0 | 0 | 0 | 1 | 1 | 0 | 1 | 3,979 |
| Purchase | 1 | 2 | 0 | 0 | 0 | 0 | 2 | 0 | 0 | 1 | 4,225 |
| **Metropolitan Counties** | 21 | 69 | 10 | 0 | 0 | 1 | | | | | |
| Dutchess | 0 | 1 | 0 | 0 | 0 | 0 | 0 | 0 | 0 | 1 | |
| Nassau | 8 | 23 | 1 | 0 | 0 | 0 | 7 | 13 | 6 | 6 | |
| Niagara | 0 | 0 | 1 | 0 | 0 | 0 | 0 | 1 | 0 | 0 | |
| Orleans | 0 | 1 | 0 | 0 | 0 | 0 | 0 | 0 | 1 | 0 | |
| Suffolk County Police Department | 13 | 44 | 8 | 0 | 0 | 1 | 8 | 24 | 18 | 16 | |
| **Nonmetropolitan Counties** | 0 | 0 | 1 | 0 | 0 | 0 | | | | | |
| Cattaraugus | 0 | 0 | 1 | 0 | 0 | 0 | 1 | 0 | 0 | 0 | |
| **State Police Agencies** | 7 | 3 | 0 | 0 | 0 | 0 | | | | | |
| Cattaraugus County | 1 | 0 | 0 | 0 | 0 | 0 | 0 | 0 | 0 | 1 | |
| Delaware County | 0 | 1 | 0 | 0 | 0 | 0 | 0 | 0 | 0 | 1 | |
| Duchess County | 1 | 0 | 0 | 0 | 0 | 0 | 0 | 0 | 1 | 0 | |
| Franklin County | 1 | 0 | 0 | 0 | 0 | 0 | 1 | 0 | 0 | 0 | |
| Monroe County | 1 | 0 | 0 | 0 | 0 | 0 | 0 | 1 | 0 | 0 | |
| Orange County | 0 | 1 | 0 | 0 | 0 | 0 | 0 | 1 | 0 | 0 | |
| St. Lawrence County | 0 | 1 | 0 | 0 | 0 | 0 | 0 | 1 | 0 | 0 | |
| Tioga County | 1 | 0 | 0 | 0 | 0 | 0 | 0 | 0 | 0 | 1 | |
| Warren County | 1 | 0 | 0 | 0 | 0 | 0 | 0 | 0 | 0 | 1 | |
| Westchester County | 1 | 0 | 0 | 0 | 0 | 0 | 0 | 1 | 0 | 0 | |

# Table 13. Hate Crime Incidents Per Bias Motivation and Quarter, by Selected State and Agency, 2015—*Continued*

(Number.)

| State/agency | Number of incidents per bias motivation | | | | | | Number of incidents per quarter | | | | Population[1] |
|---|---|---|---|---|---|---|---|---|---|---|---|
| | Race/ Ethnicity/ Ancestry | Religion | Sexual orientation | Disability | Gender | Gender Identity | 1st quarter | 2nd quarter | 3rd quarter | 4th quarter | |
| **Other Agencies** | 5 | 8 | 0 | 0 | 0 | 0 | | | | | |
| New York City Metropolitan Transportation Authority | 4 | 8 | 0 | 0 | 0 | 0 | 5 | 5 | 2 | 0 | |
| State Park, New York City Region | 1 | 0 | 0 | 0 | 0 | 0 | 1 | 0 | 0 | 0 | |
| **NORTH CAROLINA** | | | | | | | | | | | |
| **Total** | 106 | 17 | 37 | 2 | 0 | 0 | | | | | |
| **Cities** | 82 | 14 | 33 | 2 | 0 | 0 | | | | | |
| Apex | 2 | 0 | 1 | 0 | 0 | 0 | 0 | 0 | 3 | 0 | 45,593 |
| Asheville | 3 | 1 | 3 | 0 | 0 | 0 | 2 | 2 | 3 | 0 | 89,003 |
| Boone | 0 | 1 | 0 | 0 | 0 | 0 | 0 | 1 | 0 | 0 | 18,394 |
| Brevard | 1 | 0 | 0 | 0 | 0 | 0 | 0 | 0 | 0 | 1 | 7,695 |
| Carrboro | 1 | 0 | 0 | 0 | 0 | 0 | 0 | 0 | 1 | 0 | 21,340 |
| Charlotte-Mecklenburg | 16 | 3 | 9 | 1 | 0 | 0 | 3 | 9 | 12 | 5 | 877,817 |
| Dunn | 0 | 0 | 2 | 0 | 0 | 0 | 0 | 0 | 2 | 0 | 9,809 |
| Durham | 4 | 1 | 0 | 0 | 0 | 0 | 0 | 0 | 4 | 1 | 257,911 |
| Erwin | 1 | 0 | 0 | 0 | 0 | 0 | 1 | 0 | 0 | 0 | 4,661 |
| Fayetteville | 3 | 1 | 0 | 1 | 0 | 0 | 1 | 1 | 2 | 1 | 204,731 |
| Gastonia | 6 | 0 | 0 | 0 | 0 | 0 | 3 | 0 | 3 | 0 | 74,196 |
| Granite Falls | 1 | 0 | 0 | 0 | 0 | 0 | 0 | 0 | 0 | 1 | 4,661 |
| Greensboro[3] | 4 | 2 | 4 | 0 | 0 | 0 | 0 | 2 | 3 | 4 | 285,950 |
| Greenville | 2 | 0 | 0 | 0 | 0 | 0 | 1 | 0 | 1 | 0 | 91,114 |
| Hickory | 2 | 0 | 0 | 0 | 0 | 0 | 0 | 1 | 1 | 0 | 40,162 |
| High Point | 1 | 0 | 0 | 0 | 0 | 0 | 1 | 0 | 0 | 0 | 109,669 |
| Hillsborough | 1 | 0 | 0 | 0 | 0 | 0 | 0 | 0 | 1 | 0 | 6,460 |
| Hope Mills | 1 | 0 | 0 | 0 | 0 | 0 | 0 | 0 | 0 | 1 | 16,466 |
| Jacksonville | 1 | 0 | 1 | 0 | 0 | 0 | 0 | 1 | 1 | 0 | 68,614 |
| Mars Hill | 1 | 0 | 0 | 0 | 0 | 0 | 1 | 0 | 0 | 0 | 2,300 |
| Mayodan | 1 | 0 | 1 | 0 | 0 | 0 | 0 | 1 | 1 | 0 | 2,461 |
| Mint Hill | 0 | 0 | 1 | 0 | 0 | 0 | 0 | 0 | 1 | 0 | 25,664 |
| Mocksville | 1 | 0 | 0 | 0 | 0 | 0 | 0 | 1 | 0 | 0 | 5,114 |
| Newton | 1 | 0 | 1 | 0 | 0 | 0 | 0 | 0 | 2 | 0 | 13,014 |
| Oxford | 1 | 0 | 0 | 0 | 0 | 0 | 0 | 1 | 0 | 0 | 8,771 |
| Raleigh | 12 | 4 | 6 | 0 | 0 | 0 | 4 | 11 | 3 | 4 | 448,722 |
| Reidsville | 2 | 0 | 0 | 0 | 0 | 0 | 0 | 0 | 2 | 0 | 13,983 |
| Rocky Mount | 0 | 0 | 1 | 0 | 0 | 0 | 1 | 0 | 0 | 0 | 55,978 |
| Roxboro | 1 | 0 | 0 | 0 | 0 | 0 | 0 | 0 | 1 | 0 | 8,293 |
| Salisbury | 3 | 0 | 0 | 0 | 0 | 0 | 0 | 1 | 2 | 0 | 33,761 |
| Siler City | 2 | 0 | 0 | 0 | 0 | 0 | 0 | 0 | 1 | 1 | 8,368 |
| Smithfield | 2 | 0 | 0 | 0 | 0 | 0 | 0 | 1 | 0 | 1 | 11,924 |
| Wilmington | 3 | 1 | 3 | 0 | 0 | 0 | 0 | 2 | 2 | 3 | 115,434 |
| Wilson | 2 | 0 | 0 | 0 | 0 | 0 | 0 | 2 | 0 | 0 | 49,442 |
| **Universities and Colleges** | 6 | 0 | 3 | 0 | 0 | 0 | | | | | |
| Duke University | 1 | 0 | 1 | 0 | 0 | 0 | 0 | 0 | 0 | 2 | 15,856 |
| East Carolina University | 1 | 0 | 0 | 0 | 0 | 0 | 0 | 0 | 0 | 1 | 27,511 |
| Elizabeth City State University | 1 | 0 | 0 | 0 | 0 | 0 | 0 | 0 | 0 | 1 | 1,867 |
| North Carolina School of the Arts | 2 | 0 | 0 | 0 | 0 | 0 | 1 | 0 | 0 | 1 | 958 |
| University of North Carolina: | | | | | | | | | | | |
| Greensboro | 1 | 0 | 0 | 0 | 0 | 0 | 1 | 0 | 0 | 0 | 18,647 |
| Pembroke | 0 | 0 | 2 | 0 | 0 | 0 | 2 | 0 | 0 | 0 | 6,269 |
| **Metropolitan Counties** | 15 | 3 | 0 | 0 | 0 | 0 | | | | | |
| Cabarrus | 0 | 1 | 0 | 0 | 0 | 0 | 0 | 0 | 0 | 1 | |
| Caldwell | 0 | 1 | 0 | 0 | 0 | 0 | 0 | 0 | 1 | 0 | |
| Currituck | 1 | 0 | 0 | 0 | 0 | 0 | 0 | 1 | 0 | 0 | |
| Forsyth | 5 | 0 | 0 | 0 | 0 | 0 | 1 | 0 | 3 | 1 | |
| Franklin | 4 | 0 | 0 | 0 | 0 | 0 | 0 | 0 | 2 | 2 | |
| Gaston County Police Department | 1 | 0 | 0 | 0 | 0 | 0 | 0 | 0 | 0 | 1 | |
| Guilford | 0 | 1 | 0 | 0 | 0 | 0 | 0 | 1 | 0 | 0 | |
| New Hanover | 1 | 0 | 0 | 0 | 0 | 0 | 0 | 1 | 0 | 0 | |
| Pitt | 3 | 0 | 0 | 0 | 0 | 0 | 0 | 1 | 1 | 1 | |
| **Nonmetropolitan Counties** | 3 | 0 | 1 | 0 | 0 | 0 | | | | | |
| Bladen | 1 | 0 | 0 | 0 | 0 | 0 | 0 | 0 | 1 | 0 | |
| Cleveland | 1 | 0 | 0 | 0 | 0 | 0 | 0 | 0 | 1 | 0 | |
| Rutherford | 1 | 0 | 1 | 0 | 0 | 0 | 2 | 0 | 0 | 0 | |

(Number.)

| State/agency | Number of incidents per bias motivation | | | | | | Number of incidents per quarter | | | | Population[1] |
|---|---|---|---|---|---|---|---|---|---|---|---|
| | Race/Ethnicity/Ancestry | Religion | Sexual orientation | Disability | Gender | Gender Identity | 1st quarter | 2nd quarter | 3rd quarter | 4th quarter | |
| **NORTH DAKOTA** | | | | | | | | | | | |
| Total ............................ | 29 | 3 | 4 | 0 | 0 | 0 | | | | | |
| **Cities** .............................. | 23 | 2 | 2 | 0 | 0 | 0 | | | | | |
| Belfield ............................ | 1 | 0 | 0 | 0 | 0 | 0 | 0 | 0 | 0 | 1 | 1,092 |
| Bismarck ........................... | 8 | 0 | 0 | 0 | 0 | 0 | 4 | 3 | 1 | 0 | 70,873 |
| Devils Lake......................... | 1 | 0 | 0 | 0 | 0 | 0 | 0 | 1 | 0 | | 7,326 |
| Dickinson........................... | 0 | 0 | 1 | 0 | 0 | 0 | 0 | 1 | 0 | 0 | 23,564 |
| Fargo.................................. | 8 | 1 | 0 | 0 | 0 | 0 | 2 | 3 | 3 | 1 | 118,490 |
| Grand Forks........................ | 1 | 0 | 0 | 0 | 0 | 0 | 0 | 1 | 0 | 0 | 56,861 |
| Mandan.............................. | 1 | 0 | 0 | 0 | 0 | 0 | 0 | 1 | 0 | 0 | 21,448 |
| Minot ................................ | 1 | 0 | 0 | 0 | 0 | 0 | 0 | 1 | 0 | 0 | 49,842 |
| Rugby................................. | 1 | 0 | 0 | 0 | 0 | 0 | 0 | 0 | 0 | 1 | 2,919 |
| Wahpeton........................... | 1 | 0 | 0 | 0 | 0 | 0 | 0 | 0 | 0 | 1 | 7,940 |
| Watford City ...................... | 0 | 1 | 0 | 0 | 0 | 0 | 0 | 0 | 1 | 0 | 5,235 |
| Williston ............................ | 0 | 0 | 1 | 0 | 0 | 0 | 0 | 0 | 0 | 1 | 27,324 |
| **Universities and Colleges** ........ | 0 | 0 | 1 | 0 | 0 | 0 | | | | | |
| University of North Dakota......... | 0 | 0 | 1 | 0 | 0 | 0 | 0 | 0 | 0 | 1 | 14,906 |
| **Metropolitan Counties** ............ | 0 | 1 | 0 | 0 | 0 | 0 | | | | | |
| Morton ............................... | 0 | 1 | 0 | 0 | 0 | 0 | 0 | 0 | 1 | 0 | |
| **Nonmetropolitan Counties**...... | 6 | 0 | 1 | 0 | 0 | 0 | | | | | |
| Barnes ............................... | 1 | 0 | 0 | 0 | 0 | 0 | 0 | 0 | 1 | 0 | |
| McKenzie............................ | 2 | 0 | 0 | 0 | 0 | 0 | 0 | 0 | 2 | 0 | |
| McLean............................... | 1 | 0 | 0 | 0 | 0 | 0 | 0 | 1 | 0 | 0 | |
| Ramsey............................... | 1 | 0 | 1 | 0 | 0 | 0 | 1 | 0 | 0 | 1 | |
| Richland.............................. | 1 | 0 | 0 | 0 | 0 | 0 | 0 | 1 | 0 | 0 | |
| **OHIO** | | | | | | | | | | | |
| Total ............................... | 309 | 39 | 58 | 10 | 0 | 0 | | | | | |
| **Cities** .............................. | 276 | 27 | 52 | 9 | 0 | 0 | | | | | |
| Akron................................. | 4 | 0 | 0 | 0 | 0 | 0 | 1 | 3 | 0 | 0 | 197,587 |
| Athens................................ | 0 | 1 | 0 | 0 | 0 | 0 | 0 | 0 | 0 | 1 | 23,960 |
| Barberton........................... | 5 | 0 | 1 | 0 | 0 | 0 | 3 | 2 | 1 | 0 | 26,242 |
| Bellefontaine...................... | 2 | 0 | 0 | 0 | 0 | 0 | 1 | 1 | 0 | 0 | 13,124 |
| Blue Ash ............................ | 2 | 0 | 0 | 0 | 0 | 0 | 0 | 1 | 0 | 1 | 12,159 |
| Boardman........................... | 4 | 0 | 0 | 0 | 0 | 0 | 0 | 1 | 2 | 1 | 39,887 |
| Bowling Green.................... | 1 | 0 | 0 | 0 | 0 | 0 | 1 | 0 | 0 | 0 | 31,878 |
| Butler Township .................. | 2 | 0 | 0 | 0 | 0 | 0 | 0 | 1 | 1 | 0 | 7,857 |
| Celina................................. | 1 | 0 | 0 | 0 | 0 | 0 | 0 | 0 | 1 | 0 | 10,366 |
| Cheviot............................... | 1 | 0 | 0 | 0 | 0 | 0 | 0 | 1 | 0 | 0 | 8,314 |
| Cincinnati........................... | 23 | 4 | 6 | 0 | 0 | 0 | 7 | 8 | 10 | 8 | 298,478 |
| Cleveland............................ | 6 | 1 | 0 | 1 | 0 | 0 | 1 | 5 | 2 | 0 | 387,921 |
| Coldwater........................... | 1 | 0 | 0 | 0 | 0 | 0 | 0 | 0 | 1 | 0 | 4,459 |
| Columbus............................ | 114 | 9 | 14 | 0 | 0 | 0 | 15 | 39 | 56 | 27 | 847,745 |
| Columbus Grove................... | 1 | 0 | 0 | 0 | 0 | 0 | 0 | 0 | 1 | 0 | 2,071 |
| Conneaut............................ | 0 | 0 | 0 | 5 | 0 | 0 | | | 5 | | 12,809 |
| Cortland............................. | 1 | 0 | 0 | 0 | 0 | 0 | 0 | 0 | 1 | 0 | 6,931 |
| Dayton................................ | 4 | 1 | 0 | 0 | 0 | 0 | 2 | 0 | 2 | 1 | 140,683 |
| Defiance ............................ | 1 | 0 | 0 | 0 | 0 | 0 | 0 | 1 | 0 | 0 | 16,698 |
| Elmwood Place ................... | 7 | 0 | 0 | 0 | 0 | 0 | 0 | 7 | 0 | 0 | 2,170 |
| Fairborn............................. | 1 | 1 | 0 | 0 | 0 | 0 | 0 | 1 | 1 | 0 | 33,423 |
| Forest Park......................... | 1 | 0 | 0 | 0 | 0 | 0 | 0 | 0 | 0 | 1 | 18,726 |
| Fostoria.............................. | 1 | 0 | 0 | 0 | 0 | 0 | 1 | 0 | 0 | 0 | 13,126 |
| Gahanna............................. | 1 | 0 | 0 | 0 | 0 | 0 | 0 | 0 | 0 | 1 | 34,508 |
| Garfield Heights.................. | 1 | 0 | 0 | 0 | 0 | 0 | 1 | 0 | 0 | | 28,088 |
| Glouster.............................. | 1 | 0 | 0 | 0 | 0 | 0 | 0 | 1 | 0 | 0 | 1,787 |
| Greenhills ........................... | 2 | 0 | 0 | 0 | 0 | 0 | 0 | 0 | 1 | 1 | 3,592 |
| Grove City .......................... | 3 | 0 | 0 | 0 | 0 | 0 | 0 | 2 | 0 | 1 | 39,251 |
| Hamilton............................. | 6 | 0 | 4 | 1 | 0 | 0 | 2 | 2 | 3 | 4 | 62,526 |
| Haskins............................... | 1 | 0 | 0 | 0 | 0 | 0 | 0 | 1 | 0 | 0 | 1,232 |
| Heath ................................. | 4 | 0 | 1 | 0 | 0 | 0 | 1 | 2 | 1 | 1 | 10,496 |
| Holland............................... | 2 | 0 | 0 | 0 | 0 | 0 | 0 | 0 | 1 | 1 | 1,702 |
| Howland Township ............. | 1 | 0 | 0 | 0 | 0 | 0 | 0 | 0 | 1 | 0 | 16,857 |
| Huber Heights...................... | 2 | 0 | 0 | 0 | 0 | 0 | 1 | 1 | 0 | 0 | 38,164 |
| Independence ..................... | 1 | 0 | 1 | 0 | 0 | 0 | 0 | 0 | 2 | 0 | 7,139 |

# Table 13. Hate Crime Incidents Per Bias Motivation and Quarter, by Selected State and Agency, 2015—*Continued*

(Number.)

| State/agency | Number of incidents per bias motivation | | | | | | Number of incidents per quarter | | | | Population[1] |
|---|---|---|---|---|---|---|---|---|---|---|---|
| | Race/ Ethnicity/ Ancestry | Religion | Sexual orientation | Disability | Gender | Gender Identity | 1st quarter | 2nd quarter | 3rd quarter | 4th quarter | |
| Jackson Township, Stark County . | 2 | 0 | 1 | 0 | 0 | 0 | 0 | 2 | 1 | 0 | 40,779 |
| Lakewood | 9 | 0 | 0 | 0 | 0 | 0 | 9 | 0 | | | 50,653 |
| Lancaster | 0 | 0 | 1 | 0 | 0 | 0 | 0 | 0 | 1 | 0 | 39,793 |
| Lorain | 1 | 0 | 0 | 0 | 0 | 0 | 0 | 0 | 1 | | 63,700 |
| Lyndhurst | 0 | 1 | 0 | 0 | 0 | 0 | 0 | 0 | 1 | 0 | 13,672 |
| Madison Township, Franklin County | 2 | 0 | 1 | 0 | 0 | 0 | 0 | 1 | 2 | 0 | 18,260 |
| Mansfield | 3 | 0 | 0 | 0 | 0 | 0 | 0 | 1 | 2 | 0 | 46,605 |
| Massillon | 1 | 0 | 0 | 0 | 0 | 0 | 0 | 0 | 1 | 0 | 32,301 |
| Maumee | 0 | 0 | 1 | 0 | 0 | 0 | 0 | 1 | 0 | 0 | 13,978 |
| Medina Township | 0 | 1 | 0 | 0 | 0 | 0 | 0 | 0 | 1 | 0 | 8,961 |
| Mentor | 1 | 0 | 0 | 0 | 0 | 0 | 0 | 0 | 0 | 1 | 46,802 |
| Miamisburg | 0 | 0 | 0 | 1 | 0 | 0 | 1 | 0 | 0 | 0 | 20,064 |
| Miami Township, Montgomery County | 1 | 1 | 0 | 0 | 0 | 0 | 0 | 0 | 0 | 2 | 29,134 |
| Monroe | 4 | 0 | 0 | 0 | 0 | 0 | 2 | 1 | 1 | 0 | 15,814 |
| Montpelier | 2 | 0 | 0 | 0 | 0 | 0 | 0 | 0 | 2 | 0 | 4,010 |
| Montville Township | 0 | 1 | 0 | 0 | 0 | 0 | 0 | 1 | 0 | 0 | 11,738 |
| Moraine | 2 | 0 | 0 | 0 | 0 | 0 | 1 | 1 | 0 | 0 | 6,378 |
| Mount Healthy | 1 | 0 | 0 | 0 | 0 | 0 | 0 | 1 | 0 | 0 | 6,053 |
| Mount Vernon | 1 | 0 | 0 | 0 | 0 | 0 | 0 | 1 | 0 | 0 | 16,727 |
| Newton Falls | 0 | 0 | 2 | 0 | 0 | 0 | 1 | 0 | 1 | 0 | 4,656 |
| Niles | 4 | 2 | 0 | 0 | 0 | 0 | 1 | 2 | 1 | 2 | 18,667 |
| North Canton | 1 | 0 | 0 | 0 | 0 | 0 | 0 | 0 | 1 | 0 | 17,496 |
| Norton | 2 | 0 | 1 | 0 | 0 | 0 | 0 | 1 | 1 | 1 | 12,031 |
| Parma | 1 | 0 | 0 | 0 | 0 | 0 | 0 | 0 | 0 | 1 | 79,655 |
| Portsmouth | 0 | 0 | 1 | 0 | 0 | 0 | 0 | 0 | 1 | 0 | 20,346 |
| Sidney | 0 | 0 | 1 | 0 | 0 | 0 | 0 | 0 | 0 | 1 | 20,836 |
| Springfield Township, Hamilton County | 1 | 0 | 2 | 0 | 0 | 0 | 2 | 1 | 0 | 0 | 36,574 |
| Streetsboro | 0 | 0 | 1 | 0 | 0 | 0 | 1 | 0 | 0 | 0 | 16,286 |
| Sugarcreek Township | 1 | 0 | 0 | 0 | 0 | 0 | 0 | 0 | 0 | 1 | 8,212 |
| Sunbury | 1 | 0 | 0 | 0 | 0 | 0 | 0 | 0 | 0 | 1 | 5,037 |
| Toledo[3] | 13 | 1 | 5 | 0 | 0 | 0 | 3 | 3 | 12 | 1 | 279,552 |
| Upper Arlington | 1 | 1 | 0 | 0 | 0 | 0 | 0 | 1 | 1 | 0 | 34,838 |
| Urbana | 2 | 1 | 0 | 0 | 0 | 0 | 0 | 1 | 2 | 0 | 11,453 |
| Vandalia | 1 | 0 | 0 | 0 | 0 | 0 | 0 | 0 | 0 | 1 | 15,106 |
| Van Wert | 0 | 0 | 1 | 0 | 0 | 0 | 0 | 0 | 0 | 1 | 10,755 |
| Vienna Township | 0 | 0 | 0 | 1 | 0 | 0 | 0 | 0 | 0 | 1 | 3,844 |
| Wadsworth | 1 | 0 | 5 | 0 | 0 | 0 | 0 | 0 | 0 | 6 | 21,966 |
| Washington Court House | 0 | 0 | 1 | 0 | 0 | 0 | 0 | 0 | 1 | 0 | 14,060 |
| Weathersfield | 1 | 0 | 0 | 0 | 0 | 0 | 0 | 0 | 1 | 0 | 8,091 |
| Wellston | 1 | 0 | 0 | 0 | 0 | 0 | 1 | 0 | 0 | 0 | 5,503 |
| West Carrollton | 1 | 0 | 0 | 0 | 0 | 0 | | | | 1 | 12,983 |
| West Chester Township | 1 | 0 | 0 | 0 | 0 | 0 | 1 | 0 | 0 | 0 | 60,365 |
| Wilmington | 2 | 0 | 0 | 0 | 0 | 0 | 0 | 1 | 1 | 0 | 12,350 |
| Wooster | 1 | 0 | 0 | 0 | 0 | 0 | 0 | 1 | 0 | 0 | 26,651 |
| Worthington | 1 | 0 | 0 | 0 | 0 | 0 | 0 | 0 | 1 | 0 | 14,594 |
| Youngstown | 1 | 1 | 0 | 0 | 0 | 0 | 0 | 1 | 0 | 1 | 64,608 |
| Zanesville | 0 | 0 | 1 | 0 | 0 | 0 | 0 | 0 | 1 | 0 | 25,337 |
| **Universities and Colleges** | 5 | 2 | 0 | 0 | 0 | 0 | | | | | |
| Bowling Green State University ... | 1 | 0 | 0 | 0 | 0 | 0 | 0 | 0 | 1 | 0 | 16,554 |
| Capital University | 1 | 1 | 0 | 0 | 0 | 0 | 0 | 0 | 1 | 1 | 3,494 |
| Lakeland Community College | 1 | 0 | 0 | 0 | 0 | 0 | 0 | 1 | 0 | 0 | 8,250 |
| Miami University | 1 | 0 | 0 | 0 | 0 | 0 | 0 | 0 | 0 | 1 | 18,620 |
| Ohio State University, Columbus . | 1 | 1 | 0 | 0 | 0 | 0 | 1 | 1 | 0 | 0 | 58,322 |
| **Metropolitan Counties** | 16 | 10 | 4 | 0 | 0 | 0 | | | | | |
| Butler | 3 | 0 | 1 | 0 | 0 | 0 | 2 | 1 | 0 | 1 | |
| Fairfield | 1 | 0 | 0 | 0 | 0 | 0 | 1 | 0 | 0 | 0 | |
| Greene | 6 | 4 | 0 | 0 | 0 | 0 | 3 | 6 | 0 | 1 | |
| Lawrence | 0 | 0 | 1 | 0 | 0 | 0 | 0 | 0 | 0 | 1 | |
| Lorain | 1 | 0 | 0 | 0 | 0 | 0 | 0 | 0 | 1 | 0 | |
| Lucas | 1 | 0 | 0 | 0 | 0 | 0 | 1 | 0 | 0 | 0 | |
| Montgomery | 1 | 2 | 1 | 0 | 0 | 0 | 1 | 1 | 0 | 2 | |
| Stark | 2 | 4 | 1 | 0 | 0 | 0 | 1 | 2 | 4 | 0 | |
| Warren | 1 | 0 | 0 | 0 | 0 | 0 | 1 | 0 | 0 | 0 | |

| State/agency | Number of incidents per bias motivation | | | | | | Number of incidents per quarter | | | | Population[1] |
|---|---|---|---|---|---|---|---|---|---|---|---|
| | Race/ Ethnicity/ Ancestry | Religion | Sexual orientation | Disability | Gender | Gender Identity | 1st quarter | 2nd quarter | 3rd quarter | 4th quarter | |
| **Nonmetropolitan Counties......** | 8 | 0 | 1 | 1 | 0 | 0 | | | | | |
| Ashland ......................... | 1 | 0 | 0 | 0 | 0 | 0 | 0 | 0 | 0 | 1 | |
| Ashtabula ...................... | 1 | 0 | 0 | 0 | 0 | 0 | 0 | 0 | 1 | 0 | |
| Athens........................... | 1 | 0 | 0 | 0 | 0 | 0 | 0 | 1 | 0 | 0 | |
| Gallia............................. | 0 | 0 | 1 | 0 | 0 | 0 | 0 | 0 | 1 | 0 | |
| Marion............................ | 0 | 0 | 0 | 1 | 0 | 0 | 0 | 1 | 0 | 0 | |
| Preble ............................ | 1 | 0 | 0 | 0 | 0 | 0 | 0 | 0 | 0 | 1 | |
| Ross ............................... | 1 | 0 | 0 | 0 | 0 | 0 | 0 | 1 | 0 | 0 | |
| Scioto ............................ | 1 | 0 | 0 | 0 | 0 | 0 | 0 | 1 | 0 | 0 | |
| Shelby............................ | 1 | 0 | 0 | 0 | 0 | 0 | 0 | 1 | 0 | 0 | |
| Washington .................... | 1 | 0 | 0 | 0 | 0 | 0 | 0 | 1 | 0 | 0 | |
| **State Police Agencies...............** | | | | | | | | | | | |
| Ohio State Highway Patrol ......... | 2 | 0 | 1 | 0 | 0 | 0 | 1 | 1 | 0 | 1 | |
| **Other Agencies.........................** | 2 | 0 | 0 | 0 | 0 | 0 | | | | | |
| Cleveland Metropolitan Park District | 1 | 0 | 0 | 0 | 0 | 0 | 0 | 1 | 0 | 0 | |
| Hamilton County Park District ..... | 1 | 0 | 0 | 0 | 0 | 0 | 0 | 0 | 0 | 1 | |
| **OKLAHOMA** | | | | | | | | | | | |
| **Total ............................** | 27 | 3 | 7 | 0 | 0 | 0 | | | | | |
| **Cities ..........................** | 19 | 3 | 6 | 0 | 0 | 0 | | | | | |
| Apache........................... | 1 | 0 | 0 | 0 | 0 | 0 | 0 | 0 | 0 | 1 | 1,424 |
| Broken Bow ..................... | 1 | 0 | 0 | 0 | 0 | 0 | 0 | 0 | 0 | 1 | 4,134 |
| Catoosa.......................... | 1 | 0 | 0 | 0 | 0 | 0 | 1 | 0 | 0 | 0 | 7,105 |
| Chickasha....................... | 2 | 0 | 1 | 0 | 0 | 0 | 1 | 1 | 1 | 0 | 16,408 |
| Choctaw......................... | 0 | 1 | 0 | 0 | 0 | 0 | 0 | 1 | 0 | 0 | 12,196 |
| Edmond.......................... | 0 | 1 | 0 | 0 | 0 | 0 | 0 | 0 | 0 | 1 | 90,418 |
| Elk City .......................... | 1 | 0 | 0 | 0 | 0 | 0 | 0 | 0 | 1 | 0 | 12,951 |
| Enid ............................... | 2 | 0 | 0 | 0 | 0 | 0 | 0 | 0 | 0 | 2 | 51,870 |
| Guymon .......................... | 0 | 1 | 0 | 0 | 0 | 0 | 0 | 1 | 0 | 0 | 12,281 |
| Jenks ............................. | 0 | 0 | 1 | 0 | 0 | 0 | 0 | 0 | 1 | 0 | 20,710 |
| Lawton ........................... | 1 | 0 | 0 | 0 | 0 | 0 | 0 | 1 | 0 | 0 | 96,801 |
| McAlester ....................... | 0 | 0 | 1 | 0 | 0 | 0 | 0 | 0 | 1 | 0 | 18,215 |
| Muskogee........................ | 3 | 0 | 0 | 0 | 0 | 0 | 0 | 3 | 0 | 0 | 38,451 |
| Norman .......................... | 1 | 0 | 0 | 0 | 0 | 0 | 1 | 0 | | | 119,767 |
| Oklahoma City................. | 1 | 0 | 2 | 0 | 0 | 0 | 0 | 2 | 1 | 0 | 630,621 |
| Purcell............................ | 1 | 0 | 0 | 0 | 0 | 0 | 0 | 0 | 0 | 1 | 6,376 |
| Sallisaw.......................... | 1 | 0 | 0 | 0 | 0 | 0 | 0 | 1 | 0 | 0 | 8,581 |
| Sayre ............................. | 1 | 0 | 0 | 0 | 0 | 0 | 1 | 0 | 0 | 0 | 4,846 |
| Stigler ............................ | 0 | 0 | 1 | 0 | 0 | 0 | 0 | 0 | 1 | 0 | 2,755 |
| Stilwell........................... | 1 | 0 | 0 | 0 | 0 | 0 | 0 | 1 | 0 | 0 | 4,019 |
| Woodward ....................... | 1 | 0 | 0 | 0 | 0 | 0 | 1 | 0 | 0 | 0 | 13,240 |
| **Metropolitan Counties ............** | 3 | 0 | 1 | 0 | 0 | 0 | | | | | |
| Lincoln............................ | 1 | 0 | 0 | 0 | 0 | 0 | 1 | 0 | 0 | 0 | |
| Tulsa .............................. | 1 | 0 | 1 | 0 | 0 | 0 | 1 | 0 | 1 | 0 | |
| Wagoner.......................... | 1 | 0 | 0 | 0 | 0 | 0 | 0 | 0 | 1 | 0 | |
| **Nonmetropolitan Counties......** | 5 | 0 | 0 | 0 | 0 | 0 | | | | | |
| Carter............................. | 1 | 0 | 0 | 0 | 0 | 0 | 0 | 1 | 0 | 0 | |
| Craig .............................. | 1 | 0 | 0 | 0 | 0 | 0 | 0 | 0 | 1 | 0 | |
| Hughes............................ | 1 | 0 | 0 | 0 | 0 | 0 | 0 | 0 | 0 | 1 | |
| Kiowa ............................. | 1 | 0 | 0 | 0 | 0 | 0 | 0 | 0 | 1 | 0 | |
| Payne.............................. | 1 | 0 | 0 | 0 | 0 | 0 | 0 | 0 | 0 | 1 | |
| **OREGON** | | | | | | | | | | | |
| **Total ............................** | 41 | 9 | 11 | 5 | 0 | 0 | | | | | |
| **Cities ..........................** | 34 | 9 | 9 | 4 | 0 | 0 | | | | | |
| Ashland .......................... | 0 | 1 | 1 | 0 | 0 | 0 | 1 | 1 | 0 | 0 | 20,834 |
| Corvallis.......................... | 2 | 1 | 0 | 1 | 0 | 0 | 0 | 0 | 3 | 1 | 55,100 |
| Eugene[3]......................... | 25 | 6 | 7 | 2 | 0 | 0 | 9 | 12 | 10 | 8 | 161,608 |
| Hood River....................... | 1 | 0 | 0 | 0 | 0 | 0 | 0 | 1 | 0 | 0 | 7,556 |
| La Grande........................ | 0 | 0 | 0 | 1 | 0 | 0 | 1 | 0 | 0 | 0 | 13,010 |
| Salem ............................. | 4 | 1 | 1 | 0 | 0 | 0 | 0 | 2 | 3 | 1 | 163,320 |
| Springfield ...................... | 1 | 0 | 0 | 0 | 0 | 0 | 0 | 0 | 0 | 1 | 60,485 |
| Sutherlin......................... | 1 | 0 | 0 | 0 | 0 | 0 | 0 | 1 | 0 | 0 | 7,749 |

(Number.)

| State/agency | Number of incidents per bias motivation | | | | | | Number of incidents per quarter | | | | Population[1] |
|---|---|---|---|---|---|---|---|---|---|---|---|
| | Race/ Ethnicity/ Ancestry | Religion | Sexual orientation | Disability | Gender | Gender Identity | 1st quarter | 2nd quarter | 3rd quarter | 4th quarter | |
| **Metropolitan Counties** ............ | 1 | 0 | 1 | 0 | 0 | 0 | | | | | |
| Deschutes.................................. | 1 | 0 | 0 | 0 | 0 | 0 | 0 | 0 | 1 | 0 | |
| Jackson..................................... | 0 | 0 | 1 | 0 | 0 | 0 | 1 | 0 | 0 | 0 | |
| **Nonmetropolitan Counties......** | 2 | 0 | 0 | 1 | 0 | 0 | | | | | |
| Hood River................................ | 1 | 0 | 0 | 0 | 0 | 0 | 0 | 0 | 1 | 0 | |
| Lincoln...................................... | 0 | 0 | 0 | 1 | 0 | 0 | 1 | 0 | 0 | | |
| Umatilla..................................... | 1 | 0 | 0 | 0 | 0 | 0 | 0 | 0 | 0 | 1 | |
| **PENNSYLVANIA** | | | | | | | | | | | |
| **Total** ........................ | 40 | 12 | 11 | 0 | 0 | 1 | | | | | |
| **Cities** ................................... | 40 | 12 | 11 | 0 | 0 | 1 | | | | | |
| Brighton Township..................... | 1 | 0 | 0 | 0 | 0 | 0 | 0 | 0 | | 1 | 8,365 |
| Columbia................................... | 1 | 0 | 0 | 0 | 0 | 0 | 1 | 0 | | 0 | 10,379 |
| Economy................................... | 1 | 0 | 0 | 0 | 0 | 0 | 0 | 0 | 0 | 1 | 9,371 |
| Lancaster................................... | 1 | 0 | 1 | 0 | 0 | 0 | 0 | 0 | 0 | 2 | 59,295 |
| New Cumberland........................ | 1 | 0 | 0 | 0 | 0 | 0 | 0 | 0 | 1 | 0 | 7,268 |
| New Garden Township................ | 0 | 0 | 1 | 0 | 0 | 0 | 0 | 1 | | | 12,121 |
| Philadelphia.............................. | 6 | 5 | 3 | 0 | 0 | 0 | 3 | 5 | 2 | 4 | 1,567,810 |
| Pittsburgh................................. | 11 | 0 | 3 | 0 | 0 | 0 | 3 | 4 | 2 | 5 | 306,870 |
| Reading..................................... | 1 | 0 | 0 | 0 | 0 | 1 | 0 | 1 | | 1 | 87,744 |
| Scranton................................... | 1 | 1 | 0 | 0 | 0 | 0 | 0 | 0 | | 2 | 75,087 |
| State College............................. | 2 | 0 | 1 | 0 | 0 | 0 | 1 | 1 | | 1 | 57,710 |
| Throop...................................... | 1 | 0 | 0 | 0 | 0 | 0 | 0 | 1 | | 0 | 4,039 |
| Washington Township, Franklin County ...................................... | 0 | 1 | 1 | 0 | 0 | 0 | 1 | 0 | 1 | 0 | 14,559 |
| **Universities and Colleges** ........ | 4 | 5 | 1 | 0 | 0 | 0 | | | | | |
| Elizabethtown College ............... | 1 | 0 | 0 | 0 | 0 | 0 | 0 | 0 | | 1 | 1,822 |
| Lehigh University........................ | 0 | 0 | 1 | 0 | 0 | 0 | 0 | 0 | | 1 | 7,119 |
| Pennsylvania State University, University Park .......................... | 2 | 1 | 0 | 0 | 0 | 0 | 2 | 0 | | 1 | 47,040 |
| University of Pittsburgh.............. | | | | | | | | | | | |
| Johnstown........................... | 0 | 4 | 0 | 0 | 0 | 0 | 0 | 0 | | 4 | 2,869 |
| Pittsburgh............................. | 1 | 0 | 0 | 0 | 0 | 0 | 1 | 0 | | 0 | 28,617 |
| **State Police Agencies**............... | 7 | 0 | 0 | 0 | 0 | 0 | | | | | |
| Elizabethville............................. | 2 | 0 | 0 | 0 | 0 | 0 | 1 | 0 | 1 | | |
| Fulton County............................ | 1 | 0 | 0 | 0 | 0 | 0 | 0 | 1 | | 0 | |
| Juniata County........................... | 1 | 0 | 0 | 0 | 0 | 0 | 0 | 0 | | 1 | |
| Monroe County ......................... | 1 | 0 | 0 | 0 | 0 | 0 | 0 | 1 | | 0 | |
| Skippack County......................... | 1 | 0 | 0 | 0 | 0 | 0 | | 1 | | 0 | |
| Washington County.................... | 1 | 0 | 0 | 0 | 0 | 0 | 0 | 0 | | 1 | |
| **Other Agencies**........................ | 2 | 0 | 0 | 0 | 0 | 0 | | | | | |
| Allegheny County Port Authority. | 1 | 0 | 0 | 0 | 0 | 0 | 0 | 1 | | | |
| Delaware County Park ............... | 1 | 0 | 0 | 0 | 0 | 0 | 0 | 0 | | 1 | |
| **RHODE ISLAND** | | | | | | | | | | | |
| **Total** ........................ | 6 | 7 | 5 | 0 | 0 | 0 | | | | | |
| **Cities** ................................... | 5 | 7 | 5 | 0 | 0 | 0 | | | | | |
| East Providence.......................... | 0 | 0 | 1 | 0 | 0 | 0 | 0 | 1 | 0 | 0 | 47,428 |
| Newport .................................... | 0 | 0 | 1 | 0 | 0 | 0 | 0 | 0 | 1 | 0 | 23,887 |
| Pawtucket.................................. | 0 | 1 | 0 | 0 | 0 | 0 | 0 | 0 | 0 | 1 | 71,624 |
| Providence................................. | 4 | 4 | 3 | 0 | 0 | 0 | 0 | 3 | 4 | 4 | 179,522 |
| Richmond .................................. | 1 | 0 | 0 | 0 | 0 | 0 | 0 | 0 | 0 | 1 | 7,592 |
| West Warwick............................ | 0 | 1 | 0 | 0 | 0 | 0 | 1 | 0 | 0 | 0 | 28,828 |
| Woonsocket .............................. | 0 | 1 | 0 | 0 | 0 | 0 | 0 | 0 | 1 | 0 | 41,261 |
| **Universities and Colleges** ........ | 1 | 0 | 0 | 0 | 0 | 0 | | | | | |
| University of Rhode Island........... | 1 | 0 | 0 | 0 | 0 | 0 | 0 | 1 | 0 | 0 | 16,571 |
| **SOUTH CAROLINA** | | | | | | | | | | | |
| **Total** ........................ | 44 | 2 | 7 | 2 | 0 | 0 | | | | | |
| **Cities** ................................... | 27 | 0 | 5 | 0 | 0 | 0 | | | | | |
| Belton....................................... | 2 | 0 | 0 | 0 | 0 | 0 | 0 | 1 | 1 | 0 | 4,324 |
| Blacksburg................................. | 1 | 0 | 0 | 0 | 0 | 0 | 1 | 0 | 0 | 0 | 1,880 |

| State/agency | Number of incidents per bias motivation | | | | | | Number of incidents per quarter | | | | |
|---|---|---|---|---|---|---|---|---|---|---|---|
| | Race/ Ethnicity/ Ancestry | Religion | Sexual orientation | Disability | Gender | Gender Identity | 1st quarter | 2nd quarter | 3rd quarter | 4th quarter | Population[1] |
| Cayce .............................. | 2 | 0 | 0 | 0 | 0 | 0 | 2 | 0 | 0 | 0 | 13,055 |
| Charleston .......................... | 3 | 0 | 1 | 0 | 0 | 0 | 0 | 2 | 0 | 2 | 132,585 |
| Cheraw .............................. | 1 | 0 | 0 | 0 | 0 | 0 | 0 | 0 | 1 | 0 | 5,781 |
| Chester .............................. | 1 | 0 | 0 | 0 | 0 | 0 | 0 | 0 | 1 | 0 | 5,467 |
| Columbia ............................ | 1 | 0 | 0 | 0 | 0 | 0 | 0 | 0 | 1 | 0 | 132,495 |
| Darlington ......................... | 0 | 0 | 1 | 0 | 0 | 0 | 0 | 0 | 0 | 1 | 6,186 |
| Easley ............................... | 1 | 0 | 0 | 0 | 0 | 0 | 0 | 0 | 0 | 1 | 20,676 |
| Elgin ................................ | 2 | 0 | 0 | 0 | 0 | 0 | 0 | 1 | 1 | 0 | 1,452 |
| Georgetown ........................ | 0 | 0 | 1 | 0 | 0 | 0 | 0 | 0 | 1 | 0 | 9,028 |
| Greenville .......................... | 1 | 0 | 0 | 0 | 0 | 0 | 0 | 0 | 1 | 0 | 63,011 |
| Hemingway ......................... | 1 | 0 | 0 | 0 | 0 | 0 | 0 | 0 | 0 | 1 | 428 |
| Honea Path ......................... | 2 | 0 | 0 | 0 | 0 | 0 | 0 | 2 | 0 | 0 | 3,697 |
| Mauldin ............................. | 1 | 0 | 0 | 0 | 0 | 0 | 1 | 0 | 0 | 0 | 25,246 |
| Mount Pleasant ..................... | 1 | 0 | 0 | 0 | 0 | 0 | 0 | 1 | 0 | 0 | 80,446 |
| Myrtle Beach ....................... | 1 | 0 | 0 | 0 | 0 | 0 | 0 | 0 | 0 | 1 | 30,731 |
| North Charleston ................... | 0 | 0 | 1 | 0 | 0 | 0 | 0 | 0 | 1 | 0 | 109,051 |
| North Myrtle Beach ................. | 1 | 0 | 0 | 0 | 0 | 0 | 1 | 0 | 0 | 0 | 15,518 |
| Orangeburg ........................ | 1 | 0 | 0 | 0 | 0 | 0 | 0 | 0 | 1 | 0 | 13,459 |
| Saluda .............................. | 0 | 0 | 1 | 0 | 0 | 0 | 0 | 0 | 1 | 0 | 3,618 |
| Santee .............................. | 1 | 0 | 0 | 0 | 0 | 0 | 0 | 0 | 0 | 1 | 940 |
| Summerville ......................... | 2 | 0 | 0 | 0 | 0 | 0 | 1 | 0 | 1 | 0 | 48,071 |
| Surfside Beach ...................... | 1 | 0 | 0 | 0 | 0 | 0 | 0 | 0 | 1 | 0 | 4,276 |
| **Universities and Colleges** ....... | 2 | 0 | 0 | 1 | 0 | 0 | | | | | |
| Trident Technical College............. | 0 | 0 | 0 | 1 | 0 | 0 | 1 | 0 | 0 | 0 | 16,136 |
| University of South Carolina:....... | | | | | | | | | | | |
| Columbia................................. | 1 | 0 | 0 | 0 | 0 | 0 | 0 | 0 | 1 | 0 | 32,971 |
| Upstate.................................. | 1 | 0 | 0 | 0 | 0 | 0 | 0 | 0 | 0 | 1 | 5,585 |
| **Metropolitan Counties** ............ | 10 | 1 | 1 | 0 | 0 | 0 | | | | | |
| Berkeley.................................. | 1 | 0 | 0 | 0 | 0 | 0 | 1 | 0 | 0 | 0 | |
| Charleston ............................... | 1 | 0 | 0 | 0 | 0 | 0 | 0 | 0 | 1 | 0 | |
| Greenville ............................... | 1 | 0 | 0 | 0 | 0 | 0 | 0 | 1 | 0 | 0 | |
| Horry County Police Department. | 4 | 1 | 0 | 0 | 0 | 0 | 2 | 3 | 0 | 0 | |
| Lexington................................. | 1 | 0 | 0 | 0 | 0 | 0 | 0 | 0 | 1 | 0 | |
| Richland.................................. | 0 | 0 | 1 | 0 | 0 | 0 | 1 | 0 | 0 | 0 | |
| Sumter.................................... | 1 | 0 | 0 | 0 | 0 | 0 | 0 | 0 | 1 | 0 | |
| Union .................................... | 1 | 0 | 0 | 0 | 0 | 0 | 0 | 0 | 1 | 0 | |
| **Nonmetropolitan Counties......** | 4 | 0 | 1 | 1 | 0 | 0 | | | | | |
| Cherokee................................. | 0 | 0 | 0 | 1 | 0 | 0 | 1 | 0 | 0 | 0 | |
| Colleton.................................. | 1 | 0 | 1 | 0 | 0 | 0 | 1 | 0 | 1 | 0 | |
| Georgetown ............................. | 2 | 0 | 0 | 0 | 0 | 0 | 2 | 0 | 0 | 0 | |
| Hampton ................................ | 1 | 0 | 0 | 0 | 0 | 0 | 0 | 0 | 0 | 1 | |
| **Other Agencies.......................** | 1 | 1 | 0 | 0 | 0 | 0 | | | | | |
| United States Department of | | | | | | | | | | | |
| Energy, Savannah River Plant....... | 1 | 1 | 0 | 0 | 0 | 0 | 0 | 0 | 2 | 0 | |
| **SOUTH DAKOTA** | | | | | | | | | | | |
| **Total .........................................** | 9 | 2 | 5 | 0 | 0 | 0 | | | | | |
| **Cities .....................................** | 8 | 2 | 5 | 0 | 0 | 0 | | | | | |
| Aberdeen................................. | 1 | 0 | 0 | 0 | 0 | 0 | 0 | 0 | 0 | 1 | 28,219 |
| Beresford................................. | 2 | 0 | 0 | 0 | 0 | 0 | 0 | 2 | 0 | 0 | 2,029 |
| Brookings ................................ | 2 | 1 | 0 | 0 | 0 | 0 | 1 | 0 | 0 | 2 | 23,501 |
| Gettysburg............................... | 1 | 0 | 1 | 0 | 0 | 0 | 0 | 0 | 1 | 1 | 1,174 |
| Rapid City ............................... | 0 | 1 | 1 | 0 | 0 | 0 | 2 | 0 | 0 | 0 | 73,801 |
| Spearfish.................................. | 1 | 0 | 0 | 0 | 0 | 0 | 1 | 0 | 0 | 0 | 11,225 |
| Sturgis .................................... | 0 | 0 | 3 | 0 | 0 | 0 | 0 | 0 | 3 | 0 | 6,767 |
| Vermillion ............................... | 1 | 0 | 0 | 0 | 0 | 0 | 0 | 0 | 1 | 0 | 10,732 |
| **Nonmetropolitan Counties......** | 1 | 0 | 0 | 0 | 0 | 0 | | | | | |
| Brown..................................... | 1 | 0 | 0 | 0 | 0 | 0 | 0 | 0 | 1 | 0 | |

# Table 13. Hate Crime Incidents Per Bias Motivation and Quarter, by Selected State and Agency, 2015—*Continued*

(Number.)

| State/agency | Race/ Ethnicity/ Ancestry | Religion | Sexual orientation | Disability | Gender | Gender Identity | 1st quarter | 2nd quarter | 3rd quarter | 4th quarter | Population[1] |
|---|---|---|---|---|---|---|---|---|---|---|---|
| **TENNESSEE** | | | | | | | | | | | |
| **Total** | 157 | 28 | 26 | 5 | 1 | 4 | | | | | |
| | | | | | | | | | | | |
| **Cities** | 83 | 17 | 22 | 5 | 1 | 1 | | | | | |
| Atoka | 8 | 0 | 0 | 1 | 0 | 0 | 0 | 5 | 2 | 2 | 9,042 |
| Chapel Hill | 0 | 0 | 0 | 1 | 0 | 0 | 0 | 1 | 0 | 0 | 1,464 |
| Chattanooga | 10 | 6 | 0 | 0 | 0 | 0 | 2 | 1 | 6 | 7 | 174,969 |
| Clarksville | 10 | 3 | 2 | 1 | 0 | 0 | 4 | 4 | 4 | 4 | 150,319 |
| Cleveland | 4 | 0 | 0 | 0 | 0 | 0 | 0 | 1 | 2 | 1 | 43,650 |
| Cookeville | 0 | 1 | 0 | 0 | 0 | 0 | 0 | 0 | 1 | 0 | 31,509 |
| Cowan | 0 | 0 | 0 | 1 | 0 | 0 | 0 | 0 | 1 | 0 | 1,713 |
| Crossville | 1 | 0 | 1 | 0 | 0 | 0 | 0 | 0 | 2 | 0 | 11,445 |
| Dover | 1 | 0 | 0 | 0 | 0 | 0 | 1 | 0 | 0 | 0 | 1,433 |
| Dunlap | 1 | 0 | 0 | 0 | 0 | 0 | 0 | 0 | 1 | 0 | 5,131 |
| Dyersburg | 2 | 0 | 0 | 0 | 0 | 0 | 0 | 1 | 1 | 0 | 16,766 |
| Elizabethton | 4 | 0 | 0 | 0 | 0 | 0 | 1 | 1 | 2 | 0 | 14,265 |
| Fairview | 2 | 0 | 0 | 0 | 0 | 0 | 0 | 0 | 0 | 2 | 8,331 |
| Germantown | 0 | 0 | 0 | 0 | 1 | 0 | 0 | 1 | 0 | 0 | 39,361 |
| Greeneville | 5 | 0 | 0 | 0 | 0 | 0 | 2 | 2 | 0 | 1 | 15,031 |
| Harriman | 0 | 0 | 1 | 0 | 0 | 0 | 1 | 0 | 0 | 0 | 6,182 |
| Huntland | 1 | 0 | 0 | 0 | 0 | 0 | 0 | 1 | 0 | 0 | 858 |
| Johnson City | 1 | 0 | 0 | 0 | 0 | 0 | 1 | 0 | 0 | 0 | 66,369 |
| Jonesborough | 1 | 0 | 0 | 0 | 0 | 0 | 0 | 0 | 0 | 1 | 5,283 |
| Kingsport | 1 | 0 | 0 | 0 | 0 | 0 | 1 | 0 | 0 | 0 | 53,091 |
| Knoxville | 2 | 1 | 0 | 0 | 0 | 0 | 2 | 0 | 0 | 1 | 185,638 |
| Lafayette | 2 | 0 | 0 | 0 | 0 | 0 | 0 | 0 | 2 | 0 | 5,075 |
| Lawrenceburg | 0 | 0 | 1 | 0 | 0 | 0 | 0 | 1 | 0 | 0 | 10,514 |
| Lebanon | 1 | 0 | 0 | 0 | 0 | 0 | 1 | 0 | 0 | 0 | 30,266 |
| Manchester | 0 | 1 | 0 | 0 | 0 | 0 | 0 | 0 | 1 | 0 | 10,404 |
| Mason | 1 | 0 | 0 | 0 | 0 | 0 | 1 | 0 | 0 | 0 | 1,598 |
| McMinnville | 2 | 0 | 0 | 0 | 0 | 0 | 0 | 1 | 0 | 1 | 13,622 |
| Memphis | 7 | 1 | 8 | 0 | 0 | 1 | 3 | 4 | 7 | 3 | 657,936 |
| Millington | 3 | 0 | 0 | 0 | 0 | 0 | 0 | 2 | 0 | 1 | 11,061 |
| Moscow | 1 | 0 | 0 | 1 | 0 | 0 | 1 | 0 | 1 | 0 | 534 |
| Munford | 2 | 0 | 0 | 0 | 0 | 0 | 0 | 0 | 0 | 2 | 6,082 |
| Nashville Metropolitan | 7 | 2 | 6 | 0 | 0 | 0 | 1 | 6 | 6 | 2 | 658,029 |
| Niota | 0 | 1 | 0 | 0 | 0 | 0 | 0 | 0 | 0 | 1 | 718 |
| Portland | 0 | 1 | 0 | 0 | 0 | 0 | 0 | 0 | 0 | 1 | 12,396 |
| Rockwood | 1 | 0 | 0 | 0 | 0 | 0 | 0 | 0 | 0 | 1 | 5,396 |
| Savannah | 1 | 0 | 0 | 0 | 0 | 0 | 0 | 0 | 1 | 0 | 7,069 |
| Smithville | 0 | 0 | 2 | 0 | 0 | 0 | 0 | 0 | 2 | 0 | 4,694 |
| Winchester | 1 | 0 | 1 | 0 | 0 | 0 | 0 | 1 | 1 | 0 | 8,555 |
| | | | | | | | | | | | |
| **Universities and Colleges** | 3 | 4 | 1 | 0 | 0 | 0 | | | | | |
| East Tennessee State University | 1 | 1 | 0 | 0 | 0 | 0 | 0 | 0 | 2 | 0 | 14,434 |
| Tennessee Technological University | 0 | 0 | 1 | 0 | 0 | 0 | 0 | 1 | 0 | 0 | 11,339 |
| University of Tennessee, Chattanooga | 1 | 1 | 0 | 0 | 0 | 0 | 1 | 0 | 0 | 1 | 11,670 |
| Vanderbilt University | 1 | 2 | 0 | 0 | 0 | 0 | 1 | 0 | 0 | 2 | 12,686 |
| | | | | | | | | | | | |
| **Metropolitan Counties** | 59 | 6 | 3 | 0 | 0 | 0 | | | | | |
| Blount | 1 | 0 | 0 | 0 | 0 | 0 | 0 | 0 | 1 | 0 | |
| Bradley | 0 | 1 | 0 | 0 | 0 | 0 | 0 | 0 | 0 | 1 | |
| Cheatham | 1 | 0 | 0 | 0 | 0 | 0 | 0 | 0 | 0 | 1 | |
| Hamilton | 3 | 1 | 1 | 0 | 0 | 0 | 3 | 1 | 0 | 1 | |
| Hickman | 1 | 0 | 0 | 0 | 0 | 0 | 1 | 0 | 0 | 0 | |
| Jefferson | 1 | 0 | 0 | 0 | 0 | 0 | 0 | 1 | 0 | 0 | |
| Knox | 1 | 0 | 0 | 0 | 0 | 0 | 0 | 0 | 0 | 1 | |
| Roane | 0 | 1 | 2 | 0 | 0 | 0 | 0 | 0 | 1 | 2 | |
| Robertson | 1 | 0 | 0 | 0 | 0 | 0 | 0 | 0 | 0 | 1 | |
| Rutherford | 1 | 0 | 0 | 0 | 0 | 0 | 0 | 1 | 0 | 0 | |
| Shelby | 28 | 2 | 0 | 0 | 0 | 0 | 12 | 6 | 2 | 10 | |
| Sullivan | 1 | 0 | 0 | 0 | 0 | 0 | 0 | 1 | 0 | 0 | |
| Tipton | 2 | 0 | 0 | 0 | 0 | 0 | 0 | 1 | 1 | 0 | |
| Washington | 18 | 0 | 0 | 0 | 0 | 0 | 9 | 8 | 1 | 0 | |
| Williamson | 0 | 1 | 0 | 0 | 0 | 0 | 0 | 1 | 0 | 0 | |
| Lewis | 0 | 0 | 1 | 0 | 0 | 0 | 0 | 0 | 1 | 0 | |
| Monroe | 0 | 0 | 0 | 0 | 0 | 0 | 0 | 0 | 1 | 0 | |
| Overton | 1 | 0 | 0 | 0 | 0 | 0 | 0 | 0 | 0 | 1 | |
| Van Buren | 0 | 0 | 0 | 0 | 0 | 0 | 0 | 0 | 2 | 0 | |

| State/agency | Race/Ethnicity/Ancestry | Religion | Sexual orientation | Disability | Gender | Gender Identity | 1st quarter | 2nd quarter | 3rd quarter | 4th quarter | Population[1] |
|---|---|---|---|---|---|---|---|---|---|---|---|
| **Nonmetropolitan Counties......** | 3 | 0 | 0 | 0 | 0 | 0 | | | | | |
| Bedford ...................... | 1 | 0 | 0 | 0 | 0 | 0 | 1 | 0 | 0 | 0 | |
| Gibson.......................... | 1 | 0 | 0 | 0 | 0 | 0 | 0 | 0 | 1 | 0 | |
| Lawrence ..................... | 1 | 0 | 0 | 0 | 0 | 0 | 1 | 0 | 0 | 0 | |
| **State Police Agencies..............** | 9 | 1 | 0 | 0 | 0 | 3 | | | | | |
| Department of Safety................. | 9 | 1 | 0 | 0 | 0 | 3 | 4 | 2 | 2 | 5 | |
| **TEXAS** | | | | | | | | | | | |
| **Total .........................** | 107 | 36 | 41 | 1 | 1 | 5 | | | | | |
| **Cities .....................** | 86 | 35 | 33 | 1 | 1 | 5 | | | | | |
| Austin...... | 5 | 2 | 4 | 0 | 0 | 2 | 3 | 6 | 3 | 1 | 938,728 |
| Baytown.................. | 0 | 1 | 0 | 0 | 0 | 0 | | 1 | | | 77,145 |
| Beaumont................. | 7 | 1 | 0 | 0 | 0 | 0 | 5 | 1 | 1 | 1 | 117,635 |
| Bedford ..................... | 6 | 0 | 0 | 0 | 0 | 0 | 0 | 2 | 3 | 1 | 49,377 |
| Burkburnett ................. | 0 | 1 | 0 | 0 | 0 | 0 | 1 | | | | 11,224 |
| Carrollton ..................... | 1 | 0 | 0 | 0 | 0 | 0 | | 1 | | | 130,676 |
| Cedar Park................. | 4 | 0 | 0 | 0 | 0 | 0 | 2 | 1 | | 1 | 66,724 |
| Center ......................... | 4 | 0 | 0 | 0 | 0 | 0 | 1 | | 3 | | 5,246 |
| Cisco ......................... | 1 | 0 | 0 | 0 | 0 | 0 | | 1 | | | 3,746 |
| Commerce.................... | 1 | 0 | 0 | 0 | 0 | 0 | | 1 | | | 8,732 |
| Corpus Christi............... | 0 | 0 | 1 | 0 | 0 | 0 | | | | 1 | 324,326 |
| Dalhart ....................... | 0 | 0 | 1 | 0 | 0 | 0 | | 1 | | | 8,416 |
| Dallas.......................... | 4 | 3 | 2 | 0 | 0 | 2 | 2 | 5 | 2 | 2 | 1,301,977 |
| Denton ........................ | 1 | 0 | 1 | 1 | 0 | 0 | 0 | 1 | 2 | 0 | 131,194 |
| Dublin.......................... | 1 | 0 | 0 | 0 | 0 | 0 | | | | 1 | 3,616 |
| El Paso ........................ | 0 | 3 | 0 | 0 | 0 | 0 | 1 | | 2 | | 686,077 |
| Fairfield....................... | 1 | 0 | 0 | 0 | 0 | 0 | | | | 1 | 2,899 |
| Fort Worth................... | 11 | 5 | 4 | 0 | 0 | 0 | 6 | 7 | 5 | 2 | 829,731 |
| Frisco .......................... | 0 | 1 | 0 | 0 | 0 | 0 | 0 | 0 | 0 | 1 | 152,678 |
| Galveston .................... | 1 | 0 | 0 | 0 | 0 | 0 | 0 | 1 | 0 | 0 | 50,065 |
| Gilmer ......................... | 1 | 0 | 0 | 0 | 0 | 0 | | 1 | | | 5,224 |
| Grand Prairie................ | 0 | 1 | 0 | 0 | 0 | 0 | 1 | | | | 187,901 |
| Houston...................... | 12 | 3 | 10 | 0 | 1 | 1 | 2 | 13 | 10 | 2 | 2,275,221 |
| Hurst........................... | 1 | 0 | 0 | 0 | 0 | 0 | 0 | 0 | 1 | 0 | 39,069 |
| La Grange.................... | 1 | 0 | 0 | 0 | 0 | 0 | | | | 1 | 4,679 |
| La Porte....................... | 1 | 0 | 0 | 0 | 0 | 0 | | 1 | | | 35,336 |
| Lewisville ..................... | 0 | 1 | 0 | 0 | 0 | 0 | 1 | 0 | 0 | 0 | 104,741 |
| Longview...................... | 2 | 1 | 1 | 0 | 0 | 0 | 0 | 1 | 0 | 3 | 81,842 |
| Madisonville................. | 1 | 0 | 0 | 0 | 0 | 0 | | | 1 | | 4,589 |
| McKinney ..................... | 2 | 0 | 1 | 0 | 0 | 0 | 0 | 2 | 1 | 0 | 163,406 |
| Missouri City................. | 1 | 0 | 0 | 0 | 0 | 0 | | 1 | | | 72,879 |
| Odessa......................... | 2 | 0 | 2 | 0 | 0 | 0 | 2 | 2 | | | 118,606 |
| Pearland ...................... | 2 | 0 | 0 | 0 | 0 | 0 | 0 | 0 | 0 | 2 | 106,850 |
| Plano .......................... | 3 | 1 | 0 | 0 | 0 | 0 | 0 | 1 | 2 | 1 | 282,968 |
| Port Lavaca .................. | 1 | 0 | 0 | 0 | 0 | 0 | 0 | 0 | 1 | 0 | 12,446 |
| Rusk............................. | 1 | 0 | 0 | 0 | 0 | 0 | 0 | 0 | 1 | 0 | 5,585 |
| Sachse.......................... | 0 | 0 | 1 | 0 | 0 | 0 | 0 | 0 | 0 | 1 | 24,564 |
| San Angelo.................... | 0 | 1 | 0 | 0 | 0 | 0 | 0 | 0 | 1 | 0 | 100,356 |
| San Antonio.................. | 2 | 8 | 2 | 0 | 0 | 0 | 2 | 2 | 7 | 1 | 1,463,586 |
| Schertz......................... | 0 | 0 | 1 | 0 | 0 | 0 | | | 1 | | 38,201 |
| Tyler............................ | 2 | 1 | 1 | 0 | 0 | 0 | 0 | 0 | 1 | 3 | 102,481 |
| University Park ............. | 1 | 1 | 0 | 0 | 0 | 0 | 1 | | 1 | | 24,729 |
| Victoria........................ | 1 | 0 | 0 | 0 | 0 | 0 | 0 | 1 | 0 | 0 | 66,988 |
| Weatherford ................ | 1 | 0 | 1 | 0 | 0 | 0 | 1 | 1 | | | 28,379 |
| **Universities and Colleges ........** | 6 | 1 | 4 | 0 | 0 | 0 | | | | | |
| Alamo Community College District..................... | 0 | 0 | 2 | 0 | 0 | 0 | | | 2 | | 55,967 |
| Texas Christian University ........... | 1 | 0 | 0 | 0 | 0 | 0 | 1 | | | | 10,033 |
| Texas Tech University, Lubbock .... | 2 | 1 | 0 | 0 | 0 | 0 | | 3 | | | 35,158 |
| University of Texas..................... | | | | | | | | | | | |
| Arlington ............................. | 1 | 0 | 0 | 0 | 0 | 0 | | 1 | | | 39,740 |
| Austin................................. | 2 | 0 | 0 | 0 | 0 | 0 | | | 2 | | 51,313 |
| Houston.............................. | 0 | 0 | 1 | 0 | 0 | 0 | | | | 1 | 4,859 |
| Pan American ..................... | 0 | 0 | 1 | 0 | 0 | 0 | | | 1 | | 21,015 |

# Table 13. Hate Crime Incidents Per Bias Motivation and Quarter, by Selected State and Agency, 2015—*Continued*

(Number.)

| State/agency | Number of incidents per bias motivation | | | | | | Number of incidents per quarter | | | | Population[1] |
|---|---|---|---|---|---|---|---|---|---|---|---|
| | Race/Ethnicity/Ancestry | Religion | Sexual orientation | Disability | Gender | Gender Identity | 1st quarter | 2nd quarter | 3rd quarter | 4th quarter | |
| **Metropolitan Counties** ............ | 10 | 0 | 4 | 0 | 0 | 0 | | | | | |
| Brazoria .................................. | 1 | 0 | 0 | 0 | 0 | 0 | | 1 | | | |
| Galveston ................................ | 3 | 0 | 0 | 0 | 0 | 0 | | | 2 | 1 | |
| Lubbock ................................... | 2 | 0 | 0 | 0 | 0 | 0 | 1 | 0 | 0 | 1 | |
| Martin ..................................... | 1 | 0 | 0 | 0 | 0 | 0 | | | | 1 | |
| Parker ..................................... | 1 | 0 | 0 | 0 | 0 | 0 | 1 | 0 | 0 | 0 | |
| Smith ...................................... | 2 | 0 | 0 | 0 | 0 | 0 | | | | 2 | |
| Travis ...................................... | 0 | 0 | 4 | 0 | 0 | 0 | 2 | 2 | | | |
| **Nonmetropolitan Counties** ...... | | | | | | | | | | | |
| Gray ........................................ | 1 | 0 | 0 | 0 | 0 | 0 | | | | 1 | |
| Young ...................................... | 1 | 0 | 0 | 0 | 0 | 0 | | | | 1 | |
| Zavala ..................................... | 2 | 0 | 0 | 0 | 0 | 0 | | | 1 | 1 | |
| **Other Agencies** ........................ | 1 | 0 | 0 | 0 | 0 | 0 | | | | | |
| Hospital District, Dallas County ... | 1 | 0 | 0 | 0 | 0 | 0 | | | 1 | | |
| **UTAH** | | | | | | | | | | | |
| Total ....................................... | 29 | 11 | 7 | 0 | 0 | 0 | | | | | |
| **Cities** ...................................... | 22 | 9 | 5 | 0 | 0 | 0 | | | | | |
| Bountiful .................................. | 2 | 0 | 0 | 0 | 0 | 0 | 1 | 0 | 1 | 0 | 43,570 |
| Farmington .............................. | 1 | 0 | 0 | 0 | 0 | 0 | 0 | 1 | 0 | 0 | 23,198 |
| Grantsville ............................... | 0 | 2 | 0 | 0 | 0 | 0 | 0 | 0 | 0 | 2 | 10,071 |
| Ogden ..................................... | 0 | 2 | 0 | 0 | 0 | 0 | 0 | 0 | 2 | 0 | 84,642 |
| Price ....................................... | 2 | 0 | 0 | 0 | 0 | 0 | 1 | 0 | 0 | 1 | 8,269 |
| Roosevelt ................................. | 2 | 0 | 0 | 0 | 0 | 0 | 0 | 0 | 1 | 1 | 6,970 |
| Salt Lake City ........................... | 1 | 1 | 2 | 0 | 0 | 0 | 0 | 3 | 1 | 0 | 191,992 |
| Sandy ...................................... | 2 | 0 | 0 | 0 | 0 | 0 | 0 | 0 | 0 | 2 | 92,013 |
| Saratoga Springs ....................... | 1 | 0 | 0 | 0 | 0 | 0 | 0 | 0 | 1 | 0 | 26,260 |
| South Salt Lake ......................... | 1 | 0 | 1 | 0 | 0 | 0 | 1 | 0 | 1 | 0 | 25,020 |
| St. George ............................... | 1 | 0 | 1 | 0 | 0 | 0 | 0 | 0 | 0 | 2 | 79,984 |
| Tooele ..................................... | 2 | 2 | 0 | 0 | 0 | 0 | 0 | 1 | 2 | 1 | 32,789 |
| Vernal ..................................... | 0 | 1 | 0 | 0 | 0 | 0 | 1 | 0 | 0 | 0 | 11,346 |
| West Bountiful .......................... | 2 | 0 | 0 | 0 | 0 | 0 | 0 | 1 | 1 | 0 | 5,488 |
| West Jordan ............................. | 1 | 0 | 0 | 0 | 0 | 0 | 0 | 0 | 0 | 1 | 112,687 |
| West Valley .............................. | 4 | 1 | 1 | 0 | 0 | 0 | 2 | 0 | 0 | 4 | 135,744 |
| **Universities and Colleges** ........ | 1 | 1 | 0 | 0 | 0 | 0 | | | | | |
| Brigham Young University ........... | 1 | 1 | 0 | 0 | 0 | 0 | 0 | 2 | 0 | 0 | 30,484 |
| **Metropolitan Counties** ............ | 2 | 1 | 1 | 0 | 0 | 0 | | | | | |
| Davis ....................................... | 1 | 0 | 0 | 0 | 0 | 0 | 0 | 0 | 0 | 1 | |
| Washington .............................. | 1 | 1 | 1 | 0 | 0 | 0 | 1 | 0 | 2 | 0 | |
| **Nonmetropolitan Counties** ...... | 1 | 0 | 1 | 0 | 0 | 0 | | | | | |
| Duchesne .................................. | 1 | 0 | 0 | 0 | 0 | 0 | 0 | 1 | 0 | 0 | |
| Uintah ..................................... | 0 | 0 | 1 | 0 | 0 | 0 | 0 | 0 | 1 | 0 | |
| **Other Agencies** ........................ | 3 | 0 | 0 | 0 | 0 | 0 | | | | | |
| Utah Transit Authority ............... | 3 | 0 | 0 | 0 | 0 | 0 | 2 | 0 | 1 | 0 | |
| **VERMONT** | | | | | | | | | | | |
| Total ....................................... | 5 | 0 | 2 | 0 | 0 | 1 | | | | | |
| **Cities** ...................................... | 4 | 0 | 1 | 0 | 0 | 0 | | | | | |
| Burlington ................................ | 4 | 0 | 0 | 0 | 0 | 0 | 0 | 2 | 0 | 2 | 42,160 |
| South Burlington ....................... | 0 | 0 | 1 | 0 | 0 | 0 | 0 | 0 | 0 | 1 | 18,946 |
| **Universities and Colleges** ........ | 1 | 0 | 0 | 0 | 0 | 0 | | | | | |
| University of Vermont ................ | 1 | 0 | 0 | 0 | 0 | 0 | 0 | 0 | 0 | 1 | 12,856 |
| **Nonmetropolitan Counties** ...... | 0 | 0 | 0 | 0 | 0 | 1 | | | | | |
| Windham .................................. | 0 | 0 | 0 | 0 | 0 | 1 | 0 | 0 | 1 | 0 | |
| **State Police Agencies** .............. | 0 | 0 | 1 | 0 | 0 | 0 | | | | | |
| State Police, Brattleboro ............. | 0 | 0 | 1 | 0 | 0 | 0 | 0 | 1 | 0 | 0 | |

# Table 13. Hate Crime Incidents Per Bias Motivation and Quarter, by Selected State and Agency, 2015—*Continued*

(Number.)

| State/agency | Number of incidents per bias motivation | | | | | | Number of incidents per quarter | | | | Population[1] |
|---|---|---|---|---|---|---|---|---|---|---|---|
| | Race/ Ethnicity/ Ancestry | Religion | Sexual orientation | Disability | Gender | Gender Identity | 1st quarter | 2nd quarter | 3rd quarter | 4th quarter | |
| **VIRGINIA** | | | | | | | | | | | |
| Total | 108 | 24 | 24 | 2 | 0 | 0 | | | | | |
| **Cities** | 53 | 5 | 15 | 1 | 0 | 0 | | | | | |
| Alexandria | 1 | 0 | 0 | 0 | 0 | 0 | 0 | 0 | 1 | 0 | 152,710 |
| Altavista | 1 | 0 | 0 | 0 | 0 | 0 | 0 | 0 | 1 | 0 | 3,462 |
| Bedford | 1 | 0 | 0 | 0 | 0 | 0 | 0 | 0 | 0 | 1 | 6,437 |
| Charlottesville | 1 | 0 | 0 | 0 | 0 | 0 | 1 | 0 | 0 | 0 | 45,997 |
| Chesapeake | 15 | 0 | 0 | 0 | 0 | 0 | 1 | 2 | 3 | 9 | 235,273 |
| Chilhowie | 0 | 1 | 0 | 0 | 0 | 0 | 0 | 0 | 1 | 0 | 1,741 |
| Danville | 1 | 0 | 0 | 0 | 0 | 0 | 0 | 0 | 1 | 0 | 42,210 |
| Emporia | 1 | 0 | 0 | 0 | 0 | 0 | 1 | 0 | 0 | 0 | 5,339 |
| Fairfax City | 1 | 0 | 0 | 0 | 0 | 0 | 1 | 0 | 0 | 0 | 24,911 |
| Front Royal | 2 | 0 | 0 | 0 | 0 | 0 | 0 | 1 | 1 | 0 | 15,184 |
| Galax | 1 | 0 | 0 | 0 | 0 | 0 | 0 | 0 | 1 | 0 | 6,980 |
| Hampton | 4 | 0 | 0 | 0 | 0 | 0 | 1 | 1 | 2 | 0 | 136,381 |
| Herndon | 0 | 1 | 0 | 0 | 0 | 0 | 0 | 0 | 1 | 0 | 24,849 |
| Hopewell | 1 | 0 | 0 | 0 | 0 | 0 | 0 | 0 | 0 | 1 | 22,027 |
| Kenbridge | 1 | 0 | 0 | 0 | 0 | 0 | 0 | 0 | 1 | 0 | 1,236 |
| Leesburg | 1 | 0 | 0 | 0 | 0 | 0 | 0 | 1 | 0 | 0 | 51,254 |
| Lynchburg | 2 | 0 | 0 | 0 | 0 | 0 | 0 | 0 | 2 | 0 | 79,675 |
| Manassas | 0 | 0 | 1 | 0 | 0 | 0 | 0 | 0 | 1 | 0 | 42,977 |
| Marion | 0 | 0 | 1 | 0 | 0 | 0 | 0 | 1 | 0 | 0 | 5,852 |
| Newport News | 2 | 0 | 1 | 0 | 0 | 0 | 1 | 0 | 0 | 2 | 182,975 |
| Norfolk | 4 | 1 | 9 | 1 | 0 | 0 | 0 | 1 | 9 | 5 | 245,400 |
| Richmond | 2 | 0 | 1 | 0 | 0 | 0 | 0 | 2 | 0 | 1 | 220,802 |
| Roanoke | 2 | 0 | 0 | 0 | 0 | 0 | 0 | 0 | 1 | 1 | 99,827 |
| Smithfield | 0 | 0 | 1 | 0 | 0 | 0 | 0 | 0 | 1 | 0 | 8,336 |
| Staunton | 1 | 0 | 0 | 0 | 0 | 0 | 0 | 0 | 0 | 1 | 24,654 |
| Vinton | 3 | 0 | 0 | 0 | 0 | 0 | 0 | 2 | 1 | 0 | 8,210 |
| Virginia Beach | 5 | 2 | 1 | 0 | 0 | 0 | 1 | 0 | 4 | 3 | 452,797 |
| **Universities and Colleges** | 7 | 5 | 1 | 0 | 0 | 0 | | | | | |
| Christopher Newport University | 1 | 0 | 0 | 0 | 0 | 0 | 0 | 0 | 0 | 1 | 5,221 |
| College of William and Mary | 0 | 1 | 0 | 0 | 0 | 0 | 1 | 0 | 0 | 0 | 8,437 |
| George Mason University | 1 | 1 | 0 | 0 | 0 | 0 | 0 | 1 | 0 | 1 | 33,729 |
| Longwood University | 1 | 0 | 1 | 0 | 0 | 0 | 0 | 2 | 0 | 0 | 5,096 |
| Norfolk State University | 1 | 0 | 0 | 0 | 0 | 0 | 0 | 0 | 0 | 1 | 6,027 |
| Northern Virginia Community College | 1 | 2 | 0 | 0 | 0 | 0 | 1 | 0 | 0 | 2 | 51,487 |
| University of Richmond | 1 | 0 | 0 | 0 | 0 | 0 | 1 | 0 | 0 | 0 | 4,182 |
| University of Virginia | 1 | 0 | 0 | 0 | 0 | 0 | 0 | 0 | 1 | 0 | 23,732 |
| Virginia Polytechnic Institute and State University | 0 | 1 | 0 | 0 | 0 | 0 | 0 | 0 | 0 | 1 | 31,224 |
| **Metropolitan Counties** | 43 | 14 | 6 | 1 | 0 | 0 | | | | | |
| Albemarle County Police Department | 6 | 0 | 0 | 0 | 0 | 0 | 1 | 2 | 3 | 0 | |
| Appomattox | 0 | 1 | 0 | 0 | 0 | 0 | 0 | 0 | 0 | 1 | |
| Arlington County Police Department | 5 | 0 | 1 | 0 | 0 | 0 | 3 | 0 | 1 | 2 | |
| Chesterfield County Police Department | 1 | 2 | 2 | 0 | 0 | 0 | 1 | 2 | 2 | 0 | |
| Dinwiddie | 3 | 0 | 0 | 0 | 0 | 0 | 0 | 1 | 2 | 0 | |
| Fairfax County Police Department | 16 | 8 | 2 | 0 | 0 | 0 | 3 | 6 | 9 | 8 | |
| Franklin | 0 | 0 | 1 | 0 | 0 | 0 | 0 | 0 | 0 | 1 | |
| Henrico County Police Department | 3 | 0 | 0 | 0 | 0 | 0 | 2 | 1 | 0 | 0 | |
| James City County Police Department | 1 | 0 | 0 | 0 | 0 | 0 | 0 | 0 | 0 | 1 | |
| Loudoun | 2 | 1 | 0 | 0 | 0 | 0 | 1 | 0 | 1 | 1 | |
| Mathews | 1 | 0 | 0 | 0 | 0 | 0 | 0 | 0 | 0 | 1 | |
| Roanoke County Police Department | 0 | 1 | 0 | 1 | 0 | 0 | 2 | 0 | 0 | 0 | |
| Rockingham | 2 | 0 | 0 | 0 | 0 | 0 | 1 | 0 | 1 | 0 | |
| Spotsylvania | 2 | 1 | 0 | 0 | 0 | 0 | 2 | 0 | 0 | 1 | |
| Washington | 1 | 0 | 0 | 0 | 0 | 0 | 0 | 0 | 1 | 0 | |

# Table 13. Hate Crime Incidents Per Bias Motivation and Quarter, by Selected State and Agency, 2015—*Continued*

(Number.)

| State/agency | Race/ Ethnicity/ Ancestry | Religion | Sexual orientation | Disability | Gender | Gender Identity | 1st quarter | 2nd quarter | 3rd quarter | 4th quarter | Population[1] |
|---|---|---|---|---|---|---|---|---|---|---|---|
| **Nonmetropolitan Counties......** | 4 | 0 | 1 | 0 | 0 | 0 | | | | | |
| Accomack................................ | 0 | 0 | 1 | 0 | 0 | 0 | 1 | 0 | 0 | 0 | |
| Henry..................................... | 1 | 0 | 0 | 0 | 0 | 0 | 0 | 1 | 0 | 0 | |
| Madison ................................. | 1 | 0 | 0 | 0 | 0 | 0 | 0 | 1 | 0 | 0 | |
| Rockbridge ............................ | 1 | 0 | 0 | 0 | 0 | 0 | 0 | 0 | 1 | 0 | |
| Shenandoah ........................... | 1 | 0 | 0 | 0 | 0 | 0 | 0 | 0 | 1 | 0 | |
| | | | | | | | | | | | |
| **State Police Agencies ............** | 1 | 0 | 1 | 0 | 0 | 0 | | | | | |
| Hanover County....................... | 1 | 0 | 0 | 0 | 0 | 0 | 0 | 0 | 1 | 0 | |
| Pittsylvania County................... | 0 | 0 | 1 | 0 | 0 | 0 | 1 | 0 | 0 | 0 | |
| | | | | | | | | | | | |
| **WASHINGTON** | | | | | | | | | | | |
| **Total .........................** | 160 | 43 | 57 | 3 | 3 | 9 | | | | | |
| | | | | | | | | | | | |
| **Cities .........................** | 130 | 36 | 52 | 3 | 1 | 9 | | | | | |
| Aberdeen................................. | 1 | 0 | 0 | 0 | 0 | 0 | 0 | 1 | 0 | 0 | 16,100 |
| Anacortes................................ | 1 | 0 | 0 | 0 | 0 | 0 | 0 | 0 | 0 | 1 | 16,351 |
| Arlington ................................ | 1 | 0 | 0 | 0 | 0 | 0 | 0 | 0 | 0 | 1 | 19,018 |
| Auburn ................................... | 3 | 0 | 0 | 0 | 0 | 0 | 0 | 2 | 0 | 1 | 77,914 |
| Bellevue.................................. | 1 | 0 | 0 | 1 | 0 | 0 | 0 | 1 | 0 | 1 | 138,532 |
| Bellingham.............................. | 3 | 1 | 0 | 0 | 1 | 0 | 2 | 0 | 2 | 1 | 83,976 |
| Bothell ................................... | 0 | 3 | 0 | 0 | 0 | 0 | 2 | 0 | 0 | 1 | 37,346 |
| Burien .................................... | 1 | 0 | 0 | 0 | 0 | 0 | 1 | 0 | 0 | 0 | 50,701 |
| Burlington............................... | 1 | 0 | 0 | 0 | 0 | 0 | 0 | 0 | 0 | 1 | 8,610 |
| Centralia................................. | 0 | 2 | 1 | 0 | 0 | 0 | 1 | 2 | 0 | 0 | 16,632 |
| Des Moines.............................. | 1 | 0 | 0 | 0 | 0 | 0 | 0 | 0 | 1 | 0 | 31,335 |
| Edmonds ................................ | 1 | 0 | 1 | 0 | 0 | 0 | 0 | 0 | 0 | 2 | 41,187 |
| Ellensburg............................... | 0 | 0 | 1 | 0 | 0 | 0 | 0 | 0 | 1 | 0 | 18,899 |
| Everett ................................... | 1 | 0 | 1 | 0 | 0 | 0 | 0 | 0 | 0 | 2 | 107,633 |
| Federal Way ............................ | 4 | 1 | 0 | 0 | 0 | 0 | 3 | 0 | 2 | 0 | 94,424 |
| Fife ....................................... | 1 | 0 | 0 | 0 | 0 | 0 | 0 | 0 | 0 | 1 | 9,642 |
| Kelso ..................................... | 0 | 0 | 1 | 0 | 0 | 0 | 0 | 1 | 0 | 0 | 11,756 |
| Kent ...................................... | 12 | 0 | 1 | 0 | 0 | 0 | 1 | 4 | 6 | 2 | 127,259 |
| Lakewood................................ | 2 | 0 | 1 | 0 | 0 | 0 | 1 | 0 | 0 | 2 | 59,958 |
| Longview................................. | 4 | 0 | 1 | 0 | 0 | 0 | 3 | 2 | 0 | 0 | 36,401 |
| Marysville................................ | 1 | 0 | 0 | 0 | 0 | 0 | 0 | 0 | 0 | 1 | 66,374 |
| Mercer Island .......................... | 0 | 1 | 0 | 0 | 0 | 0 | 0 | 0 | 0 | 1 | 24,737 |
| Moses Lake.............................. | 2 | 0 | 0 | 0 | 0 | 0 | 0 | 1 | 1 | 0 | 22,026 |
| Mountlake Terrace .................... | 0 | 1 | 0 | 0 | 0 | 0 | 0 | 0 | 0 | 1 | 21,051 |
| Mount Vernon .......................... | 0 | 0 | 1 | 0 | 0 | 0 | 1 | 0 | 0 | 0 | 33,474 |
| Mukilteo................................. | 1 | 0 | 0 | 0 | 0 | 0 | 0 | 0 | 0 | 1 | 21,171 |
| Olympia.................................. | 2 | 0 | 2 | 0 | 0 | 0 | 0 | 1 | 2 | 1 | 49,875 |
| Omak ..................................... | 0 | 0 | 1 | 0 | 0 | 0 | 0 | 0 | 1 | 0 | 4,847 |
| Oroville.................................. | 0 | 0 | 0 | 1 | 0 | 0 | 0 | 0 | 0 | 1 | 1,676 |
| Orting.................................... | 0 | 0 | 1 | 0 | 0 | 0 | 1 | 0 | 0 | 0 | 7,401 |
| Port Angeles ........................... | 0 | 1 | 0 | 0 | 0 | 0 | 0 | 1 | 0 | 0 | 19,304 |
| Pullman ................................. | 1 | 0 | 0 | 0 | 0 | 0 | 0 | 1 | 0 | 0 | 32,174 |
| Puyallup ................................. | 1 | 0 | 0 | 0 | 0 | 0 | 0 | 0 | 1 | 0 | 39,645 |
| Redmond................................ | 1 | 5 | 0 | 0 | 0 | 0 | 3 | 0 | 0 | 3 | 60,542 |
| Renton.................................... | 3 | 1 | 0 | 0 | 0 | 0 | 0 | 2 | 0 | 2 | 100,015 |
| Republic.................................. | 0 | 0 | 0 | 0 | 0 | 1 | 0 | 1 | 0 | 0 | 1,086 |
| Richland.................................. | 1 | 0 | 0 | 0 | 0 | 0 | 1 | 0 | 0 | 0 | 54,218 |
| Sammamish ............................. | 1 | 0 | 0 | 0 | 0 | 0 | 1 | 0 | 0 | 0 | 52,365 |
| SeaTac .................................... | 0 | 0 | 1 | 0 | 0 | 0 | 1 | 0 | 0 | 0 | 28,418 |
| Seattle.................................... | 40 | 8 | 27 | 0 | 0 | 8 | 16 | 32 | 23 | 12 | 683,700 |
| Shelton................................... | 0 | 0 | 1 | 0 | 0 | 0 | 1 | 0 | 0 | 0 | 9,758 |
| Shoreline ................................ | 1 | 0 | 0 | 0 | 0 | 0 | 1 | 0 | 0 | 0 | 55,690 |
| Soap Lake................................ | 1 | 0 | 0 | 0 | 0 | 0 | 0 | 1 | 0 | 0 | 1,594 |
| Spokane[3] ............................... | 3 | 4 | 5 | 0 | 0 | 0 | 3 | 1 | 4 | 4 | 212,698 |
| Spokane Valley......................... | 3 | 1 | 1 | 0 | 0 | 0 | 2 | 2 | 1 | 0 | 92,157 |
| Steilacoom .............................. | 1 | 1 | 0 | 0 | 0 | 0 | 0 | 0 | 2 | 0 | 6,228 |
| Sunnyside ............................... | 2 | 0 | 0 | 0 | 0 | 0 | 1 | 0 | 0 | 1 | 16,198 |
| Tacoma................................... | 6 | 0 | 3 | 0 | 0 | 0 | 2 | 6 | 1 | 0 | 206,884 |
| Tukwila................................... | 2 | 2 | 0 | 0 | 0 | 0 | 0 | 2 | 2 | 0 | 20,116 |
| Vancouver............................... | 3 | 1 | 0 | 1 | 0 | 0 | 1 | 2 | 1 | 1 | 171,076 |
| Walla Walla.............................. | 11 | 0 | 0 | 0 | 0 | 0 | 3 | 3 | 1 | 4 | 31,940 |
| Washougal............................... | 1 | 0 | 0 | 0 | 0 | 0 | 0 | 1 | 0 | 0 | 15,220 |
| Woodway................................ | 1 | 0 | 0 | 0 | 0 | 0 | 0 | 0 | 0 | 1 | 1,362 |
| Yakima.................................... | 3 | 3 | 0 | 0 | 0 | 0 | 1 | 2 | 1 | 2 | 93,798 |
| Zillah..................................... | 0 | 0 | 1 | 0 | 0 | 0 | 0 | 1 | 0 | 0 | 3,138 |

| State/agency | Number of incidents per bias motivation | | | | | | Number of incidents per quarter | | | | Population[1] |
|---|---|---|---|---|---|---|---|---|---|---|---|
| | Race/ Ethnicity/ Ancestry | Religion | Sexual orientation | Disability | Gender | Gender Identity | 1st quarter | 2nd quarter | 3rd quarter | 4th quarter | |
| **Universities and Colleges** ........ | 7 | 0 | 2 | 0 | 1 | 0 | | | | | |
| Eastern Washington University .... | 2 | 0 | 0 | 0 | 0 | 0 | 0 | 1 | 0 | 1 | 13,453 |
| Evergreen State College ............. | 0 | 0 | 1 | 0 | 0 | 0 | 1 | 0 | 0 | 0 | 4,219 |
| University of Washington ........... | 4 | 0 | 0 | 0 | 1 | 0 | 3 | 1 | 1 | 0 | 44,784 |
| Washington State University, Pullman ..................................... | 0 | 0 | 1 | 0 | 0 | 0 | 0 | 1 | 0 | 0 | 28,686 |
| Western Washington University... | 1 | 0 | 0 | 0 | 0 | 0 | 0 | 0 | 0 | 1 | 15,060 |
| **Metropolitan Counties** ........... | 19 | 7 | 2 | 0 | 0 | 0 | | | | | |
| Asotin.................................... | 1 | 0 | 0 | 0 | 0 | 0 | 0 | 1 | 0 | 0 | |
| Clark...................................... | 1 | 0 | 0 | 0 | 0 | 0 | 0 | 1 | 0 | 0 | |
| Cowlitz................................... | 1 | 0 | 0 | 0 | 0 | 0 | 1 | 0 | 0 | 0 | |
| King....................................... | 3 | 2 | 0 | 0 | 0 | 0 | 1 | 1 | 1 | 2 | |
| Kitsap.................................... | 1 | 0 | 0 | 0 | 0 | 0 | 0 | 0 | 1 | 0 | |
| Pend Oreille ............................ | 2 | 0 | 0 | 0 | 0 | 0 | 1 | 0 | 0 | 1 | |
| Pierce.................................... | 0 | 1 | 0 | 0 | 0 | 0 | 0 | 0 | 1 | 0 | |
| Skagit..................................... | 1 | 0 | 0 | 0 | 0 | 0 | 0 | 0 | 1 | 0 | |
| Snohomish............................... | 2 | 0 | 1 | 0 | 0 | 0 | 0 | 0 | 0 | 3 | |
| Spokane ................................. | 2 | 1 | 0 | 0 | 0 | 0 | 2 | 1 | 0 | 0 | |
| Thurston................................. | 1 | 0 | 0 | 0 | 0 | 0 | 0 | 1 | 0 | 0 | |
| Whatcom................................. | 3 | 3 | 1 | 0 | 0 | 0 | 4 | 1 | 2 | 0 | |
| Yakima................................... | 1 | 0 | 0 | 0 | 0 | 0 | 0 | 0 | 1 | 0 | |
| **Nonmetropolitan Counties**...... | 4 | 0 | 0 | 0 | 1 | 0 | | | | | |
| Clallam .................................. | 0 | 0 | 0 | 0 | 1 | 0 | 0 | 0 | 1 | 0 | |
| Garfield .................................. | 1 | 0 | 0 | 0 | 0 | 0 | 1 | 0 | 0 | 0 | |
| Grays Harbor ........................... | 1 | 0 | 0 | 0 | 0 | 0 | 0 | 0 | 1 | 0 | |
| Lewis...................................... | 1 | 0 | 0 | 0 | 0 | 0 | 0 | 0 | 0 | 1 | |
| Okanogan................................ | 1 | 0 | 0 | 0 | 0 | 0 | 0 | 0 | 0 | 1 | |
| **Tribal Agencies** ........................ | 0 | 0 | 1 | 0 | 0 | 0 | | | | | |
| Lummi Tribal ............................ | 0 | 0 | 1 | 0 | 0 | 0 | 0 | 0 | 1 | 0 | |
| **WEST VIRGINIA** | | | | | | | | | | | |
| Total ........................ | 28 | 3 | 6 | 4 | 0 | 0 | | | | | |
| **Cities** ........................ | 16 | 1 | 3 | 2 | 0 | 0 | | | | | |
| Buckhannon ............................. | 1 | 1 | 0 | 0 | 0 | 0 | 0 | 0 | 2 | 0 | 5,690 |
| Charleston................................ | 6 | 0 | 3 | 1 | 0 | 0 | 1 | 2 | 3 | 4 | 50,176 |
| Moundsville.............................. | 6 | 0 | 0 | 1 | 0 | 0 | 2 | 3 | 2 | 0 | 8,852 |
| Oak Hill................................... | 2 | 0 | 0 | 0 | 0 | 0 | 1 | 0 | 0 | 1 | 8,138 |
| Weirton................................... | 1 | 0 | 0 | 0 | 0 | 0 | 1 | 0 | 0 | 0 | 19,273 |
| **Metropolitan Counties** ........... | 6 | 1 | 2 | 1 | 0 | 0 | | | | | |
| Berkeley.................................. | 0 | 1 | 0 | 0 | 0 | 0 | 0 | 0 | 1 | 0 | |
| Brooke.................................... | 2 | 0 | 0 | 0 | 0 | 0 | 0 | 1 | 1 | 0 | |
| Fayette.................................... | 2 | 0 | 0 | 0 | 0 | 0 | 0 | 1 | 0 | 1 | |
| Hancock ................................. | 2 | 0 | 0 | 1 | 0 | 0 | 1 | 0 | 0 | 2 | |
| Kanawha ................................. | 0 | 0 | 2 | 0 | 0 | 0 | 0 | 0 | 1 | 1 | |
| **Nonmetropolitan Counties**...... | 6 | 1 | 1 | 1 | 0 | 0 | | | | | |
| Mason .................................... | 6 | 1 | 0 | 1 | 0 | 0 | 2 | 3 | 3 | 0 | |
| McDowell ................................ | 0 | 0 | 1 | 0 | 0 | 0 | 0 | 1 | 0 | 0 | |
| **WISCONSIN** | | | | | | | | | | | |
| Total ........................ | 27 | 8 | 7 | 0 | 1 | 0 | | | | | |
| **Cities** ........................ | 21 | 7 | 4 | 0 | 1 | 0 | | | | | |
| Appleton ................................. | 0 | 1 | 1 | 0 | 0 | 0 | 1 | 1 | 0 | 0 | 74,310 |
| Ashland................................... | 0 | 1 | 0 | 0 | 0 | 0 | 0 | 0 | 0 | 1 | 8,169 |
| Beloit...................................... | 2 | 0 | 0 | 0 | 0 | 0 | 2 | 0 | 0 | 0 | 36,862 |
| Campbell Township.................... | 0 | 0 | 1 | 0 | 0 | 0 | 1 | 0 | 0 | 0 | 4,429 |
| Darlington ............................... | 1 | 0 | 0 | 0 | 0 | 0 | 0 | 1 | 0 | 0 | 2,402 |
| Fennimore ............................... | 1 | 0 | 0 | 0 | 0 | 0 | 1 | 0 | 0 | 0 | 2,471 |
| Fond du Lac............................. | 1 | 0 | 0 | 0 | 0 | 0 | 0 | 0 | 1 | 0 | 42,887 |
| Green Bay................................ | 1 | 0 | 0 | 0 | 0 | 0 | 0 | 0 | 0 | 1 | 105,119 |
| Janesville................................. | 1 | 0 | 0 | 0 | 0 | 0 | 0 | 0 | 0 | 1 | 64,122 |
| Lancaster................................. | 0 | 0 | 1 | 0 | 0 | 0 | 0 | 0 | 1 | 0 | 3,765 |
| Madison.................................. | 4 | 3 | 1 | 0 | 0 | 0 | 3 | 0 | 3 | 2 | 248,833 |

(Number.)

| State/agency | Number of incidents per bias motivation | | | | | | Number of incidents per quarter | | | | Population[1] |
|---|---|---|---|---|---|---|---|---|---|---|---|
| | Race/ Ethnicity/ Ancestry | Religion | Sexual orientation | Disability | Gender | Gender Identity | 1st quarter | 2nd quarter | 3rd quarter | 4th quarter | |
| Menomonie.................... | 2 | 0 | 0 | 0 | 0 | 0 | 2 | 0 | 0 | 0 | 16,223 |
| Milwaukee..................... | 4 | 1 | 0 | 0 | 0 | 0 | 3 | 2 | 0 | 0 | 600,400 |
| Muscoda....................... | 0 | 0 | 0 | 0 | 1 | 0 | 0 | 0 | 1 | 0 | 1,263 |
| New Berlin.................... | 1 | 0 | 0 | 0 | 0 | 0 | 0 | 1 | 0 | 0 | 39,906 |
| Onalaska...................... | 1 | 0 | 0 | 0 | 0 | 0 | 0 | 0 | 1 | 0 | 18,529 |
| Rhinelander .................. | 1 | 0 | 0 | 0 | 0 | 0 | 1 | 0 | 0 | 0 | 7,429 |
| River Falls.................... | 1 | 1 | 0 | 0 | 0 | 0 | 1 | 0 | 0 | 1 | 15,207 |
| **Universities and Colleges** ........ | 0 | 0 | 1 | 0 | 0 | 0 | | | | | |
| University of Wisconsin, Platteville ...................... | 0 | 0 | 1 | 0 | 0 | 0 | 0 | 0 | 1 | 0 | 8,901 |
| **Metropolitan Counties** ............ | 2 | 0 | 2 | 0 | 0 | 0 | | | | | |
| Fond du Lac................... | 0 | 0 | 1 | 0 | 0 | 0 | 0 | 0 | 1 | 0 | |
| Rock........................... | 2 | 0 | 0 | 0 | 0 | 0 | 0 | 1 | 1 | 0 | |
| Waukesha...................... | 0 | 0 | 1 | 0 | 0 | 0 | 0 | 0 | 0 | 1 | |
| **Nonmetropolitan Counties**...... | 4 | 1 | 0 | 0 | 0 | 0 | | | | | |
| Burnett........................ | 1 | 0 | 0 | 0 | 0 | 0 | 0 | 0 | 0 | 1 | |
| Oneida......................... | 0 | 1 | 0 | 0 | 0 | 0 | 0 | 0 | 1 | 0 | |
| Sawyer......................... | 3 | 0 | 0 | 0 | 0 | 0 | 0 | 0 | 1 | 2 | |
| **WYOMING** | | | | | | | | | | | |
| **Total** ......................... | 2 | 0 | 0 | 0 | 0 | 0 | | | | | |
| **Cities** ......................... | 2 | 0 | 0 | 0 | 0 | 0 | | | | | |
| Gillette........................ | 2 | 0 | 0 | 0 | 0 | 0 | 0 | 0 | 1 | 1 | 32,502 |
| **OTHER OUTLYING AREAS** ........ | | | | | | | | | | | |
| **Total** ......................... | 1 | 0 | 0 | 0 | 0 | 0 | | | | | |
| Guam .......................... | 1 | 0 | 0 | 0 | 0 | 0 | 0 | 1 | 0 | 0 | |

[1]Population figures are published only for the cities. The figures listed for the universities and colleges are student enrollment and were provided by the United States Department of Education for the 2014 school year, the most recent available. The enrollment figures include full-time and part-time students.
[2]Student enrollment figures were not available.
[3] Includes one incident reported with more than one bias motivation.

# METHODOLOGY

The Federal Bureau of Investigation (FBI) began the procedures for implementing, collecting, and managing hate crime data after Congress passed the Hate Crime Statistics Act in 1990. This act required the collection of data "about crimes that manifest evidence of prejudice based on race, religion, sexual orientation, or ethnicity." Beginning in 2013, law enforcement agencies could submit hate crime data in accordance with a number of program modifications. In 1994, the Hate Crime Statistics Act was amended to include bias against persons with disabilities. The Church Arson Prevention Act, which was signed into law in July 1996, removed the sunset clause from the original statute and mandated that the collection of hate crime data become a permanent part of the UCR program. In 2009, Congress further amended the Hate Crime Statistics Act by passing the Matthew Shepard and James Byrd, Jr., Hate Crime Prevention Act. The amendment includes the collection of data for crimes motivated by bias against a particular gender and gender identity, as well as for crimes committed by, and crimes directed against, juveniles. In response to the Shepard/Byrd Act, the FBI modified its data collection so that reporting agencies could indicate whether hate crimes were committed by, or directed against, juveniles.

## Definitions

Hate crimes include any crime motivated by bias against race, religion, sexual orientation, ethnicity/national origin, and/or disability. Because motivation is subjective, it is sometimes difficult to know with certainty whether a crime resulted from the offender's bias. Moreover, the presence of bias alone does not necessarily mean that a crime can be considered a hate crime. Only when law enforcement investigation reveals sufficient evidence to lead a reasonable and prudent person to conclude that the offender's actions were motivated, in whole or in part, by his or her bias should an incident be reported as a hate crime.

## Data Collection

The UCR (Uniform Crime Reporting) program collects data about both single-bias and multiple-bias hate crimes. A single-bias incident is defined as an incident in which one or more offense types are motivated by the same bias. A multiple-bias incident is defined as an incident in which more than one offense type occurs and at least two offense types are motivated by different biases.

A table enumerating the selected places in the United States covered by the data can be found at the following URL:

https://ucr.fbi.gov/hate-crime/2015/tables-and-data -declarations/participationtabledatadecpdf.

## Caution to Users

Data users should exercise care in making any direct comparison between data in this publication and those in prior issues of *Hate Crime Statistics*. Because of differing levels of participation from year to year, some data may not be comparable. In addition, data users should not rank locales because there are many factors that cause the nature and type of crime to vary from place to place. UCR statistics include only jurisdictional population figures along with reported crime, clearance, or arrest data. Rankings ignore the uniqueness of each locale.

For information about the FBI's caution against ranking, including warnings about variables affecting crime and characteristics of jurisdictions, please see https://ucr.fbi.gov/ucr-statistics-their-proper-use.

### Crimes Against Persons, Property, or Society

The UCR program's data collection guidelines stipulate that a hate crime may involve multiple offenses, victims, and offenders within one incident; therefore, the Hate Crime Statistics program is incident-based. According to UCR counting guidelines:

- One offense is counted for each victim in *crimes against persons*
- One offense is counted for each offense type in *crimes against property*
- One offense is counted for each offense type in *crimes against society*

### Victims

In the UCR program, the victim of a hate crime may be an individual, a business, an institution, or society as a whole.

### Offenders

According to the UCR program, the term *known offender* does not imply that the suspect's identity is known; rather, the term indicates that some aspect of the suspect was identified, thus distinguishing the suspect from an unknown offender. Law enforcement agencies specify the number of offenders, and when possible, the race of the offender or offenders as a group.

### Race/Ethnicity

The UCR program uses the following racial designations in its Hate Crime Statistics program: White; Black; American Indian or Alaskan Native; Asian; Native Hawaiian or Other Pacific Islander; and Multiple Races, Group. In addition, the UCR program uses the ethnic designations of Hispanic or Latino and Not Hispanic or Latino.

The law enforcement agencies that voluntarily participate in the Hate Crime Statistics program collect details about an offender's bias motivation associated with 11 offense types already being reported to the UCR program: murder and nonnegligent manslaughter, rape, aggravated assault, simple assault, and intimidation (crimes against persons); and robbery, burglary, larceny-theft, motor vehicle theft, arson, and destruction/damage/vandalism (crimes against property). The law enforcement agencies that participate in the UCR program via the National Incident-Based Reporting System (NIBRS) collect data about additional offenses for *crimes against persons* and *crimes against property*. These data appear in the category of other. These agencies also collect hate crime data for the category called *crimes against society*, which includes drug or narcotic offenses, gambling offenses, prostitution offenses, and weapon law violations.

### Changes to the Data Collection

Beginning in 2013, law enforcement agencies could submit hate crime data in accordance with a number of program modifications. Descriptions of those modifications, which are again included in the published data, follow.

### Addition of Gender and Gender Identity Bias Categories

In response to the Matthew Shepard and James Byrd Jr. Hate Crimes Prevention Act of 2009 (Shepard/Byrd Act), the FBI began accepting data on crimes motivated by gender (male and female) bias and gender identity (transgender and gender nonconforming) bias from contributors.

### Involvement of Juveniles

Also in response to the Shepard/Byrd Act, the FBI modified its data collection so that reporting agencies could indicate whether hate crimes were committed by, or directed against, juveniles. Therefore, in addition to reporting the number of individual victims, in 2013, law enforcement began reporting the number of victims who are 18 years of age or older and the number of victims under the age of 18.

### Revision of Sexual-Orientation Bias Types

Following the passage of the Shepard/Byrd Act, the FBI updated select sexual-orientation bias types at the recommendation of the Criminal Justice Information Services (CJIS) Advisory Policy Board (APB) and with input from the Hate Crime Coalition. The sexual-orientation bias types were revised from anti-male homosexual, anti-female homosexual, anti-homosexual, anti-heterosexual, and anti-bisexual to anti-gay (male); anti-lesbian; anti-lesbian, gay, bisexual, and transgender (mixed group); anti-heterosexual; and anti-bisexual.

### Additional Bias Types per Offense

At the recommendation of the CJIS APB and with the approval of the FBI Director, the UCR Program began permitting law enforcement agencies to report four additional bias types per offense instead of one.

### Revision of Race and Ethnicity Categories

To comply with a directive from the U.S. Government's Office of Management and Budget (OMB), the UCR Program expanded its race categories and changed its ethnicity categories. The race categories were expanded from four (White, Black, American Indian or Alaskan Native, and Asian or Other Pacific Islander) to five (White, Black or African American, American Indian or Alaska Native, Asian, and Native Hawaiian or Other Pacific Islander). The ethnicity categories changed from "Hispanic" and "Other Ethnicity/National Origin" to "Hispanic or Latino" and "Not Hispanic or Latino."

### Revision to the Definition of Rape

At the recommendation of the CJIS APB and with the approval of the FBI Director, the UCR Program initiated the collection of rape data under a revised definition and removed the term "forcible" from the offense name in 2013. The changes bring uniformity to the offense in both the Summary Reporting System (SRS) and the National Incident-Based Reporting System (NIBRS) by capturing data (1) without regard to gender, (2) including penetration of any bodily orifice by any object or body part, and (3) including offenses where physical force is not involved. Beginning in 2013, the UCR Program defined rape as follows:

Rape (revised definition): Penetration, no matter how slight, of the vagina or anus with any body part or object, or oral penetration by a sex organ of another person, without the consent of the victim. (This includes the offenses of rape, sodomy, and sexual assault with an object as converted from data submitted via the NIBRS.)

Rape (legacy definition): The carnal knowledge of a female forcibly and against her will.

## From the NIBRS

For all law enforcement agencies that submitted their hate crime data via the NIBRS in 2015, the UCR Program combined the agencies' totals for the offenses of rape (which includes both male and female victims), sodomy, and sexual assault with an object to derive rape figures in accordance with the broader revised definition. In addition, the UCR Program published any offenses of fondling, incest, and statutory rape submitted via the NIBRS in the crimes against persons category of *other*.

## From the SRS

The UCR Program's revised definition of rape is the same definition adopted specifically for the SRS and includes the offenses of rape, sodomy, and sexual assault with an object (without any breakdowns for individual offenses). Likewise, the UCR Program's legacy definition of rape is the same definition formerly used in the SRS as forcible rape. Although some SRS agencies were able to apply the revised definition to their data collection procedures, not all agencies were able to do so. Therefore, the UCR Program published the rape data of law enforcement agencies that submitted their hate crime data via the SRS electronic record layout, or the Microsoft Excel Workbook Tool in accordance with the rape definition (revised or legacy) the agency applied in 2015.

# PART 6

# Human Trafficking, 2015

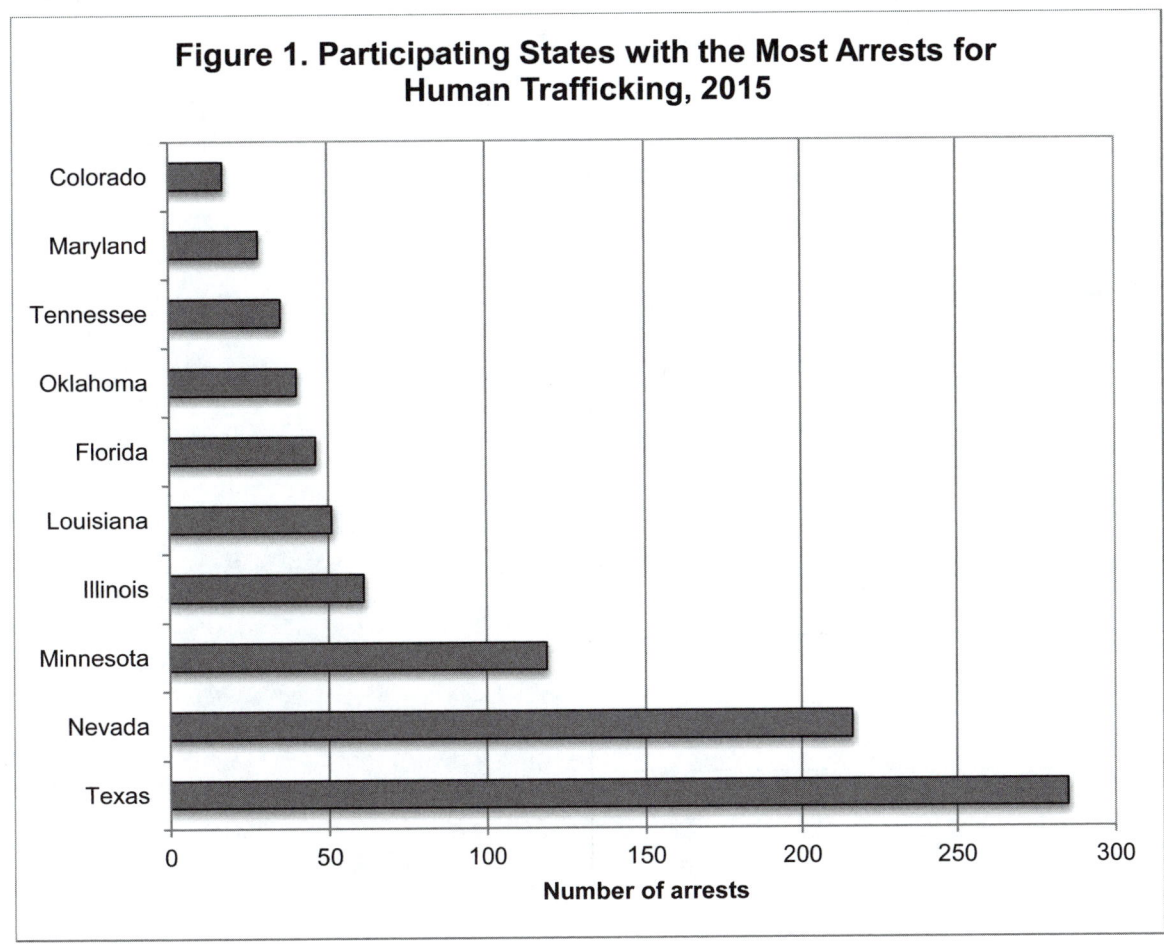

**Figure 1. Participating States with the Most Arrests for Human Trafficking, 2015**

- Of the participating states, Texas had the highest number of participating agencies in the contribution of human trafficking data (1,080), followed by Illinois (735) and Florida (698).

- Adult males represented the highest number of arrestees for human trafficking crimes.

- Texas and Minnesota had the highest incidences of arrests of persons of non—Hispanic or Latino ethnicity for human trafficking crimes (421 and 66, respectively).

# Table 1. Human Trafficking, by Participating State/Territory, 2015

(Number.)

| State | Number of participating agencies |
|---|---:|
| Alaska | 2 |
| Arkansas | 296 |
| Arizona | 124 |
| Colorado | 249 |
| Connecticut | 2 [1] |
| Delaware | 60 |
| Florida | 698 |
| Guam | 1 |
| Hawaii | 3 |
| Idaho | 3 [1] |
| Illinois | 735 |
| Indiana | 70 |
| Kansas | 6 |
| Louisiana | 176 |
| Maine | 3 [1] |
| Maryland | 155 |
| Massachusetts | 60 |
| Michigan | 657 |
| Minnesota | 39 |
| Mississippi | 52 |
| Missouri | 637 |
| Montana | 114 |
| Nebraska | 1 [1] |
| Nevada | 45 |
| North Carolina | 1 [1] |
| Ohio | 58 |
| Oklahoma | 75 |
| Oregon | 140 |
| Puerto Rico | 1 |
| Rhode Island | 2 [1] |
| South Carolina | 506 |
| South Dakota | 137 |
| Tennessee | 464 |
| Texas | 1,080 |
| U.S. Virgin Islands | 1 |
| Utah | 145 |
| Washington | 255 |
| Wisconsin | 116 |
| Wyoming | 57 |

[1] Data submitted through the Bureau of Indian Affairs.

# Table 2. Human Trafficking, Offenses and Clearances by Participating State/Territory, 2015

(Number.)

| State | Commercial sex acts | | | Involuntary servitude | | | Total | | |
|---|---|---|---|---|---|---|---|---|---|
| | Offenses | Total cleared | Clearances under 18 | Offenses | Total cleared | Clearances under 18 | Offenses | Total cleared | Clearances under 18 |
| Alaska | 10 | 1 | 0 | 0 | 0 | 0 | 10 | 1 | 0 |
| Arizona | 5 | 6 | 0 | 1 | 0 | 0 | 6 | 6 | 0 |
| Arkansas | 5 | 2 | 0 | 0 | 0 | 0 | 5 | 2 | 0 |
| Colorado | 11 | 5 | 0 | 6 | 2 | 0 | 17 | 7 | 0 |
| Connecticut | 0 | 0 | 0 | 0 | 0 | 0 | 0 | 0 | 0 |
| Delaware | 0 | 0 | 0 | 0 | 0 | 0 | 0 | 0 | 0 |
| Florida | 44 | 23 | 0 | 2 | 0 | 0 | 46 | 23 | 0 |
| Guam | 0 | 0 | 0 | 0 | 0 | 0 | 0 | 0 | 0 |
| Hawaii | 3 | 0 | 0 | 0 | 0 | 0 | 3 | 0 | 0 |
| Idaho | 0 | 0 | 0 | 0 | 0 | 0 | 0 | 0 | 0 |
| Illinois | 53 | 0 | 0 | 8 | 0 | 0 | 61 | 0 | 0 |
| Indiana | 0 | 0 | 0 | 0 | 0 | 0 | 0 | 0 | 0 |
| Kansas | 0 | 0 | 0 | 0 | 0 | 0 | 0 | 0 | 0 |
| Louisiana | 51 | 41 | 1 | 0 | 0 | 0 | 51 | 41 | 1 |
| Maine | 0 | 0 | 0 | 0 | 0 | 0 | 0 | 0 | 0 |
| Maryland | 27 | 22 | 0 | 1 | 1 | 0 | 28 | 23 | 0 |
| Massachusetts | 0 | 0 | 0 | 2 | 1 | 0 | 2 | 1 | 0 |
| Michigan | 3 | 3 | 0 | 0 | 0 | 0 | 3 | 3 | 0 |
| Minnesota | 119 | 77 | 0 | 0 | 0 | 0 | 119 | 77 | 0 |
| Mississippi | 0 | 0 | 0 | 0 | 0 | 0 | 0 | 0 | 0 |
| Missouri | 13 | 5 | 0 | 0 | 0 | 0 | 13 | 5 | 0 |
| Montana | 0 | 0 | 0 | 0 | 0 | 0 | 0 | 0 | 0 |
| Nebraska | 0 | 0 | 0 | 0 | 0 | 0 | 0 | 0 | 0 |
| Nevada | 214 | 49 | 1 | 2 | 0 | 0 | 216 | 49 | 1 |
| New York | 0 | 0 | 0 | 0 | 0 | 0 | 0 | 0 | 0 |
| North Carolina | 0 | 0 | 0 | 0 | 0 | 0 | 0 | 0 | 0 |
| Ohio | 3 | 2 | 0 | 0 | 0 | 0 | 3 | 2 | 0 |
| Oklahoma | 38 | 27 | 1 | 2 | 1 | 0 | 40 | 28 | 1 |
| Oregon | 0 | 0 | 0 | 0 | 0 | 0 | 0 | 0 | 0 |
| Puerto Rico | 0 | 0 | 0 | 0 | 0 | 0 | 2 | 0 | 0 |
| Rhode Island | 0 | 0 | 0 | 0 | 0 | 0 | 0 | 0 | 0 |
| South Carolina | 10 | 5 | 0 | 4 | 0 | 0 | 14 | 5 | 0 |
| South Dakota | 0 | 0 | 0 | 0 | 0 | 0 | 0 | 0 | 0 |
| Tennessee | 32 | 10 | 0 | 3 | 1 | 0 | 35 | 11 | 0 |
| Texas | 98 | 30 | 0 | 187 | 71 | 0 | 285 | 101 | 0 |
| U. S. Virgin Islands | 0 | 0 | 0 | 0 | 0 | 0 | 0 | 0 | 0 |
| Utah | 0 | 0 | 0 | 0 | 0 | 0 | 0 | 0 | 0 |
| Washington | 1 | 0 | 0 | 0 | 0 | 0 | 1 | 0 | 0 |
| Wisconsin | 4 | 2 | 0 | 0 | 0 | 0 | 4 | 2 | 0 |
| Wyoming | 0 | 0 | 0 | 1 | 0 | 0 | 1 | 0 | 0 |

## Table 3. Human Trafficking Arrests, by Age, State, and Participating State/Territory, 2015

(Number.)

| Area and offense | Juvenile | | Adult | |
|---|---|---|---|---|
| | Juvenile male | Juvenile female | Adult male | Adult female |
| **Alaska** | | | | |
| Commercial sex acts | 0 | 0 | 0 | 0 |
| Involuntary servitude | 0 | 0 | 0 | 0 |
| **Arizona** | | | | |
| Commercial sex acts | 0 | 0 | 0 | 0 |
| Involuntary servitude | 0 | 0 | 0 | 0 |
| **Arkansas** | | | | |
| Commercial sex acts | 0 | 0 | 0 | 0 |
| Involuntary servitude | 0 | 0 | 0 | 0 |
| **Colorado** | | | | |
| Commercial sex acts | 0 | 0 | 1 | 0 |
| Involuntary servitude | 0 | 0 | 2 | 0 |
| **Guam** | | | | |
| Commercial sex acts | 0 | 0 | 1 | 0 |
| Involuntary servitude | 0 | 0 | 0 | 0 |
| **Hawaii** | | | | |
| Commercial sex acts | 0 | 0 | 1 | 0 |
| Involuntary servitude | 0 | 0 | 0 | 0 |
| **Indiana** | | | | |
| Commercial sex acts | 1 | 1 | 0 | 0 |
| Involuntary servitude | 0 | 1 | 0 | 0 |
| **Louisiana** | | | | |
| Commercial sex acts | 0 | 0 | 4 | 0 |
| Involuntary servitude | 2 | 6 | 1 | 0 |
| **Maryland** | | | | |
| Commercial sex acts | 1 | 0 | 11 | 1 |
| Involuntary servitude | 0 | 6 | 4 | 1 |
| **Massachusetts** | | | | |
| Commercial sex acts | 0 | 0 | 0 | 0 |
| Involuntary servitude | 0 | 0 | 2 | 0 |
| **Michigan** | | | | |
| Commercial sex acts | 0 | 0 | 0 | 0 |
| Involuntary servitude | 0 | 0 | 0 | 0 |
| **Minnesota** | | | | |
| Commercial sex acts | 0 | 0 | 67 | 7 |
| Involuntary servitude | 0 | 0 | 0 | 0 |
| **Mississippi** | 0 | 0 | 0 | 0 |
| Commercial sex acts | 2 | 4 | 0 | 0 |
| Involuntary servitude | | | | |
| **Missouri** | 0 | 0 | 5 | 2 |
| Commercial sex acts | 0 | 0 | 0 | 0 |
| Involuntary servitude | | | | |
| **Nebraska** | | | | |
| Commercial sex acts | 0 | 0 | 0 | 0 |
| Involuntary servitude | 0 | 0 | 0 | 0 |
| **Nevada** | | | | |
| Commercial sex acts | 0 | 2 | 15 | 7 |
| Involuntary servitude | 0 | 0 | 7 | 1 |
| **North Dakota** | | | | |
| Commercial sex acts | 0 | 0 | 0 | 1 |
| Involuntary servitude | 0 | 0 | 0 | 0 |

# Table 3. Human Trafficking Arrests, by Age, State, and Participating State/Territory, 2015—*Continued*

(Number.)

| Area and offense | Juvenile | | Adult | |
|---|---|---|---|---|
| | Juvenile male | Juvenile female | Adult male | Adult female |
| **Ohio** | | | | |
| Commercial sex acts | 0 | 0 | 0 | 0 |
| Involuntary servitude | 0 | 0 | 0 | 0 |
| **Oklahoma** | | | | |
| Commercial sex acts | 0 | 0 | 9 | 5 |
| Involuntary servitude | 0 | 0 | 0 | 0 |
| **South Carolina** | | | | |
| Commercial sex acts | 0 | 0 | 3 | 0 |
| Involuntary servitude | 0 | 0 | 0 | 0 |
| **Tennessee** | | | | |
| Commercial sex acts | 0 | 0 | 1 | 1 |
| Involuntary servitude | 0 | 0 | 0 | 0 |
| **Texas** | | | | |
| Commercial sex acts | 3 | 54 | 350 | 131 |
| Involuntary servitude | 1 | 2 | 16 | 8 |
| **U.S. Virgin Islands** | | | | |
| Commercial sex acts | 0 | 0 | 0 | 0 |
| Involuntary servitude | 0 | 0 | 0 | 0 |
| **Utah** | | | | |
| Commercial sex acts | 0 | 0 | 0 | 0 |
| Involuntary servitude | 0 | 0 | 0 | 0 |
| **Washington** | | | | |
| Commercial sex acts | 0 | 0 | 0 | 0 |
| Involuntary servitude | 0 | 0 | 0 | 0 |
| **Wyoming** | | | | |
| Commercial sex acts | 0 | 0 | 0 | 0 |
| Involuntary servitude | 0 | 0 | 0 | 0 |

# Table 4. Human Trafficking Arrests, by Race and Participating State/Territory, 2015

(Number.)

| Area and offense | Juvenile | | | | | | Adult | | | | | |
|---|---|---|---|---|---|---|---|---|---|---|---|---|
| | White | Black or African American | American Indian or Alaska Native | Asian | Native Hawaiian or Other Pacific Islander | Total | White | Black or African American | American Indian or Alaska Native | Asian | Native Hawaiian or Other Pacific Islander | Total |
| **Alaska** | | | | | | | | | | | | |
| Commercial sex acts | 0 | 0 | 0 | 0 | 0 | 0 | 0 | 0 | 0 | 0 | 0 | 0 |
| Involuntary servitude | 0 | 0 | 0 | 0 | 0 | 0 | 0 | 0 | 0 | 0 | 0 | 0 |
| **Arizona** | | | | | | | | | | | | |
| Commercial sex acts | 0 | 0 | 0 | 0 | 0 | 0 | 0 | 0 | 0 | 0 | 0 | 0 |
| Involuntary servitude | 0 | 0 | 0 | 0 | 0 | 0 | 0 | 0 | 0 | 0 | 0 | 0 |
| **Arkansas** | | | | | | | | | | | | |
| Commercial sex acts | 0 | 0 | 0 | 0 | 0 | 0 | 0 | 0 | 0 | 0 | 0 | 0 |
| Involuntary servitude | 0 | 0 | 0 | 0 | 0 | 0 | 0 | 0 | 0 | 0 | 0 | 0 |
| **Colorado** | | | | | | | | | | | | |
| Commercial sex acts | 0 | 0 | 0 | 0 | 0 | 0 | 1 | 0 | 0 | 0 | 0 | 1 |
| Involuntary servitude | 0 | 0 | 0 | 0 | 0 | 0 | 1 | 1 | 0 | 0 | 0 | 2 |
| **Guam** | | | | | | | | | | | | |
| Commercial sex acts | 0 | 0 | 0 | 0 | 0 | 0 | 0 | 0 | 0 | 0 | 1 | 1 |
| Involuntary servitude | 0 | 0 | 0 | 0 | 0 | 0 | 0 | 0 | 0 | 0 | 0 | 0 |
| **Hawaii** | | | | | | | | | | | | |
| Commercial sex acts | 0 | 0 | 0 | 0 | 0 | 0 | 1 | 0 | 0 | 0 | 0 | 1 |
| Involuntary servitude | 0 | 0 | 0 | 0 | 0 | 0 | 0 | 0 | 0 | 0 | 0 | 0 |
| **Indiana** | | | | | | | | | | | | |
| Commercial sex acts | 2 | 0 | 0 | 0 | 0 | 2 | 0 | 0 | 0 | 0 | 0 | 0 |
| Involuntary servitude | 1 | 0 | 0 | 0 | 0 | 1 | 0 | 0 | 0 | 0 | 0 | 0 |
| **Louisiana** | | | | | | | | | | | | |
| Commercial sex acts | 0 | 0 | 0 | 0 | 0 | 0 | 0 | 4 | 0 | 0 | 0 | 4 |
| Involuntary servitude | 3 | 5 | 0 | 0 | 0 | 8 | 0 | 1 | 0 | 0 | 0 | 1 |
| **Maryland** | | | | | | | | | | | | |
| Commercial sex acts | 1 | 0 | 0 | 0 | 0 | 1 | 1 | 11 | 0 | 0 | 0 | 12 |
| Involuntary servitude | 3 | 3 | 0 | 0 | 0 | 6 | 2 | 3 | 0 | 0 | 0 | 5 |
| **Massachusetts** | | | | | | | | | | | | |
| Commercial sex acts | 0 | 0 | 0 | 0 | 0 | 0 | 0 | 0 | 0 | 0 | 0 | 0 |
| Involuntary servitude | 0 | 0 | 0 | 0 | 0 | 0 | 2 | 0 | 0 | 0 | 0 | 2 |
| **Michigan** | | | | | | | | | | | | |
| Commercial sex acts | 0 | 0 | 0 | 0 | 0 | 0 | 0 | 0 | 0 | 0 | 0 | 0 |
| Involuntary servitude | 0 | 0 | 0 | 0 | 0 | 0 | 0 | 0 | 0 | 0 | 0 | 0 |
| **Minnesota** | | | | | | | | | | | | |
| Commercial sex acts | 0 | 0 | 0 | 0 | 0 | 0 | 49 | 21 | 1 | 3 | 0 | 74 |
| Involuntary servitude | 0 | 0 | 0 | 0 | 0 | 0 | 0 | 0 | 0 | 0 | 0 | 0 |
| **Mississippi** | | | | | | | | | | | | |
| Commercial sex acts | 0 | 0 | 0 | 0 | 0 | 0 | 0 | 0 | 0 | 0 | 0 | 0 |
| Involuntary servitude | 0 | 0 | 0 | 0 | 0 | 0 | 0 | 0 | 0 | 0 | 0 | 0 |
| **Missouri** | | | | | | | | | | | | |
| Commercial sex acts | 0 | 0 | 0 | 0 | 0 | 0 | 1 | 6 | 0 | 0 | 0 | 7 |
| Involuntary servitude | 0 | 0 | 0 | 0 | 0 | 0 | 0 | 0 | 0 | 0 | 0 | 0 |
| **Nebraska** | | | | | | | | | | | | |
| Commercial sex acts | 0 | 0 | 0 | 0 | 0 | 0 | 0 | 0 | 0 | 0 | 0 | 0 |
| Involuntary servitude | 0 | 0 | 0 | 0 | 0 | 0 | 0 | 0 | 0 | 0 | 0 | 0 |
| **Nevada** | | | | | | | | | | | | |
| Commercial sex acts | 0 | 2 | 0 | 0 | 0 | 2 | 4 | 17 | 0 | 1 | 0 | 22 |
| Involuntary servitude | 0 | 0 | 0 | 0 | 0 | 0 | 1 | 7 | 0 | 0 | 0 | 8 |

## Table 4. Human Trafficking Arrests, by Race and Participating State/Territory, 2015—*Continued*

(Number.)

| Area and offense | Juvenile | | | | | | Adult | | | | | |
|---|---|---|---|---|---|---|---|---|---|---|---|---|
| | White | Black or African American | American Indian or Alaska Native | Asian | Native Hawaiian or Other Pacific Islander | Total | White | Black or African American | American Indian or Alaska Native | Asian | Native Hawaiian or Other Pacific Islander | Total |
| **North Dakota** | | | | | | | | | | | | |
| Commercial sex acts ...................... | 0 | 0 | 0 | 0 | 0 | 0 | 0 | 0 | 1 | 0 | 0 | 1 |
| Involuntary servitude..................... | 0 | 0 | 0 | 0 | 0 | 0 | 0 | 0 | 0 | 0 | 0 | 0 |
| **Ohio** | | | | | | | | | | | | |
| Commercial sex acts ...................... | 0 | 0 | 0 | 0 | 0 | 0 | 0 | 0 | 0 | 0 | 0 | 0 |
| Involuntary servitude..................... | 0 | 0 | 0 | 0 | 0 | 0 | 0 | 0 | 0 | 0 | 0 | 0 |
| **Oklahoma** | | | | | | | | | | | | |
| Commercial sex acts ...................... | 0 | 0 | 0 | 0 | 0 | 0 | 6 | 8 | 0 | 0 | 0 | 14 |
| Involuntary servitude..................... | 0 | 0 | 0 | 0 | 0 | 0 | 0 | 0 | 0 | 0 | 0 | 0 |
| **South Carolina** | | | | | | | | | | | | |
| Commercial sex acts ...................... | 0 | 0 | 0 | 0 | 0 | 0 | 0 | 3 | 0 | 0 | 0 | 3 |
| Involuntary servitude..................... | 0 | 0 | 0 | 0 | 0 | 0 | 0 | 0 | 0 | 0 | 0 | 0 |
| **Tennessee** | | | | | | | | | | | | |
| Commercial sex acts ...................... | 0 | 0 | 0 | 0 | 0 | 0 | 0 | 1 | 0 | 1 | 0 | 2 |
| Involuntary servitude..................... | 0 | 0 | 0 | 0 | 0 | 0 | 0 | 0 | 0 | 0 | 0 | 0 |
| **Texas** | | | | | | | | | | | | |
| Commercial sex acts ...................... | 24 | 33 | 0 | 0 | 0 | 57 | 379 | 100 | 0 | 1 | 1 | 481 |
| Involuntary servitude..................... | 3 | 0 | 0 | 0 | 0 | 3 | 22 | 2 | 0 | 0 | 0 | 24 |
| **U.S. Virgin Islands** | | | | | | | | | | | | |
| Commercial sex acts ...................... | 0 | 0 | 0 | 0 | 0 | 0 | 0 | 0 | 0 | 0 | 0 | 0 |
| Involuntary servitude..................... | 0 | 0 | 0 | 0 | 0 | 0 | 0 | 0 | 0 | 0 | 0 | 0 |
| **Utah** | | | | | | | | | | | | |
| Commercial sex acts ...................... | 0 | 0 | 0 | 0 | 0 | 0 | 0 | 0 | 0 | 0 | 0 | 0 |
| Involuntary servitude..................... | 0 | 0 | 0 | 0 | 0 | 0 | 0 | 0 | 0 | 0 | 0 | 0 |
| **Washington** | | | | | | | | | | | | |
| Commercial sex acts ...................... | 0 | 0 | 0 | 0 | 0 | 0 | 0 | 0 | 0 | 0 | 0 | 0 |
| Involuntary servitude..................... | 0 | 0 | 0 | 0 | 0 | 0 | 0 | 0 | 0 | 0 | 0 | 0 |
| **Wyoming** | | | | | | | | | | | | |
| Commercial sex acts ...................... | 0 | 0 | 0 | 0 | 0 | 0 | 0 | 0 | 0 | 0 | 0 | 0 |
| Involuntary servitude..................... | 0 | 0 | 0 | 0 | 0 | 0 | 0 | 0 | 0 | 0 | 0 | 0 |

## Table 5. Human Trafficking Arrests, by Ethnicity and Participating State/Territory, 2015

(Number.)

| Area and offense | Juvenile | | | Adult | | |
|---|---|---|---|---|---|---|
| | Hispanic or Latino | Not Hispanic or Latino | Total | Hispanic or Latino | Not Hispanic or Latino | Total |
| **Alaska** | | | | | | |
| Commercial sex acts | 0 | 0 | 0 | 0 | 0 | 0 |
| Involuntary servitude | 0 | 0 | 0 | 0 | 0 | 0 |
| **Arizona** | | | | | | |
| Commercial sex acts | 0 | 0 | 0 | 0 | 0 | 0 |
| Involuntary servitude | 0 | 0 | 0 | 0 | 0 | 0 |
| **Arkansas** | | | | | | |
| Commercial sex acts | 0 | 0 | 0 | 0 | 0 | 0 |
| Involuntary servitude | 0 | 0 | 0 | 0 | 0 | 0 |
| **Colorado** | | | | | | |
| Commercial sex acts | 0 | 0 | 0 | 0 | 1 | 1 |
| Involuntary servitude | 0 | 0 | 0 | 1 | 1 | 2 |
| **Guam** | | | | | | |
| Commercial sex acts | 0 | 0 | 0 | 0 | 1 | 1 |
| Involuntary servitude | 0 | 0 | 0 | 0 | 0 | 0 |
| **Indiana** | | | | | | |
| Commercial sex acts | 0 | 0 | 0 | 0 | 0 | 0 |
| Involuntary servitude | 0 | 0 | 0 | 0 | 0 | 0 |
| **Maryland** | | | | | | |
| Commercial sex acts | 0 | 1 | 1 | 0 | 12 | 12 |
| Involuntary servitude | 0 | 6 | 6 | 1 | 4 | 5 |
| **Massachusetts** | | | | | | |
| Commercial sex acts | 0 | 0 | 0 | 0 | 0 | 0 |
| Involuntary servitude | 0 | 0 | 0 | 0 | 2 | 2 |
| **Michigan** | | | | | | |
| Commercial sex acts | 0 | 0 | 0 | 0 | 0 | 0 |
| Involuntary servitude | 0 | 0 | 0 | 0 | 0 | 0 |
| **Minnesota** | | | | | | |
| Commercial sex acts | 0 | 0 | 0 | 8 | 66 | 74 |
| Involuntary servitude | 0 | 0 | 0 | 0 | 0 | 0 |
| **Mississippi** | | | | | | |
| Commercial sex acts | 0 | 0 | 0 | 0 | 0 | 0 |
| Involuntary servitude | 0 | 0 | 0 | 0 | 0 | 0 |
| **Nevada** | | | | | | |
| Commercial sex acts | 0 | 2 | 2 | 4 | 18 | 22 |
| Involuntary servitude | 0 | 0 | 0 | 0 | 8 | 8 |
| **North Dakota** | | | | | | |
| Commercial sex acts | 0 | 0 | 0 | 0 | 1 | 1 |
| Involuntary servitude | 0 | 0 | 0 | 0 | 0 | 0 |
| **Ohio** | | | | | | |
| Commercial sex acts | 0 | 0 | 0 | 0 | 0 | 0 |
| Involuntary servitude | 0 | 0 | 0 | 0 | 0 | 0 |
| **Oklahoma** | | | | | | |
| Commercial sex acts | 0 | 0 | 0 | 1 | 13 | 14 |
| Involuntary servitude | 0 | 0 | 0 | 0 | 0 | 0 |

# Table 5. Human Trafficking Arrests, by Ethnicity and Participating State/Territory, 2015—*Continued*

(Number.)

| Area and offense | Juvenile | | | Adult | | |
|---|---|---|---|---|---|---|
| | Hispanic or Latino | Not Hispanic or Latino | Total | Hispanic or Latino | Not Hispanic or Latino | Total |
| **South Carolina** | | | | | | |
| Commercial sex acts ............................................. | 0 | 0 | 0 | 0 | 3 | 3 |
| Involuntary servitude............................................. | 0 | 0 | 0 | 0 | 0 | 0 |
| **Tennessee** | | | | | | |
| Commercial sex acts ............................................. | 0 | 0 | 0 | 0 | 2 | 2 |
| Involuntary servitude............................................. | 0 | 0 | 0 | 0 | 0 | 0 |
| **Texas** | | | | | | |
| Commercial sex acts ............................................. | 15 | 42 | 57 | 102 | 379 | 481 |
| Involuntary servitude............................................. | 1 | 2 | 3 | 17 | 7 | 24 |
| **U.S. Virgin Islands** | | | | | | |
| Commercial sex acts ............................................. | 0 | 0 | 0 | 0 | 0 | 0 |
| Involuntary servitude............................................. | 0 | 0 | 0 | 0 | 0 | 0 |
| **Utah** | | | | | | |
| Commercial sex acts ............................................. | 0 | 0 | 0 | 0 | 0 | 0 |
| Involuntary servitude............................................. | 0 | 0 | 0 | 0 | 0 | 0 |
| **Washington** | | | | | | |
| Commercial sex acts ............................................. | 0 | 0 | 0 | 0 | 0 | 0 |
| Involuntary servitude............................................. | 0 | 0 | 0 | 0 | 0 | 0 |
| **Wisconsin** | | | | | | |
| Commercial sex acts ............................................. | 0 | 0 | 0 | 0 | 0 | 0 |
| Involuntary servitude............................................. | 0 | 0 | 0 | 0 | 0 | 0 |
| **Wyoming** | | | | | | |
| Commercial sex acts ............................................. | 0 | 0 | 0 | 0 | 0 | 0 |
| Involuntary servitude............................................. | 0 | 0 | 0 | 0 | 0 | 0 |

*Note:* Not all agencies provide ethnicity data; therefore, the race and ethnicity totals will not equal.

# METHODOLOGY

In January 2013, the national UCR Program began collecting offense and arrest data regarding human trafficking as authorized by the *William Wilberforce Trafficking Victims Protection Reauthorization Act of 2008*. The act requires the FBI to collect human trafficking offense data and to make distinctions between prostitution, assisting or promoting prostitution, and purchasing prostitution.

To comply with the Wilberforce Act, the national UCR Program created two additional offenses in the Summary Reporting System and the National Incident-Based Reporting System for which the UCR Program collects both offense and arrest data. The definitions for these offenses are:

**Human Trafficking/Commercial Sex Acts:** inducing a person by force, fraud, or coercion to participate in commercial sex acts, or in which the person induced to perform such act(s) has not attained 18 years of age.

**Human Trafficking/Involuntary Servitude:** the obtaining of a person(s) through recruitment, harboring, transportation, or provision, and subjecting such persons by force, fraud, or coercion into involuntary servitude, peonage, debt bondage, or slavery (not to include commercial sex acts).

The data in the tables included in this report reflect the offenses and arrests recorded by state and local law enforcement agencies (LEAs) that currently have the ability to report the data to the national UCR Program. As such, they should not be interpreted as a definitive statement of the level or characteristics of human trafficking as a whole.

In addition to the data reported to the UCR Program, it is important to note that this is only one view of a complex issue—the law enforcement perspective. The investigation of human trafficking by local, state, tribal, and federal LEAs is one facet of this crime. However, due to the nature of human trafficking, many of these crimes are never reported to law enforcement. In addition to the law enforcement facet in fighting these crimes, there are victim service organizations whose mission it is to serve the needs of the victims of human trafficking. In order to have the complete picture of human trafficking, it would be necessary to gather information from all of these sources.

## Table 1

The FBI collects these data through the Uniform Crime Reporting (UCR) Program's Summary Reporting System and National Incident- Based Reporting System. This table includes the states that have added human trafficking offenses to their data collection and the number of agencies per state participating in the UCR Program. Even though a state program included human trafficking, the individual agencies in that state may or may not have added it to their collections.

Indiana, Mississippi, and portions of Ohio have no UCR state program to manage the collection of UCR data within the state. Each law enforcement agency is responsible for reporting its crime data directly to the FBI.

This table only includes those states that have added the capability to collect human trafficking data.

## Table 2

The FBI collects these data through the Uniform Crime Reporting (UCR) Program's Summary Reporting System and National Incident- Based Reporting System. This table provides the volume of human trafficking offenses as reported by state. For UCR purposes, juveniles are individuals under the age of 18 years. Adults are 18 years of age and older.

The data used in creating this table were from all law enforcement agencies submitting one or more human trafficking incidents for at least 1 month of the calendar year. The published data, therefore, do not necessarily represent reports from each participating agency for all 12 months of the calendar year. When the FBI determines that an agency's data collection methodology does not comply with national UCR guidelines, the figure(s) for that agency's offense(s) will not be included in the table, and the discrepancy will be explained in a footnote.

## Table 3

The FBI collects these data through the Uniform Crime Reporting (UCR) Program's Summary Reporting System and National Incident-Based Reporting System.

This table provides the number of juvenile and adult male and female persons arrested for human trafficking offenses by state in 2014. These data represent the number of persons arrested; however, some persons may be arrested more than once during a year. Therefore, the statistics in this table could, in some cases, represent multiple arrests of the same person. For UCR purposes, juveniles are under the age of 18 years. Adults are 18 years of age and older. The data used in creating this table were from all law enforcement agencies submitting one or more human trafficking arrests for at least 1 month of the calendar year. The published data, therefore, do not necessarily represent reports from each participating agency for all 12 months of the calendar year.

## Table 4

The FBI collects these data through the Uniform Crime Reporting (UCR) Program's Summary Reporting System and National Incident-Based Reporting System.

This table provides the number of persons arrested for human trafficking offenses by state in 2014 broken down by race of the arrestee. These data represent the number of persons arrested; however, some persons may be arrested more than once during a year. Therefore, the statistics in this table could, in some cases, represent multiple arrests of the same person. For UCR purposes, juveniles are individuals under the age of 18 years. Adults are 18 years of age and older. The data used in creating

this table were from all law enforcement agencies submitting one or more human trafficking arrests for at least 1 month of the calendar year. The published data, therefore, do not necessarily represent reports from each participating agency for all 12 months of the calendar year.

## Table 5

This table provides the number of persons arrested for human trafficking offenses by state in 2015 broken down by ethnicity of the arrestee. These data represent the number of persons arrested; however, some persons may be arrested more than once during a year. Therefore, the statistics in this table could, in some cases, represent multiple arrests of the same person. For UCR purposes, juveniles are individuals under the age of 18 years. Adults are 18 years of age and older. The data used in creating this table were from all law enforcement agencies submitting one or more human trafficking arrests for at least 1 month of the calendar year. The published data, therefore, do not necessarily represent reports from each participating agency for all 12 months of the calendar year.

PART 7.

# Indicators of School Crime and Safety, 2015

# HIGHLIGHTS

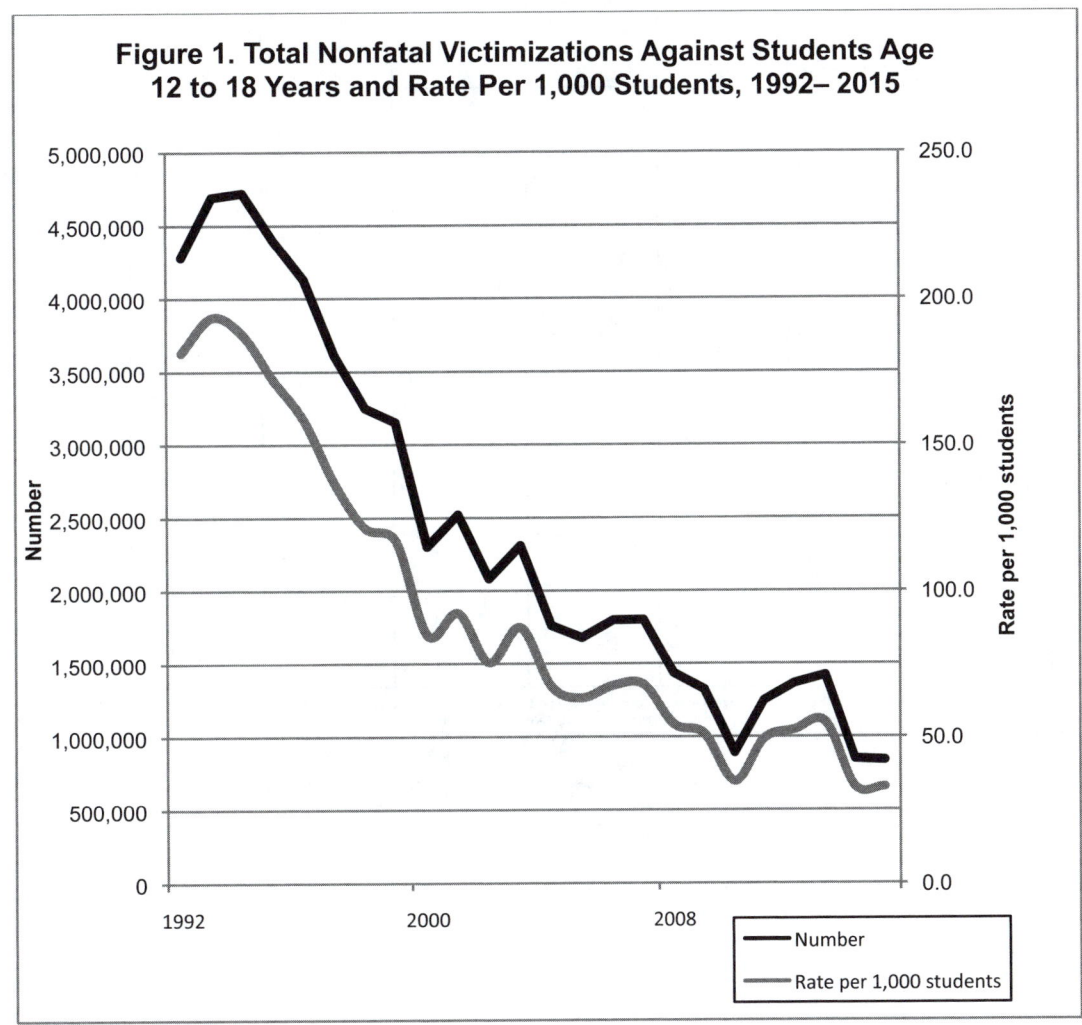

**Figure 1. Total Nonfatal Victimizations Against Students Age 12 to 18 Years and Rate Per 1,000 Students, 1992– 2015**

- Approximately 850,100 nonfatal victimization incidents of students age 12 to 18 years occurred in schools in 2014; incidents included 363,700 theft victimizations and 486,400 violent victimizations (both simple assault and serious violent victimizations).

- The 2014 rate of nonfatal victimization incidents per 1,000 students age 12 to 18 years was 33 at school and 24 away from school; the at-school rate declined 82 percent from 1992 to 2014, while the away-from-school rate dropped 86 percent.

- Rural-area students had higher rates of total victimization (53 per 1,000 students in the age group) than their suburban counterparts (28 victimizations per 1,000 students).

- During the 2012–2013 school year, the latest year for which data are available, there were 53 school-associated violent deaths of all connected persons (students, staff, and other nonstudents). Of these deaths, 41 were homicides, 11 were suicides, and 1 was due to legal interventions. That year, 31 of the homicides and 6 of the suicides occurred at school.

- In 2015, 20.8 percent of students age 12 to 18 years reported experiencing bullying. The greatest proportion of incidents came from mocking, name-calling, and insulting.

# Table 1. School-Associated Violent Deaths of All Persons, Homicides and Suicides of Youth Ages 5 to 18 Years at School, and Total Homicides and Suicides of Youth Ages 5 to 18 Years, by Type of Violent Death: 1992–1993 to 2012–2013

(Number.)

| Year | School-associated violent deaths[1] of all persons (includes students, staff, and other nonstudents) | | | | | Homicides of youth age 5 to 18 years | | Suicides of youth age 5 to 18 years | |
|---|---|---|---|---|---|---|---|---|---|
| | Total | Homicides | Suicides | Legal interventions | Unintentional firearm-related deaths | Homicides at school[2] | Total homicides | Suicides at school[2] | Total suicides[3] |
| 1992–1993 | 57 | 47 | 10 | 0 | 0 | 34 | 2,721 | 6 | 1,680 |
| 1993–1994 | 48 | 38 | 10 | 0 | 0 | 29 | 2,932 | 7 | 1,723 |
| 1994–1995 | 48 | 39 | 8 | 0 | 1 | 28 | 2,696 | 7 | 1,767 |
| 1995–1996 | 53 | 46 | 6 | 1 | 0 | 32 | 2,545 | 6 | 1,725 |
| 1996–1997 | 48 | 45 | 2 | 1 | 0 | 28 | 2,221 | 1 | 1,633 |
| 1997–1998 | 57 | 47 | 9 | 1 | 0 | 34 | 2,100 | 6 | 1,626 |
| 1998–1999 | 47 | 38 | 6 | 2 | 1 | 33 | 1,777 | 4 | 1,597 |
| 1999–2000[4] | 37[4] | 26[4] | 11[4] | 0[4] | 0[4] | 14[4] | 1,567 | 8[4] | 1,415 |
| 2000–2001 | 34[4] | 26[4] | 7[4] | 1[4] | 0[4] | 14[4] | 1,509 | 6[4] | 1,493 |
| 2001–2002 | 36[4] | 27[4] | 8[4] | 1[4] | 0[4] | 16[4] | 1,498 | 5[4] | 1,400 |
| 2002–2003 | 36[4] | 25[4] | 11[4] | 0[4] | 0[4] | 18[4] | 1,553 | 10[4] | 1,331 |
| 2003–2004 | 45[4] | 37[4] | 7[4] | 1[4] | 0[4] | 23[4] | 1,474 | 5[4] | 1,285 |
| 2004–2005 | 52[4] | 40[4] | 10[4] | 2[4] | 0[4] | 22[4] | 1,554 | 8[4] | 1,471 |
| 2005–2006 | 44[4] | 37[4] | 6[4] | 1[4] | 0[4] | 21[4] | 1,697 | 3[4] | 1,408 |
| 2006–2007 | 63[4] | 48[4] | 13[4] | 2[4] | 0[4] | 32[4] | 1,801 | 9[4] | 1,296 |
| 2007–2008 | 44[4] | 39[4] | 7[4] | 2[4] | 0[4] | 21[4] | 1,744 | 5[4] | 1,231 |
| 2008–2009 | 44[4] | 29[4] | 15[4] | 0[4] | 0[4] | 18[4] | 1,605 | 7[4] | 1,344 |
| 2009–2010 | 35[4] | 27[4] | 5[4] | 3[4] | 0[4] | 19[4] | 1,410 | 2[4] | 1,467 |
| 2010–2011 | 32[4] | 26[4] | 6[4] | 0[4] | 0[4] | 11[4] | 1,339 | 3[4] | 1,456 |
| 2011–2012 | 45[4] | 26[4] | 14 | 5[4] | 0[4] | 15[4] | 1,201 | 5[4] | 1,568 |
| 2012–2013 | 53[4] | 41[4] | 11 | 1[4] | 0[4] | 31[4] | 1,186 | 6[4] | 1,590 |

NOTE: Unless otherwise noted, data are reported for the school year, defined as July 1 through June 30. Some data have been revised from previously published figures.
[1] A school-associated violent death is defined as "a homicide, suicide, or legal intervention (involving a law enforcement officer), in which the fatal injury occurred on the campus of a functioning elementary or secondary school in the United States," while the victim was on the way to or from regular sessions at school, or while the victim was attending or traveling to or from an official school-sponsored event.
[2] "At school" includes on school property, on the way to or from regular sessions at school, and while attending or traveling to or from a school-sponsored event.
[3] Total youth suicides are reported for calendar years 1992 through 2012 (instead of school years 1992-93 through 2012-13).
[4] Data from 1999–2000 onward are subject to change until interviews with school and law enforcement officials have been completed. The details learned during the interviews can occasionally change the classification of a case.

## Table 2. Number of Nonfatal Victimizations Against Students Ages 12 to 18 Years and Rate of Victimization Per 1,000 Students, by Type of Victimization and Location, 1992–2015

(Number; rate per 1,000 students.)

| Location and year | Number of nonfatal victimizations | | | | Rate of victimization per 1,000 students | | | |
|---|---|---|---|---|---|---|---|---|
| | Total | Theft | Violent | | Total | Theft | Violent | |
| | | | All violent | Serious violent[1] | | | All violent | Serious violent[1] |
| **At School[2]** | | | | | | | | |
| 1992 | 4,281,200 | 2,679,400 | 1,601,800 | 197,600 | 181.5 | 113.6 | 67.9 | 8.4 |
| 1993 | 4,692,800 | 2,477,100 | 2,215,700 | 535,500 | 193.5 | 102.1 | 91.4 | 22.1 |
| 1994 | 4,721,000 | 2,474,100 | 2,246,900 | 459,100 | 187.7 | 98.4 | 89.3 | 18.3 |
| 1995 | 4,400,700 | 2,468,400 | 1,932,200 | 294,500 | 172.2 | 96.6 | 75.6 | 11.5 |
| 1996 | 4,130,400 | 2,205,200 | 1,925,300 | 371,900 | 158.4 | 84.5 | 73.8 | 14.3 |
| 1997 | 3,610,900 | 1,975,000 | 1,635,900 | 376,200 | 136.6 | 74.7 | 61.9 | 14.2 |
| 1998 | 3,247,300 | 1,635,100 | 1,612,200 | 314,500 | 121.3 | 61.1 | 60.2 | 11.7 |
| 1999 | 3,152,400 | 1,752,200 | 1,400,200 | 281,100 | 117.0 | 65.1 | 52.0 | 10.4 |
| 2000 | 2,301,000 | 1,331,500 | 969,500 | 214,200 | 84.9 | 49.1 | 35.8 | 7.9 |
| 2001 | 2,521,300 | 1,348,500 | 1,172,700 | 259,400 | 92.3 | 49.4 | 42.9 | 9.5 |
| 2002 | 2,082,600 | 1,088,800 | 993,800 | 173,500 | 75.4 | 39.4 | 36.0 | 6.3 |
| 2003 | 2,308,800 | 1,270,500 | 1,038,300 | 188,400 | 87.4 | 48.1 | 39.3 | 7.1 |
| 2004 | 1,762,200 | 1,065,400 | 696,800 | 107,300 | 67.2 | 40.6 | 26.6 | 4.1 |
| 2005 | 1,678,600 | 875,900 | 802,600 | 140,300 | 63.2 | 33.0 | 30.2 | 5.3 |
| 2006 [3] | 1,799,900 | 859,000 | 940,900 | 249,900 | 67.5 | 32.2 | 35.3 | 9.4 |
| 2007 | 1,801,200 | 896,700 | 904,400 | 116,100 | 67.8 | 33.7 | 34.0 | 4.4 |
| 2008 | 1,435,500 | 648,000 | 787,500 | 128,700 | 54.3 | 24.5 | 29.8 | 4.9 |
| 2009 | 1,322,800 | 594,500 | 728,300 | 233,700 | 51.0 | 22.9 | 28.1 | 9.0 |
| 2010 | 892,000 | 469,800 | 422,300 | 155,000 | 34.9 | 18.4 | 16.5 | 6.1 |
| 2011 | 1,246,200 | 647,700 | 598,600 | 89,500 | 49.3 | 25.6 | 23.7 | 3.5 |
| 2012 | 1,364,900 | 615,600 | 749,200 | 89,000 | 52.4 | 23.6 | 28.8 | 3.4 |
| 2013 | 1,420,900 | 454,900 | 966,000 | 125,500 | 55.0 | 17.6 | 37.4 | 4.9 |
| 2014 | 850,100 | 363,700 | 486,400 | 93,800 | 33.0 | 14.1 | 18.9 | 3.6 |
| 2015 | 841,100 | 309,100 | 531,900 | 99,000 | 32.9 | 12.1 | 20.8 | 3.9 |
| **Away from School** | | | | | | | | |
| 1992 | 4,084,100 | 1,857,600 | 2,226,500 | 1,025,100 | 173.1 | 78.7 | 94.4 | 43.5 |
| 1993 | 3,835,900 | 1,731,100 | 2,104,800 | 1,004,300 | 158.2 | 71.4 | 86.8 | 41.4 |
| 1994 | 4,147,100 | 1,713,900 | 2,433,200 | 1,074,900 | 164.9 | 68.1 | 96.7 | 42.7 |
| 1995 | 3,626,600 | 1,604,800 | 2,021,800 | 829,700 | 141.9 | 62.8 | 79.1 | 32.5 |
| 1996 | 3,483,200 | 1,572,700 | 1,910,600 | 870,000 | 133.5 | 60.3 | 73.3 | 33.4 |
| 1997 | 3,717,600 | 1,710,700 | 2,006,900 | 853,300 | 140.7 | 64.7 | 75.9 | 32.3 |
| 1998 | 3,047,800 | 1,408,000 | 1,639,800 | 684,900 | 113.8 | 52.6 | 61.3 | 25.6 |
| 1999 | 2,713,800 | 1,129,200 | 1,584,500 | 675,400 | 100.8 | 41.9 | 58.8 | 25.1 |
| 2000 | 2,303,600 | 1,228,900 | 1,074,800 | 402,100 | 85.0 | 45.3 | 39.6 | 14.8 |
| 2001 | 1,780,300 | 961,400 | 819,000 | 314,800 | 65.2 | 35.2 | 30.0 | 11.5 |
| 2002 | 1,619,500 | 820,100 | 799,400 | 341,200 | 58.6 | 29.7 | 28.9 | 12.4 |
| 2003 | 1,824,100 | 780,900 | 1,043,200 | 412,800 | 69.1 | 29.6 | 39.5 | 15.6 |
| 2004 | 1,371,800 | 718,000 | 653,700 | 272,500 | 52.3 | 27.4 | 24.9 | 10.4 |
| 2005 | 1,429,000 | 637,700 | 791,300 | 257,100 | 53.8 | 24.0 | 29.8 | 9.7 |
| 2006 [3] | 1,413,100 | 714,200 | 698,900 | 263,600 | 53.0 | 26.8 | 26.2 | 9.9 |
| 2007 | 1,371,700 | 614,300 | 757,400 | 337,700 | 51.6 | 23.1 | 28.5 | 12.7 |
| 2008 | 1,132,600 | 498,500 | 634,100 | 258,600 | 42.8 | 18.9 | 24.0 | 9.8 |
| 2009 | 857,200 | 484,200 | 372,900 | 176,800 | 33.1 | 18.7 | 14.4 | 6.8 |
| 2010 | 689,900 | 378,800 | 311,200 | 167,300 | 27.0 | 14.8 | 12.2 | 6.5 |
| 2011 | 966,100 | 541,900 | 424,300 | 137,600 | 38.2 | 21.4 | 16.8 | 5.4 |
| 2012 | 991,200 | 470,800 | 520,400 | 169,900 | 38.0 | 18.1 | 20.0 | 6.5 |
| 2013 | 778,500 | 403,000 | 375,500 | 151,200 | 30.1 | 15.6 | 14.5 | 5.8 |
| 2014 | 621,300 | 288,900 | 332,400 | 165,000 | 24.1 | 11.2 | 12.9 | 6.4 |
| 2015 | 545,100 | 263,100 | 281,900 | 110,900 | 21.3 | 10.3 | 11.0 | 4.3 |

NOTE: "Serious violent victimization" includes the crimes of rape, sexual assault, robbery, and aggravated assault. "All violent victimization" includes serious violent crimes as well as simple assault. "Theft" includes attempted and completed purse-snatching, completed pickpocketing, and all attempted and completed thefts, with the exception of motor vehicle thefts. Theft does not include robbery, which involves the threat or use of force and is classified as a violent crime. "Total victimization" includes theft and violent crimes. Data in this table are from the National Crime Victimization Survey (NCVS); due to differences in time coverage and administration between the NCVS and the School Crime Supplement (SCS) to the NCVS, data in this table cannot be compared with data in tables that are based on the SCS. Detail may not sum to totals because of rounding.
[1] Serious violent victimization is also included in all violent victimization.
[2] "At school" includes inside the school building, on school property, and on the way to and from school.
[3] Due to methodological differences, use caution when comparing 2006 estimates to other years.

# Table 3. Number of Nonfatal Victimizations Against Students Ages 12 to 18 Years and Rate of Victimization Per 1,000 Students, by Type of Victimization, Location, and Selected Student Characteristics, 2015

(Number; rate per 1,000 students.)

| | Number of nonfatal victimizations | | Violent | | Rate of victimization per 1,000 students | | Violent | |
|---|---|---|---|---|---|---|---|---|
| Location and year | Total | Theft | All violent | Serious violent[1] | Total | Theft | All violent | Serious violent[1] |
| **At School[2]** | | | | | | | | |
| Total .......................... | 841,100 | 309,100 | 531,900 | 99,000 | 32.9 | 12.1 | 20.8 | 3.9 |
| Sex ................................ | | | | | | | | |
| Male ........................... | 407,200 | 152,200 | 255,000 | 62,800 | 30.9 | 11.6 | 19.4 | 4.8 |
| Female.......................... | 433,800 | 157,000 | 276,900 | 36,300 | 34.9 | 12.6 | 22.3 | 2.9 |
| Age ................................ | | | | | | | | |
| 12 to 14 years................ | 501,500 | 123,800 | 377,700 | 61,200 | 41.3 | 10.2 | 31.1 | 5.0 |
| 15 to 18 years................ | 339,600 | 185,300 | 154,300 | 37,900 (!) | 25.3 | 13.8 | 11.5 | 2.8 (!) |
| Race/ethnicity[3] ..................... | | | | | | | | |
| White ........................... | 462,900 | 175,000 | 287,900 | 45,900 | 34.3 | 13.0 | 21.3 | 3.4 |
| Black............................. | 107,100 | 25,400 | 81,700 | 15,700 (!) | 29.8 | 7.1 | 22.7 | 4.4 (!) |
| Hispanic........................ | 191,800 | 80,600 | 111,200 | 29,000 (!) | 30.0 | 12.6 | 17.4 | 4.5 (!) |
| Other............................ | 79,200 | 28,100 | 51,100 | 8,400 (!) | 38.2 | 13.5 | 24.7 | 4.1 (!) |
| Urban/city[4]......................... | | | | | | | | |
| Urban ........................... | 272,300 | 109,100 | 163,200 | 26,300 (!) | 35.3 | 14.2 | 21.2 | 3.4 (!) |
| Suburban...................... | 499,100 | 169,000 | 330,100 | 67,600 | 35.9 | 12.1 | 23.7 | 4.9 |
| Rural............................. | 69,600 | 31,000 | 38,600 (!) | 5,200 (!) | 17.6 | 7.8 | 9.7 (!) | 1.3 (!) |
| Household income[5]............. | | | | | | | | |
| Less than $15,000 ......... | 90,000 | 42,600 | 47,300 | 9,400 (!) | 36.6 | 17.3 | 19.2 | 3.8 (!) |
| $15,000 to $29,999 ...... | 166,700 | 44,800 | 121,900 | 11,100 (!) | 40.3 | 10.8 | 29.5 | 2.7 (!) |
| $30,000 to $49,999 ...... | 150,100 | 63,200 | 86,900 | 18,900 (!) | 28.3 | 11.9 | 16.4 | 3.6 (!) |
| $50,000 to $74,999 ...... | 153,600 | 43,200 | 110,400 | 27,100 (!) | 36.1 | 10.1 | 25.9 | 6.4 (!) |
| $75,000 or more ........... | 280,600 | 115,300 | 165,300 | 32,500 | 29.8 | 12.2 | 17.5 | 3.5 |
| **Away from School** | | | | | | | | |
| Total ............................ | 545,100 | 263,100 | 281,900 | 110,900 | 21.3 | 10.3 | 11.0 | 4.3 |
| Sex ................................ | | | | | | | | |
| Male ........................... | 280,200 | 134,200 | 146,100 | 43,400 (!) | 21.3 | 10.2 | 11.1 | 3.3 (!) |
| Female.......................... | 264,800 | 129,000 | 135,800 | 67,500 | 21.3 | 10.4 | 10.9 | 5.4 |
| Age ................................ | | | | | | | | |
| 12 to 14 years................ | 235,900 | 100,000 | 136,000 | 62,200 | 19.4 | 8.2 | 11.2 | 5.1 |
| 15 to 18 years................ | 309,100 | 163,200 | 145,900 | 48,700 | 23.0 | 12.1 | 10.9 | 3.6 |
| Race/ethnicity[3] ..................... | | | | | | | | |
| White ........................... | 271,700 | 106,000 | 165,700 | 52,400 | 20.1 | 7.8 | 12.3 | 3.9 |
| Black............................. | 132,500 | 85,100 | 47,400 (!) | 20,800 (!) | 36.9 | 23.7 | 13.2 (!) | 5.8 (!) |
| Hispanic........................ | 117,400 | 59,800 | 57,500 | 37,800 (!) | 18.3 | 9.4 | 9.0 | 5.9 (!) |
| Other............................ | 23,400 | 12200 (!) | 11,200 (!) | NA | 11.3 | 5.9 (!) | 5.4 (!) | NA |
| Urban/city[4]......................... | | | | | | | | |
| Urban ........................... | 182,800 | 127,800 | 55,000 | 35,800 (!) | 23.7 | 16.6 | 7.1 | 4.6 (!) |
| Suburban...................... | 282,400 | 110,100 | 172,300 | 68,600 | 20.3 | 7.9 | 12.4 | 4.9 |
| Rural............................. | 79,900 | 25,200 | 54,700 | 6,500 (!) | 20.2 | 6.4 | 13.8 | 1.7 (!) |
| Household income[5]............. | | | | | | | | |
| Less than $15,000 ......... | 76,200 | 35,200 | 41,000 | 30,600 (!) | 31.0 | 14.3 | 16.7 | 12.5 (!) |
| $15,000 to $29,999 ...... | 140,800 | 79,300 | 61,500 | 30,200 (!) | 34.0 | 19.2 | 14.9 | 7.3 (!) |
| $30,000 to $49,999 ...... | 142,100 | 42,900 | 99,200 | 34,900 (!) | 26.8 | 8.1 | 18.7 | 6.6 (!) |
| $50,000 to $74,999 ...... | 94,900 | 46,700 | 48,200 (!) | 4,100 (!) | 22.3 | 11.0 | 11.3 (!) | 1.0 (!) |
| $75,000 or more ........... | 91,100 | 59,000 | 32,000 | 11,100 (!) | 9.7 | 6.3 | 3.4 | 1.2 (!) |

NOTE: "Serious violent victimization" includes the crimes of rape, sexual assault, robbery, and aggravated assault. "All violent victimization" includes serious violent crimes as well as simple assault. "Theft" includes attempted and completed purse-snatching, completed pickpocketing, and all attempted and completed thefts, with the exception of motor vehicle thefts. Theft does not include robbery, which involves the threat or use of force and is classified as a violent crime. "Total victimization" includes theft and violent crimes. Data in this table are from the National Crime Victimization Survey (NCVS) and are reported in accordance with Bureau of Justice Statistics standards. Detail may not sum to totals because of rounding and missing data on student characteristics. The population size for students ages 12-18 was 25,581,700 in 2015.
NA = Not available.
(!) = Interpret data with caution. Estimate based on 10 or fewer sample cases, or the coefficient of variation is greater than 50 percent.
[1] Serious violent victimization is also included in all violent victimization.
[2] "At school" includes inside the school building, on school property, and on the way to and from school.
[3] Race categories exclude persons of Hispanic ethnicity. "Other" includes Asians, Pacific Islanders, American Indians/Alaska Natives, and persons of two or more races.
[4] Refers to the Standard Metropolitan Statistical Area (MSA) status of the respondent's household as defined by the U.S. Census Bureau. Categories include "central city of an MSA (Urban)," "in MSA but not in central city (Suburban)," and "not MSA (Rural)."
[5] Income data for 2015 were imputed. Estimates may not be comparable to previous years. For more information, see *Criminal Victimization*, 2015 (NCJ 250180, October 2016).

# Table 4. Percentage of Students in Grades 9 to 12 Who Reported Being Threatened or Injured with a Weapon on School Property During the Previous 12 Months, by Selected Student Characteristics and Number of Times Threatened or Injured: Selected Years, 1993–2015

(Percent.)

| Number of times and year | Total | Sex | | Race/ethnicity[1] | | | | | | | Grade | | | |
|---|---|---|---|---|---|---|---|---|---|---|---|---|---|---|
| | | Male | Female | White | Black | Hispanic | Asian[2] | Pacific Islander[2] | American Indian/ Alaska Native | Two or more races[2] | 9th | 10th | 11th | 12th |
| **At Least Once** | | | | | | | | | | | | | | |
| 1993 | 7.3 | 9.2 | 5.4 | 6.3 | 11.2 | 8.6 | NA | NA | 11.7 | NA | 9.4 | 7.3 | 7.3 | 5.5 |
| 1995 | 8.4 | 10.9 | 5.8 | 7.0 | 11.0 | 12.4 | NA | NA | 11.4 (!) | NA | 9.6 | 9.6 | 7.7 | 6.7 |
| 1997 | 7.4 | 10.2 | 4.0 | 6.2 | 9.9 | 9.0 | NA | NA | 12.5 (!) | NA | 10.1 | 7.9 | 5.9 | 5.8 |
| 1999 | 7.7 | 9.5 | 5.8 | 6.6 | 7.6 | 9.8 | 7.7 | 15.6 | 13.2 (!) | 9.3 | 10.5 | 8.2 | 6.1 | 5.1 |
| 2001 | 8.9 | 11.5 | 6.5 | 8.5 | 9.3 | 8.9 | 11.3 | 24.8 | 15.2 (!) | 10.3 | 12.7 | 9.1 | 6.9 | 5.3 |
| 2003 | 9.2 | 11.6 | 6.5 | 7.8 | 10.9 | 9.4 | 11.5 | 16.3 | 22.1 | 18.7 | 12.1 | 9.2 | 7.3 | 6.3 |
| 2005 | 7.9 | 9.7 | 6.1 | 7.2 | 8.1 | 9.8 | 4.6 | 14.5 (!) | 9.8 | 10.7 | 10.5 | 8.8 | 5.5 | 5.8 |
| 2007 | 7.8 | 10.2 | 5.4 | 6.9 | 9.7 | 8.7 | 7.6 (!) | 8.1 (!) | 5.9 | 13.3 | 9.2 | 8.4 | 6.8 | 6.3 |
| 2009 | 7.7 | 9.6 | 5.5 | 6.4 | 9.4 | 9.1 | 5.5 | 12.5 | 16.5 | 9.2 | 8.7 | 8.4 | 7.9 | 5.2 |
| 2011 | 7.4 | 9.5 | 5.2 | 6.1 | 8.9 | 9.2 | 7.0 | 11.3 | 8.2 | 9.9 | 8.3 | 7.7 | 7.3 | 5.9 |
| 2013 | 6.9 | 7.7 | 6.1 | 5.8 | 8.4 | 8.5 | 5.3 | 8.7 (!) | 18.5 | 7.7 | 8.5 | 7.0 | 6.8 | 4.9 |
| 2015 | 6.0 | 7.0 | 4.6 | 4.9 | 7.9 | 6.6 | 3.6 (!) | 20.5 (!) | 8.2 (!) | 8.0 | 7.2 | 6.2 | 5.5 | 4.4 |
| **Number of Times, 2015** | | | | | | | | | | | | | | |
| 0 times | 94.0 | 93.0 | 95.4 | 95.1 | 92.1 | 93.4 | 96.4 | 79.5 | 91.8 | 92.0 | 92.8 | 93.8 | 94.5 | 95.6 |
| 1 time | 2.7 | 3.1 | 2.3 | 2.4 | 4.1 | 2.6 | X | X | X | 3.8 (!) | 3.5 | 2.9 | 2.5 | 1.8 |
| 2 or three times | 1.5 | 1.6 | 1.3 | 1.5 | 1.6 (!) | 1.4 | 0.5 (!) | X | 3.1 (!) | 1.7 (!) | 2.1 | 1.3 | 1.1 | 1.3 |
| 4 to 11 times | 1.0 | 1.3 | 0.6 | 0.6 | 1.4 (!) | 1.4 | X | X | X | 1.2 (!) | 0.9 | 1.3 | 1.1 (!) | 0.7 (!) |
| 12 or more times | 0.8 | 1.0 | 0.4 (!) | 0.4 | 0.9 (!) | 1.2 | X | X | X | 1.3 (!) | 0.6 | 0.7 | 0.8 | 0.6 |

NOTE: Survey respondents were asked about being threatened or injured "with a weapon such as a gun, knife, or club on school property." "On school property" was not defined for respondents. Detail may not sum to totals because of rounding.
NA = Not available.
(!) = Interpret data with caution.
X = Not applicable.
[1] Race categories exclude persons of Hispanic ethnicity.
[2] Before 1999, Asian students and Pacific Islander students were not categorized separately, and students could not be classified as two or more races. Because the response categories changed in 1999, caution should be used in comparing data on race from 1993, 1995, and 1997 with data from later years.

# Table 5. Number and Percentage of Public and Private School Teachers Who Reported That They Were Threatened with Injury or Physically Attacked by a Student from School During the Previous 12 Months, by Selected Teacher and School Characteristics, Selected Years, 1993–1994 through 2011–2012

(Number; percent.)

| Incident and year | Total | Sex | | Race/ethnicity[1] | | | | Instructional level[1] | | Control of school | |
|---|---|---|---|---|---|---|---|---|---|---|---|
| | | Male | Female | White | Black | Hispanic | Other[2] | Elementary | Secondary | Public[3] | Private |
| | Number of teachers | | | | | | | | | | |
| **Threatened with Injury** | | | | | | | | | | | |
| 1993–1994.............. | 342,700 | 115,900 | 226,800 | 295,700 | 23,900 | 15,900 | 7,300 | 135,200 | 207,500 | 326,800 | 15,900 |
| 1999–2000.............. | 304,900 | 95,100 | 209,800 | 252,500 | 28,300 | 17,200 | 7,000 | 148,100 | 156,900 | 287,400 | 17,500 |
| 2003–2004.............. | 252,800 | 78,400 | 174,400 | 198,900 | 32,500 | 12,400 | 9,000 | 113,600 | 139,200 | 242,100 | 10,700 |
| 2007–2008.............. | 289,900 | 88,300 | 201,600 | 234,700 | 28,700 | 17,900 | 8,600 | 130,000 | 160,000 | 276,600 | 13,300 |
| 2011–2012.............. | 352,900 | 84,500 | 268,400 | 279,900 | 34,200 | 27,100 | 11,800 | 189,800 | 163,200 | 338,400 | 14,500 |
| **Physically Attacked** | | | | | | | | | | | |
| 1993–1994.............. | 121,100 | 30,800 | 90,300 | 104,300 | 7,700 | 6,200 | 2,800 | 77,300 | 43,800 | 112,400 | 8,700 |
| 1999–2000.............. | 134,800 | 30,600 | 104,200 | 111,700 | 11,600 | 8,800 | 2,600 | 102,200 | 32,600 | 125,000 | 9,800 |
| 2003–2004.............. | 129,200 | 23,600 | 105,700 | 102,200 | 15,100 | 7,000 | 5,000 | 89,800 | 39,400 | 121,400 | 7,800 |
| 2007–2008.............. | 156,000 | 34,900 | 121,100 | 132,300 | 12,300 | 8,200 | 3,200 (!) | 114,700 | 41,300 | 146,400 | 9,600 |
| 2011–2012.............. | 209,800 | 32,500 | 177,300 | 171,300 | 18,800 | 11,800 | 7,900 | 160,700 | 49,100 | 197,400 | 12,400 |
| | Percent of teachers | | | | | | | | | | |
| **Threatened with Injury** | | | | | | | | | | | |
| 1993–1994.............. | 11.7 | 14.7 | 10.5 | 11.5 | 11.9 | 13.1 | 13.4 | 8.7 | 15.0 | 12.8 | 4.2 |
| 1999–2000.............. | 8.8 | 11.0 | 8.1 | 8.6 | 11.6 | 9.1 | 8.3 | 8.0 | 9.9 | 9.6 | 3.9 |
| 2003–2004.............. | 6.8 | 8.5 | 6.2 | 6.4 | 11.8 | 5.5 | 8.7 | 5.7 | 8.0 | 7.4 | 2.3 |
| 2007–2008.............. | 7.4 | 9.3 | 6.8 | 7.2 | 11.1 | 6.7 | 7.6 | 6.6 | 8.4 | 8.1 | 2.7 |
| 2011–2012.............. | 9.2 | 9.2 | 9.2 | 8.8 | 13.8 | 9.4 | 9.1 | 9.6 | 8.7 | 10.0 | 3.1 |
| **Physically Attacked** | | | | | | | | | | | |
| 1993–1994.............. | 4.1 | 3.9 | 4.2 | 4.1 | 3.9 | 5.2 | 5.2 | 5.0 | 3.2 | 4.4 | 2.3 |
| 1999–2000.............. | 3.9 | 3.5 | 4.0 | 3.8 | 4.8 | 4.6 | 3.1 | 5.5 | 2.1 | 4.2 | 2.2 |
| 2003–2004.............. | 3.5 | 2.6 | 3.8 | 3.3 | 5.5 | 3.1 | 4.8 | 4.5 | 2.3 | 3.7 | 1.7 |
| 2007–2008.............. | 4.0 | 3.7 | 4.1 | 4.1 | 4.7 | 3.1 | 2.8 (!) | 5.8 | 2.2 | 4.3 | 2.0 |
| 2011–2012.............. | 5.4 | 3.5 | 6.0 | 5.4 | 7.6 | 4.1 | 6.1 | 8.2 | 2.6 | 5.8 | 2.7 |

NOTE: Teachers who taught only prekindergarten students are excluded. Instructional level divides teachers into elementary or secondary based on a combination of the grades taught, main teaching assignment, and the structure of the teachers' class(es). Race categories exclude persons of Hispanic ethnicity. Detail may not sum to totals because of rounding. Some data have been revised from previously published figures.
(!) = Interpret data with caution. The coefficient of variation (CV) for this estimate is between 30 and 50 percent.
[1] Teachers were classified as elementary or secondary on the basis of the grades they taught, rather than on the level of the school in which they taught. In general, elementary teachers include those teaching prekindergarten through grade 5 and those teaching multiple grades, with a preponderance of grades taught being kindergarten through grade 6. In general, secondary teachers include those teaching any of grades 7 through 12 and those teaching multiple grades, with a preponderance of grades taught being grades 7 through 12 and usually with no grade taught being lower than grade 5.
[2] Includes American Indians/Alaska Natives, Asians, and Pacific Islanders; for 2003–2004 and later years, also includes persons of two or more races.
[3] Includes traditional public and public charter schools.

# Table 6. Percentage of Public Schools Recording Incidents of Crime at School and Reporting Incidents to Police, Number of Incidents, and Rate Per 1,000 Students, by Type of Crime, Selected Years, 1999–2000 through 2013–2014

(Percent; number; rate per 1,000 students.)

| Type of crime recorded or reported to police | Percent of schools | | | | | 2013–2014[1] | | |
|---|---|---|---|---|---|---|---|---|
| | 1999–2000 | 2003–2004 | 2005–2006 | 2007–2008 | 2009–2010 | Percent of schools | Number of incidents | Rate per 1,000 students[2] |
| **Recorded Incidents** | | | | | | | | |
| Total[3] | 86.4 | 88.5 | 85.7 | 85.5 | 85.0 | NA | NA | NA |
| | | | | | | | | |
| **Violent Incidents** | 71.4 | 81.4 | 77.7 | 75.5 | 73.8 | 65.0 | 757,000 | 15.4 |
| Serious violent incidents | 19.7 | 18.3 | 17.1 | 17.2 | 16.4 | 13.1 | 25,700 | 0.5 |
| Rape or attempted rape | 0.7 | 0.8 | 0.3 | 0.8 | 0.5 | 0.2 (!) | ‡ | ... |
| Sexual battery other than rape | 2.5 | 3.0 | 2.8 | 2.5 | 2.3 | 1.7 | 1,800 | ... |
| Physical attack or fight with a weapon | 5.2 | 4.0 | 3.0 | 3.0 | 3.9 | 1.8 | 2,900 | 0.1 |
| Threat of physical attack with a weapon | 11.1 | 8.6 | 8.8 | 9.3 | 7.7 | 8.7 | 15,100 | 0.3 |
| Robbery with a weapon | 0.5 (!) | 0.6 | 0.4 | 0.4 (!) | 0.2 | ‡ | ‡ | ‡ |
| Robbery without a weapon | 5.3 | 6.3 | 6.4 | 5.2 | 4.4 | 2.5 | 5,200 | 0.1 |
| Physical attack or fight without a weapon | 63.7 | 76.7 | 74.3 | 72.7 | 70.5 | 57.5 | 453,100 | 9.1 |
| Threat of physical attack without a weapon | 52.2 | 53.0 | 52.2 | 47.8 | 46.4 | 47.1 | 278,100 | 5.7 |
| | | | | | | | | |
| **Theft[4]** | 45.6 | 46.0 | 46.0 | 47.3 | 44.1 | NA | NA | NA |
| | | | | | | | | |
| **Other Incidents[5]** | 72.7 | 64.0 | 68.2 | 67.4 | 68.1 | NA | NA | NA |
| Possession of a firearm/ explosive device | 5.5 | 6.1 | 7.2 | 4.7 | 4.7 | NA | NA | NA |
| Possession of a knife or sharp object | 42.6 | NA | 42.8 | 40.6 | 39.7 | NA | NA | NA |
| Distribution of illegal drugs[6] | 12.3 | 12.9 | NA | NA | NA | NA | NA | NA |
| Possession or use of alcohol or illegal drugs[6] | 26.6 | 29.3 | NA | NA | NA | NA | NA | NA |
| Distribution, possession, or use of illegal drugs[7] | NA | NA | 25.9 | 23.2 | 24.6 | NA | NA | NA |
| Inappropriate distribution, possession, or use of prescription drugs[8] | NA | NA | NA | NA | 12.1 | NA | NA | NA |
| Distribution, possession, or use of alcohol[8] | NA | NA | 16.2 | 14.9 | 14.1 | NA | NA | NA |
| Sexual harassment | 36.3 | NA | NA | NA | NA | NA | NA | NA |
| Vandalism | 51.4 | 51.4 | 50.5 | 49.3 | 45.8 | NA | NA | NA |
| | | | | | | | | |
| **Reported Incidents to Police** | | | | | | | | |
| Total | 62.5 | 65.2 | 60.9 | 62.0 | 60.0 | NA | NA | NA |
| | | | | | | | | |
| **Violent Incidents** | 36.0 | 43.6 | 37.7 | 37.8 | 39.9 | NA | NA | NA |
| Serious violent incidents | 14.8 | 13.3 | 12.6 | 12.6 | 10.4 | NA | NA | NA |
| Rape or attempted rape | 0.6 | 0.8 | 0.3 | 0.8 | 0.5 | NA | NA | NA |
| Sexual battery other than rape | 2.3 | 2.6 | 2.6 | 2.1 | 1.4 | NA | NA | NA |
| Physical attack or fight with a weapon | 3.9 | 2.8 | 2.2 | 2.1 | 2.2 | NA | NA | NA |
| Threat of physical attack with a weapon | 8.5 | 6.0 | 5.9 | 5.7 | 4.5 | NA | NA | NA |
| Robbery with a weapon | 0.3 (!) | 0.6 | 0.4 | 0.4 | 0.2 | NA | NA | NA |
| Robbery without a weapon | 3.4 | 4.2 | 4.9 | 4.1 | 3.5 | NA | NA | NA |
| Physical attack or fight without a weapon | 25.8 | 35.6 | 29.2 | 28.2 | 34.3 | NA | NA | NA |
| Threat of physical attack without a weapon | 18.9 | 21.0 | 19.7 | 19.5 | 15.2 | NA | NA | NA |

## Table 6. Percentage of Public Schools Recording Incidents of Crime at School and Reporting Incidents to Police, Number of Incidents, and Rate Per 1,000 Students, by Type of Crime, Selected Years, 1999–2000 through 2013–2014—Continued

(Percent; number; rate per 1,000 students.)

| Type of crime recorded or reported to police | Percent of schools | | | | | 2013–2014[1] | | |
|---|---|---|---|---|---|---|---|---|
| | 1999–2000 | 2003–2004 | 2005–2006 | 2007–2008 | 2009–2010 | Percent of schools | Number of incidents | Rate per 1,000 students[2] |
| **Theft[4]** | 28.5 | 30.5 | 27.9 | 31.0 | 25.4 | NA | NA | NA |
| **Other Incidents[5]** | 52.0 | 50.0 | 50.6 | 48.7 | 46.3 | NA | NA | NA |
| Possession of a firearm/ explosive device | 4.5 | 4.9 | 5.5 | 3.6 | 3.1 | NA | NA | NA |
| Possession of a knife or sharp object | 23.0 | NA | 25.0 | 23.3 | 20.0 | NA | NA | NA |
| Distribution of illegal drugs[6] | 11.4 | 12.4 | NA | NA | NA | NA | NA | NA |
| Possession or use of alcohol or illegal drugs[6] | 22.2 | 26.0 | NA | NA | NA | NA | NA | NA |
| Distribution, possession, or use of illegal drugs[7] | NA | NA | 22.8 | 20.7 | 21.4 | NA | NA | NA |
| Inappropriate distribution, possession, or use of prescription drugs[8] | NA | NA | NA | NA | 9.6 | NA | NA | NA |
| Distribution, possession, or use of alcohol[8] | NA | NA | 11.6 | 10.6 | 10.0 | NA | NA | NA |
| Sexual harassment | 14.7 | NA | NA | NA | NA | NA | NA | NA |
| Vandalism | 32.7 | 34.3 | 31.9 | 30.8 | 26.8 | NA | NA | NA |

NOTE: Responses were provided by the principal or the person most knowledgeable about crime and safety issues at the school. "At school" was defined to include activities that happen in school buildings, on school grounds, on school buses, and at places that hold school-sponsored events or activities. Respondents were instructed to include incidents that occurred before, during, and after normal school hours or when school activities or events were in session. Detail may not sum to totals because of rounding and because schools that recorded or reported more than one type of crime incident were counted only once in the total percentage of schools recording or reporting incidents.
NA = Not available.
… = Rounds to zero.
(!) = Interpret data with caution. The coefficient of variation (CV) for this estimate is between 30 and 50 percent.
[1] Data for 2013-14 were collected using the Fast Response Survey System, while data for earlier years were collected using the School Survey on Crime and Safety (SSOCS). The 2013-14 survey was designed to allow comparisons with SSOCS data. However, respondents to the 2013-14 survey could choose either to complete the survey on paper (and mail it back) or to complete the survey online, whereas respondents to SSOCS did not have the option of completing the survey online. The 2013-14 survey also relied on a smaller sample. The smaller sample size and change in survey administration may have impacted 2013-14 results.
[2] Because the 2013-14 survey did not collect school enrollment counts, the rate per 1,000 students was calculated by dividing the number of incidents by the total number of students obtained from the Common Core of Data.
[3] Total not presented for 2013-14 because the survey did not collect information regarding theft and other incidents. Therefore, the total incident rate is not comparable with earlier years.
[4] Theft/larceny (taking things worth over $10 without personal confrontation) was defined for respondents as "the unlawful taking of another person's property without personal confrontation, threat, violence, or bodily harm." This includes pocket picking, stealing a purse or backpack (if left unattended or no force was used to take it from owner), theft from a building, theft from a motor vehicle or motor vehicle parts or accessories, theft of a bicycle, theft from a vending machine, and all other types of thefts.
[5] Caution should be used when making direct comparisons of "Other incidents" between years because the survey questions about alcohol and drugs changed, as outlined in footnotes 6, 7, and 8.
[6] The survey items "Distribution of illegal drugs" and "Possession or use of alcohol or illegal drugs" appear only on the 1999-2000 and 2003-04 questionnaires. Different alcohol- and drug-related survey items were used on the questionnaires for later years.
[7] The survey items "Distribution, possession, or use of illegal drugs" and "Distribution, possession, or use of alcohol" appear only on the questionnaires for 2005-06 and later years.
[8] The 2009-10 questionnaire was the first to include the survey item "Inappropriate distribution, possession, or use of prescription drugs."

**Table 7. Percentage of Students Ages 12 to 18 Years Who Reported That Gangs Were Present at School During the School Year, by Selected Student and School Characteristics and Location, Selected Years, 2001–2015**

(Percent.)

| Year and location | Total | Sex | | Race/ethnicity[1] | | | | | Grade | | | | | | | Control of school | |
|---|---|---|---|---|---|---|---|---|---|---|---|---|---|---|---|---|---|
| | | Male | Female | White | Black | Hispanic | Asian | Other | 6th | 7th | 8th | 9th | 10th | 11th | 12th | Public | Private |
| **2001 [2]** | | | | | | | | | | | | | | | | | |
| Total ................... | 20.1 | 21.4 | 18.8 | 15.5 | 28.6 | 32.0 | NA | 21.4 | 11.2 | 15.7 | 17.3 | 24.3 | 23.6 | 24.2 | 21.1 | 21.6 | 4.9 |
| Urban .............. | 28.9 | 31.9 | 25.9 | 20.5 | 32.4 | 40.3 | NA | 27.0 | 14.9 | 23.7 | 24.0 | 35.3 | 33.1 | 34.2 | 34.1 | 31.9 | 5.0 |
| Suburban......... | 18.3 | 18.9 | 17.5 | 15.4 | 25.4 | 27.1 | NA | 20.0 | 9.0 | 13.7 | 16.6 | 20.8 | 22.3 | 22.7 | 18.6 | 19.5 | 4.3 (!) |
| Rural............... | 13.3 | 14.0 | 12.5 | 12.1 | 22.5 | 16.8 (!) | NA | ‡ | 11.0 | 8.9 | 10.1 | 18.9 | 14.4 | 15.8 | 11.5 (!) | 13.7 | ‡ |
| **2003 [2]** | | | | | | | | | | | | | | | | | |
| Total ................... | 20.9 | 22.3 | 19.5 | 14.2 | 29.5 | 37.2 | NA | 22.0 | 10.9 | 16.3 | 17.9 | 26.1 | 26.3 | 23.4 | 22.2 | 22.5 | 3.9 |
| Urban .............. | 30.9 | 32.1 | 29.7 | 19.8 | 32.8 | 42.6 | NA | 30.6 | 21.6 | 25.5 | 25.2 | 38.2 | 35.3 | 34.6 | 34.8 | 33.7 | 6.0 |
| Suburban......... | 18.4 | 20.5 | 16.3 | 13.8 | 28.3 | 34.6 | NA | 18.2 | 7.5 | 13.2 | 16.2 | 24.3 | 24.1 | 20.4 | 19.3 | 19.9 | 2.4 (!) |
| Rural............... | 12.3 | 12.2 | 12.4 | 10.7 | 21.8 (!) | 12.7 (!) | NA | ‡ | ‡ | 9.4 | 10.9 (!) | 13.8 | 18.0 | 15.0 | 13.3 | 12.8 | ‡ |
| **2005 [2]** | | | | | | | | | | | | | | | | | |
| Total ................... | 24.2 | 25.3 | 22.9 | 16.8 | 37.6 | 38.9 | 20.2 | 27.7 | 12.1 | 17.3 | 19.1 | 28.3 | 32.6 | 28.0 | 27.9 | 25.8 | 4.2 |
| Urban .............. | 36.2 | 37.4 | 35.0 | 23.7 | 41.8 | 48.9 | 25.0 | 33.9 | 19.9 | 24.2 | 30.5 | 40.3 | 50.6 | 44.3 | 39.5 | 39.1 | 7.7 |
| Suburban......... | 20.8 | 22.4 | 19.1 | 16.0 | 36.2 | 32.1 | 18.1 | 29.0 | 8.9 | 14.9 | 14.6 | 24.8 | 27.9 | 25.5 | 25.1 | 22.3 | 3.0 (!) |
| Rural............... | 16.4 | 16.1 | 16.7 | 14.1 | 24.4 | 26.2 | 19.0 (!) | ‡ | 8.3 | 15.2 | 14.7 | 21.0 | 22.0 | 13.3 (!) | 15.8 (!) | 17.2 | ‡ |
| **2007** | | | | | | | | | | | | | | | | | |
| Total ................... | 23.2 | 25.1 | 21.3 | 16.0 | 37.6 | 36.1 | 17.4 | 26.4 | 15.3 | 17.4 | 20.6 | 28.0 | 28.1 | 25.9 | 24.4 | 24.9 | 5.2 |
| Urban .............. | 32.3 | 35.3 | 29.2 | 23.4 | 39.7 | 40.4 | 18.4 | 31.9 | 17.8 | 24.1 | 25.9 | 41.1 | 38.6 | 34.7 | 38.4 | 35.6 | 7.3 |
| Suburban......... | 21.0 | 23.1 | 18.9 | 15.9 | 35.5 | 33.3 | 16.3 | 29.0 | 14.0 | 15.4 | 19.6 | 23.1 | 26.6 | 23.6 | 22.4 | 22.7 | 2.8 (!) |
| Rural............... | 15.5 | 14.9 | 16.1 | 10.9 | 36.8 | 27.5 (!) | ‡ | 14.3 | 15.6 (!) | 13.1 | 14.7 | 21.7 | 15.2 | 18.7 | 7.6 (!) | 15.6 | 11.8 (!) |
| **2009** | | | | | | | | | | | | | | | | | |
| Total ................... | 20.4 | 20.9 | 19.9 | 14.1 | 31.4 | 33.0 | 17.2 | 15.3 | 11.0 | 14.8 | 15.9 | 24.9 | 27.7 | 22.6 | 21.9 | 22.0 | 2.3 (!) |
| Urban .............. | 30.7 | 32.8 | 28.6 | 19.4 | 40.0 | 38.9 | 18.9 | 23.2 | 14.5 | 21.0 | 24.4 | 34.2 | 44.8 | 34.9 | 36.0 | 33.7 | 4.1 (!) |
| Suburban......... | 16.6 | 17.2 | 16.0 | 13.5 | 20.2 | 28.3 | 14.5 | 14.8 | 9.7 | 11.2 | 11.8 | 22.4 | 21.0 | 19.4 | 17.6 | 18.1 | ‡ |
| Rural............... | 16.0 | 13.7 | 18.1 | 11.8 | 35.4 | 27.3 (!) | ‡ | ‡ | 8.3 (!) | 16.5 | 14.2 (!) | 18.8 | 19.6 | 13.4 | 17.3 (!) | 16.2 | ‡ |
| **2011** | | | | | | | | | | | | | | | | | |
| Total ................... | 17.5 | 17.5 | 17.5 | 11.1 | 32.7 | 26.4 | 9.9 | 9.9 | 8.2 | 10.2 | 11.3 | 21.7 | 23.0 | 23.2 | 21.3 | 18.9 | 1.9 (!) |
| Urban .............. | 22.8 | 23.0 | 22.6 | 13.9 | 31.6 | 31.0 | 7.6 (!) | 12.3 | 5.4 (!) | 11.7 | 16.2 | 27.5 | 31.1 | 28.1 | 32.9 | 25.7 | ‡ |
| Suburban......... | 16.1 | 16.5 | 15.6 | 11.3 | 33.5 | 23.2 | 12.0 (!) | 10.4 | 8.6 | 9.3 | 9.0 | 18.9 | 21.5 | 23.7 | 18.5 | 17.1 | 2.9 (!) |
| Rural............... | 12.1 | 10.2 | 14.1 | 7.7 | 34.5 | 22.1 (!) | ‡ | ‡ | 11.1 | 10.1 | 9.6 (!) | 19.3 | 13.9 | 10.6 | 9.2 (!) | 12.5 | ‡ |
| **2013** | | | | | | | | | | | | | | | | | |
| Total ................... | 12.4 | 12.9 | 12.0 | 7.5 | 18.6 | 20.1 | 9.4 | 14.3 | 5.0 | 7.7 | 7.8 | 13.9 | 17.7 | 17.1 | 14.6 | 13.3 | 2.3 (!) |
| Urban .............. | 18.3 | 18.6 | 18.0 | 14.3 | 20.6 | 22.6 | 10.4 | 17.9 | 9.6 | 12.0 | 13.2 | 19.6 | 24.8 | 26.7 | 18.2 | 19.9 | 4.6 (!) |
| Suburban......... | 10.8 | 11.7 | 9.8 | 6.5 | 17.3 | 19.3 | 8.2 (!) | 13.0 | 3.0 (!) | 6.6 | 6.3 | 12.2 | 15.4 | 15.1 | 14.1 | 11.7 | ‡ |
| Rural............... | 6.8 | 5.7 | 7.9 | 4.1 | 16.1 | 9.4 (!) | ‡ | 11.9 | ‡ | 4.2 (!) | ‡ | 8.0 (!) | 11.3 | 8.1 (!) | 9.0 (!) | 6.8 | ‡ |
| **2015** | | | | | | | | | | | | | | | | | |
| Total ................... | 10.7 | 10.9 | 10.4 | 7.4 | 17.1 | 15.3 | 4.1 (!) | 12.7 | 5.7 | 6.8 | 7.2 | 13.3 | 13.3 | 13.3 | 13.1 | 11.3 | 2.4 |
| Urban .............. | 15.3 | 14.8 | 15.8 | 12.3 | 19.3 | 17.8 | 5.9 (!) | 17.5 | 6.4 (!) | 9.0 | 10.9 | 19.5 | 19.8 | 21.9 | 17.3 | 16.4 | 4.4 |
| Suburban......... | 10.2 | 10.7 | 9.6 | 7.1 | 19.3 | 14.7 | ‡ | 11.4 | 6.0 | 5.8 | 6.3 | 13.4 | 12.1 | 12.1 | 13.3 | 10.7 | ‡ |
| Rural | 3.9 | 4.2 | 3.7 | 3.5 | 3.4 (!) | ‡ | ‡ | ‡ | ‡ | 5.5 | 3.2 (!) | 4.5 (!) | 5.3 (!) | ‡ | ‡ | 4.1 | ‡ |

NOTE: "Urbanicity" refers to the Standard Metropolitan Statistical Area (MSA) status of the respondent's household as defined by the U.S. Census Bureau. Categories include "central city of an MSA (Urban)," "in MSA but not in central city (Suburban)," and "not MSA (Rural)." All gangs, whether or not they are involved in violent or illegal activity, are included. "At school" includes in the school building, on school property, on a school bus, and going to and from school. NA = Not available.
(!) = Interpret data with caution. The coefficient of variation (CV) for this estimate is between 30 and 50 percent.
‡ = Reporting standards not met. Either there are too few cases for a reliable estimate or the coefficient of variation (CV) is 50 percent or greater.
[1] Race categories exclude persons of Hispanic ethnicity. "Other" includes American Indians/Alaska Natives, Asians (prior to 2005), Pacific Islanders, and, from 2003 onward, persons of Two or more races. Due to changes in racial/ethnic categories, comparisons of race/ethnicity across years should be made with caution.
[2] In 2005 and prior years, the period covered by the survey question was "during the last 6 months," whereas the period was "during this school year" beginning in 2007. Cognitive testing showed that estimates for earlier years are comparable to those for 2007 and later years.

## Table 8. Percentage of Students in Grades 9 to 12 Who Reported That Illegal Drugs Were Made Available to Them on School Property During the Previous 12 Months, by Selected Student Characteristics, Selected Years, 1993–2015

(Percent.)

| Student characteristic | 1993 | 1995 | 1997 | 1999 |
|---|---|---|---|---|
| **Total** | 24.0 | 32.1 | 31.7 | 30.2 |
| **Sex** | | | | |
| Male | 28.5 | 38.8 | 37.4 | 34.7 |
| Female | 19.1 | 24.8 | 24.7 | 25.7 |
| **Race/ethnicity[1]** | | | | |
| White | 24.1 | 31.7 | 31.0 | 28.8 |
| Black | 17.5 | 28.5 | 25.4 | 25.3 |
| Hispanic | 34.1 | 40.7 | 41.1 | 36.9 |
| Asian[2] | NA | NA | NA | 25.7 |
| Pacific Islander[2] | NA | NA | NA | 46.9 |
| American Indian/Alaska Native | 20.9 | 22.8 | 30.1 | 30.6 |
| Two or more races[2] | NA | NA | NA | 36.0 |
| **Grade** | | | | |
| 9th | 21.8 | 31.1 | 31.4 | 27.6 |
| 10th | 23.7 | 35.0 | 33.4 | 32.1 |
| 11th | 27.5 | 32.8 | 33.2 | 31.1 |
| 12th | 23.0 | 29.1 | 29.0 | 30.5 |
| **Urban/city[3]** | | | | |
| Urban | NA | NA | 31.2 | 30.3 |
| Suburban | NA | NA | 34.2 | 29.7 |
| Rural | NA | NA | 22.7 | 32.1 |

NOTE: "On school property" was not defined for survey respondents.
NA = Not available.
[1] Race categories exclude persons of Hispanic ethnicity.
[2] Before 1999, Asian students and Pacific Islander students were not categorized separately, and students could not be classified as two or more races. Because the response categories changed in 1999, caution should be used in comparing data on race from 1993, 1995, and 1997 with data from later years.
[3] Refers to the Standard Metropolitan Statistical Area (MSA) status of the respondent's household as defined by the U.S. Census Bureau. Categories include "central city of an MSA (Urban)," "in MSA but not in central city (Suburban)," and "not MSA (Rural)."

# Table 9. Percentage of Students Age 12 to 18 Years Who Reported Being the Target of Hate-Related Words and Seeing Hate-Related Graffiti at School During the School Year by Selected Student and School Characteristics and Location, Selected Years, 1999–2015

(Percent.)

| Student/school characteristic | 1999 [1] | 2001 [1] | 2003 [1] | 2005 [1] | 2007 | 2009 | 2011 | 2013 | 2015 |
|---|---|---|---|---|---|---|---|---|---|
| **HATE-RELATED WORDS** | | | | | | | | | |
| Total | NA | 12.3 | 11.7 | 11.2 | 9.7 | 8.7 | 9.1 | 6.6 | 7.2 |
| **Sex** | | | | | | | | | |
| Male | NA | 12.8 | 12.0 | 11.7 | 9.9 | 8.5 | 9.0 | 6.6 | 7.8 |
| Female | NA | 11.7 | 11.3 | 10.7 | 9.6 | 8.9 | 9.1 | 6.7 | 6.7 |
| **Race/Ethnicity[2]** | | | | | | | | | |
| White | NA | 12.1 | 10.9 | 10.3 | 8.9 | 7.2 | 8.3 | 5.3 | 6.3 |
| Black | NA | 13.9 | 14.2 | 15.1 | 11.4 | 11.1 | 10.7 | 7.8 | 9.4 |
| Hispanic | NA | 11.0 | 11.4 | 10.5 | 10.6 | 11.2 | 9.8 | 7.4 | 6.5 |
| Asian | NA | NA | NA | 10.9 | 11.1 | 10.7 | 9.0 | 10.3 | 10.8 |
| Other | NA | 13.6 | 14.1 | 14.2 | 10.6 | 10.0 | 10.4 | 11.2 | 11.4 |
| **Grade** | | | | | | | | | |
| 6th | NA | 12.1 | 11.9 | 11.1 | 12.1 | 8.3 | 9.0 | 6.7 | 10.1 |
| 7th | NA | 14.1 | 12.5 | 13.1 | 10.7 | 9.6 | 9.9 | 7.5 | 7.0 |
| 8th | NA | 13.0 | 12.8 | 11.2 | 11.0 | 10.9 | 8.4 | 7.4 | 9.2 |
| 9th | NA | 12.1 | 13.5 | 12.8 | 10.9 | 8.0 | 10.2 | 6.6 | 7.4 |
| 10th | NA | 13.1 | 11.6 | 10.9 | 9.0 | 9.7 | 9.6 | 6.4 | 6.5 |
| 11th | NA | 12.7 | 8.3 | 9.0 | 8.6 | 8.4 | 8.7 | 7.5 | 6.0 |
| 12th | NA | 7.9 | 10.8 | 9.7 | 6.0 | 5.8 | 7.5 | 4.1 | 5.4 |
| **Urban/City[3]** | | | | | | | | | |
| Urban | NA | 11.9 | 13.2 | 12.2 | 9.7 | 9.9 | 8.0 | 7.2 | 6.5 |
| Suburban | NA | 12.4 | 10.7 | 9.4 | 9.3 | 8.3 | 9.8 | 6.6 | 8.3 |
| Rural | NA | 12.4 | 12.2 | 15.5 | 11.0 | 8.1 | 8.5 | 5.7 | 4.9 |
| **Control of School** | | | | | | | | | |
| Public | NA | 12.7 | 11.9 | 11.6 | 10.1 | 8.9 | 9.3 | 6.6 | 7.6 |
| Private | NA | 8.2 | 9.7 | 6.8 | 6.1 | 6.6 | 6.9 | 6.7 | 2.8 (!) |
| **HATE-RELATED GRAFFITI** | | | | | | | | | |
| Total | 36.3 | 35.5 | 36.3 | 38.4 | 34.9 | 29.2 | 28.4 | 24.6 | 27.2 |
| **Sex** | | | | | | | | | |
| Male | 33.8 | 34.9 | 35.0 | 37.7 | 34.4 | 29.0 | 28.6 | 24.1 | 26.3 |
| Female | 38.9 | 36.1 | 37.6 | 39.1 | 35.4 | 29.3 | 28.1 | 25.1 | 28.1 |
| **Race/Ethnicity[2]** | | | | | | | | | |
| White | 36.4 | 36.2 | 35.2 | 38.5 | 35.5 | 28.3 | 28.2 | 23.7 | 28.6 |
| Black | 37.6 | 33.6 | 38.1 | 38.0 | 33.7 | 29.0 | 28.1 | 26.3 | 24.9 |
| Hispanic | 35.6 | 35.1 | 40.3 | 38.0 | 34.8 | 32.2 | 29.1 | 25.6 | 26.7 |
| Asian | NA | NA | NA | 34.5 | 28.2 | 31.2 | 29.9 | 20.8 | 17.5 |
| Other | 32.2 | 32.1 | 31.4 | 46.9 | 38.7 | 25.8 | 25.9 | 28.4 | 29.7 |
| **Grade** | | | | | | | | | |
| 6th | 30.3 | 34.9 | 35.7 | 34.0 | 35.5 | 28.1 | 25.9 | 21.9 | 30.0 |
| 7th | 34.9 | 34.9 | 37.2 | 37.0 | 32.3 | 27.9 | 26.0 | 21.7 | 24.7 |
| 8th | 35.6 | 36.7 | 34.2 | 35.7 | 33.5 | 30.8 | 25.9 | 24.0 | 27.2 |
| 9th | 39.2 | 35.7 | 37.0 | 41.6 | 34.5 | 28.1 | 28.7 | 27.2 | 28.2 |
| 10th | 38.9 | 36.2 | 40.7 | 40.7 | 36.4 | 31.0 | 33.3 | 26.0 | 28.6 |
| 11th | 37.0 | 36.1 | 36.6 | 40.2 | 35.3 | 27.4 | 32.1 | 25.8 | 26.2 |
| 12th | 35.6 | 33.0 | 32.2 | 37.8 | 37.7 | 30.4 | 25.7 | 24.2 | 26.1 |
| **Urban/City[3]** | | | | | | | | | |
| Urban | 37.0 | 35.7 | 38.6 | 40.9 | 34.4 | 31.1 | 27.5 | 27.8 | 26.4 |
| Suburban | 37.3 | 36.0 | 35.9 | 38.0 | 34.2 | 28.6 | 29.9 | 23.7 | 28.0 |
| Rural | 32.7 | 33.8 | 33.9 | 35.8 | 37.8 | 27.7 | 24.9 | 21.6 | 25.7 |
| **Control of School** | | | | | | | | | |
| Public | 38.0 | 37.3 | 37.9 | 40.0 | 36.4 | 30.7 | 29.7 | 25.6 | 28.3 |
| Private | 20.7 | 16.8 | 19.5 | 18.6 | 18.5 | 11.8 | 13.4 | 12.6 | 11.5 |

NOTE: "At school" includes in the school building, on school property, on a school bus, and, from 2001 onward, going to and from school. "Hate-related" refers to derogatory terms used by others in reference to students' personal characteristics.

NA = Not available.

(!) = Interpret data with caution. The coefficient of variation (CV) for this estimate is between 30 and 50 percent.

[1] In 2005 and prior years, the period covered by the survey question was "during the last 6 months," whereas the period was "during this school year" beginning in 2007. Cognitive testing showed that estimates for earlier years are comparable to those for 2007 and later years.

[2] Race categories exclude persons of Hispanic ethnicity. "Other" includes American Indians/Alaska Natives, Asians (prior to 2005), Pacific Islanders, and, from 2003 onward, persons of two or more races. Due to changes in racial/ethnic categories, comparisons of race/ethnicity across years should be made with caution.

[3] Refers to the Standard Metropolitan Statistical Area (MSA) status of the respondent's household as defined by the U.S. Census Bureau. Categories include "central city of an MSA (Urban)," "in MSA but not in central city (Suburban)," and "not MSA (Rural)."

# Table 10. Percentage of Students Age 12 to 18 Years Who Reported Being Bullied at School During the School Year, by Type of Bullying and Selected Student and School Characteristics, Selected Years, 2005–2015

(Percent.)

| Student/school characteristic | Total bullied at school[1] | Made fun of, called names, or insulted | Subject of rumors | Threatened with harm | Tried to make do things did not want to do | Excluded from activities on purpose | Property destroyed on purpose | Pushed, shoved, tripped, or spit on |
|---|---|---|---|---|---|---|---|---|
| **2005** [2] | | | | | | | | |
| Total ............................. | 28.1 | 18.7 | 14.7 | 4.8 | 3.5 | 4.6 | 3.4 | 9.0 |
| **Sex** | | | | | | | | |
| Male.............................. | 27.1 | 18.5 | 11.0 | 5.2 | 3.9 | 4.1 | 3.5 | 10.9 |
| Female........................... | 29.2 | 19.0 | 18.5 | 4.4 | 3.1 | 5.2 | 3.3 | 7.1 |
| **Race/Ethnicity**[3] | | | | | | | | |
| White ............................ | 30.0 | 20.1 | 15.8 | 5.1 | 3.6 | 5.3 | 3.4 | 9.7 |
| Black.............................. | 28.5 | 18.5 | 14.2 | 4.9 | 4.7 | 4.5 | 4.6 | 8.9 |
| Hispanic......................... | 22.3 | 14.7 | 12.4 | 4.6 | 2.6 | 3.0 | 2.7 | 7.6 |
| Asian............................. | NA | NA | NA | NA | NA | NA | NA | NA |
| Other............................. | 24.6 | 16.3 | 11.6 | 2.1 | 2.1 (!) | 2.5 | 2.5 (!) | 6.8 |
| **Grade** | | | | | | | | |
| 6th ............................... | 36.6 | 26.3 | 16.4 | 6.4 | 4.4 | 7.4 | 3.9 | 15.1 |
| 7th ............................... | 35.0 | 25.2 | 18.9 | 6.3 | 4.7 | 7.1 | 4.6 | 15.4 |
| 8th ............................... | 30.4 | 20.4 | 14.3 | 4.3 | 3.8 | 5.4 | 4.5 | 11.3 |
| 9th ............................... | 28.1 | 18.9 | 13.8 | 5.3 | 3.2 | 3.8 | 2.7 | 8.2 |
| 10th ............................. | 24.9 | 15.5 | 13.6 | 4.9 | 3.6 | 3.6 | 2.9 | 6.8 |
| 11th ............................. | 23.0 | 14.7 | 13.4 | 3.2 | 2.8 | 3.3 | 2.6 | 4.2 |
| 12th ............................. | 19.9 | 11.3 | 12.5 | 3.5 | 1.8 | 2.2 | 2.4 | 2.9 |
| **Urban/City**[4] | | | | | | | | |
| Urban ............................ | 26.0 | 17.7 | 13.3 | 5.5 | 4.1 | 4.9 | 3.9 | 8.5 |
| Suburban........................ | 28.9 | 18.9 | 14.6 | 4.4 | 3.1 | 4.5 | 3.0 | 9.0 |
| Rural.............................. | 29.0 | 19.8 | 17.2 | 5.0 | 3.7 | 4.5 | 3.8 | 9.9 |
| **Control of School**[5] | | | | | | | | |
| Public............................ | 28.6 | 19.0 | 14.9 | 5.1 | 3.5 | 4.5 | 3.5 | 9.3 |
| Private ........................... | 22.7 | 15.3 | 12.4 | 0.9 (!) | 3.0 (!) | 6.2 | 2.0 (!) | 5.5 |
| **2007** | | | | | | | | |
| Total ............................. | 31.7 | 21.0 | 18.1 | 5.8 | 4.1 | 5.2 | 4.2 | 11.0 |
| **Sex** | | | | | | | | |
| Male.............................. | 30.3 | 20.3 | 13.5 | 6.0 | 4.8 | 4.6 | 4.0 | 12.2 |
| Female........................... | 33.2 | 21.7 | 22.8 | 5.6 | 3.4 | 5.8 | 4.4 | 9.7 |
| **Race/Ethnicity**[3] | | | | | | | | |
| White ............................ | 34.1 | 23.5 | 20.3 | 6.3 | 4.8 | 6.1 | 4.2 | 11.5 |
| Black.............................. | 30.4 | 19.5 | 15.7 | 5.8 | 3.2 | 3.7 | 5.6 | 11.3 |
| Hispanic......................... | 27.3 | 16.1 | 14.4 | 4.9 | 3.0 | 4.0 | 3.6 | 9.9 |
| Asian............................. | 18.1 | 10.6 | 8.2 | ‡ | ‡ | ‡ | 1.8 | 3.8 (!) |
| Other............................. | 34.1 | 20.1 | 20.8 | 7.7 | 3.1 | 7.7 | 3.4 | 14.4 |
| **Grade** | | | | | | | | |
| 6th ............................... | 42.7 | 31.2 | 21.3 | 7.0 | 5.4 | 7.4 | 5.2 | 17.6 |
| 7th ............................... | 35.6 | 27.6 | 20.2 | 7.4 | 4.1 | 7.7 | 6.0 | 15.8 |
| 8th ............................... | 36.9 | 25.1 | 19.7 | 6.9 | 3.6 | 5.4 | 4.6 | 14.2 |
| 9th ............................... | 30.6 | 20.3 | 18.1 | 4.6 | 5.1 | 4.5 | 3.5 | 11.4 |
| 10th ............................. | 27.7 | 17.7 | 15.0 | 5.8 | 4.6 | 4.6 | 3.4 | 8.6 |
| 11th ............................. | 28.5 | 15.3 | 18.7 | 4.9 | 4.2 | 3.9 | 4.4 | 6.5 |
| 12th ............................. | 23.0 | 12.1 | 14.1 | 4.3 | 2.1 | 3.5 | 2.4 | 4.1 |
| **Urban/City**[4] | | | | | | | | |
| Urban ............................ | 30.7 | 20.0 | 15.5 | 5.2 | 3.6 | 4.9 | 4.2 | 9.2 |
| Suburban........................ | 31.2 | 21.1 | 17.4 | 5.7 | 4.1 | 5.0 | 4.0 | 11.2 |
| Rural.............................. | 35.2 | 22.1 | 24.1 | 7.0 | 5.1 | 6.3 | 4.9 | 13.1 |
| **Control of School**[5] | | | | | | | | |
| Public............................ | 32.0 | 21.1 | 18.3 | 6.2 | 4.2 | 5.2 | 4.1 | 11.4 |
| Private ........................... | 29.1 | 20.1 | 16.0 | 1.3 (!) | 3.6 | 5.9 | 5.0 | 6.5 |

**Table 10. Percentage of Students Age 12 to 18 Years Who Reported Being Bullied at School During the School Year, by Type of Bullying and Selected Student and School Characteristics, Selected Years, 2005–2015**—*Continued*

(Percent.)

| Student/school characteristic | Total bullied at school[1] | Type of bullying | | | | | | |
|---|---|---|---|---|---|---|---|---|
| | | Made fun of, called names, or insulted | Subject of rumors | Threatened with harm | Tried to make do things did not want to do | Excluded from activities on purpose | Property destroyed on purpose | Pushed, shoved, tripped, or spit on |
| **2009** | | | | | | | | |
| Total ................................. | 28.0 | 18.8 | 16.5 | 5.7 | 3.6 | 4.7 | 3.3 | 9.0 |
| **Sex** | | | | | | | | |
| Male ................................. | 26.6 | 18.4 | 12.8 | 5.6 | 4.0 | 3.8 | 3.4 | 10.1 |
| Female ............................... | 29.5 | 19.2 | 20.3 | 5.8 | 3.2 | 5.7 | 3.2 | 7.9 |
| **Race/Ethnicity[3]** | | | | | | | | |
| White ................................. | 29.3 | 20.5 | 17.4 | 5.4 | 3.7 | 5.2 | 3.3 | 9.1 |
| Black .................................. | 29.1 | 18.4 | 17.7 | 7.8 | 4.8 | 4.6 | 4.6 | 9.9 |
| Hispanic ............................. | 25.5 | 15.8 | 14.8 | 5.8 | 2.7 | 3.6 | 2.6 | 9.1 |
| Asian .................................. | 17.3 | 9.6 | 8.1 | ‡ | ‡ | 3.4 (!) | ‡ | 5.5 (!) |
| Other .................................. | 26.7 | 17.4 | 12.9 | 9.7 (!) | 4.5 (!) | 4.5 (!) | 3.8 (!) | 7.1 (!) |
| **Grade** | | | | | | | | |
| 6th ..................................... | 39.4 | 30.6 | 21.4 | 9.3 | 4.2 | 6.6 | 4.0 | 14.5 |
| 7th ..................................... | 33.1 | 23.6 | 17.3 | 5.7 | 4.6 | 5.6 | 4.6 | 13.1 |
| 8th ..................................... | 31.7 | 22.8 | 18.1 | 6.8 | 5.4 | 6.9 | 6.1 | 12.8 |
| 9th ..................................... | 28.0 | 19.2 | 16.6 | 7.1 | 4.0 | 4.5 | 2.9 | 9.7 |
| 10th ................................... | 26.6 | 15.0 | 17.0 | 5.8 | 3.1 | 4.0 | 2.9 | 7.3 |
| 11th ................................... | 21.1 | 13.9 | 13.9 | 4.8 | 2.5 | 3.6 | 1.5 (!) | 4.4 |
| 12th ................................... | 20.4 | 11.1 | 13.1 | 2.0 | 1.7 (!) | 2.6 | 1.3 (!) | 3.0 |
| **Urban/City[4]** | | | | | | | | |
| Urban ................................. | 27.4 | 17.0 | 16.5 | 6.6 | 4.2 | 4.0 | 4.2 | 9.0 |
| Suburban ............................ | 27.5 | 19.3 | 15.5 | 5.2 | 3.2 | 5.0 | 2.9 | 8.9 |
| Rural .................................. | 30.7 | 20.2 | 19.9 | 6.1 | 4.1 | 5.2 | 3.3 | 9.5 |
| **Control of School[5]** | | | | | | | | |
| Public ................................. | 28.8 | 19.3 | 16.9 | 5.9 | 3.8 | 4.7 | 3.4 | 9.4 |
| Private ................................ | 18.9 | 13.3 | 11.6 | 4.4 | 1.9 | 4.9 | 1.8 | 4.5 |
| **2011** | | | | | | | | |
| Total ................................. | 27.8 | 17.6 | 18.3 | 5.0 | 3.3 | 5.6 | 2.8 | 7.9 |
| **Sex** | | | | | | | | |
| Male ................................. | 24.5 | 16.2 | 13.2 | 5.0 | 3.6 | 4.8 | 3.3 | 8.9 |
| Female ............................... | 31.4 | 19.1 | 23.8 | 5.1 | 3.0 | 6.4 | 2.3 | 6.8 |
| **Race/Ethnicity[3]** | | | | | | | | |
| White ................................. | 31.5 | 20.6 | 20.3 | 5.8 | 3.3 | 7.1 | 3.1 | 8.6 |
| Black .................................. | 27.2 | 16.4 | 18.6 | 5.5 | 4.3 | 4.7 | 3.3 | 9.3 |
| Hispanic ............................. | 21.9 | 12.7 | 15.1 | 3.3 | 2.9 | 2.8 | 2.4 | 6.2 |
| Asian .................................. | 14.9 | 9.0 | 7.7 | ‡ | 2.7 | 2.9 | ‡ | 2.1 |
| Other .................................. | 23.7 | 15.0 | 17.0 | 6.5 | ‡ | 5.0 | ‡ | 7.2 |
| **Grade** | | | | | | | | |
| 6th ..................................... | 37.0 | 27.0 | 23.1 | 4.9 | 3.9 | 6.6 | 3.7 | 12.7 |
| 7th ..................................... | 30.3 | 22.4 | 18.3 | 6.9 | 4.5 | 7.8 | 4.0 | 12.6 |
| 8th ..................................... | 30.7 | 20.7 | 19.0 | 5.3 | 2.9 | 6.4 | 4.0 | 10.8 |
| 9th ..................................... | 26.5 | 16.4 | 16.3 | 5.4 | 3.3 | 4.1 | 2.5 | 7.3 |
| 10th ................................... | 28.0 | 16.9 | 19.6 | 5.1 | 3.9 | 5.3 | 2.2 | 6.7 |
| 11th ................................... | 23.8 | 12.7 | 17.1 | 4.0 | 2.4 | 4.7 | 1.8 | 3.9 |
| 12th ................................... | 22.0 | 10.6 | 16.7 | 3.5 | 2.3 | 4.3 | 1.9 | 2.7 |
| **Urban/City[4]** | | | | | | | | |
| Urban ................................. | 24.8 | 15.9 | 16.1 | 4.4 | 3.1 | 4.6 | 2.5 | 7.6 |
| Suburban ............................ | 29.0 | 18.4 | 18.7 | 5.0 | 3.2 | 6.0 | 3.0 | 8.2 |
| Rural .................................. | 29.7 | 18.4 | 21.4 | 6.3 | 3.9 | 5.8 | 3.0 | 7.3 |
| **Control of School[5]** | | | | | | | | |
| Public ................................. | 28.4 | 17.9 | 18.8 | 5.3 | 3.3 | 5.5 | 2.9 | 8.1 |
| Private ................................ | 21.5 | 13.9 | 12.6 | 1.6 | 2.9 | 5.6 | 2.1 | 4.7 |
| **2013** | | | | | | | | |
| Total ................................. | 21.5 | 13.6 | 13.2 | 3.9 | 2.2 | 4.5 | 1.6 | 6.0 |

# Table 10. Percentage of Students Age 12 to 18 Years Who Reported Being Bullied at School During the School Year, by Type of Bullying and Selected Student and School Characteristics, Selected Years, 2005–2015—*Continued*

(Percent.)

| Student/school characteristic | Total bullied at school[1] | Made fun of, called names, or insulted | Subject of rumors | Threatened with harm | Tried to make do things did not want to do | Excluded from activities on purpose | Property destroyed on purpose | Pushed, shoved, tripped, or spit on |
|---|---|---|---|---|---|---|---|---|
| **Sex** | | | | | | | | |
| Male.............. | 19.5 | 12.6 | 9.6 | 4.1 | 2.4 | 3.5 | 1.8 | 7.4 |
| Female............ | 23.7 | 14.7 | 17.0 | 3.7 | 1.9 | 5.5 | 1.3 | 4.6 |
| | | | | | | | | |
| **Race/Ethnicity[3]** | | | | | | | | |
| White.............. | 23.7 | 15.6 | 14.6 | 4.4 | 2.0 | 5.4 | 1.5 | 6.1 |
| Black.............. | 20.3 | 10.5 | 12.7 | 3.2 | 2.7 | 2.7 | 2.0 | 6.0 |
| Hispanic.......... | 19.2 | 12.1 | 11.5 | 4.0 | 1.6 | 3.5 | 1.4 | 6.3 |
| Asian.............. | 9.2 | 7.5 | 3.7 | ‡ | 3.8 (!) | 2.2 | 1.6 (!) | 2.0 (!) |
| Other.............. | 25.2 | 16.5 | 17.3 | 4.3 (!) | 4.0 (!) | 6.5 | 2.1 (!) | 8.5 |
| | | | | | | | | |
| **Grade** | | | | | | | | |
| 6th............... | 27.8 | 21.3 | 16.1 | 5.9 | 3.4 | 6.5 | 3.1 | 11.0 |
| 7th............... | 26.4 | 17.9 | 15.5 | 6.1 | 3.0 | 6.3 | 2.2 | 11.6 |
| 8th............... | 21.7 | 14.5 | 12.7 | 3.9 | 2.3 | 5.2 | 1.5 (!) | 6.5 |
| 9th............... | 23.0 | 13.7 | 13.8 | 3.6 | 2.6 | 4.3 | 1.2 (!) | 4.9 |
| 10th.............. | 19.5 | 12.9 | 12.9 | 4.3 | 1.7 | 4.6 | 1.3 | 3.7 |
| 11th.............. | 20.0 | 11.2 | 12.5 | 3.0 | 1.5 | 2.4 | 1.6 (!) | 3.4 |
| 12th.............. | 14.1 | 6.4 | 9.7 | 1.0 (!) | 1.3 (!) | 2.5 | 0.7 (!) | 3.0 |
| | | | | | | | | |
| **Urban/City[4]** | | | | | | | | |
| Urban............. | 20.7 | 12.8 | 12.7 | 3.9 | 2.7 | 4.1 | 1.4 | 5.6 |
| Suburban.......... | 22.0 | 14.2 | 13.4 | 3.9 | 2.0 | 4.7 | 1.3 | 6.4 |
| Rural............. | 21.4 | 13.2 | 13.3 | 4.1 | 1.7 | 4.2 | 2.8 | 5.8 |
| | | | | | | | | |
| **Control of School[5]** | | | | | | | | |
| Public............ | 21.5 | 13.5 | 13.2 | 3.9 | 2.2 | 4.3 | 1.6 | 6.1 |
| Private .......... | 22.4 | 15.3 | 13.4 | 3.9 | 2.7 (!) | 6.7 | 1.3 (!) | 5.2 |
| | | | | | | | | |
| **2015** | | | | | | | | |
| Total ............ | 20.8 | 13.3 | 12.3 | 3.9 | 2.5 | 5.0 | 1.8 | 5.1 |
| | | | | | | | | |
| **Sex** | | | | | | | | |
| Male.............. | 18.8 | 12.7 | 9.1 | 4.8 | 2.7 | 4.4 | 1.9 | 6.0 |
| Female............ | 22.8 | 13.9 | 15.5 | 2.9 | 2.3 | 5.7 | 1.8 | 4.2 |
| | | | | | | | | |
| **Race/Ethnicity[3]** | | | | | | | | |
| White.............. | 21.6 | 14.2 | 12.8 | 3.9 | 2.1 | 5.6 | 1.6 | 5.3 |
| Black.............. | 24.7 | 17.2 | 14.3 | 5.2 | 3.4 (!) | 4.9 | 1.6 (!) | 5.6 |
| Hispanic.......... | 17.2 | 9.5 | 10.4 | 2.9 | 2.1 (!) | 3.4 | 2.0 (!) | 3.7 |
| Asian.............. | 15.6 | 10.1 (!) | 4.9 (!) | ‡ | ‡ | ‡ | ‡ | 3.9 (!) |
| Other.............. | 25.9 | 16.4 | 18.6 | 8.9 (!) | 9.1 (!) | 9.8 (!) | ‡ | 11.2 (!) |
| | | | | | | | | |
| **Grade** | | | | | | | | |
| 6th............... | 31.0 | 21.4 | 17.7 | 7.3 | 5.2 | 10.1 | 4.0 (!) | 13.1 |
| 7th............... | 25.1 | 18.6 | 12.9 | 3.8 | 2.9 (!) | 6.4 | 2.7 (!) | 7.8 |
| 8th............... | 22.2 | 15.6 | 13.1 | 5.0 | 2.9 (!) | 5.1 | 3.0 (!) | 7.5 |
| 9th............... | 19.0 | 12.5 | 10.6 | 2.8 (!) | 2.7 (!) | 4.4 | 1.3 (!) | 4.4 |
| 10th.............. | 21.2 | 12.6 | 12.9 | 2.9 (!) | 1.7 (!) | 5.7 | 1,2 (!) | 2.2 (!) |
| 11th.............. | 15.8 | 8.8 | 10.2 | 4.2 | ‡ | 3.0 | ‡ | 2.1 (!) |
| 12th.............. | 14.9 | 6.2 | 10.8 | 2.5 (!) | 2.4 (!) | 2.4 | ‡ | 1.6 (!) |
| | | | | | | | | |
| **Urban/City[4]** | | | | | | | | |
| Urban ............ | 21.5 | 14.5 | 11.4 | 3.9 | 2.9 | 5.1 | 2.4 | 5.6 |
| Suburban.......... | 21.1 | 13.3 | 13.2 | 3.9 | 2.6 | 5.4 | 1.6 | 4.8 |
| Rural............. | 18.2 | 10.9 | 10.6 | 3.8 (!) | ‡ | 3.7 | ‡ | 5.2 |
| | | | | | | | | |
| **Control of School[5]** | | | | | | | | |
| Public............ | 21.1 | 13.4 | 12.5 | 4.0 | 2.6 | 5.0 (!) | 1.8 | 5.2 |
| Private .......... | 16.1 | 11.5 | 8.6 | ‡ | ‡ | 5.0 | ‡ | 3.6 (!) |

NOTE: "At school" includes the school building, on school property, on a school bus, and going to and from school.

NA = Not available.

(!) = Interpret data with caution. The coefficient of variation (CV) for this estimate is between 30 and 50 percent.

‡ = Reporting standards not met. Either there are too few cases for a reliable estimate or the coefficient of variation (CV) is 50 percent or greater.

[1] Students who reported experiencing more than one type of bullying at school were counted only once in the total for students bullied at school.

[2] In 2005 and prior years, the period covered by the survey question was "during the last 6 months," whereas the period was "during this school year" beginning in 2007. Cognitive testing showed that estimates for earlier years are comparable to those for 2007 and later years.

[3] Race categories exclude persons of Hispanic ethnicity. "Other" includes American Indians/Alaska Natives, Pacific Islanders, and persons of two or more races.

[4] Refers to the Standard Metropolitan Statistical Area (MSA) status of the respondent's household as defined by the U.S. Census Bureau. Categories include "central city of an MSA (Urban)," "in MSA but not in central city (Suburban)," and "not MSA (Rural)." These data by metropolitan status were based on the location of households and differ from those published in *Student Reports of Bullying and Cyber-Bullying: Results from the 2013 School Crime Supplement to the National Crime Victimization Survey*, which were based on the urban-centric measure of the location of the school that the child attended.

[5] Control of school as reported by the respondent. These data differ from those based on a matching of the respondent-reported school name to the Common Core of Data's Public Elementary/Secondary School Universe Survey or the Private School Survey, as reported in *Student Reports of Bullying and Cyber-Bullying: Results from the 2013 School Crime Supplement to the National Crime Victimization Survey*.

# METHODOLOGY

This annual report, a joint effort by the Bureau of Justice Statistics and the National Center for Education Statistics (NCES), provides the most current statistical information on the nature of crime in schools. It presents data on crime and safety at school from the perspectives of students, teachers, and principals. This report contains 23 indicators of crime and safety at school from a number of sources, including the National Crime Victimization Survey (NCVS), the School Crime Supplement to the NCVS, the Youth Risk Behavior Survey, the School Survey on Crime and Safety, and the School and Staffing Survey. Topics covered include victimization at school, teacher injury, bullying and cyber-bullying, school conditions, fights, weapons, availability and student use of drugs and alcohol, student perceptions of personal safety at school, and crime at postsecondary institutions. For more information or to access the full report, please see < http://www.bjs.gov/index.cfm?ty=pbdetail&iid=5599>.

## Data

The Bureau of Justice Statistics' (BJS) **National Crime Victimization Survey (NCVS)** is the nation's primary source of information on criminal victimization. Each year, data are obtained from a nationally representative sample of about 90,000 households, comprising nearly 160,000 persons, on the frequency, characteristics, and consequences of criminal victimization in the United States. The NCVS collects information on nonfatal personal crimes (rape or sexual assault, robbery, aggravated and simple assault, and personal larceny) and household property crimes (burglary, motor vehicle theft, and other theft) both reported and not reported to police. Survey respondents provide information about themselves (e.g., age, sex, race and Hispanic origin, marital status, education level, and income) and whether they experienced a victimization. For each victimization incident, the NCVS collects information about the offender (e.g., age, race and Hispanic origin, sex, and victim-offender relationship), characteristics of the crime (including time and place of occurrence, use of weapons, nature of injury, and economic consequences), whether the crime was reported to police, reasons the crime was or was not reported, and victim experiences with the criminal justice system.

The National Crime Victimization Survey (NCVS) is an annual data collection conducted by the U.S. Census Bureau for the Bureau of Justice Statistics (BJS). The NCVS is a self-report survey in which interviewed persons are asked about the number and characteristics of victimizations experienced during the prior 6 months. The NCVS collects information on nonfatal personal crimes (rape or sexual assault, robbery, aggravated and simple assault, and personal larceny) and household property crimes (burglary, motor vehicle theft, and other theft) both reported and not reported to police. In addition to providing annual level and change estimates on criminal victimization, the NCVS is the primary source of information on the nature of criminal victimization incidents.

Survey respondents provide information about themselves (e.g., age, sex, race and Hispanic origin, marital status, education level, and income) and whether they experienced a victimization. The NCVS collects information for each victimization incident about the offender (e.g., age, race and Hispanic origin, sex, and victim-offender relationship), characteristics of the crime (including time and place of occurrence, use of weapons, nature of injury, and economic consequences), whether the crime was reported to police, reasons the crime was or was not reported, and victim experiences with the criminal justice system.

The NCVS is administered to persons age 12 or older from a nationally representative sample of households in the United States. The NCVS defines a household as a group of persons who all reside at a sampled address. Persons are considered household members when the sampled address is their usual place of residence at the time of the interview and when they have no usual place of residence elsewhere. Once selected, households remain in the sample for 3 years, and eligible persons in these households are interviewed every 6 months either in person or over the phone for a total of seven interviews.

## Nonresponse and weighting adjustments

In 2015, 95,760 households and 163,880 persons age 12 or older were interviewed for the NCVS. Each household was interviewed twice during the year. The response rate was 82 percent for households and 86 percent for eligible persons. Victimizations that occurred outside of the United States were excluded from this report.

In 2015, less than 1 percent of the unweighted victimizations occurred outside of the United States and were excluded from the analyses.

Estimates in NCVS reports generally use data from the 1993 to 2015 NCVS data files, weighted to produce annual estimates of victimization for persons age 12 or older living in U.S. households. Because the NCVS relies on a sample rather than a census of the entire U.S. population, weights are designed to inflate sample point estimates to known population totals and to compensate for survey nonresponse and other aspects of the sample design.

The NCVS data files include both person and household weights. Person weights provide an estimate of the population represented by each person in the sample. Household weights provide an estimate of the U.S. household population represented by each household in the sample. After proper adjustment, both household and person weights are also typically used to form the denominator in calculations of crime rates.

Victimization weights used in this analysis account for the number of persons present during an incident and for high frequency repeat victimizations (i.e., series victimizations). Series victimizations are similar in type but occur with such frequency that a victim is unable to recall each individual event or describe each event in detail. Survey procedures allow NCVS interviewers to identify and classify these similar victimizations as series victimizations and to collect detailed information on only the most recent incident in the series.

The **School-Associated Violent Deaths Study (SAVD)** is an epidemiological study developed by the Centers for Disease Control and Prevention in conjunction with the U.S. Department of Education and the U.S. Department of Justice. SAVD seeks to describe the epidemiology of school-associated violent deaths, identify common features of these deaths, estimate the rate of school-associated violent deaths in the United States, and identify potential risk factors for these deaths. The study includes descriptive data on all school-associated violent deaths in the United States, including all homicides, suicides, or legal intervention deaths in which the fatal injury occurred on the campus of a functioning elementary or secondary school; while the victim was on the way to or from regular sessions at such a school; or while attending or on the way to or from an official school-sponsored event. Victims of such incidents include nonstudents, as well as students and staff members. SAVD includes descriptive information about the school, event, victim(s), and offender(s). The SAVD study has collected data from July 1, 1992, through the present.

SAVD uses a four-step process to identify and collect data on school-associated violent deaths. Cases are initially identified through a search of the LexisNexis newspaper and media database. Then law enforcement officials from the office that investigated the deaths are contacted to confirm the details of the case and to determine if the event meets the case definition. Once a case is confirmed, a law enforcement official and a school official are interviewed regarding details about the school, event,

victim(s), and offender(s). A copy of the full law enforcement report is also sought for each case. The information obtained on schools includes school demographics, attendance/absentee rates, suspensions/expulsions and mobility, school history of weapon-carrying incidents, security measures, violence prevention activities, school response to the event, and school policies about weapon carrying. Event information includes the location of injury, the context of injury (while classes were being held, during break, etc.), motives for injury, method of injury, and school and community events happening around the time period. Information obtained on victim(s) and offender(s) includes demographics, circumstances of the event (date/time, alcohol or drug use, number of persons involved), types and origins of weapons, criminal history, psychological risk factors, school-related problems, extracurricular activities, and family history, including structure and stressors.

For several reasons, all data for years from 1999 to the present are flagged as preliminary. For some recent data, the interviews with school and law enforcement officials to verify case details have not been completed. The details learned during the interviews can occasionally change the classification of a case. Also, new cases may be identified because of the expansion of the scope of the media files used for case identification. Sometimes other cases not identified during earlier data years using the independent case finding efforts (which focus on nonmedia sources of information) will be discovered. Also, other cases may occasionally be identified while the law enforcement and school interviews are being conducted to verify known cases.

Created as a supplement to the NCVS and co-designed by the National Center for Education Statistics and Bureau of Justice Statistics, the School Crime Supplement (SCS) survey has been conducted in 1989, 1995, and biennially since 1999 to collect additional information about school-related victimizations on a national level. This report includes data from the 1995, 1999, 2001, 2003, 2005, 2007, 2009, 2011, and 2013 collections. The 1989 data are not included in this report as a result of methodological changes to the NCVS and SCS. The SCS was designed to assist policymakers, as well as academic researchers and practitioners at federal, state, and local levels, to make informed decisions concerning crime in schools. The survey asks students a number of key questions about their experiences with and perceptions of crime and violence that occurred inside their school, on school grounds, on the school bus, or on the way to or from school. Students are asked additional questions about security measures used by their school, students' participation in after-school activities, students' perceptions of school rules, the presence of weapons and gangs in school, the presence of hate-related words and graffiti in school, student reports of bullying and reports of rejection at school, and the availability of drugs and alcohol in school. Students are also asked attitudinal questions relating to fear of victimization and avoidance behavior at school.

The SCS survey was conducted for a 6-month period from January through June in all households selected for the NCVS (see discussion above for information about the NCVS sampling design and changes to the race/ethnicity variable beginning in 2003). Within these households, the eligible respondents for the SCS were those household members who had attended school at any time during the 6 months preceding the interview, were enrolled in grades 6–12, and were not homeschooled. In 2007, the questionnaire was changed and household members who attended school sometime during the school year of the interview were included. The age range of students covered in this report is 12–18 years of age. Eligible respondents were asked the supplemental questions in the SCS only after completing their entire NCVS interview. It should be noted that the first or unbounded NCVS interview has always been included in analysis of the SCS data and may result in the reporting of events outside of the requested reference period.

A total of about 9,700 students participated in the 1995 SCS, 8,400 in 1999, 8,400 in 2001, 7,200 in 2003, 6,300 in 2005, 5,600 in 2007, 5,000 in 2009, 6,500 in 2011, and 5,700 in 2013. In the 2013 SCS, the household completion rate was 86 percent.

**The Youth Risk Behavior Surveillance System (YRBSS) is** an epidemiological surveillance system developed by the Centers for Disease Control and Prevention (CDC) to monitor the prevalence of youth behaviors that most influence health. The YRBSS focuses on priority health-risk behaviors established during youth that result in the most significant mortality, morbidity, disability, and social problems during both youth and adulthood. The YRBSS includes a national school-based Youth Risk Behavior Survey (YRBS) as well as surveys conducted in states and large urban school districts. This report uses 1993, 1995, 1997, 1999, 2001, 2003, 2005, 2007, 2009, 2011, and 2013 YRBSS data.

The national YRBS uses a three-stage cluster sampling design to produce a nationally representative sample of students in grades 9–12 in the United States. The target population consisted of all public and private school students in grades 9–12 in the 50 states and the District of Columbia. The first-stage sampling frame included selecting primary sampling units (PSUs) from strata formed on the basis of urbanization and the relative percentage of Black and Hispanic students in the PSU. These PSUs are either counties; subareas of large counties; or groups of smaller, adjacent counties. At the second stage, schools were selected with probability proportional to school enrollment size.

The final stage of sampling consisted of randomly selecting, in each chosen school and in each of grades 9–12, one or two classrooms from either a required subject, such as English or social studies, or a required period, such as homeroom or second period. All students in selected classes were eligible

to participate. In surveys conducted before 2013, three strategies were used to oversample Black and Hispanic students: (1) larger sampling rates were used to select PSUs that are in high-Black and high- Hispanic strata; (2) a modified measure of size was used that increased the probability of selecting schools with a disproportionately high minority enrollment; and (3) two classes per grade, rather than one, were selected in schools with a high percentage of combined Black, Hispanic, Asian/Pacific Islander, or American Indian/Alaska Native enrollment. In 2013, only selection of two classes per grade was needed to achieve an adequate precision with minimum variance. Approximately 16,300 students participated in the 1993 survey, 10,900 students participated in the 1995 survey, 16,300 students participated in the 1997 survey, 15,300 students participated in the 1999 survey, 13,600 students participated in the 2001 survey, 15,200 students participated in the 2003 survey, 13,900 students participated in the 2005 survey, 14,000 students participated in the 2007 survey, 16,400 students participated in the 2009 survey, 15,400 participated in the 2011 survey, and 13,600 participated in the 2013 survey.

The overall response rate was 70 percent for the 1993 survey, 60 percent for the 1995 survey, 69 percent for the 1997 survey, 66 percent for the 1999 survey, 63 percent for the 2001 survey, 67 percent for the 2003 survey, 67 percent for the 2005 survey, 68 percent for the 2007 survey, 71 percent for the 2009 survey, 71 percent for the 2011 survey, and 68 percent for the 2013 survey. NCES standards call for response rates of 85 percent or better for cross-sectional surveys, and bias analyses are required by NCES when that percentage is not achieved. For YRBS data, a full nonresponse bias analysis has not been done because the data necessary to do the analysis are not available. The weights were developed to adjust for nonresponse and the oversampling of Black and Hispanic students in the sample. The final weights were constructed so that only weighted proportions of students (not weighted counts of students) in each grade matched national population projections.

**The School Survey on Crime and Safety (SSOCS) is** managed by the National Center for Education Statistics (NCES) on behalf of the U.S. Department of Education. SSOCS collects extensive crime and safety data from principals and school administrators of U.S. public schools. Data from this collection can be used to examine the relationship between school characteristics and violent and serious violent crimes in primary schools, middle schools, high schools, and combined schools. In addition, data from SSOCS can be used to assess what crime prevention programs, practices, and policies are used by schools. SSOCS has been conducted in school years 1999–2000, 2003–04, 2005–06, 2007–08, and 2009–10.

SSOCS was developed by NCES and is funded by the Office of Safe and Drug-Free Schools of the U.S. Department of Education. The 2009–10 SSOCS (SSOCS: 2010) was conducted by the U.S. Census Bureau. Data collection began on February

24, 2010, when questionnaire packets were mailed to sampled schools, and continued through June 11, 2010.

## Definitions

### General Terms

**Crime** Any violation of a statute or regulation or any act that the government has determined is injurious to the public, including felonies and misdemeanors. Such violation may or may not involve violence, and it may affect individuals or property.

**Incident** A specific criminal act or offense involving one or more victims and one or more offenders.

**Multistage sampling** A survey sampling technique in which there is more than one wave of sampling. That is, one sample of units is drawn, and then another sample is drawn within that sample. For example, at the first stage, a number of Census blocks may be sampled out of all the Census blocks in the United States. At the second stage, households are sampled within the previously sampled Census blocks.

**Prevalence** The percentage of the population directly affected by crime in a given period. This rate is based upon specific information elicited directly from the respondent regarding crimes committed against his or her person, against his or her property, or against an individual bearing a unique relationship to him or her. It is not based upon perceptions and beliefs about, or reactions to, criminal acts.

**School** An education institution consisting of one or more of grades K–12.

**School crime** Any criminal activity that is committed on school property.

**School year** The 12-month period of time denoting the beginning and ending dates for school accounting purposes, usually from July 1 through June 30.

**Stratification** A survey sampling technique in which the target population is divided into mutually exclusive groups or strata based on some variable or variables (e.g., metropolitan area) and sampling of units occurs separately within each stratum.

**Unequal probabilities** A survey sampling technique in which sampled units do not have the same probability of selection into the sample. For example, the investigator may oversample rural students in order to increase the sample sizes of rural students. Rural students would then be more likely than other students to be sampled.

## Specific Terms Used in Various Surveys

### School-Associated Violent Deaths Study (SAVD)

**Homicide** An act involving a killing of one person by another resulting from interpersonal violence.

**Legal intervention death** An act involving the killing of one person by a law enforcement agent in the course of arresting or attempting to arrest a lawbreaker, suppressing a disturbance, maintaining order, or engaging in another legal action.

**School-associated violent death** A homicide or suicide in which the fatal injury occurred on the campus of a functioning elementary or secondary school in the United States, while the victim was on the way to or from regular sessions at such a school, or while the victim was attending or traveling to or from an official school-sponsored event. Victims included nonstudents as well as students and staff members.

**Suicide** An act of taking one's own life voluntarily and intentionally.

### National Crime Victimization Survey (NCVS)

**Aggravated assault** Attack or attempted attack with a weapon, regardless of whether or not an injury occurs, and attack without a weapon when serious injury results.

**At school (students)** Inside the school building, on school property (school parking area, play area, school bus, etc.), or on the way to or from school.

**Metropolitan Statistical Areas (MSAs)** Geographic entities defined by the U.S. Office of Management and Budget (OMB) for use by federal statistical agencies in collecting, tabulating, and publishing federal statistics.

**Rape** Forced sexual intercourse including both psychological coercion as well as physical force. Forced sexual intercourse means vaginal, anal, or oral penetration by the offender(s). Includes attempts and verbal threats of rape. This category also includes incidents where the penetration is from a foreign object, such as a bottle.

**Robbery** Completed or attempted theft, directly from a person, of property or cash by force or threat of force, with or without a weapon, and with or without injury.

**Serious violent victimization** Rape, sexual assault, robbery, or aggravated assault.

**Sexual assault** A wide range of victimizations, separate from rape or attempted rape. These crimes include attacks or attempted attacks generally involving unwanted sexual contact between the victim and offender. Sexual assault may or may not involve force and includes such things as grabbing or fondling. Sexual assault also includes verbal threats.

**Simple assault** Attack without a weapon resulting either in no injury, minor injury, or an undetermined injury requiring less than 2 days of hospitalization. Also includes attempted assault without a weapon.

**Theft** Completed or attempted theft of property or cash without personal contact. Indicators of School Crime and Safety: 2015.

**Victimization** A crime as it affects one individual person or household. For personal crimes, the number of victimizations is equal to the number of victims involved. The number of victimizations may be greater than the number of incidents because more than one person may be victimized during an incident.

**Victimization rate** A measure of the occurrence of victimizations among a specific population group. For personal crimes, the number of victimizations is equal to the number of victims involved. Each victimization that is reported by the respondents is counted, so there may be one incident with two victims, which would be counted as two victimizations. The number of victimizations may be greater than the number of incidents because more than one person may be victimized during an incident.

**Violent victimization** Includes serious violent victimization, rape, sexual assault, robbery, aggravated assault, or simple assault.

## School Crime Supplement (SCS)

**At school** In the school building, on school property, on a school bus, or going to or from school.

**Bullied** Students were asked if any student had bullied them at school in one or more ways during the school year. Specifically, students were asked if another student had made fun of them, called them names, or insulted them; spread rumors about them; threatened them with harm; pushed, shoved, tripped, or spit on them; tried to make them to do something they did not want to do; excluded them from activities on purpose; or destroyed their property on purpose.

**Gang** Street gangs, fighting gangs, crews, or something else. Gangs may use common names, signs, symbols, or colors. All gangs, whether or not they are involved in violent or illegal activity, are included.

**Hate-related graffiti** Hate-related words or symbols written in school classrooms, school bathrooms, school hallways, or on the outside of the school building.

**Hate-related words** Students were asked if anyone called them an insulting or bad name at school having to do with their race, religion, ethnic background or national origin, disability, gender, or sexual orientation.

**Serious violent victimization** Rape, sexual assault, robbery, or aggravated assault.

**Total victimization** Combination of violent victimization and theft. If a student reported an incident of either type, he or she is counted as having experienced any victimization. If the student reported having experienced both, he or she is counted once under "total victimization."

**Violent victimization** Includes serious violent victimization, rape, sexual assault, robbery, aggravated assault, or simple assault.

## Youth Risk Behavior Survey (YRBS)

**On school property** On school property is included in the question wording, but was not defined for respondents.

**Rural school** A school located outside a Metropolitan Statistical Area (MSA).

**Suburban school** A school located inside an MSA, but outside the "central city."

**Urban school** A school located inside an MSA and inside the "central city."

**Weapon** Examples of weapons appearing in the questionnaire include guns, knives, and clubs.

## School Survey on Crime and Safety (SSOCS)

**Gang** An ongoing loosely organized association of three or more persons, whether formal or informal, that has a common name, signs, symbols, or colors, whose members engage, either individually or collectively, in violent or other forms of illegal behavior.

**Hate crime** A criminal offense or threat against a person, property, or society that is motivated, in whole or in part, by the offender's bias against a race, color, national origin, ethnicity, gender, religion, disability, or sexual orientation.

**Intimidation** To frighten, compel, or deter by actual or implied threats. It includes bullying and sexual harassment.

(Intimidation was not defined in the front of the questionnaire in 2005–06.)

**Physical attack or fight** An actual and intentional touching or striking of another person against his or her will, or the intentional causing of bodily harm to an individual.

**Rape** Forced sexual intercourse (vaginal, anal, or oral penetration). Includes penetration from a foreign object.

**Robbery** The taking or attempting to take anything of value that is owned by another person or organization, under confrontational circumstances by force or threat of force or violence and/or by putting the victim in fear. A key difference between robbery and theft/larceny is that a threat or battery is involved in robbery.

**Serious violent incidents** Include rape, sexual battery other than rape, physical attacks or fights with a weapon, threats of physical attack with a weapon, and robbery with or without a weapon.

**Sexual battery** An incident that includes threatened rape, fondling, indecent liberties, child molestation, or sodomy. Principals were instructed that classification of these incidents should take into consideration the age and developmentally appropriate behavior of the offenders.

**Sexual harassment** Unsolicited, offensive behavior that inappropriately asserts sexuality over another person. The behavior may be verbal or nonverbal.

**Theft/larceny** Taking things valued at over $10 without personal confrontation. Specifically, the unlawful taking of another person's property without personal confrontation, threat, violence, or bodily harm. Included are pocket picking, stealing purse or backpack (if left unattended or no force was used to take it from owner), theft from a building, theft from a motor vehicle or motor vehicle parts or accessories, theft of bicycles, theft from vending machines, and all other types of thefts.

**Vandalism** The willful damage or destruction of school property, including bombing, arson, graffiti, and other acts that cause property damage. Includes damage caused by computer hacking.

**Violent incidents** Include rape, sexual battery other than rape, physical attacks or fights with or without a weapon, threats of physical attack with or without a weapon, and robbery with or without a weapon.

**Weapon** Any instrument or object used with the intent to threaten, injure, or kill. Includes look-alikes if they are used to threaten others.

# PART 8

# Jail Inmates in Midyear, 2015

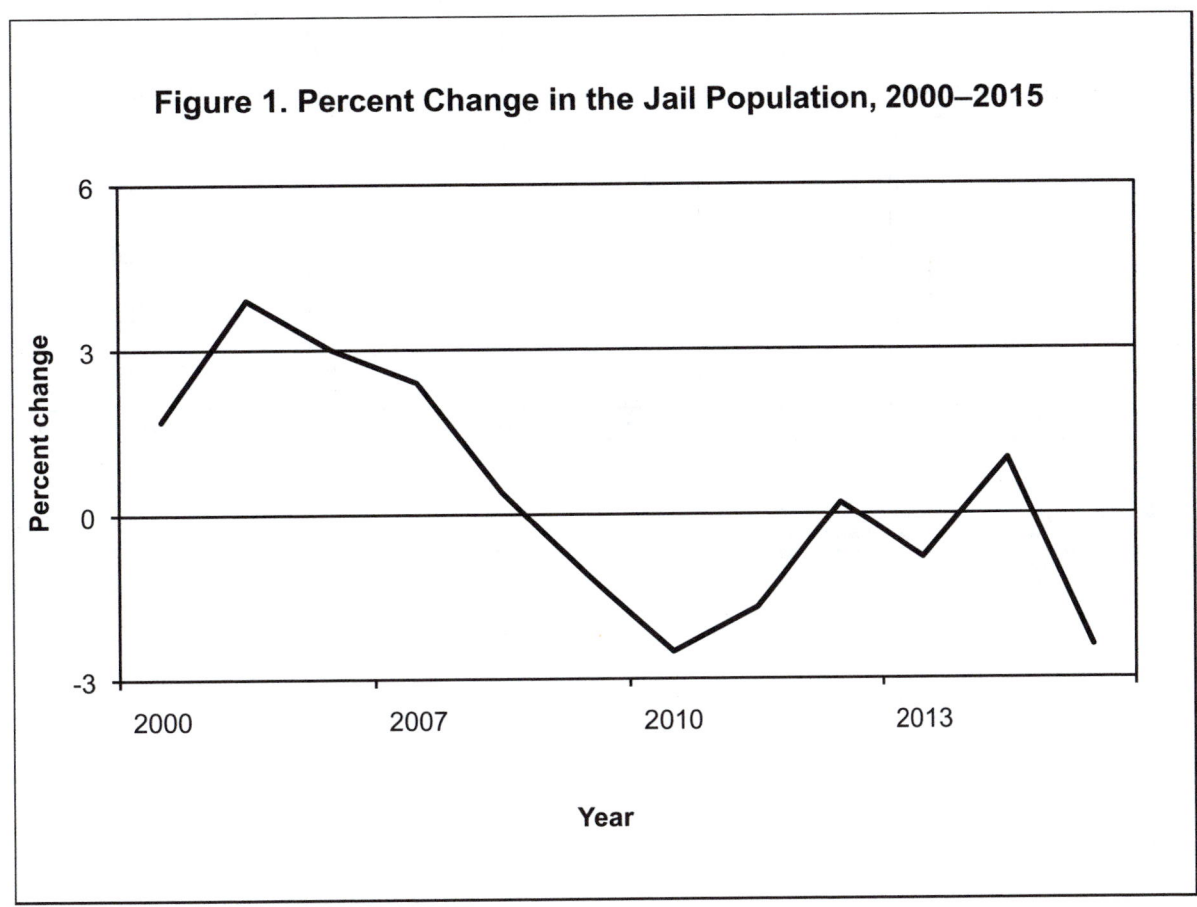

Figure 1. Percent Change in the Jail Population, 2000–2015

- The number of inmates confined in county and city jails was an estimated 721,300 at midyear 2015, lower than the peak of 776,600 inmates on an average day in 2008.

- At midyear 2015, the jail incarceration rate had decreased from a peak of 340 per 100,000 population in 2006 through 2008 to about 300 per 100,000 population, representing a steady total from 2013 onward.

- Approximately 10.9 million admissions to jail occurred in 2015, continuing the trend of steady decline that has been experienced since 2008.

- Fewer than 4,000 juveniles age 17 years or younger were held in local jails at midyear 2015; this was significantly below the peak of about 7,600 in 2000 and 2010.

## Table 1. Inmates Confined in Local Jails at Midyear, Average Daily Population and Incarceration Rates, 2000 and 2005–2015

(Number; percent.)

| Year | Inmates confined at midyear[1] | | Average daily population[2] | | Jail incarceration rate[3] | |
|---|---|---|---|---|---|---|
| | Total (number) | Year-to-year percent change (percent) | Total | Year-to-year percent change (percent) | Adults and juveniles | Adults only |
| 2000................................. | 621,100 | 2.5 | 618,300 | 1.7 | 220 | 290 |
| 2005................................. | 747,500 | 4.7 | 733,400 | 3.9 | 250 | 330 |
| 2006................................. | 765,800 | 2.4 | 755,300 | 3.0 | 260 | 340 |
| 2007................................. | 780,200 | 1.9 | 773,100 | 2.4 | 260 | 340 |
| 2008................................. | 785,500 | 0.7 | 776,600 | 0.4 | 260 | 340 |
| 2009................................. | 767,400 | -2.3 | 768,100 | -1.1 | 250 | 330 |
| 2010................................. | 748,700 | -2.4 | 748,600 | -2.5 | 240 | 320 |
| 2011................................. | 735,600 | -1.8 | 735,600 | -1.7 | 240 | 310 |
| 2012................................. | 744,500 | 1.2 | 737,400 | 0.2 | 240 | 310 |
| 2013................................. | 731,200 | -1.8 | 731,400 | -0.8 | 230 | 300 |
| 2014................................. | 744,600 | 1.8 | 739,000 | 1.0 | 230 | 300 |
| 2015*................................. | 728,200 | -2.2 | NC | NC | 230 | Ö |
| 2015 [4]................................. | 693,300^ | ^ | 721,300 | -2.4 | ^ | ^ |

*Note:* Data are adjusted for nonresponse and rounded to the nearest 100 for confined inmates and average daily population. Starting in 2015, the Annual Survey Jails collects data on the number of inmates confined on the last weekday in June (midyear) and on December 31 (yearend). Italics indicate that the difference with comparison year (total) or the year-to-year change (percent) is significant at the 95% confidence level.
^ = Not compared because the jail population goes through seasonal variation, typically with fewer inmates at yearend than at midyear.
* = Comparison year on confined inmates and average daily population.
NC = Not calculated.
Ö = Not collected.
[1] Unless noted for a specific year, data are based on the number of inmates confined on the last weekday in June.
[2] Sum of all inmates in jail each day for a year, divided by the number of days in the year.
[3] Number of confined inmates per 100,000 U.S. residents. Adults are defined as persons age 18 or older, and juveniles are defined as persons age 17 or younger.
[4] Data are based on the number of inmates confined on December 31, 2015.

## Table 2. Number of Confined Inmates in Local Jails, by Characteristics, Midyear 2000, 2005, and 2013–2014 and Yearend 2015

(Number.)

| Characteristic | Midyear | | | | | | | Yearend |
|---|---|---|---|---|---|---|---|---|
| | 2000 | 2005 | 2010 | 2011 | 2012 | 2013 | 2014* | 2015 |
| **Total** | 621,100 | 747,500 | 748,700 | 735,600 | 744,500 | 731,200 | 744,600 | 693,300 ^ |
| **Sex** | | | | | | | | |
| Male | 550,200 | 653,000 | 656,400 | 642,300 | 645,900 | 628,900 | 635,500 | 594,200 ^ |
| Female | 71,000 | 94,600 | 92,400 | 93,300 | 98,600 | 102,400 | 109,100 | 99,100 ^ |
| **Adult** | 613,500 | 740,800 | 741,200 | 729,700 | 739,100 | 726,600 | 740,400 | 689,900 ^ |
| Male | 543,100 | 646,800 | 649,300 | 636,900 | 640,900 | 624,700 | 631,600 | 591,100 ^ |
| Female | 70,400 | 94,000 | 91,900 | 92,800 | 98,100 | 101,900 | 108,800 | 98,800 ^ |
| **Juvenile[1]** | 7,600 | 6,800 | 7,600 | 5,900 | 5,400 | 4,600 | 4,200 | 3,500 ^ |
| Held as adult[2] | 6,100 | 5,800 | 5,600 | 4,600 | 4,600 | 3,500 | 3,700 | 3,200 ^ |
| Held as juvenile | 1,500 | 1,000 | 1,900 | 1,400 | 900 | 1,100 | 500 | 300 ^ |
| **Race/Hispanic Origin** | | | | | | | | |
| White[3] | 260,500 | 331,000 | 331,600 | 329,400 | 341,100 | 344,900 | 352,800 | 335,100 ^ |
| Black/African American[3] | 256,300 | 290,500 | 283,200 | 276,400 | 274,600 | 261,500 | 263,800 | 243,400 ^ |
| Hispanic/Latino | 94,100 | 111,900 | 118,100 | 113,900 | 112,700 | 107,900 | 110,600 | 99,000 ^ |
| American Indian/Alaska Native[3] | 5,500 | 7,600 | 9,900 | 9,400 | 9,300 | 10,200 | 10,400 | 8,600 ^ |
| Asian/Native Hawaiian/ Other Pacific Islander[3] | 4,700 | 5,400 | 5,100 | 5,300 | 5,400 | 5,100 | 6,000 | 5,800 ^ |
| Two or more races[3] | Ö | 1,000 | 800 | 1,200 | 1,500 | 1,600 | 1,000 | 1,500 ^ |
| **Conviction Status[4,5]** | | | | | | | | |
| Convicted | 271,300 | 284,400 | 291,300 | 289,600 | 293,100 | 278,000 | 277,100 | 258,800 ^ |
| Unconvicted | 349,800 | 463,200 | 457,400 | 446,000 | 451,400 | 453,200 | 467,500 | 434,600 ^ |

*Note:* Detail may not sum to total because of rounding. Data are adjusted for nonresponse and rounded to the nearest 100. Midyear estimates are based on the number of inmates confined on the last weekday in June, and yearend estimates are based on the number of inmates confined on December 31. In 2015, the ASJ collected characteristic data at yearend. Italics indicate that the difference with comparison year is significant at the 95% confidence level.
^ = Not compared because the jail population goes through seasonal variation, typically with fewer inmates at yearend than at midyear.
* = Comparison year for each characteristic.
Ö = Not collected.
[1] Persons age 17 or younger.
[2] Includes juveniles who were tried or awaiting trial as adults.
[3] Excludes persons of Hispanic or Latino origin, unless specified.
[4] Reports prior to 2014 combined American Indians and Alaska Natives and Asians, Native Hawaiians, and Other Pacific Islanders into an other race category.
[5] Includes juveniles who were tried or awaiting trial as adults.

## Table 3. Percent of Confined Inmates in Local Jails, by Characteristics, Midyear 2000, 2005, 2010–2014, and Yearend 2015

(Percent.)

| Characteristic | Midyear | | | | | | | Yearend |
|---|---|---|---|---|---|---|---|---|
| | 2000 | 2005 | 2010 | 2011 | 2012 | 2013 | 2014* | 2015 |
| **Sex** | | | | | | | | |
| Male.................... | 88.6 | 87.3 | 87.7 | 87.3 | 86.8 | 86 | 85.3 | 85.7 ^ |
| Female.................. | 11.4 | 12.7 | 12.3 | 12.7 | 13.2 | 14 | 14.7 | 14.3 ^ |
| **Adult**.................. | 98.8 | 99.1 | 99 | 99.2 | 99.3 | 99.4 | 99.4 | 99.5 ^ |
| Male.................... | 87.4 | 86.5 | 86.7 | 86.6 | 86.1 | 85.4 | 84.8 | 85.2 ^ |
| Female.................. | 11.3 | 12.6 | 12.3 | 12.6 | 13.2 | 13.9 | 14.6 | 14.3 ^ |
| **Juvenile**[1].............. | 1.2 | 0.9 | 1 | 0.8 | 0.7 | 0.6 | 0.6 | 0.5 ^ |
| Held as adult[2]......... | 1 | 0.8 | 0.8 | 0.6 | 0.6 | 0.5 | 0.5 | 0.5 ^ |
| Held as juvenile......... | 0.2 | 0.1 | 0.3 | 0.2 | 0.1 | 0.1 | 0.1 | ... |
| **Race/Hispanic Origin** | | | | | | | | |
| White[3]................. | 41.9 | 44.3 | 44.3 | 44.8 | 45.8 | 47.2 | 47.4 | 48.3 ^ |
| Black/African American[3]..... | 41.3 | 38.9 | 37.8 | 37.6 | 36.9 | 35.8 | 35.4 | 35.1 ^ |
| Hispanic/Latino.......... | 15.2 | 15 | 15.8 | 15.5 | 15.1 | 14.8 | 14.9 | 14.3 ^ |
| American Indian/Alaska Native[3,4]...... | 0.9 | 1 | 1.3 | 1.3 | 1.2 | 1.4 | 1.4 | 1.2 ^ |
| Asian/Native Hawaiian/Other Pacific Islander[3,4] .... | 0.8 | 0.7 | 0.7 | 0.7 | 0.7 | 0.7 | 0.8 | 0.8 ^ |
| Two or more races[3,4]......... | ... | 0.1 | 0.1 | 0.2 | 0.2 | 0.2 | 0.1 | 0.2 ^ |
| **Conviction Status**[5] | | | | | | | | |
| Convicted............... | 44 | 38 | 38.9 | 39.4 | 39.4 | 38 | 37.2 | 37.3 ^ |
| Unconvicted............. | 56 | 62 | 61.1 | 60.6 | 60.6 | 62 | 62.8 | 62.7 ^ |

*Note:* Percentages are based on the total number of confined inmates in table 3. Detail may not sum to total due to rounding. Midyear estimates are based on the number of inmates confined on the last weekday in June, and yearend estimates are based on the number of inmates confined on December 31. In 2015, the ASJ collected characteristic data at yearend. Italics indicate that the difference with comparison year is significant at the 95% confidence level.
... = Less than 0.05 percent.
Ö = Not collected.
^ = Not compared because the jail population goes through seasonal change, typically with fewer inmates at yearend than at midyear.
[1] Persons age 17 or younger at midyear.
[2] Includes juveniles who were tried or awaiting trial as adults.
[3] Excludes persons of Hispanic or Latino origin, unless specified.
[4] Reports prior to 2014 combined American Indians and Alaska Natives and Asians, Native Hawaiians, and Other Pacific Islanders into an other race category.
[5] Includes juveniles who were tried or awaiting trial as adults.

# Table 4. Rated Capacity of Local Jails and Percent of Capacity Occupied, 2000 and 2005–2015

(Number; percent.)

| Year[1] | Rated capacity[2] | Year-to-year change in rated capacity[2] | Percent of capacity occupied based on:[3] | |
|---|---|---|---|---|
| | | | Confined one-day population[4] | Average daily population[5] |
| 2000............................................. | 677,800 | 3.9 | 92 | 91.2 |
| 2005............................................. | 787,000 | 4.1 | 95 | 93.2 |
| 2006............................................. | 795,000 | 1 | 96.3 | 95 |
| 2007............................................. | 810,500 | 2 | 96.3 | 95.4 |
| 2008............................................. | 828,700 | 2.2 | 94.8 | 93.7 |
| 2009............................................. | 849,900 | 2.6 | 90.3 | 90.4 |
| 2010............................................. | 857,900 | 0.9 | 87.3 | 87.3 |
| 2011............................................. | 870,400 | 1.5 | 84.5 | 84.5 |
| 2012............................................. | 877,400 | 0.8 | 84.9 | 84 |
| 2013............................................. | 872,900 | -0.5 | 83.8 | 83.8 |
| 2014*............................................ | 890,500 | 2 | 83.6 | 83 |
| 2015 [6]........................................ | 904,900 | 1.6 | 76.6 ^ | 79.7 |
| Average annual change 2000–2015........................................... | | 1.9 | | |

*Note:* Data are adjusted for nonresponse and rounded to the nearest 100. Italics indicate that the difference with comparison year is significant at the 95% confidence level.
^ = Not compared because the jail population goes through seasonal variation, typically with fewer inmates at yearend than at midyear.
*Comparison year on rated capacity and percent of capacity occupied.
[1] Data are based on the number of inmates confined on the last weekday in June, except for 2015, which was based on December 31, 2015.
[2] Maximum number of beds or inmates assigned by a rating official to a facility, excluding separate temporary holding areas.
[3] Based on the inmate population divided by the rated capacity.
[4] Data are based on the number of inmates confined on the last weekday in June, except for 2015, which was based on December 31, 2015.
[5] Sum of all inmates in jail each day for a year, divided by the number of days in the year.
[6] Data are based on the rated capacity for December 31, 2015.

## Table 5. Percent of Jail Capacity Occupied Based on Average Daily Population, by Size of Jurisdiction, 2014–2015

(Percent.)

| Jurisdiction size | Percent of capacity occupied | | Percent of jail jurisdictions operating over 100% of capacity | |
|---|---|---|---|---|
| | 2014 | 2015* | 2014 | 2015* |
| Total ................................................................................ | *83.0* | 79.7 | 12.8 | 12.0 |
| 49 or fewer........................................................................ | 57.3 | 55.3 | 3.8 | 4.1 |
| 50 to 99 ............................................................................. | 68.0 | 71.0 | 11.7 | 12.3 |
| 100 to 249 .......................................................................... | *78.7* | 83.7 | 20.2 | 18.9 |
| 250 to 499 .......................................................................... | 83.3 | 80.0 | 21.0 | 17.9 |
| 500 to 999 .......................................................................... | *84.1* | 79.2 | 19.6 | 17.6 |
| 1,000 to 2,499 .................................................................... | *88.8* | 85.8 | *28.9* | 24.1 |
| 2,500 or more ..................................................................... | *87.0* | 79.5 | *22.9* | 17.4 |

Note: The average daily population (ADP) is divided by the rated capacity. For 2014, the jurisdiction size was based on the ADP during the 12-month period ending June 30, 2014. For yearend 2015, the jurisdiction size is based on the ADP during the 12-month period ending December 31, 2015. *Italics* indicate difference with comparison year is significant at the 95% confidence level.
* = Comparison year for jurisdiction size.

## Table 6. Mean and Proportion of the Average Daily Jail Population, by Size of Jurisdiction, 2014–2015

(Number; percent.)

| Jurisdiction size[1] | Mean ADP[2] | | Percent change in ADP | |
|---|---|---|---|---|
| | 2014 | 2015* | 2014 | 2015* |
| Total ................................................................................ | *269* | 253 | 100.0 | 100.0 |
| 49 or fewer........................................................................ | 20 | 22 | 2.8 | 3.4 |
| 50 to 99 ............................................................................. | 72 | 72 | 4.9 | 4.9 |
| 100 to 249 .......................................................................... | 162 | 162 | *11.6* | 14.1 |
| 250 to 499 .......................................................................... | 346 | 354 | 14.6 | 14.5 |
| 500 to 999 .......................................................................... | 702 | 695 | 18.2 | 18.2 |
| 1,000 to 2,499 .................................................................... | 1,444 | 1,423 | 23.1 | 24.1 |
| 2,500 and over ................................................................... | 5,109 | 4,942 | *24.8* | 20.8 |

Note: Detail may not sum to total because of rounding. Italics indicate that the difference with comparison year is significant at the 95% confidence level.
* = Comparison year for jurisdiction size.
[1] Sum of all inmates in jail each day for a year, divided by the number of days in the year.
[2] For 2014, the jurisdiction size was based on the ADP during the 12-month period ending June 30, 2014. For 2015, the jurisdiction size was based on the ADP during the 12-month period ending December 31, 2015.

## Table 7. Average Daily Jail Population, Admissions, and Turnover Rate, by Size of Jurisdiction, 2014–2015

(Number; rate.[1])

| Jurisdiction size[2] | ADP[3] | | Estimated number of admissions during last week of June | | Weekly turnover rate[1] | |
|---|---|---|---|---|---|---|
| | 2014 | 2015* | 2014 [4] | 2015*[5] | 2014 | 2015* |
| Total ............................. | 739,000 | 721,300 | 11,400,000 | 10,900,000 | 58.1 | 57.0 |
| 49 or fewer.................................. | 20,600 | 24,300 | 653,800 | 902,000 | 119.0 | 139.6 |
| 50 to 99 ..................................... | 36,500 | 35,000 | 899,800 | 694,200 | 88.0 | 73.9 |
| 100 to 249 .................................. | 85,400 | 101,100 | 1,588,600 | 1,820,300 | 69.9 | 67.4 |
| 250 to 499 .................................. | 107,700 | 105,000 | 1,864,100 | 1,716,600 | 65.0 | 62.2 |
| 500 to 999 .................................. | 134,500 | 131,600 | 1,940,100 | 1,857,600 | 54.5 | 53.6 |
| 1,000 to 2,499 ............................ | 170,900 | 173,900 | 2,327,800 | 2,200,800 | 52.5 | 48.6 |
| 2,500 and over ............................ | 183,400 | 150,100 | 2,141,200 | 1,661,700 | 43.7 | 41.8 |

*Note:* Detail may not sum to total because of rounding. All comparisons by average daily population are not significant at the 95%-confidence level; however, italics indicate that difference with comparison year is significant at the 95% confidence level.
*Comparison year on admissions and weekly turnover rate.
[1] Calculated by adding weekly admissions and releases, dividing by the average daily population (ADP). To calculate weekly admissions for 2015, the annual number of admissions was divided by the number of weeks in 2015.
[2] For 2014, the jurisdiction size was based on the ADP during the 12-month period ending June 30, 2014. For 2015, the jurisdiction size is based on the ADP during the 12-month period ending December 31, 2015, the first year in the current ASJ sample.
[3] Sum of all inmates in jail each day for a year, divided by the number of days in the year.
[4] The 2014 ASJ collected data on weekly admissions during the last week in June. The number of annual admissions was calculated by multiplying the weekly admissions by 365 days and dividing by 7 days.
[5] Starting in 2015, the ASJ collects annual admissions.


## Table 8. Number of Annual Admissions to Local Jails, 1999 and 2007–2015

(Number; percent.)

| Year | Estimated total number of annual admissions[1] | Year-to-year percent change |
|---|---|---|
| 1999.................................................................... | 11,400,000 | Ö |
| 2007.................................................................... | 13,100,000 | Ö |
| 2008.................................................................... | 13,600,000 | 3.8 |
| 2009.................................................................... | 12,800,000 | -5.9 |
| 2010.................................................................... | 12,900,000 | 0.8 |
| 2011.................................................................... | 11,800,000 | -8.5 |
| 2012.................................................................... | 11,600,000 | -1.7 |
| 2013.................................................................... | 11,700,000 | 0.9 |
| 2014.................................................................... | 11,400,000 | -2.6 |
| 2015*.................................................................. | 10,900,000 | -4.4 |
| Average annual change | | |
| 1999–2014............................................................ | 0.0 | |
| 2014–2015............................................................ | -4.4 | |

*Note:* Data are adjusted for nonresponse and rounded to the nearest 100,000. Italics indicate that the difference with comparison year or the year-to-year percent change is significant at the 95% confidence level.
* = Comparison year on annual admissions.
Ö = Not collected.
[1] In 2015, the ASJ collected annual admissions. The 1999 Census of Jails and the 2007ñ2014 ASJ collected data on weekly admissions during the last week in June. The number of annual admissions was calculated by multiplying the weekly admissions by 365 days and dividing by 7 days.

## Table 9. Persons Under Jail Supervision, by Confinement Status, 2000 and 2006–2015

(Number.)

| Year | Total | Held in jail[1] | Supervised outside of a jail facility[2] |
|---|---|---|---|
| 2000................................................... | 687,000 | 621,100 | 65,900 |
| 2006................................................... | 826,000 | 765,800 | 60,200 |
| 2007................................................... | 848,400 | 780,200 | 68,200 |
| 2008................................................... | 858,400 | 785,500 | 72,900 |
| 2009................................................... | 837,600 | 767,400 | 70,200 |
| 2010................................................... | 809,400 | 748,700 | 60,600 |
| 2011................................................... | 798,400 | 735,600 | 62,800 |
| 2012................................................... | 808,600 | 744,500 | 64,100 |
| 2013................................................... | 790,600 | 731,200 | 59,400 |
| 2014*................................................. | 808,100 | 744,600 | 63,500 |
| 2015................................................... | 750,500 ^ | 693,300 ^ | 57,100 ^ |

Note: Data are adjusted for nonresponse and rounded to the nearest 100. Detail may not sum to total due to rounding. Italics indicate difference with comparison year is significant at the 95% confidence level.
* = Comparison year on confined inmates and inmates supervised outside of jail.
^ = Not compared because the jail population goes through seasonal change, typically with fewer inmates at yearend than at midyear.
[1] Unless noted for a specific year, data are based on the number of inmates confined on the last weekday in June.
[2] Unless noted for a specific year, the number of persons under jail supervision but not confined is based on the last weekday in June. Excludes persons supervised by a probation or parole agency. Includes offenders that served their sentences of confinement on weekends only (i.e., Friday to Sunday), persons under electronic monitoring, persons in work release programs, work gangs, and other alternative work programs, and persons in drug, alcohol, mental health, and other medical treatment.

## Table 10. Staff Employed in Local Jails, by Sex, December 2013 and 2015

(Number; percent.)

| Job function | Number | | Percent | |
|---|---|---|---|---|
| | 2013 | 2015* | 2013 | 2015 |
| **Job Function** ..................................... | | | | |
| Total ..................................................... | 220,000 | 213,300 | 100.0 | 100.0 |
| **Correctional Officers**[1]....................... | 173,900 | 169,200 | 79.0 | 79.3 |
| Male.......................................... | 123,400 | 117,300 | 56.1 | 55.0 |
| Female...................................... | 50,500 | 52,000 | 23.0 | 24.4 |
| **All Other Staff**[2].................................. | 46,100 | 44,000 | 21.0 | 20.6 |
| Male.......................................... | 20,800 | 20,000 | 9.5 | 9.4 |
| Female...................................... | 25,200 | 24,000 | 11.5 | 11.3 |
| **Inmate to Correctional Officer Ratio**[3]..................................... | 4.2 | 4.1 | | |

NOTE: Data are adjusted for nonresponse and rounded to the nearest 100. Detail may not sum to total due to rounding. Italics indicate that the difference with comparison year is significant at the 95% confidence level.
* = Comparison year on staff.
[1] Includes deputies, monitors, and other custody staff who spend more than 50% of their time with the incarcerated population.
[2] Includes administrators, clerical and maintenance staff, educational staff, professional and technical staff, and other unspecified staff who spend more than 50% of their time in the facility.
[3] Number of confined inmates per correctional officer.

# METHODOLOGY

## About the Report

This report presents information on the change in the number of jail inmates between 2000 and 2015 by sex, race, Hispanic origin, and conviction status. This report also provides estimates of year-to-year changes from 2000 to 2015 in the average daily population, rated capacity of local jails, and percent of capacity occupied. It also includes statistics, by jurisdiction size, on changes in the number of inmates, number of admissions, and weekly turnover rate between 2014 and 2015. Estimates and standard errors were based on BJS's *Annual Survey of Jails*.

One change for the 2015 data is the use of yearend, rather than midyear, data. This distinction has been pointed out in the relevant tables.

BJS periodically conducts census data collections from all local jails in the United States. In years between census collections, BJS conducts the Annual Survey of Jails (ASJ). The survey collects data annually from a sample of local jails and uses the data to estimate the number and characteristics of inmates in local jails nationwide.

The Bureau of Justice Statistics drew a sample of local jail jurisdictions for the 2015 Annual Survey of Jails, based on information from the 2013 Census of Jails. Local jail jurisdictions include counties (parishes in Louisiana) or municipal governments that administered one or more local jails. All jail jurisdictions were grouped into 10 strata based on their average daily population and presence of juveniles in 2013. In 8 of the 10 strata, a random sample of jail jurisdictions was selected. The remaining two strata were certainty strata, where all jurisdictions were selected with probability 1. One stratum consisted of all jails that were operated jointly by two or more jurisdictions (referred to as multijurisdictional jails). The other stratum consisted of all jail jurisdictions that:

- held juvenile inmates at the time of the 2013 Census of Jails and had an average daily population of 500 or more inmates during the 12 months ending December 31, 2013
- held only adult inmates and had an average daily population of 750 or more
- were located in California.

The ASJ sample includes all California jail jurisdictions. This sampling feature was introduced in 2013 in response to the enactment of California AB 109 and AB 117, aimed to reduce the number of inmates housed in state prisons starting on October 1, 2011. After the enactment of these two laws, the jail population in California experienced an unusual increase, which was atypical of the rest of the United States. For this reason, the ASJ sampling design was modified to include all California jail jurisdictions in a certainty (self-representing) stratum (see Methodology in *Jail Inmates at Midyear 2014* (NCJ 248629, BJS web, June 2015). The inclusion of all California jail jurisdictions resulted in an additional 21 jurisdictions.

For more information, please see http://www.bjs.gov/index.cfm?ty=pbdetail&iid=5872.

## Terms and Definitions

**Admissions:** Persons who are officially booked and housed in jails by formal legal document and the authority of the courts or some other official agency. Jail admissions include persons sentenced to weekend programs and those who are booked into the facility for the first time. Excluded from jail admissions are inmates re-entering the facility after an escape, work release, medical appointment or treatment facility appointment, and bail and court appearances. BJS collects jail admissions for the last 7 days in June.

**Average daily population (ADP):** The average is derived by the sum of inmates in jail each day for a year, divided by the number of days in the year.

**Average annual change:** The mean average change across a 12-month time period.

**Calculating annual admissions:** Annual jail admissions are calculated by multiplying weekly admissions by the sum of 365 days divided by 7 days.

**Calculating weekly jail turnover rate:** This rate is calculated by adding admissions and releases and dividing by the average daily population.

**Inmates confined:** The number of inmates held in custody.

**Jail incarceration rate:** The number of inmates held in the custody of local jails, per 100,000 U.S. residents.

**Percent of capacity occupied:** This percentage is calculated by taking the number of inmates, dividing by the rated capacity, and multiplying by 100.

**Rated capacity:** The number of beds or inmates assigned by a rating official to a facility, excluding separate temporary holding areas.

**Releases:** Persons released after a period of confinement (e.g., sentence completion, bail or bond releases, other pretrial releases, transfers to other jurisdictions, and deaths). Releases include those persons who have completed their weekend program and who are leaving the facility for the last time. Excluded from jail releases are temporary discharges including work release, medical appointment or treatment center, court appearance, furlough, day reporting, and transfers to other facilities within the jail's jurisdiction.

**Standard errors and tests of significance:** As with any survey, the ASJ estimates are subject to error arising from sampling rather than using a complete enumeration of the jail population. A common way to express this sampling variability is to construct a 95% confidence interval around each survey estimate. Typically, multiplying the standard error by 1.96 and then adding or subtracting the result from the estimate produces the confidence interval. This interval expresses the range of values that could result among 95% of the different samples that could be drawn.

**Under jail supervision but not confined:** This classification includes all persons in community-based programs operated by a jail facility. These programs include electronic monitoring, house arrest, community service, day reporting, and work programs. The classification excludes persons on pretrial release and who are not in a community-based program run by the jail, as well as persons under supervision of probation, parole, or other agencies; inmates on weekend programs; and inmates who participate in work release programs and return to the jail at night.

**Weekend programs:** Offenders in these programs are allowed to serve their sentences of confinement only on weekends (i.e., Friday to Sunday).

# PART 9

# Law Enforcement Officers Killed and Assaulted, 2015

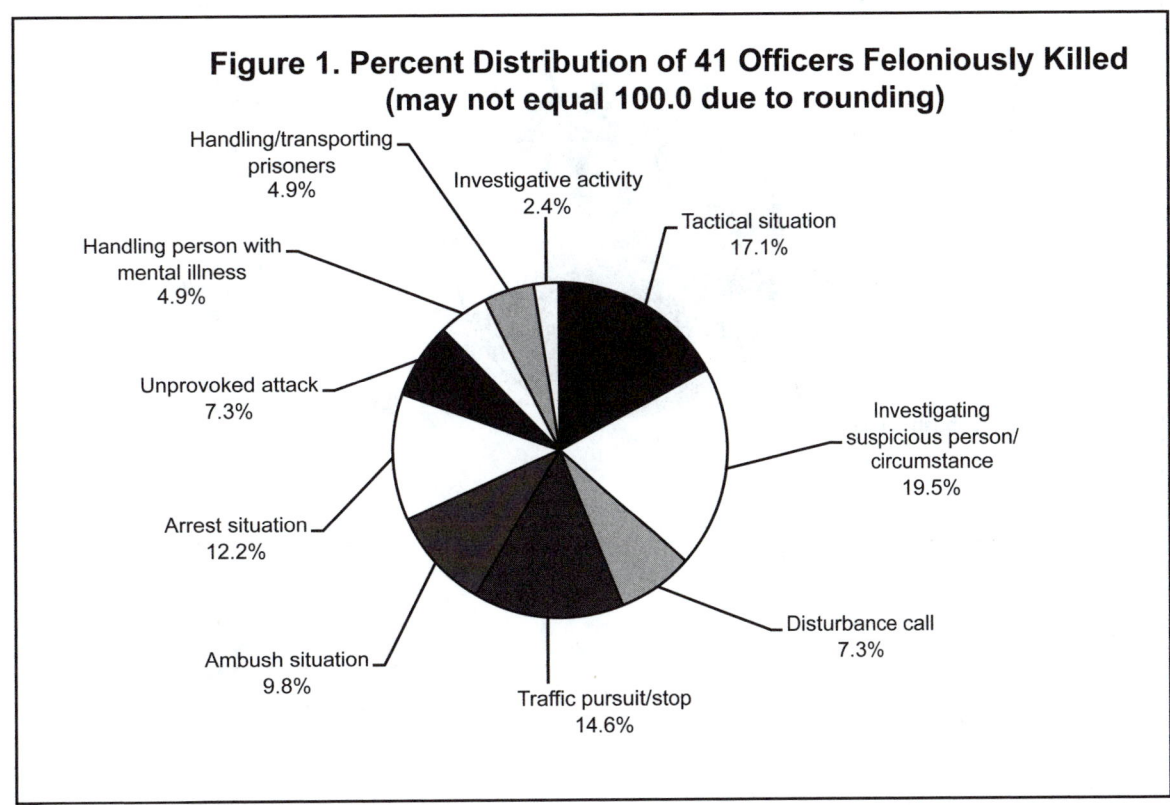

**Figure 1. Percent Distribution of 41 Officers Feloniously Killed (may not equal 100.0 due to rounding)**

- Handling/transporting prisoners 4.9%
- Investigative activity 2.4%
- Tactical situation 17.1%
- Handling person with mental illness 4.9%
- Unprovoked attack 7.3%
- Investigating suspicious person/circumstance 19.5%
- Arrest situation 12.2%
- Disturbance call 7.3%
- Ambush situation 9.8%
- Traffic pursuit/stop 14.6%

- In 2015, 41 law enforcement officers died from injuries incurred in the line of duty during felonious incidents. Of the officers feloniously killed, 24 were employed by city police departments, including 10 who were members of law enforcement agencies in cities with 250,000 or more inhabitants.

- Line-of-duty deaths in 2015 occurred in 21 states and Puerto Rico. By region, 19 officers were feloniously killed in the South, 9 officers in the West, 5 officers in the Midwest, 4 officers in the Northeast, and 4 officers in Puerto Rico.

- The average age of the officers who died in 2015 was 40 years old. The slain officers' average length of law enforcement service was 12 years. Of these officers, 38 were male and 3 were female.

- In 2015, 45 law enforcement officers died as the result of accidents that occurred in the line of duty, unchanged from 2014. Accidental line-of-duty deaths of law enforcement officers occurred in 21 states.

- Law enforcement agencies (11,961 participated, representing 507,852 employed officers and 75.1 percent of the nation's population) reported that 50,212 officers were assaulted while performing their duties in 2015.

- The U.S. Department of Justice employed 4 of the federal officers killed between 2011 and 2015, including the only federal officer killed in 2015; the other 5 fatalities were employed with the U.S. Department of Homeland Security (3) and the U.S. Department of the Interior (2).

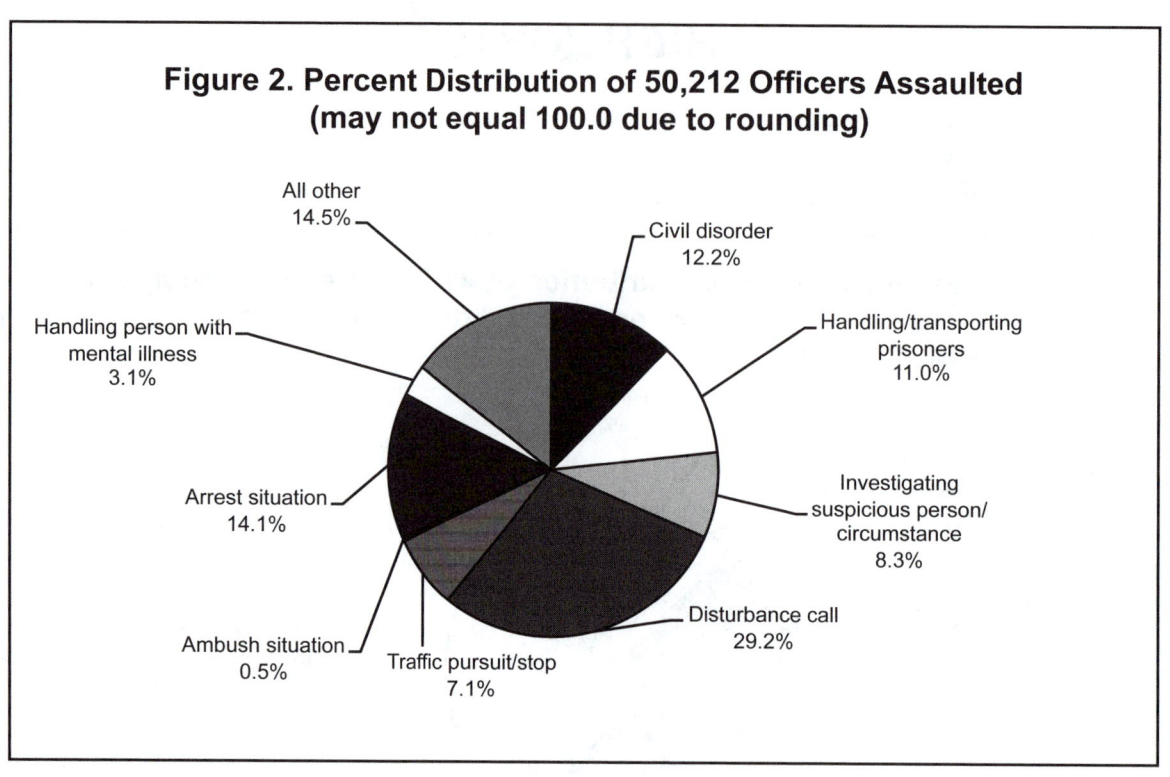

**Figure 2. Percent Distribution of 50,212 Officers Assaulted (may not equal 100.0 due to rounding)**

All other
14.5%

Civil disorder
12.2%

Handling/transporting
prisoners
11.0%

Handling person with
mental illness
3.1%

Investigating
suspicious person/
circumstance
8.3%

Arrest situation
14.1%

Disturbance call
29.2%

Ambush situation
0.5%

Traffic pursuit/stop
7.1%

# Table 1. Law Enforcement Officers Feloniously Killed, by Region, Geographic Division, and State/Territory, 2006–2015

(Number.)

| Area | Total | 2006 | 2007 | 2008 | 2009 | 2010 | 2011 | 2012 | 2013 | 2014 | 2015 |
|---|---|---|---|---|---|---|---|---|---|---|---|
| **Number of Victim Officers** | 491 | 48 | 58 | 41 | 48 | 56 | 72 | 49 | 27 | 51 | 41 |
| Northeast | 57 | 7 | 7 | 3 | 7 | 3 | 10 | 6 | 2 | 8 | 4 |
| New England | 8 | 1 | 2 | 0 | 0 | 1 | 0 | 2 | 1 | 1 | 0 |
| Connecticut | 0 | 0 | 0 | 0 | 0 | 0 | 0 | 0 | 0 | 0 | 0 |
| Maine | 0 | 0 | 0 | 0 | 0 | 0 | 0 | 0 | 0 | 0 | 0 |
| Massachusetts | 4 | 0 | 1 | 0 | 0 | 1 | 0 | 1 | 1 | 0 | 0 |
| New Hampshire | 4 | 1 | 1 | 0 | 0 | 0 | 0 | 1 | 0 | 1 | 0 |
| Rhode Island | 0 | 0 | 0 | 0 | 0 | 0 | 0 | 0 | 0 | 0 | 0 |
| Vermont | 0 | 0 | 0 | 0 | 0 | 0 | 0 | 0 | 0 | 0 | 0 |
| Middle Atlantic | 49 | 6 | 5 | 3 | 7 | 2 | 10 | 4 | 1 | 7 | 4 |
| New Jersey | 7 | 1 | 2 | 0 | 1 | 0 | 2 | 0 | 0 | 1 | 0 |
| New York | 19 | 3 | 2 | 0 | 0 | 0 | 4 | 2 | 1 | 5 | 2 |
| Pennsylvania | 23 | 2 | 1 | 3 | 6 | 2 | 4 | 2 | 0 | 1 | 2 |
| Midwest | 83 | 6 | 9 | 9 | 5 | 10 | 21 | 6 | 4 | 8 | 5 |
| East North Central | 54 | 5 | 8 | 6 | 2 | 8 | 12 | 2 | 3 | 5 | 3 |
| Illinois | 15 | 2 | 1 | 3 | 2 | 4 | 1 | 0 | 1 | 0 | 1 |
| Indiana | 10 | 1 | 3 | 0 | 0 | 0 | 2 | 0 | 1 | 3 | 0 |
| Michigan | 12 | 1 | 1 | 1 | 0 | 3 | 4 | 1 | 1 | 0 | 0 |
| Ohio | 13 | 1 | 2 | 2 | 0 | 1 | 4 | 1 | 0 | 1 | 1 |
| Wisconsin | 4 | 0 | 1 | 0 | 0 | 0 | 1 | 0 | 0 | 1 | 1 |
| West North Central | 29 | 1 | 1 | 3 | 3 | 2 | 9 | 4 | 1 | 3 | 2 |
| Iowa | 2 | 0 | 0 | 0 | 0 | 0 | 1 | 0 | 1 | 0 | 0 |
| Kansas | 6 | 1 | 0 | 0 | 1 | 0 | 1 | 2 | 0 | 1 | 0 |
| Minnesota | 7 | 0 | 0 | 0 | 1 | 2 | 1 | 1 | 0 | 1 | 1 |
| Missouri | 9 | 0 | 1 | 3 | 0 | 0 | 3 | 1 | 0 | 1 | 0 |
| Nebraska | 1 | 0 | 0 | 0 | 0 | 0 | 0 | 0 | 0 | 0 | 1 |
| North Dakota | 1 | 0 | 0 | 0 | 0 | 0 | 1 | 0 | 0 | 0 | 0 |
| South Dakota | 3 | 0 | 0 | 0 | 1 | 0 | 2 | 0 | 0 | 0 | 0 |
| South | 219 | 22 | 32 | 20 | 21 | 22 | 29 | 22 | 15 | 17 | 19 |
| South Atlantic | 102 | 11 | 14 | 13 | 7 | 11 | 18 | 10 | 5 | 10 | 3 |
| Delaware | 2 | 0 | 0 | 0 | 1 | 0 | 1 | 0 | 0 | 0 | 0 |
| District of Columbia | 1 | 1 | 0 | 0 | 0 | 0 | 0 | 0 | 0 | 0 | 0 |
| Florida | 34 | 3 | 6 | 3 | 3 | 4 | 6 | 2 | 2 | 4 | 1 |
| Georgia | 16 | 2 | 0 | 2 | 0 | 5 | 3 | 1 | 0 | 2 | 1 |
| Maryland | 5 | 0 | 2 | 1 | 0 | 1 | 0 | 0 | 1 | 0 | 0 |
| North Carolina | 16 | 0 | 3 | 2 | 3 | 1 | 2 | 3 | 0 | 2 | 0 |
| South Carolina | 10 | 0 | 3 | 2 | 0 | 0 | 2 | 1 | 0 | 1 | 1 |
| Virginia | 12 | 4 | 0 | 3 | 0 | 0 | 3 | 0 | 1 | 1 | 0 |
| West Virginia | 6 | 1 | 0 | 0 | 0 | 0 | 1 | 3 | 1 | 0 | 0 |
| East South Central | 37 | 4 | 3 | 2 | 5 | 4 | 6 | 5 | 3 | 0 | 5 |
| Alabama | 11 | 2 | 1 | 0 | 4 | 1 | 1 | 2 | 0 | 0 | 0 |
| Kentucky | 6 | 0 | 1 | 1 | 0 | 0 | 0 | 1 | 1 | 0 | 2 |
| Mississippi | 10 | 1 | 0 | 0 | 0 | 3 | 1 | 1 | 2 | 0 | 2 |
| Tennessee | 10 | 1 | 1 | 1 | 1 | 0 | 4 | 1 | 0 | 0 | 1 |
| West South Central | 80 | 7 | 15 | 5 | 9 | 7 | 5 | 7 | 7 | 7 | 11 |
| Arkansas | 8 | 1 | 1 | 0 | 1 | 2 | 1 | 0 | 0 | 1 | 1 |
| Louisiana | 22 | 2 | 5 | 2 | 0 | 3 | 0 | 2 | 1 | 1 | 6 |
| Oklahoma | 3 | 1 | 0 | 0 | 2 | 0 | 0 | 0 | 0 | 0 | 0 |
| Texas | 47 | 3 | 9 | 3 | 6 | 2 | 4 | 5 | 6 | 5 | 4 |
| West | 108 | 11 | 9 | 9 | 13 | 18 | 10 | 9 | 6 | 14 | 9 |
| Mountain | 48 | 4 | 4 | 2 | 2 | 11 | 5 | 5 | 1 | 7 | 7 |
| Arizona | 18 | 0 | 3 | 2 | 0 | 5 | 3 | 2 | 0 | 3 | 0 |
| Colorado | 9 | 2 | 0 | 0 | 1 | 1 | 2 | 1 | 0 | 0 | 2 |
| Idaho | 2 | 0 | 1 | 0 | 0 | 0 | 0 | 0 | 0 | 0 | 1 |
| Montana | 3 | 0 | 0 | 0 | 0 | 2 | 0 | 0 | 0 | 1 | 0 |
| Nevada | 6 | 1 | 0 | 0 | 0 | 1 | 0 | 1 | 0 | 2 | 1 |
| New Mexico | 5 | 1 | 0 | 0 | 1 | 0 | 0 | 0 | 0 | 0 | 3 |
| Utah | 5 | 0 | 0 | 0 | 0 | 2 | 0 | 1 | 1 | 1 | 0 |
| Wyoming | 0 | 0 | 0 | 0 | 0 | 0 | 0 | 0 | 0 | 0 | 0 |
| Pacific | 60 | 7 | 5 | 7 | 11 | 7 | 5 | 4 | 5 | 7 | 2 |
| Alaska | 4 | 0 | 0 | 0 | 0 | 2 | 0 | 0 | 0 | 2 | 0 |
| California | 40 | 6 | 4 | 3 | 5 | 5 | 3 | 2 | 5 | 5 | 2 |
| Hawaii | 1 | 0 | 1 | 0 | 0 | 0 | 0 | 0 | 0 | 0 | 0 |
| Oregon | 4 | 0 | 0 | 2 | 0 | 0 | 2 | 0 | 0 | 0 | 0 |
| Washington | 11 | 1 | 0 | 2 | 6 | 0 | 0 | 2 | 0 | 0 | 0 |
| Puerto Rico and other outlying areas | 24 | 2 | 1 | 0 | 2 | 3 | 2 | 6 | 0 | 4 | 4 |
| American Samoa | 0 | 0 | 0 | 0 | 0 | 0 | 0 | 0 | 0 | 0 | 0 |
| Guam | 0 | 0 | 0 | 0 | 0 | 0 | 0 | 0 | 0 | 0 | 0 |
| Mariana Islands | 0 | 0 | 0 | 0 | 0 | 0 | 0 | 0 | 0 | 0 | 0 |
| Puerto Rico | 23 | 2 | 1 | 0 | 2 | 3 | 2 | 5 | 0 | 4 | 4 |
| U.S. Virgin Islands | 1 | 0 | 0 | 0 | 0 | 0 | 0 | 1 | 0 | 0 | 0 |

## Table 2. Law Enforcement Officers Feloniously Killed, by Population Group/Agency Type, 2006–2015

(Number.)

| Area | Total | 2006 | 2007 | 2008 | 2009 | 2010 | 2011 | 2012 | 2013 | 2014 | 2015 |
|---|---|---|---|---|---|---|---|---|---|---|---|
| **Number of Victim Officers** ................ | 491 | 48 | 58 | 41 | 48 | 56 | 72 | 49 | 27 | 51 | 41 |
| Group I (cities 250,000 and over) ......... | 101 | 8 | 12 | 12 | 15 | 13 | 13 | 6 | 4 | 8 | 10 |
| Group II (cities 100,000–249,999) ........ | 43 | 4 | 9 | 1 | 3 | 3 | 9 | 4 | 2 | 6 | 2 |
| Group III (cities 50,000–99,999) ........... | 31 | 2 | 5 | 1 | 4 | 3 | 9 | 2 | 2 | 2 | 1 |
| Group IV (25,000–49,999) .................... | 32 | 3 | 2 | 5 | 1 | 6 | 4 | 2 | 3 | 2 | 4 |
| Group V (cities 10,000–24,999) ........... | 30 | 3 | 3 | 3 | 3 | 2 | 5 | 3 | 2 | 4 | 2 |
| Group VI (cities under 10,000) ............. | 46 | 3 | 5 | 0 | 6 | 5 | 10 | 4 | 3 | 5 | 5 |
| Metropolitan counties ......................... | 99 | 15 | 11 | 9 | 8 | 9 | 14 | 11 | 6 | 11 | 5 |
| Nonmetropolitan counties .................... | 39 | 3 | 4 | 4 | 4 | 6 | 4 | 5 | 3 | 4 | 2 |
| State agencies ................................... | 34 | 4 | 6 | 3 | 1 | 5 | 0 | 5 | 2 | 4 | 4 |
| Federal agencies ................................ | 12 | 1 | 0 | 3 | 1 | 1 | 2 | 1 | 0 | 1 | 2 |
| Puerto Rico and other outlying areas ..... | 24 | 2 | 1 | 0 | 2 | 3 | 2 | 6 | 0 | 4 | 4 |

## Table 3. Law Enforcement Officers Feloniously Killed, by Time of Incident, 2006–2015

(Number.)

| Time of day | Total | 2006 | 2007 | 2008 | 2009 | 2010 | 2011 | 2012 | 2013 | 2014 | 2015 |
|---|---|---|---|---|---|---|---|---|---|---|---|
| **Number of Victim Officers** ........... | 491 | 48 | 58 | 41 | 48 | 56 | 72 | 49 | 27 | 51 | 41 |
| Total A.M. hours ............................ | 224 | 17 | 24 | 24 | 21 | 23 | 36 | 24 | 13 | 20 | 22 |
| 12:01 a.m.–2 a.m. ............. | 60 | 5 | 13 | 9 | 3 | 7 | 7 | 5 | 3 | 4 | 4 |
| 2:01 a.m.–4 a.m. ............... | 44 | 4 | 4 | 4 | 1 | 4 | 9 | 3 | 3 | 6 | 6 |
| 4:01 a.m.–6 a.m. ............... | 22 | 3 | 0 | 2 | 2 | 3 | 2 | 3 | 3 | 3 | 1 |
| 6:01 a.m.–8 a.m. ............... | 21 | 2 | 2 | 0 | 5 | 2 | 5 | 3 | 0 | 1 | 1 |
| 8:01 a.m.–10 a.m. ............. | 30 | 0 | 1 | 4 | 8 | 1 | 3 | 4 | 1 | 0 | 8 |
| 10:01 a.m.–noon ............... | 47 | 3 | 4 | 5 | 2 | 6 | 10 | 6 | 3 | 6 | 2 |
| Total P.M. hours ............................ | 263 | 30 | 34 | 17 | 27 | 33 | 36 | 23 | 14 | 31 | 18 |
| 12:01 p.m.–2 p.m. ............. | 36 | 5 | 6 | 0 | 5 | 2 | 5 | 2 | 3 | 7 | 1 |
| 2:01 p.m.–4 p.m. ............... | 44 | 4 | 6 | 4 | 3 | 4 | 6 | 3 | 3 | 9 | 2 |
| 4:01 p.m.–6 p.m. ............... | 36 | 5 | 2 | 2 | 3 | 4 | 8 | 3 | 1 | 6 | 2 |
| 6:01 p.m.–8 p.m. ............... | 41 | 4 | 7 | 4 | 3 | 4 | 5 | 6 | 2 | 1 | 5 |
| 8:01 p.m.–10 p.m. ............. | 58 | 5 | 9 | 2 | 10 | 10 | 3 | 6 | 2 | 4 | 7 |
| 10:01 p.m.–midnight .......... | 48 | 7 | 4 | 5 | 3 | 9 | 9 | 3 | 3 | 4 | 1 |
| Not reported ................................. | 4 | 1 | 0 | 0 | 0 | 0 | 0 | 2 | 0 | 0 | 1 |

## Table 4. Law Enforcement Officers Feloniously Killed, by Day of Incident, 2006–2015

(Number.)

| Day of the week | Total | 2006 | 2007 | 2008 | 2009 | 2010 | 2011 | 2012 | 2013 | 2014 | 2015 |
|---|---|---|---|---|---|---|---|---|---|---|---|
| **Number of Victim Officers** ........... | 491 | 48 | 58 | 41 | 48 | 56 | 72 | 49 | 27 | 51 | 41 |
| Sunday ......................................... | 62 | 2 | 4 | 6 | 9 | 5 | 13 | 7 | 2 | 9 | 5 |
| Monday ........................................ | 60 | 11 | 4 | 1 | 5 | 6 | 12 | 5 | 3 | 7 | 6 |
| Tuesday ........................................ | 71 | 3 | 7 | 7 | 6 | 11 | 11 | 10 | 5 | 5 | 6 |
| Wednesday .................................... | 70 | 11 | 8 | 6 | 4 | 12 | 8 | 5 | 3 | 4 | 9 |
| Thursday ....................................... | 80 | 11 | 10 | 7 | 7 | 11 | 9 | 9 | 6 | 7 | 3 |
| Friday ........................................... | 68 | 5 | 12 | 8 | 4 | 6 | 11 | 5 | 5 | 8 | 4 |
| Saturday ....................................... | 80 | 5 | 13 | 6 | 13 | 5 | 8 | 8 | 3 | 11 | 8 |

## Table 5. Law Enforcement Officers Feloniously Killed, by Month of Incident, 2006–2015

(Number.)

| Month | Total | 2006 | 2007 | 2008 | 2009 | 2010 | 2011 | 2012 | 2013 | 2014 | 2015 |
|---|---|---|---|---|---|---|---|---|---|---|---|
| **Number of Victim Officers** ............ | 491 | 48 | 58 | 41 | 48 | 56 | 72 | 49 | 27 | 51 | 41 |
| January ............................................. | 39 | 1 | 6 | 8 | 1 | 4 | 9 | 6 | 2 | 2 | 0 |
| February ............................................ | 33 | 6 | 5 | 4 | 1 | 4 | 3 | 4 | 5 | 1 | 0 |
| March ................................................ | 49 | 5 | 8 | 0 | 6 | 5 | 9 | 1 | 1 | 8 | 6 |
| April .................................................. | 31 | 2 | 2 | 1 | 8 | 1 | 9 | 4 | 3 | 1 | 0 |
| May ................................................... | 48 | 6 | 7 | 2 | 0 | 7 | 3 | 3 | 1 | 9 | 10 |
| June .................................................. | 43 | 4 | 4 | 6 | 6 | 4 | 6 | 4 | 2 | 4 | 3 |
| July ................................................... | 40 | 0 | 6 | 4 | 7 | 7 | 8 | 2 | 1 | 4 | 1 |
| August ............................................... | 50 | 7 | 5 | 4 | 4 | 4 | 7 | 8 | 2 | 3 | 6 |
| September .......................................... | 43 | 5 | 7 | 6 | 4 | 1 | 1 | 5 | 4 | 6 | 4 |
| October ............................................. | 33 | 6 | 4 | 1 | 2 | 5 | 5 | 1 | 1 | 4 | 4 |
| November .......................................... | 27 | 1 | 0 | 1 | 4 | 6 | 2 | 4 | 0 | 5 | 4 |
| December .......................................... | 55 | 5 | 4 | 4 | 5 | 8 | 10 | 7 | 5 | 4 | 3 |

## Table 6. Law Enforcement Officers Feloniously Killed, by Age Group of Victim Officer, 2006–2015

(Number.)

| Age group | Total | 2006 | 2007 | 2008 | 2009 | 2010 | 2011 | 2012 | 2013 | 2014 | 2015 |
|---|---|---|---|---|---|---|---|---|---|---|---|
| **Number of Victim Officers** ............ | 491 | 48 | 58 | 41 | 48 | 56 | 72 | 49 | 27 | 51 | 41 |
| Under 25 years ................................. | 25 | 1 | 7 | 2 | 1 | 3 | 2 | 2 | 0 | 5 | 2 |
| 25–30 years ...................................... | 79 | 9 | 7 | 7 | 9 | 12 | 17 | 8 | 2 | 3 | 5 |
| 31–35 years ...................................... | 107 | 10 | 17 | 7 | 8 | 13 | 11 | 12 | 9 | 11 | 9 |
| 36–40 years ...................................... | 92 | 17 | 8 | 11 | 11 | 9 | 12 | 8 | 7 | 7 | 2 |
| 41–45 years ...................................... | 73 | 3 | 4 | 3 | 13 | 7 | 10 | 8 | 4 | 12 | 9 |
| 46–50 years ...................................... | 61 | 3 | 7 | 4 | 3 | 5 | 13 | 6 | 1 | 9 | 10 |
| 51–55 years ...................................... | 31 | 4 | 5 | 5 | 0 | 1 | 4 | 5 | 2 | 3 | 2 |
| 56–60 years ...................................... | 15 | 0 | 1 | 2 | 3 | 4 | 3 | 0 | 1 | 0 | 1 |
| Over 60 years ................................... | 8 | 1 | 2 | 0 | 0 | 2 | 0 | 0 | 1 | 1 | 1 |
| Average age (years) .......................... | 38 | 38 | 38 | 39 | 38 | 38 | 38 | 38 | 39 | 39 | 40 |

## Table 7. Law Enforcement Officers Feloniously Killed, by Years of Service of Victim Officer, 2006–2015

(Number.)

| Years of service | Total | 2006 | 2007 | 2008 | 2009 | 2010 | 2011 | 2012 | 2013 | 2014 | 2015 |
|---|---|---|---|---|---|---|---|---|---|---|---|
| **Number of Victim Officers** ............ | 491 | 48 | 58 | 41 | 48 | 56 | 72 | 49 | 27 | 51 | 41 |
| Less than 1 ....................................... | 11 | 0 | 2 | 0 | 0 | 1 | 0 | 2 | 0 | 2 | 4 |
| 1–5 ................................................... | 135 | 16 | 17 | 15 | 13 | 22 | 17 | 12 | 4 | 11 | 8 |
| 6–10 ................................................. | 132 | 13 | 17 | 11 | 12 | 13 | 24 | 13 | 10 | 8 | 11 |
| 11–15 ............................................... | 73 | 9 | 7 | 7 | 6 | 9 | 6 | 8 | 5 | 8 | 11 | 4 |
| 16–20 ............................................... | 65 | 4 | 7 | 2 | 6 | 9 | 8 | 10 | 1 | 13 | 5 |
| 21–25 ............................................... | 42 | 4 | 5 | 4 | 3 | 1 | 12 | 1 | 1 | 5 | 6 |
| 26–30 ............................................... | 21 | 1 | 3 | 3 | 4 | 1 | 1 | 4 | 2 | 0 | 2 |
| More than 30 .................................... | 9 | 1 | 0 | 0 | 0 | 3 | 2 | 1 | 1 | 1 | 0 |
| Not reported .................................... | 3 | 0 | 0 | 0 | 1 | 0 | 0 | 1 | 0 | 0 | 1 |
| Average years of service .................... | 11 | 11 | 10 | 10 | 12 | 10 | 12 | 12 | 13 | 13 | 12 |

## Table 8. Law Enforcement Officers Feloniously Killed, by Profile of Victim Officer, Averages, 1996–2015

(Number.)

| Characteristic | 2015 | 5-year averages | | 10-year averages | |
|---|---|---|---|---|---|
| | | 2006–2010 | 2011–2015 | 1996–2005 | 2006–2015 |
| Age ........................................ | 40 | 38 | 39 | 37 | 38 |
| Years of service ..................... | 12 | 11 | 12 | 10 | 11 |
| Height ..................................... | 5'10" | 5'11" | 5'10" | 5'11" | 5'11" |
| Weight .................................... | 200 | 201 | 204 | 199 | 202 |

Note: The deaths of the 72 law enforcement officers that resulted from the events of September 11, 2001, are not included in this table.


## Table 9. Law Enforcement Officers Feloniously Killed, by Race and Sex of Victim Officer, 2006–2015

(Number.)

| Characteristic | Total | 2006 | 2007 | 2008 | 2009 | 2010 | 2011 | 2012 | 2013 | 2014 | 2015 |
|---|---|---|---|---|---|---|---|---|---|---|---|
| **Number of Victim Officers** ............ | 491 | 48 | 58 | 41 | 48 | 56 | 72 | 49 | 27 | 51 | 41 |
| Race ...................................... | | | | | | | | | | | |
| White ....................................... | 421 | 41 | 48 | 30 | 42 | 48 | 68 | 43 | 25 | 47 | 29 |
| Black/African American ............. | 55 | 5 | 9 | 10 | 3 | 7 | 3 | 6 | 2 | 2 | 8 |
| American Indian/Alaska Native ... | 7 | 1 | 0 | 1 | 2 | 0 | 1 | 0 | 0 | 0 | 2 |
| Asian/Native Hawaiian/Other Pacific Islander ................................ | 8 | 1 | 1 | 0 | 1 | 1 | 0 | 0 | 0 | 2 | 2 |
| Sex ......................................... | | | | | | | | | | | |
| Male ........................................ | 468 | 45 | 58 | 37 | 47 | 54 | 69 | 44 | 25 | 51 | 38 |
| Female ..................................... | 23 | 3 | 0 | 4 | 1 | 2 | 3 | 5 | 2 | 0 | 3 |

# Table 10. Law Enforcement Officers Feloniously Killed, by Use of Weapon by Victim Officer, Assisting Officer, and Offender During Incident, 2006–2015

(Number; percent.)

| Characteristic | Total | 2006 | 2007 | 2008 | 2009 | 2010 | 2011 | 2012 | 2013 | 2014 | 2015 |
|---|---|---|---|---|---|---|---|---|---|---|---|
| **Number of victim officers** | 491 | 48 | 58 | 41 | 48 | 56 | 72 | 49 | 27 | 51 | 41 |
| Average number of rounds fired by victim officers | 1.3 | 1.6 | 0.7 | 1.8 | 0.8 | 1.9 | 2.0 | 0.7 | 0.9 | 0.9 | 1.7 |
| Average number of victim officer's rounds that struck offender(s) | 1.3 | 2.3 | 0.5 | 0.9 | 1.5 | 1.2 | 0.8 | 1.5 | 0.7 | 4.0 | 0.7 |
| Average number of rounds fired by assisting officers | 9.0 | 6.5 | 7.8 | 5.3 | 10.4 | 7.3 | 11.1 | 9.3 | 3.3 | 14.3 | 9.5 |
| Average number of rounds fired by offender(s) | 6.6 | 9.0 | 7.7 | 7.7 | 3.9 | 4.5 | 5.2 | 10.0 | 5.3 | 5.8 | 6.3 |
| | | | | | | | | | | | |
| **Number of victim officers who fired own weapon** | 103 | 11 | 11 | 11 | 12 | 17 | 18 | 6 | 6 | 5 | 6 |
| Average number of rounds fired by victim officers | 7.3 | 7.4 | 4.4 | 7.0 | 4.1 | 7.1 | 9.7 | 6.0 | 5.8 | 9.6 | 11.2 |
| Average number of victim officer's rounds that struck offender(s) | 1.3 | 2.3 | 0.5 | 0.9 | 1.5 | 1.2 | 0.8 | 1.5 | 0.7 | 4.0 | 0.7 |
| Percent hit rate of victim officer's rounds striking offender(s) | 18.7 | 33.3 | 7.5 | 12.9 | 50.0 | 19.4 | 6.3 | 40.0 | 13.3 | 41.7 | 6.0 |
| Average number of rounds fired by assisting officers | 5.8 | 5.0 | 4.8 | 6.4 | 3.6 | 3.2 | 7.4 | 14.7 | 2.7 | 2.5 | 2.0 |
| Average number of rounds fired by offender(s) | 8.4 | 20.8 | 2.6 | 7.1 | 4.0 | 6.7 | 9.5 | 8.2 | 6.7 | 4.4 | 10.0 |
| | | | | | | | | | | | |
| **Number of victim officers who attempted to (but did not) use own weapon** | 73 | 7 | 17 | 4 | 9 | 7 | 10 | 2 | 3 | 8 | 6 |
| Average number of rounds fired by assisting officers | 10.1 | 4.5 | 9.0 | 11.3 | 14.2 | 12.4 | 6.7 | 0.0 | 1.0 | 15.2 | 7.6 |
| Average number of rounds fired by offender(s) | 8.4 | 3.2 | 14.8 | 33.0 | 7.6 | 3.3 | 2.4 | 2.0 | 2.3 | 9.3 | 3.4 |
| | | | | | | | | | | | |
| **Number of victim officers who did not use and did not attempt to use own weapon** | 259 | 22 | 25 | 14 | 18 | 20 | 43 | 38 | 18 | 36 | 25 |
| Average number of rounds fired by assisting officers | 8.9 | 8.3 | 9.0 | 5.0 | 4.5 | 8.0 | 12.8 | 7.2 | 3.9 | 13.8 | 3.8 |
| Average number of rounds fired by offender(s) | 6.4 | 11.7 | 5.0 | 4.5 | 4.1 | 4.2 | 4.6 | 10.5 | 5.6 | 4.6 | 6.2 |
| | | | | | | | | | | | |
| **Number of victim officers who did not use own weapon, but attempt to use own weapon information was not reported** | 48 | 6 | 4 | 12 | 8 | 12 | 0 | 1 | 0 | 2 | 3 |
| Average number of rounds fired by assisting officers[1] | 8.0 | 2.0 | 5.5 | 1.2 | 15.2 | 4.8 | 0.0 | | 0.0 | 41.0 | |
| Average number of rounds fired by offender(s)[1] | 4.2 | 3.5 | 3.0 | 3.2 | 3.3 | 4.0 | 0.0 | | 0.0 | 15.0 | |
| | | | | | | | | | | | |
| **Number of victim officers in which victim officer's use of weapon was not reported** | 8 | 2 | 1 | 0 | 1 | 0 | 1 | 2 | 0 | 0 | 1 |

NOTE: When calculating the averages presented in this table, the FBI's Law Enforcement Officers Killed and Assaulted Program used all available data for each incident. For example, in a specific incident, if the number of rounds fired by the victim officer is known, but the number of rounds fired by the offender is not known, the known number was included in the calculation for the average number of rounds fired by victim officers.
[1] For 2012 and 2015, number of rounds data were not available for inclusion in these averages.

## Table 11. Law Enforcement Officers Feloniously Killed, by Victim Officer Killed with Own Weapon, Disarmed[1] of Weapon by Offender, and Weapon Stolen[2] by Offender, 2006–2015

(Number.)

| Characteristic | Total | 2006 | 2007 | 2008 | 2009 | 2010 | 2011 | 2012 | 2013 | 2014 | 2015 |
|---|---|---|---|---|---|---|---|---|---|---|---|
| **Number of victim officers** ..................... | 491 | 48 | 58 | 41 | 48 | 56 | 72 | 49 | 27 | 51 | 41 |
| **Killed with own weapon** ....................... | 24 | 1 | 2 | 4 | 2 | 6 | 3 | 1 | 1 | 1 | 3 |
| Disarmed ............................................. | 22 | 1 | 1 | 3 | 2 | 6 | 3 | 1 | 1 | 1 | 3 |
|   Weapon stolen ................................ | 9 | 0 | 1 | 1 | 1 | 4 | 1 | 0 | 0 | 0 | 1 |
|   Weapon not stolen ......................... | 13 | 1 | 0 | 2 | 1 | 2 | 2 | 1 | 1 | 1 | 2 |
|   Weapon stolen information not reported ............................................ | 0 | 0 | 0 | 0 | 0 | 0 | 0 | 0 | 0 | 0 | 0 |
| Not disarmed ....................................... | 2 | 0 | 1 | 1 | 0 | 0 | 0 | 0 | 0 | 0 | 0 |
|   Weapon stolen ................................ | 1 | 0 | 1 | 0 | 0 | 0 | 0 | 0 | 0 | 0 | 0 |
|   Weapon not stolen ......................... | 1 | 0 | 0 | 1 | 0 | 0 | 0 | 0 | 0 | 0 | 0 |
|   Weapon stolen information not reported ............................................ | 0 | 0 | 0 | 0 | 0 | 0 | 0 | 0 | 0 | 0 | 0 |
| Disarmed information not reported .......... | 0 | 0 | 0 | 0 | 0 | 0 | 0 | 0 | 0 | 0 | 0 |
|   Weapon stolen ................................ | 0 | 0 | 0 | 0 | 0 | 0 | 0 | 0 | 0 | 0 | 0 |
|   Weapon not stolen ......................... | 0 | 0 | 0 | 0 | 0 | 0 | 0 | 0 | 0 | 0 | 0 |
|   Weapon stolen information not reported ............................................ | 0 | 0 | 0 | 0 | 0 | 0 | 0 | 0 | 0 | 0 | 0 |
| **Killed with weapon other than own** .... | 465 | 46 | 56 | 37 | 45 | 50 | 69 | 48 | 26 | 50 | 38 |
| Disarmed ............................................. | 42 | 2 | 1 | 3 | 3 | 3 | 10 | 5 | 3 | 7 | 5 |
|   Weapon stolen ................................ | 26 | 2 | 1 | 2 | 3 | 1 | 4 | 3 | 2 | 6 | 2 |
|   Weapon not stolen ......................... | 16 | 0 | 0 | 1 | 0 | 2 | 6 | 2 | 1 | 1 | 3 |
|   Weapon stolen information not reported ............................................ | 0 | 0 | 0 | 0 | 0 | 0 | 0 | 0 | 0 | 0 | 0 |
| Not disarmed ....................................... | 421 | 44 | 54 | 34 | 42 | 47 | 58 | 43 | 23 | 43 | 33 |
|   Weapon stolen ................................ | 9 | 2 | 1 | 2 | 2 | 2 | 0 | 0 | 0 | 0 | 0 |
|   Weapon not stolen ......................... | 411 | 42 | 53 | 32 | 40 | 44 | 58 | 43 | 23 | 43 | 33 |
|   Weapon stolen information not reported ............................................ | 1 | 0 | 0 | 0 | 0 | 1 | 0 | 0 | 0 | 0 | 0 |
| Disarmed information not reported .......... | 2 | 0 | 1 | 0 | 0 | 0 | 1 | 0 | 0 | 0 | 0 |
|   Weapon stolen ................................ | 0 | 0 | 0 | 0 | 0 | 0 | 0 | 0 | 0 | 0 | 0 |
|   Weapon not stolen ......................... | 1 | 0 | 0 | 0 | 0 | 0 | 1 | 0 | 0 | 0 | 0 |
|   Weapon stolen information not reported ............................................ | 1 | 0 | 1 | 0 | 0 | 0 | 0 | 0 | 0 | 0 | 0 |
| **Killed with weapon information not reported** ............................................ | 2 | 1 | 0 | 0 | 1 | 0 | 0 | 0 | 0 | 0 | 0 |
| Disarmed ............................................. | 1 | 0 | 0 | 0 | 1 | 0 | 0 | 0 | 0 | 0 | 0 |
|   Weapon stolen ................................ | 1 | 0 | 0 | 0 | 1 | 0 | 0 | 0 | 0 | 0 | 0 |
|   Weapon not stolen ......................... | 0 | 0 | 0 | 0 | 0 | 0 | 0 | 0 | 0 | 0 | 0 |
|   Weapon stolen information not reported ............................................ | 0 | 0 | 0 | 0 | 0 | 0 | 0 | 0 | 0 | 0 | 0 |
| Not disarmed ....................................... | 0 | 0 | 0 | 0 | 0 | 0 | 0 | 0 | 0 | 0 | 0 |
|   Weapon stolen ................................ | 0 | 0 | 0 | 0 | 0 | 0 | 0 | 0 | 0 | 0 | 0 |
|   Weapon not stolen ......................... | 0 | 0 | 0 | 0 | 0 | 0 | 0 | 0 | 0 | 0 | 0 |
|   Weapon stolen information not reported ............................................ | 0 | 0 | 0 | 0 | 0 | 0 | 0 | 0 | 0 | 0 | 0 |
| Disarmed information not reported .......... | 1 | 1 | 0 | 0 | 0 | 0 | 0 | 0 | 0 | 0 | 0 |
|   Weapon stolen ................................ | 0 | 0 | 0 | 0 | 0 | 0 | 0 | 0 | 0 | 0 | 0 |
|   Weapon not stolen ......................... | 0 | 0 | 0 | 0 | 0 | 0 | 0 | 0 | 0 | 0 | 0 |
|   Weapon stolen information not reported ............................................ | 1 | 1 | 0 | 0 | 0 | 0 | 0 | 0 | 0 | 0 | 0 |

NOTE: Weapon is inclusive of all weapon types that may be issued to a law enforcement officer.
[1]The term "disarmed" indicates the victim officer was physically disarmed by the offender(s) of one or more of their weapons during the incident.
[2]The term "stolen" indicates a weapon issued to the victim officer was taken from the scene of the incident by the offender(s).

(Number.)

| Type of weapon | Total | 2006 | 2007 | 2008 | 2009 | 2010 | 2011 | 2012 | 2013 | 2014 | 2015 |
|---|---|---|---|---|---|---|---|---|---|---|---|
| **Number of Victim Officers Killed with Own Weapon** | 24 | 1 | 2 | 4 | 2 | 6 | 3 | 1 | 1 | 1 | 3 |
| Total, handgun | 23 | 1 | 2 | 4 | 2 | 5 | 3 | 1 | 1 | 1 | 3 |
| .38 caliber | 2 | 0 | 0 | 1 | 0 | 0 | 1 | 0 | 0 | 0 | 0 |
| .40 caliber | 11 | 1 | 1 | 3 | 1 | 1 | 2 | 0 | 0 | 1 | 1 |
| .45 caliber | 1 | 0 | 0 | 0 | 0 | 1 | 0 | 0 | 0 | 0 | 0 |
| 9 millimeter | 7 | 0 | 1 | 0 | 1 | 3 | 0 | 0 | 1 | 0 | 1 |
| Not reported | 2 | 0 | 0 | 0 | 0 | 0 | 0 | 1 | 0 | 0 | 1 |
| Rifle, total | 0 | 0 | 0 | 0 | 0 | 0 | 0 | 0 | 0 | 0 | 0 |
| Shotgun, total | 1 | 0 | 0 | 0 | 0 | 1 | 0 | 0 | 0 | 0 | 0 |
| 12 gauge | 1 | 0 | 0 | 0 | 0 | 1 | 0 | 0 | 0 | 0 | 0 |

## Table 13. Law Enforcement Officers Feloniously Killed, Time of Incident, by Type of Assignment, 2015

(Number.)

| Characteristic and time | Total | 2-officer vehicle | 1-officer vehicle | | Foot patrol | | Other[1] | | Off duty |
|---|---|---|---|---|---|---|---|---|---|
| | | | Alone | Assisted | Alone | Assisted | Alone | Assisted | |
| **Number of Victim Officers** | 41 | 8 | 11 | 10 | 0 | 0 | 4 | 6 | 2 |
| Total A.M. hours | 22 | 4 | 2 | 6 | 0 | 0 | 4 | 4 | 2 |
| 12:01 a.m.–2 a.m. | 4 | 1 | 1 | 1 | 0 | 0 | 0 | 0 | 1 |
| 2:01 a.m.–4 a.m. | 6 | 1 | 0 | 3 | 0 | 0 | 1 | 0 | 1 |
| 4:01 a.m.–6 a.m. | 1 | 0 | 0 | 0 | 0 | 0 | 1 | 0 | 0 |
| 6:01 a.m.–8 a.m. | 1 | 1 | 0 | 0 | 0 | 0 | 0 | 0 | 0 |
| 8:01 a.m.–10 a.m. | 8 | 1 | 1 | 1 | 0 | 0 | 2 | 3 | 0 |
| 10:01 a.m.–noon | 2 | 0 | 0 | 1 | 0 | 0 | 0 | 1 | 0 |
| Total P.M. hours | 18 | 3 | 9 | 4 | 0 | 0 | 0 | 2 | 0 |
| 12:01 p.m.–2 p.m. | 1 | 0 | 0 | 0 | 0 | 0 | 0 | 1 | 0 |
| 2:01 p.m.–4 p.m. | 2 | 0 | 2 | 0 | 0 | 0 | 0 | 0 | 0 |
| 4:01 p.m.–6 p.m. | 2 | 1 | 1 | 0 | 0 | 0 | 0 | 0 | 0 |
| 6:01 p.m.–8 p.m. | 5 | 1 | 1 | 2 | 0 | 0 | 0 | 1 | 0 |
| 8:01 p.m.–10 p.m. | 7 | 1 | 4 | 2 | 0 | 0 | 0 | 0 | 0 |
| 10:01 p.m.–midnight | 1 | 0 | 1 | 0 | 0 | 0 | 0 | 0 | 0 |
| Not reported | 1 | 1 | 0 | 0 | 0 | 0 | 0 | 0 | 0 |

[1] Includes detectives, officers on special assignments, undercover officers, and officers on other types of assignments not listed.

# Table 14. Law Enforcement Officers Feloniously Killed, by Circumstance at Scene of Incident, 2006–2015

(Number.)

| Circumstance | Total | 2006 | 2007 | 2008 | 2009 | 2010 | 2011 | 2012 | 2013 | 2014 | 2015 |
|---|---|---|---|---|---|---|---|---|---|---|---|
| **Number of Victim Officers** ....................... | 491 | 48 | 58 | 41 | 48 | 56 | 72 | 49 | 27 | 51 | 41 |
| Disturbance call ........................................ | 58 | 8 | 5 | 1 | 6 | 6 | 10 | 4 | 4 | 11 | 3 |
|   Disturbance (bar fight, person with firearm, etc.) ........... | 37 | 6 | 3 | 1 | 4 | 2 | 5 | 3 | 3 | 10 | 0 |
|   Domestic disturbance (family quarrel, etc.) ...................... | 21 | 2 | 2 | 0 | 2 | 4 | 5 | 1 | 1 | 1 | 3 |
| Arrest situation ........................................ | 92 | 12 | 17 | 9 | 8 | 14 | 10 | 7 | 6 | 4 | 5 |
|   Burglary in progress/pursuing burglary suspect .............. | 9 | 0 | 1 | 2 | 1 | 3 | 0 | 1 | 0 | 0 | 1 |
|   Robbery in progress/pursuing robbery suspect ................ | 38 | 6 | 7 | 1 | 3 | 6 | 6 | 3 | 3 | 0 | 3 |
|   Drug-related matter ................................................ | 8 | 2 | 1 | 1 | 0 | 1 | 0 | 2 | 0 | 1 | 0 |
|   Attempting other arrest .......................................... | 37 | 4 | 8 | 5 | 4 | 4 | 4 | 1 | 3 | 3 | 1 |
| Civil disorder (mass disobedience, riot, etc.) ......................... | 0 | 0 | 0 | 0 | 0 | 0 | 0 | 0 | 0 | 0 | 0 |
| Handling, transporting, custody of prisoner ......................... | 12 | 1 | 1 | 1 | 2 | 1 | 1 | 3 | 0 | 0 | 2 |
| Investigating suspicious person/circumstance ....................... | 70 | 6 | 4 | 7 | 4 | 8 | 12 | 8 | 5 | 8 | 8 |
| Ambush (entrapment/premeditation) ..................................... | 36 | 1 | 9 | 1 | 6 | 2 | 2 | 3 | 1 | 7 | 4 |
| Unprovoked attack ........................................ | 56 | 9 | 7 | 5 | 9 | 11 | 6 | 1 | 4 | 1 | 3 |
| Investigative activity (surveillance, search, interview, etc.) ....... | 22 | 0 | 1 | 2 | 0 | 2 | 4 | 6 | 1 | 5 | 1 |
| Handling person with mental illness ......................... | 9 | 1 | 0 | 0 | 0 | 0 | 0 | 3 | 0 | 3 | 2 |
| Traffic pursuit/stop ........................................ | 83 | 8 | 11 | 8 | 8 | 9 | 14 | 9 | 2 | 8 | 6 |
|   Felony vehicle stop ................................................ | 29 | 0 | 5 | 5 | 2 | 3 | 7 | 5 | 0 | 1 | 1 |
|   Traffic violation stop .............................................. | 54 | 8 | 6 | 3 | 6 | 6 | 7 | 4 | 2 | 7 | 5 |
| Tactical situation (barricaded offender, hostage taking, high-risk entry, etc.) ............................................... | 53 | 2 | 3 | 7 | 5 | 3 | 13 | 5 | 4 | 4 | 7 |

# Table 15. Law Enforcement Officers Feloniously Killed, by Circumstance at Scene of Incident, by Type of Assignment, 2006–2015

(Number.)

| Circumstance | Total | 2-officer vehicle | 1-officer vehicle | | Foot patrol | | Other[1] | | Off duty |
|---|---|---|---|---|---|---|---|---|---|
| | | | Alone | Assisted | Alone | Assisted | Alone | Assisted | |
| **Number of Victim Officers** ......................................... | 491 | 50 | 126 | 153 | 1 | 1 | 23 | 90 | 47 |
| Disturbance call ....................................................... | 58 | 3 | 14 | 30 | 0 | 1 | 1 | 3 | 6 |
|    Disturbance (bar fight, person with firearm, etc.) ......................... | 37 | 2 | 8 | 16 | 0 | 1 | 1 | 3 | 6 |
|    Domestic disturbance (family quarrel, etc.) .................................... | 21 | 1 | 6 | 14 | 0 | 0 | 0 | 0 | 0 |
| Arrest situation ......................................................... | 92 | 14 | 15 | 25 | 0 | 0 | 3 | 17 | 18 |
|    Burglary in progress/pursuing burglary suspect .......................... | 9 | 4 | 2 | 1 | 0 | 0 | 0 | 1 | 1 |
|    Robbery in progress/pursuing robbery suspect ............................ | 38 | 7 | 7 | 7 | 0 | 0 | 0 | 1 | 16 |
|    Drug-related matter ...................................................... | 8 | 0 | 0 | 0 | 0 | 0 | 0 | 8 | 0 |
|    Attempting other arrest .................................................. | 37 | 3 | 6 | 17 | 0 | 0 | 3 | 7 | 1 |
| Civil disorder (mass disobedience, riot, etc.) ............................. | 0 | 0 | 0 | 0 | 0 | 0 | 0 | 0 | 0 |
| Handling, transporting, custody of prisoner ............................. | 12 | 5 | 4 | 0 | 0 | 0 | 2 | 0 | 1 |
| Investigating suspicious person/circumstance ......................... | 70 | 9 | 29 | 14 | 1 | 0 | 3 | 8 | 6 |
| Ambush (entrapment/premeditation) ................................... | 36 | 3 | 6 | 14 | 0 | 0 | 3 | 1 | 9 |
| Unprovoked attack ..................................................... | 56 | 6 | 24 | 10 | 0 | 0 | 7 | 7 | 2 |
| Investigative activity (surveillance, search, interview, etc.) .................... | 22 | 1 | 3 | 5 | 0 | 0 | 0 | 11 | 2 |
| Handling person with mental illness ...................................... | 9 | 2 | 0 | 4 | 0 | 0 | 2 | 1 | 0 |
| Traffic pursuit/stop ..................................................... | 83 | 5 | 31 | 38 | 0 | 0 | 2 | 5 | 2 |
|    Felony vehicle stop ...................................................... | 29 | 1 | 2 | 20 | 0 | 0 | 1 | 4 | 1 |
|    Traffic violation stop .................................................... | 54 | 4 | 29 | 18 | 0 | 0 | 1 | 1 | 1 |
| Tactical situation (barricaded offender, hostage taking, high-risk entry, etc.) ...................................................... | 53 | 2 | 0 | 13 | 0 | 0 | 0 | 37 | 1 |

[1] Includes detectives, officers on special assignments, undercover officers, and officers on other types of assignments not listed.

# Table 16. Law Enforcement Officers Feloniously Killed, by Circumstance at Scene of Incident, by Type of Assignment, 2015

(Number.)

| Circumstance | Total | 2-officer vehicle | 1-officer vehicle | | Foot patrol | | Other[1] | | Off duty |
|---|---|---|---|---|---|---|---|---|---|
| | | | Alone | Assisted | Alone | Assisted | Alone | Assisted | |
| **Number of Victim Officers** | 41 | 8 | 11 | 10 | 0 | 0 | 4 | 6 | 2 |
| Disturbance call | 3 | 0 | 1 | 2 | 0 | 0 | 0 | 0 | 0 |
| Disturbance (bar fight, person with firearm, etc.) | 0 | 0 | 0 | 0 | 0 | 0 | 0 | 0 | 0 |
| Domestic disturbance (family quarrel, etc.) | 3 | 0 | 1 | 2 | 0 | 0 | 0 | 0 | 0 |
| Arrest situation | 5 | 3 | 1 | 0 | 0 | 0 | 1 | 0 | 0 |
| Burglary in progress/pursuing burglary suspect | 1 | 1 | 0 | 0 | 0 | 0 | 0 | 0 | 0 |
| Robbery in progress/pursuing robbery suspect | 3 | 2 | 1 | 0 | 0 | 0 | 0 | 0 | 0 |
| Drug-related matter | 0 | 0 | 0 | 0 | 0 | 0 | 0 | 0 | 0 |
| Attempting other arrest | 1 | 0 | 0 | 0 | 0 | 0 | 1 | 0 | 0 |
| Civil disorder (mass disobedience, riot, etc.) | 0 | 0 | 0 | 0 | 0 | 0 | 0 | 0 | 0 |
| Handling, transporting, custody of prisoner | 2 | 0 | 1 | 0 | 0 | 0 | 1 | 0 | 0 |
| Investigating suspicious person/circumstance | 8 | 2 | 4 | 0 | 0 | 0 | 0 | 1 | 1 |
| Ambush (entrapment/premeditation) | 4 | 0 | 1 | 2 | 0 | 0 | 0 | 0 | 1 |
| Unprovoked attack | 3 | 1 | 1 | 0 | 0 | 0 | 1 | 0 | 0 |
| Investigative activity (surveillance, search, interview, etc.) | 1 | 1 | 0 | 0 | 0 | 0 | 0 | 0 | 0 |
| Handling person with mental illness | 2 | 1 | 0 | 0 | 0 | 0 | 1 | 0 | 0 |
| Traffic pursuit/stop | 6 | 0 | 2 | 4 | 0 | 0 | 0 | 0 | 0 |
| Felony vehicle stop | 1 | 0 | 0 | 1 | 0 | 0 | 0 | 0 | 0 |
| Traffic violation stop | 5 | 0 | 2 | 3 | 0 | 0 | 0 | 0 | 0 |
| Tactical situation (barricaded offender, hostage taking, high-risk entry, etc.) | 7 | 0 | 0 | 2 | 0 | 0 | 0 | 5 | 0 |

[1] Includes detectives, officers on special assignments, undercover officers, and officers on other types of assignments not listed.

# Table 17. Law Enforcement Officers Feloniously Killed, by Type of Weapon, 2006–2015

(Number.)

| Type of weapon | Total | 2006 | 2007 | 2008 | 2009 | 2010 | 2011 | 2012 | 2013 | 2014 | 2015 |
|---|---|---|---|---|---|---|---|---|---|---|---|
| **Number of Victim Officers** | 491 | 48 | 58 | 41 | 48 | 56 | 72 | 49 | 27 | 51 | 41 |
| Total firearms | 454 | 46 | 56 | 35 | 45 | 55 | 63 | 44 | 26 | 46 | 38 |
| Handgun | 330 | 36 | 39 | 25 | 28 | 38 | 50 | 34 | 18 | 33 | 29 |
| Rifle | 88 | 8 | 8 | 6 | 15 | 15 | 7 | 7 | 5 | 10 | 7 |
| Shotgun | 34 | 2 | 8 | 4 | 2 | 2 | 6 | 3 | 3 | 3 | 1 |
| Type of firearm not reported | 2 | 0 | 1 | 0 | 0 | 0 | 0 | 0 | 0 | 0 | 1 |
| Knife or other cutting instrument | 2 | 0 | 0 | 0 | 0 | 0 | 1 | 1 | 0 | 0 | 0 |
| Bomb | 2 | 0 | 0 | 2 | 0 | 0 | 0 | 0 | 0 | 0 | 0 |
| Blunt instrument | 0 | 0 | 0 | 0 | 0 | 0 | 0 | 0 | 0 | 0 | 0 |
| Personal weapons | 5 | 0 | 0 | 0 | 0 | 0 | 2 | 2 | 0 | 1 | 0 |
| Vehicle | 28 | 2 | 2 | 4 | 3 | 1 | 6 | 2 | 1 | 4 | 3 |
| Other | 0 | 0 | 0 | 0 | 0 | 0 | 0 | 0 | 0 | 0 | 0 |
| **Number of Victim Officers Who Had Prior Knowledge That a Weapon Might Be Involved in the Incident** | 156 | 15 | 19 | 12 | 21 | 20 | 24 | 6 | 8 | 15 | 16 |

**Table 18. Law Enforcement Officers Feloniously Killed, by Number of Victim Officers Wearing Uniform, Body Armor, or Holster, 2006–2015**

(Number.)

| Characteristic | Total | 2006 | 2007 | 2008 | 2009 | 2010 | 2011 | 2012 | 2013 | 2014 | 2015 |
|---|---|---|---|---|---|---|---|---|---|---|---|
| **Number of Victim Officers** ................ | 491 | 48 | 58 | 41 | 48 | 56 | 72 | 49 | 27 | 51 | 41 |
| Wearing body armor ............................ | 335 | 27 | 36 | 32 | 36 | 38 | 51 | 26 | 19 | 40 | 30 |
| In uniform ........................................ | 305 | 22 | 33 | 26 | 32 | 35 | 46 | 25 | 18 | 40 | 28 |
| Not in uniform ................................. | 29 | 4 | 3 | 6 | 4 | 3 | 5 | 1 | 1 | 0 | 2 |
| Wearing uniform not reported ......... | 1 | 1 | 0 | 0 | 0 | 0 | 0 | 0 | 0 | 0 | 0 |
| Wearing holster ..................................... | 450 | 43 | 52 | 37 | 45 | 53 | 67 | 43 | 27 | 48 | 35 |
| In uniform ........................................ | 381 | 32 | 40 | 30 | 39 | 46 | 59 | 40 | 20 | 43 | 32 |
| Not in uniform ................................. | 67 | 10 | 12 | 7 | 6 | 7 | 8 | 3 | 7 | 5 | 2 |
| Wearing uniform not reported ......... | 2 | 1 | 0 | 0 | 0 | 0 | 0 | 0 | 0 | 0 | 1 |

**Table 19. Law Enforcement Officers Feloniously Killed, Age Group of Known Offender, 2006–2015**

(Number.)

| Age group | Total | 2006 | 2007 | 2008 | 2009 | 2010 | 2011 | 2012 | 2013 | 2014 | 2015 |
|---|---|---|---|---|---|---|---|---|---|---|---|
| **Number of Known Offenders** ..... | 543 | 59 | 66 | 42 | 45 | 80 | 76 | 51 | 28 | 59 | 37 |
| Under 18 ...................................... | 26 | 4 | 7 | 3 | 2 | 1 | 5 | 1 | 0 | 3 | 0 |
| 18–24 ............................................ | 159 | 26 | 26 | 8 | 14 | 24 | 20 | 15 | 9 | 13 | 4 |
| 25–30 ............................................ | 129 | 9 | 10 | 10 | 6 | 23 | 19 | 14 | 7 | 17 | 14 |
| 31–35 ............................................ | 78 | 7 | 6 | 4 | 9 | 12 | 9 | 6 | 6 | 10 | 9 |
| 36–40 ............................................ | 47 | 2 | 4 | 5 | 5 | 8 | 7 | 4 | 2 | 9 | 1 |
| 41–45 ............................................ | 36 | 6 | 3 | 7 | 5 | 6 | 3 | 5 | 0 | 1 | 0 |
| 46–50 ............................................ | 21 | 1 | 2 | 3 | 1 | 0 | 5 | 2 | 3 | 3 | 1 |
| 51–55 ............................................ | 21 | 2 | 3 | 1 | 2 | 3 | 4 | 1 | 1 | 1 | 3 |
| 56–60 ............................................ | 14 | 1 | 2 | 1 | 0 | 2 | 4 | 0 | 0 | 2 | 2 |
| Over 60 ........................................ | 3 | 0 | 0 | 0 | 1 | 1 | 0 | 1 | 0 | 0 | 0 |
| Not reported ................................. | 9 | 1 | 3 | 0 | 0 | 0 | 0 | 2 | 0 | 0 | 3 |
| Average age ................................. | 31 | 28 | 28 | 32 | 31 | 31 | 32 | 31 | 31 | 31 | 33 |

**Table 20. Law Enforcement Officers Feloniously Killed, by Profile of Known Offender, Averages, 1996–2015**

(Number.)

| Characteristic | 2015 | 5-year averages | | 10-year averages | |
|---|---|---|---|---|---|
| | | 2006–2010 | 2011–2015 | 1996–2005 | 2006–2015 |
| Age ................................................................ | 33 | 30 | 31 | 29 | 31 |
| Height ........................................................... | 5'11" | 5'10" | 5'10" | 5'10" | 5'10" |
| Weight .......................................................... | 188 | 179 | 181 | 175 | 180 |

Note: The 14 known offenders involved in the events of September 11, 2001, are not included in this table.

## Table 21. Law Enforcement Officers Feloniously Killed, by Race and Sex of Known Offender, 2006–2015

(Number.)

| Characteristic | Total | 2006 | 2007 | 2008 | 2009 | 2010 | 2011 | 2012 | 2013 | 2014 | 2015 |
|---|---|---|---|---|---|---|---|---|---|---|---|
| **Number of Known Offenders** ..... | 543 | 59 | 66 | 42 | 45 | 80 | 76 | 51 | 28 | 59 | 37 |
| Race ................................................ | | | | | | | | | | | |
|   White ...................................... | 289 | 25 | 35 | 20 | 28 | 32 | 44 | 32 | 15 | 42 | 16 |
|   Black/African American .......... | 222 | 31 | 26 | 21 | 17 | 39 | 28 | 17 | 12 | 14 | 17 |
|   American Indian/Alaska Native | 10 | 0 | 0 | 0 | 0 | 4 | 2 | 1 | 0 | 2 | 1 |
|   Asian/Native Hawaiian/Other Pacific Islander ........................... | 10 | 0 | 4 | 1 | 0 | 2 | 1 | 1 | 0 | 1 | 0 |
|   Not reported ........................... | 12 | 3 | 1 | 0 | 0 | 3 | 1 | 0 | 1 | 0 | 3 |
| Sex .................................................. | | | | | | | | | | | |
|   Male ........................................ | 525 | 58 | 65 | 40 | 43 | 78 | 74 | 49 | 27 | 54 | 37 |
|   Female .................................... | 18 | 1 | 1 | 2 | 2 | 2 | 2 | 2 | 1 | 5 | 0 |

## Table 22. Law Enforcement Officers Feloniously Killed, by Status of Known Offender at Time of Incident, 2006–2015

(Number.)

| Characteristic | Total | 2006 | 2007 | 2008 | 2009 | 2010 | 2011 | 2012 | 2013 | 2014 | 2015 |
|---|---|---|---|---|---|---|---|---|---|---|---|
| **Number of Known Offenders** .................... | 543 | 59 | 66 | 42 | 45 | 80 | 76 | 51 | 28 | 59 | 37 |
| Under judicial supervision ............................. | | | | | | | | | | | |
|   Total ................................................. | 131 | 15 | 19 | 12 | 13 | 19 | 17 | 10 | 6 | 11 | 9 |
|   Probation ......................................... | 58 | 5 | 10 | 4 | 7 | 9 | 7 | 5 | 2 | 5 | 4 |
|   Parole ............................................... | 44 | 5 | 7 | 5 | 3 | 8 | 4 | 3 | 2 | 5 | 2 |
|   Halfway house ................................. | 1 | 0 | 0 | 0 | 0 | 0 | 1 | 0 | 0 | 0 | 0 |
|   Escapee from penal institution ............... | 4 | 3 | 0 | 0 | 0 | 1 | 0 | 0 | 0 | 0 | 0 |
|   Conditional release, pending criminal prosecution ................................................ | 24 | 2 | 2 | 3 | 3 | 1 | 5 | 2 | 2 | 1 | 3 |
| Known to agency as: ...................................... | | | | | | | | | | | |
|   User of controlled substance ................... | 89 | 9 | 9 | 11 | 10 | 19 | 13 | 6 | 3 | 8 | 1 |
|   Dealer of controlled substance ............... | 69 | 11 | 9 | 5 | 5 | 7 | 9 | 6 | 4 | 11 | 2 |
|   Possessor of controlled substance .......... | 70 | 7 | 12 | 9 | 2 | 12 | 9 | 5 | 2 | 10 | 2 |
| Use of controlled substance .......................... | | | | | | | | | | | |
|   Under influence ............................... | 69 | 5 | 8 | 3 | 1 | 11 | 8 | 11 | 1 | 11 | 10 |
|   Not under influence ......................... | 89 | 8 | 14 | 11 | 9 | 10 | 15 | 5 | 5 | 5 | 7 |
|   Unknown to victim officer's agency ........ | 349 | 40 | 41 | 28 | 29 | 54 | 48 | 28 | 21 | 42 | 18 |
|   Not reported ................................... | 36 | 6 | 3 | 0 | 6 | 5 | 5 | 7 | 1 | 1 | 2 |
| Use of alcohol ................................................ | | | | | | | | | | | |
|   Intoxicated/under influence .................... | 51 | 4 | 11 | 2 | 2 | 7 | 7 | 7 | 3 | 2 | 6 |
|   Not intoxicated/under influence .............. | 115 | 10 | 11 | 13 | 11 | 16 | 16 | 9 | 4 | 14 | 11 |
|   Unknown to victim officer's agency ........ | 340 | 39 | 41 | 27 | 26 | 52 | 48 | 27 | 20 | 42 | 18 |
|   Not reported ................................... | 37 | 6 | 3 | 0 | 6 | 5 | 5 | 8 | 1 | 1 | 2 |
| Known to agency as having prior mental disorders ......................................................... | 29 | 4 | 4 | 2 | 3 | 2 | 7 | 2 | 2 | 1 | 2 |
| Relationship between victim officer and offender ........................................................... | | | | | | | | | | | |
|   Through law enforcement .................... | 52 | 5 | 6 | 5 | 3 | 8 | 11 | 4 | 3 | 3 | 4 |
|   Through non-law enforcement .............. | 5 | 1 | 1 | 0 | 0 | 1 | 0 | 0 | 2 | 0 | 0 |
|   No known relationship ......................... | 449 | 46 | 56 | 37 | 33 | 66 | 60 | 41 | 23 | 56 | 31 |
|   Unknown to victim officer's agency ........ | 1 | 1 | 0 | 0 | 0 | 0 | 0 | 0 | 0 | 0 | 0 |
|   Not reported ................................... | 36 | 6 | 3 | 0 | 9 | 5 | 5 | 6 | 0 | 0 | 2 |

## Table 23. Law Enforcement Officers Feloniously Killed, by Criminal History of Known Offender, 2006–2015

(Number.)

| Characteristic | Total | 2006 | 2007 | 2008 | 2009 | 2010 | 2011 | 2012 | 2013 | 2014 | 2015 |
|---|---|---|---|---|---|---|---|---|---|---|---|
| **Number of Known Offenders** ................... | 543 | 59 | 66 | 42 | 45 | 80 | 76 | 51 | 28 | 59 | 37 |
| Prior criminal arrest ................................ | 455 | 43 | 60 | 36 | 35 | 71 | 67 | 40 | 22 | 50 | 31 |
| Convicted on prior criminal charge .............. | 349 | 31 | 46 | 24 | 28 | 55 | 53 | 32 | 15 | 37 | 28 |
| Received juvenile conviction on prior criminal charge .... | 95 | 9 | 14 | 6 | 8 | 10 | 19 | 8 | 2 | 10 | 9 |
| Received parole/probation on prior criminal charge ...... | 266 | 22 | 39 | 18 | 26 | 41 | 44 | 20 | 9 | 29 | 18 |
| Prior arrest for ...................................... | | | | | | | | | | | |
| Crime of violence ............................. | 256 | 26 | 32 | 17 | 23 | 44 | 39 | 18 | 12 | 22 | 23 |
| Murder ........................................... | 24 | 3 | 2 | 1 | 2 | 7 | 3 | 2 | 0 | 1 | 3 |
| Drug law violation ............................. | 240 | 27 | 38 | 19 | 13 | 39 | 28 | 20 | 8 | 34 | 14 |
| Assaulting an officer/resisting arrest .......... | 132 | 11 | 20 | 6 | 9 | 20 | 23 | 9 | 5 | 16 | 13 |
| Weapons violation ............................. | 231 | 25 | 29 | 14 | 18 | 40 | 36 | 17 | 7 | 26 | 19 |

## Table 24. Law Enforcement Officers Feloniously Killed, by Disposition of Known Offender, 2004–2013

(Number.)

| Disposition | 2004–2008 | 2009–2013 | 2004–2013 |
|---|---|---|---|
| **Number of Known Offenders** ........................................ | 284 | 280 | 564 |
| **Fugitive** ................................................................ | 0 | 3 | 3 |
| **Arrested and charged** ............................................... | 204 | 170 | 374 |
| Guilty of murder ................................................... | 148 | 99 | 247 |
| Received death sentence ..................................... | 47 | 13 | 60 |
| Received life imprisonment ................................. | 77 | 60 | 137 |
| Received prison term (ranging from 5 years to 999 years) ............. | 24 | 26 | 50 |
| Sentence not reported ........................................ | 0 | 1 | 1 |
| Guilty of lesser offense related to murder ................ | 18 | 16 | 34 |
| Guilty of crime other than murder ........................ | 13 | 9 | 22 |
| Acquitted/dismissed/nolle prosequi ...................... | 15 | 16 | 31 |
| Indeterminate charge and sentence ...................... | 1 | 0 | 1 |
| Committed to psychiatric institution ..................... | 4 | 5 | 9 |
| Case pending/disposition unknown ...................... | 3 | 23 | 26 |
| Died in custody prior to sentencing ...................... | 2 | 1 | 3 |
| **Not arrested** ......................................................... | 80 | 105 | 185 |
| Justifiably killed ................................................... | 50 | 63 | 113 |
| Justifiably killed by victim officer ......................... | 19 | 18 | 37 |
| Justifiably killed by person(s) other than victim officer ............ | 31 | 45 | 76 |
| Committed suicide ................................................ | 25 | 36 | 61 |
| Murdered while at large ........................................ | 0 | 0 | 0 |
| Died under other circumstance ............................. | 3 | 4 | 7 |
| Other ................................................................ | 2 | 2 | 4 |
| **Not reported** ......................................................... | 0 | 2 | 2 |

# Table 25. Law Enforcement Officers Accidentally Killed, by Region, Geographic Division, and State/Territory, 2006–2015

(Number.)

| Area | Total | 2006 | 2007 | 2008 | 2009 | 2010 | 2011 | 2012 | 2013 | 2014 | 2015 |
|---|---|---|---|---|---|---|---|---|---|---|---|
| **Number of Victim Officers** | 577 | 66 | 83 | 68 | 48 | 72 | 53 | 48 | 49 | 45 | 45 |
| Northeast | 71 | 5 | 6 | 11 | 6 | 8 | 8 | 9 | 5 | 8 | 5 |
| New England | 16 | 1 | 2 | 1 | 2 | 3 | 2 | 4 | 0 | 1 | 0 |
| Connecticut | 4 | 1 | 0 | 1 | 0 | 2 | 0 | 0 | 0 | 0 | 0 |
| Maine | 1 | 0 | 0 | 0 | 0 | 0 | 1 | 0 | 0 | 0 | 0 |
| Massachusetts | 10 | 0 | 2 | 0 | 2 | 1 | 1 | 3 | 0 | 1 | 0 |
| New Hampshire | 0 | 0 | 0 | 0 | 0 | 0 | 0 | 0 | 0 | 0 | 0 |
| Rhode Island | 1 | 0 | 0 | 0 | 0 | 0 | 0 | 1 | 0 | 0 | 0 |
| Vermont | 0 | 0 | 0 | 0 | 0 | 0 | 0 | 0 | 0 | 0 | 0 |
| Middle Atlantic | 55 | 4 | 4 | 10 | 4 | 5 | 6 | 5 | 5 | 7 | 5 |
| New Jersey | 16 | 1 | 2 | 2 | 0 | 4 | 1 | 1 | 0 | 2 | 3 |
| New York | 24 | 2 | 2 | 3 | 3 | 1 | 5 | 2 | 3 | 3 | 0 |
| Pennsylvania | 15 | 1 | 0 | 5 | 1 | 0 | 0 | 2 | 2 | 2 | 2 |
| Midwest | 77 | 14 | 11 | 5 | 9 | 14 | 7 | 3 | 4 | 4 | 6 |
| East North Central | 54 | 14 | 5 | 5 | 6 | 7 | 3 | 3 | 4 | 3 | 4 |
| Illinois | 15 | 6 | 1 | 0 | 0 | 3 | 0 | 1 | 2 | 1 | 1 |
| Indiana | 11 | 2 | 2 | 2 | 2 | 2 | 0 | 0 | 0 | 1 | 0 |
| Michigan | 9 | 2 | 0 | 0 | 2 | 0 | 1 | 0 | 1 | 1 | 2 |
| Ohio | 13 | 3 | 2 | 2 | 1 | 1 | 2 | 1 | 1 | 0 | 0 |
| Wisconsin | 6 | 1 | 0 | 1 | 1 | 1 | 0 | 1 | 0 | 0 | 1 |
| West North Central | 23 | 0 | 6 | 0 | 3 | 7 | 4 | 0 | 0 | 1 | 2 |
| Iowa | 2 | 0 | 1 | 0 | 0 | 0 | 1 | 0 | 0 | 0 | 0 |
| Kansas | 3 | 0 | 1 | 0 | 0 | 2 | 0 | 0 | 0 | 0 | 0 |
| Minnesota | 1 | 0 | 1 | 0 | 0 | 0 | 0 | 0 | 0 | 0 | 0 |
| Missouri | 15 | 0 | 3 | 0 | 2 | 4 | 3 | 0 | 0 | 1 | 2 |
| Nebraska | 1 | 0 | 0 | 0 | 1 | 0 | 0 | 0 | 0 | 0 | 0 |
| North Dakota | 0 | 0 | 0 | 0 | 0 | 0 | 0 | 0 | 0 | 0 | 0 |
| South Dakota | 1 | 0 | 0 | 0 | 0 | 1 | 0 | 0 | 0 | 0 | 0 |
| South | 298 | 26 | 46 | 32 | 21 | 39 | 27 | 28 | 31 | 19 | 29 |
| South Atlantic | 130 | 11 | 22 | 14 | 12 | 16 | 16 | 14 | 9 | 4 | 12 |
| Delaware | 0 | 0 | 0 | 0 | 0 | 0 | 0 | 0 | 0 | 0 | 0 |
| District of Columbia | 2 | 0 | 1 | 0 | 0 | 1 | 0 | 0 | 0 | 0 | 0 |
| Florida | 25 | 2 | 8 | 4 | 1 | 4 | 1 | 2 | 1 | 1 | 1 |
| Georgia | 32 | 3 | 3 | 3 | 2 | 3 | 6 | 4 | 2 | 1 | 5 |
| Maryland | 16 | 0 | 2 | 3 | 0 | 3 | 2 | 3 | 0 | 0 | 3 |
| North Carolina | 17 | 0 | 4 | 2 | 3 | 0 | 4 | 2 | 1 | 1 | 0 |
| South Carolina | 12 | 1 | 1 | 1 | 2 | 2 | 1 | 0 | 2 | 0 | 2 |
| Virginia | 24 | 5 | 2 | 1 | 3 | 3 | 2 | 3 | 3 | 1 | 1 |
| West Virginia | 2 | 0 | 1 | 0 | 1 | 0 | 0 | 0 | 0 | 0 | 0 |
| East South Central | 55 | 6 | 6 | 4 | 4 | 6 | 3 | 3 | 7 | 7 | 9 |
| Alabama | 17 | 1 | 3 | 2 | 1 | 0 | 2 | 1 | 3 | 2 | 2 |
| Kentucky | 7 | 2 | 1 | 0 | 0 | 1 | 0 | 1 | 0 | 0 | 2 |
| Mississippi | 16 | 1 | 2 | 1 | 2 | 2 | 0 | 0 | 4 | 2 | 2 |
| Tennessee | 15 | 2 | 0 | 1 | 1 | 3 | 1 | 1 | 0 | 3 | 3 |
| West South Central | 113 | 9 | 18 | 14 | 5 | 17 | 8 | 11 | 15 | 8 | 8 |
| Arkansas | 8 | 1 | 0 | 2 | 1 | 0 | 0 | 0 | 4 | 0 | 0 |
| Louisiana | 21 | 2 | 4 | 0 | 1 | 3 | 3 | 2 | 3 | 1 | 2 |
| Oklahoma | 13 | 1 | 0 | 3 | 1 | 1 | 0 | 2 | 2 | 2 | 1 |
| Texas | 71 | 5 | 14 | 9 | 2 | 13 | 5 | 7 | 6 | 5 | 5 |
| West | 124 | 20 | 19 | 17 | 12 | 11 | 10 | 8 | 9 | 13 | 5 |
| Mountain | 57 | 9 | 10 | 6 | 8 | 4 | 4 | 6 | 4 | 4 | 2 |
| Arizona | 17 | 4 | 2 | 2 | 1 | 1 | 2 | 1 | 2 | 2 | 0 |
| Colorado | 9 | 0 | 2 | 0 | 0 | 0 | 0 | 4 | 0 | 1 | 2 |
| Idaho | 2 | 0 | 0 | 0 | 2 | 0 | 0 | 0 | 0 | 0 | 0 |
| Montana | 6 | 2 | 1 | 1 | 1 | 0 | 1 | 0 | 0 | 0 | 0 |
| Nevada | 5 | 0 | 1 | 1 | 2 | 0 | 0 | 0 | 1 | 0 | 0 |
| New Mexico | 11 | 1 | 4 | 1 | 2 | 1 | 0 | 0 | 1 | 1 | 0 |
| Utah | 5 | 1 | 0 | 1 | 0 | 2 | 0 | 1 | 0 | 0 | 0 |
| Wyoming | 2 | 1 | 0 | 0 | 0 | 0 | 1 | 0 | 0 | 0 | 0 |
| Pacific | 67 | 11 | 9 | 11 | 4 | 7 | 6 | 2 | 5 | 9 | 3 |
| Alaska | 1 | 0 | 0 | 0 | 0 | 0 | 0 | 0 | 1 | 0 | 0 |
| California | 55 | 9 | 7 | 11 | 3 | 6 | 5 | 0 | 3 | 9 | 2 |
| Hawaii | 4 | 1 | 0 | 0 | 0 | 0 | 1 | 2 | 0 | 0 | 0 |
| Oregon | 2 | 0 | 1 | 0 | 0 | 0 | 0 | 0 | 0 | 0 | 1 |
| Washington | 5 | 1 | 1 | 0 | 1 | 1 | 0 | 0 | 1 | 0 | 0 |
| Puerto Rico and other outlying areas | 7 | 1 | 1 | 3 | 0 | 0 | 1 | 0 | 0 | 1 | 0 |
| American Samoa | 0 | 0 | 0 | 0 | 0 | 0 | 0 | 0 | 0 | 0 | 0 |
| Guam | 1 | 0 | 1 | 0 | 0 | 0 | 0 | 0 | 0 | 0 | 0 |
| Mariana Islands | 0 | 0 | 0 | 0 | 0 | 0 | 0 | 0 | 0 | 0 | 0 |
| Puerto Rico | 5 | 1 | 0 | 2 | 0 | 0 | 1 | 0 | 0 | 1 | 0 |
| U.S. Virgin Islands | 1 | 0 | 0 | 1 | 0 | 0 | 0 | 0 | 0 | 0 | 0 |

# Table 26. Law Enforcement Officers Accidentally Killed, by Population Group/Agency Type, 2006–2015

(Number.)

| Area | Total | 2006 | 2007 | 2008 | 2009 | 2010 | 2011 | 2012 | 2013 | 2014 | 2015 |
|---|---|---|---|---|---|---|---|---|---|---|---|
| **Number of Victim Officers** | 577 | 66 | 83 | 68 | 48 | 72 | 53 | 48 | 49 | 45 | 45 |
| Group I (cities 250,000 and over) | 63 | 7 | 4 | 10 | 4 | 9 | 5 | 9 | 5 | 6 | 4 |
| Group II (cities 100,000–249,999) | 38 | 6 | 7 | 5 | 3 | 3 | 3 | 3 | 4 | 1 | 3 |
| Group III (cities 50,000–99,999) | 34 | 3 | 6 | 4 | 3 | 2 | 5 | 1 | 5 | 2 | 3 |
| Group IV (25,000–49,999) | 29 | 2 | 5 | 2 | 1 | 6 | 3 | 6 | 1 | 2 | 1 |
| Group V (cities 10,000–24,999) | 19 | 2 | 4 | 3 | 1 | 2 | 0 | 1 | 3 | 2 | 1 |
| Group VI (cities under 10,000) | 58 | 5 | 8 | 8 | 4 | 4 | 7 | 2 | 6 | 7 | 7 |
| Metropolitan counties | 129 | 19 | 19 | 14 | 10 | 13 | 11 | 12 | 10 | 10 | 11 |
| Nonmetropolitan counties | 58 | 4 | 6 | 5 | 11 | 9 | 3 | 4 | 5 | 7 | 4 |
| State agencies | 113 | 15 | 14 | 13 | 10 | 19 | 12 | 6 | 8 | 5 | 11 |
| Federal agencies | 29 | 2 | 9 | 1 | 1 | 5 | 3 | 4 | 2 | 2 | 0 |
| Puerto Rico and other outlying areas | 7 | 1 | 1 | 3 | 0 | 0 | 1 | 0 | 0 | 1 | 0 |

# Table 27. Law Enforcement Officers Accidentally Killed, by Time of Incident, 2006–2015

(Number.)

| Time of day | Total | 2006 | 2007 | 2008 | 2009 | 2010 | 2011 | 2012 | 2013 | 2014 | 2015 |
|---|---|---|---|---|---|---|---|---|---|---|---|
| **Number of Victim Officers** | 577 | 66 | 83 | 68 | 48 | 72 | 53 | 48 | 49 | 45 | 45 |
| Total A.M. hours | 262 | 26 | 37 | 32 | 23 | 39 | 22 | 25 | 16 | 25 | 17 |
| 12:01 a.m.–2 a.m. | 63 | 5 | 8 | 10 | 8 | 10 | 5 | 6 | 3 | 6 | 2 |
| 2:01 a.m.–4 a.m. | 58 | 5 | 9 | 7 | 2 | 8 | 9 | 5 | 5 | 4 | 4 |
| 4:01 a.m.–6 a.m. | 31 | 4 | 3 | 5 | 4 | 4 | 3 | 4 | 1 | 1 | 2 |
| 6:01 a.m.–8 a.m. | 40 | 5 | 2 | 3 | 3 | 5 | 3 | 5 | 3 | 7 | 4 |
| 8:01 a.m.–10 a.m. | 31 | 2 | 8 | 3 | 2 | 4 | 1 | 4 | 2 | 3 | 2 |
| 10:01 a.m.–noon | 39 | 5 | 7 | 4 | 4 | 8 | 1 | 1 | 2 | 4 | 3 |
| Total P.M. hours | 309 | 40 | 46 | 36 | 25 | 32 | 31 | 23 | 30 | 19 | 27 |
| 12:01 p.m.–2 p.m. | 53 | 9 | 10 | 6 | 4 | 4 | 6 | 3 | 3 | 4 | 4 |
| 2:01 p.m.–4 p.m. | 46 | 3 | 7 | 5 | 3 | 5 | 6 | 5 | 4 | 4 | 4 |
| 4:01 p.m.–6 p.m. | 47 | 10 | 6 | 4 | 3 | 3 | 7 | 2 | 4 | 3 | 5 |
| 6:01 p.m.–8 p.m. | 30 | 3 | 3 | 3 | 3 | 5 | 4 | 2 | 3 | 2 | 2 |
| 8:01 p.m.–10 p.m. | 64 | 6 | 12 | 7 | 8 | 6 | 3 | 5 | 10 | 2 | 5 |
| 10:01 p.m.–midnight | 69 | 9 | 8 | 11 | 4 | 9 | 5 | 6 | 6 | 4 | 7 |
| Not reported | 6 | 0 | 0 | 0 | 0 | 1 | 0 | 0 | 3 | 1 | 1 |

## Table 28. Law Enforcement Officers Accidentally Killed, by Day and Time of Incident, 2006–2015

(Number.)

| Time of day | Total | Sunday | Monday | Tuesday | Wednesday | Thursday | Friday | Saturday |
|---|---|---|---|---|---|---|---|---|
| **Number of Victim Officers** ............................. | 577 | 83 | 75 | 77 | 65 | 85 | 104 | 88 |
| Total A.M. hours ............................................. | 262 | 50 | 34 | 29 | 27 | 43 | 40 | 39 |
|     12:01 a.m.–2 a.m. ...................................... | 63 | 15 | 8 | 7 | 9 | 8 | 6 | 10 |
|     2:01 a.m.–4 a.m. ........................................ | 58 | 17 | 5 | 6 | 3 | 8 | 8 | 11 |
|     4:01 a.m.–6 a.m. ........................................ | 31 | 6 | 5 | 3 | 0 | 7 | 2 | 8 |
|     6:01 a.m.–8 a.m. ........................................ | 40 | 4 | 6 | 5 | 7 | 4 | 9 | 5 |
|     8:01 a.m.–10 a.m. ...................................... | 31 | 2 | 3 | 6 | 5 | 5 | 7 | 3 |
|     10:01 a.m.–noon ......................................... | 39 | 6 | 7 | 2 | 3 | 11 | 8 | 2 |
| Total P.M. hours ............................................. | 309 | 33 | 38 | 48 | 38 | 41 | 62 | 49 |
|     12:01 p.m.–2 p.m. ...................................... | 53 | 5 | 7 | 12 | 7 | 8 | 5 | 9 |
|     2:01 p.m.–4 p.m. ........................................ | 46 | 2 | 10 | 7 | 10 | 5 | 7 | 5 |
|     4:01 p.m.–6 p.m. ........................................ | 47 | 4 | 5 | 8 | 6 | 7 | 12 | 5 |
|     6:01 p.m.–8 p.m. ........................................ | 30 | 3 | 4 | 4 | 4 | 5 | 6 | 4 |
|     8:01 p.m.–10 p.m. ...................................... | 64 | 11 | 4 | 6 | 7 | 9 | 19 | 8 |
|     10:01 p.m.–midnight ................................... | 69 | 8 | 8 | 11 | 4 | 7 | 13 | 18 |
| Not reported ................................................. | 6 | 0 | 3 | 0 | 0 | 1 | 2 | 0 |

## Table 29. Law Enforcement Officers Accidentally Killed, by Day of Incident, 2006–2015

(Number.)

| Day of the week | Total | 2006 | 2007 | 2008 | 2009 | 2010 | 2011 | 2012 | 2013 | 2014 | 2015 |
|---|---|---|---|---|---|---|---|---|---|---|---|
| **Number of Victim Officers** ......... | 577 | 66 | 83 | 68 | 48 | 72 | 53 | 48 | 49 | 45 | 45 |
| Sunday ......................................... | 83 | 12 | 11 | 10 | 5 | 11 | 7 | 6 | 6 | 9 | 6 |
| Monday ....................................... | 75 | 4 | 6 | 12 | 8 | 8 | 7 | 7 | 6 | 5 | 12 |
| Tuesday ....................................... | 77 | 12 | 11 | 8 | 5 | 7 | 10 | 5 | 7 | 9 | 3 |
| Wednesday .................................. | 65 | 7 | 17 | 7 | 7 | 8 | 2 | 2 | 6 | 4 | 5 |
| Thursday ..................................... | 85 | 11 | 11 | 11 | 9 | 10 | 10 | 8 | 4 | 5 | 6 |
| Friday .......................................... | 104 | 14 | 16 | 11 | 7 | 17 | 7 | 8 | 12 | 8 | 4 |
| Saturday ...................................... | 88 | 6 | 11 | 9 | 7 | 11 | 10 | 12 | 8 | 5 | 9 |

## Table 30. Law Enforcement Officers Accidentally Killed, by Month of Incident, 2006–2015

(Number.)

| Month | Total | 2006 | 2007 | 2008 | 2009 | 2010 | 2011 | 2012 | 2013 | 2014 | 2015 |
|---|---|---|---|---|---|---|---|---|---|---|---|
| **Number of Victim Officers** ............ | 577 | 66 | 83 | 68 | 48 | 72 | 53 | 48 | 49 | 45 | 45 |
| January ......................................... | 53 | 6 | 2 | 7 | 9 | 8 | 4 | 4 | 1 | 6 | 6 |
| February ....................................... | 39 | 6 | 6 | 6 | 4 | 9 | 4 | 1 | 0 | 2 | 1 |
| March ........................................... | 42 | 5 | 6 | 3 | 2 | 3 | 8 | 3 | 5 | 2 | 5 |
| April ............................................. | 50 | 6 | 14 | 0 | 5 | 6 | 1 | 3 | 5 | 5 | 5 |
| May .............................................. | 58 | 4 | 9 | 6 | 6 | 4 | 8 | 4 | 9 | 6 | 2 |
| June .............................................. | 50 | 3 | 8 | 4 | 3 | 15 | 5 | 4 | 2 | 1 | 5 |
| July .............................................. | 40 | 4 | 4 | 3 | 3 | 3 | 5 | 8 | 6 | 1 | 3 |
| August .......................................... | 44 | 8 | 6 | 8 | 4 | 4 | 3 | 2 | 3 | 1 | 5 |
| September ..................................... | 46 | 5 | 3 | 9 | 2 | 6 | 4 | 6 | 3 | 5 | 3 |
| October ........................................ | 63 | 7 | 14 | 9 | 4 | 10 | 2 | 4 | 5 | 6 | 2 |
| November ..................................... | 47 | 8 | 7 | 9 | 2 | 1 | 3 | 5 | 3 | 4 | 5 |
| December ..................................... | 45 | 4 | 4 | 4 | 4 | 3 | 6 | 4 | 7 | 6 | 3 |

## Table 31. Law Enforcement Officers Accidentally Killed, by Age Group of Victim Officer, 2006–2015

(Number.)

| Age group | Total | 2006 | 2007 | 2008 | 2009 | 2010 | 2011 | 2012 | 2013 | 2014 | 2015 |
|---|---|---|---|---|---|---|---|---|---|---|---|
| **Number of Victim Officers** .......... | 577 | 66 | 83 | 68 | 48 | 72 | 53 | 48 | 49 | 45 | 45 |
| Under 25 ...................................... | 39 | 1 | 10 | 2 | 7 | 2 | 2 | 2 | 2 | 4 | 7 |
| 25–30 ......................................... | 116 | 21 | 11 | 17 | 13 | 15 | 10 | 6 | 6 | 7 | 10 |
| 31–35 ......................................... | 98 | 15 | 20 | 11 | 8 | 15 | 3 | 9 | 4 | 9 | 4 |
| 36–40 ......................................... | 101 | 10 | 15 | 14 | 7 | 13 | 11 | 6 | 10 | 8 | 7 |
| 41–45 ......................................... | 79 | 9 | 9 | 10 | 4 | 5 | 8 | 13 | 9 | 5 | 7 |
| 46–50 ......................................... | 60 | 2 | 10 | 6 | 7 | 8 | 9 | 8 | 5 | 3 | 2 |
| 51–55 ......................................... | 42 | 4 | 2 | 4 | 2 | 6 | 5 | 3 | 8 | 5 | 3 |
| 56–60 ......................................... | 25 | 2 | 5 | 3 | 0 | 5 | 2 | 1 | 2 | 2 | 3 |
| Over 60 ...................................... | 12 | 2 | 1 | 1 | 0 | 2 | 3 | 0 | 0 | 2 | 1 |
| Not reported ................................. | 5 | 0 | 0 | 0 | 0 | 1 | 0 | 0 | 3 | 0 | 1 |
| Average age (years) ........................ | 38 | 36 | 37 | 38 | 35 | 39 | 41 | 40 | 41 | 39 | 37 |

## Table 32. Law Enforcement Officers Accidentally Killed, by Years of Service of Victim Officer, 2006–2015

(Number.)

| Years of service | Total | 2006 | 2007 | 2008 | 2009 | 2010 | 2011 | 2012 | 2013 | 2014 | 2015 |
|---|---|---|---|---|---|---|---|---|---|---|---|
| **Number of Victim Officers** ......... | 577 | 66 | 83 | 68 | 48 | 72 | 53 | 48 | 49 | 45 | 45 |
| Less than 1 ................................. | 31 | 3 | 4 | 3 | 2 | 4 | 2 | 2 | 2 | 5 | 4 |
| 1–5 ........................................... | 183 | 24 | 32 | 19 | 20 | 24 | 13 | 9 | 9 | 15 | 18 |
| 6–10 ......................................... | 146 | 20 | 24 | 18 | 12 | 18 | 13 | 14 | 12 | 12 | 3 |
| 11–15 ........................................ | 67 | 5 | 7 | 9 | 4 | 8 | 7 | 9 | 8 | 3 | 7 |
| 16–20 ........................................ | 71 | 9 | 8 | 9 | 4 | 8 | 6 | 8 | 7 | 3 | 9 |
| 21–25 ........................................ | 27 | 1 | 4 | 3 | 2 | 2 | 5 | 3 | 5 | 0 | 2 |
| 26–30 ........................................ | 29 | 1 | 1 | 3 | 4 | 4 | 3 | 3 | 3 | 5 | 2 |
| More than 30 .............................. | 20 | 3 | 2 | 3 | 0 | 4 | 4 | 0 | 2 | 2 | 0 |
| Not reported ................................. | 3 | 0 | 1 | 1 | 0 | 0 | 0 | 0 | 1 | 0 | 0 |
| Average years of service ............... | 11 | 10 | 9 | 11 | 9 | 11 | 13 | 12 | 13 | 10 | 9 |

## Table 33. Law Enforcement Officers Accidentally Killed, by Profile of Victim Officer, Averages, 1996–2015

(Number.)

| Characteristic | 2015 | 5-year averages | | 10-year averages | |
|---|---|---|---|---|---|
| | | 2006–2010 | 2011–2015 | 1996–2005 | 2006–2015 |
| Age ............................................. | 37 | 37 | 40 | 37 | 38 |
| Years of service ........................... | 9 | 10 | 12 | 10 | 11 |
| Height ......................................... | 5'10" | 5'11" | 5'11" | 5'11" | 5'11" |
| Weight[1] ...................................... | 209 | 202 | 211 | 196 | 206 |

## Table 34. Law Enforcement Officers Accidentally Killed, by Race and Sex of Victim Officer, 2006–2015

(Number.)

| Characteristic | Total | 2006 | 2007 | 2008 | 2009 | 2010 | 2011 | 2012 | 2013 | 2014 | 2015 |
|---|---|---|---|---|---|---|---|---|---|---|---|
| **Number of Victim Officers** ......... | 577 | 66 | 83 | 68 | 48 | 72 | 53 | 48 | 49 | 45 | 45 |
| Race ................................................ | | | | | | | | | | | |
| White .................................... | 490 | 59 | 70 | 59 | 44 | 60 | 45 | 36 | 41 | 43 | 33 |
| Black ..................................... | 63 | 4 | 8 | 7 | 4 | 8 | 7 | 10 | 6 | 0 | 9 |
| American Indian/Alaska Native | 2 | 0 | 0 | 0 | 0 | 2 | 0 | 0 | 0 | 0 | 0 |
| Asian/Native Hawaiian/Other | | | | | | | | | | | |
| Pacific Islander ........................... | 12 | 3 | 1 | 1 | 0 | 1 | 1 | 2 | 0 | 2 | 1 |
| Not reported ........................... | 10 | 0 | 4 | 1 | 0 | 1 | 0 | 0 | 2 | 0 | 2 |
| Sex ................................................ | | | | | | | | | | | |
| Male ...................................... | 547 | 64 | 79 | 61 | 48 | 67 | 50 | 46 | 49 | 42 | 41 |
| Female ................................... | 30 | 2 | 4 | 7 | 0 | 5 | 3 | 2 | 0 | 3 | 4 |

## Table 35. Law Enforcement Officers Accidentally Killed, by Circumstance at Scene of Incident, 2006–2015

(Number.)

| Circumstance | Total | 2006 | 2007 | 2008 | 2009 | 2010 | 2011 | 2012 | 2013 | 2014 | 2015 |
|---|---|---|---|---|---|---|---|---|---|---|---|
| **Number of Victim Officers** ............................................. | 577 | 66 | 83 | 68 | 48 | 72 | 53 | 48 | 49 | 45 | 45 |
| Automobile accident ................................................ | 338 | 38 | 49 | 39 | 34 | 45 | 30 | 23 | 23 | 28 | 29 |
| Motorcycle accident ................................................ | 54 | 8 | 6 | 6 | 3 | 7 | 4 | 6 | 4 | 6 | 4 |
| Aircraft accident ................................................ | 17 | 3 | 3 | 2 | 1 | 2 | 1 | 3 | 1 | 0 | 1 |
| Struck by vehicle ................................................ | 93 | 13 | 12 | 13 | 7 | 11 | 5 | 10 | 9 | 6 | 7 |
| Traffic stop, roadblock, etc. ........................................ | 28 | 4 | 7 | 1 | 3 | 4 | 3 | 2 | 1 | 1 | 2 |
| Directing traffic, assisting motorist, etc. ..................... | 65 | 9 | 5 | 12 | 4 | 7 | 2 | 8 | 8 | 5 | 5 |
| Accidental shooting ................................................ | 27 | 4 | 4 | 2 | 2 | 3 | 4 | 2 | 2 | 2 | 2 |
| Crossfire, mistaken for subject, firearm mishap ......... | 21 | 3 | 4 | 2 | 2 | 1 | 3 | 2 | 2 | 1 | 1 |
| Training session ................................................ | 3 | 0 | 0 | 0 | 0 | 1 | 0 | 0 | 0 | 1 | 1 |
| Self-inflicted, cleaning mishap (not apparent or confirmed suicide) ................................................ | 3 | 1 | 0 | 0 | 0 | 1 | 1 | 0 | 0 | 0 | 0 |
| Drowning ................................................ | 9 | 0 | 2 | 1 | 0 | 0 | 3 | 0 | 2 | 1 | 0 |
| Fall ................................................ | 12 | 0 | 1 | 0 | 0 | 1 | 2 | 3 | 4 | 0 | 1 |
| Other accidental ................................................ | 27 | 0 | 6 | 5 | 1 | 3 | 4 | 1 | 4 | 2 | 1 |

## Table 36. Law Enforcement Officers Accidentally Killed, by Circumstance at Scene of Incident, by Type of Assignment, 2015

(Number.)

| Circumstance | Total | 2-officer vehicle | 1-officer vehicle | | Foot patrol | | Other[1] | | Off duty |
|---|---|---|---|---|---|---|---|---|---|
| | | | Alone | Assisted | Alone | Assisted | Alone | Assisted | |
| **Number of Victim Officers** .................... | 45 | 5 | 18 | 4 | 1 | 0 | 8 | 6 | 3 |
| Automobile accident ................... | 29 | 4 | 17 | 1 | 0 | 0 | 5 | 1 | 1 |
| Wearing seatbelt ................... | 18 | 1 | 13 | 0 | 0 | 0 | 3 | 0 | 1 |
| Not wearing seatbelt ................... | 8 | 2 | 2 | 1 | 0 | 0 | 2 | 1 | 0 |
| Seatbelt usage not reported ................... | 3 | 1 | 2 | 0 | 0 | 0 | 0 | 0 | 0 |
| Motorcycle accident ................... | 4 | 0 | 1 | 0 | 0 | 0 | 0 | 3 | 0 |
| Aircraft accident ................... | 1 | 0 | 0 | 0 | 0 | 0 | 1 | 0 | 0 |
| Struck by vehicle ................... | 7 | 1 | 0 | 2 | 1 | 0 | 1 | 0 | 2 |
| Traffic stop, roadblock, etc. ................... | 2 | 0 | 0 | 1 | 0 | 0 | 1 | 0 | 0 |
| Directing traffic, assisting motorist, etc. ................... | 5 | 1 | 0 | 1 | 1 | 0 | 0 | 0 | 2 |
| Accidental shooting ................... | 2 | 0 | 0 | 0 | 0 | 0 | 0 | 2 | 0 |
| Crossfire, mistaken for subject, firearm mishap ................... | 1 | 0 | 0 | 0 | 0 | 0 | 0 | 1 | 0 |
| Training session ................... | 1 | 0 | 0 | 0 | 0 | 0 | 0 | 1 | 0 |
| Self-inflicted, cleaning mishap (not apparent or confirmed suicide) .......... | 0 | 0 | 0 | 0 | 0 | 0 | 0 | 0 | 0 |
| Drowning ................... | 0 | 0 | 0 | 0 | 0 | 0 | 0 | 0 | 0 |
| Fall ................... | 1 | 0 | 0 | 1 | 0 | 0 | 0 | 0 | 0 |
| Other accidental ................... | 1 | 0 | 0 | 0 | 0 | 0 | 1 | 0 | 0 |

[1] Includes detectives, officers on special assignments, undercover officers, and officers on other types of assignments not listed.

## Table 37. Law Enforcement Officers Assaulted, by Region and Geographic Division, 2015

(Number; rate.)

| Characteristic | Total[1] | Rate per 100 officers | Assaults with injury | Rate per 100 officers | Number of reporting agencies | Population covered | Number of officers employed |
|---|---|---|---|---|---|---|---|
| **Number of Victim Officers** .................... | 50,212 | 9.9 | 14,281 | 2.8 | 11,961 | 241,382,351 | 507,852 |
| Northeast ................... | 7,767 | 7.7 | 2,534 | 2.5 | 2,892 | 44,823,303 | 101,011 |
| New England ................... | 3,521 | 11.9 | 894 | 3.0 | 910 | 14,166,413 | 29,678 |
| Middle Atlantic ................... | 4,246 | 6.0 | 1,640 | 2.3 | 1,982 | 30,656,890 | 71,333 |
| Midwest ................... | 6,722 | 8.9 | 2,114 | 2.8 | 2,933 | 38,767,397 | 75,757 |
| East North Central ................... | 2,784 | 7.6 | 989 | 2.7 | 1,218 | 19,474,830 | 36,409 |
| West North Central ................... | 3,938 | 10.0 | 1,125 | 2.9 | 1,715 | 19,292,567 | 39,348 |
| South ................... | 18,963 | 9.6 | 4,638 | 2.3 | 4,291 | 86,938,822 | 198,151 |
| South Atlantic ................... | 12,520 | 10.3 | 2,601 | 2.1 | 2,076 | 51,053,258 | 121,678 |
| East South Central ................... | 2,539 | 8.7 | 857 | 3.0 | 848 | 12,907,198 | 29,019 |
| West Soiuth Central ................... | 3,904 | 8.2 | 1,180 | 2.5 | 1,367 | 22,978,366 | 47,454 |
| West ................... | 16,760 | 12.6 | 4,995 | 3.8 | 1,845 | 70,852,829 | 132,933 |
| Mountain ................... | 4,973 | 12.0 | 1,463 | 3.5 | 770 | 21,408,662 | 41,278 |
| Pacific ................... | 11,787 | 12.9 | 3,532 | 3.9 | 1,075 | 49,444,167 | 91,655 |

[1] Regional and divisional totals do not include data for Alaska, which were not available for inclusion in this table.

## Table 38. Law Enforcement Officers Assaulted, by Population Group, 2015

(Number; rate.)

| Characteristic | Total | Rate per 100 officers | Assaults with injury | Rate per 100 officers | Number of reporting agencies | Population covered | Number of officers employed |
|---|---|---|---|---|---|---|---|
| **Number of Victim Officers** .................................. | 50,212 | 9.9 | 14,281 | 2.8 | 11,961 | 241,382,351 | 507,852 |
| Group I (cities 250,000 and over) .......................... | 12,799 | 13.9 | 3,231 | 3.5 | 67 | 41,818,592 | 92,290 |
| Group II (cities 100,000–249,999) .......................... | 6,496 | 15.4 | 1,918 | 4.5 | 180 | 26,746,492 | 42,280 |
| Group III (cities 50,000–99,999) .......................... | 6,100 | 14.6 | 1,921 | 4.6 | 419 | 29,180,916 | 41,828 |
| Group IV (cities 25,000–49,999) .......................... | 4,122 | 10.9 | 1,283 | 3.4 | 685 | 23,638,790 | 37,913 |
| Group V (cities 10,000–24,999) .......................... | 3,784 | 9.1 | 1,117 | 2.7 | 1,445 | 23,069,940 | 41,368 |
| Group VI (cities under 10,000)[1] .......................... | 3,865 | 5.8 | 1,194 | 1.8 | 5,891 | 18,516,489 | 66,293 |
| Metropolitan counties[1] .................................. | 11,102 | 7.6 | 3,061 | 2.1 | 1,370 | 58,404,530 | 146,188 |
| Nonmetropolitan counties[1] .................................. | 1,944 | 4.9 | 556 | 1.4 | 1,904 | 20,006,602 | 39,692 |

[1] Includes universities and colleges, state police agencies, and/or other agencies to which no population is attributed.

# Table 39. Law Enforcement Officers Assaulted, by Time of Incident, Number of Assaults, and Percent Distribution, 2006–2015

(Number; percent.)

| Characteristic | Total | Percent distribution | 2006 Total | 2006 Percent distribution | 2007 Total | 2007 Percent distribution | 2008 Total | 2008 Percent distribution | 2009 Total | 2009 Percent distribution | 2010 Total | 2010 Percent distribution |
|---|---|---|---|---|---|---|---|---|---|---|---|---|
| **Total Number of Victim Officers** ........ | 556,095 | 100.0 | 59,396 | 100.0 | 61,257 | 100.0 | 61,087 | 100.0 | 58,364 | 100.0 | 56,491 | 100.0 |
| Total A.M. hours ..................... | 223,786 | 40.2 | 23,964 | 40.3 | 24,488 | 40.0 | 24,637 | 40.3 | 23,586 | 40.4 | 22,807 | 40.4 |
| 12:01 a.m.–2 a.m. ............... | 84,081 | 15.1 | 8,823 | 14.9 | 9,318 | 15.2 | 9,585 | 15.7 | 9,323 | 16.0 | 8,829 | 15.6 |
| 2:01 a.m.–4 a.m. .............. | 51,408 | 9.2 | 5,505 | 9.3 | 5,862 | 9.6 | 5,879 | 9.6 | 5,653 | 9.7 | 5,390 | 9.5 |
| 4:01 a.m.–6 a.m. .............. | 19,796 | 3.6 | 2,169 | 3.7 | 2,157 | 3.5 | 2,114 | 3.5 | 2,082 | 3.6 | 1,987 | 3.5 |
| 6:01 a.m.–8 a.m. .............. | 14,219 | 2.6 | 1,548 | 2.6 | 1,476 | 2.4 | 1,480 | 2.4 | 1,389 | 2.4 | 1,428 | 2.5 |
| 8:01 a.m.–10 a.m. ............. | 23,570 | 4.2 | 2,621 | 4.4 | 2,489 | 4.1 | 2,376 | 3.9 | 2,192 | 3.8 | 2,291 | 4.1 |
| 10:01 a.m.–noon ............... | 30,712 | 5.5 | 3,298 | 5.6 | 3,186 | 5.2 | 3,203 | 5.2 | 2,947 | 5.0 | 2,882 | 5.1 |
| Total P.M. hours ..................... | 332,309 | 59.8 | 35,432 | 59.7 | 36,769 | 60.0 | 36,450 | 59.7 | 34,778 | 59.6 | 33,684 | 59.6 |
| 12:01 p.m.–2 p.m. ............... | 34,352 | 6.2 | 3,599 | 6.1 | 3,659 | 6.0 | 3,558 | 5.8 | 3,414 | 5.8 | 3,307 | 5.9 |
| 2:01 p.m.–4 p.m. .............. | 42,085 | 7.6 | 4,508 | 7.6 | 4,464 | 7.3 | 4,286 | 7.0 | 4,232 | 7.3 | 4,361 | 7.7 |
| 4:01 p.m.–6 p.m. .............. | 50,413 | 9.1 | 5,307 | 8.9 | 5,573 | 9.1 | 5,274 | 8.6 | 5,315 | 9.1 | 5,045 | 8.9 |
| 6:01 p.m.–8 p.m. .............. | 59,301 | 10.7 | 6,309 | 10.6 | 6,372 | 10.4 | 6,611 | 10.8 | 6,269 | 10.7 | 6,088 | 10.8 |
| 8:01 p.m.–10 p.m. ............. | 69,713 | 12.5 | 7,487 | 12.6 | 7,825 | 12.8 | 7,853 | 12.9 | 7,337 | 12.6 | 7,195 | 12.7 |
| 10:01 p.m.–midnight ........... | 76,445 | 13.7 | 8,222 | 13.8 | 8,876 | 14.5 | 8,868 | 14.5 | 8,211 | 14.1 | 7,688 | 13.6 |

(Number; percent.)

| Characteristic | 2011 Total | 2011 Percent distribution | 2012 Total | 2012 Percent distribution | 2013 Total | 2013 Percent distribution | 2014 Total | 2014 Percent distribution | 2015 Total | 2015 Percent distribution |
|---|---|---|---|---|---|---|---|---|---|---|
| **Total Number of Victim Officers** ................................. | 55,631 | 100.0 | 53,867 | 100.0 | 50,802 | 100.0 | 48,988 | 100.0 | 50,212 | 100.0 |
| Total A.M. hours ....................................... | 22,703 | 40.8 | 22,056 | 40.9 | 20,662 | 40.7 | 19,381 | 39.6 | 19,502 | 38.8 |
| 12:01 a.m.–2 a.m. ..................................... | 8,555 | 15.4 | 8,188 | 15.2 | 7,679 | 15.1 | 6,983 | 14.3 | 6,798 | 13.5 |
| 2:01 a.m.–4 a.m. ..................................... | 5,293 | 9.5 | 5,212 | 9.7 | 4,623 | 9.1 | 4,091 | 8.4 | 3,900 | 7.8 |
| 4:01 a.m.–6 a.m. ..................................... | 2,126 | 3.8 | 1,973 | 3.7 | 1,817 | 3.6 | 1,631 | 3.3 | 1,740 | 3.5 |
| 6:01 a.m.–8 a.m. ..................................... | 1,438 | 2.6 | 1,367 | 2.5 | 1,258 | 2.5 | 1,343 | 2.7 | 1,492 | 3.0 |
| 8:01 a.m.–10 a.m. ..................................... | 2,213 | 4.0 | 2,272 | 4.2 | 2,336 | 4.6 | 2,377 | 4.9 | 2,403 | 4.8 |
| 10:01 a.m.–noon ..................................... | 3,078 | 5.5 | 3,044 | 5.7 | 2,949 | 5.8 | 2,956 | 6.0 | 3,169 | 6.3 |
| Total P.M. hours ....................................... | 32,928 | 59.2 | 31,811 | 59.1 | 30,140 | 59.3 | 29,607 | 60.4 | 30,710 | 61.2 |
| 12:01 p.m.–2 p.m. ..................................... | 3,297 | 5.9 | 3,395 | 6.3 | 3,303 | 6.5 | 3,318 | 6.8 | 3,502 | 7.0 |
| 2:01 p.m.–4 p.m. ..................................... | 4,145 | 7.5 | 4,083 | 7.6 | 3,828 | 7.5 | 4,018 | 8.2 | 4,160 | 8.3 |
| 4:01 p.m.–6 p.m. ..................................... | 4,826 | 8.7 | 4,839 | 9.0 | 4,654 | 9.2 | 4,726 | 9.6 | 4,854 | 9.7 |
| 6:01 p.m.–8 p.m. ..................................... | 6,032 | 10.8 | 5,603 | 10.4 | 5,434 | 10.7 | 5,045 | 10.3 | 5,538 | 11.0 |
| 8:01 p.m.–10 p.m. ..................................... | 6,808 | 12.2 | 6,684 | 12.4 | 6,177 | 12.2 | 6,102 | 12.5 | 6,245 | 12.4 |
| 10:01 p.m.–midnight ..................................... | 7,820 | 14.1 | 7,207 | 13.4 | 6,744 | 13.3 | 6,398 | 13.1 | 6,411 | 12.8 |

*Note:* Assault figures published in prior years' editions of Law Enforcement Officers Killed and Assaulted have been updated for inclusion in this table. Because of rounding, percentages may not add to 100.0

# Table 40. Law Enforcement Officers Assaulted, by Type of Weapon and Percent Injured, 2006–2015

(Number; percent.)

| Characteristic | Total | Percent injured | Firearm Total | Firearm Percent injured | Knife or other cutting instrument Total | Knife or other cutting instrument Percent injured | Other dangerous weapon Total | Other dangerous weapon Percent injured | Personal weapons Total | Personal weapons Percent injured | Number of reporting agencies | Population covered | Number of officers employed |
|---|---|---|---|---|---|---|---|---|---|---|---|---|---|
| **Total Number of Victim Officers** ............ | 556,095 | 27.1 | 21,539 | 9.4 | 9,541 | 12.8 | 78,054 | 23.7 | 446,961 | 28.8 | | | |
| 2006 ........................... | 59,396 | 26.7 | 2,290 | 9.5 | 1,055 | 12.7 | 8,611 | 23.6 | 47,440 | 28.4 | 10,596 | 227,360,586 | 504,147 |
| 2007 ........................... | 61,257 | 25.9 | 2,216 | 8.7 | 1,028 | 10.5 | 8,692 | 22.2 | 49,321 | 27.6 | 10,973 | 234,734,286 | 523,944 |
| 2008 ........................... | 61,087 | 26.0 | 2,292 | 8.3 | 958 | 13.0 | 8,466 | 22.8 | 49,371 | 27.7 | 10,835 | 238,730,830 | 541,906 |
| 2009 ........................... | 58,364 | 26.0 | 2,007 | 8.1 | 886 | 12.4 | 7,966 | 23.5 | 47,505 | 27.4 | 11,691 | 245,925,716 | 560,387 |
| 2010 ........................... | 56,491 | 26.5 | 1,925 | 11.1 | 918 | 12.1 | 7,413 | 23.8 | 46,235 | 27.8 | 11,826 | 248,726,641 | 557,884 |
| 2011 ........................... | 55,631 | 26.6 | 2,240 | 9.0 | 1,003 | 15.0 | 7,856 | 22.4 | 44,532 | 28.5 | 12,031 | 254,534,862 | 539,282 |
| 2012 ........................... | 53,867 | 27.7 | 2,276 | 9.9 | 909 | 13.1 | 7,435 | 24.2 | 43,247 | 29.6 | 11,794 | 250,150,500 | 525,217 |
| 2013 ........................... | 50,802 | 29.1 | 2,299 | 10.7 | 901 | 14.0 | 7,042 | 27.0 | 40,560 | 30.8 | 11,958 | 256,689,224 | 551,893 |
| 2014 ........................... | 48,988 | 28.5 | 1,976 | 9.2 | 966 | 12.6 | 6,976 | 23.9 | 39,070 | 30.7 | 11,235 | 246,680,861 | 543,331 |
| 2015 ........................... | 50,212 | 28.4 | 2,018 | 9.5 | 917 | 12.3 | 7,597 | 24.7 | 39,680 | 30.5 | 11,961 | 241,382,351 | 507,852 |

*Note:* Assault figures published in prior years' editions of *Law Enforcement Officers Killed and Assaulted* have been updated for inclusion in this table.

# Table 41. Law Enforcement Officers Assaulted, by Region, Geographic Division, and State, by Type of Weapon, 2015

(Number.)

| Characteristic | Total | Firearm | Knife or other cutting instrument | Other dangerous weapon | Personal weapons | Number of reporting agencies | Population covered | Number of officers employed |
|---|---|---|---|---|---|---|---|---|
| Total Number of Victim Officers ............... | 50,212 | 2,018 | 917 | 7,597 | 39,680 | 11,961 | 241,382,351 | 507,852 |
| Northeast ......................................... | 7,767 | 116 | 130 | 925 | 6,596 | 2,892 | 44,823,303 | 101,011 |
| New England ................................ | 3,521 | 22 | 62 | 528 | 2,909 | 910 | 14,166,413 | 29,678 |
| Connecticut ............................ | 616 | 1 | 4 | 76 | 535 | 102 | 3,518,098 | 7,741 |
| Maine .................................... | 184 | 0 | 1 | 12 | 171 | 181 | 1,324,696 | 1,972 |
| Massachusetts ........................ | 2,101 | 17 | 46 | 383 | 1,655 | 332 | 6,448,573 | 14,151 |
| New Hampshire ...................... | 252 | 3 | 1 | 22 | 226 | 163 | 1,227,634 | 2,224 |
| Rhode Island .......................... | 286 | 1 | 3 | 31 | 251 | 49 | 1,056,298 | 2,441 |
| Vermont ................................ | 82 | 0 | 7 | 4 | 71 | 83 | 591,114 | 1,149 |
| Middle Atlantic ............................ | 4,246 | 94 | 68 | 397 | 3,687 | 1,982 | 30,656,890 | 71,333 |
| New Jersey ............................ | 1,542 | 13 | 30 | 115 | 1,384 | 550 | 8,639,473 | 26,459 |
| New York .............................. | 710 | 6 | 8 | 71 | 625 | 452 | 10,281,246 | 25,001 |
| Pennsylvania .......................... | 1,994 | 75 | 30 | 211 | 1,678 | 980 | 11,736,171 | 19,873 |
| Midwest ........................................ | 6,722 | 346 | 123 | 996 | 5,257 | 2,933 | 38,767,397 | 75,757 |
| East North Central ...................... | 2,784 | 154 | 50 | 332 | 2,248 | 1,218 | 19,474,830 | 36,409 |
| Illinois[1] .................................. | 92 | 12 | 0 | 10 | 70 | 1 | 148,178 | 280 |
| Indiana .................................. | 925 | 40 | 14 | 80 | 791 | 168 | 2,923,088 | 5,117 |
| Michigan ................................ | 867 | 61 | 27 | 137 | 642 | 600 | 9,656,510 | 16,660 |
| Ohio ...................................... | 147 | 7 | 0 | 19 | 121 | 69 | 1,219,794 | 2,428 |
| Wisconsin .............................. | 753 | 34 | 9 | 86 | 624 | 380 | 5,527,260 | 11,924 |
| West North Central ...................... | 3,938 | 192 | 73 | 664 | 3,009 | 1,715 | 19,292,567 | 39,348 |
| Iowa ...................................... | 573 | 9 | 16 | 99 | 449 | 229 | 3,027,329 | 4,589 |
| Kansas .................................. | 281 | 6 | 5 | 29 | 241 | 177 | 1,735,445 | 4,817 |
| Minnesota .............................. | 401 | 16 | 5 | 93 | 287 | 373 | 5,469,764 | 9,170 |
| Missouri ................................ | 2,141 | 147 | 35 | 359 | 1,600 | 526 | 5,856,810 | 14,286 |
| Nebraska ................................ | 65 | 3 | 1 | 12 | 49 | 213 | 1,779,678 | 3,477 |
| North Dakota .......................... | 222 | 3 | 1 | 20 | 198 | 107 | 755,337 | 1,651 |
| South Dakota .......................... | 255 | 8 | 10 | 52 | 185 | 90 | 668,204 | 1,358 |
| South ........................................... | 18,963 | 837 | 335 | 3,004 | 14,787 | 4,291 | 86,938,822 | 198,151 |
| South Atlantic ............................ | 12,520 | 458 | 192 | 1,690 | 10,180 | 2,076 | 51,053,258 | 121,678 |
| Delaware ................................ | 382 | 18 | 6 | 78 | 280 | 56 | 944,670 | 2,239 |
| District of Columbia[2] .............. | 971 | 25 | 20 | 201 | 725 | 1 | 672,228 | 3,826 |
| Florida .................................. | 5,000 | 169 | 69 | 705 | 4,057 | 271 | 15,426,782 | 36,264 |
| Georgia .................................. | 953 | 58 | 33 | 138 | 724 | 322 | 7,624,641 | 18,870 |
| Maryland ................................ | 1,249 | 30 | 8 | 126 | 1,085 | 132 | 3,482,747 | 10,237 |
| North Carolina ........................ | 1,755 | 64 | 23 | 102 | 1,566 | 305 | 8,438,400 | 19,575 |
| South Carolina ........................ | 516 | 39 | 10 | 99 | 368 | 358 | 4,594,077 | 11,063 |
| Virginia .................................. | 1,204 | 32 | 11 | 166 | 995 | 410 | 8,377,319 | 16,787 |
| West Virginia .......................... | 490 | 23 | 12 | 75 | 380 | 221 | 1,492,394 | 2,817 |
| East South Central ...................... | 2,539 | 212 | 75 | 594 | 1,658 | 848 | 12,907,198 | 29,019 |
| Alabama ................................ | 54 | 2 | 0 | 3 | 49 | 94 | 1,832,494 | 4,858 |
| Kentucky ................................ | 767 | 41 | 12 | 157 | 557 | 286 | 3,828,749 | 6,009 |
| Mississippi ............................ | 50 | 6 | 3 | 7 | 34 | 46 | 703,707 | 1,810 |
| Tennessee .............................. | 1,668 | 163 | 60 | 427 | 1,018 | 422 | 6,542,248 | 16,342 |
| West South Central ...................... | 3,904 | 167 | 68 | 720 | 2,949 | 1,367 | 22,978,366 | 47,454 |
| Arkansas ................................ | 193 | 11 | 1 | 28 | 153 | 256 | 2,693,322 | 5,327 |
| Louisiana .............................. | 1,080 | 43 | 4 | 385 | 648 | 80 | 2,048,917 | 5,874 |
| Oklahoma .............................. | 758 | 34 | 27 | 131 | 566 | 346 | 3,777,046 | 7,278 |
| Texas .................................... | 1,873 | 79 | 36 | 176 | 1,582 | 685 | 14,459,081 | 28,975 |
| West ............................................. | 16,760 | 719 | 329 | 2,672 | 13,040 | 1,845 | 70,852,829 | 132,933 |
| Mountain .................................... | 4,973 | 310 | 128 | 812 | 3,723 | 770 | 21,408,662 | 41,278 |
| Arizona .................................. | 1,900 | 104 | 36 | 285 | 1,475 | 91 | 6,748,833 | 12,260 |
| Colorado ................................ | 1,136 | 125 | 51 | 197 | 763 | 220 | 5,389,082 | 11,696 |
| Idaho .................................... | 312 | 18 | 10 | 58 | 226 | 102 | 1,642,012 | 2,692 |
| Montana ................................ | 372 | 6 | 7 | 40 | 319 | 101 | 1,006,559 | 1,559 |
| Nevada .................................. | 427 | 50 | 4 | 106 | 267 | 42 | 2,890,845 | 6,253 |
| New Mexico ............................ | 138 | 1 | 5 | 20 | 112 | 38 | 365,923 | 902 |
| Utah ...................................... | 600 | 2 | 14 | 93 | 491 | 120 | 2,825,160 | 4,630 |
| Wyoming ................................ | 88 | 4 | 1 | 13 | 70 | 56 | 540,248 | 1,286 |
| Pacific ........................................ | 11,787 | 409 | 201 | 1,860 | 9,317 | 1,075 | 49,444,167 | 91,655 |
| Alaska[3] ................................ | | | | | | | | |
| California .............................. | 9,967 | 343 | 156 | 1,569 | 7,899 | 683 | 38,983,164 | 76,351 |
| Hawaii[4] ................................ | 335 | 5 | 5 | 40 | 285 | 2 | 1,164,233 | 2,361 |
| Oregon .................................. | 329 | 10 | 7 | 39 | 273 | 150 | 2,142,413 | 3,861 |
| Washington ............................ | 1,156 | 51 | 33 | 212 | 860 | 240 | 7,154,357 | 9,082 |

[1] Data represents the number of assaults on officers reported by the Rockford Police Department.
[2] Data represents the number of assaults on officers reported by the Metropolitan Police Department.
[3] Data for Alaska were not available for inclusion in this table.
[4] Data represents the number of assaults on officers reported by the Honolulu Police Department and the Maui Police Department.

## Table 42. Law Enforcement Officers Assaulted, by Circumstance at Scene of Incident, by Type of Weapon and Percent Distribution, 2015

(Number; percent.)

| Circumstance | Total | Percent distribution | Firearm Total | Firearm Percent distribution | Knife or other cutting instrument Total | Knife or other cutting instrument Percent distribution | Other dangerous weapon Total | Other dangerous weapon Percent distribution | Personal weapons Total | Personal weapons Percent distribution |
|---|---|---|---|---|---|---|---|---|---|---|
| **Total Number of Victim Officers** .......................... | 50,212 | 100.0 | 2,018 | 4.0 | 917 | 1.8 | 7,597 | 15.1 | 39,680 | 79.0 |
| Disturbance call ...................................................... | 16,256 | 100.0 | 657 | 4.0 | 386 | 2.4 | 1,758 | 10.8 | 13,455 | 82.8 |
| Burglary in progress/pursuing burglary suspect ......... | 840 | 100.0 | 63 | 7.5 | 25 | 3.0 | 198 | 23.6 | 554 | 66.0 |
| Robbery in progress/pursuing robbery suspect .......... | 398 | 100.0 | 48 | 12.1 | 12 | 3.0 | 64 | 16.1 | 274 | 68.8 |
| Attempting other arrest ......................................... | 7,820 | 100.0 | 226 | 2.9 | 99 | 1.3 | 944 | 12.1 | 6,551 | 83.8 |
| Civil disorder (mass disobedience, riot, etc.) ............ | 677 | 100.0 | 12 | 1.8 | 7 | 1.0 | 198 | 29.2 | 460 | 67.9 |
| Handling, transporting, custody of prisoner .............. | 6,143 | 100.0 | 17 | 0.3 | 19 | 0.3 | 647 | 10.5 | 5,460 | 88.9 |
| Investigating suspicious person/circumstance ........... | 4,647 | 100.0 | 229 | 4.9 | 113 | 2.4 | 681 | 14.7 | 3,624 | 78.0 |
| Ambush situation .................................................... | 240 | 100.0 | 86 | 12.0 | 1 | 0.4 | 61 | 25.4 | 92 | 38.3 |
| Handling person with mental illness ........................ | 1,710 | 100.0 | 69 | 4.0 | 101 | 5.9 | 203 | 11.9 | 1,337 | 78.2 |
| Traffic pursuit/stop ................................................ | 3,972 | 100.0 | 247 | 6.2 | 31 | 0.8 | 1,474 | 37.1 | 2,220 | 55.9 |
| All other ................................................................ | 7,509 | 100.0 | 364 | 4.8 | 123 | 1.6 | 1,369 | 18.2 | 5,653 | 75.3 |

Note: Because of rounding, percentages may not add to 100.0

## Table 43. Federal Officers Killed and Assaulted, by Department and Agency, by Number of Victim Officers and Known Offenders, 2014 and 2015

(Number; percent.)

| Department/agency | Victim officers 2014 | Victim officers 2015 | Known offenders 2014 | Known offenders 2015 |
|---|---|---|---|---|
| **Total Number of Victim Officers/Known Offenders** ................... | 1,410 | 1,336 | 892 | 832 |
| U.S. Capitol Police ......................................................... | 3 | 13 | 2 | 10 |
| U.S. Department of Homeland Security ............................................. | 535 | 488 | 111 | 109 |
|   U.S. Customs and Border Protection (CBP) ................................. | 500 | 454 | 80 | 83 |
|     CBP, Office of Air and Marine ........................... | 11 | 19 | 1 | 2 |
|     CBP, Office of Border Patrol[1] ........................... | 373 | 349 | | |
|     CBP, Office of Field Operations ........................... | 116 | 86 | 79 | 81 |
|   U.S. Immigration and Customs Enforcement ........................ | 8 | 8 | 5 | 6 |
|   U.S. Secret Service ........................................... | 27 | 26 | 26 | 20 |
| U.S. Department of the Interior ........................................... | 607 | 570 | 594 | 534 |
|   Bureau of Indian Affairs ........................................... | 550 | 505 | 544 | 471 |
|   Bureau of Land Management ........................................... | 5 | 3 | 5 | 4 |
|   National Park Service ........................................... | 47 | 54 | 43 | 54 |
|   U.S. Fish and Wildlife Service (FWS) ........................... | 5 | 8 | 2 | 5 |
|     FWS, National Wildlife Refuge System ........................... | 5 | 8 | 2 | 5 |
|     FWS, Office of Law Enforcement ........................... | 0 | 0 | 0 | 0 |
| U.S. Department of Justice ........................................... | 257 | 260 | 178 | 175 |
|   Bureau of Alcohol, Tobacco, Firearms and Explosives ................ | 10 | 11 | 11 | 7 |
|   Federal Bureau of Investigation ........................................... | 11 | 22 | 6 | 14 |
|   U.S. Drug Enforcement Administration ........................................... | 6 | 11 | 10 | 15 |
|   U.S. Marshals Service ........................................... | 230 | 216 | 151 | 139 |
| U.S. Department of the Treasury ........................................... | 1 | 1 | 2 | 1 |
|   Internal Revenue Service ........................................... | 1 | 0 | 2 | 0 |
|   Treasury Inspector General for Tax Administration ................... | 0 | 1 | 0 | 1 |
| U.S. Postal Inspection Service ........................................... | 7 | 4 | 5 | 3 |

[1] For 2013 and 2014, known offender data were not reported by the CBP, Office of Border Patrol.

# Table 44. Federal Officers Killed and Assaulted, by Department and Agency, by Extent of Injury to Victim Officer, 2011–2015

(Number; percent.)

| Department/agency | 2011 | | | 2012 | | | 2013 | | | 2014 | | | 2015 | | |
|---|---|---|---|---|---|---|---|---|---|---|---|---|---|---|---|
| | Killed | Injured | Not injured | Killed | Injured | Not injured | Killed | Injured | Not injured | Killed | Injured | Not injured | Killed | Injured | Not injured |
| **Total Number of Victim Officers/Known Offenders** | 3 | 254 | 1,432 | 1 | 206 | 1,096 | 4 | 292 | 1,478 | 0 | 170 | 867 | 1 | 172 | 814 |
| U.S. Capitol Police | 0 | 8 | 13 | 0 | 1 | 3 | 0 | 6 | 7 | 0 | 0 | 3 | 0 | 5 | 8 |
| U.S. Department of Homeland Security | 1 | 90 | 745 | 0 | 20 | 83 | 2 | 122 | 466 | 0 | 39 | 123 | 0 | 36 | 103 |
| U.S. Customs and Border Protection (CBP) | 0 | 82 | 720 | 0 | 12 | 40 | 2 | 121 | 432 | 0 | 18 | 109 | 0 | 24 | 81 |
| CBP, Office of Air and Marine | 0 | 0 | 25 | 0 | 0 | 9 | 0 | 0 | 27 | 0 | 0 | 11 | 0 | 0 | 19 |
| CBP, Office of Border Patrol[1,2,3,4] | 0 | 71 | 628 | | | | 2 | 98 | 368 | | | | | | |
| CBP, Office of Field Operations | 0 | 11 | 67 | 0 | 12 | 31 | 0 | 23 | 37 | 0 | 18 | 98 | 0 | 24 | 62 |
| U.S. Immigration and Customs Enforcement[5,6] | 1 | 4 | 0 | 0 | 6 | 6 | | | | 0 | 7 | 1 | 0 | 4 | 4 |
| U.S. Secret Service | 0 | 4 | 25 | 0 | 2 | 37 | 0 | 1 | 34 | 0 | 14 | 13 | 0 | 8 | 18 |
| U.S. Department of the Interior | 0 | 113 | 423 | 1 | 151 | 709 | 1 | 106 | 768 | 0 | 84 | 523 | 0 | 85 | 485 |
| Bureau of Indian Affairs[7] | 0 | 88 | 337 | 0 | 112 | 604 | 1 | 94 | 711 | 0 | 69 | 481 | 0 | 74 | 431 |
| Bureau of Land Management | 0 | 0 | 7 | 0 | 0 | 5 | 0 | 0 | 5 | 0 | 1 | 4 | 0 | 1 | 2 |
| National Park Service | 0 | 25 | 76 | 1 | 37 | 99 | 0 | 12 | 47 | 0 | 13 | 34 | 0 | 7 | 47 |
| U.S. Fish and Wildlife Service (FWS) | 0 | 0 | 3 | 0 | 2 | 1 | 0 | 0 | 5 | 0 | 1 | 4 | 0 | 3 | 5 |
| FWS, National Wildlife Refuge System | 0 | 0 | 3 | 0 | 1 | 1 | 0 | 0 | 5 | 0 | 1 | 4 | 0 | 3 | 5 |
| FWS, Office of Law Enforcement | 0 | 0 | 0 | 0 | 1 | 0 | 0 | 0 | 0 | 0 | 0 | 0 | 0 | 0 | 0 |
| U.S. Department of Justice | 2 | 41 | 246 | 0 | 32 | 297 | 1 | 58 | 234 | 0 | 46 | 211 | 1 | 45 | 214 |
| Bureau of Alcohol, Tobacco, Firearms and Explosives | 0 | 2 | 22 | 0 | 0 | 20 | 0 | 2 | 12 | 0 | 5 | 5 | 0 | 1 | 10 |
| Federal Bureau of Investigation | 0 | 7 | 22 | 0 | 2 | 22 | 0 | 11 | 20 | 0 | 3 | 8 | 0 | 5 | 17 |
| U.S. Drug Enforcement Administration[8] | 0 | 0 | 0 | 0 | 0 | 0 | 1 | 0 | 6 | 0 | 0 | 6 | 0 | 1 | 10 |
| U.S. Marshals Service | 2 | 32 | 202 | 0 | 30 | 255 | 0 | 45 | 196 | 0 | 38 | 192 | 1 | 38 | 177 |
| U.S. Department of the Treasury | 0 | 0 | 0 | 0 | 2 | 0 | 0 | 0 | 0 | 0 | 0 | 1 | 0 | 0 | 1 |
| Internal Revenue Service | 0 | 0 | 0 | 0 | 2 | 0 | 0 | 0 | 0 | 0 | 0 | 1 | 0 | 0 | 0 |
| Treasury Inspector General for Tax Administration | 0 | 0 | 0 | 0 | 0 | 0 | 0 | 0 | 0 | 0 | 0 | 0 | 0 | 0 | 1 |
| U.S. Postal Inspection Service | 0 | 2 | 5 | 0 | 0 | 4 | 0 | 0 | 3 | 0 | 1 | 6 | 0 | 1 | 3 |

[1] For 2012, extent of injury data for 555 victim officers were not reported by the CBP, Office of Border Patrol.
[2] For 2013, detailed incident data were not reported by the CBP, Office of Border Patrol, for the 2 killed victim officers; therefore, the deaths were not represented in the feloniously killed section of this publication.
[3] For 2014, extent of injury data for 373 victim officers were not reported by the CBP, Office of Border Patrol.
[4] For 2015, extent of injury data for 349 victim officers were not reported by the CBP, Office of Border Patrol.
[5] For 2011, detailed incident data were not reported by the U.S. Immigration and Customs Enforcement for the killed victim officer; therefore, the death was not represented in the feloniously killed section of this publication.
[6] For 2013, data were not reported by the U.S. Immigration and Customs Enforcement.
[7] For 2013, detailed incident data were not reported by the Bureau of Indian Affairs for the killed victim officer; therefore, the death was not represented in the feloniously killed section of this publication.
[8] For 2013, detailed incident data were not reported by the U.S. Drug Enforcement Administration for the killed victim officer; therefore, the death was not represented in the feloniously killed section of this publication.

# METHODOLOGY

## Officers Killed

When an officer is killed in the line of duty, the FBI gathers data about circumstances pertaining to the death. The data come from various sources:

- City, university and college, county, state, tribal, and federal law enforcement agencies participating in the Uniform Crime Reporting Program may report line-of-duty deaths that occur in their jurisdictions

- FBI field offices report line-of-duty deaths of law enforcement officers that occur in the United States and its outlying areas

- Several nonprofit organizations, such as the Concerns of Police Survivors and the National Law Enforcement Officers Memorial Fund, which provide various services to the families of fallen officers, also furnish information about line-of-duty deaths

When the FBI receives notification of a line-of-duty death, the Law Enforcement Officers Killed and Assaulted (LEOKA) Program's staff works with FBI field offices to contact the fallen officer's employing agency and request additional details about the fatal incident. The LEOKA staff also obtains criminal history data from the FBI's Interstate Identification Index about individuals who are identified in connection with line-of-duty felonious deaths.

## Officers Assaulted

The Uniform Crime Reporting (UCR) Program collects information monthly about assaults on duly sworn city, university and college, county, state, and tribal law enforcement officers. The agencies that employ these officers collect and submit data either through their state UCR Programs or, for non-Program states, directly to the FBI. For assault data to be included in this publication, law enforcement agencies must have submitted information for all 12 months of 2015 regarding their sworn officers who were assaulted as well as the number of officers and civilians their agencies employed full time for the reporting year.

Law enforcement agencies report to the UCR Program the number of assaults resulting in injuries to their officers or instances in which an offender used a weapon that could have caused injury or death. Law enforcement agencies report other assaults (i.e., those not causing injury) if they involved more than verbal abuse or minor resistance to an arrest.

## Federal Law Enforcement Officers Killed and Assaulted

Data published by the FBI concerning federal officers who were killed or assaulted in the line of duty are provided by the following six federal departments:

- U.S. Capitol Police

- U.S. Department of Homeland Security

- U.S. Department of the Interior

- U.S. Department of Justice

- U.S. Department of the Treasury

- U.S. Postal Inspection Service

Within these departments are the agencies, bureaus, and services that employ most of the personnel who are responsible for protecting government officials and enforcing and investigating violations of federal law. Every year, the FBI contacts these agencies and requests information about the officers who were killed or assaulted in the line of duty.

The information concerning federal officers differs slightly from the data regarding assaults on city, university and college, county, state, and tribal law enforcement officers. First, the data regarding federal officers include all reports of assaults regardless of the extent (or the absence) of personal injury. Second, the circumstance categories are tailored to represent the unique duties of federal law enforcement personnel.

The data in *Law Enforcement Officers Killed and Assaulted* pertain to felonious deaths, accidental deaths, and assaults of duly sworn city, university and college, county, state, tribal, and federal law enforcement officers who, at the time of the incident, met the following criteria.

- They were working in an official capacity, whether on or off duty

- They had full arrest powers

- They ordinarily wore/carried a badge and a firearm

- They were paid from governmental funds set aside specifically for payment of sworn law enforcement representatives

Officers who died are included if their deaths are directly related to injuries received during the incidents.

The FBI publishes *Law Enforcement Officers Killed and Assaulted* each year to provide information about officers who were killed, feloniously or accidentally, and officers who were assaulted while performing their duties. The FBI collects these data through the Uniform Crime Reporting (UCR) Program.

## Data Considerations

When reviewing the tables, charts, and summaries presented in this publication, readers should be aware of certain features of the Law Enforcement Officers Killed and Assaulted (LEOKA) data collection process that could affect their interpretation of the information.

- The data in the tables and charts reflect the number of victim officers, not the number of incidents or weapons used

- The UCR Program considers any parts of the body that can be used as weapons (such as hands, fists, or feet) to be personal weapons and designates them as such in its data

- Law enforcement agencies use a different methodology for collecting and reporting data about officers who were killed than the methodology used for those who were assaulted. As a result, information about officers killed and information about officers assaulted reside in two separate databases, and the data are not comparable

- **Because the information in the tables of this publication is updated each year, the FBI cautions readers against making comparisons between the data in this publication and those in prior editions**

## History

Beginning in 1937, the FBI's UCR Program collected and published statistics on law enforcement officers killed in the line of duty in its annual publication, *Crime in the United States*. Statistics regarding assaults on officers were added in 1960. In June 1971, executives from the law enforcement conference, "Prevention of Police Killings," called for an increase in the FBI's involvement in preventing and investigating officers' deaths. In response to this directive, the UCR Program expanded its collection of data to include more details about the incidents in which law enforcement officers were killed and assaulted.

Using this comprehensive set of data, the FBI began in 1972 to produce two reports annually, the *Law Enforcement Officers Killed Summary* and the *Analysis of Assaults on Federal Officers*. These two reports were combined in 1982 to create the annual publication, *Law Enforcement Officers Killed and Assaulted*.

## Definitions

### Type of Incident

**Feloniously Killed** – Incident type in which an officer, while engaged in or on account of the performance of their official duties, was fatally injured as a direct result of a willful and intentional act by an offender.

**Accidentally Killed** – Incident type in which an officer was fatally injured as a result of an accident or negligence that occurred while the officer was acting in an official capacity. Due to the hazardous nature of the law enforcement profession, deaths of law enforcement officers are considered accidental if the act causing the death is found not to be willful and intentional.

**Assaulted** – An unlawful attack by one person upon another for the purpose of inflicting severe or aggravated bodily injury. This type of assault is accompanied by the use of a weapon or by a means likely to produce death or great bodily injury.

**Detailed Assault Data** – The detailed data collection is limited to officers who are assaulted and injured with firearms or knives/other cutting instruments. – Incident type in which an officer, while engaged in or on account of the performance of their official duties, received nonfatal injuries as a direct result of a willful and intentional act by an offender.

### Race

**White** – A person having origins in any of the original peoples of Europe, the Middle East, or North Africa.

**Black/African American** – A person having origins in any of the black racial groups of Africa. Terms such as "Haitian" or "Negro" can be used in addition to "Black or African American."

**Asian** – Included within "Asian/Pacific Islander" in LEOKA publication tables referring to Race – A person having origins in any of the original peoples of the Far East, Southeast Asia, or the Indian subcontinent, including, for example, Cambodia, China, India, Japan, Korea, Malaysia, Pakistan, the Philippine Islands, Thailand, and Vietnam.

**Native Hawaiian/Other Pacific Islands** – Included within "Asian/Pacific Islander" in LEOKA publication tables referring to Race – A person having origins in any of the original peoples of Hawaii, Guam, Samoa, or other Pacific Islands, e.g., individuals who are Carolinian, Fijian, Kosraean, Melanesian, Micronesian, Northern Mariana Islander, Palauan, Papua New Guinean, Ponapean (Pohnpelan), Polynesian, Solomon Islander, Tahitian, Tarawa Islander, Tokelauan, Tongan, Trukese (Chuukese), and Yapese. (NOTE: The term "Native Hawaiian" does not include individuals who are native to the state of Hawaii simply by virtue of being born there.)

**American Indian/Alaska Native** – A person having origins in any of the original peoples of North and South America (including Central America), and who maintains tribal affiliation or community attachment.

## Type of Assignment

**2-Officer vehicle** – An assignment where the officer is on patrol and is accompanied by another law enforcement officer(s) in the agency's marked patrol vehicle.

**1-Officer vehicle** – An assignment where the officer is on patrol and is not accompanied by another officer in the agency's marked patrol vehicle.

**Foot patrol** – An assignment where the officer is patrolling a designated route on foot.

**Administrative** – Included within "Other" in LEOKA publication tables referring to Type of Assignment – An assignment in which an officer is working management, performance, or executive duties of the local, state, or federal jurisdiction. Examples include, but are not limited to:

- handling, transporting, or maintaining custody of persons who are in the custodial care of a law enforcement agency subsequent to an arrest and/or while dealing with persons who are being detained in accordance with the law;

- attending community meetings, crime preventive programs, or other organized functions as an official representative of a law enforcement agency;

- performing duties and recreational activities associated with agency sanctioned programs such as D.A.R.E., Boys and Girls Clubs, or other youth programs; or

- serving of writs, notices, summonses, subpoenas, hearing notices, notifications, and other civil processes; and transporting of papers, equipment, or persons associated with official agency sanctioned activities, functions, and programs.

**Investigative/detective** – Included within "Other" in LEOKA publication tables referring to Type of Assignment – An officer whose occupation is mainly to investigate and solve crimes.

**Plainclothes assignment** – Included within "Other" in LEOKA publication tables referring to Type of Assignment – A non-uniformed assignment where the officer's role and identity as a sworn law enforcement officer is not intended to be confidential or clandestine.

**Tactical assignment (uniformed)** – Included within "Other" in LEOKA publication tables referring to Type of Assignment – A uniformed assignment where an officer is strategically deployed in order to achieve a specific goal or objective. These are typically high-risk assignments.

**Undercover** – Included within "Other" in LEOKA publication tables referring to Type of Assignment – A non-uniformed assignment where the officer requires anonymity or blending into a group or environment to gather evidence or intelligence. The disclosure of the officer's identity would pose a significant safety risk.

**Off duty** – An officer who is off duty at the time of incident, but is acting in such a way which is sanctioned by, recognized by, or derived from authority.

## Circumstances at Scene of Incident

**Disturbance (bar fight, person with firearm, etc.)** – A breach of the peace type of circumstance resulting in a call for law enforcement to respond. Examples include, but are not limited to: curfew violations, disorderly persons, drinking in public, fights, fireworks violations, gambling in public space, persons under the influence, landlord/tenant disputes, loitering, loud noise of any type (excluding animal disturbance complaints by a citizen), littering, nuisance complaints, prostitution offenses, trespassing or unwanted guests, vagrancy violations, and verbal altercations.

**Domestic disturbance (family quarrel, etc.)** – A breach of the peace or crime against a person occurring within a family, families, or other relatives or members of the household. Examples include, but are not limited to: family disputes, family intimidations, family arguments, and assisting citizens with the removal of legally owned possessions at locations where prior domestic disturbances or other related offenses have occurred. (Family includes a current or former spouse, parent, or guardian of the victim; a person with whom the victim shares a child in common; a person who is or has been in a social relationship of a romantic or intimate nature with the victim; a person who is cohabiting with or has cohabited with the victim as a spouse, parent, or guardian; or by a person who is or has been similarly situated to a spouse, parent, or guardian of the victim.)

**Domestic violence** – Included within "Domestic disturbance (family quarrels, etc.)" in LEOKA publication tables referring to Circumstance at Scene of Incident – The use, attempted use, or threatened use of physical force, or a weapon; or the use of coercion or intimidation; or committing a crime against property by a current or former spouse, parent, or guardian of the victim; a person with whom the victim shares a child in common; a person who is or has been in a social relationship of a romantic or intimate nature with the victim; a person who is cohabiting with or has cohabited with the victim as a spouse, parent, or guardian; or by a person who is or has been similarly situated to a spouse, parent, or guardian of the victim.

**Burglary** – The unlawful entry of a structure with the intent to commit a felony or a theft.

**Burglary in progress/pursuing burglary suspect** – Situation where an officer is pursuing, arresting, or attempting to arrest an offender involved in a burglary.

**Robbery** – The taking, or attempting to take, anything of value under confrontational circumstances from the care, custody, or control of a person by force, threat of force, or violence and/or by putting the victim in fear of immediate harm.

**Robbery in progress/pursuing robbery suspect** – Situation where an officer is pursuing, arresting, or attempting to arrest an offender involved in a robbery.

**Drug-related matter** – Situation where an officer is pursuing, arresting, or attempting to arrest an offender involved in a drug-related matter, such as, drug busts, buys, etc.

**Drug complaint** – Included within "Drug-related matter" in LEOKA publication tables referring to Circumstance at Scene of Incident – Incident where a citizen reports the use or presence of illegal drugs or drug paraphernalia. Examples include, but are not limited to, the possession, buying, or selling of illegal drugs or drug paraphernalia.

**Attempting other arrest** – Situation where an officer is arresting or attempting to arrest an offender either through verbal advisement or through physical contact, such as, attempting to restrain, control, or handcuff the offender.

**Civil disorder (mass disobedience, riot, etc.)** – An activity where an officer is to control, disperse, or terminate a riot or mass disobedience.

**Handling, transporting, custody of prisoner** – Situation where an officer is handling, transporting, or maintaining custody of persons who are in the custodial care of a law enforcement agency subsequent to an arrest and/or while dealing with persons who are being detained in accordance with the law.

**Investigating suspicious person/circumstance** – An activity where an officer's intent is to investigate an unusual occurrence, an out-of-the-ordinary condition, or a suspicious person or circumstance.

**Ambush** – Situation where an officer is assaulted, unexpectedly, as the result of premeditated design by the perpetrator.

**Ambush (entrapment/premeditation)** – Situation where an unsuspecting officer was targeted or lured into danger as the result of conscious consideration and planning by the offender.

**Unprovoked attack** – An attack on an officer not prompted by official contact at the time of the incident between the officer and the offender.

**Investigative activity (surveillance, search, interview, etc.)** – An activity where an officer is making official inquiries relating to prior criminal offenses and/or perpetrators. Examples include, but are not limited to, obtaining follow-up information or additional information relating to any crime (excluding drug offense complaints) or interviewing a citizen relating to any criminal matter (excluding drug offenses).

**Handling person with mental illness** – Situation where an officer is handling a person who is known or suspected to be suffering from a mental illness that impairs judgment, behavior, perceptions of reality, or their ability to cope with the ordinary demands of life. Examples include, but are not limited to: mental patients, suicidal persons, service of commitment orders, and calls to investigate persons or activities where it is suspected that a person is suffering from a mental illness.

**Felony vehicle stop** – A vehicle stop made by an officer that is considered to be high-risk in nature.

**Traffic violation stop** – A vehicle stop made by an officer due to a motorist's violation of traffic rules and regulations.

**Tactical situation (barricaded offender, hostage taking, high-risk entry, etc.)** – Situation where an officer is strategically deployed in order to achieve a specific goal or objective. Examples include, but are not limited to: serving search warrants, hostage situations, barricaded offenders, search warrants for drug violations, and any other situations that could be deemed "high-risk," such as, serving an arrest warrant on a known armed felon.

# PART 10

# Probation and Parole in the United States, 2015

# HIGHLIGHTS

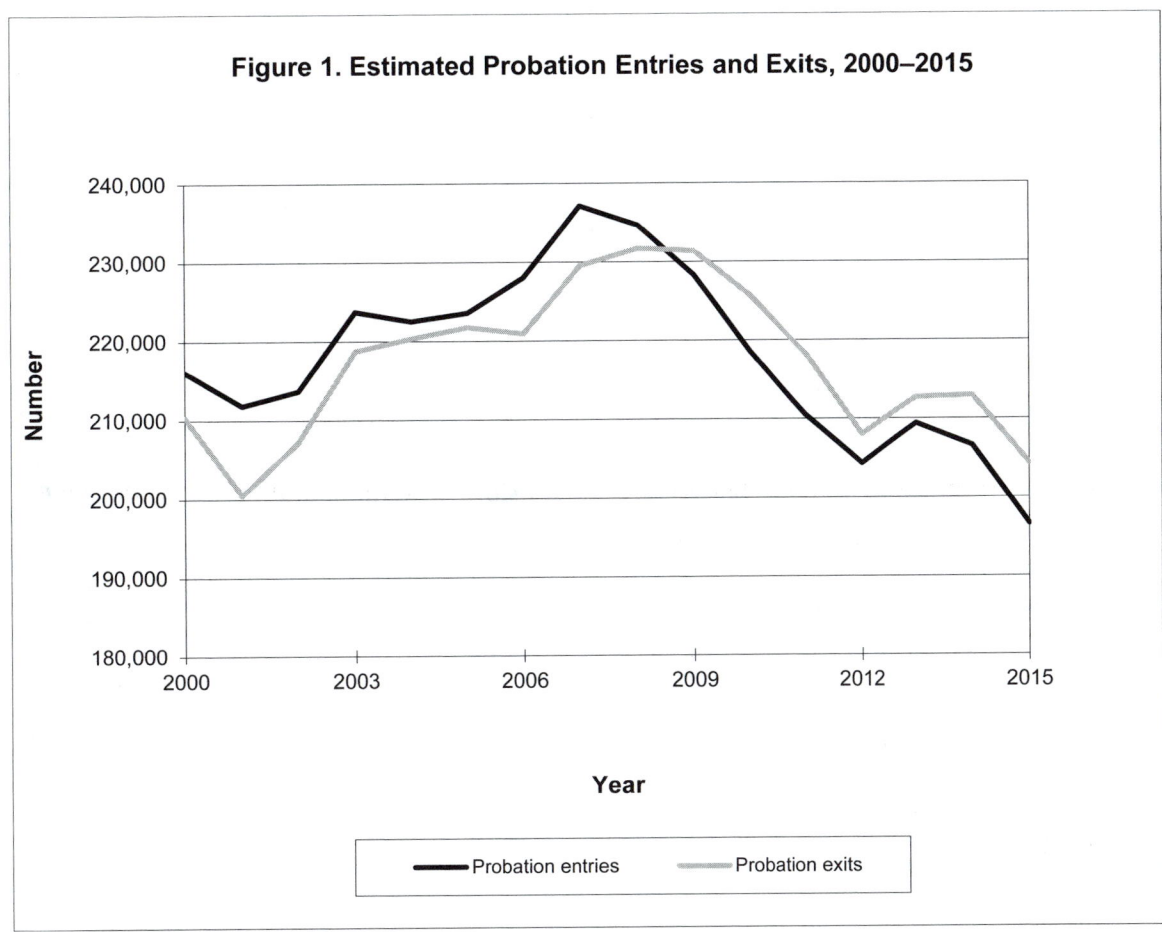

**Figure 1. Estimated Probation Entries and Exits, 2000–2015**

- At yearend 2015, an estimated 4,650,900 adults were under community supervision, down by about 62,300 offenders from yearend 2014.

- Approximately 1 in 53 adults in the United States was under community supervision at yearend 2015.

- Between yearend 2014 and 2015, the adult probation population declined by approximately 2.0 percent (about 78,700 offenders), dropping to an estimated 3,789,800 offenders at yearend 2015.

- The adult parole population increased by 12,800 offenders between yearend 2014 and 2015 to an estimated 870,500

offenders; this represented a 1.6 percent increase from yearend 2014.

- Parole entries increased for the first time in seven years (rising from an estimated 461,100 in 2014 to 475,200 in 2015), while parole exits increased for the first time in six years (growing from 450,800 in 2014 to 463,700 in 2015).

- The reincarceration rate among parolees at risk of violating their conditions of supervision remained unchanged from 2013 and 2014 at 14 exits per 100 parolees but declined overall from the 2005 rate (25 per 100 parolees).

# Table 1. Adults Under Community Supervision on Probation or Parole, Yearend 2005–2015

(Number; percent.)

| Year | Total | Probation | Parole |
|------|-------|-----------|--------|
| 2005 | 4,946,600 | 4,162,300 | 784,400 |
| 2006 | 5,035,000 | 4,236,800 | 798,200 |
| 2007 | 5,119,000 | 4,293,000 | 826,100 |
| 2008 | 5,093,400 | 4,271,200 | 826,100 |
| 2009 | 5,019,900 | 4,199,800 | 824,600 |
| 2010 | 4,888,500 | 4,055,900 | 840,800 |
| 2011 | 4,818,300 | 3,973,800 | 855,500 |
| 2012 | 4,790,700 | 3,944,900 | 858,400 |
| 2013 | 4,749,800 | 3,912,900 | 849,500 |
| 2014 | 4,713,200 | 3,868,400 | 857,700 |
| 2015 | 4,650,900 | 3,789,800 | 870,500 |
| Percent change, 2005–2015 | -6.0 | -8.9 | -11.0 |
| Percent change, 2014–2015 | -1.3 | -2.0 | -1.5 |

*Note:* Counts are rounded to the nearest 100. Detail may not sum to total due to rounding. Estimates are based on most recent data and may differ from previously published statistics. Reporting methods for some probation agencies changed over time.

# Table 2. Rates of U.S. Adult Residents on Community Supervision, Probation, and Parole, 2005–2015

(Number; rate.)

| Year | Number per 100,000 U.S. adult residents | | | U.S. adult residents on: | | |
|------|---------------------|-----------|--------|---------------------|-----------|--------|
| | Community supervision[1] | Probation | Parole | Community supervision[2] | Probation | Parole |
| 2005 | 2,215 | 1,864 | 351 | 1 in 45 | 1 in 54 | 1 in 285 |
| 2006 | 2,228 | 1,875 | 353 | 1 in 45 | 1 in 53 | 1 in 283 |
| 2007 | 2,239 | 1,878 | 361 | 1 in 45 | 1 in 53 | 1 in 277 |
| 2008 [3] | 2,202 | 1,847 | 357 | 1 in 45 | 1 in 54 | 1 in 280 |
| 2009 | 2,148 | 1,797 | 353 | 1 in 47 | 1 in 56 | 1 in 283 |
| 2010 | 2,067 | 1,715 | 356 | 1 in 48 | 1 in 58 | 1 in 281 |
| 2011 | 2,017 | 1,663 | 358 | 1 in 50 | 1 in 60 | 1 in 279 |
| 2012 | 1,984 | 1,634 | 356 | 1 in 50 | 1 in 61 | 1 in 281 |
| 2013 | 1,946 | 1,603 | 348 | 1 in 51 | 1 in 62 | 1 in 287 |
| 2014 | 1,911 | 1568 | 348 | 1 in 52 | 1 in 64 | 1 in 288 |
| 2015 | 1,868 | 1,522 | 350 | 1 in 53 | 1 in 66 | 1 in 286 |

*Note:* Detail may not sum to total due to rounding. Rates are based on most recent data available and may differ from previously published statistics. Rates are based on the total community supervision, probation, and parole population counts as of December 31 of the reporting year and the estimated U.S. adult resident population on January 1 of each subsequent year.
[1] Includes adults on probation and adults on parole. For 2008 to 2015, detail does not sum to total because the community supervision rate was adjusted to exclude parolees who were also on probation.
[2] Includes adults on probation and adults on parole.
[3] See Methodology for estimating change in population counts.

## Table 3. Rate of Probation Exits, by Type of Exit, 2005 and 2010–2015

(Rate per 100 probationers.)

| Type of exit | 2005 | 2010 | 2011 | 2012 | 2013 | 2014 | 2015 |
|---|---|---|---|---|---|---|---|
| Total exit rate[1] .............................. | 53 | 55 | 54 | 52 | 54 | 55 | 53 |
| Completion................................. | 32 | 36 | 36 | 36 | 36 | 35 | 33 |
| Incarceration[2]............................. | 8 | 9 | 9 | 8 | 8 | 8 | 8 |
| Absconder .................................... | 2 | 1 | 1 | 1 | 1 | 1 | 1 |
| Other unsatisfactory[3] .................... | 7 | 6 | 5 | 5 | 6 | 7 | 7 |
| Other[4]........................................ | 4 | 2 | 2 | 2 | 2 | 2 | 2 |

Note: Detail may not sum to total due to rounding. Rates based on most recent data and may differ from previously published statistics.
...– = Less than 0.5 per 100 probationers.
[1] The ratio of the number of probationers exiting supervision during the year to the average daily probation population (i.e., average of the January 1 and December 31 populations within the reporting year). Includes 1 per 100 probationers or fewer who were discharged to custody, detainer, or warrant; 1 per 100 who were transferred to another probation agency; and fewer than 0.5 per 100 who died.
[2] Includes probationers who were incarcerated for a new offense and those who had their current probation sentence revoked (e.g., violating a condition of supervision).
[3] Includes probationers discharged from supervision who failed to meet all conditions of supervision, including some with only financial conditions remaining, some who had their probation sentence revoked but were not incarcerated because their sentence was immediately reinstated, and other types of unsatisfactory exits. Includes some early terminations and expirations of sentence.
[4] Includes, but not limited to, probationers who were discharged from supervision through a legislative mandate because they were deported or transferred to the jurisdiction of Immigration and Customs Enforcement; were transferred to another state through an interstate compact agreement; had their sentence dismissed or overturned by the court through an appeal; had their sentence administratively closed, deferred, or terminated by the court; were awaiting a hearing; and were released on bond.


## Table 4. Rate of Parole Exits, by Type of Exit, 2005 and 2010–2015

(Rate per 100 parolees.)

| Type of exit | 2005 | 2010 | 2011 | 2012 | 2013 [1] | 2014 [1] | 2015 [1] |
|---|---|---|---|---|---|---|---|
| Total exit rate[2] ........................... | 66 | 67 | 63 | 58 | 54 | 53 | 54 |
| Completion................................. | 30 | 35 | 34 | 34 | 32 | 33 | 33 |
| Returned to incarceration.............. | 25 | 23 | 20 | 15 | 14 | 14 | 14 |
| With new sentence.................. | 8 | 6 | 6 | 5 | 4 | 4 | 4 |
| With revocation ..................... | 16 | 16 | 13 | 8 | 9 | 8 | 8 |
| Other/unknown ...................... | 1 | 1 | 2 | 1 | 1 | 1 | 2 |
| Absconder ..................................... | 7 | 6 | 6 | 6 | 4 | 3 | 4 |
| Other unsatisfactory[3] .................... | 1 | 1 | 1 | 1 | 1 | 1 | 1 |
| Transferred to another state .......... | 1 | 1 | 1 | 1 | 0 | 0 | 0 |
| Death ........................................... | 1 | 1 | 1 | 1 | 1 | 1 | 1 |
| Other[4].......................................... | 1 | 1 | 1 | 1 | 1 | 1 | 2 |

Note: Detail may not sum to total due to rounding.
[1] Includes imputed data for California, based on information provided for 2012.
[2] The ratio of the number of parolees exiting supervision during the year to the average daily parole population (i.e., average of the January 1 and December 31 populations within the reporting year).
[3] Includes parolees discharged from supervision who failed to meet all conditions of supervision, including some who had their parole sentence revoked but were not incarcerated because their sentence was immediately reinstated, and other types of unsatisfactory exits. Includes some early terminations and expirations of sentence reported as unsatisfactory exits.
[4] Includes, but not limited to, parolees discharged from supervision because they were deported or transferred to the jurisdiction of Immigration and Customs Enforcement, had their sentence terminated by the court through an appeal, or were transferred to another state through an interstate compact agreement and discharged to probation supervision.


## Table 5. Parolees on Probation Excluded from the January 1 and December 31 Community Supervision Populations, 2008–2015

(Number.)

| Year | January 1st[1] | December 31st |
|---|---|---|
| 2008............................................................... | 3,562 | 3,905 |
| 2009............................................................... | 3,905 | 4,959 |
| 2010............................................................... | 8,259 | 8,259 |
| 2011............................................................... | 8,259 | 10,958 |
| 2012............................................................... | 10,958 | 12,672 |
| 2013............................................................... | 12,672 | 12,511 |
| 2014............................................................... | 12,511 | 12,919 |
| 2015............................................................... | 12,919 | 9,375 |

Note: Counts are based on most recent data and may differ from previously published statistics. Excluded from community supervision population to avoid double counting those individuals being supervised on both probation and parole.
[1] For 2011 through 2015, data are based on the December 31 count of the prior reporting year. For 2010, the December 31, 2010, count was used as a proxy because additional states reported these data in 2010.

## Table 6. Change in the Number of Adults on Probation, Based on Reporting Changes, 2005–2015

(Number.)

| Year | December 31st probation population | Change[1] |
|---|---|---|
| 2005 | 4,162,286 | 4,262 |
| 2006 | 4,236,827 | -21,662 |
| 2007 | 4,292,950 | -59,275 |
| 2008 | 4,271,237 | -33,666 |
| 2009 | 4,199,751 | -73,122 |
| 2010 | 4,055,928 | -2,399 |
| 2011 | 3,973,756 | 9,771 |
| 2012 | 3,944,937 | 2,955 |
| 2013 | 3,912,882 | 20,983 |
| 2014 | 3,868,448 | 9,749 |
| 2015 | 3,789,785 | NA |

*Note:* Counts based on most recent data and may differ from previously published statistics.
NA = Not available.
[1] Calculated as the difference between the December 31 probation population in the reporting year and the January 1 probation population in the following year.

## Table 7. Change in the Number of Adults on Parole, Based on Reporting Changes, 2005–2015

(Number.)

| Year | December 31st probation population | Change[1] |
|---|---|---|
| 2005 | 784,354 | -3,738 |
| 2006 | 798,202 | 1,673 |
| 2007 | 826,097 | -4,920 |
| 2008 | 826,074 | 1,391 |
| 2009 | 824,584 | 13,703 |
| 2010 | 840,824 | -78 |
| 2011 | 855,458 | -2,830 |
| 2012 | 858,385 | -23,636 |
| 2013 | 849,467 | 535 |
| 2014 | 857,686 | 172 |
| 2015 | 870,526 | NA |

*Note:* Counts based on most recent data and may differ from previously published statistics.
NA = Not available.
[1] Calculated as the difference between the January 1 parole population in the year of the reporting change and the December 31 parole population in the year prior to the reporting change.

# Table 8. Adults Under Community Supervision, 2015

(Number; percent.)

| Jurisdiction | Community supervision population, 1/1/15[1] | Entries Reported | Entries Imputed[2] | Exits Reported | Exits Imputed[2] | Community supervision population, 12/31/15[1] | Change, 2015 Number | Change, 2015 Percent | Number under community supervision per 100,000 adult residents, 12/31/15[3] |
|---|---|---|---|---|---|---|---|---|---|
| U.S. Total............................ | 4,723,100 | 2,244,000 | 2,441,200 | 2,307,800 | 2,507,000 | 4,650,900 | -72,200 | -1.5 | 1,868 |
| Federal................................ | 128,400 | 58,600 | 58,600 | 55,600 | 555,600 | 132,800 | 4,400 | 3.4 | 53 |
| State................................... | 4,594,700 | 2,185,400 | 2,382,600 | 2,252,300 | 2,451,400 | 4,518,100 | -76,600 | -1.7 | 1,814 |
| Alabama.......................... | 60,900 | 20,500 | 20,500 | 16,900 | 16,900 | 64,600 | 3,700 | 6.0 | 1,714 |
| Alaska.............................. | U | U | U | U | U | U | U | U | U |
| Arizona............................ | 80,700 | 38,100 | 38,100 | 35,500 | 35,500 | 83,300 | 2,600 | 3.2 | 1,589 |
| Arkansas.......................... | 49,200 | 20,800 | 20,800 | 18,800 | 18,800 | 51,500 | 2,200 | 4.5 | 2,256 |
| California......................... | 372,800 | 182,500 | 208,000 | 192,700 | 217,300 | 349,600 | -23,200 | -6.2 | 1,158 |
| Colorado[4] | 89,100 | 62,000 | 62,900 | 62,900 | 62,900 | 89,200 | 100 | 0.1 | 2,102 |
| Connecticut .................... | 45,600 | 25,000 | 25,000 | 23,700 | 23,700 | 45,300 | -400 | -0.8 | 1,598 |
| Delaware ......................... | 16,300 | 12,800 | 12,800 | 13,100 | 13,100 | 16,100 | -300 | -1.7 | 2,155 |
| District of Columbia........ | 11,100 | 5,700 | 5,700 | 7,100 | 7,100 | 9,900 | -1,100 | -10.3 | 1,776 |
| Florida[4] | 232,100 | 155,100 | 159,900 | 161,600 | 167,100 | 225,400 | -6,700 | -2.9 | 1,381 |
| Georgia .......................... | 502,200 | 267,700 | 267,700 | 324,100 | 324,100 | 451,800 | -50,300 | -10.0 | 5,823 |
| Hawaii ............................ | 22,500 | 5,700 | 5,700 | 6,000 | 6,000 | 22,500 | 0 | -0.1 | 1,996 |
| Idaho.............................. | 37,700 | 15,600 | 15,600 | 15,500 | 15,500 | 37,800 | 100 | 0.2 | 3,071 |
| Illinois ............................ | 151,800 | U | 79,700 | U | 80,200 | 151,300 | -600 | -0.4 | 1,526 |
| Indiana............................ | 126,100 | 83,600 | 83,600 | 87,200 | 87,200 | 122,500 | -3,600 | -2.8 | 2,423 |
| Iowa ............................... | 35,400 | 18,000 | 18,000 | 17,700 | 17,700 | 35,600 | 200 | 0.7 | 1,481 |
| Kansas............................. | 20,400 | 25,200 | 25,200 | 24,700 | 24,700 | 20,900 | 500 | 2.6 | 951 |
| Kentucky ......................... | 70,700 | 37,800 | 37,800 | 37,800 | 37,800 | 70,600 | 0 | -0.1 | 2,063 |
| Louisiana ........................ | 70,600 | 29,800 | 29,800 | 28,400 | 28,400 | 71,900 | 1,300 | 1.8 | 2,014 |
| Maine.............................. | 6,600 | 3,300 | 3,300 | 3,200 | 3,200 | 6,700 | 100 | 2.2 | 626 |
| Maryland ........................ | 91,100 | 42,900 | 42,900 | 46,600 | 46,600 | 87,400 | -3,700 | -4.0 | 1,870 |
| Massachusetts ................. | 70,200 | 68,800 | 68,800 | 72,100 | 72,100 | 66,900 | -3,300 | -4.7 | 1,232 |
| Michigan[4] | 192,700 | 104,500 | 118,100 | 104,600 | 116,600 | 193,900 | 1,200 | 0.6 | 2,507 |
| Minnesota ...................... | 103,700 | 55,200 | 55,200 | 53,800 | 53,800 | 105,100 | 1,400 | 1.3 | 2,489 |
| Mississippi....................... | 44,300 | 17,800 | 17,800 | 17,300 | 17,300 | 44,800 | 500 | 1.1 | 1,972 |
| Missouri.......................... | 65,600 | 37,800 | 37,800 | 40,800 | 40,800 | 62,600 | -3,000 | -4.6 | 1,329 |
| Montana.......................... | 9,800 | 4,400 | 4,600 | 4,600 | 4,600 | 9,700 | -100 | -0.6 | 1,198 |
| Nebraska ......................... | 13,700 | 10,500 | 10,500 | 10,500 | 10,500 | 13,700 | 0 | -0.1 | 955 |
| Nevada ............................ | 18,000 | 9,700 | 9,700 | 8,400 | 8,400 | 19,200 | 1,300 | 7.1 | 858 |
| New Hampshire ............... | 6,300 | 4,100 | 4,100 | 4,100 | 4,100 | 6,300 | 0 | 0.1 | 590 |
| New Jersey....................... | 152,000 | 33,200 | 33,200 | 33,900 | 33,900 | 151,300 | -700 | -0.5 | 2,167 |
| New Mexico..................... | 17,600 | 8,200 | 9,800 | 7,900 | 9,700 | 16,800 | -900 | -4.9 | 1,054 |
| New York......................... | 150,300 | 45,800 | 45,800 | 50,600 | 50,600 | 145,600 | -4,800 | -3.2 | 931 |
| North Carolina ................ | 99,300 | 63,700 | 63,700 | 64,400 | 64,400 | 97,400 | -1,900 | -1.9 | 1,249 |
| North Dakota................... | 6,200 | 5,600 | 5,600 | 4,900 | 4,900 | 6,900 | 700 | 11.8 | 1,179 |
| Ohio ............................... | 258,400 | 131,200 | 145,600 | 129,700 | 143,500 | 262,000 | 3,600 | 1.4 | 2,908 |
| Oklahoma........................ | 31,100 | 13,000 | 13,000 | 10,700 | 10,700 | 33,400 | 2,300 | 7.3 | 1,126 |
| Oregon ........................... | U | U | U | U | U | U | U | U | U |
| Pennsylvania ................... | 281,400 | 177,700 | 177,700 | 162,800 | 162,800 | 296,200 | 14,900 | 5.3 | 2,923 |
| Rhode Island.................... | 24,000 | 300 | 4,900 | 200 | 4,500 | 24,400 | 400 | 1.6 | 2,873 |
| South Carolina................. | 39,600 | 16,100 | 16,100 | 17,200 | 17,200 | 38,500 | -1,000 | -2.6 | 1,006 |
| South Dakota................... | 9,300 | 5,200 | 5,200 | 4,700 | 4,700 | 9,800 | 500 | 5.6 | 1,505 |
| Tennessee ....................... | 77,800 | 26,400 | 26,400 | 28,800 | 28,800 | 75,400 | -2,400 | -3.1 | 1,470 |
| Texas............................... | 496,900 | 182,600 | 182,600 | 191,300 | 191,300 | 488,800 | -8,000 | -1.6 | 2,390 |
| Utah ............................... | 15,100 | 7,900 | 7,900 | 7,300 | 7,300 | 15,700 | 600 | 3.8 | 746 |
| Vermont .......................... | 6,300 | | 3,500 | U | 3,500 | 6,300 | 0 | ... | 1,236 |
| Virginia ........................... | 56,700 | 29,900 | 29,900 | 29,600 | 29,600 | 57,000 | 400 | 0.6 | 873 |
| Washington[4] | 105,000 | 44,900 | 56,100 | 38,900 | 55,400 | 104,700 | -300 | -0.2 | 1,870 |
| West Virginia[4] | 9,900 | 2,000 | 2,800 | 2,600 | 2,600 | 10,100 | 200 | 2.1 | 692 |
| Wisconsin ....................... | 65,900 | U | 29,200 | 200 | 29,500 | 65,600 | -300 | -0.5 | 1,462 |
| Wyoming ......................... | 5,700 | 3,000 | 3,000 | 2,800 | 2,800 | 5,900 | 200 | 4.0 | 1,323 |

*Note:* Counts are rounded to the nearest hundred. Detail may not sum to total due to rounding. Due to nonresponse or incomplete data, the community supervision population for some jurisdictions on December 31, 2015, does not equal the population on January 1, 2015, plus entries, minus exits.
... = Less than 0.05%.
U = Not known.
[1] The January 1 population excludes 12,919 offenders and the December 31 population excludes 9,375 offenders under community supervision who were on both probation and parole. See <http://www.bjs.gov/content/pub/pdf/ppus15.pdf> for more detail.
[2] Reflects reported data, excluding jurisdictions for which data were unavailable.
[3] Rates were computed using the estimated number of U.S. residents age 15 or older in each jurisdiction on January 1, 2016.
[4] See <http://www.bjs.gov/content/pub/pdf/ppus15.pdf> for more detail.

# Table 9. Adults on Probation, 2015

(Number; percent.)

| Jurisdiction | Probation population, 1/1/15[1] | Entries | | Exits | | Probation population, 12/31/15[1] | Change, 2015 | | Number under Probation per 100,000 adult residents, 12/31/15[2] |
|---|---|---|---|---|---|---|---|---|---|
| | | Reported | Imputed[2] | Reported | Imputed[2] | | Number | Percent | |
| U.S. Total.............................. | 3,878,197 | 1,812,310 | 1,966,100 | 1,887,556 | 2,043,200 | 3,789,785 | -88,412 | -2.0 | 1,522 |
| Federal .................................. | 19,062 | 8,646 | 8,646 | 9,253 | 9,253 | 18,368 | -694 | -4.0 | 7 |
| State..................................... | 3,859,135 | 1,803,664 | 1,957,400 | 1,878,303 | 2,034,000 | 3,771,417 | -87,718 | -2.0 | 1,514 |
| | | | | | | | | | |
| Alabama........................... | 53,132 | 18,155 | 18,155 | 14,587 | 14,587 | 56,700 | 3,568 | 7.0 | 1,505 |
| Alaska............................... | U | U | U | U | U | U | U | U | U |
| Arizona............................. | 73,232 | 26,163 | 26,163 | 23,390 | 23,390 | 76,005 | 2,773 | 3.8 | 1,449 |
| Arkansas........................... | 28,157 | 10,258 | 10,258 | 9,603 | 9,603 | 28,900 | 743 | 2.6 | 1,267 |
| California........................... | 285681 | 152,909 | 152,909 | 161166 | 161,166 | 263,531 | -22,150 | -7.8 | 873 |
| | | | | | | | | | |
| Colorado[3] ....................... | 78,988 | 53,671 | 54,500 | 54,707 | 54,800 | 78,883 | -105 | -0.1 | 1,860 |
| Connecticut ..................... | 43,084 | 22,489 | 22,489 | 21,631 | 21,631 | 42,346 | -738 | -1.7 | 1,494 |
| Delaware .......................... | 15,665 | 12,761 | 12,761 | 12,780 | 12,780 | 15,646 | -19 | -0.1 | 2,098 |
| District of Columbia .......... | 6,356 | 4,282 | 4,282 | 5,102 | 5,102 | 5,536 | -820 | -12.9 | 990 |
| Florida[3] ........................... | 227,540 | 148,775 | 153,600 | 155,313 | 160,800 | 220,769 | -6,771 | -3.0 | 1,353 |
| | | | | | | | | | |
| Georgia ............................ | 481,339 | 257,482 | 257,482 | 312,381 | 312,381 | 432,235 | -49,104 | -10.2 | 5,570 |
| Hawaii ............................. | 20,931 | 5,042 | 5,042 | 5,061 | 5,061 | 20,912 | -19 | -0.1 | 1,859 |
| Idaho............................... | 33,466 | 12,931 | 12,931 | 13,498 | 13,498 | 32,898 | -568 | -1.7 | 2,675 |
| Illinois ............................. | 122,184 | U | 55,900 | U | 55,900 | 122,125 | -59 | 0.0 | 1,232 |
| Indiana ............................ | 116,595 | 75,769 | 75,769 | 79,288 | 79,288 | 113,076 | -3,519 | -3.0 | 2,236 |
| | | | | | | | | | |
| Iowa ................................ | 29,815 | 14,375 | 14,375 | 14,315 | 14,315 | 29,875 | 60 | 0.2 | 1,243 |
| Kansas ............................. | 16,328 | 21,280 | 21,280 | 21,020 | 21,020 | 16,588 | 260 | 1.6 | 754 |
| Kentucky .......................... | 53,923 | 26,531 | 26,531 | 26,405 | 26,405 | 54,049 | 126 | 0.2 | 1,579 |
| Louisiana ......................... | 40,979 | 12,615 | 12,615 | 12,830 | 12,830 | 40,764 | -215 | -0.5 | 1,143 |
| Maine............................... | 6,562 | 3,317 | 3,317 | 3,171 | 3,171 | 6,708 | 146 | 2.2 | 624 |
| | | | | | | | | | |
| Maryland .......................... | 79,539 | 38,204 | 38,204 | 41,238 | 41,238 | 76,505 | -3,034 | -3.8 | 1,637 |
| Massachusetts .................. | 68,274 | 66,461 | 66,461 | 69,801 | 69,801 | 64,934 | -3,340 | -4.9 | 1,195 |
| Michigan[3] ....................... | 174,239 | 93,859 | 107,500 | 93,493 | 105,500 | 175,965 | 1,726 | 1.0 | 2,276 |
| Minnesota ........................ | 97,036 | 48,847 | 48,847 | 47,625 | 47,625 | 98,258 | 1,222 | 1.3 | 2,328 |
| Mississippi........................ | 34,398 | 11,885 | 11,885 | 9,950 | 9,950 | 36,333 | 1,935 | 5.6 | 1,601 |
| | | | | | | | | | |
| Missouri............................ | 47,082 | 24,824 | 24,824 | 27,030 | 27,030 | 44,876 | -2,206 | -4.7 | 953 |
| Montana........................... | 8,667 | 3,774 | 4,000 | 4,035 | 4,035 | 8,610 | -57 | -0.7 | 1,063 |
| Nebraska .......................... | 12,612 | 9,028 | 9,028 | 9,014 | 9,014 | 12,626 | 14 | 0.1 | 882 |
| Nevada ............................. | 12,027 | 5,169 | 5,169 | 3,472 | 3,472 | 13,724 | 1,697 | 14.1 | 612 |
| New Hampshire ................. | 3,920 | 2,585 | 2,585 | 2,644 | 2,644 | 3,861 | -59 | -1.5 | 361 |
| | | | | | | | | | |
| New Jersey........................ | 137,124 | 27,372 | 27,372 | 28,359 | 28,359 | 136,137 | -987 | -0.7 | 1,949 |
| New Mexico....................... | 15,588 | 6,625 | 8,200 | 6,995 | 8,700 | 15,048 | -540 | -3.5 | 946 |
| New York .......................... | 105,458 | 25,870 | 25,870 | 30,332 | 30,332 | 100,996 | -4,462 | -4.2 | 646 |
| North Carolina ................. | 90,918 | 50,862 | 50,862 | 53,474 | 53,474 | 85,634 | -5,284 | -5.8 | 1,098 |
| North Dakota.................... | 5,647 | 4,364 | 4,364 | 3,708 | 3,708 | 6,303 | 656 | 11.6 | 1,069 |
| | | | | | | | | | |
| Ohio[3] .............................. | 241,080 | 123,393 | 137,800 | 122,881 | 136,700 | 243,710 | 2,630 | 1.1 | 2,706 |
| Oklahoma......................... | 28,568 | 12,634 | 12,634 | 9,921 | 9,921 | 31,281 | 2,713 | 9.5 | 1,055 |
| Oregon ............................. | U | U | U | U | U | U | U | U | U |
| Pennsylvania .................... | 176,737 | 106,677 | 106,677 | 99,546 | 99,546 | 183,868 | 7,131 | 4.0 | 1,814 |
| Rhode Island..................... | 23,595 | U | 4,600 | U | 4,300 | 23,920 | 325 | 1.4 | 2,822 |
| | | | | | | | | | |
| South Carolina.................. | 34,753 | 13,605 | 13,605 | 14,515 | 14,515 | 33,843 | -910 | -2.6 | 883 |
| South Dakota.................... | 6,648 | 3,626 | 3,626 | 3,156 | 3,156 | 7,118 | 470 | 7.1 | 1,096 |
| Tennessee ........................ | 64,223 | 22,355 | 22,355 | 24,253 | 24,253 | 62,325 | -1,898 | -3.0 | 1,215 |
| Texas................................ | 388,101 | 146,787 | 146,787 | 155,951 | 155,951 | 378,937 | -9,164 | -2.4 | 1,853 |
| Utah ................................ | 11,805 | 5,597 | 5,597 | 5,221 | 5,221 | 12,181 | 376 | 3.2 | 579 |
| | | | | | | | | | |
| Vermont ........................... | 5,170 | U | 3,000 | U | 3,000 | 5,170 | 0 | ... | 1,021 |
| Virginia ............................ | 54,966 | 29,391 | 29,391 | 28,885 | 28,885 | 55,472 | 506 | 0.9 | 849 |
| Washington[3]..................... | 94,069 | 38,606 | 49,800 | 33,161 | 49,700 | 93,535 | -534 | -0.6 | 1,670 |
| West Virginia .................... | 7,174 | U | 800 | 969 | 969 | 7,008 | -166 | -2.3 | 478 |
| Wisconsin[4]....................... | 45,766 | U | 22,700 | 86 | 22,400 | 46,144 | 378 | 0.8 | 1,028 |
| Wyoming .......................... | 4,994 | 2,459 | 2,459 | 2,340 | 2,340 | 5,113 | 119 | 2.4 | 1,142 |

Note: Due to nonresponse or incomplete data, the probation population for some jurisdictions on December 31, 2015, does not equal the population on January 1, 2015, plus entries, minus exits. Counts may not be actual as reporting agencies may provide estimates on some or all detailed data.
... = Less than 0.05%.
U = Not known.
[1] Reflects reported data except for jurisdictions in which data were not available. Detail may not sum to total due to rounding.
[2] Rates were computed using the estimated U.S. adult resident population in each jurisdiction on January 1, 2016.
[3] See <http://www.bjs.gov/content/pub/pdf/ppus15.pdf> for more detail.
[4] The only exits reported were deaths.

# Table 10. Characteristics of Adults on Probation, 2005, 2014, and 2015

(Percent.)

| Characteristic | 2005 | 2014 | 2015 |
|---|---|---|---|
| **Total** ........................................................................... | 100.0 | 100.0 | 100.0 |
| Sex ..................................................................................... | | | |
| Male.................................................................................... | 77.0 | 75.0 | 75.0 |
| Female.................................................................................. | 23.0 | 25.0 | 25.0 |
| Race/Hispanic origin.......................................................... | 100.0 | 100.0 | 100.0 |
| White[1] ............................................................................... | 55.0 | 54.0 | 55.0 |
| Black/African American[1] ....................................................... | 30.0 | 30.0 | 30.0 |
| Hispanic/Latino ................................................................... | 13.0 | 13.0 | 13.0 |
| American Indian/Alaska Native[1]............................................. | 1.0 | 1.0 | 1.0 |
| Asian/Native Hawaiian/Other Pacific Islander[1] ........................ | 1.0 | 1.0 | 1.0 |
| Two or more races[1] .............................................................. | ... | ... | ... |
| Status of supervision ........................................................... | 100.0 | 100.0 | 100.0 |
| Active ................................................................................. | 72.0 | 73.0 | 76.0 |
| Residential/other treatment program...................................... | 1.0 | 1.0 | 1.0 |
| Financial conditions remaining .............................................. | NA | 1.0 | 2.0 |
| Inactive .............................................................................. | 9.0 | 5.0 | 4.0 |
| Absconder .......................................................................... | 10.0 | 8.0 | 7.0 |
| Supervised out of jurisdiction ............................................... | 2.0 | 6.0 | 2.0 |
| Warrant status .................................................................... | 6.0 | 2.0 | 5.0 |
| Other.................................................................................. | ... | 4.0 | 4.0 |
| Type of offense .................................................................. | 100.0 | 100.0 | 100.0 |
| Felony................................................................................. | 50.0 | 56.0 | 57.0 |
| Misdemeanor....................................................................... | 49.0 | 42.0 | 41.0 |
| Other infractions ................................................................. | 1.0 | 2.0 | 2.0 |
| Most serious offense............................................................ | 100.0 | 100.0 | 100.0 |
| Violent................................................................................. | 18.0 | 19.0 | 20.0 |
| Domestic violence ......................................................... | 6.0 | 4.0 | 4.0 |
| Sex offense ................................................................... | 3.0 | 3.0 | 4.0 |
| Other violent offense ..................................................... | 10.0 | 12.0 | 13.0 |
| Property.............................................................................. | 23.0 | 28.0 | 28.0 |
| Drug ................................................................................... | 25.0 | 25.0 | 25.0 |
| Public order ........................................................................ | | | |
| DWI/DUI .............................................................................. | 19.0 | 16.0 | 15.0 |
| Other traffic offense ............................................................. | 14.0 | 14.0 | 13.0 |
| Other.................................................................................. | 5.0 | 2.0 | 2.0 |

Note: Detail may not sum to total due to rounding. Counts based on most recent data and may differ from previously published statistics. See Methodology. Characteristics based on probationers with known type of status.
... = Less than 0.5%.
NA = Not available.
[1] Excludes persons of Hispanic or Latino origin, unless specified.

# Table 11. Adults on Parole, 2015

(Number; percent.)

| Jurisdiction | Parole population, 1/1/15 | Entries | | Exits | | Parole population, 12/31/15[1] | Change, 2015 | | Number on parole per 100,000 adult residents, 12/31/15[2] |
|---|---|---|---|---|---|---|---|---|---|
| | | Reported | Imputed[1] | Reported | Imputed[1] | | Number | Percent | |
| U.S. Total............................................. | 857,858 | 431,695 | 475,200 | 420,291 | 463,700 | 870,526 | 12668 | 1.5 | 350 |
| Federal................................................ | 109,365 | 49,988 | 49,988 | 46,315 | 46,315 | 114,471 | 5,106 | 4.7 | 46 |
| State................................................... | 748,493 | 381,707 | 425,200 | 373,976 | 417,400 | 756,055 | 7,562 | 1.0 | 304 |
| Alabama............................................ | 8,065 | 2,360 | 2,360 | 2,287 | 2,287 | 8,138 | 73 | 0.9 | 216 |
| Alaska............................................... | U | U | U | U | U | U | U | U | U |
| Arizona............................................. | 7,502 | 11,946 | 11,946 | 12,069 | 12,069 | 7,379 | -123 | -1.6 | 141 |
| Arkansas........................................... | 21,745 | 10,497 | 10,497 | 9,213 | 9,213 | 23,093 | 1348 | 6.0 | 1,012 |
| California[3]......................................... | 87,111 | 29,614 | 55,100 | 31,502 | 56,200 | 86,053 | -1058 | -1.0 | 285 |
| Colorado........................................... | 10,067 | 8,369 | 8,369 | 8,167 | 8,167 | 10,269 | 202 | 2.0 | 242 |
| Connecticut ...................................... | 2,564 | 2,487 | 2,487 | 2,112 | 2,112 | 2,939 | 375 | 15.0 | 104 |
| Delaware .......................................... | 676 | 31 | 31 | 282 | 282 | 425 | -251 | -37.1 | 57 |
| District of Columbia.......................... | 5,125 | 1,465 | 1,465 | 1,996 | 1,996 | 4,594 | -531 | -10.0 | 822 |
| Florida .............................................. | 4,526 | 6,325 | 6,325 | 6,240 | 6,240 | 4,611 | 85 | 2.0 | 28 |
| Georgia ............................................ | 25,577 | 10,249 | 10,249 | 11,696 | 11,696 | 24,130 | -1447 | -5.7 | 311 |
| Hawaii .............................................. | 1,545 | 667 | 667 | 897 | 897 | 1,540 | -5 | -0.3 | 137 |
| Idaho ............................................... | 4,217 | 2,695 | 2,695 | 2,037 | 2,037 | 4,875 | 658 | 15.6 | 396 |
| Illinois .............................................. | 29,644 | 23,830 | 23,830 | 24,328 | 24,328 | 29,146 | -498 | -2.0 | 294 |
| Indiana ............................................. | 9,481 | 7,829 | 7,829 | 7,876 | 7,876 | 9,434 | -47 | -1.0 | 187 |
| Iowa ................................................. | 5,741 | 3,588 | 3,588 | 3,411 | 3,411 | 5,918 | 177 | 3.0 | 246 |
| Kansas .............................................. | 4,051 | 3,957 | 3,957 | 3,677 | 3,677 | 4,331 | 280 | 6.9 | 197 |
| Kentucky ........................................... | 16,731 | 11,249 | 11,249 | 11,417 | 11,417 | 16,563 | -168 | -1.0 | 484 |
| Louisiana .......................................... | 29,619 | 17,158 | 17,158 | 15,590 | 15,590 | 31,187 | 1568 | 5.3 | 874 |
| Maine ............................................... | 20 | 1 | 1 | 0 | 0 | 21 | 1 | 5.0 | 2 |
| Maryland ........................................... | 11,537 | 4,690 | 4,690 | 5,340 | 5,340 | 10,887 | -650 | -5.6 | 233 |
| Massachusetts ................................... | 1,914 | 2,318 | 2,318 | 2,254 | 2,254 | 1,978 | 64 | 3.0 | 36 |
| Michigan ........................................... | 18,413 | 10,621 | 10,621 | 11,125 | 11,125 | 17,909 | -504 | -2.7 | 232 |
| Minnesota ......................................... | 6,644 | 6,346 | 6,346 | 6,182 | 6,182 | 6,808 | 164 | 2.5 | 161 |
| Mississippi......................................... | 9,883 | 5,923 | 5,923 | 7,382 | 7,382 | 8,424 | -1459 | -14.8 | 371 |
| Missouri............................................ | 18,489 | 12,991 | 12,991 | 13,786 | 13,786 | 17,694 | -795 | -4.3 | 376 |
| Montana............................................ | 1,094 | 584 | 584 | 586 | 586 | 1,092 | -2 | -0.2 | 135 |
| Nebraska ........................................... | 1,067 | 1,430 | 1,430 | 1,454 | 1,454 | 1,043 | -24 | -2.0 | 73 |
| Nevada ............................................. | 5,927 | 4,502 | 4,502 | 4,922 | 4,922 | 5,507 | -420 | -7.1 | 246 |
| New Hampshire ................................. | 2,385 | 1,503 | 1,503 | 1,437 | 1,437 | 2,451 | 66 | 2.8 | 229 |
| New Jersey......................................... | 14,889 | 5,877 | 5,877 | 5,586 | 5,586 | 15,180 | 291 | 2.0 | 217 |
| New Mexico........................................ | 2,255 | 1,577 | 1,577 | 944 | 944 | 2,888 | 633 | 28.1 | 182 |
| New York........................................... | 44,889 | 19,922 | 19,922 | 20,249 | 20,249 | 44,562 | -327 | -1.0 | 285 |
| North Carolina .................................. | 10,025 | 12,856 | 12,856 | 10,905 | 10,905 | 11,744 | 1719 | 17.1 | 151 |
| North Dakota..................................... | 564 | 1,269 | 1,269 | 1,189 | 1,189 | 644 | 80 | 14.0 | 109 |
| Ohio................................................. | 17,321 | 7,777 | 7,777 | 6,814 | 6,814 | 18,284 | 963 | 5.6 | 203 |
| Oklahoma.......................................... | 2,560 | 345 | 345 | 789 | 789 | 2,116 | -444 | -17.3 | 71 |
| Oregon.............................................. | U | U | U | U | U | U | U | U | U |
| Pennsylvania ..................................... | 104,629 | 70,985 | 70,985 | 63,263 | 63,263 | 112,351 | 7722 | 7.4 | 1,109 |
| Rhode Island ..................................... | 383 | 254 | 254 | 204 | 204 | 433 | 50 | 13.1 | 51 |
| South Carolina................................... | 5,177 | 2,485 | 2,485 | 2,641 | 2,641 | 5,021 | -156 | -3.0 | 131 |
| South Dakota..................................... | 2,608 | 1,616 | 1,616 | 1,572 | 1,572 | 2,652 | 44 | 1.7 | 408 |
| Tennessee ......................................... | 13,606 | 4,060 | 4,060 | 4,573 | 4,573 | 13,093 | -513 | -3.8 | 255 |
| Texas................................................ | 111,412 | 35,834 | 35,834 | 35,354 | 35,354 | 111,892 | 480 | 0.0 | 547 |
| Utah................................................. | 3,301 | 2,263 | 2,263 | 2,058 | 2,058 | 3,506 | 205 | 6.2 | 167 |
| Vermont ............................................ | 1,090 | U | 600 | U | 600 | 1,090 | 0 | ... | 215 |
| Virginia ............................................. | 1,732 | 511 | 511 | 667 | 667 | 1,576 | -156 | -9.0 | 24 |
| Washington ....................................... | 10,926 | 6,254 | 6,254 | 5,725 | 5,725 | 11,198 | 272 | 2.5 | 200 |
| West Virginia ..................................... | 2,749 | 2,028 | 2,028 | 1,654 | 1,654 | 3,123 | 374 | 13.6 | 213 |
| Wisconsin[4]........................................ | 20,141 | U | 6,500 | 65 | 7,200 | 19,453 | -688 | -3.4 | 434 |
| Wyoming .......................................... | 702 | 569 | 569 | 459 | 459 | 812 | 110 | 15.7 | 181 |

Note: Due to nonresponse or incomplete data, the parole population for some jurisdictions on December 31, 2015, does not equal the population on January 1, 2015, plus entries, minus exits. Counts may not be actual as reporting agencies may provide estimates on some or all detailed data.

... = Less than 0.05%.

U = Not known.

[1] Reflects reported data except for jurisdictions in which data were not available. Detail may not sum to total due to rounding.

[2] Rates were computed using the estimated U.S. adult resident population in each jurisdiction on January 1, 2016.

[3] Includes Post-Release Community Supervision and Mandatory Supervision parolees: 46,575 on January 1, 2015; and 29,614 entries, 31,502 exits, and 44,687 on December 31, 2015.

[4] The only exits reported were deaths.

# Table 12. Characteristics of Adults on Parole, 2005, 2014, and 2015

(Percent.)

| Characteristic | 2005 | 2014 | 2015 |
|---|---|---|---|
| **Total** ....................................................... | 100.0 | 100.0 | 100.0 |
| **Sex** | | | |
| Male............................................................ | 88.0 | 88.0 | 87.0 |
| Female........................................................ | 12.0 | 12.0 | 13.0 |
| **Race/Hispanic origin**..................................... | 100.0 | 100.0 | 100.0 |
| White ......................................................... | 41.0 | 43.0 | 44.0 |
| Black/African American ............................. | 40.0 | 39.0 | 38.0 |
| Hispanic/Latino ........................................ | 18.0 | 16.0 | 16.0 |
| American Indian/Alaska Native ................. | 1.0 | 1.0 | 1.0 |
| Asian/Native Hawaiian/other Pacific Islander............ | 1.0 | 1.0 | 1.0 |
| Two or more races .................................... | 0.0 | ... | ... |
| **Status of supervision** ................................... | 100.0 | 100.0 | 100.0 |
| Active ........................................................ | 83.0 | 84.0 | 83.0 |
| Inactive...................................................... | 4.0 | 5.0 | 5.0 |
| Absconder ................................................. | 7.0 | 6.0 | 6.0 |
| Supervised out of state ............................. | 4.0 | 4.0 | 4.0 |
| Financial conditions remaining ................. | NA | 0.0 | 0.0 |
| Other.......................................................... | 2.0 | 2.0 | 3.0 |
| **Maximum sentence to incarceration**.............. | 100.0 | 100.0 | 100.0 |
| Less than 1 year ........................................ | 3.0 | 6.0 | 6.0 |
| 1 year or more .......................................... | 97.0 | 94.0 | 94.0 |
| **Most serious offense**................................... | 100.0 | 100.0 | 100.0 |
| Violent........................................................ | 26.0 | 31.0 | 32.0 |
| Sex offense ........................................... | NA | 7.0 | 8.0 |
| Other violent offense ........................... | NA | 24.0 | 24.0 |
| Property...................................................... | 24.0 | 22.0 | 21.0 |
| Drug ......................................................... | 37.0 | 31.0 | 31.0 |
| Weapon....................................................... | NA | 4.0 | 4.0 |
| Other.......................................................... | 13.0 | 12.0 | 13.0 |

*Note:* Detail may not sum to total due to rounding. Counts based on most recent data and may differ from previously published statistics. See Methodology. Characteristics based on parolees with known type of status.
... = Less than 0.5%.
NA = Not available.

# METHODOLOGY

## About the Data

The Bureau of Justice Statistics' (BJS) Annual Probation Survey and Annual Parole Survey began in 1980 and collect data from probation and parole agencies in the United States that supervise adults. In these data, adults are persons subject to the jurisdiction of an adult court or correctional agency. Juveniles prosecuted as adults in a criminal court are considered adults. Juveniles under the jurisdiction of a juvenile court or correctional agency are excluded from these data.

The National Criminal Justice Information and Statistics Service of the Law Enforcement Assistance Administration, BJS's predecessor agency, began a statistical series on parole in 1976 and on probation in 1979. The two surveys collect data on the total number of adults supervised in the community on January 1 and December 31 each year, the number of entries and exits to supervision during the reporting year, and characteristics of the population at yearend.

Both surveys cover all 50 states, the District of Columbia, and the federal system. BJS depends on the voluntary participation of state central reporters and separate state, county, and court agencies for these data. During 2013, Westat (Rockville, MD) served as BJS's collection agent for the 50 states and the District of Columbia. Data for the federal system were provided directly to BJS from the Office of Probation and Pretrial Services, Administrative Office of the United States Courts through the Federal Justice Statistics Program.

## Probation

The 2014 Annual Probation Survey was sent to 467 respondents: 35 central state reporters; 426 separate state, county, or court agencies, including the state probation agency in Pennsylvania, which also provided data for 65 counties in Pennsylvania; the District of Columbia; and the federal system. States with multiple reporters were Alabama (3), Colorado (8), Florida (41), Georgia (2), Idaho (2), Kentucky (3), Michigan (131), Missouri (2), Montana (4), New Mexico (2), Ohio (186), Oklahoma (3), Pennsylvania (2), Tennessee (3), and Washington (32). Of the 461 agencies on the agency frame, 1 locality in Alabama, 1 in Colorado, 6 in Florida, 14 in Michigan, 1 in Montana, 17 in Ohio, and 5 in Washington did not provide data for the 2014 collection. For these localities, the agency's most recent December 31 population was used to estimate the populations on January 1 and December 31, 2014.

## Parole

The 2014 Annual Parole Survey was sent to 53 respondents: 50 central state reporters, including the state parole agency in Pennsylvania, which also provided one separate summary record for the state's 65 counties; the District of Columbia; and the federal system. Data for the federal system were provided directly to the BJS Federal Justice Statistics Program, which obtained data from the Office of Probation and Pretrial Services, Administrative Office of the United States Courts. In this report, federal parole includes a term of supervised release from prison, mandatory release, parole, military parole, and special parole. A term of supervised release is ordered at the time of sentencing by a federal judge, and it is served after release from a federal prison sentence.

In each collection year, respondents are asked to provide both the January 1 and December 31 population counts. At times, the January 1 count may differ from the December 31 count of the prior year. The difference reported may have resulted from administrative changes, such as implementing new information systems, leading to data review and cleanup; reconciling probationer records; reclassifying offenders, including those on probation to parole and offenders on dual community supervision statuses; and including certain probation populations not previously reported (e.g., supervised for an offense of driving while intoxicated or under the influence, some probationers who had absconded, and some on an inactive status). The discrepancy between the yearend 2013 and the beginning year 2014 probation counts resulted in an increase of 19,163 probationers. The discrepancy between the yearend and beginning year parole population count resulted in a decrease of 15,681 parolees from December 31, 2013 to January 1, 2014.

The number of probation agencies included in the survey expanded in 1998 and continued to expand through 1999 to include misdemeanor probation agencies in a few states that fell within the scope of this survey. For a discussion of this expansion, see *Probation and Parole in the United States, 2010* (NCJ 236019, BJS web, November 2011).

Technically, the change in the probation and parole populations from the beginning of the year to the end of the year should equal the difference between entries and exits during the year. However, those numbers may not be equal. Some probation and parole information systems track the number of cases that enter and exit community supervision, not the number of offenders. This means that entries and exits may include case counts as opposed to counts of offenders, while the beginning and yearend population counts represent individuals. Additionally, all of the data on entries and exits may not have been logged into the information systems, or the information systems may not have fully processed all of the data before the data were submitted to BJS. At the national level, 7,851 probationers were the difference between the change in the probation population measured by the difference between January 1 and December 31, 2014, populations and the difference between probation entries and exits during 2014. For parole, 5,927 parolees were the difference between the change in the parole population measured by the difference between January 1 and December 31, 2014, populations and the difference between parole entries and exits during 2014.

**Estimating change in population counts**

Technically, the change in the probation and parole populations from the beginning of the year to the end of the year should equal the difference between entries and exits during the year. However, those numbers may not be equal. Some probation and parole information systems track the number of cases that enter and exit community supervision, not the number of offenders. This means that entries and exits may include case counts as opposed to counts of individuals, while the beginning and yearend population counts represent individuals. Some individuals are being supervised for more than one charge or case simultaneously. Additionally, all of the data on entries and exits may not have been logged into the information systems, or the information systems may not have fully processed all of the data before the data were submitted to BJS.

At the national level, 11,312 probationers were the difference between the change in the probation population measured by the difference between January 1 and December 31, 2015, populations and the difference between probation entries and exits during 2015. For parole, 1,168 parolees were the difference between the change in the parole population measured by the difference between January 1 and December 31, 2015, populations and the difference between parole entries and exits during 2015.

Estimates of annual change reported were calculated in some tables as the difference between the January 1 and December 31 populations within the reporting year.

Jurisdiction counts reported for January 1 may differ from the December 31 counts reported in the previous year. As a result, the direction of change based on yearend data could be in the opposite direction of the within-year change.

# Appendix A: Sources for Tables

(Table number is followed by source)

## Part 1. Correctional Populations in the United States, 2014

1. Bureau of Justice Statistics, Annual Probation Survey, Annual Parole Survey, Annual Survey of Jails, Census of Jail Inmates, and National Prisoner Statistics program, 2000, 2005–2010, and 2013–2014.

2. Bureau of Justice Statistics, Annual Probation Survey, Annual Parole Survey, Annual Survey of Jails, Census of Jail Inmates, and National Prisoner Statistics program, 2000, 2005–2014; and U.S. Census Bureau, postcensal estimated resident population for January 1 of the following year, 2001, and 2006–2015.

3. Bureau of Justice Statistics, Annual Probation Survey, Annual Parole Survey, Annual Survey of Jails, and National Prisoner Statistics program, 2007 and 2014.

4. Bureau of Justice Statistics, Annual Probation Survey, Annual Parole Survey, Annual Survey of Jails, and National Prisoner Statistics program, 2000–2014.

5. Bureau of Justice Statistics, Annual Probation Survey, Annual Parole Survey, Deaths in Custody Reporting Program, and National Prisoner Statistics program, 2014; and U.S. Census Bureau, unpublished U.S. resident population estimates within jurisdiction on January 1, 2015.

6. Bureau of Justice Statistics, Annual Probation Survey, Annual Parole Survey, and National Prisoner Statistics program, 2000–2014.

7. Bureau of Justice Statistics, Annual Probation Survey, Annual Parole Survey, Deaths in Custody Reporting Program, and National Prisoner Statistics program, 2014; and U.S. Census Bureau, unpublished U.S. resident population estimates within jurisdiction on January 1, 2015.

8. Bureau of Justice Statistics, Annual Survey of Jails, and National Prisoner Statistics program, 2000 and 2013ñ2014; and U.S. Census Bureau, postcensal estimated resident populations for January 1 of the following year, 2001, 2014, and 2015.

9. Bureau of Justice Statistics, National Prisoner Statistics program and Survey of Jails in Indian Country, 2000, 2005, and 2013–2014.

10. Bureau of Justice Statistics, National Prisoner Statistics program, Census of Jail Inmates, and Annual Survey of Jails, 2004–2014; and U.S. Census Bureau, postcensal estimated resident population for January 1 of the following year, 2005–2015.

## Part 2. Crime in the United States, 2015
Tables 1 through 45 are from United States Department of Justice, Federal Bureau of Investigation, Uniform Crime Reports, 2015.

## Part 3. Crimes Against Persons with Disabilities, 2010–2014
Tables 1 through 13 are from Bureau of Justice Statistics, National Crime Victimization Survey, 2010–2014; and U.S. Census Bureau, American Community Survey, 2010–2014.

## Part 4. Criminal Victimization, 2015
Tables 1 through 12 are from Bureau of Justice Statistics, National Crime Victimization Survey, 2014 and 2015. Table 11 is also from the Preliminary Semiannual Uniform Crime Report, January-June 2015

## Part 5. Hate Crime Statistics, 2015
Tables 1 through 13 are from Federal Bureau of Investigation, Hate Crime Statistics, 2015

## Part 6. Human Trafficking, 2015

Tables 1 through 5 are from United States Department of Justice, Federal Bureau of Investigation, Uniform Crime Reports, 2015

## Part 7. Indicators of School Crime and Safety, 2015

1    Centers for Disease Control and Prevention (CDC), 1992-2013 School-Associated Violent Deaths Surveillance Study (SAVD) (partially funded by the U.S. Department of Education, Office of Safe and Healthy Students), previously unpublished tabulation (December 2015); CDC, National Center for Injury Prevention and Control, Web-based Injury Statistics Query and Reporting System Fatal (WISQARS™ Fatal), 1999–2012, retrieved September 2015 from http://www.cdc.gov/injury/wisqars/index.html; and Federal Bureau of Investigation and Bureau of Justice Statistics, Supplementary Homicide Reports (SHR), preliminary data (November 2015).

2    U.S. Department of Justice, Bureau of Justice Statistics, National Crime Victimization Survey (NCVS), 1992 through 2015.

3    U.S. Department of Justice, Bureau of Justice Statistics, National Crime Victimization Survey (NCVS), 2015.

4    Centers for Disease Control and Prevention, Division of Adolescent and School Health, Youth Risk Behavior Surveillance System (YRBSS), 1993 through 2015.

5    U.S. Department of Education, National Center for Education Statistics, Schools and Staffing Survey (SASS), "Public School Teacher Data File" and "Private School Teacher Data File," 1993-94, 1999-2000, 2003-04, 2007-08, and 2011-12; and "Charter School Teacher Data File," 1999-2000.

6    U.S. Department of Education, National Center for Education Statistics, 1999–2000, 2003–04, 2005–06, 2007–08, and 2009–10 School Survey on Crime and Safety (SSOCS), 2000, 2004, 2006, 2008, and 2010; Fast Response Survey System (FRSS), "School Safety and Discipline: 2013-14," FRSS 106, 2014; and Common Core of Data (CCD), "Public Elementary/Secondary School Universe Survey," 2013-14

7    U.S. Department of Justice, Bureau of Justice Statistics, School Crime Supplement (SCS) to the National Crime Victimization Survey, 2001 through 2015.

8    Centers for Disease Control and Prevention, Division of Adolescent and School Health, Youth Risk Behavior Surveillance System (YRBSS), 1993 through 2015.

9    U.S. Department of Justice, Bureau of Justice Statistics, School Crime Supplement (SCS) to the National Crime Victimization Survey, 1999 through 2015.

10    U.S. Department of Justice, Bureau of Justice Statistics, School Crime Supplement (SCS) to the National Crime Victimization Survey, selected years, 2005 through 2015.

## Part 8. Jail Inmates in 2015

1    Bureau of Justice Statistics, Annual Survey of Jails, 2000 and 2005–2014; and Census of Jail Inmates, midyear 2005.

2-4    Bureau of Justice Statistics, Annual Survey of Jails, 2000, 2005, 2013–2014, and 2015; and Census of Jail Inmates.

5-7    Bureau of Justice Statistics, Annual Survey of Jails, 2014–2015.

8    Bureau of Justice Statistics, Annual Survey of Jails, 1999 and 2007–2015; and Census of Jail Inmates.

9    Bureau of Justice Statistics, Annual Survey of Jails, midyear 2000 and 2006–2015.

10    Bureau of Justice Statistics, Annual Survey of Jails, 2013 and 2015.

## Part 9. Law Enforcement Officers Killed and Assaulted, 2015

Tables 1 through 44 are from United States Department of Justice, Federal Bureau of Investigation, Uniform Crime Reports, 2015.

**Part 10. Probation and Parole, 2015**

1    Bureau of Justice Statistics, Annual Probation Survey and Annual Parole Survey, 2005–2015.

2    Bureau of Justice Statistics, Annual Probation Survey and Annual Parole Survey, 2005–2015; and U.S. Census Bureau, National Intercensal Estimates, 2006–2010, and Population Estimates, January 1, 2011–2016.

3    Bureau of Justice Statistics, Annual Probation Survey and Annual Parole Survey, 2005 and 2010–2015.

4    Bureau of Justice Statistics, Annual Parole Survey, 2005 and 2010–2015.

5    Bureau of Justice Statistics, Annual Probation Survey and Annual Parole Survey, 2008–2015.

6    Bureau of Justice Statistics, Annual Parole Survey, 2005–2015.

7    Bureau of Justice Statistics, Annual Parole Survey, 2005–2015.

8    Bureau of Justice Statistics, Annual Probation Survey and Annual Parole Survey, 2015.

9    Bureau of Justice Statistics, Annual Probation Survey and Annual Parole Survey, 2015.

10   Bureau of Justice Statistics, Annual Probation Survey, 2005, 2014, and 2015.

11   Bureau of Justice Statistics, Annual Parole Survey, 2015.

12   Bureau of Justice Statistics, Annual Parole Survey, 2015.

13   Bureau of Justice Statistics, Annual Parole Survey, 2005, 2014, and 2015.

14   Bureau of Justice Statistics, Annual Parole Survey, 2015.

# Appendix B. Capital Punishment

## Table B1. Number of Persons Executed, 1930–2015

| (Number.) | | | (Number.) | |
|---|---|---|---|---|
| Year | Executions | | Year | Executions |
| 1930 | 155 | | 1975 | 0 |
| 1931 | 153 | | 1976 | 0 |
| 1932 | 140 | | 1977 | 1 |
| 1933 | 160 | | 1978 | 0 |
| 1934 | 168 | | 1979 | 2 |
| 1935 | 199 | | 1980 | 0 |
| 1936 | 195 | | 1981 | 1 |
| 1937 | 147 | | 1982 | 2 |
| 1938 | 190 | | 1983 | 5 |
| 1939 | 160 | | 1984 | 21 |
| 1940 | 124 | | 1985 | 18 |
| 1941 | 123 | | 1986 | 18 |
| 1942 | 147 | | 1987 | 25 |
| 1943 | 131 | | 1988 | 11 |
| 1944 | 120 | | 1989 | 16 |
| 1945 | 117 | | 1990 | 23 |
| 1946 | 131 | | 1991 | 14 |
| 1947 | 153 | | 1992 | 31 |
| 1948 | 119 | | 1993 | 38 |
| 1949 | 119 | | 1994 | 31 |
| 1950 | 82 | | 1995 | 56 |
| 1951 | 105 | | 1996 | 45 |
| 1952 | 83 | | 1997 | 74 |
| 1953 | 62 | | 1998 | 68 |
| 1954 | 81 | | 1999 | 98 |
| 1955 | 76 | | 2000 | 85 |
| 1956 | 65 | | 2001 | 66 |
| 1957 | 65 | | 2002 | 71 |
| 1958 | 49 | | 2003 | 65 |
| 1959 | 49 | | 2004 | 59 |
| 1960 | 56 | | 2005 | 60 |
| 1961 | 42 | | 2006 | 53 |
| 1962 | 47 | | 2007 | 42 |
| 1963 | 21 | | 2008 | 37 |
| 1964 | 15 | | 2009 | 52 |
| 1965 | 7 | | 2010 | 46 |
| 1966 | 1 | | 2011 | 43 |
| 1967 | 2 | | 2012 | 43 |
| 1968 | 0 | | 2013 | 39 |
| 1969 | 0 | | 2014 | 35 |
| 1970 | 0 | | 2015 | 28 |
| 1971 | 0 | | | |
| 1972 | 0 | | | |
| 1973 | 0 | | | |
| 1974 | 0 | | | |

## Table B2. Number of Persons Under Sentence of Death, 1953–2015

| (Number.) | | | (Number.) | |
|---|---|---|---|---|
| Year | Number of prisoners under sentence of death | | Year | Number of prisoners under sentence of death |
| 1953 | 131 | | 1983 | 1,209 |
| 1954 | 147 | | 1984 | 1,420 |
| 1955 | 125 | | 1985 | 1,575 |
| 1956 | 146 | | 1986 | 1,800 |
| 1957 | 151 | | 1987 | 1,967 |
| 1958 | 147 | | 1988 | 2,117 |
| 1959 | 164 | | 1989 | 2,243 |
| 1960 | 212 | | 1990 | 2,346 |
| 1961 | 257 | | 1991 | 2,465 |
| 1962 | 267 | | 1992 | 2,580 |
| 1963 | 297 | | 1993 | 2,727 |
| 1964 | 315 | | 1994 | 2,905 |
| 1965 | 331 | | 1995 | 3,064 |
| 1966 | 406 | | 1996 | 3,242 |
| 1967 | 435 | | 1997 | 3,328 |
| 1968 | 517 | | 1998 | 3,465 |
| 1969 | 575 | | 1999 | 3,527 |
| 1970 | 631 | | 2000 | 3,601 |
| 1971 | 642 | | 2001 | 3,577 |
| 1972 | 334 | | 2002 | 3,562 |
| 1973 | 134 | | 2003 | 3,377 |
| 1974 | 244 | | 2004 | 3,320 |
| 1975 | 488 | | 2005 | 3,245 |
| 1976 | 420 | | 2006 | 3,228 |
| 1977 | 423 | | 2007 | 3,215 |
| 1978 | 482 | | 2008 | 3,210 |
| 1979 | 593 | | 2009 | 3,173 |
| 1980 | 692 | | 2010 | 3,139 |
| 1981 | 860 | | 2011 | 3,065 |
| 1982 | 1,066 | | 2012 | 3,011 |
| | | | 2013 | 2,983 |
| | | | 2014 | 2,942 |
| | | | 2015 | 2,881 |

# Table B3. Status of the Death Penalty, 2014–2015

(Number.)

| State | Executions | | Number of prisoners under sentence of death on 12/31 | |
|---|---|---|---|---|
| | 2014 | 2015 | 2014 | 2015 |
| **Total** ............................................. | 35 | 28 | 2,942 | 2,881 |
| Alabama.......................................... | 0 | 0 | 193 | 187 |
| Arizona........................................... | 1 | 0 | 117 | 119 |
| California........................................ | 0 | 0 | 740 | 739 |
| Federal Bureau of Prisons ............... | 0 | 0 | 58 | 59 |
| Florida ........................................... | 8 | 2 | 394 | 390 |
| Georgia .......................................... | 2 | 5 | 79 | 71 |
| Louisiana ........................................ | 0 | 0 | 85 | 82 |
| Mississippi....................................... | 0 | 0 | 47 | 47 |
| Missouri.......................................... | 10 | 6 | NA | NA |
| Nevada ........................................... | 0 | 0 | 80 | 82 |
| North Carolina ................................ | 0 | 0 | 150 | 147 |
| Ohio ............................................... | 1 | 0 | 138 | 137 |
| Oklahoma........................................ | 3 | 1 | 47 | 47 |
| Pennsylvania ................................... | 0 | 0 | 186 | 181 |
| Tennessee ....................................... | 0 | 0 | 69 | 67 |
| Texas.............................................. | 10 | 13 | 271 | 254 |
| Virginia........................................... | 0 | 1 | NA | NA |
| Other jurisdictions.......................... | 0 | 0 | 288 (20 jurisdictions) | 272 (19 jurisdictions) |

NOTE: Jurisdictions without the death penalty in 2015 include Alaska, District of Columbia, Hawaii, Illinois, Iowa, Maine, Maryland, Massachusetts, Michigan, Minnesota, New Jersey, North Dakota, Rhode Island, Vermont, West Virginia, and Wisconsin. New Mexico repealed the death penalty for offenses committed after July 1, 2009. Connecticut repealed the death penalty for offenses committed after April 25, 2012. Maryland repealed the death penalty effective October 1, 2013. As of December 31, 2014, 2 men in New Mexico, 11 men in Connecticut, and 4 men in Maryland were under previously imposed death sentences. In 2015, the governor of Maryland commuted the death sentences of the remaining four inmates under sentence of death. The Nebraska legislature passed a bill to repeal the death penalty, but an appeal successfully stayed enactment until the state could hold a referendum on the issue. As of December 31, 2015, 2 men in New Mexico, 11 men in Connecticut, and 10 men in Nebraska were under previously imposed death sentences.

# Table B4. Admissions to and Removal From Under Sentence of Death, 1973–2015

(Number.)

| Year | Admissions | Removals |
|------|-----------:|---------:|
| 1973 | 44 | 240 |
| 1974 | 161 | 55 |
| 1975 | 318 | 67 |
| 1976 | 249 | 317 |
| 1977 | 159 | 156 |
| 1978 | 211 | 150 |
| 1979 | 172 | 61 |
| 1980 | 202 | 101 |
| 1981 | 249 | 84 |
| 1982 | 287 | 79 |
| 1983 | 266 | 123 |
| 1984 | 305 | 90 |
| 1985 | 291 | 130 |
| 1986 | 320 | 109 |
| 1987 | 311 | 142 |
| 1988 | 317 | 165 |
| 1989 | 275 | 149 |
| 1990 | 270 | 152 |
| 1991 | 285 | 159 |
| 1992 | 300 | 173 |
| 1993 | 299 | 162 |
| 1994 | 330 | 153 |
| 1995 | 325 | 171 |
| 1996 | 323 | 155 |
| 1997 | 283 | 187 |
| 1998 | 310 | 174 |
| 1999 | 287 | 221 |
| 2000 | 235 | 173 |
| 2001 | 164 | 194 |
| 2002 | 172 | 191 |
| 2003 | 156 | 346 |
| 2004 | 140 | 198 |
| 2005 | 143 | 216 |
| 2006 | 125 | 145 |
| 2007 | 129 | 140 |
| 2008 | 122 | 136 |
| 2009 | 118 | 165 |
| 2010 | 116 | 143 |
| 2011 | 85 | 152 |
| 2012 | 84 | 127 |
| 2013 | 85 | 115 |
| 2014 | 69 | 110 |
| 2015 | 49 | 110 |

# Table B5. Advance Count of Executions, January 1–December 31, 2016

(Number.)

| Year | Number of executions |
|------|---------------------:|
| Total | 20 |
| Alabama | 2 |
| Florida | 1 |
| Georgia | 9 |
| Missouri | 1 |
| Texas | 7 |

# INDEX